NEIL GAIMAN

TEKNOPHAGE™

Based on a concept created by NEIL GAIMAN

RICK VEITCH

PAUL JENKINS

NEIL GAIMAN

C. J. HENDERSON

JOHN NEY RIEBER

JAMES VANCE

Writers

BRYAN TALBOT	ANGUS McKIE
AL DAVISON	AL DAVISON
MICHAEL NETZER	JOHN COULTHART
SHEA ANTON PENSA	KELLY KRANTZ
TED SLAMPYAK	MICHAEL NETZER
Pencilers	ART NICHOLS
	BRYAN TALBOT
	Inkers

SUPER GENIUS

GRAPHIC NOVELS AVAILABLE FROM SUPER GENIUS

COMING SOON   COMING SOON

NEIL GAIMAN'S
LADY JUSTICE
Volume One

NEIL GAIMAN'S
TEKNOPHAGE
Volume One

NEIL GAIMAN'S
MR. HERO
Volume One

WWE SUPERSTARS
#1
"Money in the Bank"

WWE SUPERSTARS
#2
"Haze of Glory!"

WWE SUPERSTARS
#3
"Legends"

WWE SUPERSTARS
#4
"Last Man Standing"

NEIL GAIMAN'S TEKNOPHAGE™
VOLUME ONE
Copyright c 1995, 1996 Hollywood Media Corp., formerly known as BIG Entertainment, Inc. All rights reserved. Neil Gaiman's Teknophage, Neil Gaiman's Wheel of Worlds, Neil Gaiman's Lady Justice, Neil Gaiman's Mr. Hero, and Neil Gaiman's Adam Cain, including all characters featured and the names and distinct likenesses thereof, are trademarks of Hollywood Media Corp., formerly known as BIG Entertainment, Inc. Published under license from Hollywood Media Corp., 2255 Glades Rd, Suite 221A, Boca Raton, FL 33431.

Dawn Guzzo – Design & Production
Ed Polgardy – Original Editor
Julie Riddle – Original Associate Editor
Dr. Martin Greenberg – Original Senior Editor
Albert Rodriguez – Original Production Director
Ben Spoont – Associate Producer (Hollywood Media Corp.)
David Silvers – Associate Producer (Hollywood Media Corp.)
Mitchell Rubenstein – Co-Founder of Tekno•Comix
Laurie Silvers – Co-Founder of Tekno•Comix
Jeff Whitman – Production Coordinator
Bethany Bryan – Associate Editor
Jim Salicrup
Editor-in-Chief

ISBN: 978-1-62991-277-6 Paperback Edition
ISBN: 978-1-62991-295-0 Hardcover Edition

Printed in the USA.

Super Genius books may be purchased for business or promotional use. For information on bulk purchases please contact Macmillan Corporate and Premium Sales Department at (800) 221-7945 x5442.

DISTRIBUTED BY MACMILLAN
FIRST SUPER GENIUS PRINTING

Table of Contents

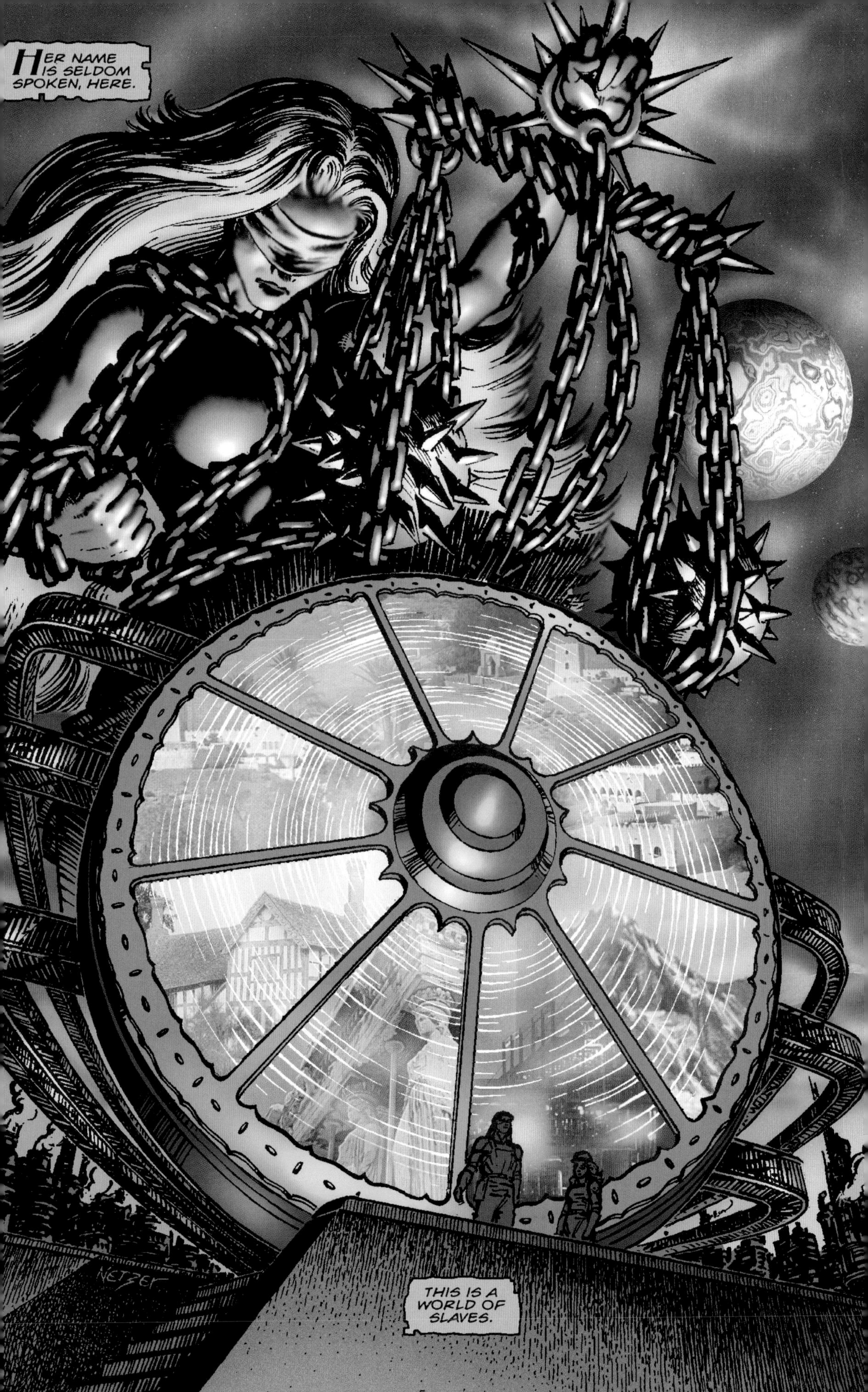
HER NAME IS SELDOM SPOKEN, HERE.
THIS IS A WORLD OF SLAVES.
NETZER

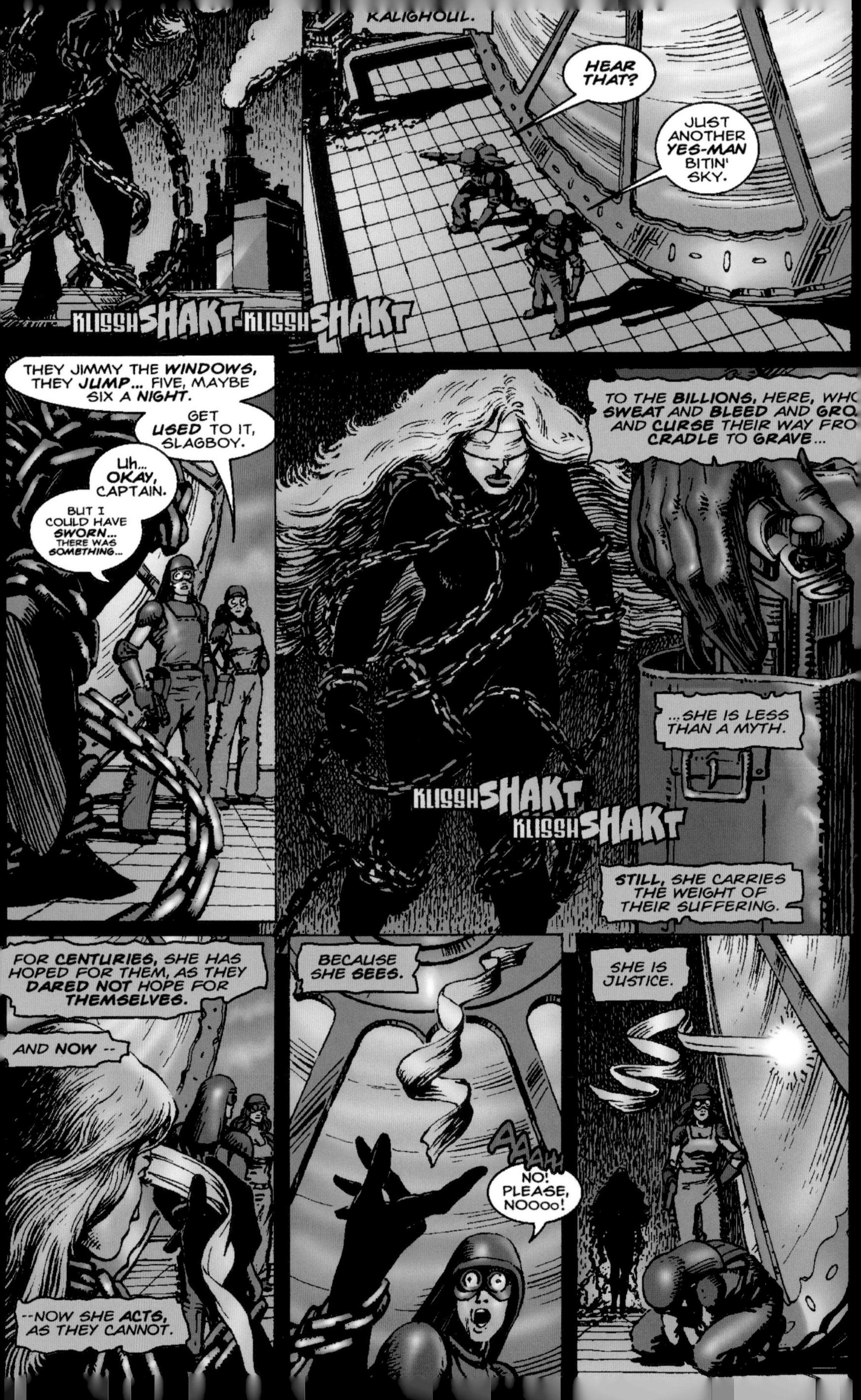

KALIGHOUL.
HEAR THAT?
JUST ANOTHER YES-MAN BITIN' SKY.
KLISSHSHAKT-KLISSHSHAKT
THEY JIMMY THE WINDOWS, THEY JUMP... FIVE, MAYBE SIX A NIGHT.
GET USED TO IT, SLAGBOY.
Uh... OKAY, CAPTAIN.
BUT I COULD HAVE SWORN... THERE WAS SOMETHING...
TO THE BILLIONS, HERE, WHO SWEAT AND BLEED AND GRO AND CURSE THEIR WAY FRO CRADLE TO GRAVE...
...SHE IS LESS THAN A MYTH.
KLISSHSHAKT KLISSHSHAKT
STILL, SHE CARRIES THE WEIGHT OF THEIR SUFFERING.
FOR CENTURIES, SHE HAS HOPED FOR THEM, AS THEY DARED NOT HOPE FOR THEMSELVES.
AND NOW --
--NOW SHE ACTS, AS THEY CANNOT.
BECAUSE SHE SEES.
AAAH
NO! PLEASE, NOOOo!
SHE IS JUSTICE.

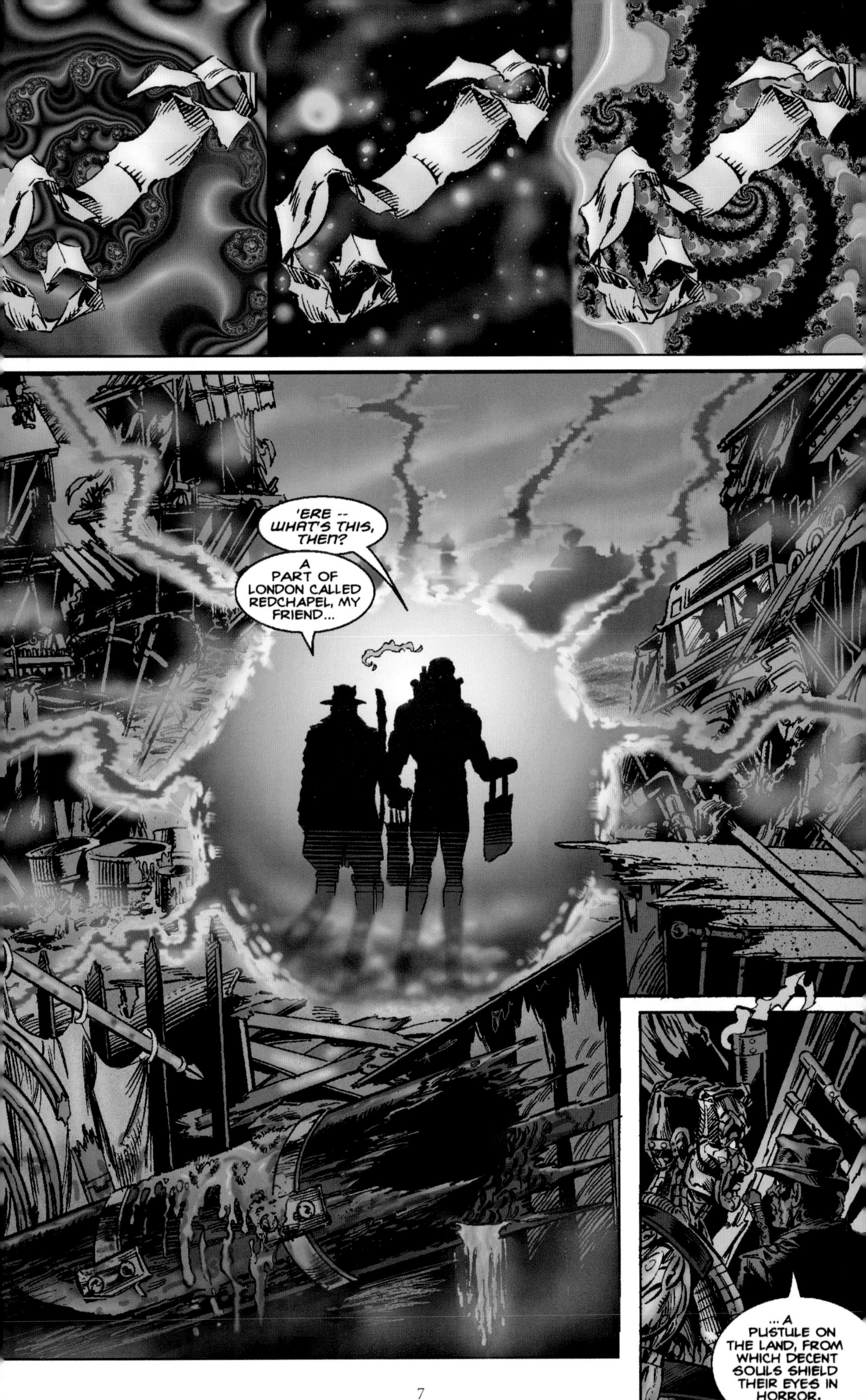
'ERE -- WHAT'S THIS, THEN?
A PART OF LONDON CALLED REDCHAPEL, MY FRIEND...
...A PUSTULE ON THE LAND, FROM WHICH DECENT SOULS SHIELD THEIR EYES IN HORROR.

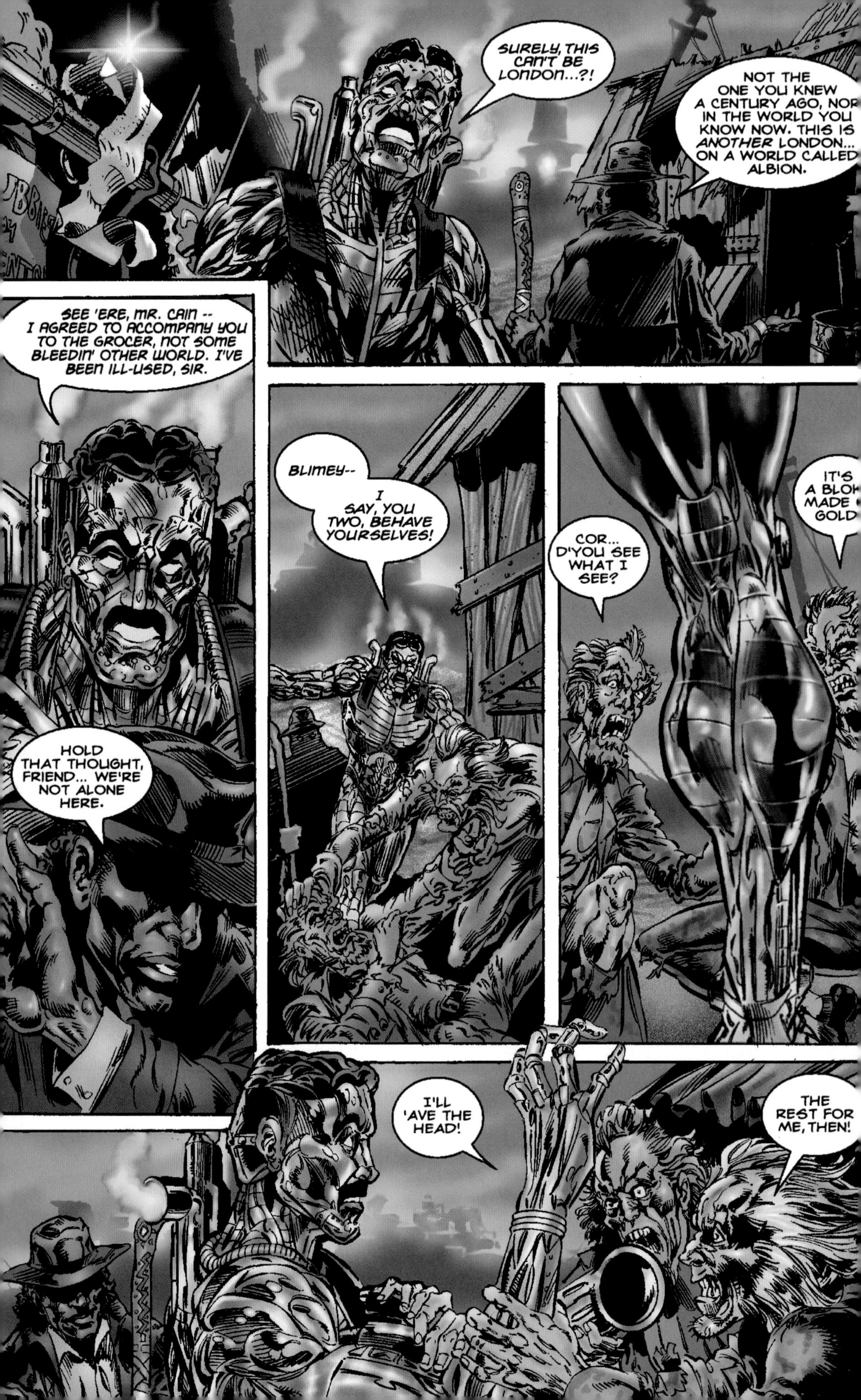

SURELY, THIS CAN'T BE LONDON...?!
NOT THE ONE YOU KNEW A CENTURY AGO, NOR IN THE WORLD YOU KNOW NOW. THIS IS *ANOTHER* LONDON... ON A WORLD CALLED ALBION.
SEE 'ERE, MR. CAIN -- I AGREED TO ACCOMPANY YOU TO THE GROCER, NOT SOME BLEEDIN' OTHER WORLD. I'VE BEEN ILL-USED, SIR.
HOLD THAT THOUGHT, FRIEND... WE'RE NOT ALONE HERE.
BLIMEY--
I SAY, YOU TWO, *BEHAVE* YOURSELVES!
COR... D'YOU SEE WHAT I SEE?
IT'S A BLOK MADE GOLD
I'LL 'AVE THE HEAD!
THE REST FOR ME, THEN!

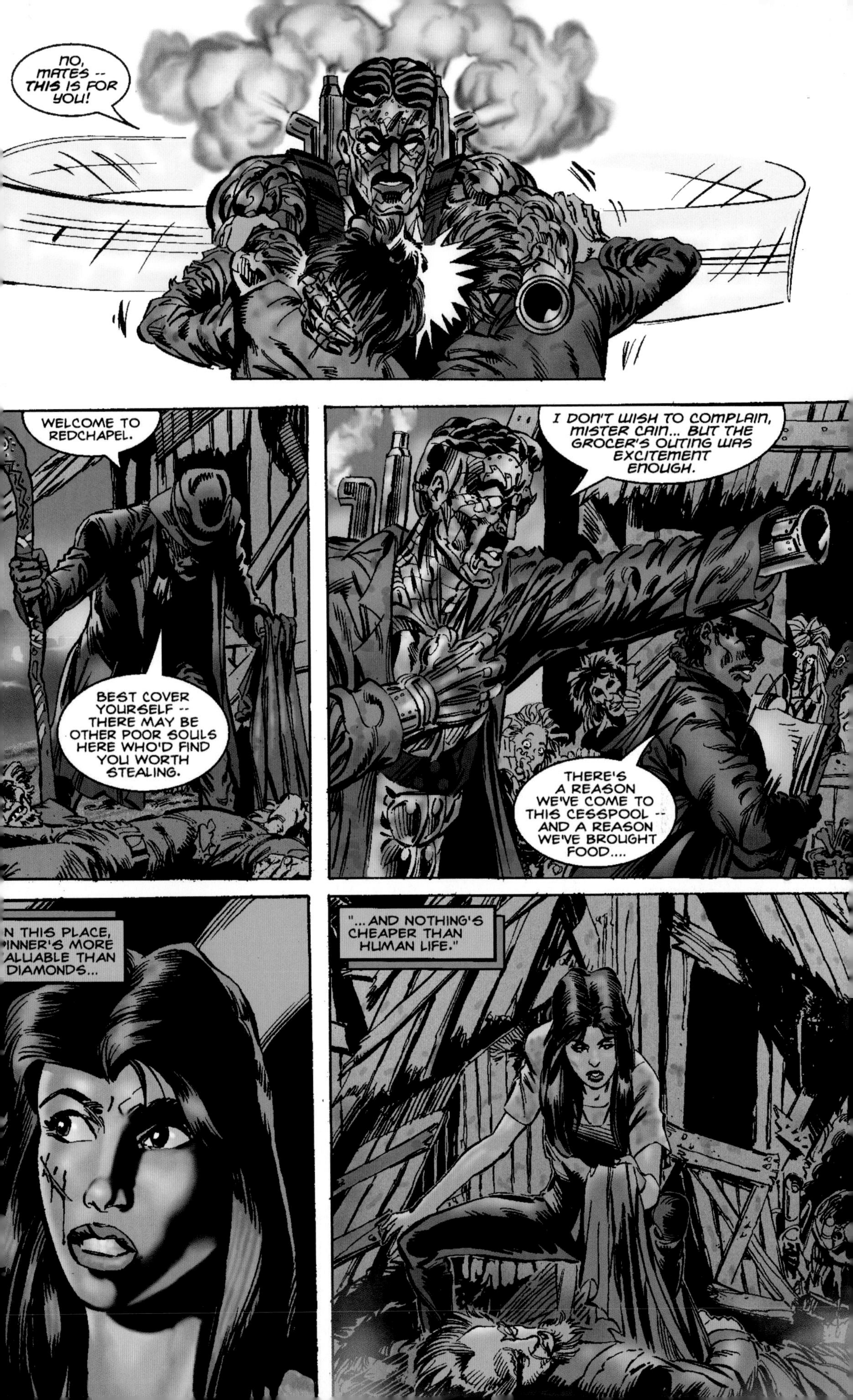
NO, MATES -- THIS IS FOR YOU!
WELCOME TO REDCHAPEL.
BEST COVER YOURSELF -- THERE MAY BE OTHER POOR SOULS HERE WHO'D FIND YOU WORTH STEALING.
I DON'T WISH TO COMPLAIN, MISTER CAIN... BUT THE GROCER'S OUTING WAS EXCITEMENT ENOUGH.
THERE'S A REASON WE'VE COME TO THIS CESSPOOL -- AND A REASON WE'VE BROUGHT FOOD....
N THIS PLACE, INNER'S MORE ALUABLE THAN DIAMONDS...
"...AND NOTHING'S CHEAPER THAN HUMAN LIFE."

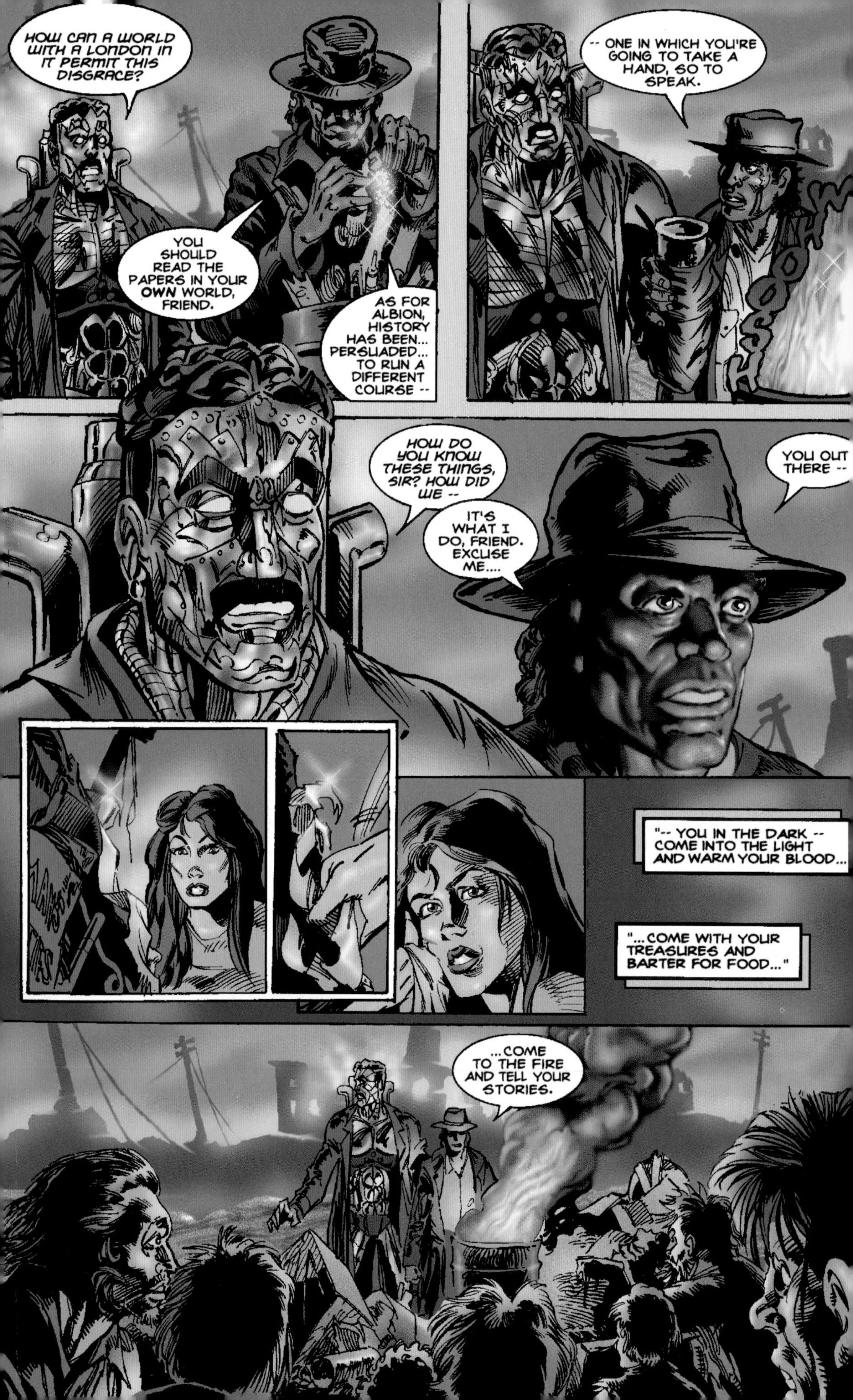
HOW CAN A WORLD WITH A LONDON IN IT PERMIT THIS DISGRACE?
YOU SHOULD READ THE PAPERS IN YOUR **OWN** WORLD, FRIEND.
AS FOR ALBION, HISTORY HAS BEEN... PERSUADED... TO RUN A DIFFERENT COURSE --
-- ONE IN WHICH YOU'RE GOING TO TAKE A HAND, SO TO SPEAK.
WHOOSH
HOW DO YOU KNOW THESE THINGS, SIR? HOW DID WE --
IT'S WHAT I DO, FRIEND. EXCUSE ME....
YOU OUT THERE --
"-- YOU IN THE DARK -- COME INTO THE LIGHT AND WARM YOUR BLOOD...
"...COME WITH YOUR TREASURES AND BARTER FOR FOOD..."
...COME TO THE FIRE AND TELL YOUR STORIES.

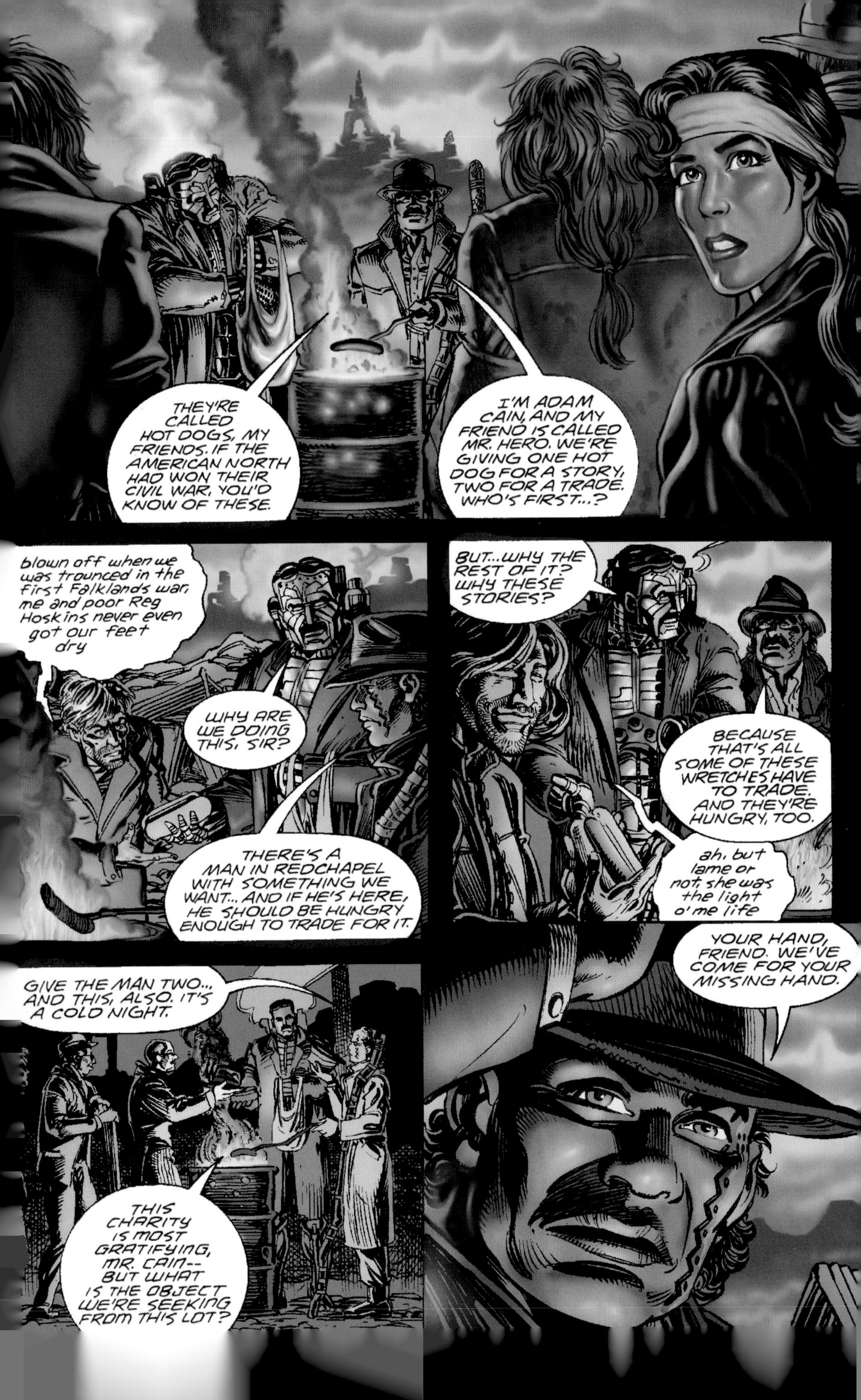
THEY'RE CALLED HOT DOGS, MY FRIENDS. IF THE AMERICAN NORTH HAD WON THEIR CIVIL WAR, YOU'D KNOW OF THESE.
I'M ADAM CAIN, AND MY FRIEND IS CALLED MR. HERO. WE'RE GIVING ONE HOT DOG FOR A STORY, TWO FOR A TRADE. WHO'S FIRST...?
blown off when we was trounced in the first Falklands war, me and poor Reg Hoskins never even got our feet dry
WHY ARE WE DOING THIS, SIR?
THERE'S A MAN IN REDCHAPEL WITH SOMETHING WE WANT... AND IF HE'S HERE, HE SHOULD BE HUNGRY ENOUGH TO TRADE FOR IT.
BUT... WHY THE REST OF IT? WHY THESE STORIES?
BECAUSE THAT'S ALL SOME OF THESE WRETCHES HAVE TO TRADE. AND THEY'RE HUNGRY, TOO.
ah, but lame or not, she was the light o' me life
GIVE THE MAN TWO... AND THIS, ALSO. IT'S A COLD NIGHT.
THIS CHARITY IS MOST GRATIFYING, MR. CAIN-- BUT WHAT IS THE OBJECT WE'RE SEEKING FROM THIS LOT?
YOUR HAND, FRIEND. WE'VE COME FOR YOUR MISSING HAND.

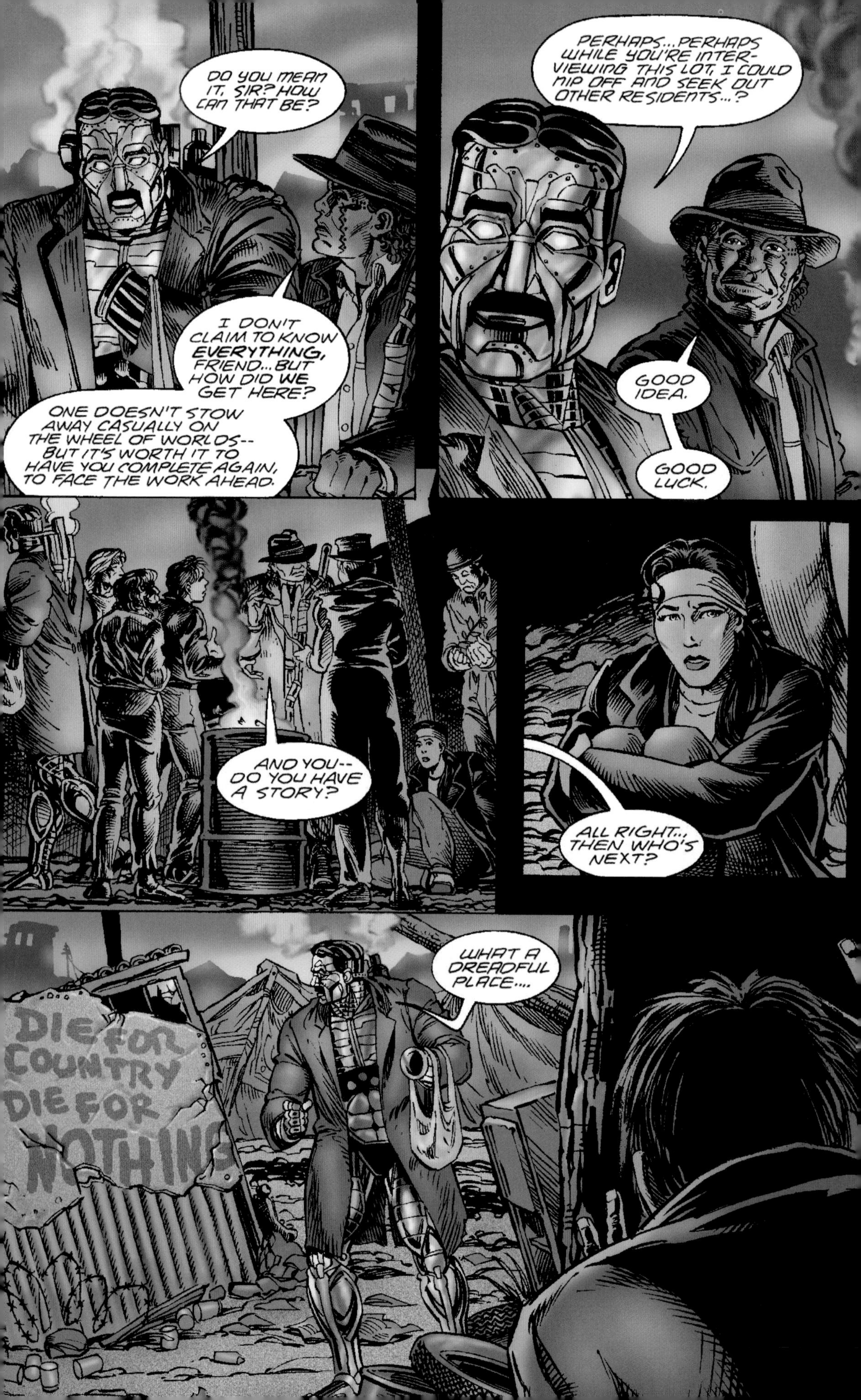
DO YOU MEAN IT, SIR? HOW CAN THAT BE?
I DON'T CLAIM TO KNOW EVERYTHING, FRIEND...BUT HOW DID WE GET HERE?
ONE DOESN'T STOW AWAY CASUALLY ON THE WHEEL OF WORLDS--BUT IT'S WORTH IT TO HAVE YOU COMPLETE AGAIN, TO FACE THE WORK AHEAD.
PERHAPS...PERHAPS WHILE YOU'RE INTER-VIEWING THIS LOT, I COULD NIP OFF AND SEEK OUT OTHER RESIDENTS...?
GOOD IDEA.
GOOD LUCK.
AND YOU--DO YOU HAVE A STORY?
ALL RIGHT... THEN WHO'S NEXT?
DIE FOR COUNTRY DIE FOR NOTHING
WHAT A DREADFUL PLACE....

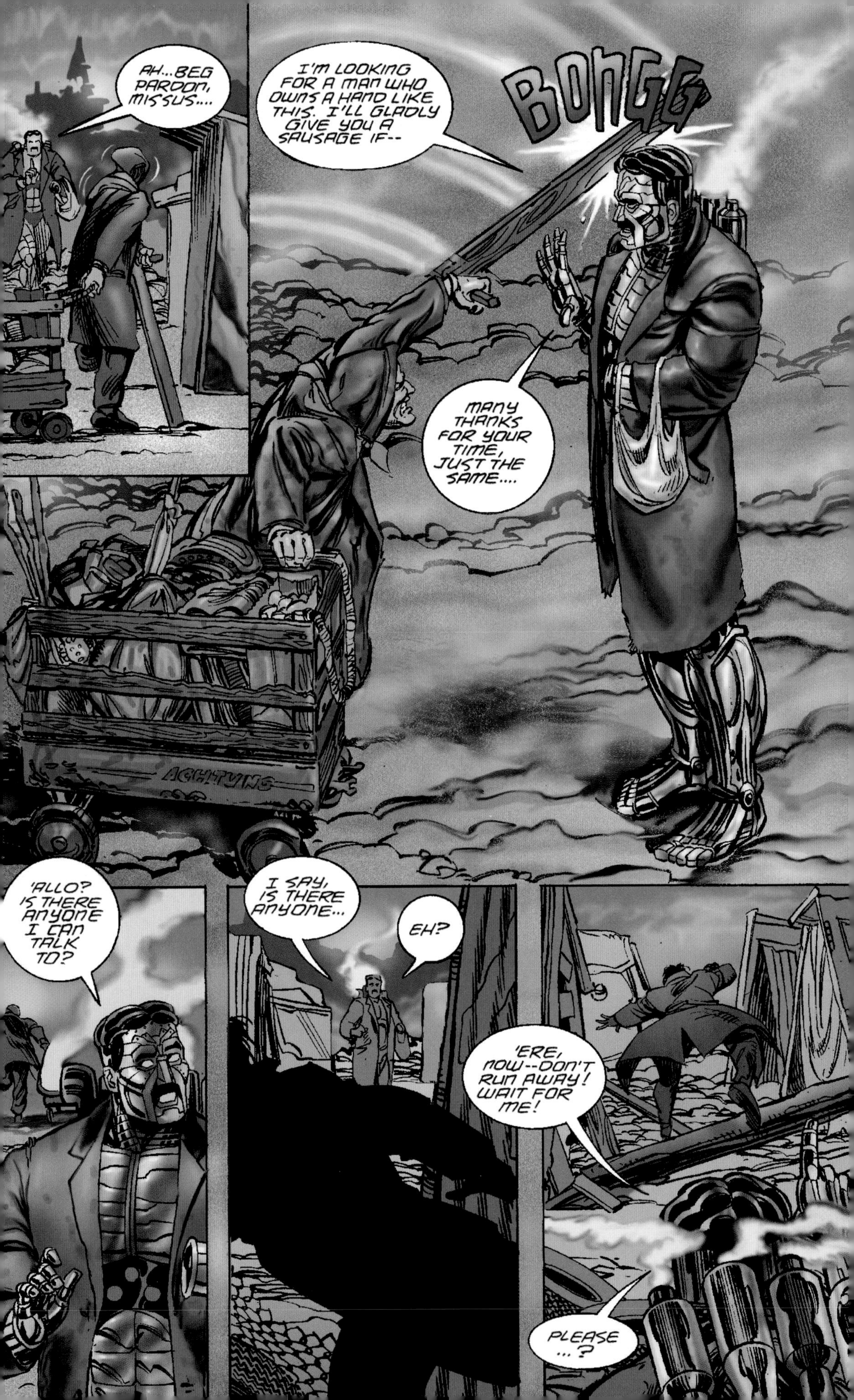
AH...BEG PARDON, MISSUS....
I'M LOOKING FOR A MAN WHO OWNS A HAND LIKE THIS. I'LL GLADLY GIVE YOU A SAUSAGE IF--
BONGG
MANY THANKS FOR YOUR TIME, JUST THE SAME....
ACHTUNG
'ALLO? IS THERE ANYONE I CAN TALK TO?
I SAY, IS THERE ANYONE...
EH?
'ERE, NOW--DON'T RUN AWAY! WAIT FOR ME!
PLEASE ...?

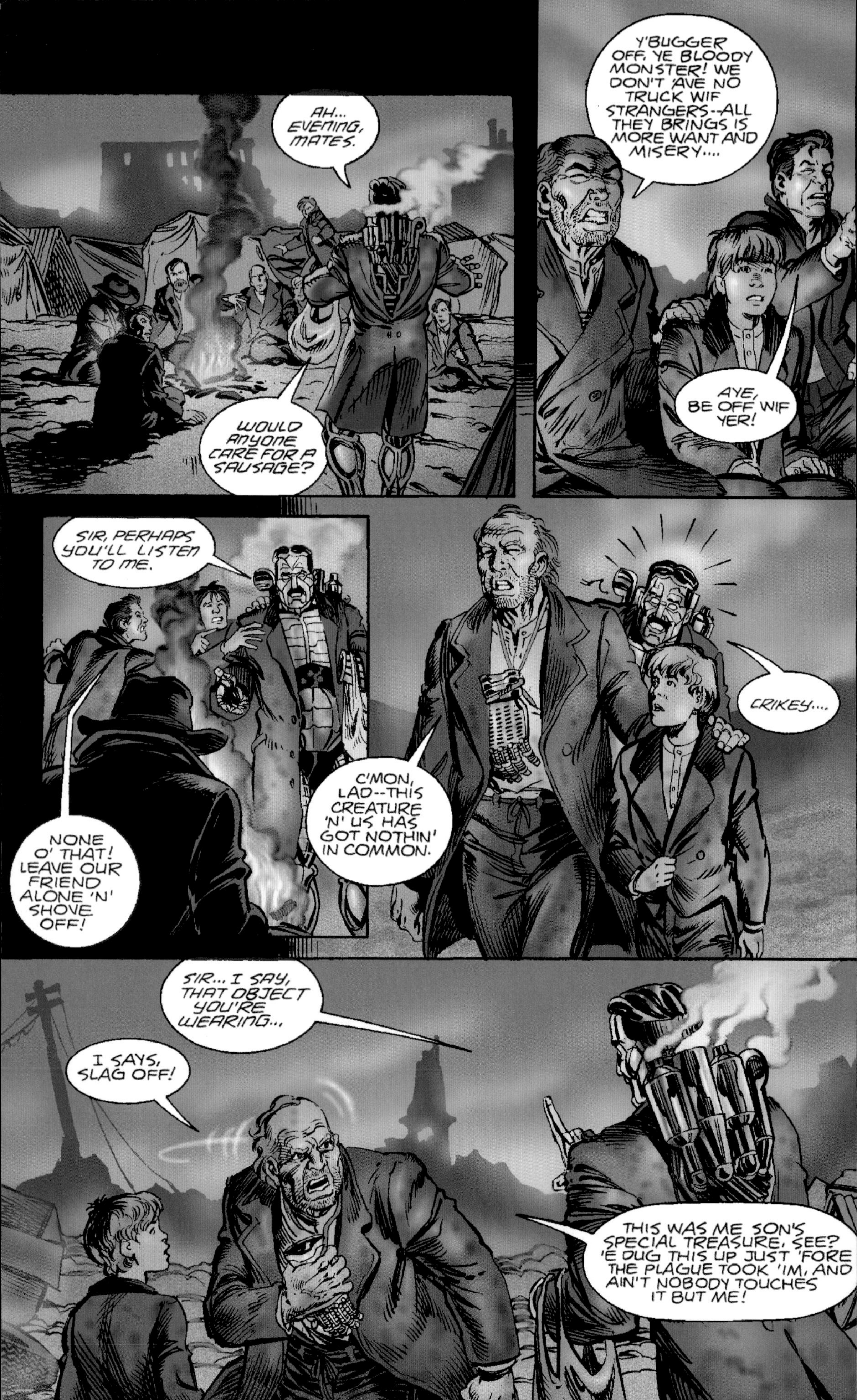
AH... EVENING, MATES.
WOULD ANYONE CARE FOR A SAUSAGE?
Y'BUGGER OFF, YE BLOODY MONSTER! WE DON'T 'AVE NO TRUCK WIF STRANGERS--ALL THEY BRINGS IS MORE WANT AND MISERY....
AYE, BE OFF WIF YER!
SIR, PERHAPS YOU'LL LISTEN TO ME.
NONE O' THAT! LEAVE OUR FRIEND ALONE 'N' SHOVE OFF!
C'MON, LAD--THIS CREATURE 'N' US HAS GOT NOTHIN' IN COMMON.
CRIKEY....
SIR... I SAY, THAT OBJECT YOU'RE WEARING...
I SAYS, SLAG OFF!
THIS WAS ME SON'S SPECIAL TREASURE, SEE? 'E DUG THIS UP JUST 'FORE THE PLAGUE TOOK 'IM, AND AIN'T NOBODY TOUCHES IT BUT ME!

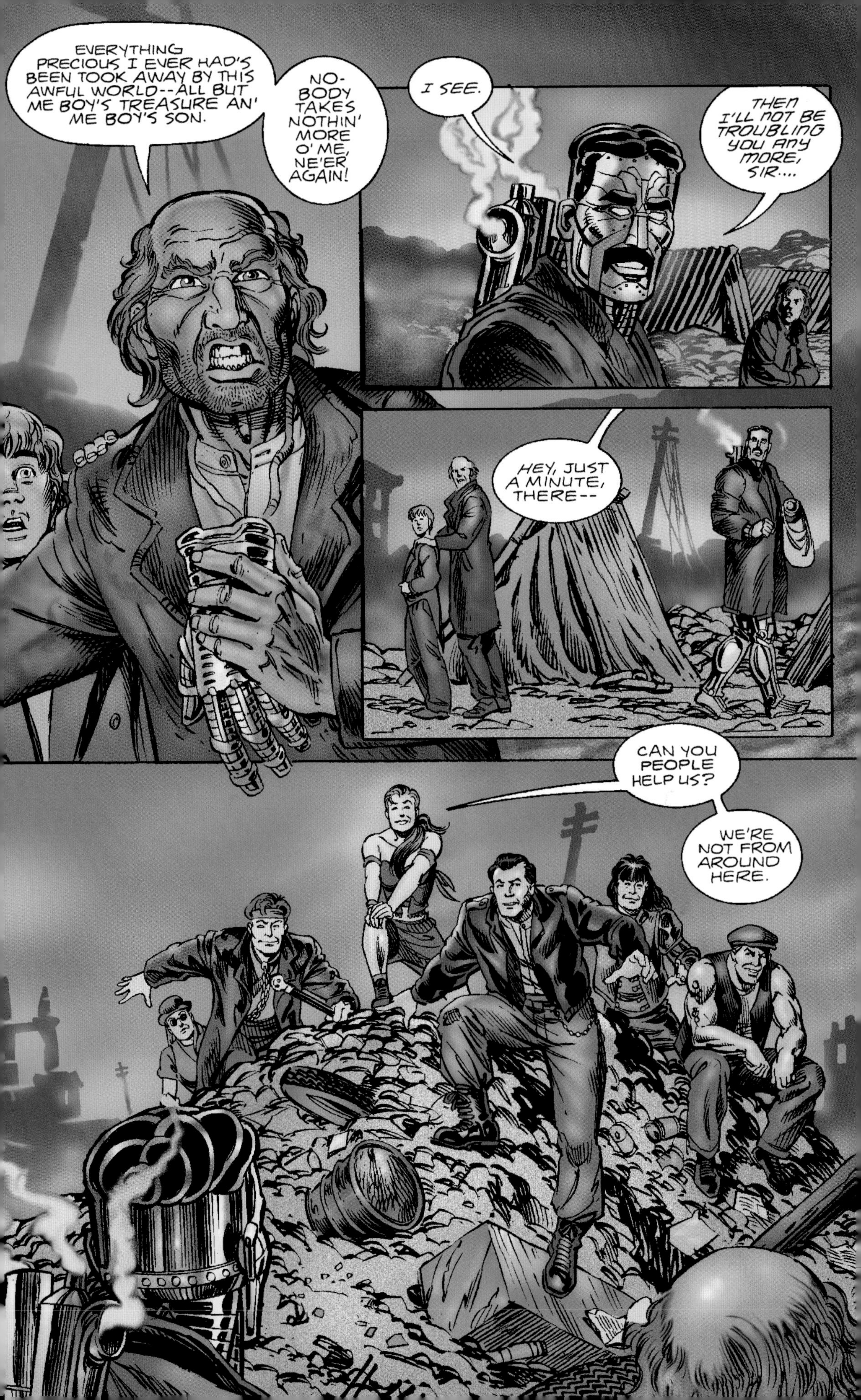
EVERYTHING PRECIOUS I EVER HAD'S BEEN TOOK AWAY BY THIS AWFUL WORLD--ALL BUT ME BOY'S TREASURE AN' ME BOY'S SON.
NO-BODY TAKES NOTHIN' MORE O' ME, NE'ER AGAIN!
I SEE.
THEN I'LL NOT BE TROUBLING YOU ANY MORE, SIR....
HEY, JUST A MINUTE, THERE--
CAN YOU PEOPLE HELP US?
WE'RE NOT FROM AROUND HERE.

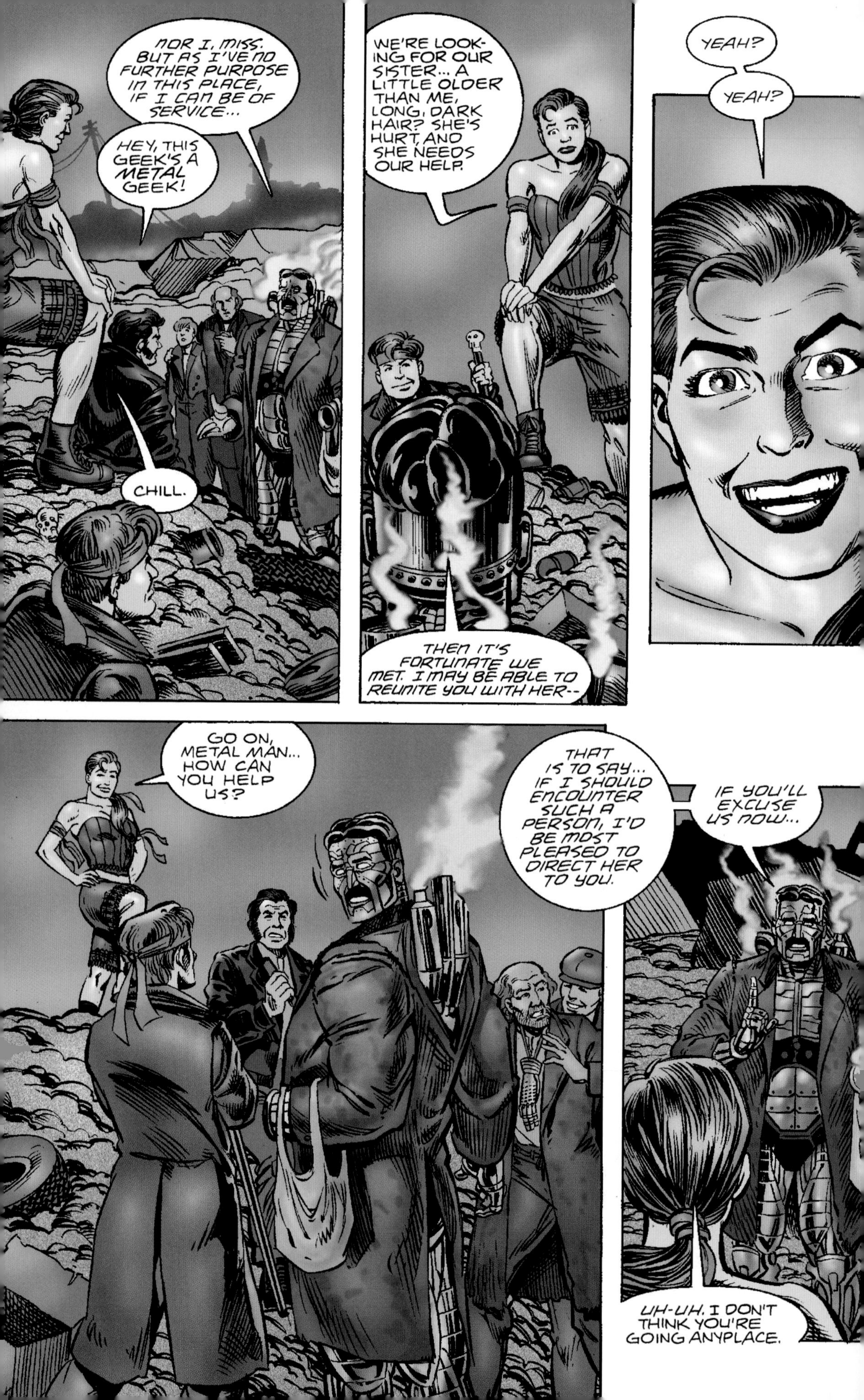
NOR I, MISS. BUT AS I'VE NO FURTHER PURPOSE IN THIS PLACE, IF I CAN BE OF SERVICE...
HEY, THIS GEEK'S A METAL GEEK!
CHILL.
WE'RE LOOKING FOR OUR SISTER... A LITTLE OLDER THAN ME, LONG, DARK HAIR? SHE'S HURT, AND SHE NEEDS OUR HELP.
THEN IT'S FORTUNATE WE MET. I MAY BE ABLE TO REUNITE YOU WITH HER--
YEAH?
YEAH?
GO ON, METAL MAN... HOW CAN YOU HELP US?
THAT IS TO SAY... IF I SHOULD ENCOUNTER SUCH A PERSON, I'D BE MOST PLEASED TO DIRECT HER TO YOU.
IF YOU'LL EXCUSE US NOW...
UH-UH. I DON'T THINK YOU'RE GOING ANYPLACE.

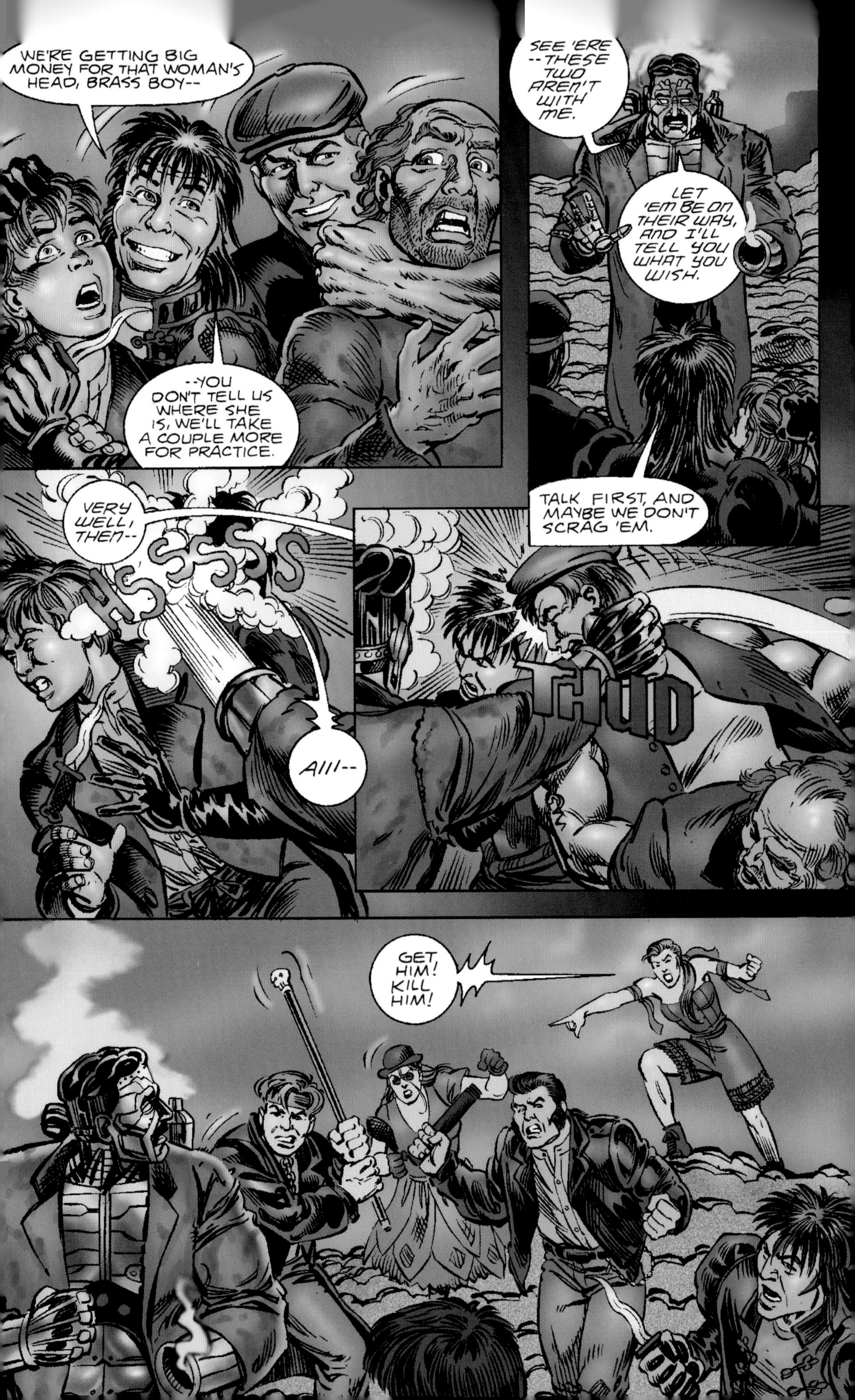
WE'RE GETTING BIG MONEY FOR THAT WOMAN'S HEAD, BRASS BOY--
--YOU DON'T TELL US WHERE SHE IS, WE'LL TAKE A COUPLE MORE FOR PRACTICE.
SEE 'ERE --THESE TWO AREN'T WITH ME.
LET 'EM BE ON THEIR WAY, AND I'LL TELL YOU WHAT YOU WISH.
TALK FIRST, AND MAYBE WE DON'T SCRAG 'EM.
VERY WELL, THEN--
HSSSSS
AIII--
THUD
GET HIM! KILL HIM!

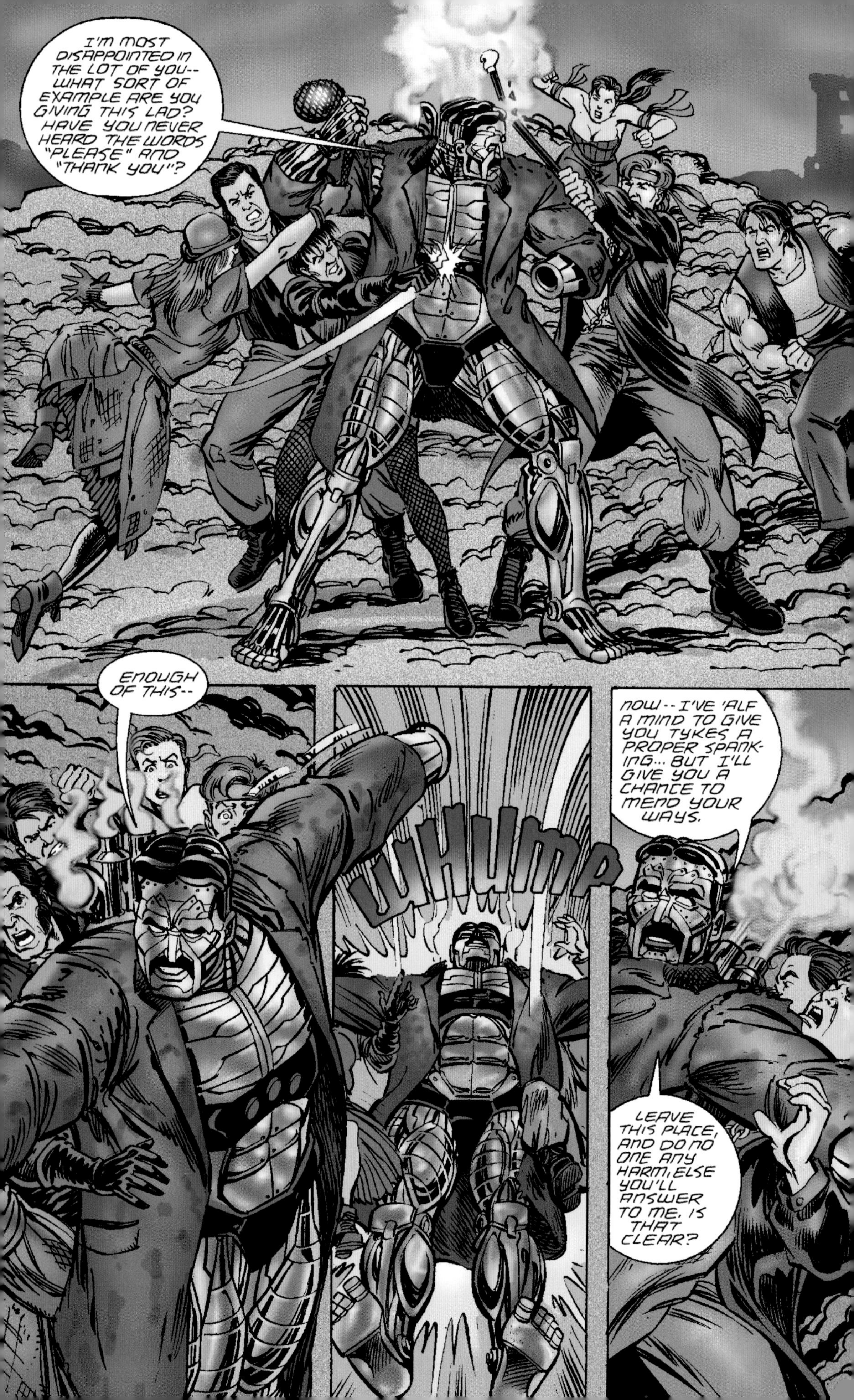
I'M MOST DISAPPOINTED IN THE LOT OF YOU-- WHAT SORT OF EXAMPLE ARE YOU GIVING THIS LAD? HAVE YOU NEVER HEARD THE WORDS "PLEASE" AND "THANK YOU"?
ENOUGH OF THIS--
WHUMP
NOW--I'VE 'ALF A MIND TO GIVE YOU TYKES A PROPER SPANKING... BUT I'LL GIVE YOU A CHANCE TO MEND YOUR WAYS.
LEAVE THIS PLACE, AND DO NO ONE ANY HARM, ELSE YOU'LL ANSWER TO ME. IS THAT CLEAR?

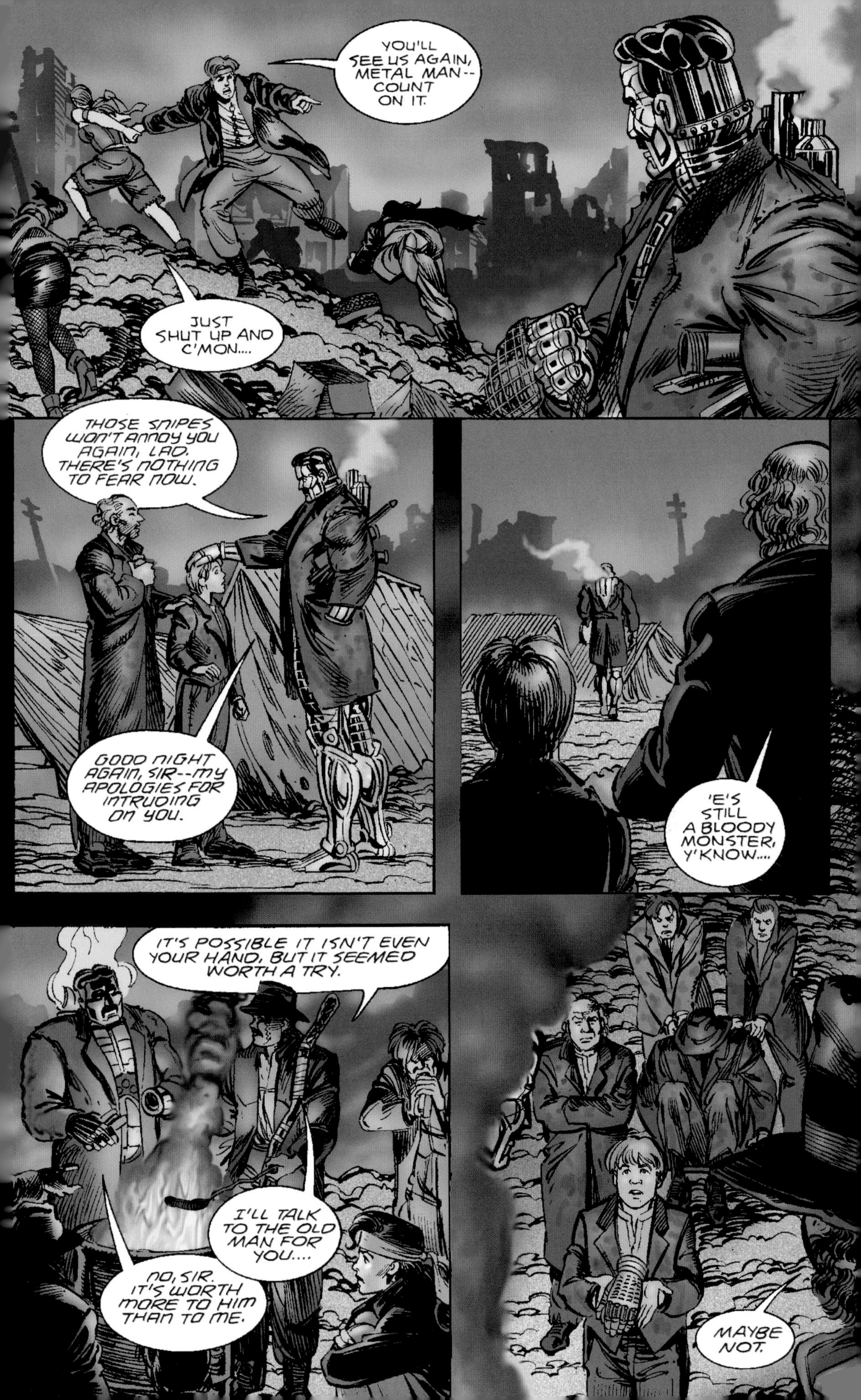
YOU'LL SEE US AGAIN, METAL MAN-- COUNT ON IT.
JUST SHUT UP AND C'MON....
THOSE SNIPES WON'T ANNOY YOU AGAIN, LAD. THERE'S NOTHING TO FEAR NOW.
GOOD NIGHT AGAIN, SIR--MY APOLOGIES FOR INTRUDING ON YOU.
'E'S STILL A BLOODY MONSTER, Y'KNOW....
IT'S POSSIBLE IT ISN'T EVEN YOUR HAND, BUT IT SEEMED WORTH A TRY.
I'LL TALK TO THE OLD MAN FOR YOU....
NO, SIR. IT'S WORTH MORE TO HIM THAN TO ME.
MAYBE NOT.

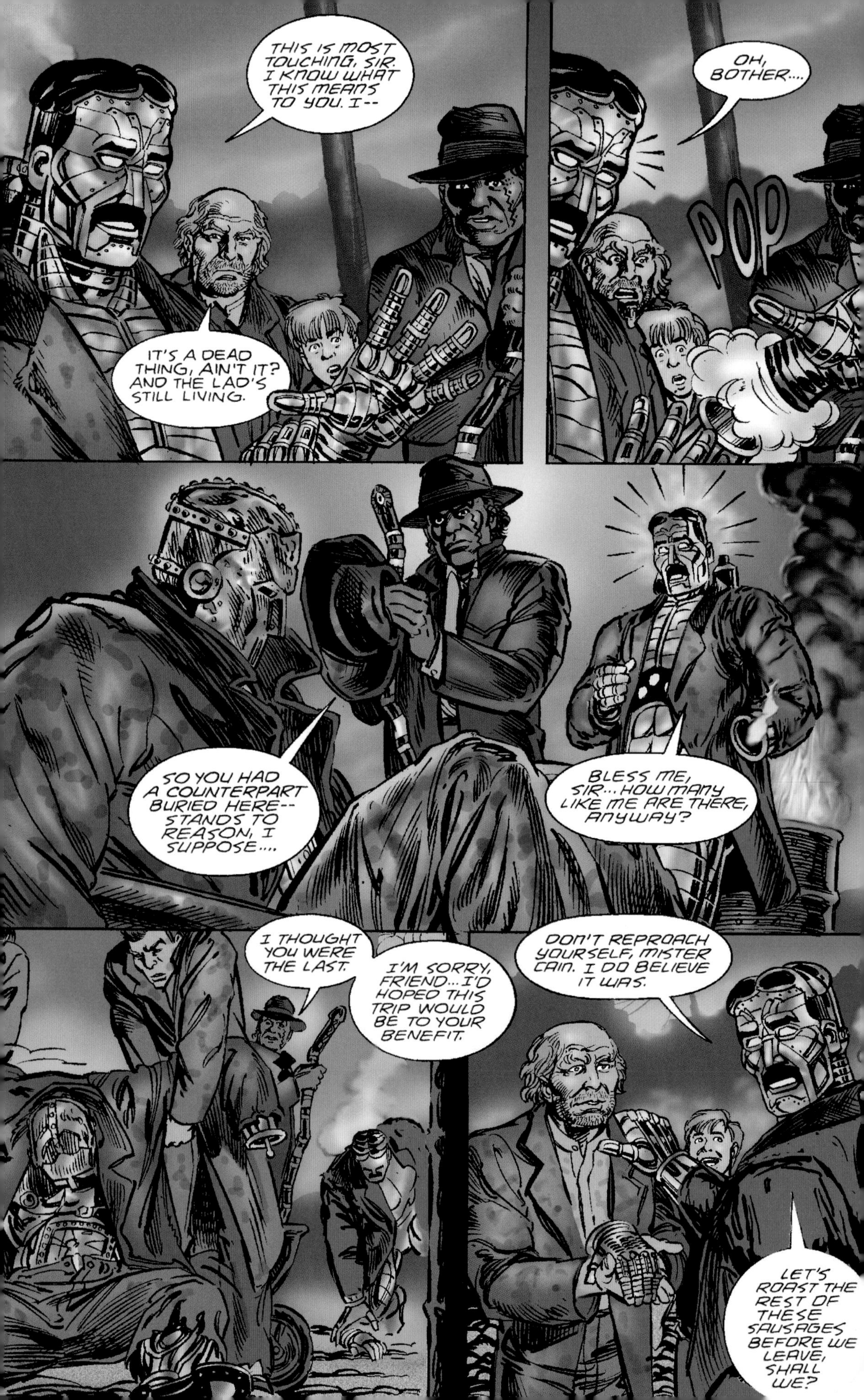
THIS IS MOST TOUCHING, SIR. I KNOW WHAT THIS MEANS TO YOU. I--
IT'S A DEAD THING, AIN'T IT? AND THE LAD'S STILL LIVING.
OH, BOTHER....
POP
SO YOU HAD A COUNTERPART BURIED HERE-- STANDS TO REASON, I SUPPOSE....
BLESS ME, SIR... HOW MANY LIKE ME ARE THERE, ANYWAY?
I THOUGHT YOU WERE THE LAST.
I'M SORRY, FRIEND... I'D HOPED THIS TRIP WOULD BE TO YOUR BENEFIT.
DON'T REPROACH YOURSELF, MISTER CAIN. I DO BELIEVE IT WAS.
LET'S ROAST THE REST OF THESE SAUSAGES BEFORE WE LEAVE, SHALL WE?

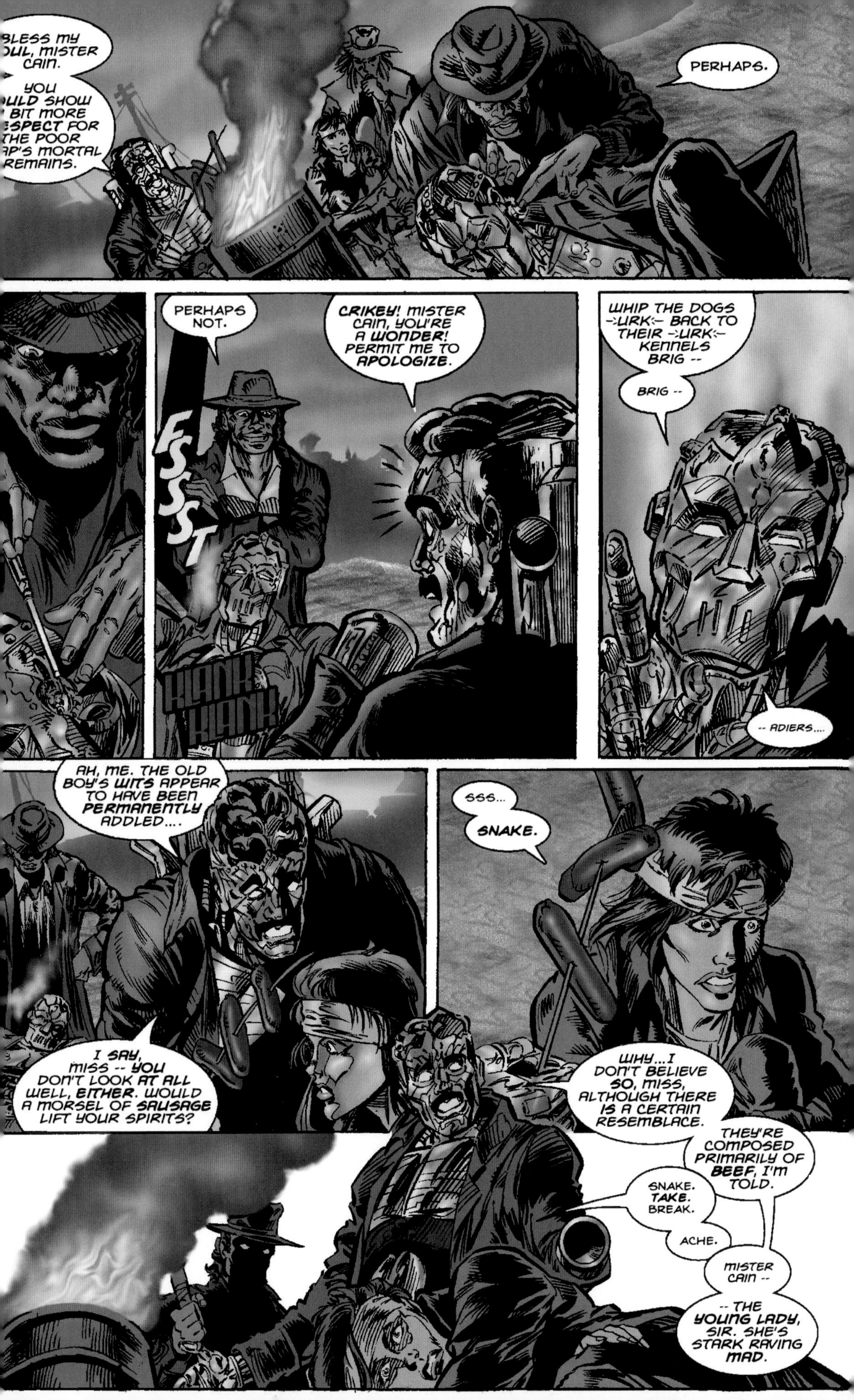
BLESS MY OUL, MISTER CAIN.
YOU ULD SHOW BIT MORE ESPECT FOR THE POOR AP'S MORTAL REMAINS.
PERHAPS.
PERHAPS NOT.
FSSST
KLANK KLANK
CRIKEY! MISTER CAIN, YOU'RE A WONDER! PERMIT ME TO APOLOGIZE.
WHIP THE DOGS -URK- BACK TO THEIR -URK- KENNELS BRIG --
BRIG --
-- ADIERS....
AH, ME. THE OLD BOY'S WITS APPEAR TO HAVE BEEN PERMANENTLY ADDLED....
I SAY, MISS -- YOU DON'T LOOK AT ALL WELL, EITHER. WOULD A MORSEL OF SAUSAGE LIFT YOUR SPIRITS?
SSS...
SNAKE.
WHY...I DON'T BELIEVE SO, MISS, ALTHOUGH THERE IS A CERTAIN RESEMBLACE.
THEY'RE COMPOSED PRIMARILY OF BEEF, I'M TOLD.
SNAKE. TAKE. BREAK.
ACHE.
MISTER CAIN --
-- THE YOUNG LADY, SIR. SHE'S STARK RAVING MAD.

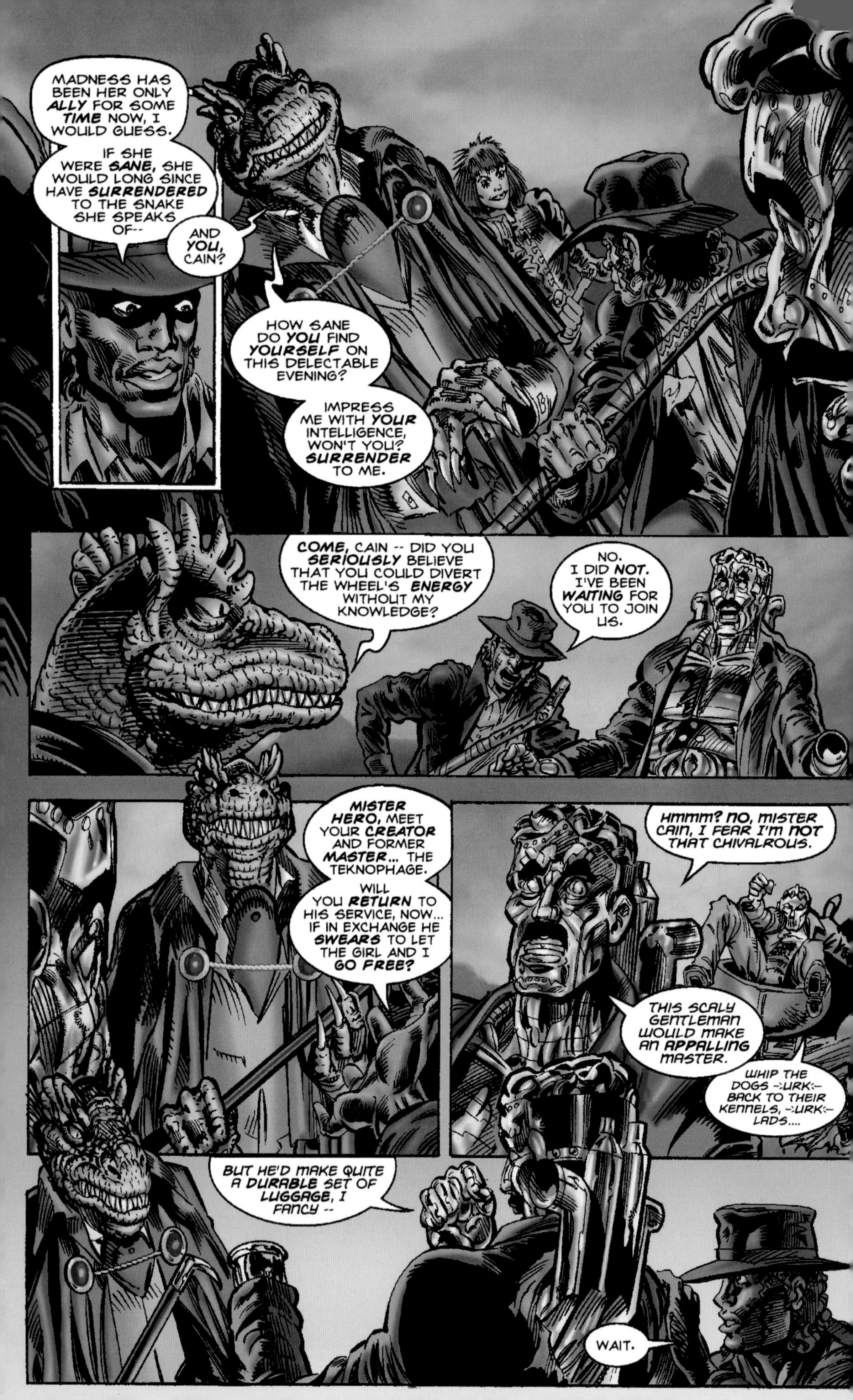
MADNESS HAS BEEN HER ONLY ALLY FOR SOME TIME NOW, I WOULD GUESS.
IF SHE WERE SANE, SHE WOULD LONG SINCE HAVE SURRENDERED TO THE SNAKE SHE SPEAKS OF--
AND YOU, CAIN?
HOW SANE DO YOU FIND YOURSELF ON THIS DELECTABLE EVENING?
IMPRESS ME WITH YOUR INTELLIGENCE, WON'T YOU? SURRENDER TO ME.
COME, CAIN -- DID YOU SERIOUSLY BELIEVE THAT YOU COULD DIVERT THE WHEEL'S ENERGY WITHOUT MY KNOWLEDGE?
NO. I DID NOT. I'VE BEEN WAITING FOR YOU TO JOIN US.
MISTER HERO, MEET YOUR CREATOR AND FORMER MASTER... THE TEKNOPHAGE.
WILL YOU RETURN TO HIS SERVICE, NOW... IF IN EXCHANGE HE SWEARS TO LET THE GIRL AND I GO FREE?
HMMM? NO, MISTER CAIN, I FEAR I'M NOT THAT CHIVALROUS.
THIS SCALY GENTLEMAN WOULD MAKE AN APPALLING MASTER.
WHIP THE DOGS -URK- BACK TO THEIR KENNELS, -URK- LADS....
BUT HE'D MAKE QUITE A DURABLE SET OF LUGGAGE, I FANCY --
WAIT.

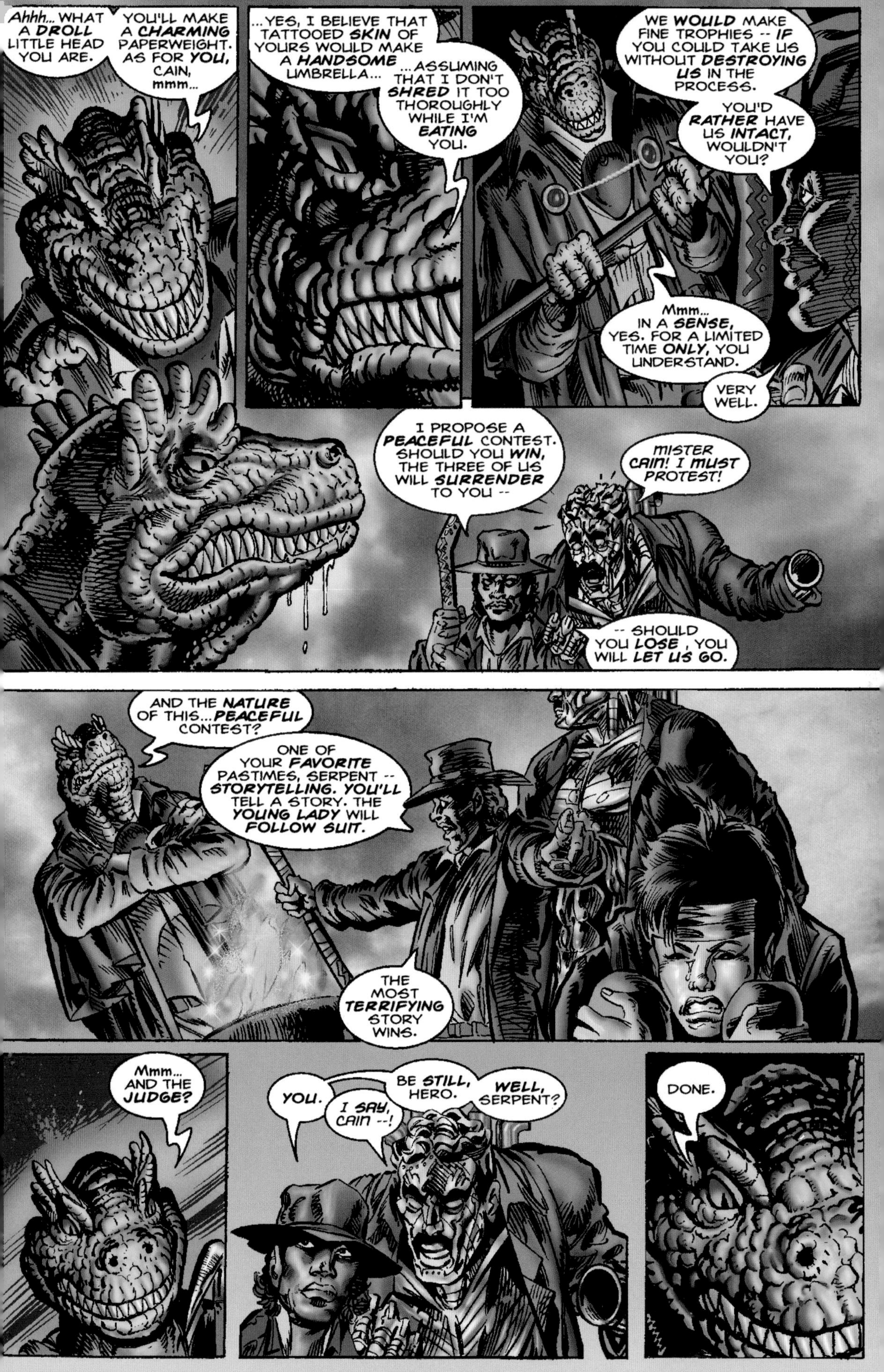
Ahhh... WHAT A DROLL LITTLE HEAD YOU ARE.
YOU'LL MAKE A CHARMING PAPERWEIGHT. AS FOR YOU, CAIN, mmm...
...YES, I BELIEVE THAT TATTOOED SKIN OF YOURS WOULD MAKE A HANDSOME UMBRELLA...
...ASSUMING THAT I DON'T SHRED IT TOO THOROUGHLY WHILE I'M EATING YOU.
WE WOULD MAKE FINE TROPHIES -- IF YOU COULD TAKE US WITHOUT DESTROYING US IN THE PROCESS.
YOU'D RATHER HAVE US INTACT, WOULDN'T YOU?
Mmm... IN A SENSE, YES. FOR A LIMITED TIME ONLY, YOU UNDERSTAND.
VERY WELL.
I PROPOSE A PEACEFUL CONTEST. SHOULD YOU WIN, THE THREE OF US WILL SURRENDER TO YOU --
MISTER CAIN! I MUST PROTEST!
-- SHOULD YOU LOSE , YOU WILL LET US GO.
AND THE NATURE OF THIS...PEACEFUL CONTEST?
ONE OF YOUR FAVORITE PASTIMES, SERPENT -- STORYTELLING. YOU'LL TELL A STORY. THE YOUNG LADY WILL FOLLOW SUIT.
THE MOST TERRIFYING STORY WINS.
Mmm... AND THE JUDGE?
YOU.
I SAY, CAIN --!
BE STILL, HERO.
WELL, SERPENT?
DONE.

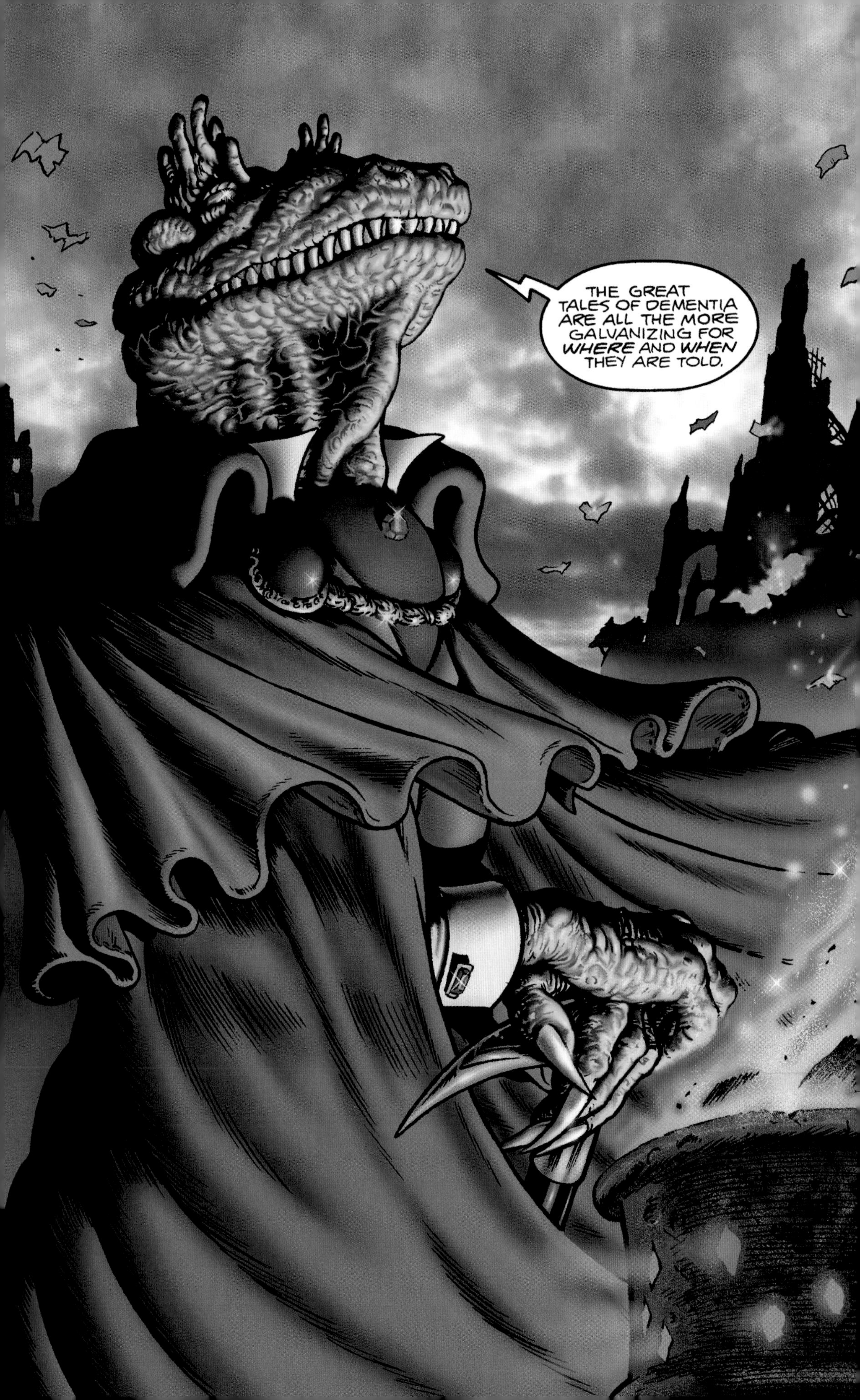
THE GREAT TALES OF DEMENTIA ARE ALL THE MORE GALVANIZING FOR *WHERE* AND *WHEN* THEY ARE TOLD.

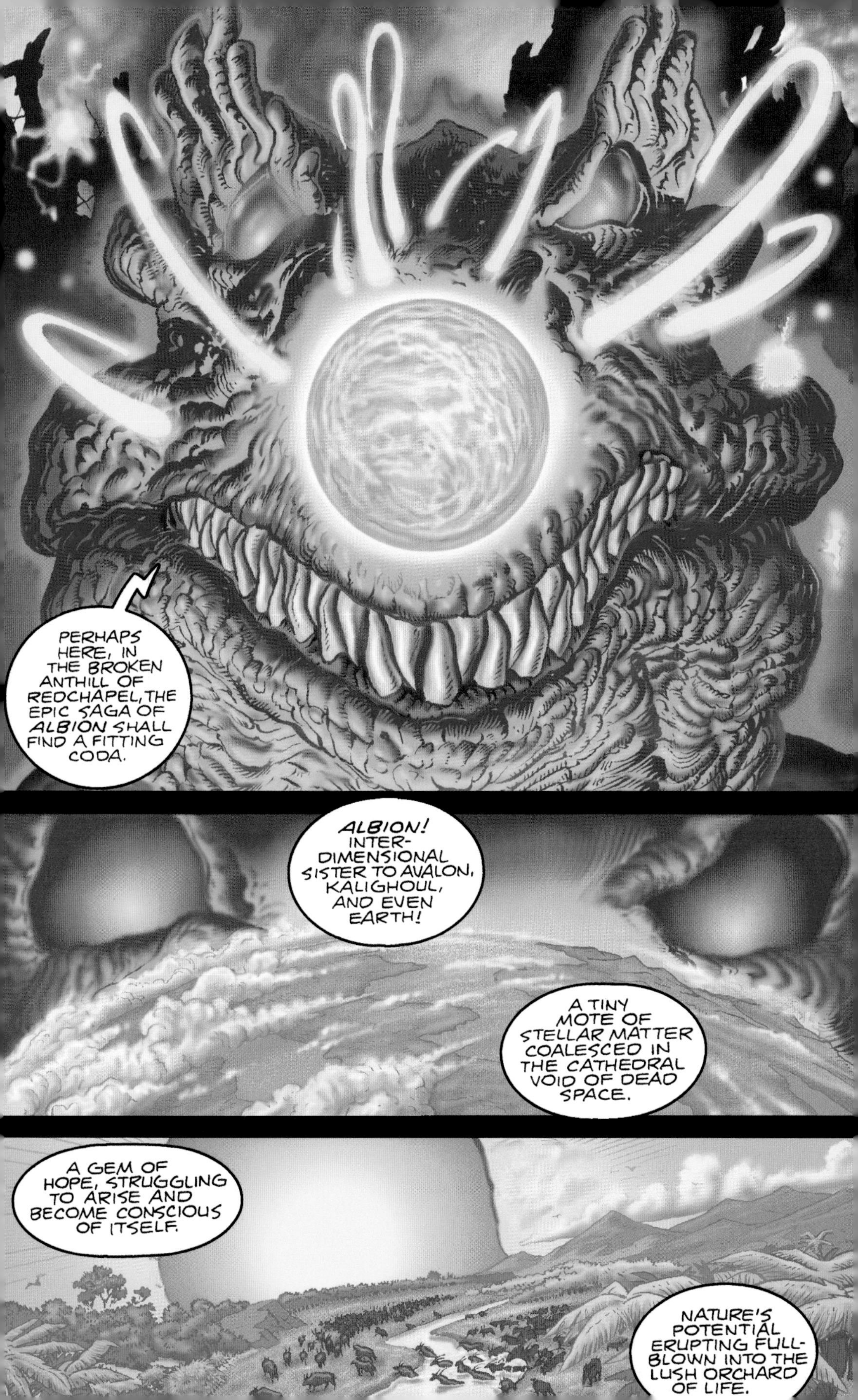
PERHAPS HERE, IN THE BROKEN ANTHILL OF REDCHAPEL, THE EPIC SAGA OF ALBION SHALL FIND A FITTING CODA.
ALBION! INTER-DIMENSIONAL SISTER TO AVALON, KALIGHOUL, AND EVEN EARTH!
A TINY MOTE OF STELLAR MATTER COALESCED IN THE CATHEDRAL VOID OF DEAD SPACE.
A GEM OF HOPE, STRUGGLING TO ARISE AND BECOME CONSCIOUS OF ITSELF.
NATURE'S POTENTIAL ERUPTING FULL-BLOWN INTO THE LUSH ORCHARD OF LIFE.

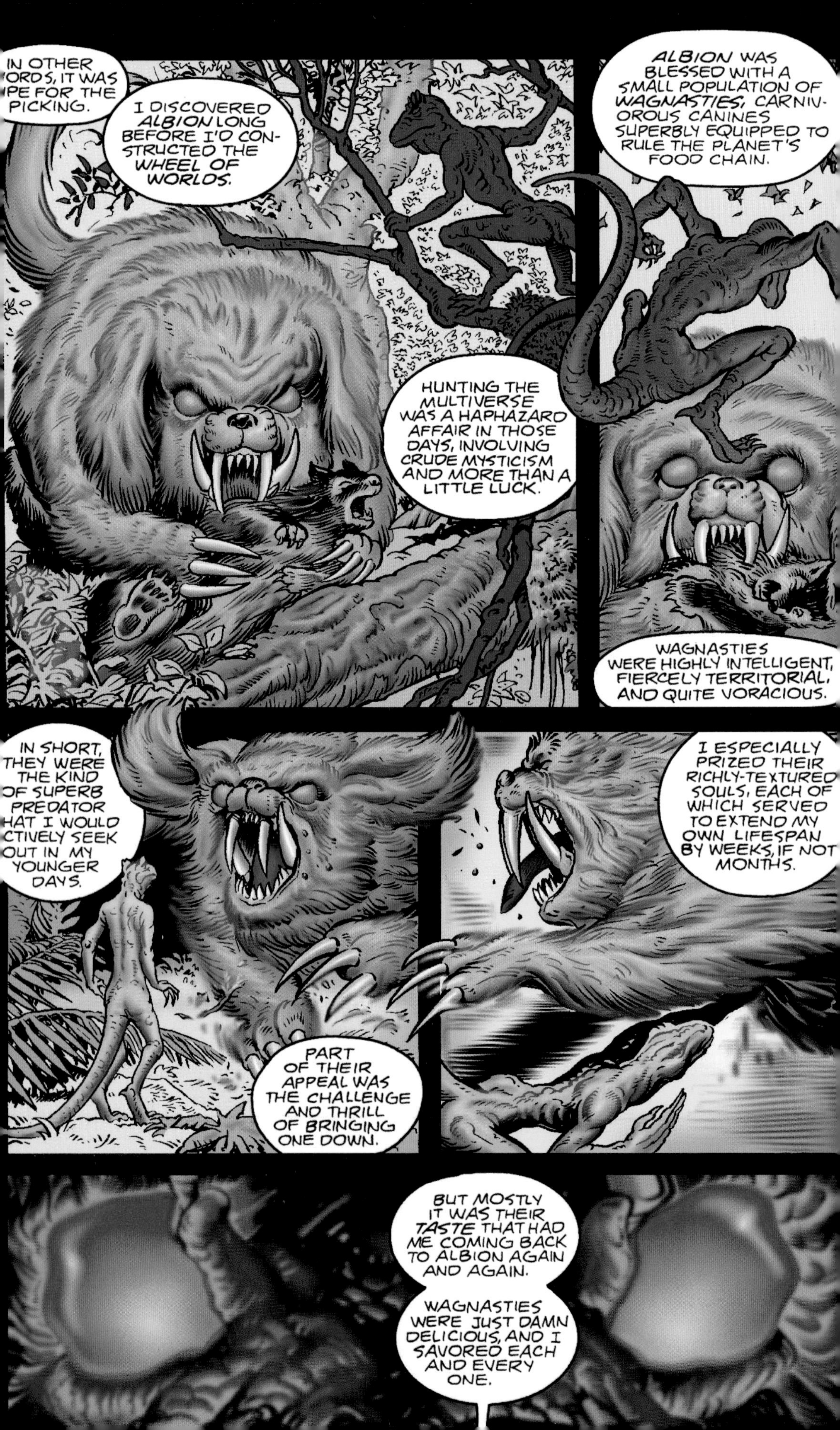
IN OTHER ORDS, IT WAS IPE FOR THE PICKING.
I DISCOVERED ALBION LONG BEFORE I'D CONSTRUCTED THE WHEEL OF WORLDS.
ALBION WAS BLESSED WITH A SMALL POPULATION OF WAGNASTIES, CARNIVOROUS CANINES SUPERBLY EQUIPPED TO RULE THE PLANET'S FOOD CHAIN.
HUNTING THE MULTIVERSE WAS A HAPHAZARD AFFAIR IN THOSE DAYS, INVOLVING CRUDE MYSTICISM AND MORE THAN A LITTLE LUCK.
WAGNASTIES WERE HIGHLY INTELLIGENT, FIERCELY TERRITORIAL, AND QUITE VORACIOUS.
IN SHORT, THEY WERE THE KIND OF SUPERB PREDATOR HAT I WOULD CTIVELY SEEK OUT IN MY YOUNGER DAYS.
I ESPECIALLY PRIZED THEIR RICHLY-TEXTURED SOULS, EACH OF WHICH SERVED TO EXTEND MY OWN LIFESPAN BY WEEKS, IF NOT MONTHS.
PART OF THEIR APPEAL WAS THE CHALLENGE AND THRILL OF BRINGING ONE DOWN.
BUT MOSTLY IT WAS THEIR TASTE THAT HAD ME COMING BACK TO ALBION AGAIN AND AGAIN.
WAGNASTIES WERE JUST DAMN DELICIOUS, AND I SAVORED EACH AND EVERY ONE.

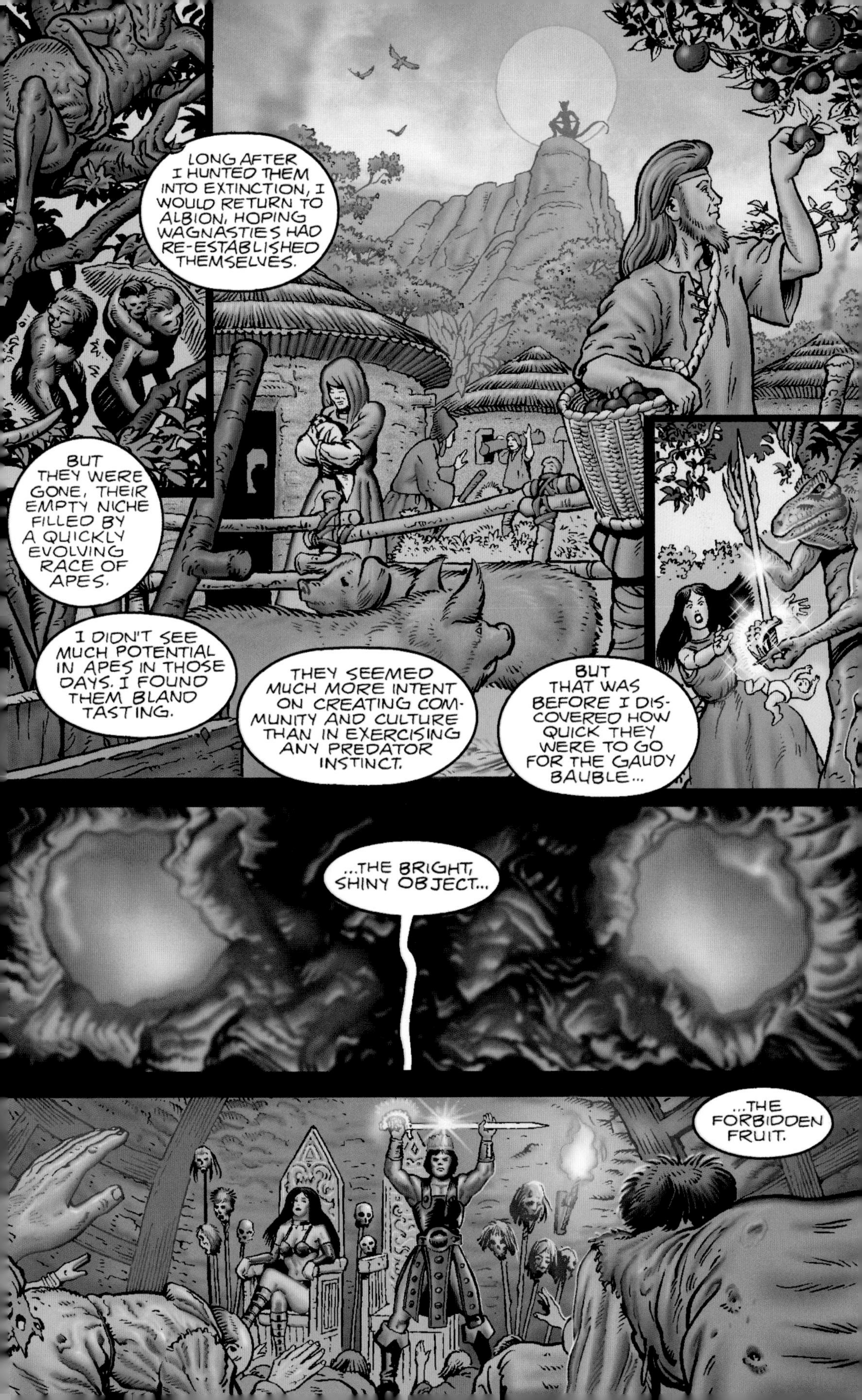
LONG AFTER I HUNTED THEM INTO EXTINCTION, I WOULD RETURN TO ALBION, HOPING WAGNASTIES HAD RE-ESTABLISHED THEMSELVES.
BUT THEY WERE GONE, THEIR EMPTY NICHE FILLED BY A QUICKLY EVOLVING RACE OF APES.
I DIDN'T SEE MUCH POTENTIAL IN APES IN THOSE DAYS. I FOUND THEM BLAND TASTING.
THEY SEEMED MUCH MORE INTENT ON CREATING COM-MUNITY AND CULTURE THAN IN EXERCISING ANY PREDATOR INSTINCT.
BUT THAT WAS BEFORE I DIS-COVERED HOW QUICK THEY WERE TO GO FOR THE GAUDY BAUBLE...
...THE BRIGHT, SHINY OBJECT...
...THE FORBIDDEN FRUIT.

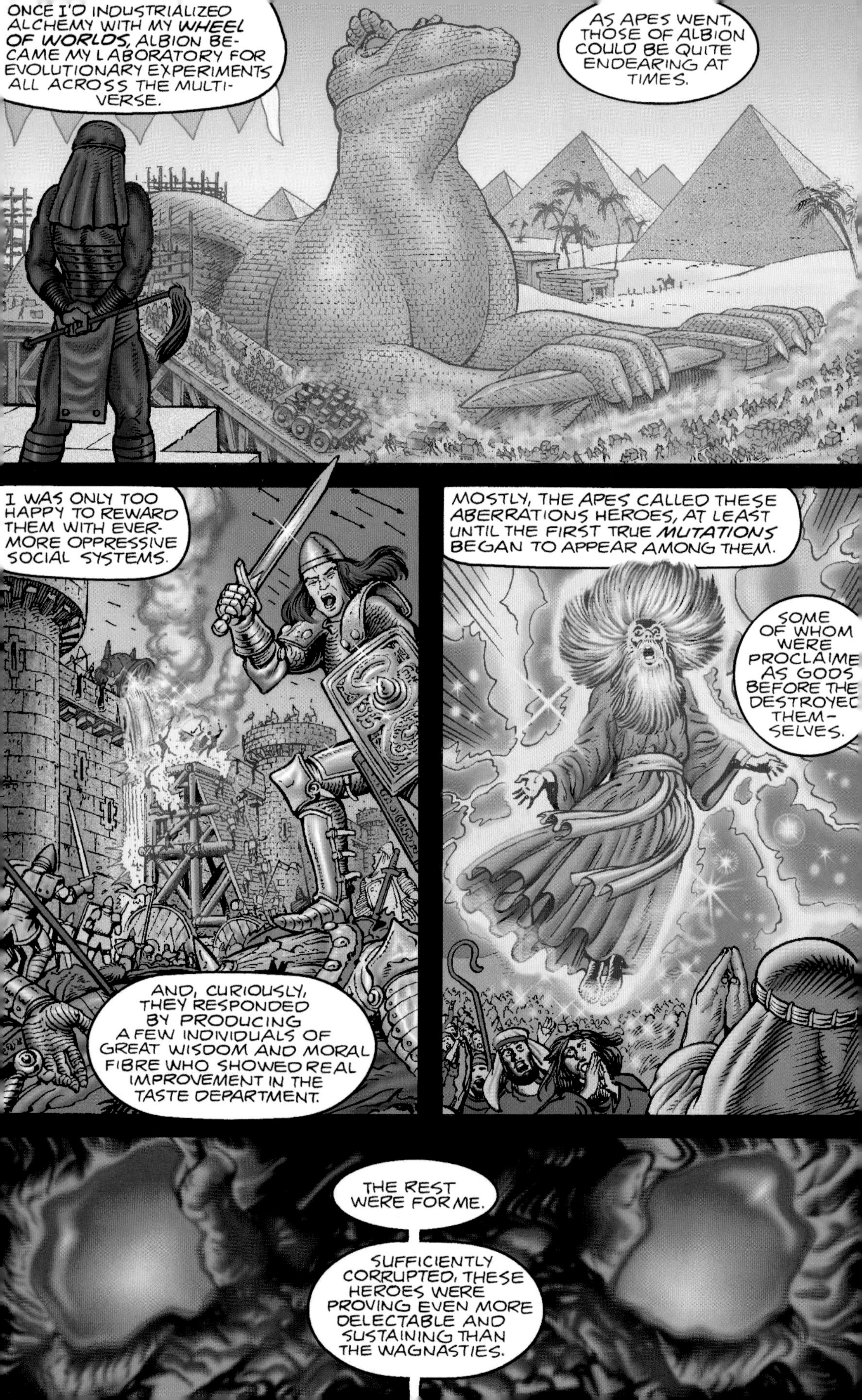

ONCE I'D INDUSTRIALIZED ALCHEMY WITH MY *WHEEL OF WORLDS*, ALBION BECAME MY LABORATORY FOR EVOLUTIONARY EXPERIMENTS ALL ACROSS THE MULTIVERSE.
AS APES WENT, THOSE OF ALBION COULD BE QUITE ENDEARING AT TIMES.
I WAS ONLY TOO HAPPY TO REWARD THEM WITH EVERMORE OPPRESSIVE SOCIAL SYSTEMS.
AND, CURIOUSLY, THEY RESPONDED BY PRODUCING A FEW INDIVIDUALS OF GREAT WISDOM AND MORAL FIBRE WHO SHOWED REAL IMPROVEMENT IN THE TASTE DEPARTMENT.
MOSTLY, THE APES CALLED THESE ABERRATIONS HEROES, AT LEAST UNTIL THE FIRST TRUE *MUTATIONS* BEGAN TO APPEAR AMONG THEM.
SOME OF WHOM WERE PROCLAIME AS GODS BEFORE THE DESTROYE THEM-SELVES.
THE REST WERE FOR ME.
SUFFICIENTLY CORRUPTED, THESE HEROES WERE PROVING EVEN MORE DELECTABLE AND SUSTAINING THAN THE WAGNASTIES.

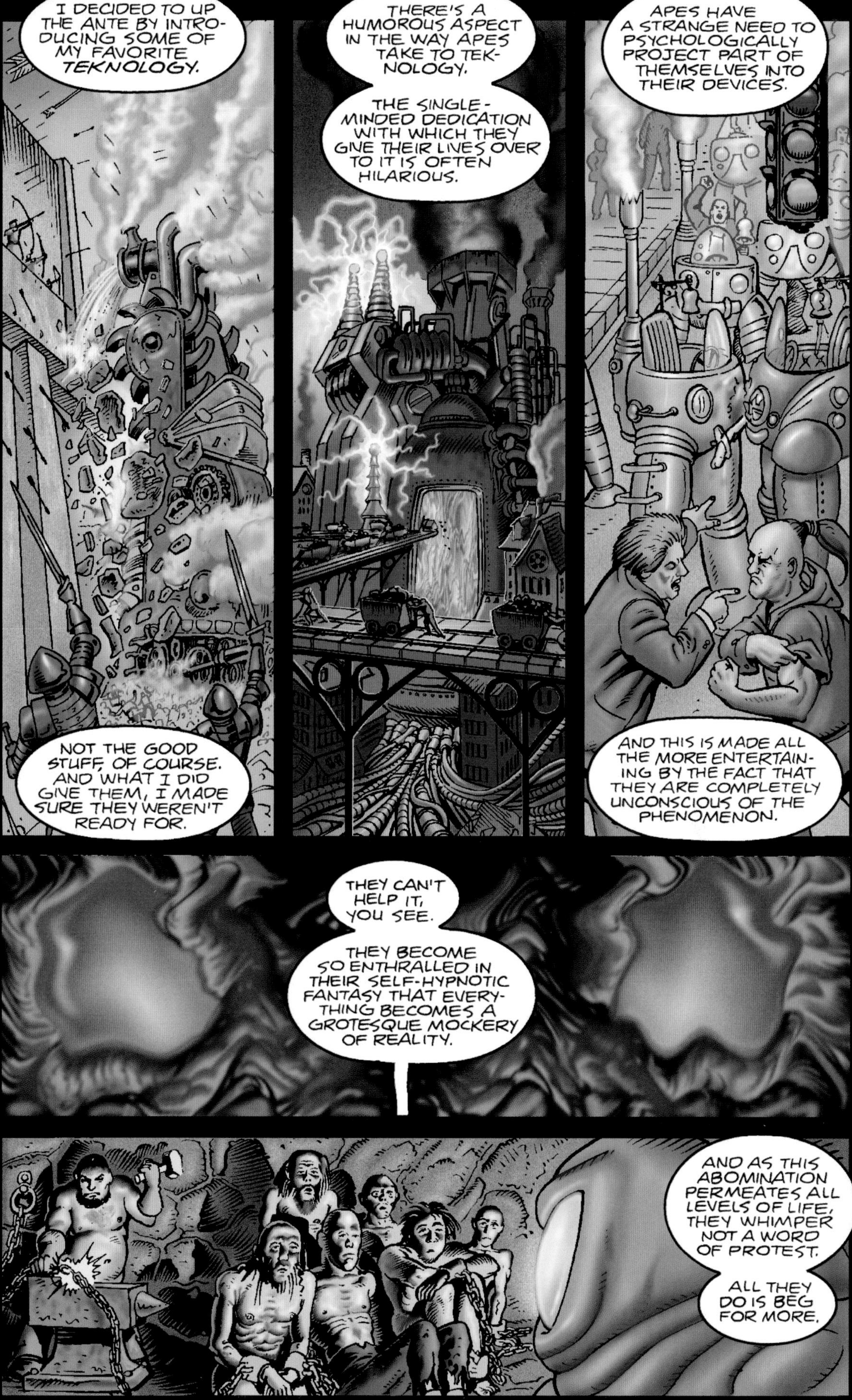
I DECIDED TO UP THE ANTE BY INTRODUCING SOME OF MY FAVORITE TEKNOLOGY.
NOT THE GOOD STUFF, OF COURSE. AND WHAT I DID GIVE THEM, I MADE SURE THEY WEREN'T READY FOR.
THERE'S A HUMOROUS ASPECT IN THE WAY APES TAKE TO TEKNOLOGY.
THE SINGLE-MINDED DEDICATION WITH WHICH THEY GIVE THEIR LIVES OVER TO IT IS OFTEN HILARIOUS.
APES HAVE A STRANGE NEED TO PSYCHOLOGICALLY PROJECT PART OF THEMSELVES INTO THEIR DEVICES.
AND THIS IS MADE ALL THE MORE ENTERTAINING BY THE FACT THAT THEY ARE COMPLETELY UNCONSCIOUS OF THE PHENOMENON.
THEY CAN'T HELP IT, YOU SEE.
THEY BECOME SO ENTHRALLED IN THEIR SELF-HYPNOTIC FANTASY THAT EVERYTHING BECOMES A GROTESQUE MOCKERY OF REALITY.
AND AS THIS ABOMINATION PERMEATES ALL LEVELS OF LIFE, THEY WHIMPER NOT A WORD OF PROTEST.
ALL THEY DO IS BEG FOR MORE.

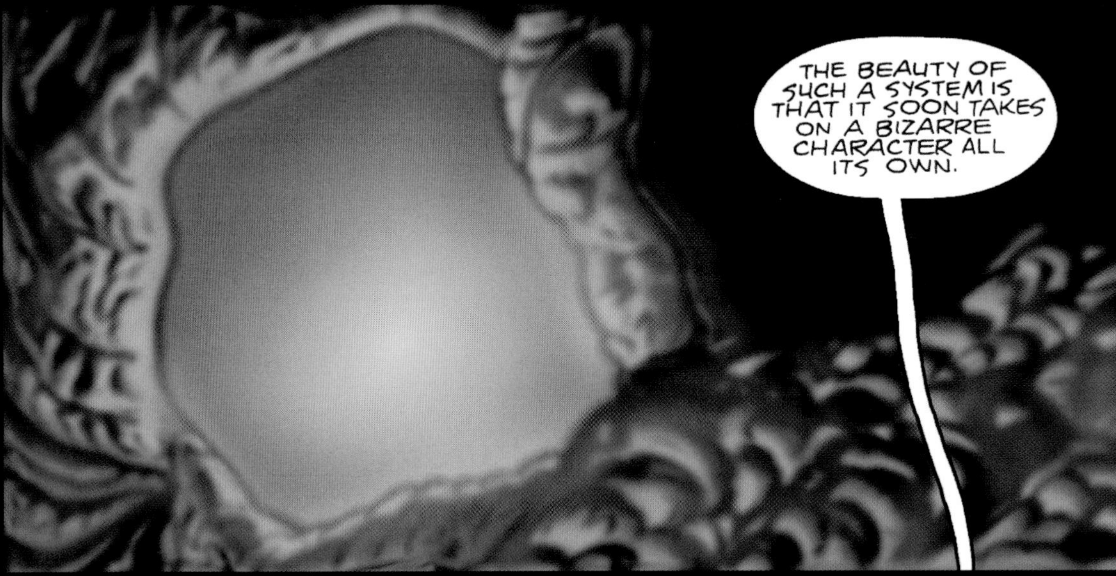
THE BEAUTY OF SUCH A SYSTEM IS THAT IT SOON TAKES ON A BIZARRE CHARACTER ALL ITS OWN.

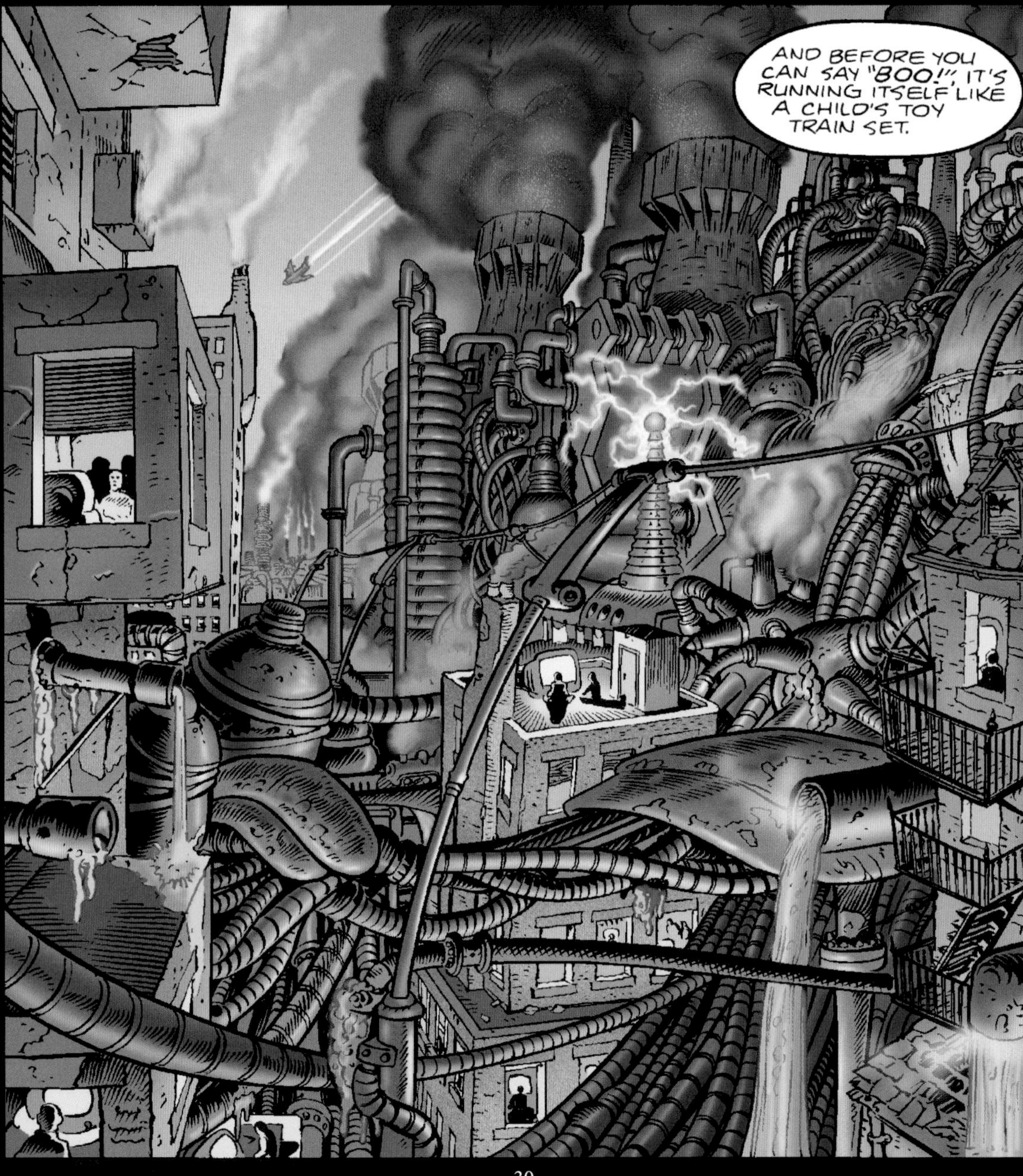
AND BEFORE YOU CAN SAY "BOO!," IT'S RUNNING ITSELF LIKE A CHILD'S TOY TRAIN SET.

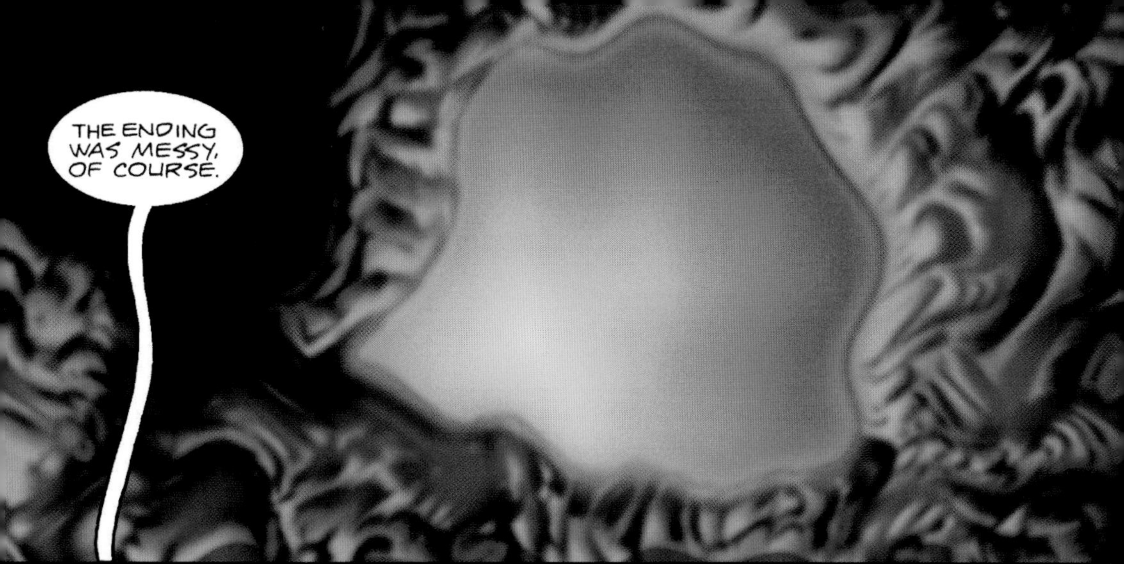
THE ENDING WAS MESSY, OF COURSE.

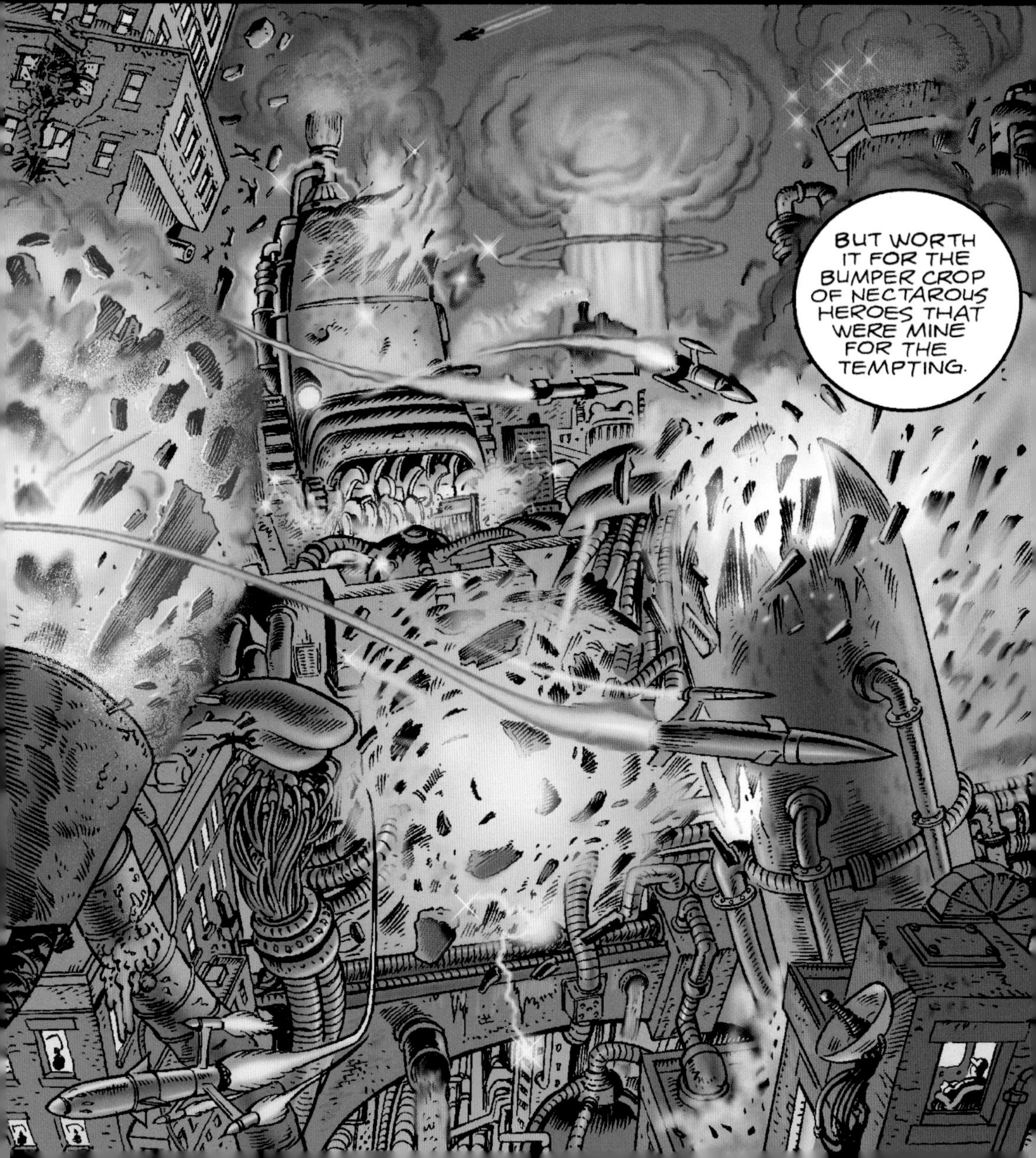
BUT WORTH IT FOR THE BUMPER CROP OF NECTAROUS HEROES THAT WERE MINE FOR THE TEMPTING.

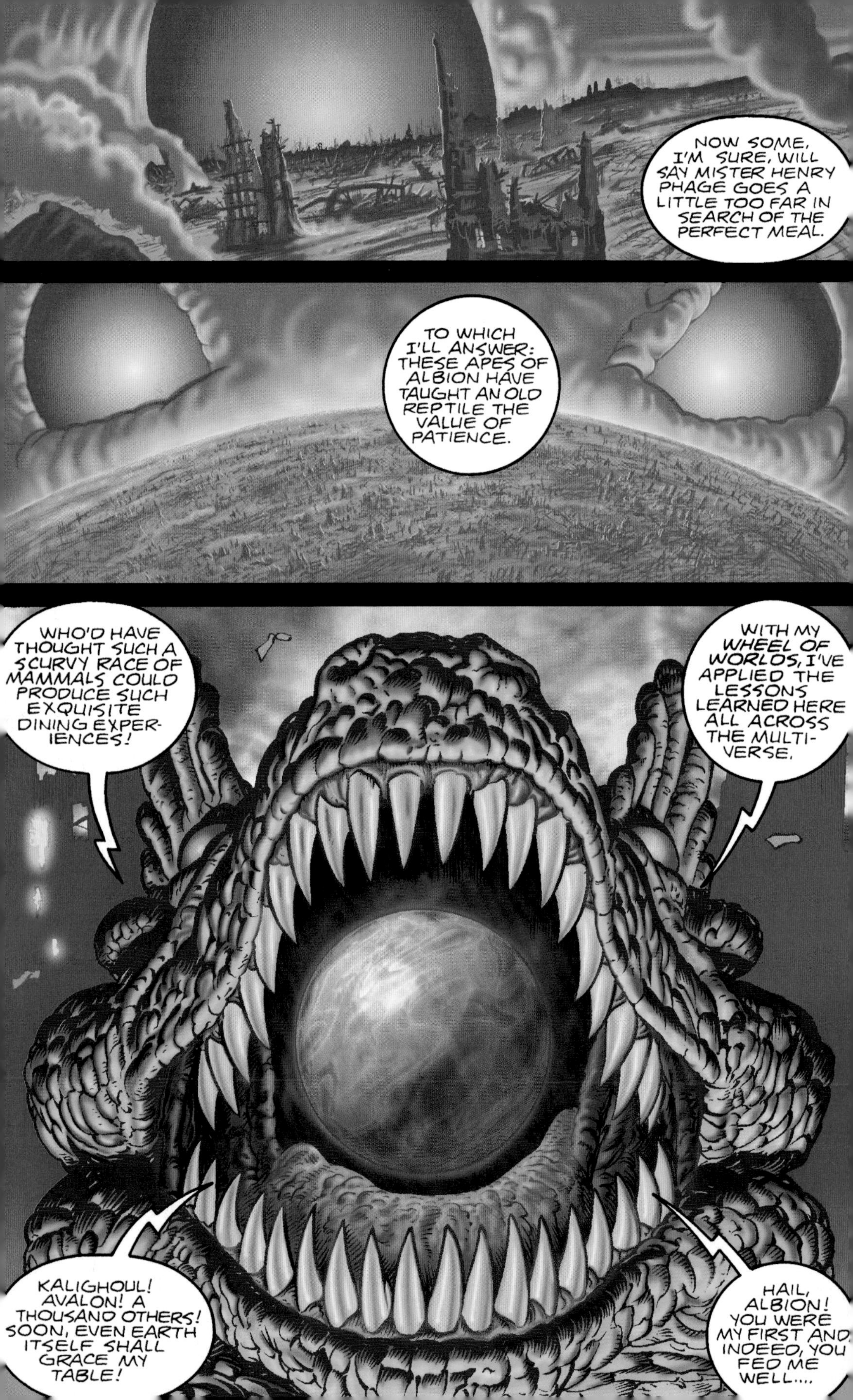
NOW SOME, I'M SURE, WILL SAY MISTER HENRY PHAGE GOES A LITTLE TOO FAR IN SEARCH OF THE PERFECT MEAL.
TO WHICH I'LL ANSWER: THESE APES OF ALBION HAVE TAUGHT AN OLD REPTILE THE VALUE OF PATIENCE.
WHO'D HAVE THOUGHT SUCH A SCURVY RACE OF MAMMALS COULD PRODUCE SUCH EXQUISITE DINING EXPER-IENCES!
WITH MY WHEEL OF WORLDS, I'VE APPLIED THE LESSONS LEARNED HERE ALL ACROSS THE MULTI-VERSE.
KALIGHOUL! AVALON! A THOUSAND OTHERS! SOON, EVEN EARTH ITSELF SHALL GRACE MY TABLE!
HAIL, ALBION! YOU WERE MY FIRST AND, INDEED, YOU FED ME WELL....

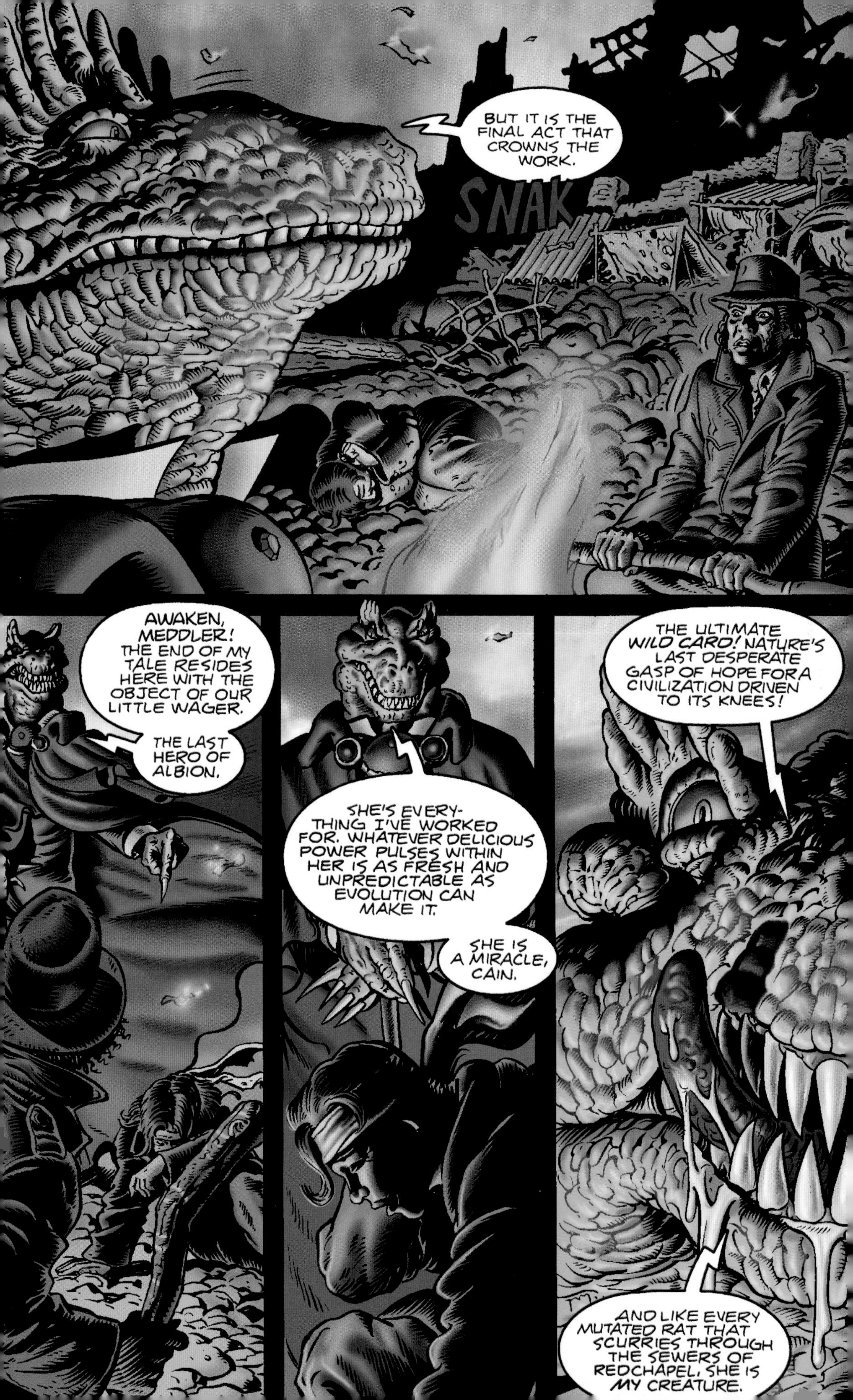
BUT IT IS THE FINAL ACT THAT CROWNS THE WORK.
SNAK
AWAKEN, MEDDLER! THE END OF MY TALE RESIDES HERE WITH THE OBJECT OF OUR LITTLE WAGER.
THE LAST HERO OF ALBION.
SHE'S EVERY-THING I'VE WORKED FOR. WHATEVER DELICIOUS POWER PULSES WITHIN HER IS AS FRESH AND UNPREDICTABLE AS EVOLUTION CAN MAKE IT.
SHE IS A MIRACLE, CAIN.
THE ULTIMATE *WILD CARD!* NATURE'S LAST DESPERATE GASP OF HOPE FOR A CIVILIZATION DRIVEN TO ITS KNEES!
AND LIKE EVERY MUTATED RAT THAT SCURRIES THROUGH THE SEWERS OF REDCHAPEL, SHE IS *MY* CREATURE.

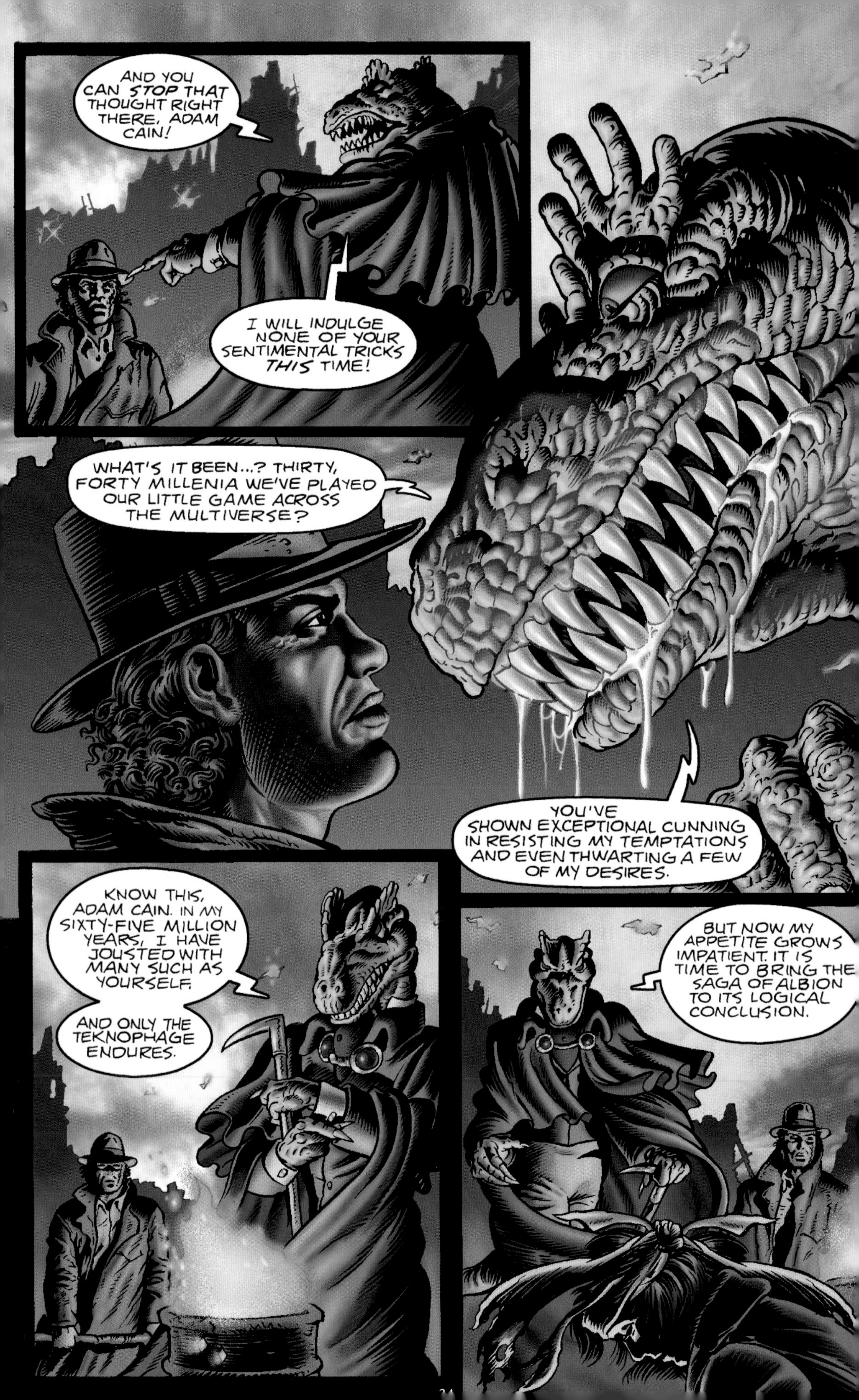
AND YOU CAN STOP THAT THOUGHT RIGHT THERE, ADAM CAIN!
I WILL INDULGE NONE OF YOUR SENTIMENTAL TRICKS THIS TIME!
WHAT'S IT BEEN...? THIRTY, FORTY MILLENIA WE'VE PLAYED OUR LITTLE GAME ACROSS THE MULTIVERSE?
YOU'VE SHOWN EXCEPTIONAL CUNNING IN RESISTING MY TEMPTATIONS AND EVEN THWARTING A FEW OF MY DESIRES.
KNOW THIS, ADAM CAIN. IN MY SIXTY-FIVE MILLION YEARS, I HAVE JOUSTED WITH MANY SUCH AS YOURSELF.
AND ONLY THE TEKNOPHAGE ENDURES.
BUT NOW MY APPETITE GROWS IMPATIENT. IT IS TIME TO BRING THE SAGA OF ALBION TO ITS LOGICAL CONCLUSION.

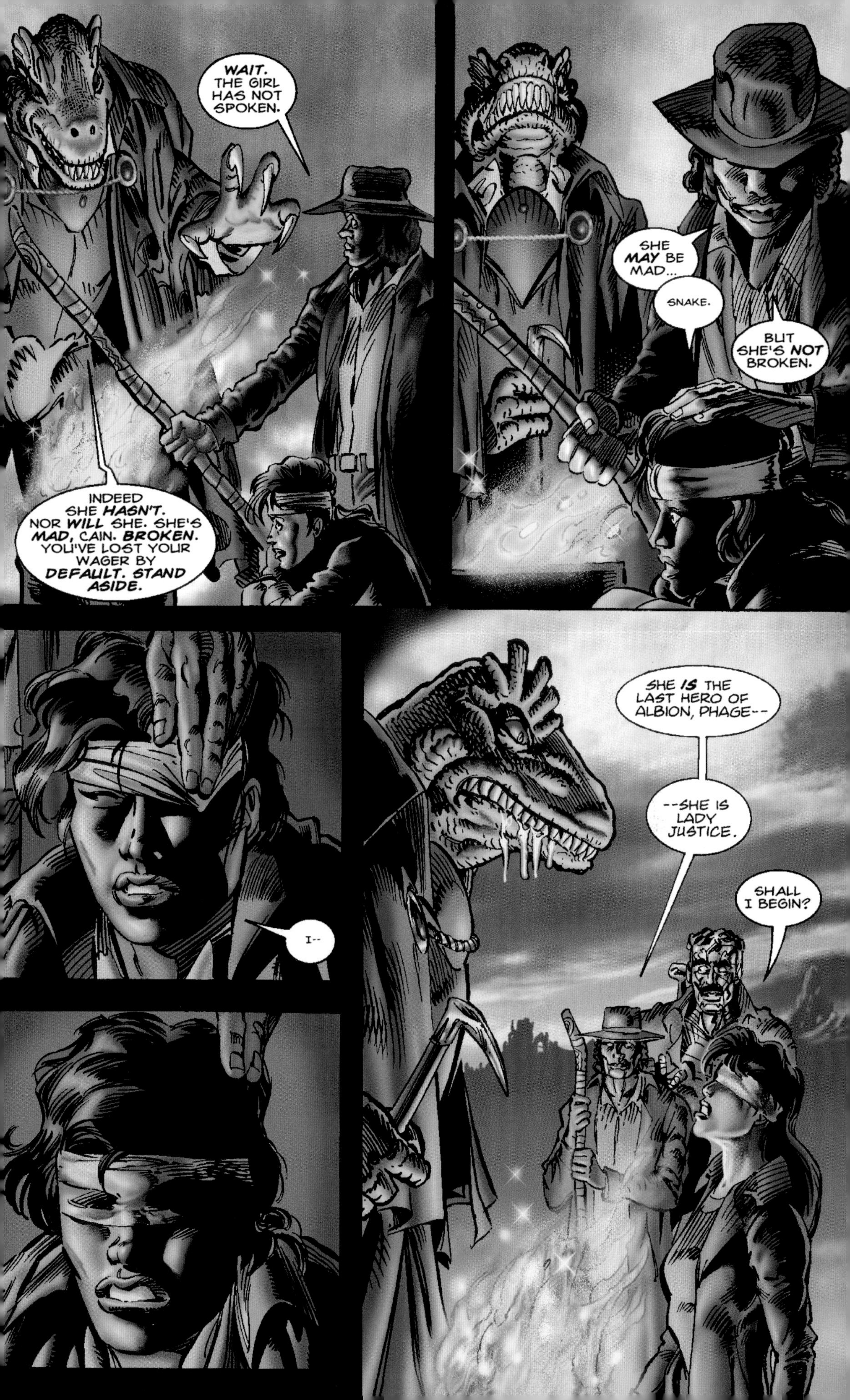

WAIT. THE GIRL HAS NOT SPOKEN.
INDEED SHE HASN'T. NOR WILL SHE. SHE'S MAD, CAIN. BROKEN. YOU'VE LOST YOUR WAGER BY DEFAULT. STAND ASIDE.
SHE MAY BE MAD...
SNAKE.
BUT SHE'S NOT BROKEN.
I--
SHE IS THE LAST HERO OF ALBION, PHAGE--
--SHE IS LADY JUSTICE.
SHALL I BEGIN?

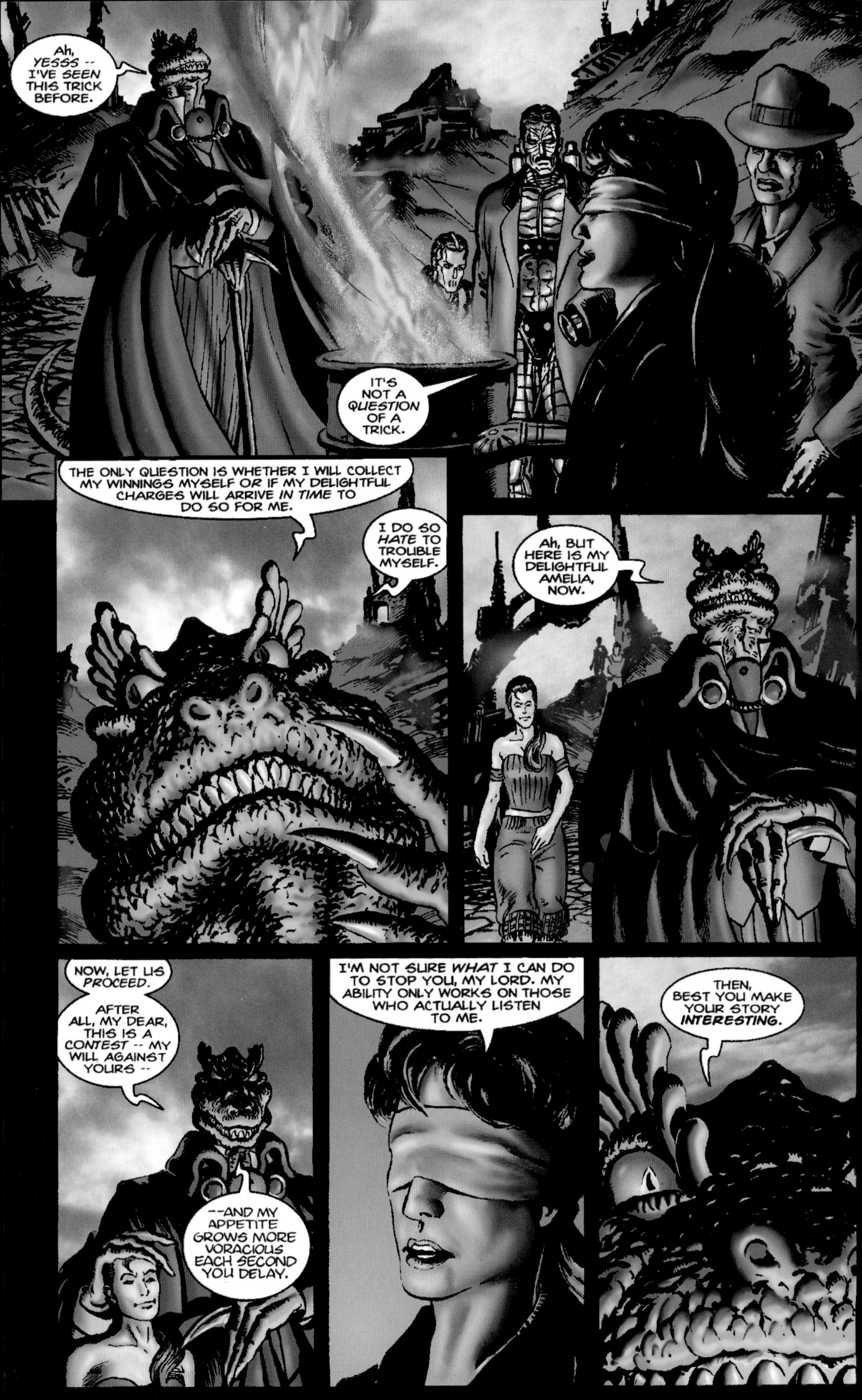

Ah, YESSS -- I'VE SEEN THIS TRICK BEFORE.
IT'S NOT A QUESTION OF A TRICK.
THE ONLY QUESTION IS WHETHER I WILL COLLECT MY WINNINGS MYSELF OR IF MY DELIGHTFUL CHARGES WILL ARRIVE IN TIME TO DO SO FOR ME.
I DO SO HATE TO TROUBLE MYSELF.
Ah, BUT HERE IS MY DELIGHTFUL AMELIA, NOW.
NOW, LET US PROCEED.
AFTER ALL, MY DEAR, THIS IS A CONTEST -- MY WILL AGAINST YOURS --
--AND MY APPETITE GROWS MORE VORACIOUS EACH SECOND YOU DELAY.
I'M NOT SURE WHAT I CAN DO TO STOP YOU, MY LORD. MY ABILITY ONLY WORKS ON THOSE WHO ACTUALLY LISTEN TO ME.
THEN, BEST YOU MAKE YOUR STORY INTERESTING.

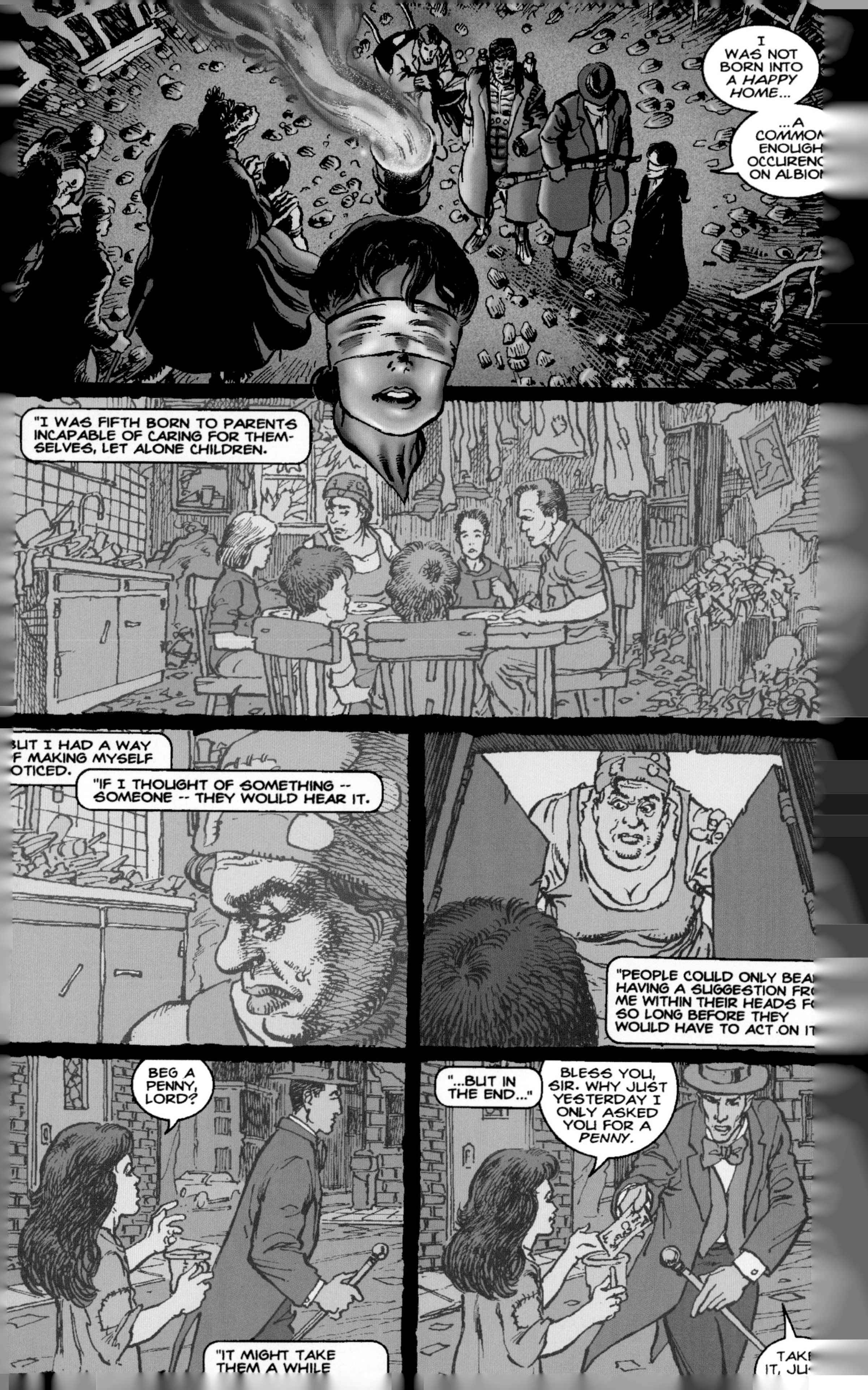
I WAS NOT BORN INTO A HAPPY HOME...
...A COMMON ENOUGH OCCURENC ON ALBIO
"I WAS FIFTH BORN TO PARENTS INCAPABLE OF CARING FOR THEMSELVES, LET ALONE CHILDREN.
UT I HAD A WAY F MAKING MYSELF OTICED.
"IF I THOUGHT OF SOMETHING -- SOMEONE -- THEY WOULD HEAR IT.
"PEOPLE COULD ONLY BEA HAVING A SUGGESTION FR ME WITHIN THEIR HEADS F SO LONG BEFORE THEY WOULD HAVE TO ACT ON IT
BEG A PENNY, LORD?
"IT MIGHT TAKE THEM A WHILE
"...BUT IN THE END..."
BLESS YOU, SIR. WHY JUST YESTERDAY I ONLY ASKED YOU FOR A PENNY.
TAK IT, JU

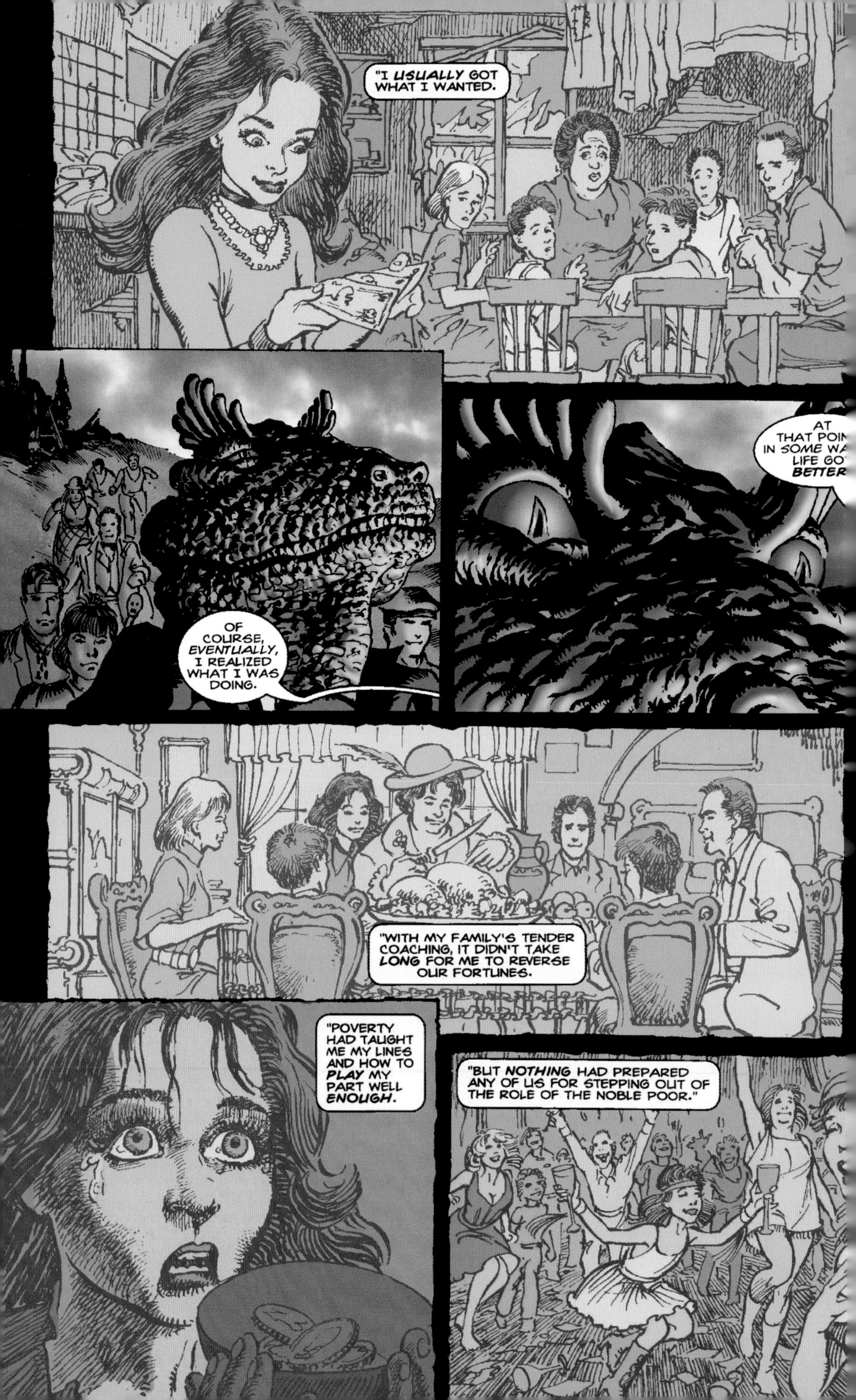
"I USUALLY GOT WHAT I WANTED.
OF COURSE, EVENTUALLY, I REALIZED WHAT I WAS DOING.
AT THAT POIN IN SOME WA LIFE GO BETTER
"WITH MY FAMILY'S TENDER COACHING, IT DIDN'T TAKE LONG FOR ME TO REVERSE OUR FORTUNES.
"POVERTY HAD TAUGHT ME MY LINES AND HOW TO PLAY MY PART WELL ENOUGH.
"BUT NOTHING HAD PREPARED ANY OF US FOR STEPPING OUT OF THE ROLE OF THE NOBLE POOR."

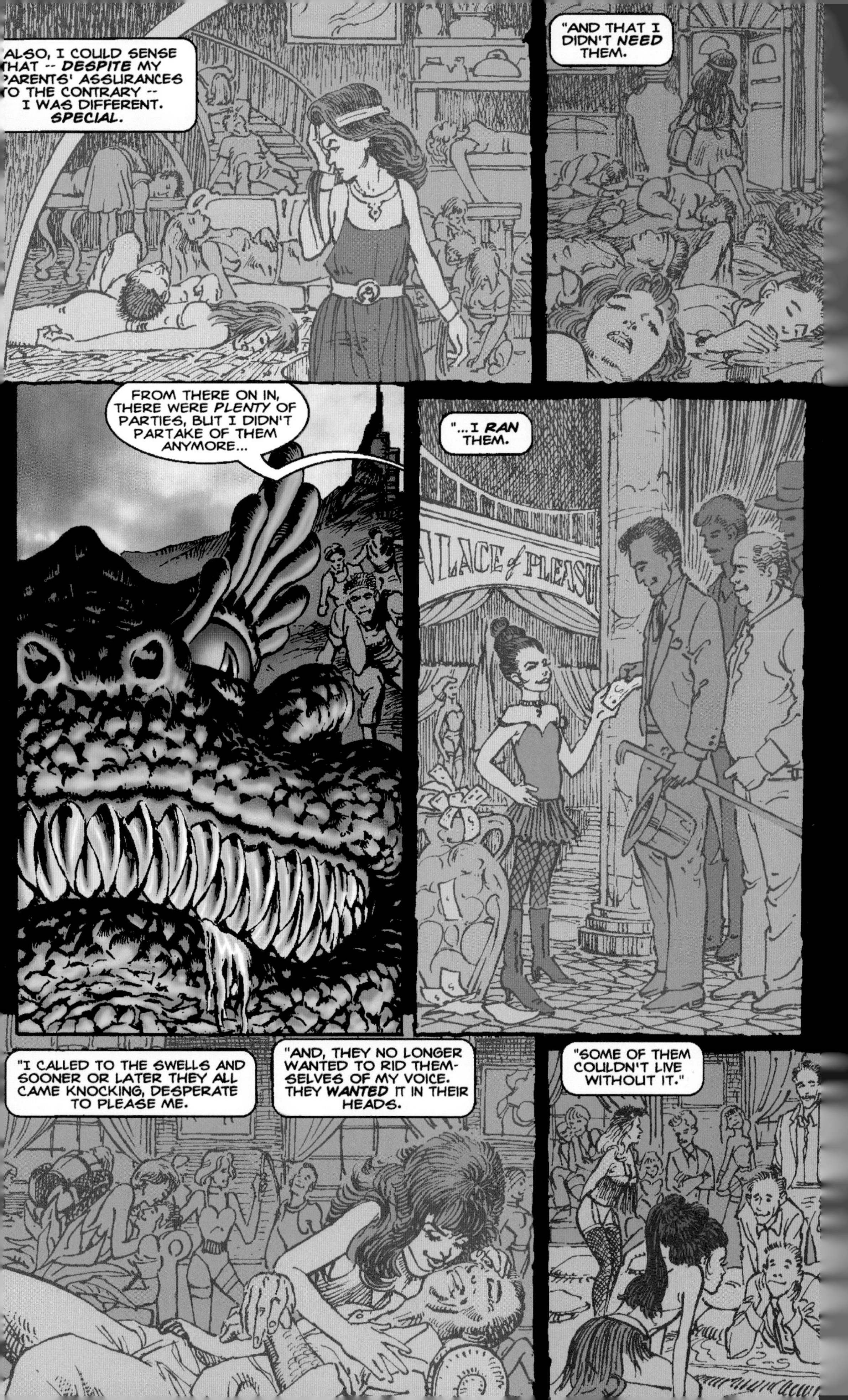
ALSO, I COULD SENSE THAT -- DESPITE MY PARENTS' ASSURANCES TO THE CONTRARY -- I WAS DIFFERENT. SPECIAL.
"AND THAT I DIDN'T NEED THEM.
FROM THERE ON IN, THERE WERE PLENTY OF PARTIES, BUT I DIDN'T PARTAKE OF THEM ANYMORE...
"...I RAN THEM.
ALACE of PLEASU
"I CALLED TO THE SWELLS AND SOONER OR LATER THEY ALL CAME KNOCKING, DESPERATE TO PLEASE ME.
"AND, THEY NO LONGER WANTED TO RID THEMSELVES OF MY VOICE. THEY WANTED IT IN THEIR HEADS.
"SOME OF THEM COULDN'T LIVE WITHOUT IT."

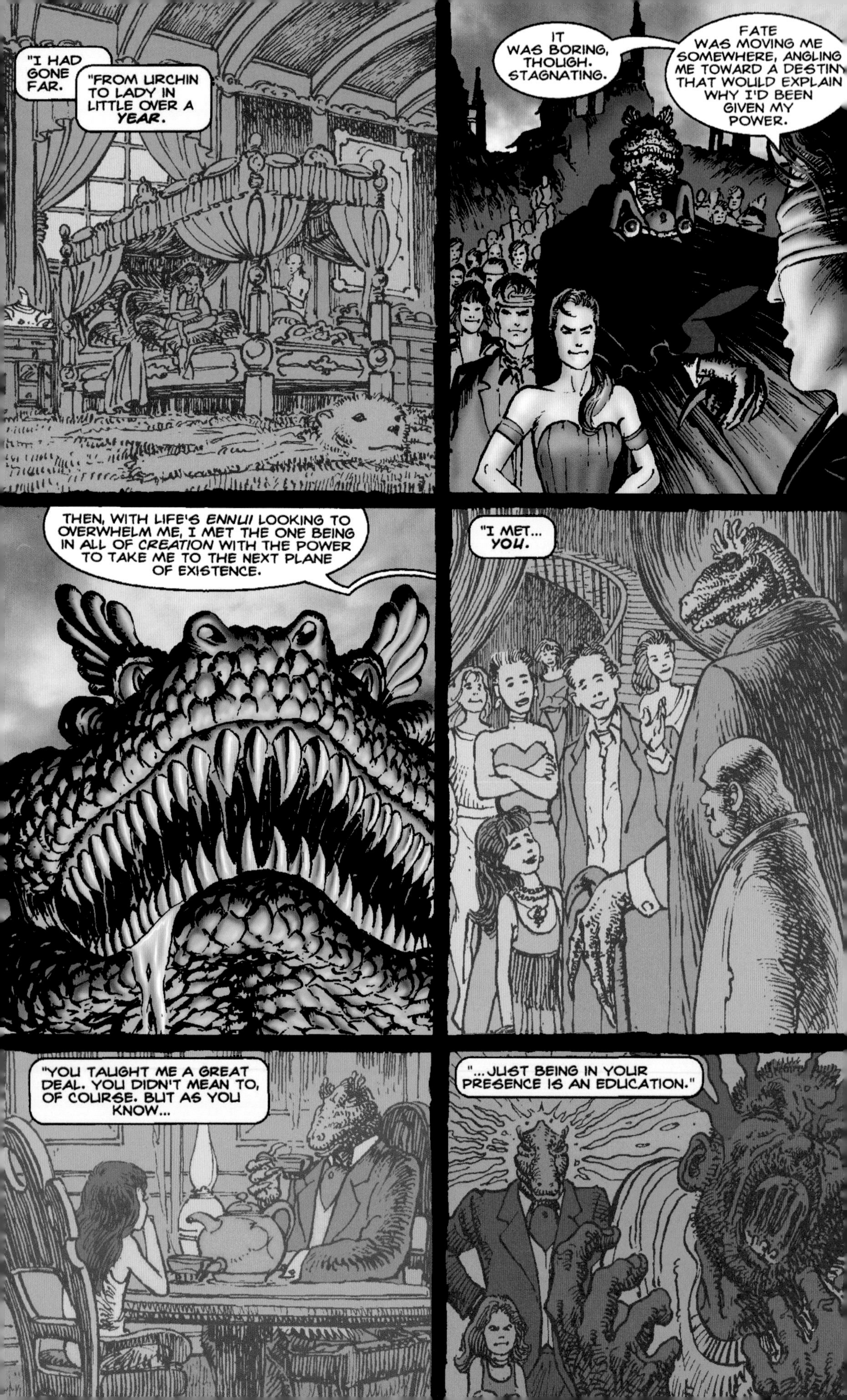
"I HAD GONE FAR.
"FROM URCHIN TO LADY IN LITTLE OVER A *YEAR*.
IT WAS BORING, THOUGH. STAGNATING.
FATE WAS MOVING ME SOMEWHERE, ANGLING ME TOWARD A DESTINY THAT WOULD EXPLAIN WHY I'D BEEN GIVEN MY POWER.
THEN, WITH LIFE'S *ENNUI* LOOKING TO OVERWHELM ME, I MET THE ONE BEING IN ALL OF *CREATION* WITH THE POWER TO TAKE ME TO THE NEXT PLANE OF EXISTENCE.
"I MET... *YOU*.
"YOU TAUGHT ME A GREAT DEAL. YOU DIDN'T MEAN TO, OF COURSE. BUT AS YOU KNOW...
"...JUST BEING IN YOUR PRESENCE IS AN EDUCATION."

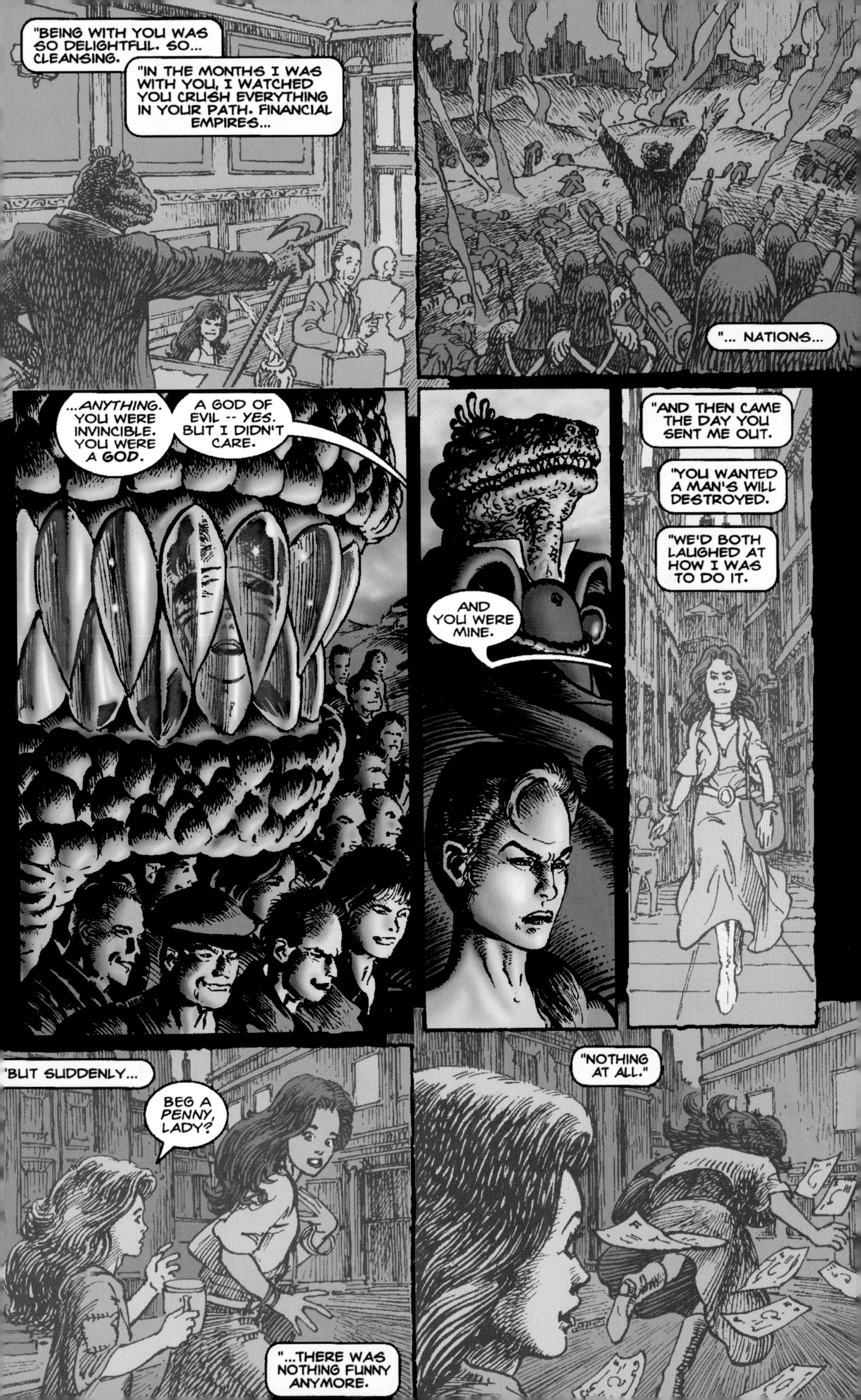
"BEING WITH YOU WAS SO DELIGHTFUL. SO... CLEANSING.
"IN THE MONTHS I WAS WITH YOU, I WATCHED YOU CRUSH EVERYTHING IN YOUR PATH. FINANCIAL EMPIRES...
"... NATIONS...
...ANYTHING. YOU WERE INVINCIBLE. YOU WERE A GOD.
A GOD OF EVIL -- YES. BUT I DIDN'T CARE.
AND YOU WERE MINE.
"AND THEN CAME THE DAY YOU SENT ME OUT.
"YOU WANTED A MAN'S WILL DESTROYED.
"WE'D BOTH LAUGHED AT HOW I WAS TO DO IT.
"BUT SUDDENLY...
BEG A PENNY, LADY?
"...THERE WAS NOTHING FUNNY ANYMORE.
"NOTHING AT ALL."

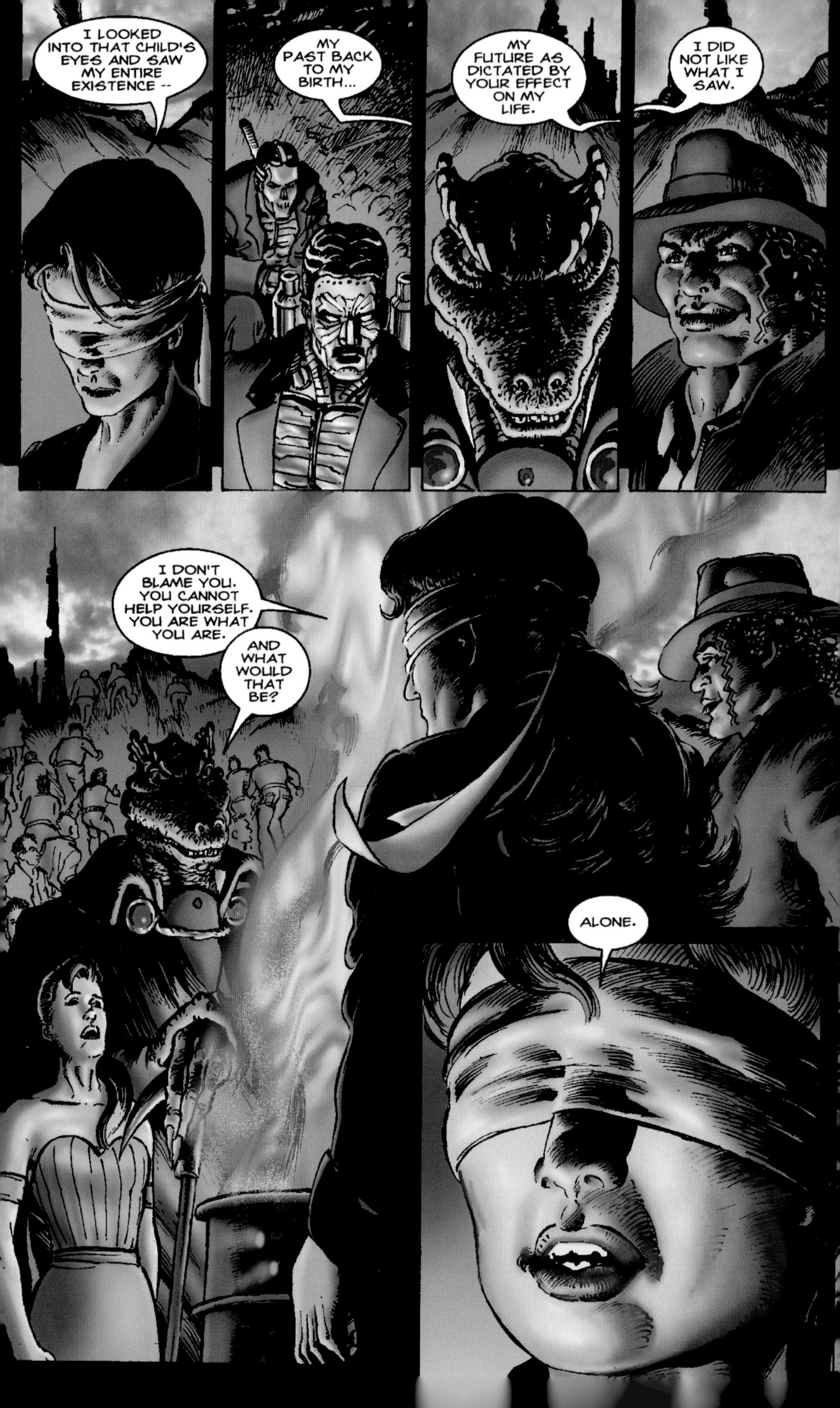
I LOOKED INTO THAT CHILD'S EYES AND SAW MY ENTIRE EXISTENCE --
MY PAST BACK TO MY BIRTH...
MY FUTURE AS DICTATED BY YOUR EFFECT ON MY LIFE.
I DID NOT LIKE WHAT I SAW.
I DON'T BLAME YOU. YOU CANNOT HELP YOURSELF. YOU ARE WHAT YOU ARE.
AND WHAT WOULD THAT BE?
ALONE.

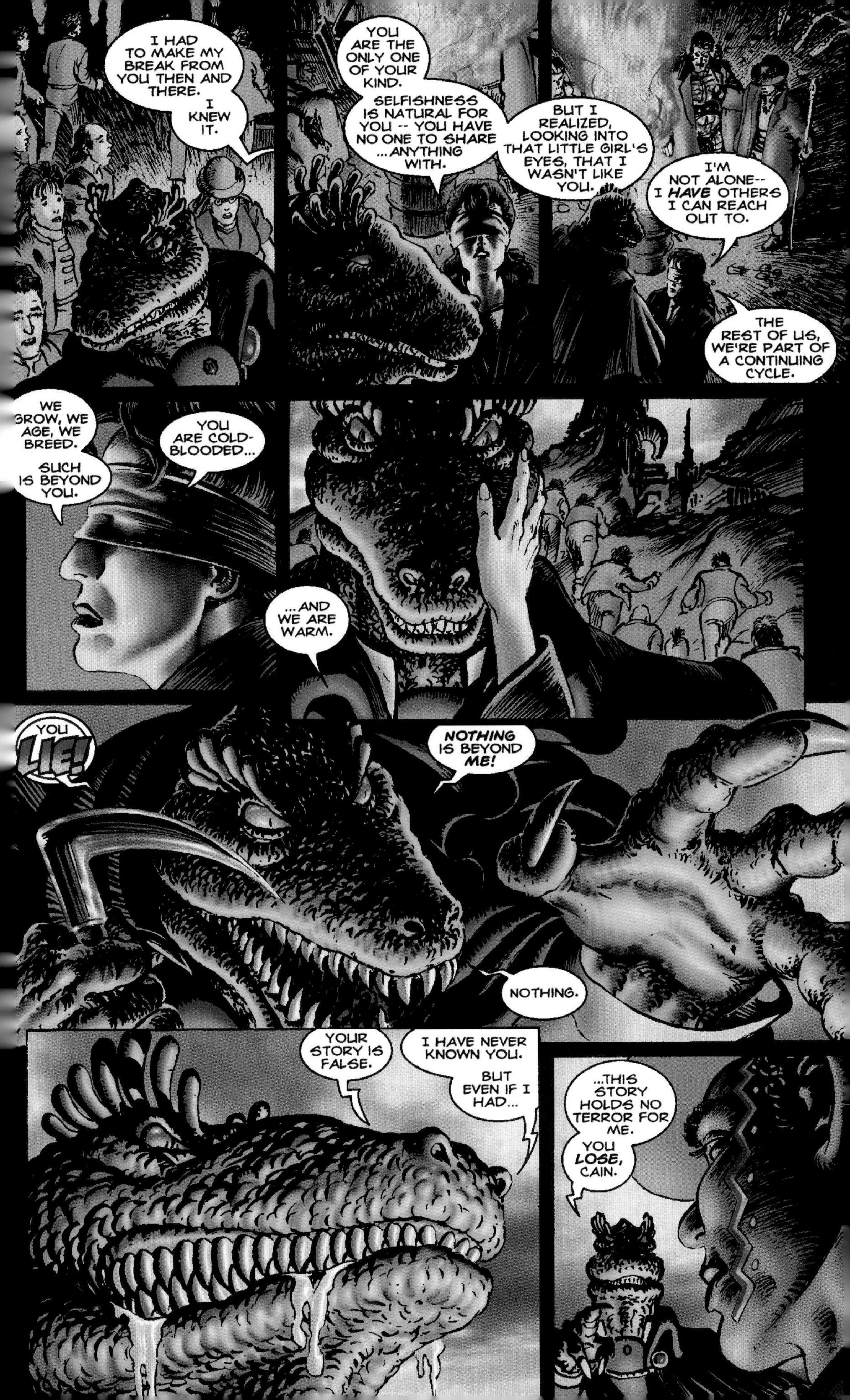
I HAD TO MAKE MY BREAK FROM YOU THEN AND THERE.
I KNEW IT.
YOU ARE THE ONLY ONE OF YOUR KIND.
SELFISHNESS IS NATURAL FOR YOU -- YOU HAVE NO ONE TO SHARE ...ANYTHING WITH.
BUT I REALIZED, LOOKING INTO THAT LITTLE GIRL'S EYES, THAT I WASN'T LIKE YOU.
I'M NOT ALONE-- I HAVE OTHERS I CAN REACH OUT TO.
THE REST OF US, WE'RE PART OF A CONTINUING CYCLE.
WE GROW, WE AGE, WE BREED.
SUCH IS BEYOND YOU.
YOU ARE COLD-BLOODED...
...AND WE ARE WARM.
YOU LIE!
NOTHING IS BEYOND ME!
NOTHING.
YOUR STORY IS FALSE.
I HAVE NEVER KNOWN YOU.
BUT EVEN IF I HAD...
...THIS STORY HOLDS NO TERROR FOR ME.
YOU LOSE, CAIN.

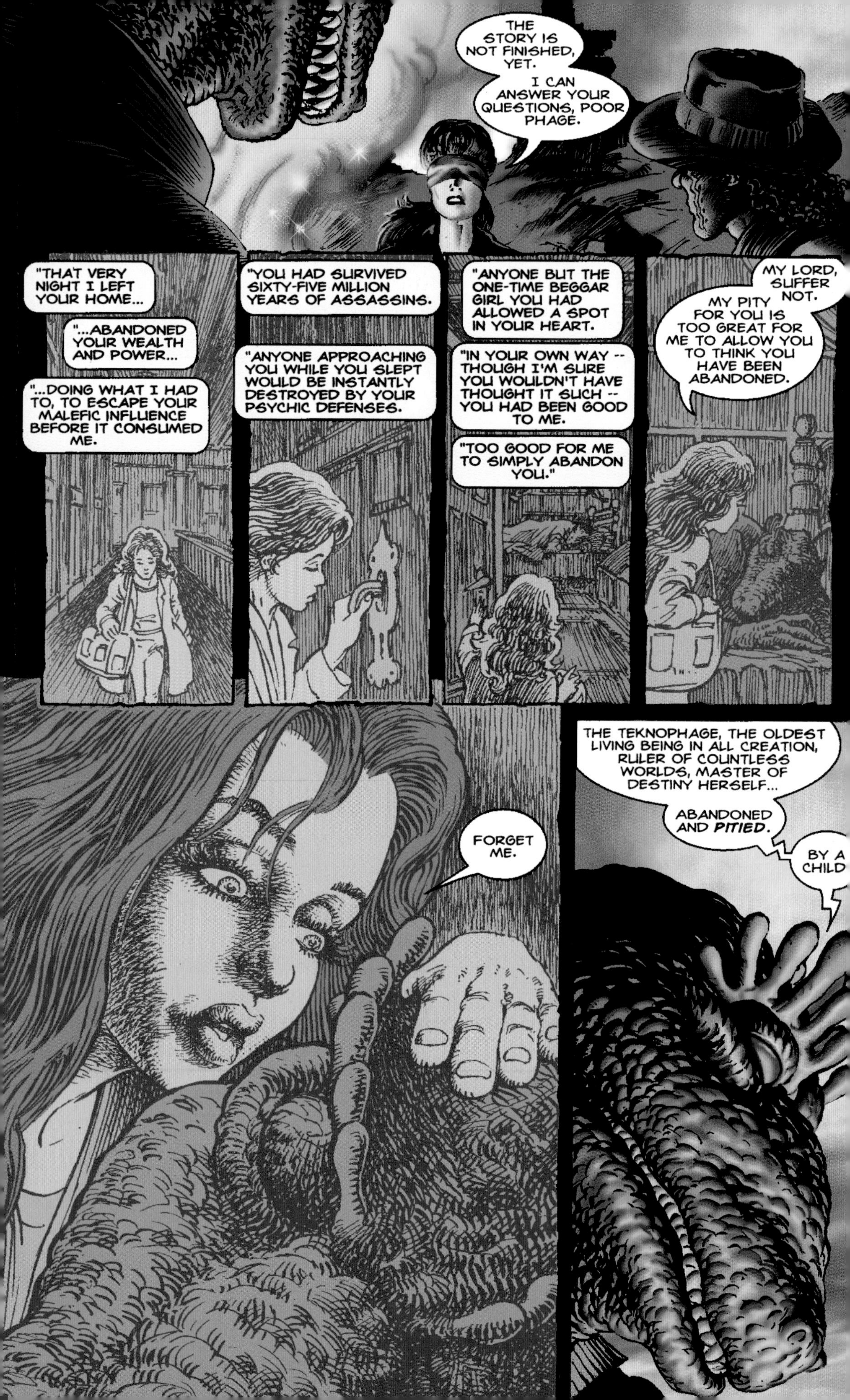
THE STORY IS NOT FINISHED, YET.
I CAN ANSWER YOUR QUESTIONS, POOR PHAGE.
"THAT VERY NIGHT I LEFT YOUR HOME...
"...ABANDONED YOUR WEALTH AND POWER...
"...DOING WHAT I HAD TO, TO ESCAPE YOUR MALEFIC INFLUENCE BEFORE IT CONSUMED ME.
"YOU HAD SURVIVED SIXTY-FIVE MILLION YEARS OF ASSASSINS.
"ANYONE APPROACHING YOU WHILE YOU SLEPT WOULD BE INSTANTLY DESTROYED BY YOUR PSYCHIC DEFENSES.
"ANYONE BUT THE ONE-TIME BEGGAR GIRL YOU HAD ALLOWED A SPOT IN YOUR HEART.
"IN YOUR OWN WAY -- THOUGH I'M SURE YOU WOULDN'T HAVE THOUGHT IT SUCH -- YOU HAD BEEN GOOD TO ME.
"TOO GOOD FOR ME TO SIMPLY ABANDON YOU."
MY LORD, SUFFER NOT.
MY PITY FOR YOU IS TOO GREAT FOR ME TO ALLOW YOU TO THINK YOU HAVE BEEN ABANDONED.
FORGET ME.
THE TEKNOPHAGE, THE OLDEST LIVING BEING IN ALL CREATION, RULER OF COUNTLESS WORLDS, MASTER OF DESTINY HERSELF...
ABANDONED AND *PITIED*.
BY A CHILD

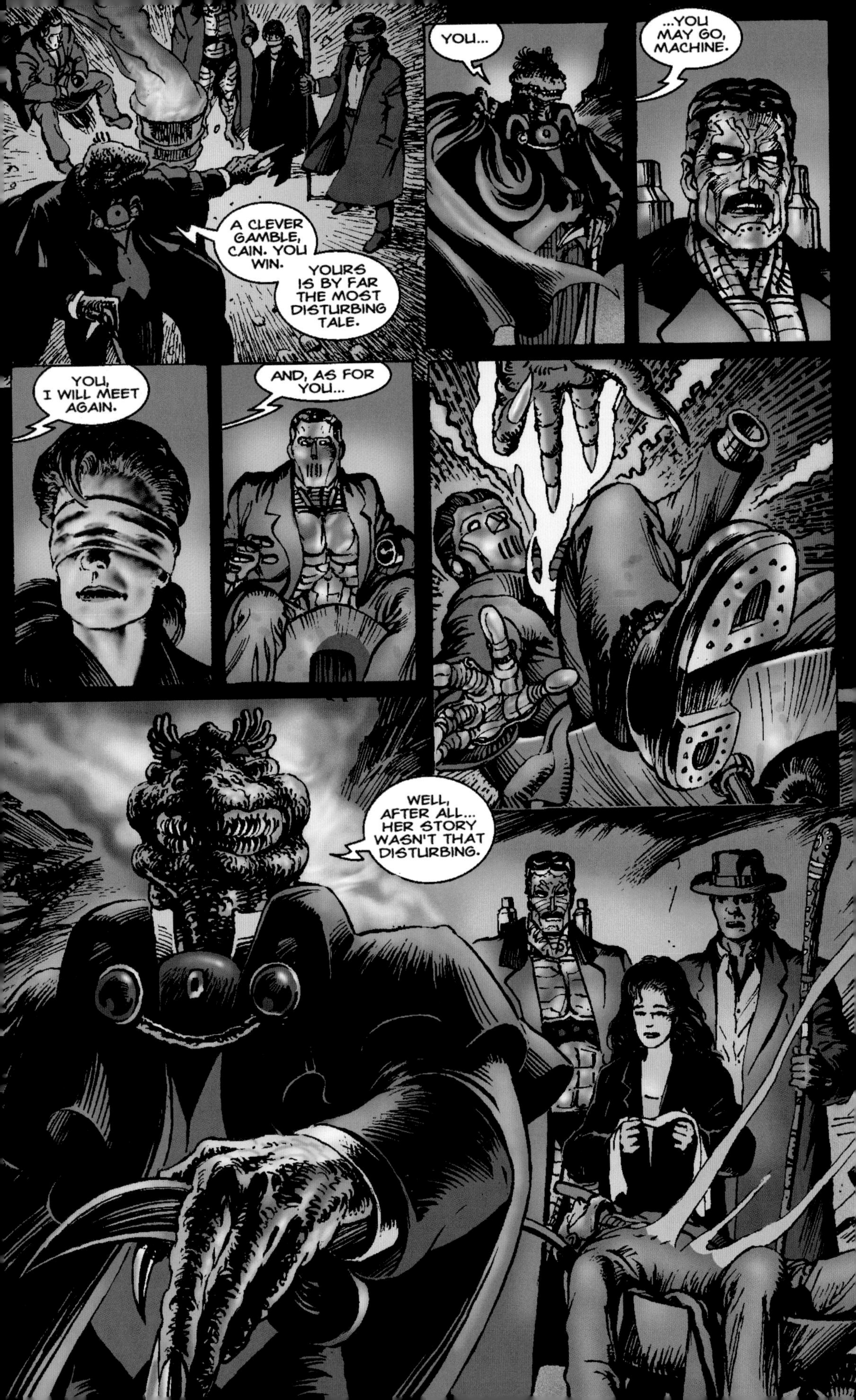
A CLEVER GAMBLE, CAIN. YOU WIN.
YOURS IS BY FAR THE MOST DISTURBING TALE.
YOU...
...YOU MAY GO, MACHINE.
YOU, I WILL MEET AGAIN.
AND, AS FOR YOU...
WELL, AFTER ALL... HER STORY WASN'T THAT DISTURBING.

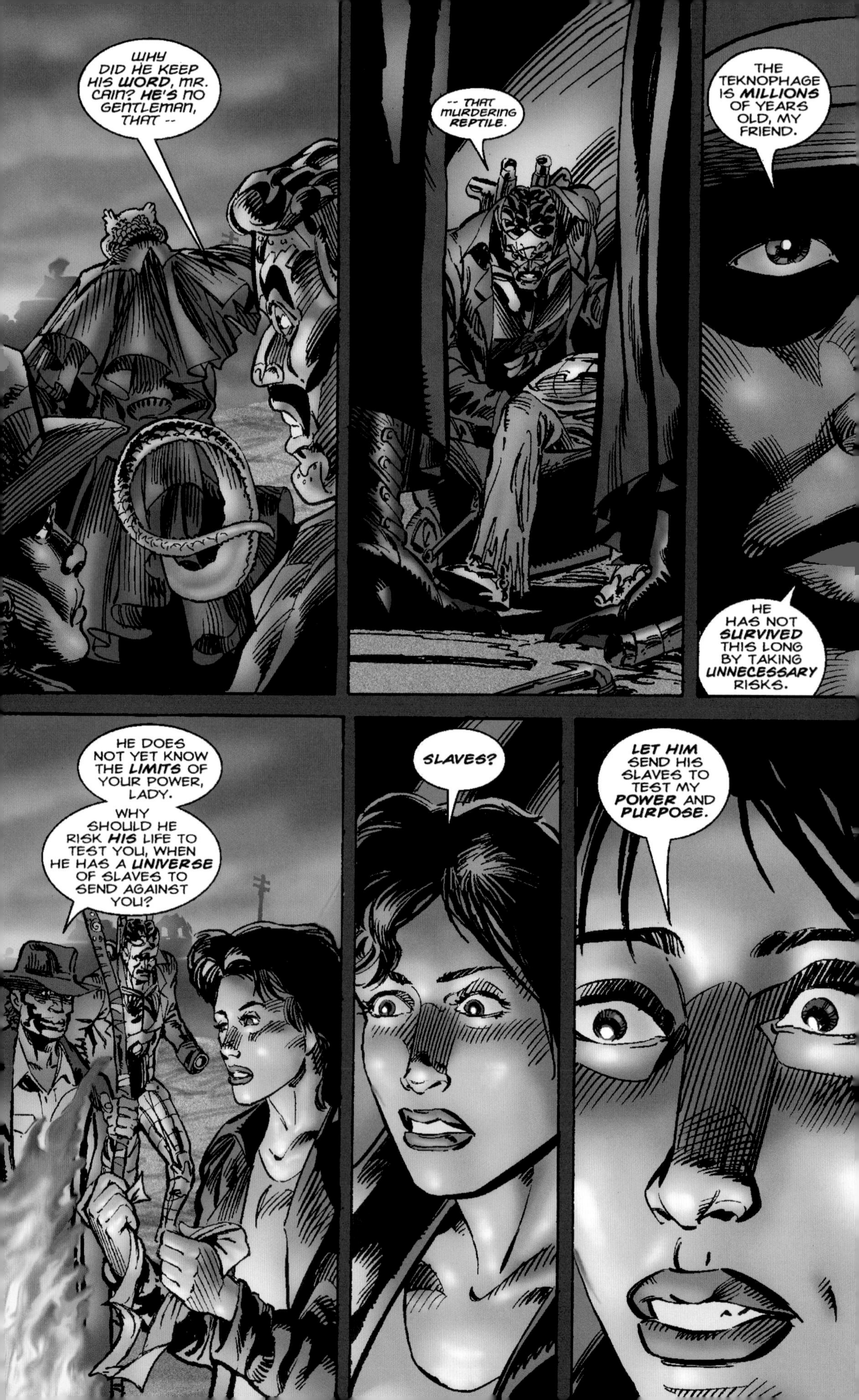

WHY DID HE KEEP HIS WORD, MR. CAIN? HE'S NO GENTLEMAN, THAT --
-- THAT MURDERING REPTILE.
THE TEKNOPHAGE IS MILLIONS OF YEARS OLD, MY FRIEND.
HE HAS NOT SURVIVED THIS LONG BY TAKING UNNECESSARY RISKS.
HE DOES NOT YET KNOW THE LIMITS OF YOUR POWER, LADY.
WHY SHOULD HE RISK HIS LIFE TO TEST YOU, WHEN HE HAS A UNIVERSE OF SLAVES TO SEND AGAINST YOU?
SLAVES?
LET HIM SEND HIS SLAVES TO TEST MY POWER AND PURPOSE.

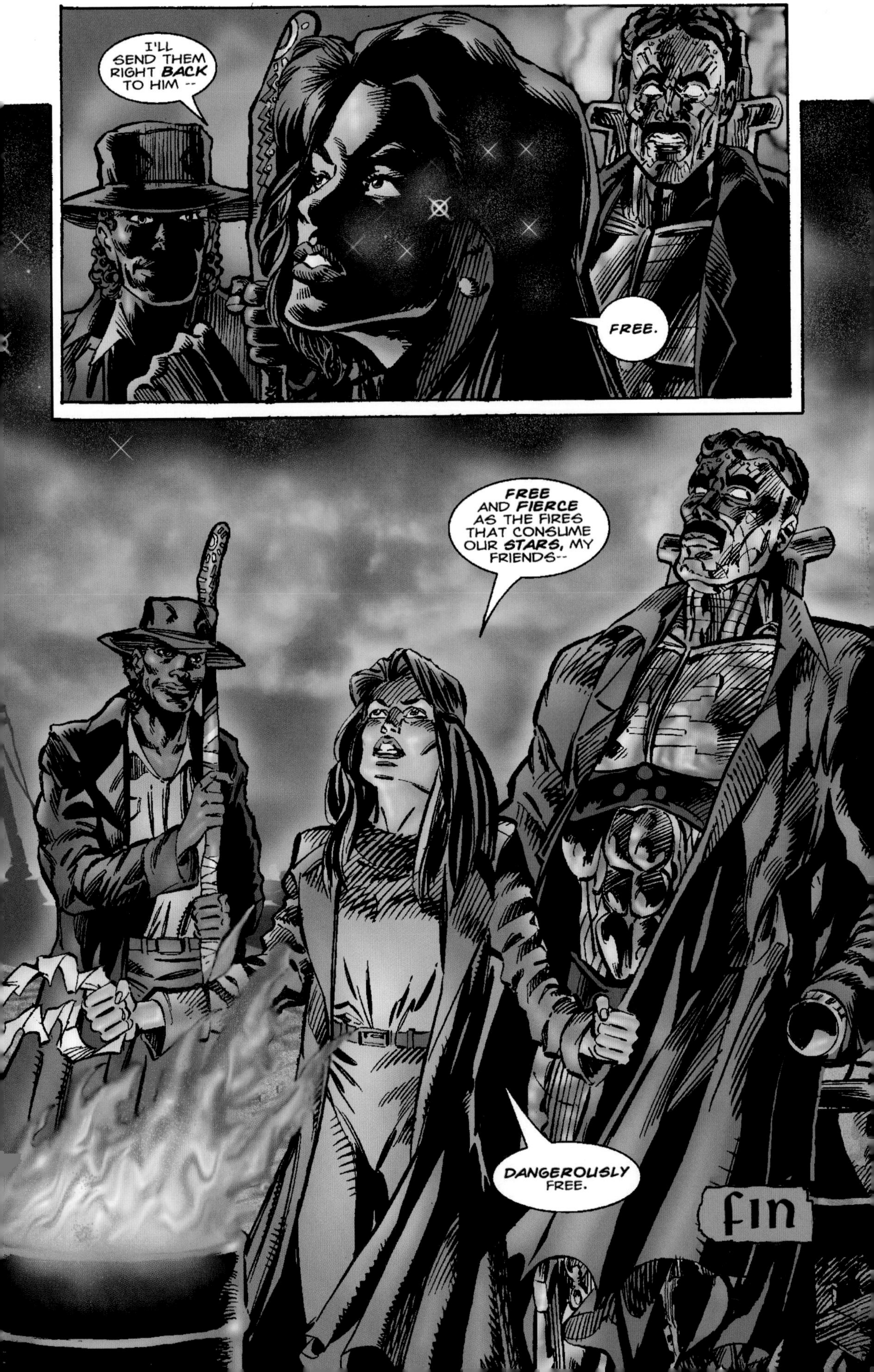
I'LL SEND THEM RIGHT BACK TO HIM --
FREE.
FREE AND FIERCE AS THE FIRES THAT CONSUME OUR STARS, MY FRIENDS--
DANGEROUSLY FREE.
fin

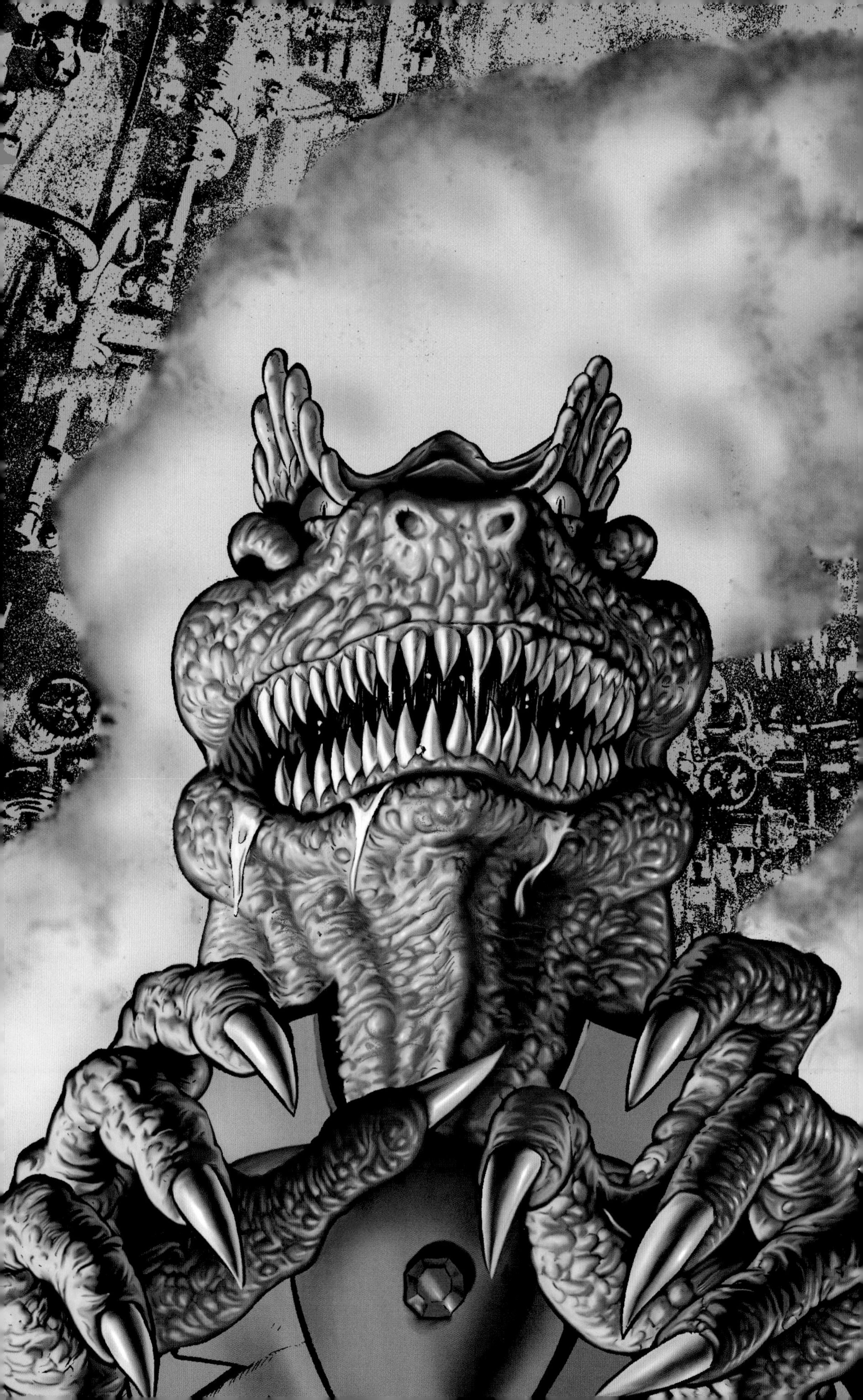

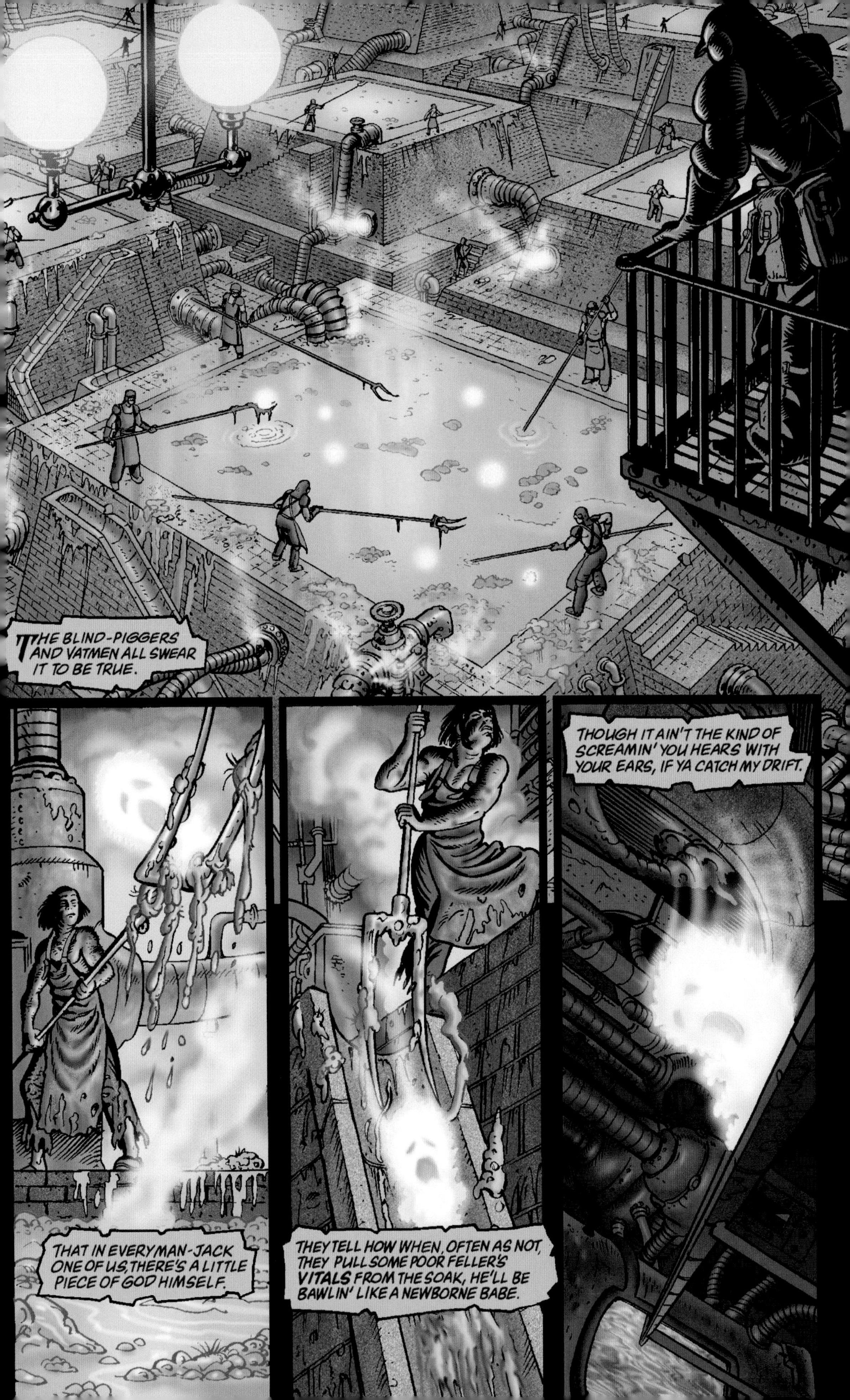
THE BLIND-PIGGERS AND VATMEN ALL SWEAR IT TO BE TRUE.
THAT IN EVERYMAN-JACK ONE OF US, THERE'S A LITTLE PIECE OF GOD HIMSELF.
THEY TELL HOW WHEN, OFTEN AS NOT, THEY PULL SOME POOR FELLER'S VITALS FROM THE SOAK, HE'LL BE BAWLIN' LIKE A NEWBORNE BABE.
THOUGH IT AIN'T THE KIND OF SCREAMIN' YOU HEARS WITH YOUR EARS, IF YA CATCH MY DRIFT.

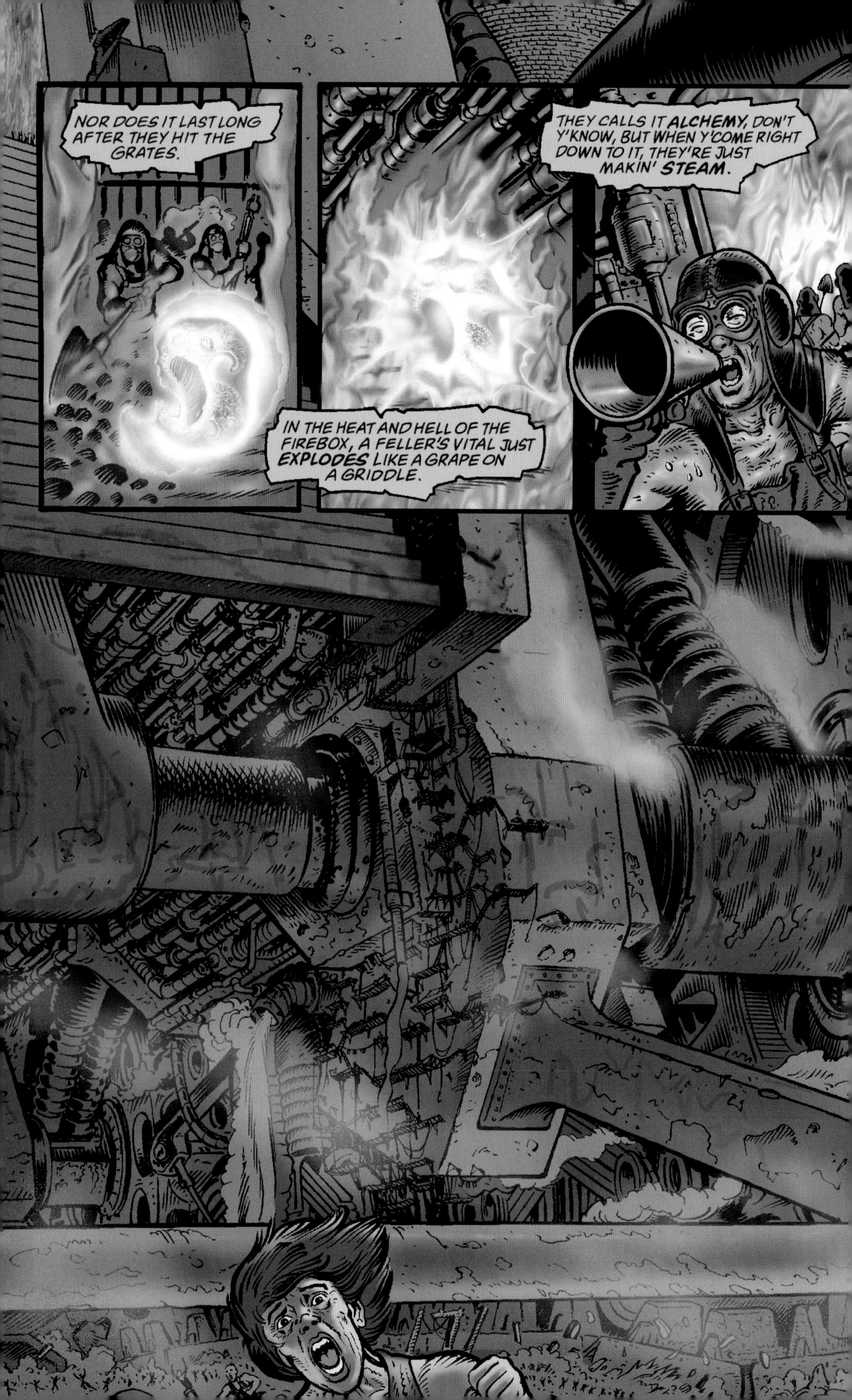
NOR DOES IT LAST LONG AFTER THEY HIT THE GRATES.
IN THE HEAT AND HELL OF THE FIREBOX, A FELLER'S VITAL JUST EXPLODES LIKE A GRAPE ON A GRIDDLE.
THEY CALLS IT ALCHEMY, DON'T Y'KNOW, BUT WHEN Y'COME RIGHT DOWN TO IT, THEY'RE JUST MAKIN' STEAM.

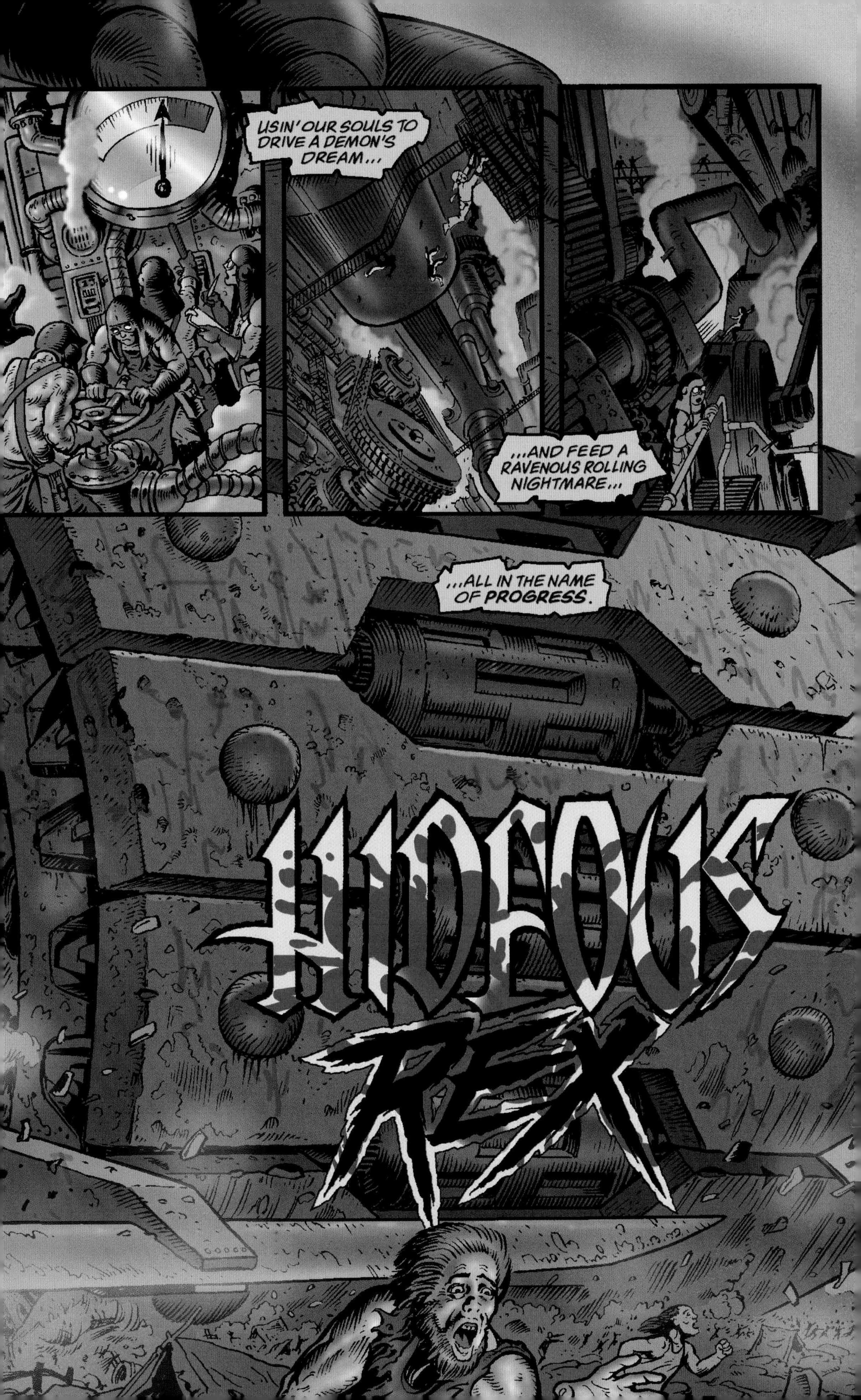
USIN' OUR SOULS TO DRIVE A DEMON'S DREAM...
...AND FEED A RAVENOUS ROLLING NIGHTMARE...
...ALL IN THE NAME OF PROGRESS.
REX

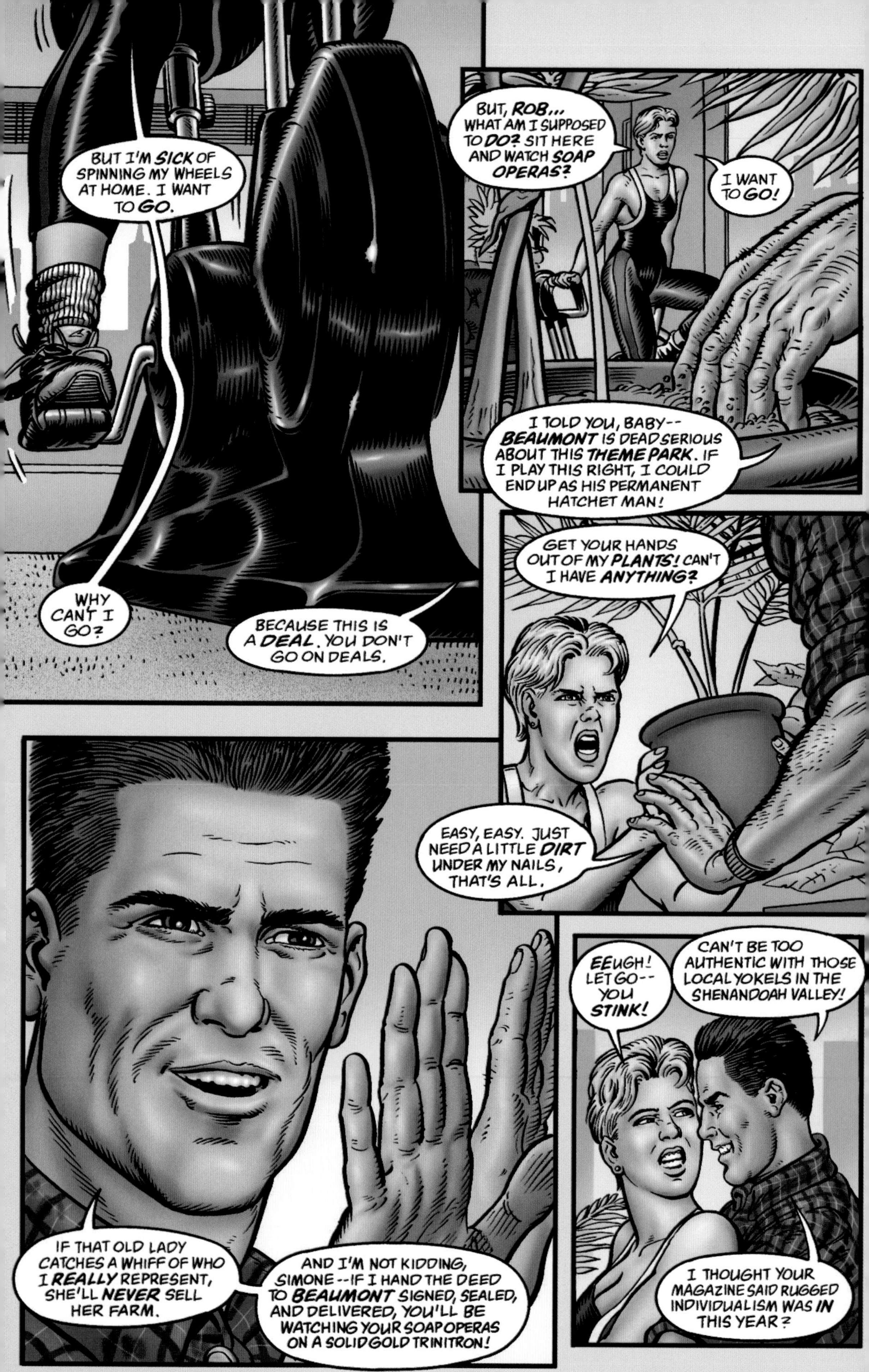

BUT I'M SICK OF SPINNING MY WHEELS AT HOME. I WANT TO GO.
WHY CAN'T I GO?
BECAUSE THIS IS A DEAL. YOU DON'T GO ON DEALS.
BUT, ROB... WHAT AM I SUPPOSED TO DO? SIT HERE AND WATCH SOAP OPERAS?
I WANT TO GO!
I TOLD YOU, BABY-- BEAUMONT IS DEAD SERIOUS ABOUT THIS THEME PARK. IF I PLAY THIS RIGHT, I COULD END UP AS HIS PERMANENT HATCHET MAN!
GET YOUR HANDS OUT OF MY PLANTS! CAN'T I HAVE ANYTHING?
EASY, EASY. JUST NEED A LITTLE DIRT UNDER MY NAILS, THAT'S ALL.
IF THAT OLD LADY CATCHES A WHIFF OF WHO I REALLY REPRESENT, SHE'LL NEVER SELL HER FARM.
AND I'M NOT KIDDING, SIMONE--IF I HAND THE DEED TO BEAUMONT SIGNED, SEALED, AND DELIVERED, YOU'LL BE WATCHING YOUR SOAP OPERAS ON A SOLID GOLD TRINITRON!
EEUGH! LET GO-- YOU STINK!
CAN'T BE TOO AUTHENTIC WITH THOSE LOCAL YOKELS IN THE SHENANDOAH VALLEY!
I THOUGHT YOUR MAGAZINE SAID RUGGED INDIVIDUALISM WAS IN THIS YEAR?

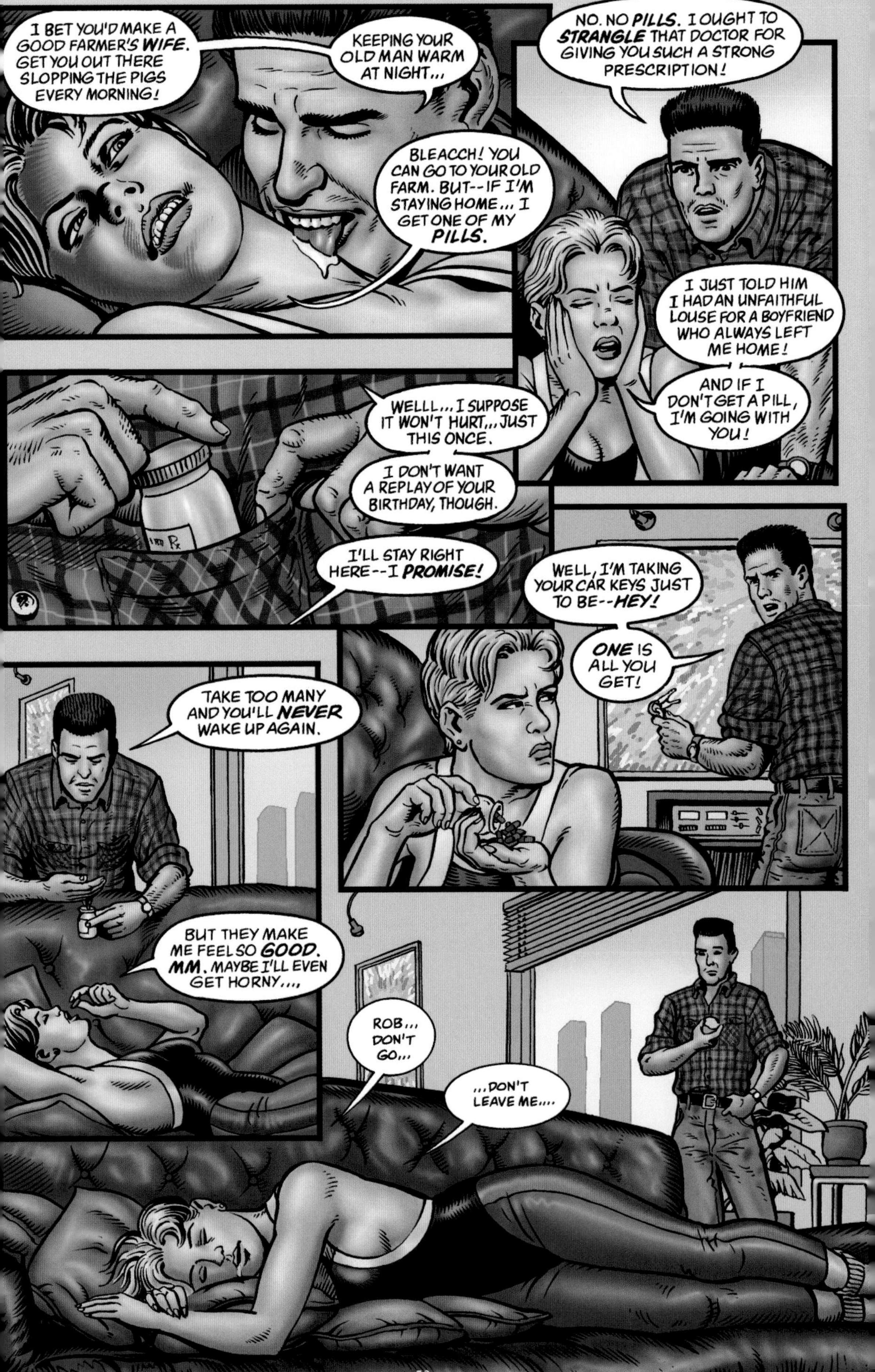
I BET YOU'D MAKE A GOOD FARMER'S WIFE. GET YOU OUT THERE SLOPPING THE PIGS EVERY MORNING!
KEEPING YOUR OLD MAN WARM AT NIGHT...
BLEACCH! YOU CAN GO TO YOUR OLD FARM. BUT--IF I'M STAYING HOME... I GET ONE OF MY PILLS.
NO. NO PILLS. I OUGHT TO STRANGLE THAT DOCTOR FOR GIVING YOU SUCH A STRONG PRESCRIPTION!
I JUST TOLD HIM I HAD AN UNFAITHFUL LOUSE FOR A BOYFRIEND WHO ALWAYS LEFT ME HOME!
AND IF I DON'T GET A PILL, I'M GOING WITH YOU!
WELLL... I SUPPOSE IT WON'T HURT... JUST THIS ONCE.
I DON'T WANT A REPLAY OF YOUR BIRTHDAY, THOUGH.
I'LL STAY RIGHT HERE--I PROMISE!
WELL, I'M TAKING YOUR CAR KEYS JUST TO BE--HEY!
ONE IS ALL YOU GET!
TAKE TOO MANY AND YOU'LL NEVER WAKE UP AGAIN.
BUT THEY MAKE ME FEEL SO GOOD. MM. MAYBE I'LL EVEN GET HORNY...,
ROB... DON'T GO...
...DON'T LEAVE ME....

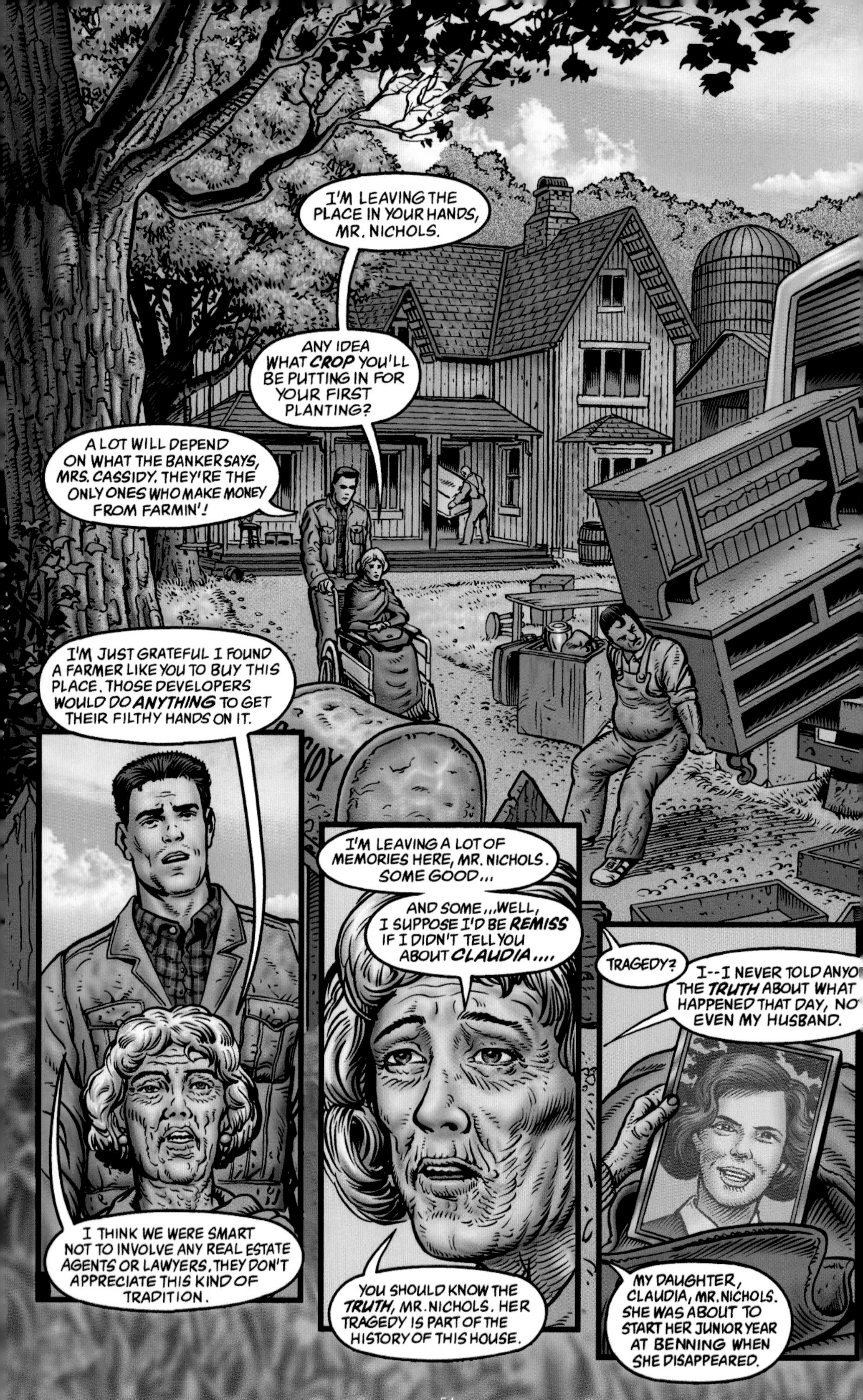
I'M LEAVING THE PLACE IN YOUR HANDS, MR. NICHOLS.
ANY IDEA WHAT CROP YOU'LL BE PUTTING IN FOR YOUR FIRST PLANTING?
A LOT WILL DEPEND ON WHAT THE BANKER SAYS, MRS. CASSIDY. THEY'RE THE ONLY ONES WHO MAKE MONEY FROM FARMIN'!
I'M JUST GRATEFUL I FOUND A FARMER LIKE YOU TO BUY THIS PLACE. THOSE DEVELOPERS WOULD DO ANYTHING TO GET THEIR FILTHY HANDS ON IT.
I THINK WE WERE SMART NOT TO INVOLVE ANY REAL ESTATE AGENTS OR LAWYERS, THEY DON'T APPRECIATE THIS KIND OF TRADITION.
I'M LEAVING A LOT OF MEMORIES HERE, MR. NICHOLS. SOME GOOD...
AND SOME ...WELL, I SUPPOSE I'D BE REMISS IF I DIDN'T TELL YOU ABOUT CLAUDIA....
YOU SHOULD KNOW THE TRUTH, MR. NICHOLS. HER TRAGEDY IS PART OF THE HISTORY OF THIS HOUSE.
TRAGEDY?
I--I NEVER TOLD ANYO THE TRUTH ABOUT WHAT HAPPENED THAT DAY, NO EVEN MY HUSBAND.
MY DAUGHTER, CLAUDIA, MR. NICHOLS. SHE WAS ABOUT TO START HER JUNIOR YEAR AT BENNING WHEN SHE DISAPPEARED.

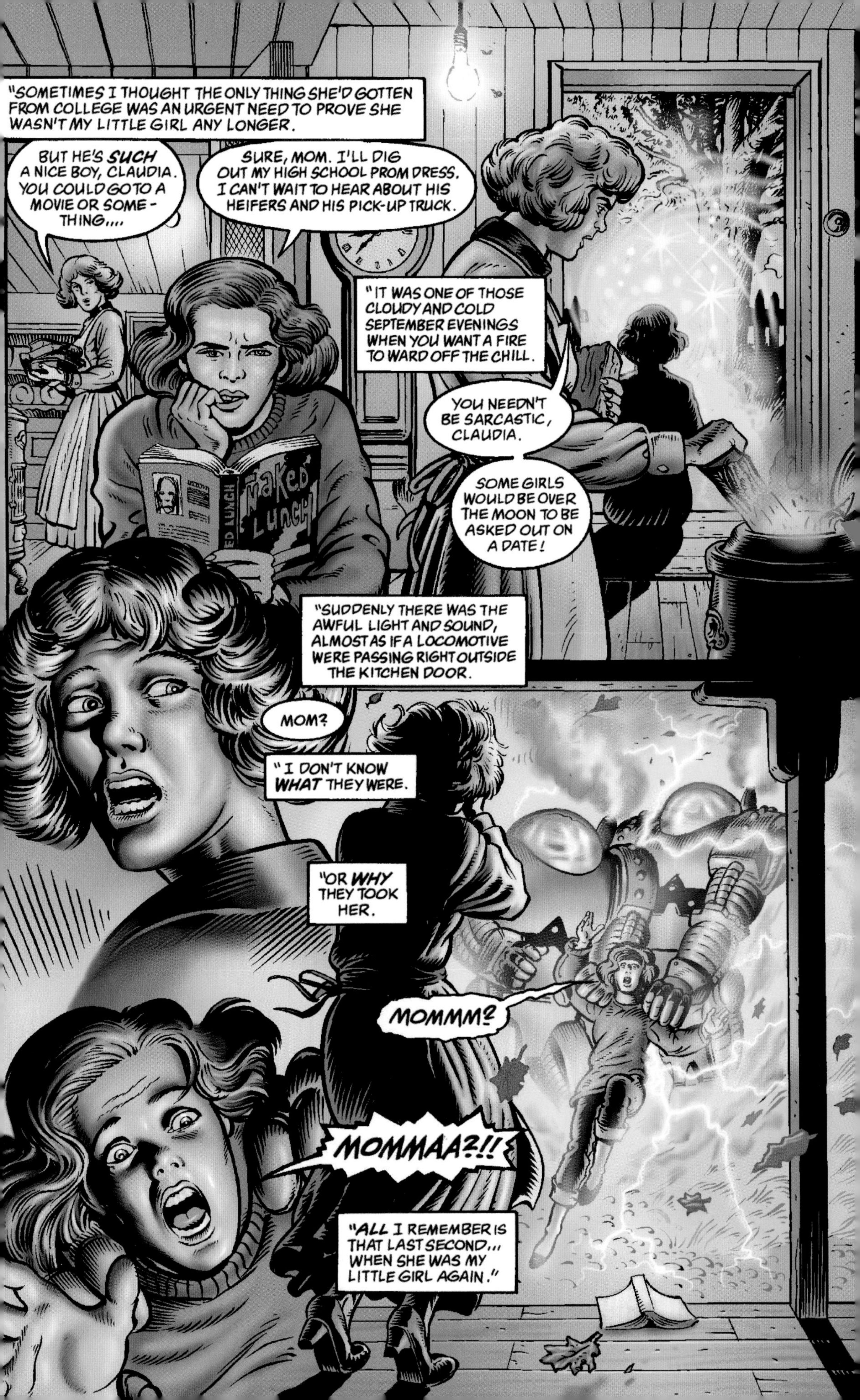

"SOMETIMES I THOUGHT THE ONLY THING SHE'D GOTTEN FROM COLLEGE WAS AN URGENT NEED TO PROVE SHE WASN'T MY LITTLE GIRL ANY LONGER.
BUT HE'S SUCH A NICE BOY, CLAUDIA. YOU COULD GO TO A MOVIE OR SOME-THING,...
SURE, MOM. I'LL DIG OUT MY HIGH SCHOOL PROM DRESS. I CAN'T WAIT TO HEAR ABOUT HIS HEIFERS AND HIS PICK-UP TRUCK.
NAKED LUNCH
"IT WAS ONE OF THOSE CLOUDY AND COLD SEPTEMBER EVENINGS WHEN YOU WANT A FIRE TO WARD OFF THE CHILL.
YOU NEEDN'T BE SARCASTIC, CLAUDIA.
SOME GIRLS WOULD BE OVER THE MOON TO BE ASKED OUT ON A DATE!
"SUDDENLY THERE WAS THE AWFUL LIGHT AND SOUND, ALMOST AS IF A LOCOMOTIVE WERE PASSING RIGHT OUTSIDE THE KITCHEN DOOR.
MOM?
"I DON'T KNOW WHAT THEY WERE.
"OR WHY THEY TOOK HER.
MOMMM?
MOMMAA?!!
"ALL I REMEMBER IS THAT LAST SECOND... WHEN SHE WAS MY LITTLE GIRL AGAIN."

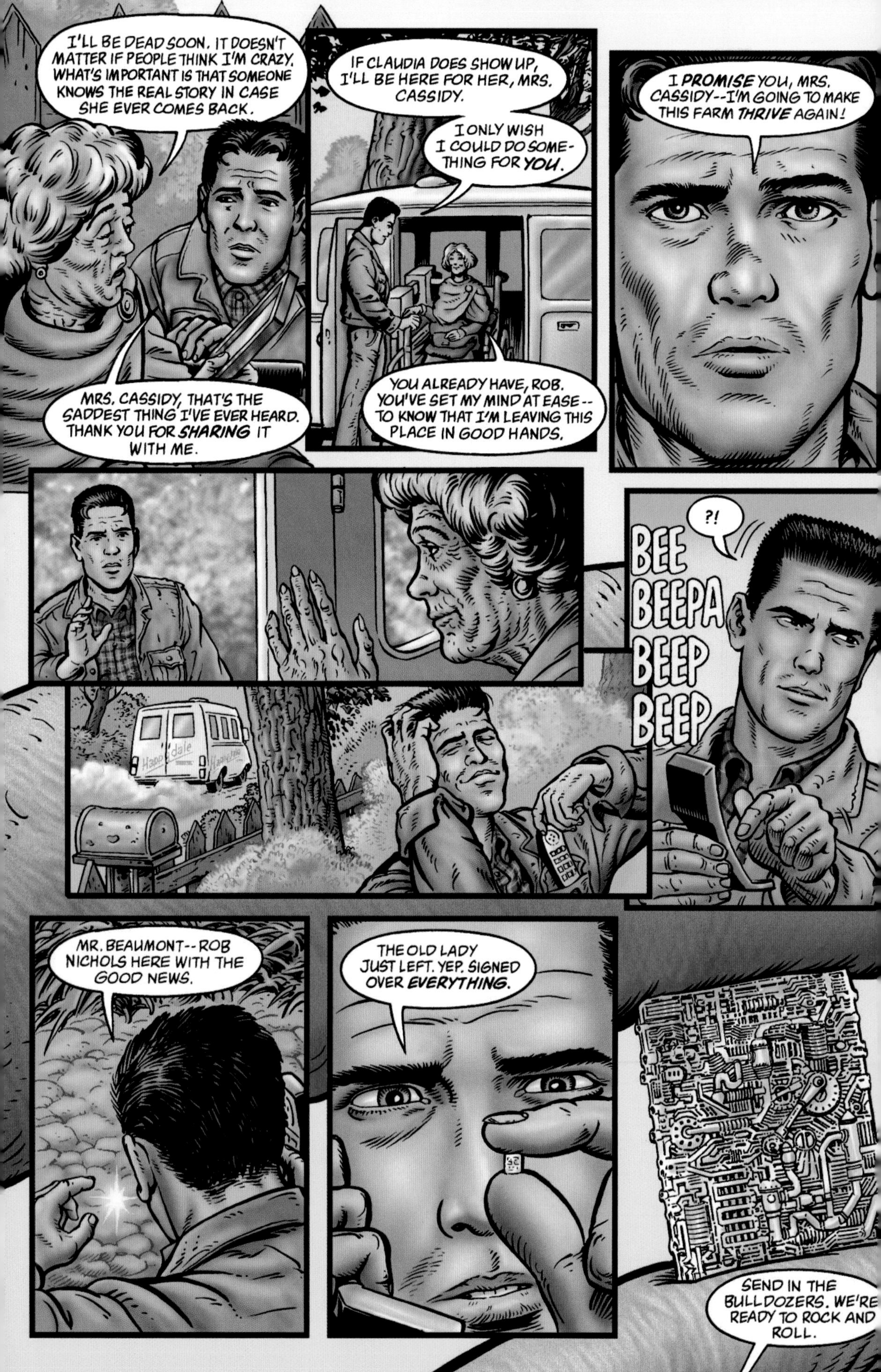
I'LL BE DEAD SOON. IT DOESN'T MATTER IF PEOPLE THINK I'M CRAZY. WHAT'S IMPORTANT IS THAT SOMEONE KNOWS THE REAL STORY IN CASE SHE EVER COMES BACK.
MRS. CASSIDY, THAT'S THE SADDEST THING I'VE EVER HEARD. THANK YOU FOR SHARING IT WITH ME.
IF CLAUDIA DOES SHOW UP, I'LL BE HERE FOR HER, MRS. CASSIDY.
I ONLY WISH I COULD DO SOMETHING FOR YOU.
YOU ALREADY HAVE, ROB. YOU'VE SET MY MIND AT EASE-- TO KNOW THAT I'M LEAVING THIS PLACE IN GOOD HANDS.
I PROMISE YOU, MRS. CASSIDY--I'M GOING TO MAKE THIS FARM THRIVE AGAIN!
?!
BEE BEEPA BEEP BEEP
MR. BEAUMONT--ROB NICHOLS HERE WITH THE GOOD NEWS.
THE OLD LADY JUST LEFT. YEP. SIGNED OVER EVERYTHING.
SEND IN THE BULLDOZERS. WE'RE READY TO ROCK AND ROLL.

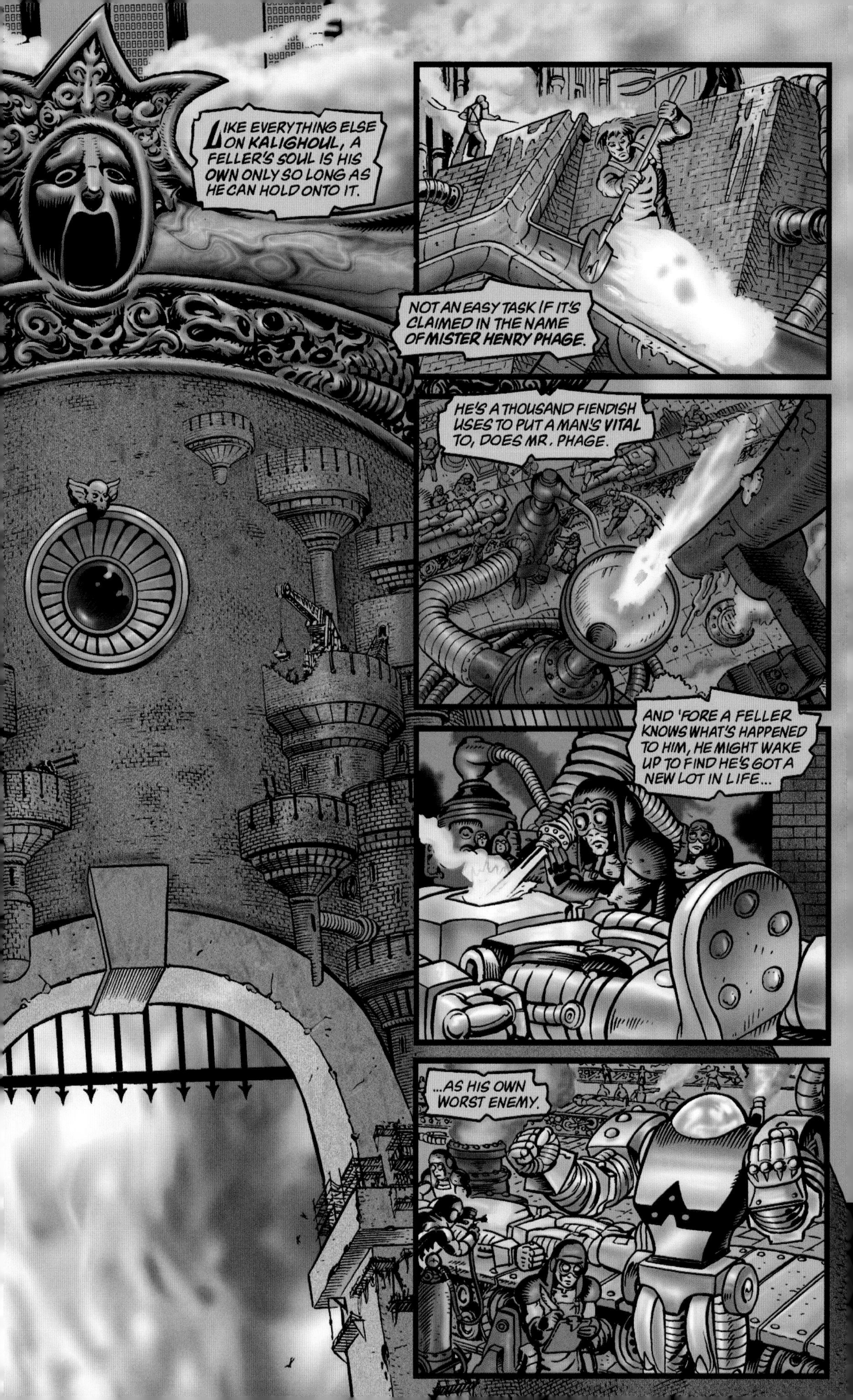
LIKE EVERYTHING ELSE ON KALIGHOUL, A FELLER'S SOUL IS HIS OWN ONLY SO LONG AS HE CAN HOLD ONTO IT.
NOT AN EASY TASK IF IT'S CLAIMED IN THE NAME OF MISTER HENRY PHAGE.
HE'S A THOUSAND FIENDISH USES TO PUT A MAN'S VITAL TO, DOES MR. PHAGE.
AND 'FORE A FELLER KNOWS WHAT'S HAPPENED TO HIM, HE MIGHT WAKE UP TO FIND HE'S GOT A NEW LOT IN LIFE...
...AS HIS OWN WORST ENEMY.

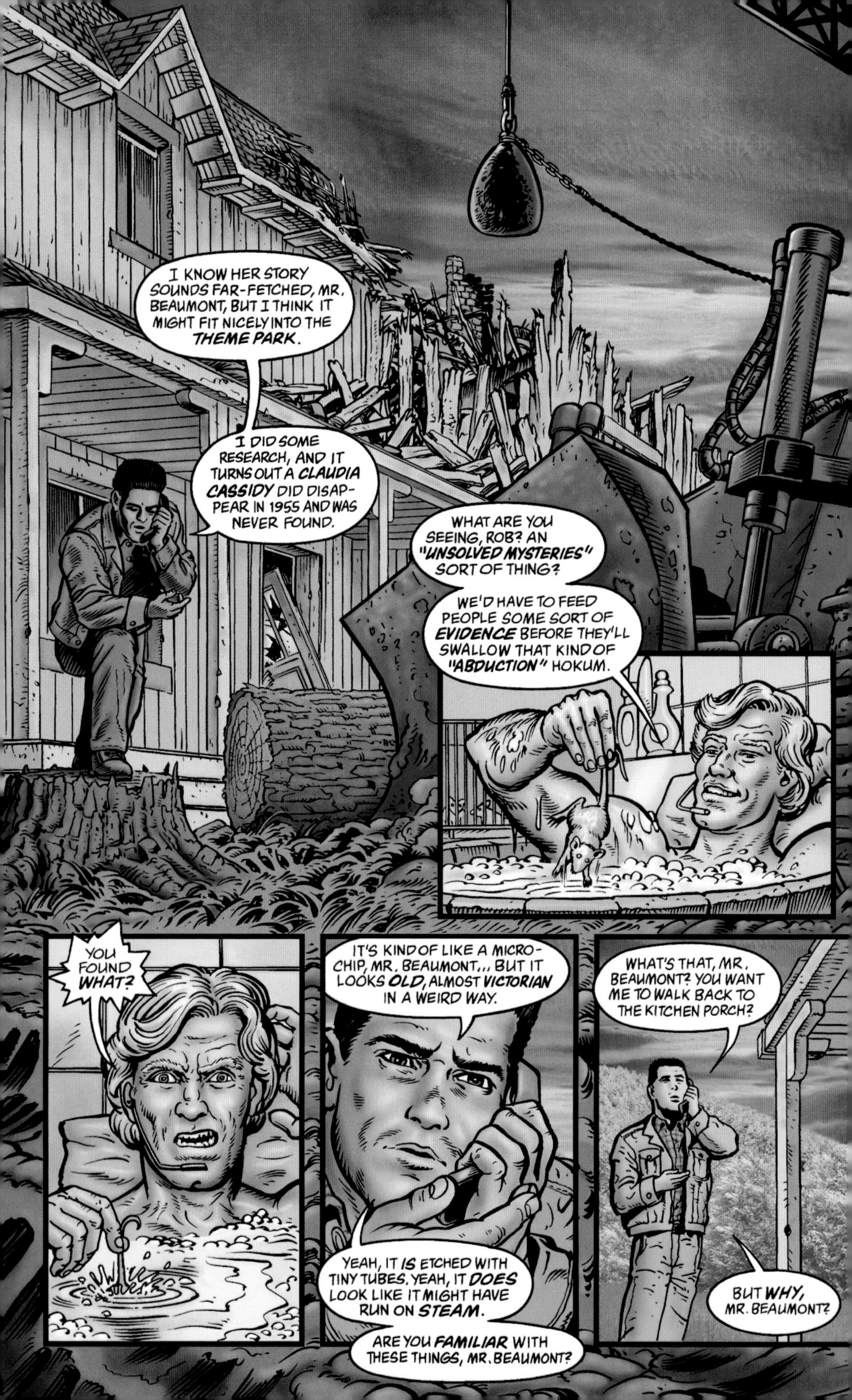
I KNOW HER STORY SOUNDS FAR-FETCHED, MR. BEAUMONT, BUT I THINK IT MIGHT FIT NICELY INTO THE THEME PARK.
I DID SOME RESEARCH, AND IT TURNS OUT A CLAUDIA CASSIDY DID DISAPPEAR IN 1955 AND WAS NEVER FOUND.
WHAT ARE YOU SEEING, ROB? AN "UNSOLVED MYSTERIES" SORT OF THING?
WE'D HAVE TO FEED PEOPLE SOME SORT OF EVIDENCE BEFORE THEY'LL SWALLOW THAT KIND OF "ABDUCTION" HOKUM.
YOU FOUND WHAT?
IT'S KIND OF LIKE A MICRO-CHIP, MR. BEAUMONT... BUT IT LOOKS OLD, ALMOST VICTORIAN IN A WEIRD WAY.
YEAH, IT IS ETCHED WITH TINY TUBES. YEAH, IT DOES LOOK LIKE IT MIGHT HAVE RUN ON STEAM.
ARE YOU FAMILIAR WITH THESE THINGS, MR. BEAUMONT?
WHAT'S THAT, MR. BEAUMONT? YOU WANT ME TO WALK BACK TO THE KITCHEN PORCH?
BUT WHY, MR. BEAUMONT?

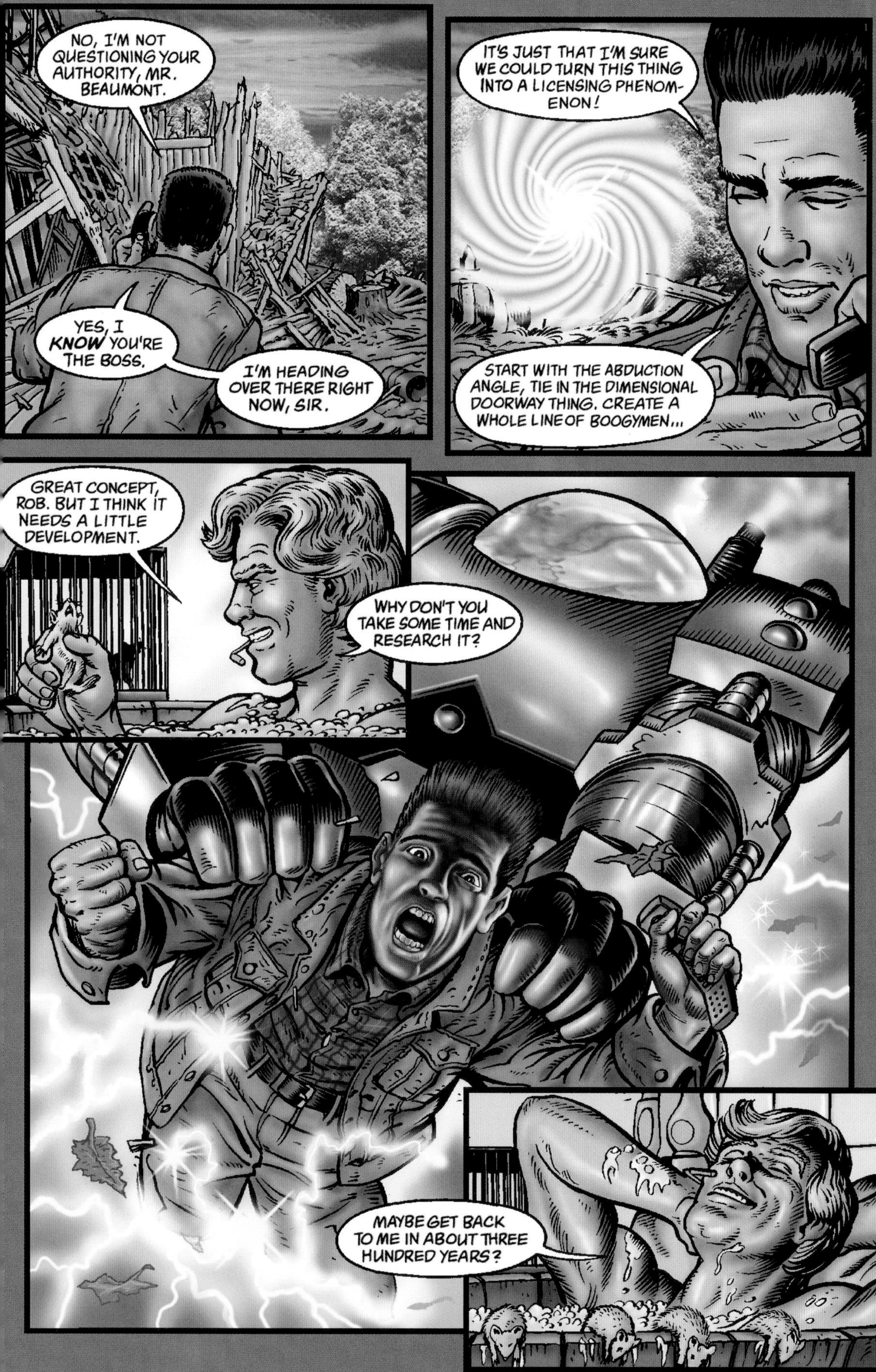
NO, I'M NOT QUESTIONING YOUR AUTHORITY, MR. BEAUMONT.
YES, I KNOW YOU'RE THE BOSS.
I'M HEADING OVER THERE RIGHT NOW, SIR.
IT'S JUST THAT I'M SURE WE COULD TURN THIS THING INTO A LICENSING PHENOM-ENON!
START WITH THE ABDUCTION ANGLE, TIE IN THE DIMENSIONAL DOORWAY THING. CREATE A WHOLE LINE OF BOOGYMEN...
GREAT CONCEPT, ROB. BUT I THINK IT NEEDS A LITTLE DEVELOPMENT.
WHY DON'T YOU TAKE SOME TIME AND RESEARCH IT?
MAYBE GET BACK TO ME IN ABOUT THREE HUNDRED YEARS?

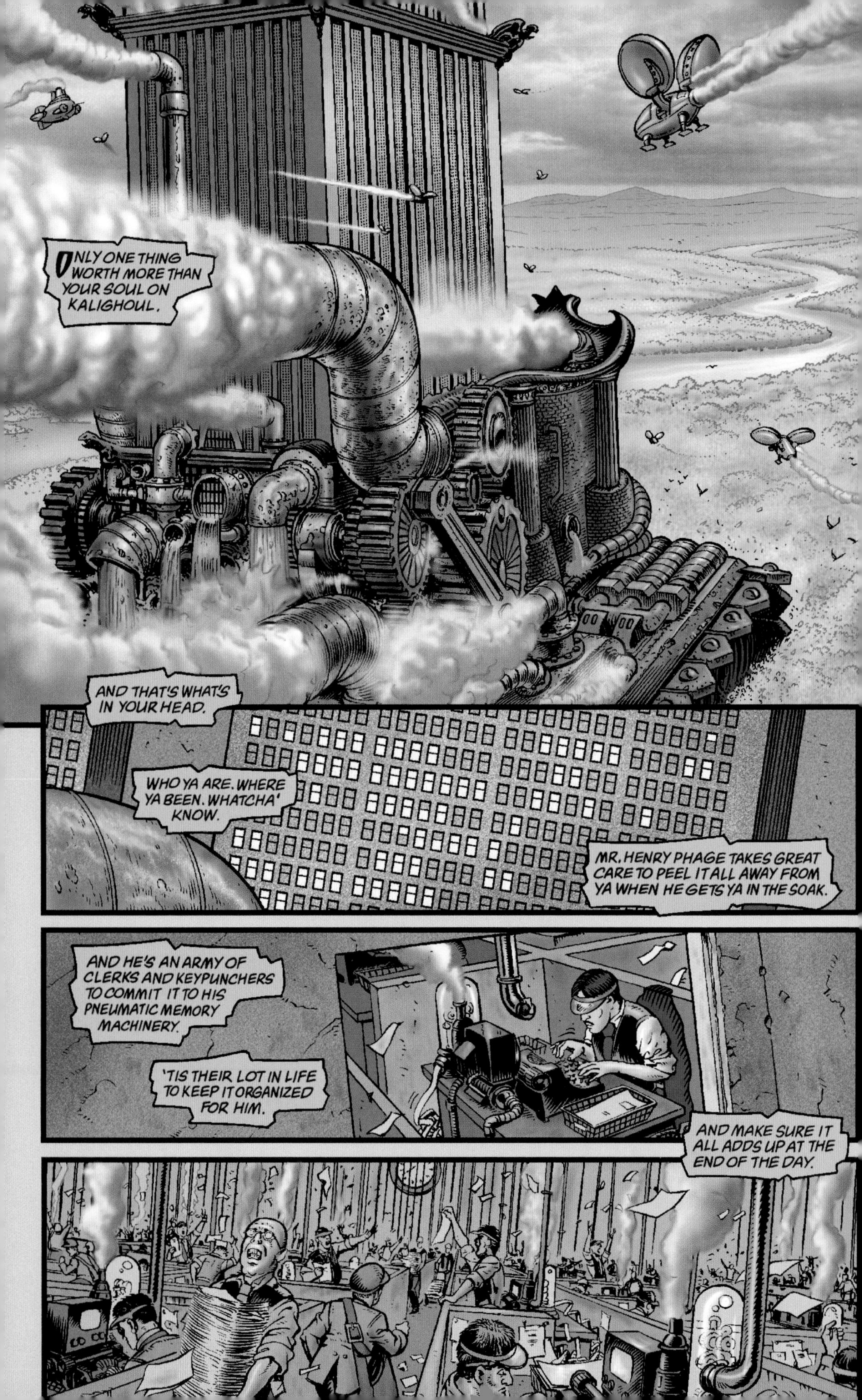
ONLY ONE THING WORTH MORE THAN YOUR SOUL ON KALIGHOUL.
AND THAT'S WHAT'S IN YOUR HEAD.
WHO YA ARE. WHERE YA BEEN. WHATCHA' KNOW.
MR. HENRY PHAGE TAKES GREAT CARE TO PEEL IT ALL AWAY FROM YA WHEN HE GETS YA IN THE SOAK.
AND HE'S AN ARMY OF CLERKS AND KEYPUNCHERS TO COMMIT IT TO HIS PNEUMATIC MEMORY MACHINERY.
'TIS THEIR LOT IN LIFE TO KEEP IT ORGANIZED FOR HIM.
AND MAKE SURE IT ALL ADDS UP AT THE END OF THE DAY.

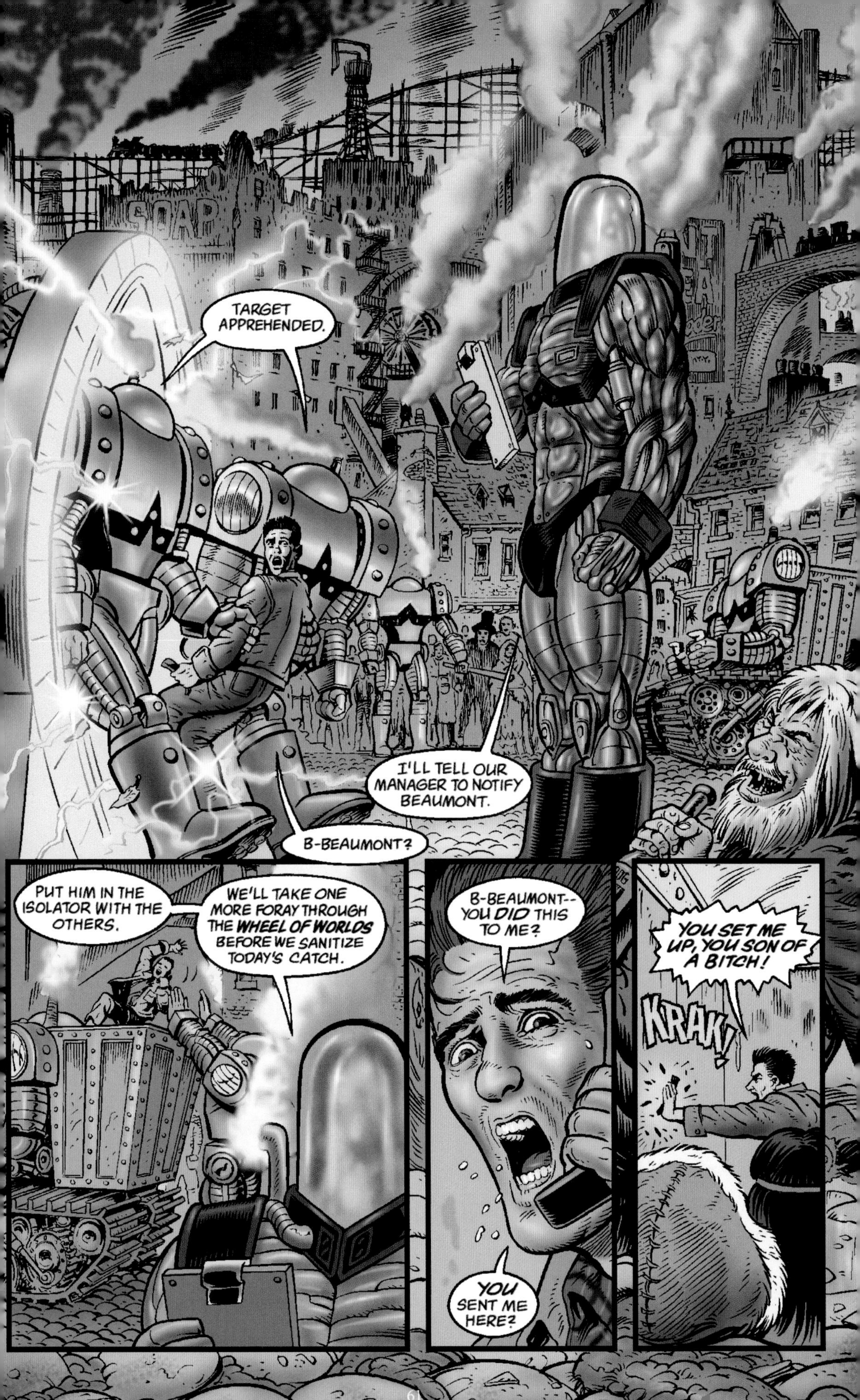
TARGET APPREHENDED.
I'LL TELL OUR MANAGER TO NOTIFY BEAUMONT.
B-BEAUMONT?
PUT HIM IN THE ISOLATOR WITH THE OTHERS.
WE'LL TAKE ONE MORE FORAY THROUGH THE WHEEL OF WORLDS BEFORE WE SANITIZE TODAY'S CATCH.
B-BEAUMONT-- YOU DID THIS TO ME?
YOU SENT ME HERE?
YOU SET ME UP, YOU SON OF A BITCH!
KRAK!

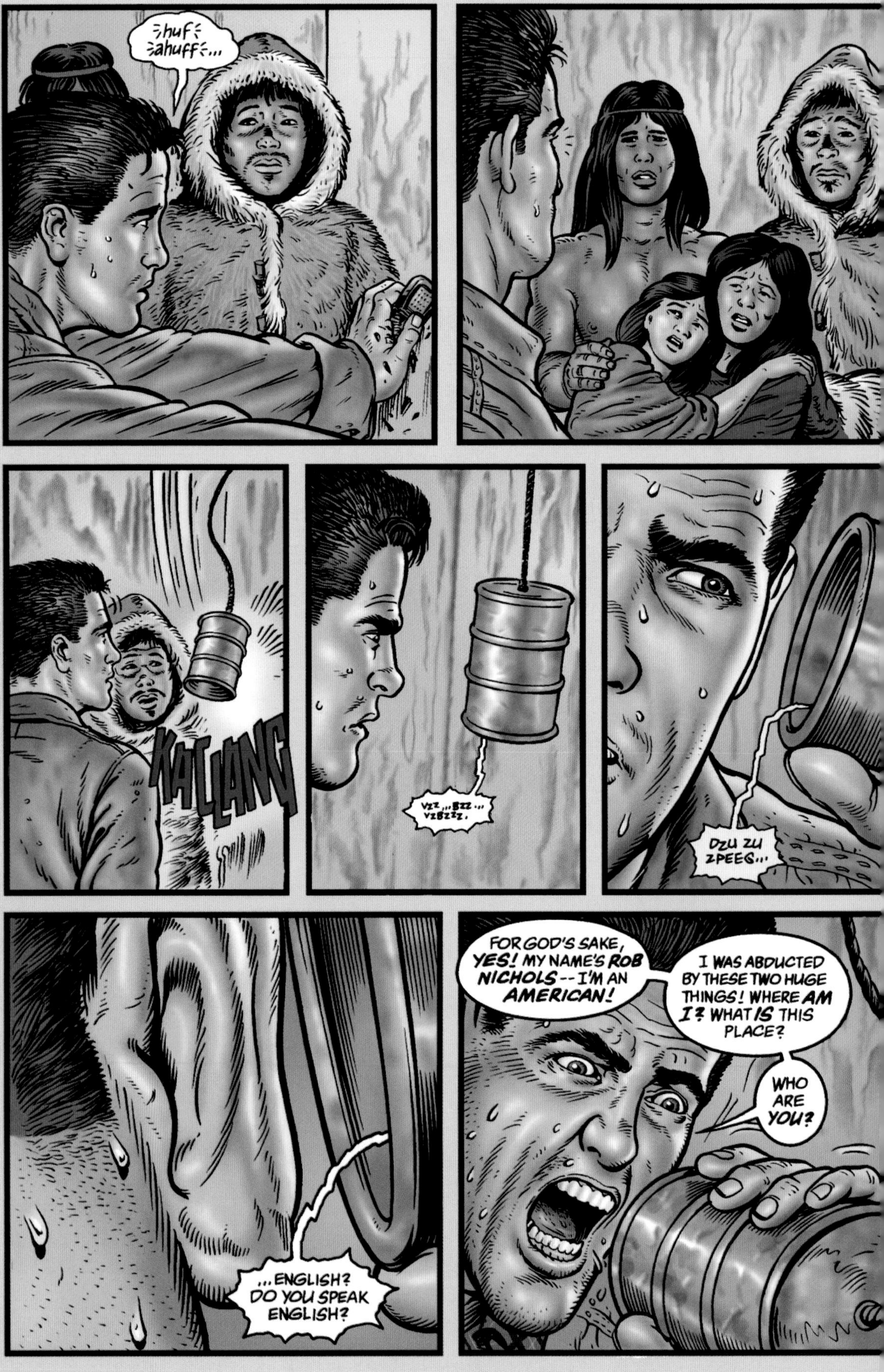
huf
ahuff...
KALLANG
VZZ...BZZ...
VZBZZZ.
DZU ZU
ZPEEG...
...ENGLISH?
DO YOU SPEAK
ENGLISH?
FOR GOD'S SAKE, YES! MY NAME'S ROB NICHOLS -- I'M AN AMERICAN!
I WAS ABDUCTED BY THESE TWO HUGE THINGS! WHERE AM I? WHAT IS THIS PLACE?
WHO ARE YOU?

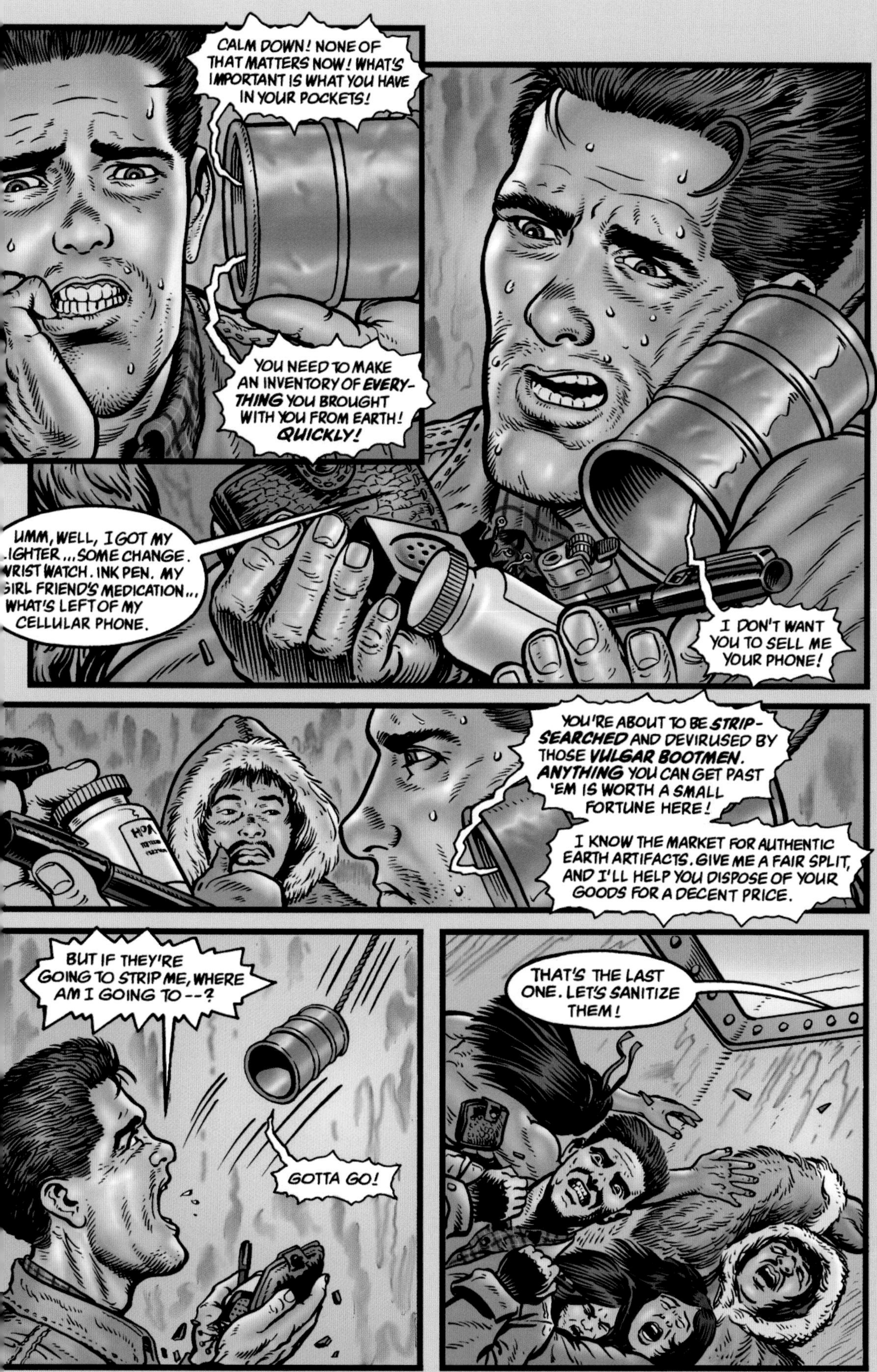
CALM DOWN! NONE OF THAT MATTERS NOW! WHAT'S IMPORTANT IS WHAT YOU HAVE IN YOUR POCKETS!
YOU NEED TO MAKE AN INVENTORY OF EVERY-THING YOU BROUGHT WITH YOU FROM EARTH! QUICKLY!
UMM, WELL, I GOT MY LIGHTER... SOME CHANGE. WRIST WATCH. INK PEN. MY GIRL FRIEND'S MEDICATION... WHAT'S LEFT OF MY CELLULAR PHONE.
I DON'T WANT YOU TO SELL ME YOUR PHONE!
YOU'RE ABOUT TO BE STRIP-SEARCHED AND DEVIRUSED BY THOSE VULGAR BOOTMEN. ANYTHING YOU CAN GET PAST 'EM IS WORTH A SMALL FORTUNE HERE!
I KNOW THE MARKET FOR AUTHENTIC EARTH ARTIFACTS. GIVE ME A FAIR SPLIT, AND I'LL HELP YOU DISPOSE OF YOUR GOODS FOR A DECENT PRICE.
BUT IF THEY'RE GOING TO STRIP ME, WHERE AM I GOING TO --?
GOTTA GO!
THAT'S THE LAST ONE. LET'S SANITIZE THEM!

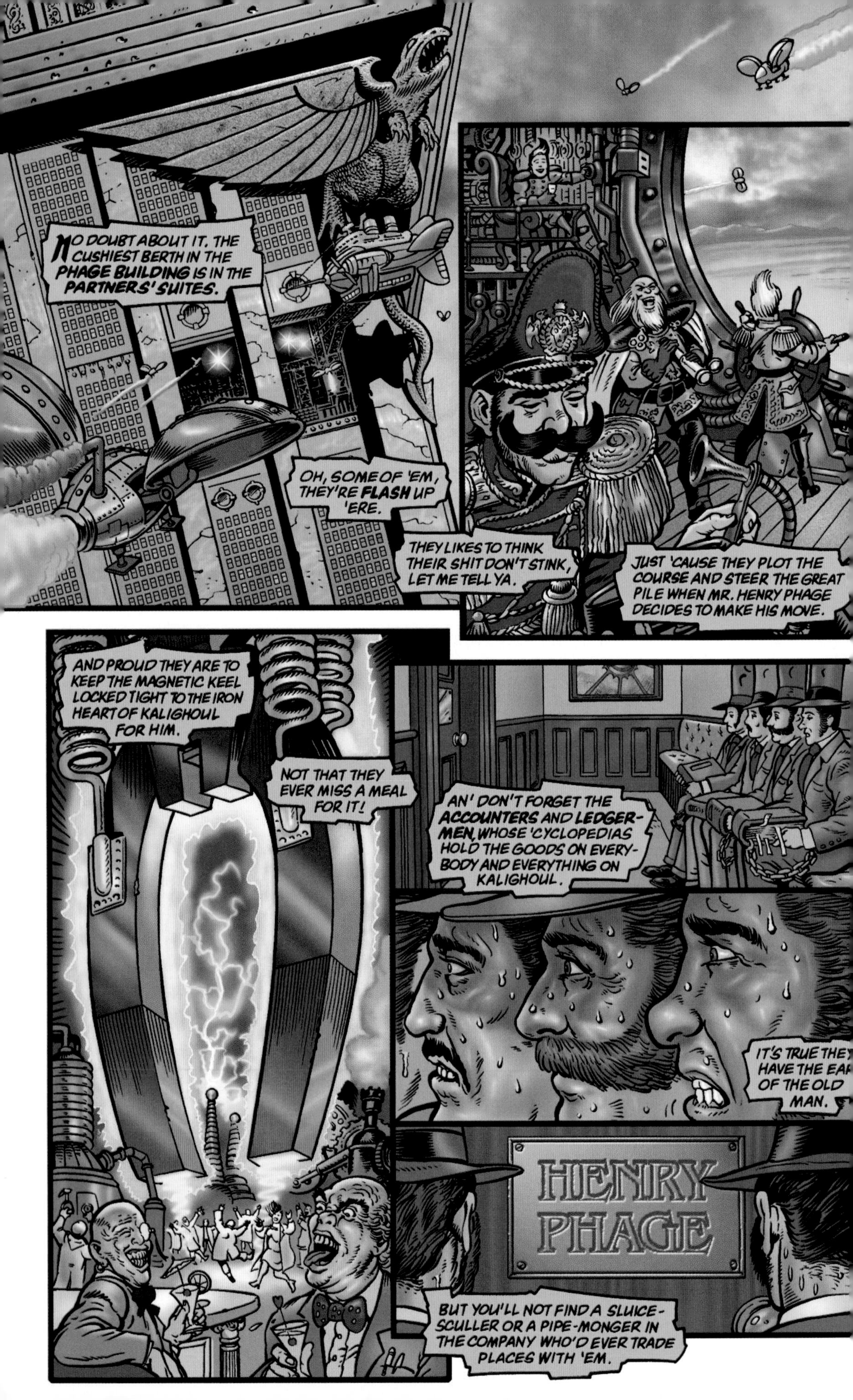
NO DOUBT ABOUT IT. THE CUSHIEST BERTH IN THE PHAGE BUILDING IS IN THE PARTNERS' SUITES.
OH, SOME OF 'EM, THEY'RE FLASH UP 'ERE.
THEY LIKES TO THINK THEIR SHIT DON'T STINK, LET ME TELL YA.
JUST 'CAUSE THEY PLOT THE COURSE AND STEER THE GREAT PILE WHEN MR. HENRY PHAGE DECIDES TO MAKE HIS MOVE.
AND PROUD THEY ARE TO KEEP THE MAGNETIC KEEL LOCKED TIGHT TO THE IRON HEART OF KALIGHOUL FOR HIM.
NOT THAT THEY EVER MISS A MEAL FOR IT!
AN' DON'T FORGET THE ACCOUNTERS AND LEDGERMEN, WHOSE 'CYCLOPEDIAS HOLD THE GOODS ON EVERYBODY AND EVERYTHING ON KALIGHOUL.
IT'S TRUE THEY HAVE THE EAR OF THE OLD MAN.
HENRY PHAGE
BUT YOU'LL NOT FIND A SLUICE-SCULLER OR A PIPE-MONGER IN THE COMPANY WHO'D EVER TRADE PLACES WITH 'EM.

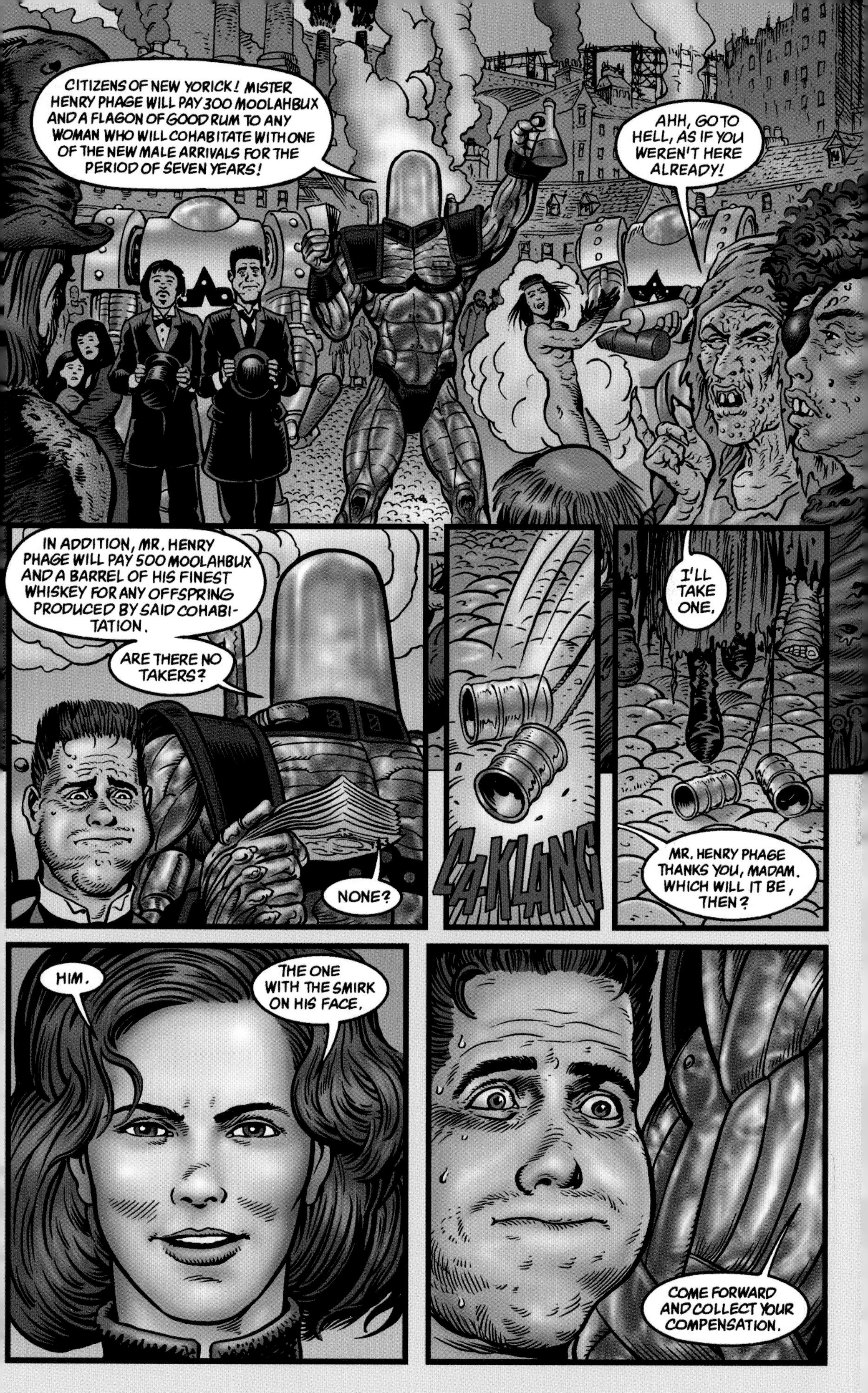
CITIZENS OF NEW YORICK! MISTER HENRY PHAGE WILL PAY 300 MOOLAHBUX AND A FLAGON OF GOOD RUM TO ANY WOMAN WHO WILL COHABITATE WITH ONE OF THE NEW MALE ARRIVALS FOR THE PERIOD OF SEVEN YEARS!
AHH, GO TO HELL, AS IF YOU WEREN'T HERE ALREADY!
IN ADDITION, MR. HENRY PHAGE WILL PAY 500 MOOLAHBUX AND A BARREL OF HIS FINEST WHISKEY FOR ANY OFFSPRING PRODUCED BY SAID COHABITATION.
ARE THERE NO TAKERS?
NONE?
CA-KLANG
I'LL TAKE ONE.
MR. HENRY PHAGE THANKS YOU, MADAM. WHICH WILL IT BE, THEN?
HIM.
THE ONE WITH THE SMIRK ON HIS FACE.
COME FORWARD AND COLLECT YOUR COMPENSATION.

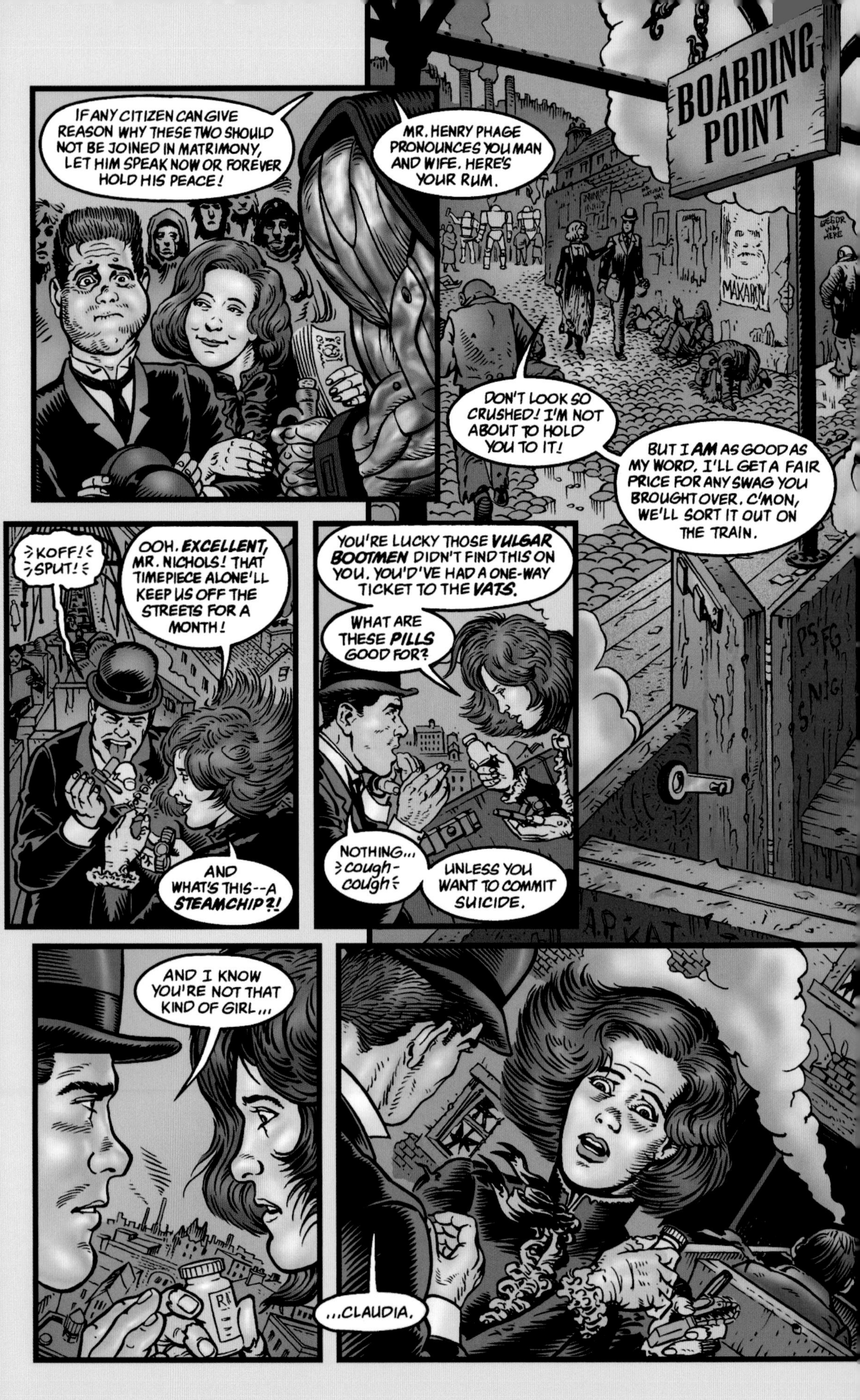
BOARDING POINT
IF ANY CITIZEN CAN GIVE REASON WHY THESE TWO SHOULD NOT BE JOINED IN MATRIMONY, LET HIM SPEAK NOW OR FOREVER HOLD HIS PEACE!
MR. HENRY PHAGE PRONOUNCES YOU MAN AND WIFE. HERE'S YOUR RUM.
MAKAROV
DON'T LOOK SO CRUSHED! I'M NOT ABOUT TO HOLD YOU TO IT!
BUT I AM AS GOOD AS MY WORD. I'LL GET A FAIR PRICE FOR ANY SWAG YOU BROUGHT OVER. C'MON, WE'LL SORT IT OUT ON THE TRAIN.
KOFF! SPUT!
OOH. EXCELLENT, MR. NICHOLS! THAT TIMEPIECE ALONE'LL KEEP US OFF THE STREETS FOR A MONTH!
AND WHAT'S THIS--A STEAMCHIP?!
YOU'RE LUCKY THOSE VULGAR BOOTMEN DIDN'T FIND THIS ON YOU. YOU'D'VE HAD A ONE-WAY TICKET TO THE VATS.
WHAT ARE THESE PILLS GOOD FOR?
NOTHING... cough-cough
UNLESS YOU WANT TO COMMIT SUICIDE.
AND I KNOW YOU'RE NOT THAT KIND OF GIRL...
...CLAUDIA.

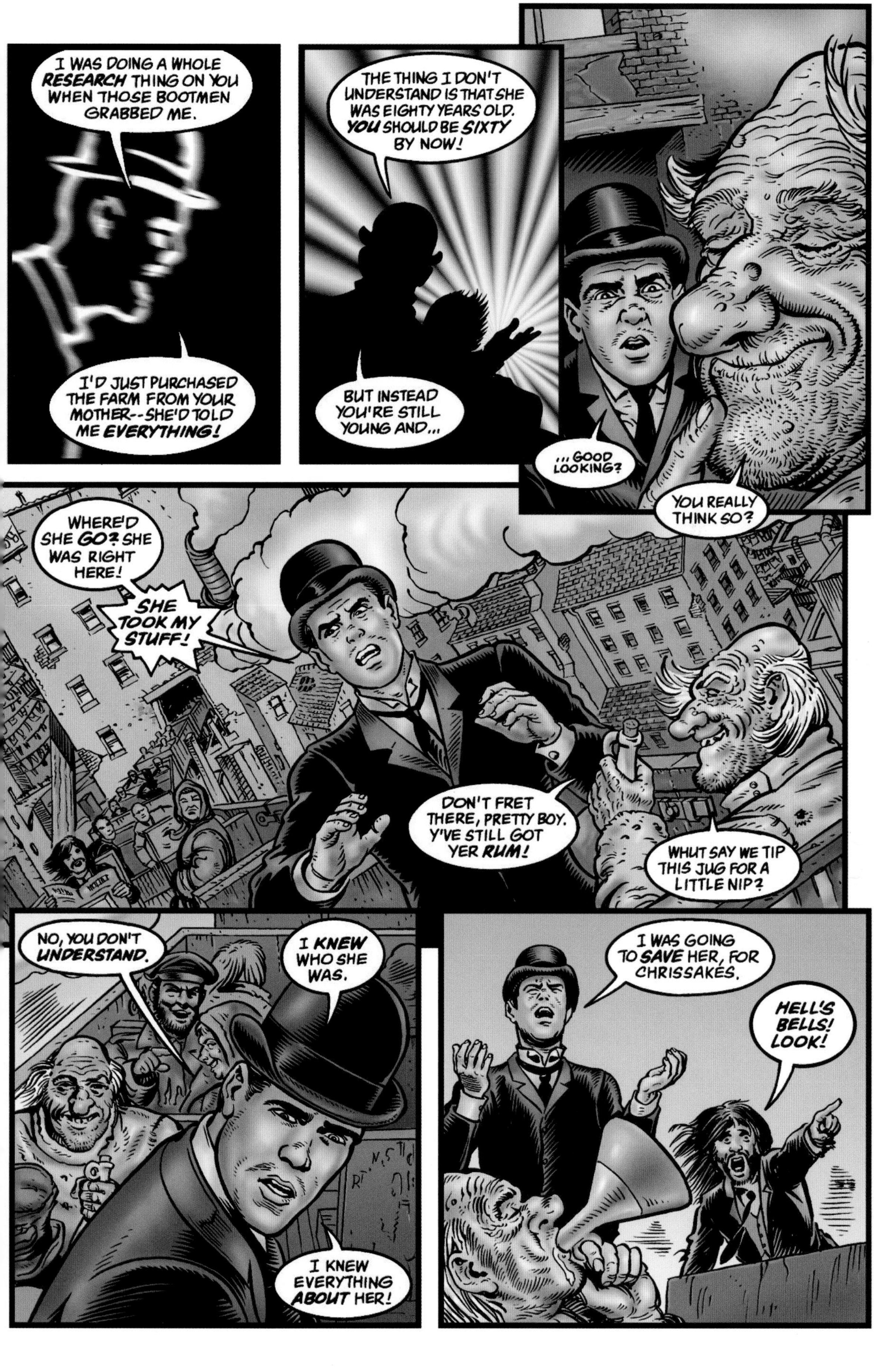

I WAS DOING A WHOLE RESEARCH THING ON YOU WHEN THOSE BOOTMEN GRABBED ME.
I'D JUST PURCHASED THE FARM FROM YOUR MOTHER--SHE'D TOLD ME EVERYTHING!
THE THING I DON'T UNDERSTAND IS THAT SHE WAS EIGHTY YEARS OLD. YOU SHOULD BE SIXTY BY NOW!
BUT INSTEAD YOU'RE STILL YOUNG AND...
...GOOD LOOKING?
YOU REALLY THINK SO?
WHERE'D SHE GO? SHE WAS RIGHT HERE!
SHE TOOK MY STUFF!
DON'T FRET THERE, PRETTY BOY. Y'VE STILL GOT YER RUM!
WHUT SAY WE TIP THIS JUG FOR A LITTLE NIP?
NO, YOU DON'T UNDERSTAND.
I KNEW WHO SHE WAS.
I KNEW EVERYTHING ABOUT HER!
I WAS GOING TO SAVE HER, FOR CHRISSAKES.
HELL'S BELLS! LOOK!

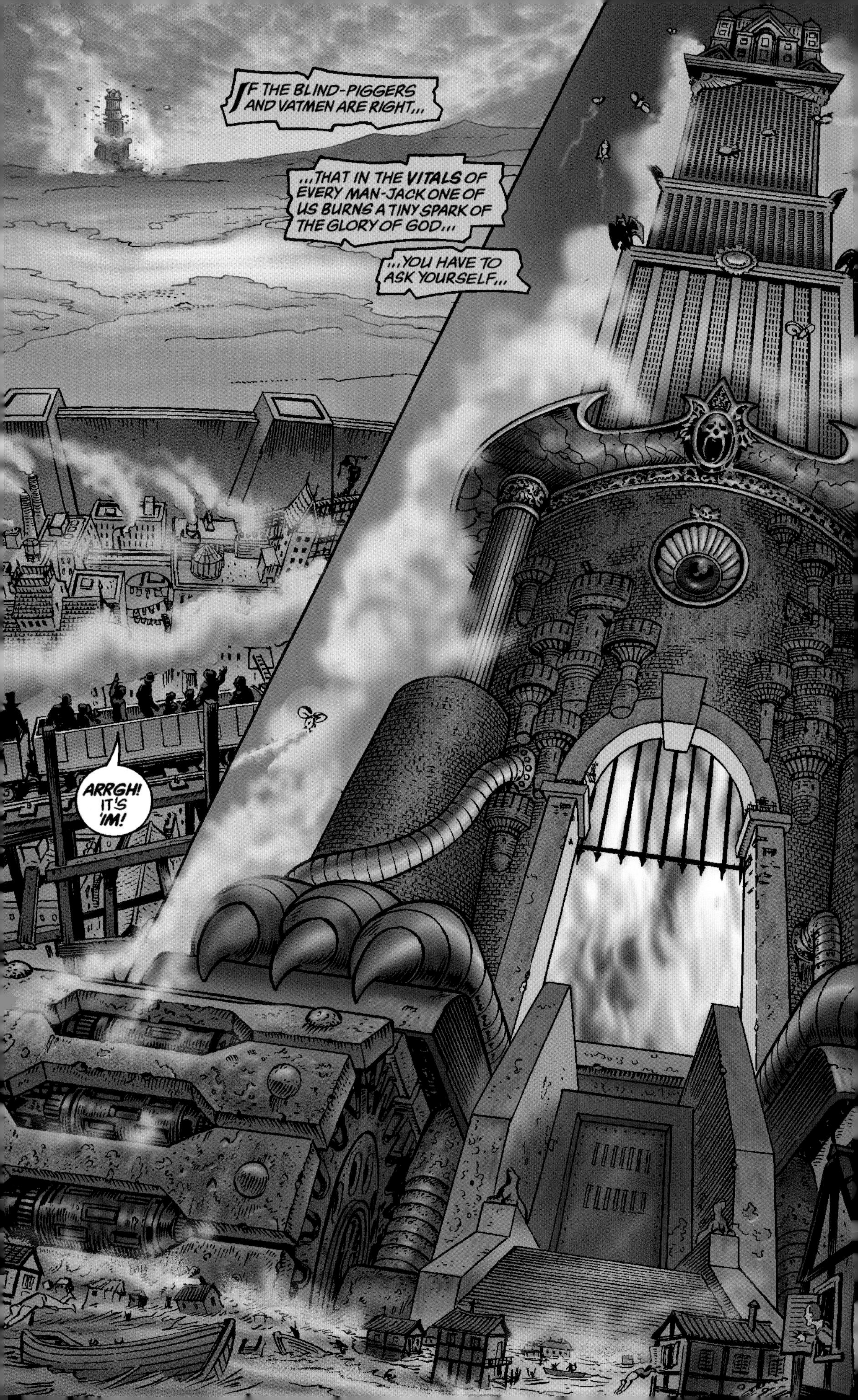
IF THE BLIND-PIGGERS AND VATMEN ARE RIGHT,,,
,,,THAT IN THE VITALS OF EVERY MAN-JACK ONE OF US BURNS A TINY SPARK OF THE GLORY OF GOD,,,
,,,YOU HAVE TO ASK YOURSELF,,,
ARRGH! IT'S 'IM!

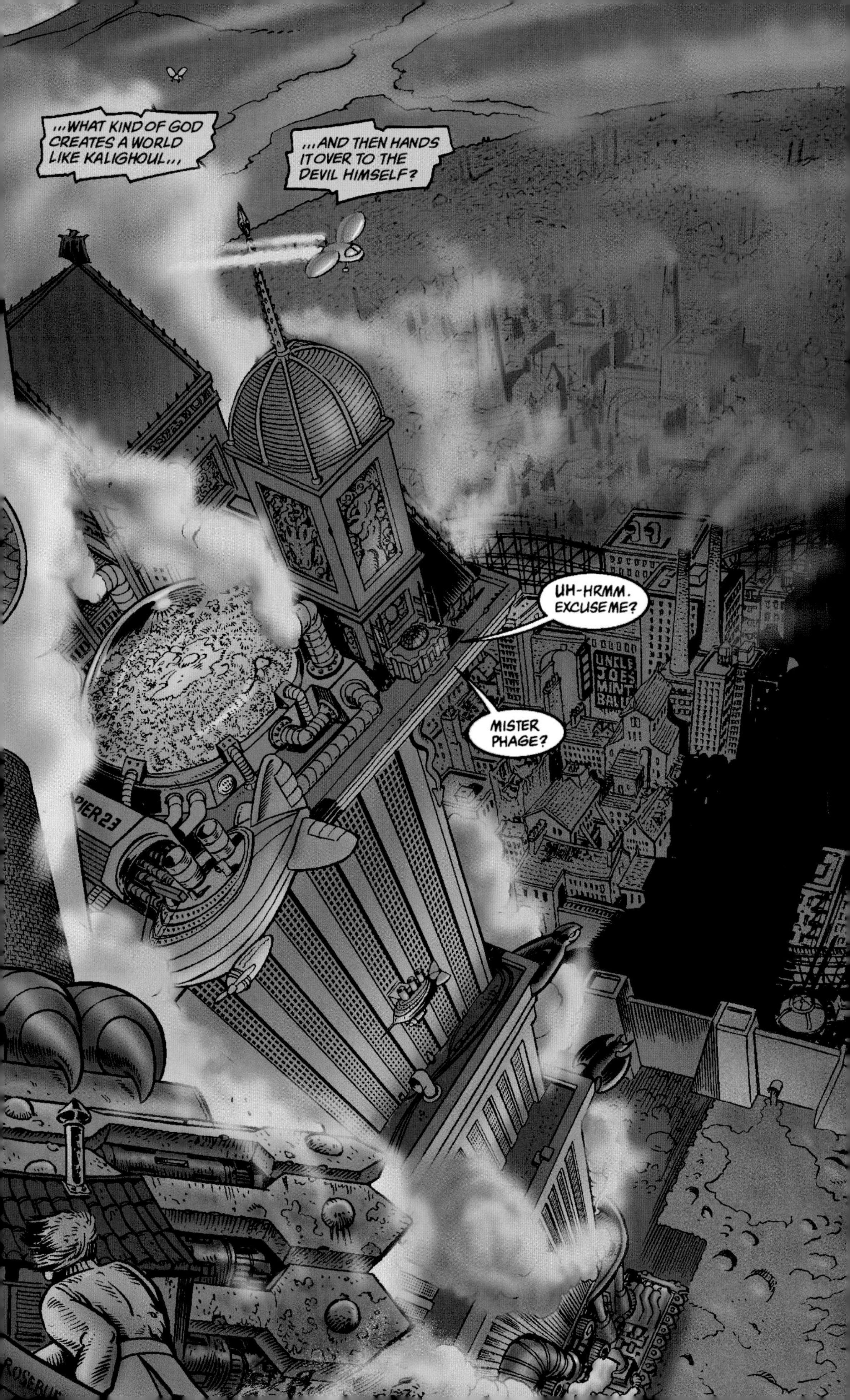
...WHAT KIND OF GOD CREATES A WORLD LIKE KALIGHOUL...
...AND THEN HANDS IT OVER TO THE DEVIL HIMSELF?
UH-HRMM. EXCUSE ME?
MISTER PHAGE?
PIER 23
UNKLE JOES MINT BALL

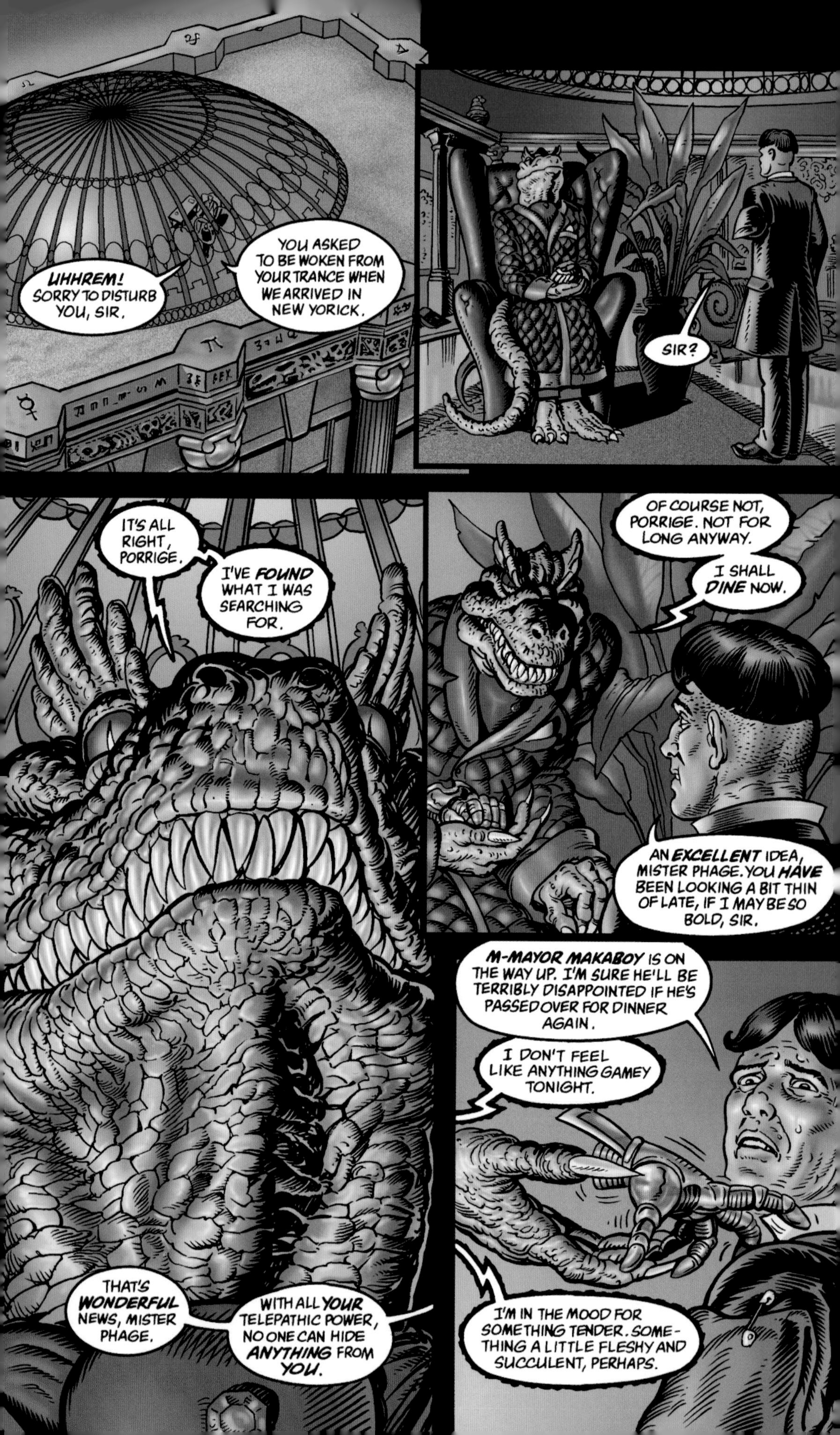
UHHREM! SORRY TO DISTURB YOU, SIR.
YOU ASKED TO BE WOKEN FROM YOUR TRANCE WHEN WE ARRIVED IN NEW YORICK.
SIR?
IT'S ALL RIGHT, PORRIGE.
I'VE FOUND WHAT I WAS SEARCHING FOR.
THAT'S WONDERFUL NEWS, MISTER PHAGE.
WITH ALL YOUR TELEPATHIC POWER, NO ONE CAN HIDE ANYTHING FROM YOU.
OF COURSE NOT, PORRIGE. NOT FOR LONG ANYWAY.
I SHALL DINE NOW.
AN EXCELLENT IDEA, MISTER PHAGE. YOU HAVE BEEN LOOKING A BIT THIN OF LATE, IF I MAY BE SO BOLD, SIR.
M-MAYOR MAKABOY IS ON THE WAY UP. I'M SURE HE'LL BE TERRIBLY DISAPPOINTED IF HE'S PASSED OVER FOR DINNER AGAIN.
I DON'T FEEL LIKE ANYTHING GAMEY TONIGHT.
I'M IN THE MOOD FOR SOMETHING TENDER. SOME-THING A LITTLE FLESHY AND SUCCULENT, PERHAPS.

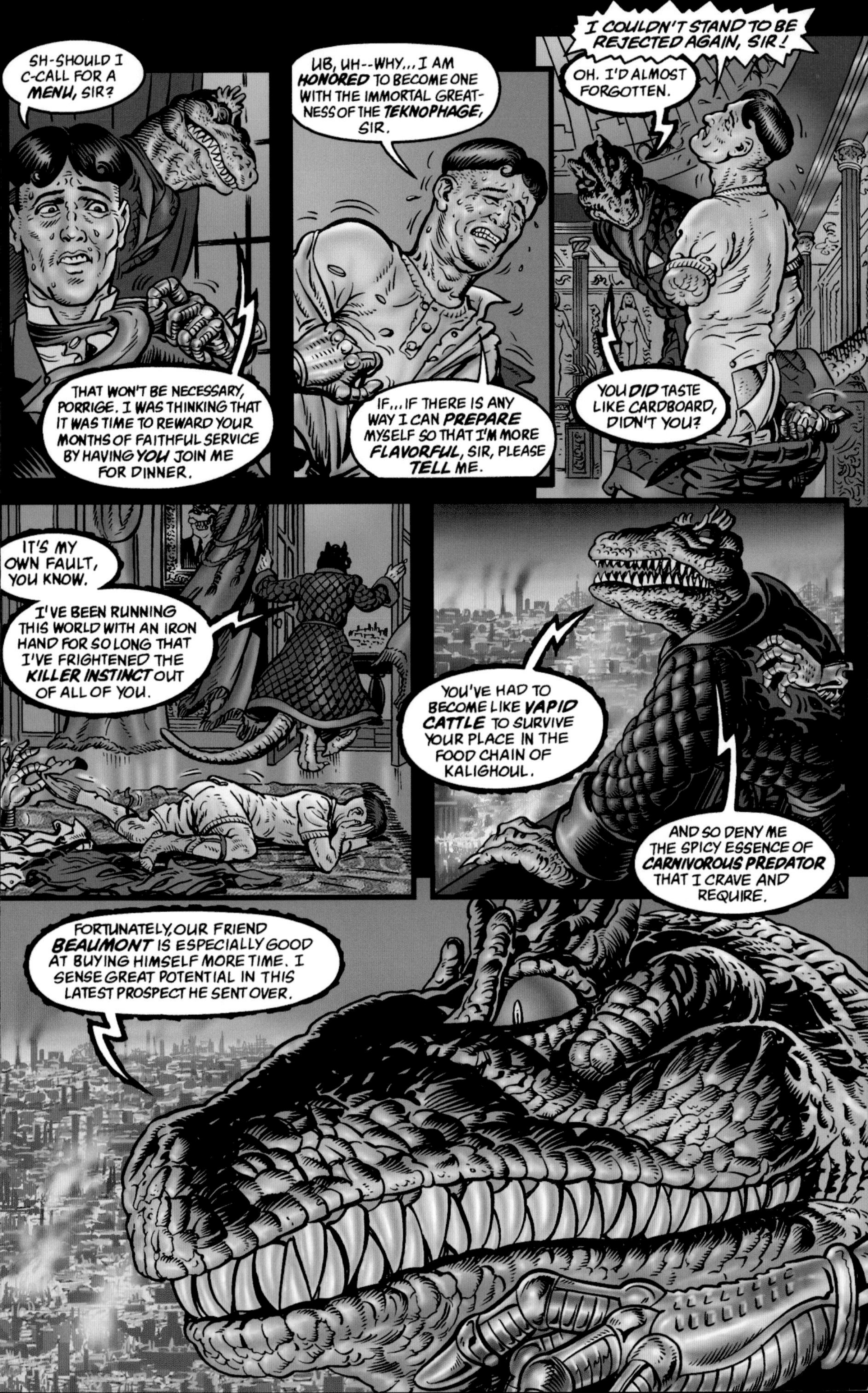
SH-SHOULD I C-CALL FOR A MENU, SIR?
THAT WON'T BE NECESSARY, PORRIGE. I WAS THINKING THAT IT WAS TIME TO REWARD YOUR MONTHS OF FAITHFUL SERVICE BY HAVING YOU JOIN ME FOR DINNER.
UB, UH--WHY... I AM HONORED TO BECOME ONE WITH THE IMMORTAL GREATNESS OF THE TEKNOPHAGE, SIR.
IF... IF THERE IS ANY WAY I CAN PREPARE MYSELF SO THAT I'M MORE FLAVORFUL, SIR, PLEASE TELL ME.
I COULDN'T STAND TO BE REJECTED AGAIN, SIR!
OH. I'D ALMOST FORGOTTEN.
YOU DID TASTE LIKE CARDBOARD, DIDN'T YOU?
IT'S MY OWN FAULT, YOU KNOW.
I'VE BEEN RUNNING THIS WORLD WITH AN IRON HAND FOR SO LONG THAT I'VE FRIGHTENED THE KILLER INSTINCT OUT OF ALL OF YOU.
YOU'VE HAD TO BECOME LIKE VAPID CATTLE TO SURVIVE YOUR PLACE IN THE FOOD CHAIN OF KALIGHOUL.
AND SO DENY ME THE SPICY ESSENCE OF CARNIVOROUS PREDATOR THAT I CRAVE AND REQUIRE.
FORTUNATELY, OUR FRIEND BEAUMONT IS ESPECIALLY GOOD AT BUYING HIMSELF MORE TIME. I SENSE GREAT POTENTIAL IN THIS LATEST PROSPECT HE SENT OVER.

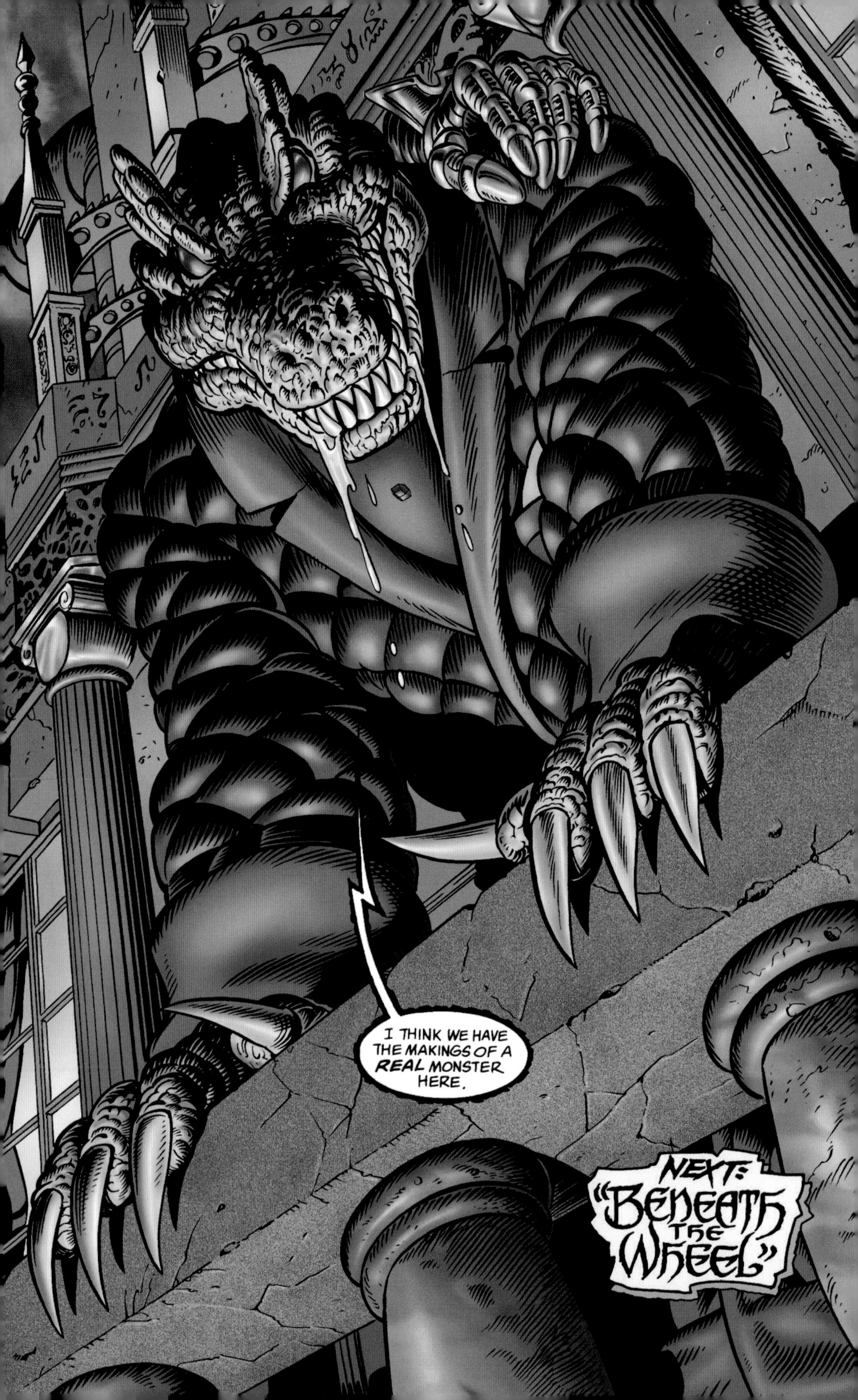
I THINK WE HAVE THE MAKINGS OF A *REAL* MONSTER HERE.
NEXT: "BENEATH THE WHEEL"

MAKING MOOLAHBUX

A Vatman's Guide to the Creation of Currency on Kalighoul

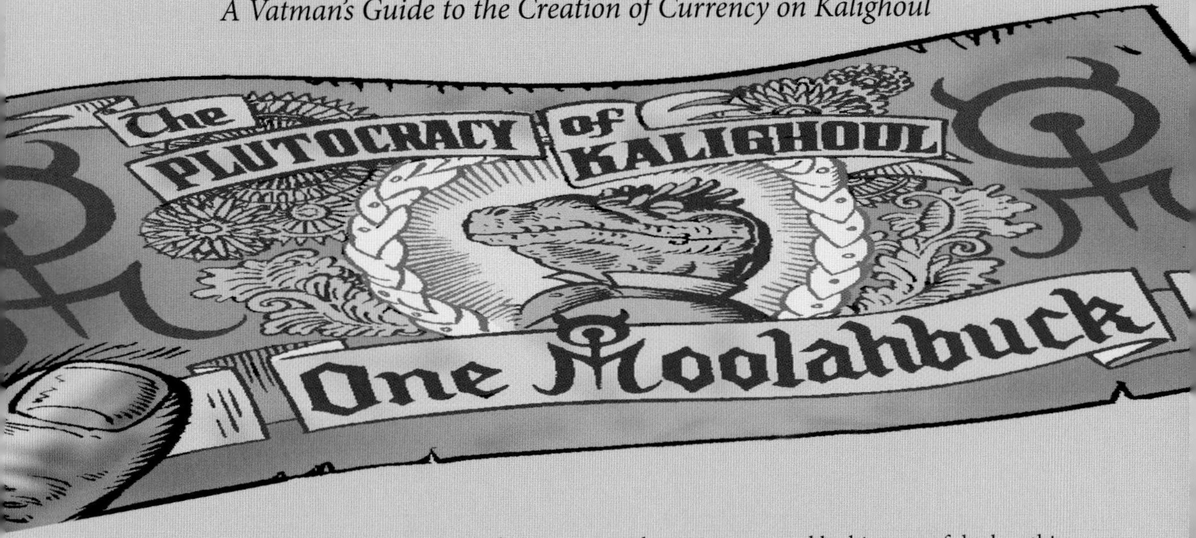
The
PLUTOCRACY
of
KALIGHOUL
One Moolahbuck

Symbols – they're important to us humans. And Mr. Henry Phage knows that the right emblem can work wonders in mass manipulation.

So when we needed to come up with the icon for the Moolahbuck, the paper currency on the greed-blasted planet of Kalighoul (also called the "Steambuck" in New Yorick slang), we knew it had to be a design that would tell the locals what the rules of their world were; a symbol that could make a desperate planetful of us "furry apes" claw over each other's corpses to get ahead.

Rick Veitch, in his script for TEKNOPHAGE #2, called for "a Moolahbuck icon that we can exploit later on, something as primal and visually catchy as the U. S. Dollar sign ($), if you can swing it. How about something with horns on it, or some sort of mystic devil symbol? Or, possibly, something adapted from an ancient alchemical symbol."

Hmmm… something as viscerally evocative and powerful as the slashed 'S' of the U. S. Dollar ('S' for Soul?), but specific to the Dark Alchemical world of Kalighoul.

Well, the dollar was founded on gold and backed by a leap of faith, a belief that everything, from art and mountains to Homo sapiens, can be melted down into '$'-value. The gold is gone, but the faith is still there. In the real world, a quivering mass psychology puts an ever-wavering value on the engraved paper. A power-current pulses through the currency. You have to boost your own '$'-value. The gold is gone, and if you run out of '$', things get cold fast.
On our Earth, as things stand, '$' means Life. But, on Kalighoul, the Steambuck is backed by the extracted souls of the Phage's victims, and sustained by the mass hysteria generated by his powerful telepathic abilities. When people viciously compete with each other for Moolahbux, they're actually filling their wallets with paper shares of that great cauldron of boiled soul-stuff, trying to get a piece of the Vat in order to stay out of it.
Entirely different… right? I went looking through my tome of alchemical symbols, on the hunt for a Moonbuck…Now represents life essence, that elusive quintessence, or "fifth" essence, after the four elements of earth, fire, water and air, that alchemists throughout the millennia have been trying to extract from matter. Sucked from the bodies of the unfortunate, this soul-force is the fuel that feeds the Phage's machinery.

Ψ

And is the symbol for gold, another long sought-after substance for the alchemists. Unlike the U. S. Treasury, Phage Industries has all the gold it needs to keep solvent (perhaps through an alchemical lead-to-gold process? Or just from the booty of an interdimensional empire?).

☉

So I stuck the two symbols together, came up with and ran it by Roarin' Rick and Bryan Talbot.

Bryan flipped the symbol, put horns on it, and, with an inspired flourish, used the lower part of the icon as the "M" in "Moolahbuck" on the Kalighoulian legal tender.

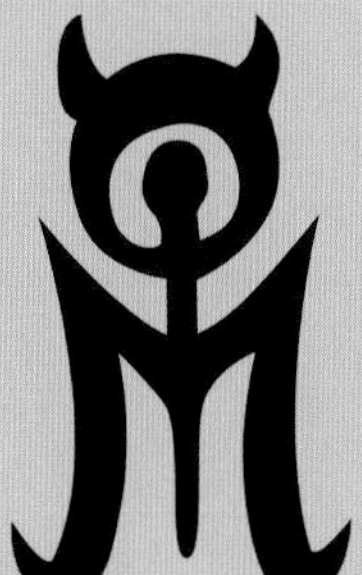

And so, a Symbol was born. Consume and Enjoy!

-L. M. Bogad

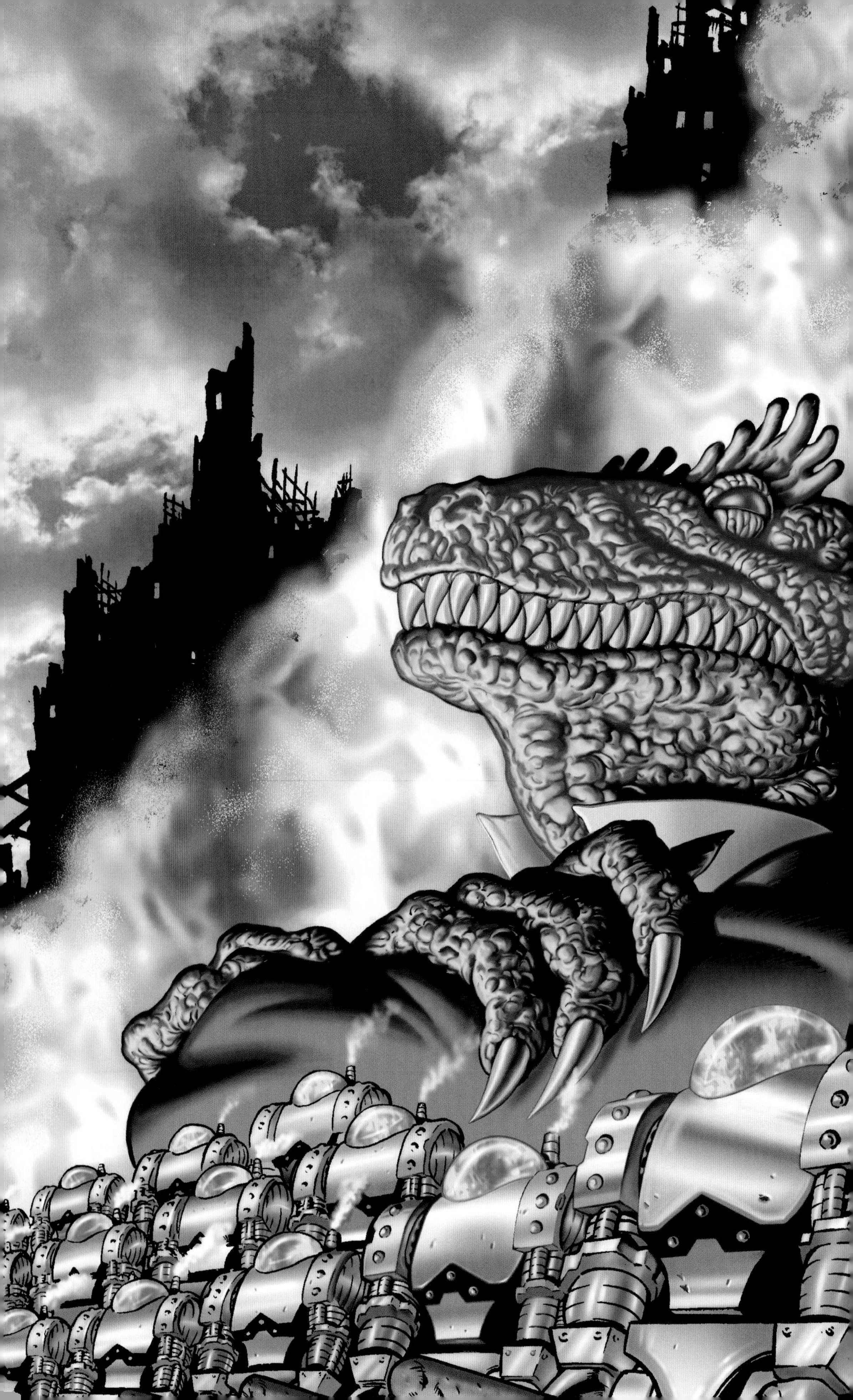

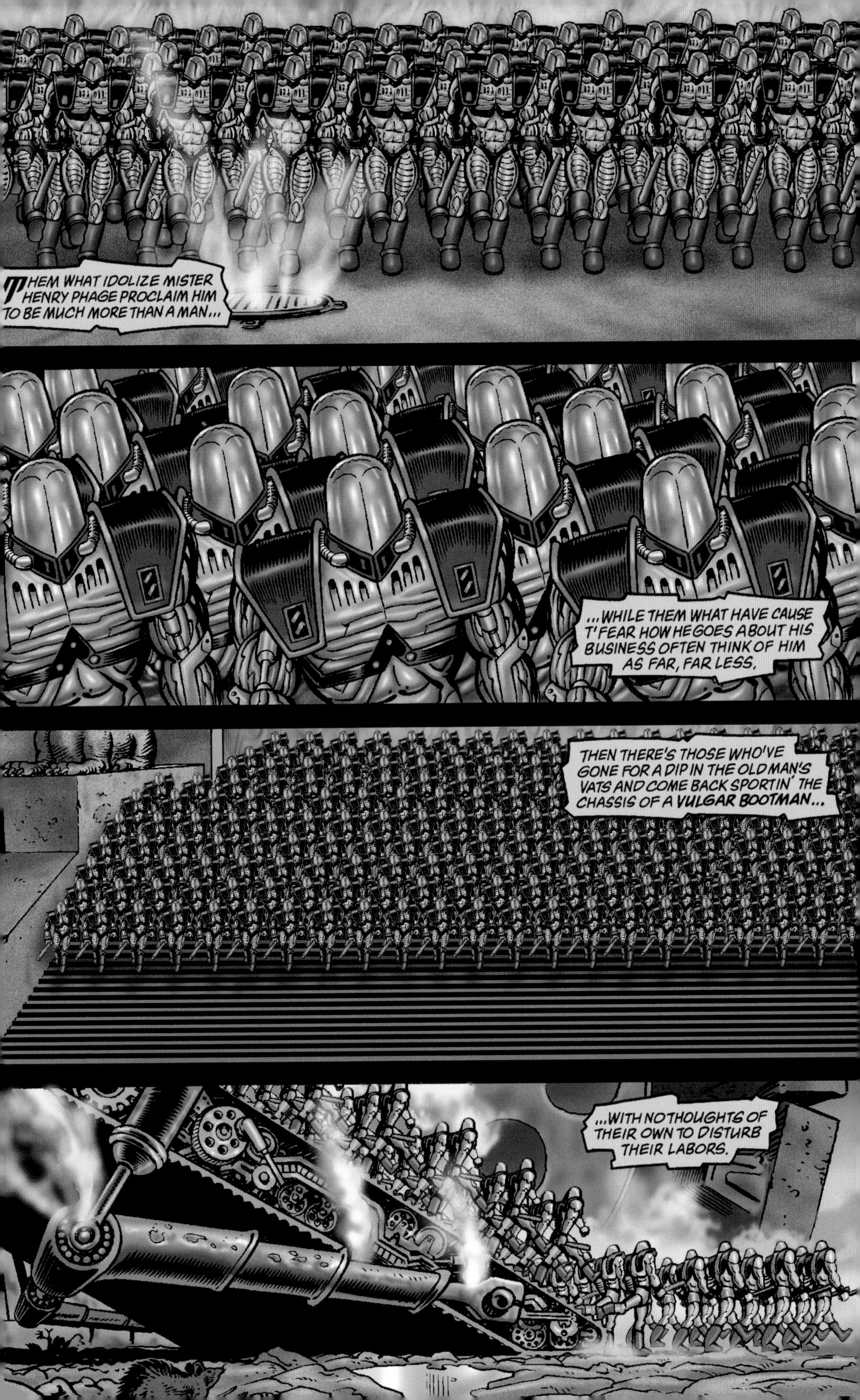
THEM WHAT IDOLIZE MISTER HENRY PHAGE PROCLAIM HIM TO BE MUCH MORE THAN A MAN...
...WHILE THEM WHAT HAVE CAUSE T' FEAR HOW HE GOES ABOUT HIS BUSINESS OFTEN THINK OF HIM AS FAR, FAR LESS.
THEN THERE'S THOSE WHO'VE GONE FOR A DIP IN THE OLD MAN'S VATS AND COME BACK SPORTIN' THE CHASSIS OF A VULGAR BOOTMAN...
...WITH NO THOUGHTS OF THEIR OWN TO DISTURB THEIR LABORS.

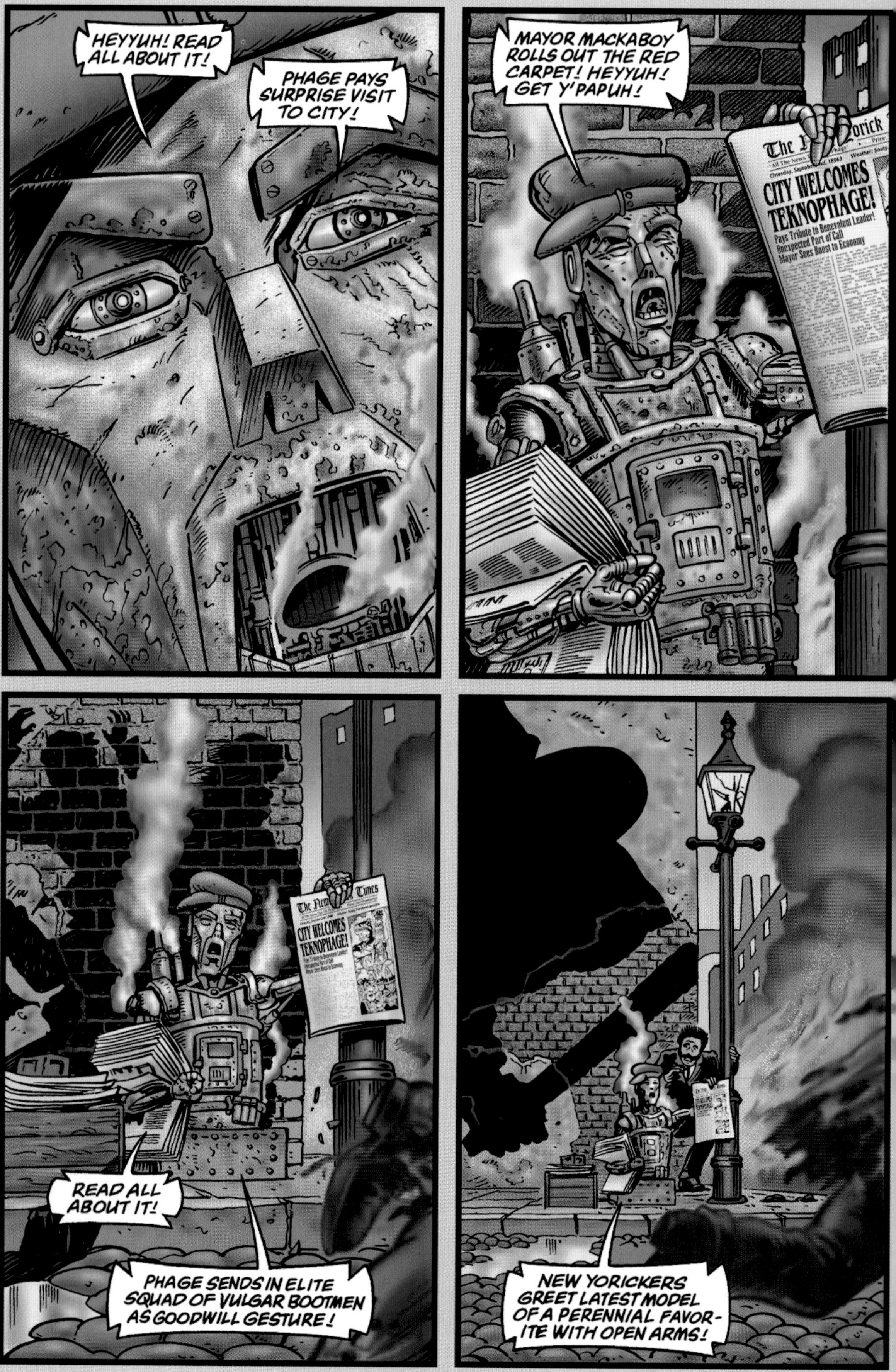
HEYYUH! READ ALL ABOUT IT!
PHAGE PAYS SURPRISE VISIT TO CITY!
MAYOR MACKABOY ROLLS OUT THE RED CARPET! HEYYUH! GET Y'PAPUH!
CITY WELCOMES TEKNOPHAGE!
Pays Tribute to Benevolent Leader!
Unexpected Port of Call
Mayor Sees Boost to Economy
READ ALL ABOUT IT!
PHAGE SENDS IN ELITE SQUAD OF VULGAR BOOTMEN AS GOODWILL GESTURE!
NEW YORICKERS GREET LATEST MODEL OF A PERENNIAL FAVOR-ITE WITH OPEN ARMS!

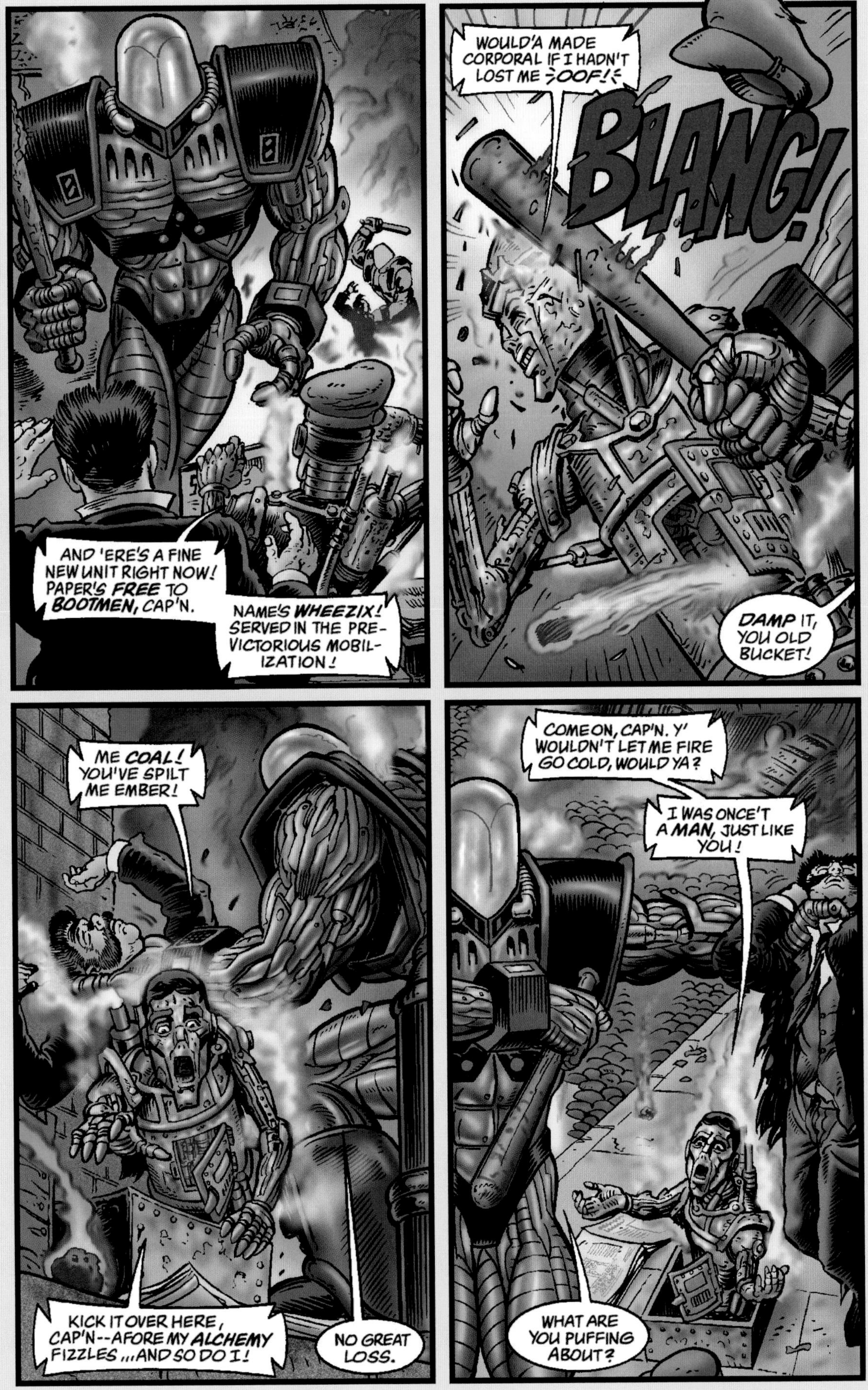
AND 'ERE'S A FINE NEW UNIT RIGHT NOW! PAPER'S FREE TO BOOTMEN, CAP'N.
NAME'S WHEEZIX! SERVED IN THE PRE-VICTORIOUS MOBIL-IZATION!
WOULD'A MADE CORPORAL IF I HADN'T LOST ME OOF!
BLANG!
DAMP IT, YOU OLD BUCKET!
ME COAL! YOU'VE SPILT ME EMBER!
KICK IT OVER HERE, CAP'N--AFORE MY ALCHEMY FIZZLES...AND SO DO I!
NO GREAT LOSS.
COME ON, CAP'N. Y' WOULDN'T LET ME FIRE GO COLD, WOULD YA?
I WAS ONCE'T A MAN, JUST LIKE YOU!
WHAT ARE YOU PUFFING ABOUT?

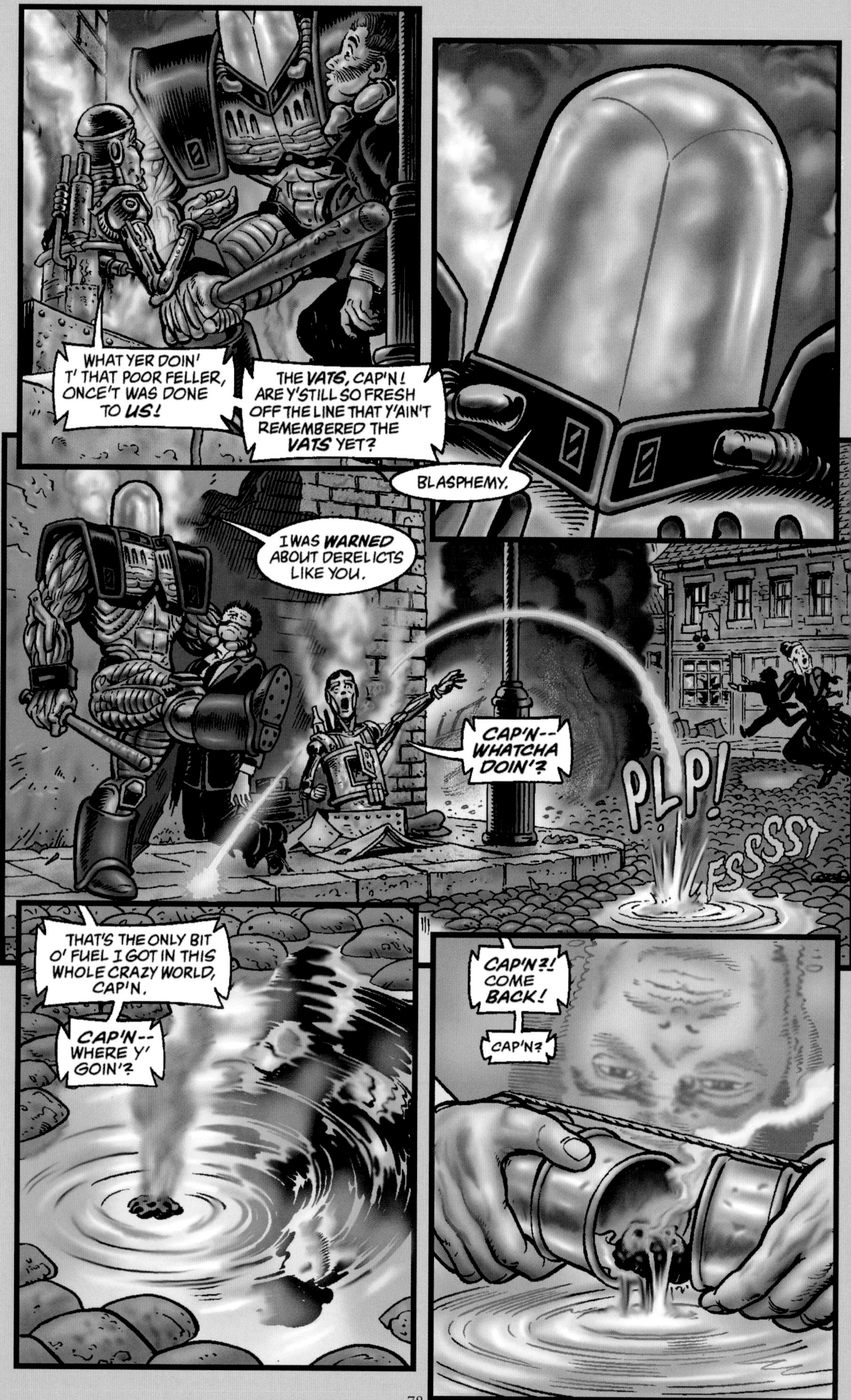
WHAT YER DOIN' T' THAT POOR FELLER, ONCE'T WAS DONE TO US!
THE VATS, CAP'N! ARE Y'STILL SO FRESH OFF THE LINE THAT Y'AIN'T REMEMBERED THE VATS YET?
BLASPHEMY.
I WAS WARNED ABOUT DERELICTS LIKE YOU.
CAP'N-- WHATCHA DOIN'?
PLP!
FSSSST
THAT'S THE ONLY BIT O' FUEL I GOT IN THIS WHOLE CRAZY WORLD, CAP'N.
CAP'N-- WHERE Y' GOIN'?
CAP'N?! COME BACK!
CAP'N?

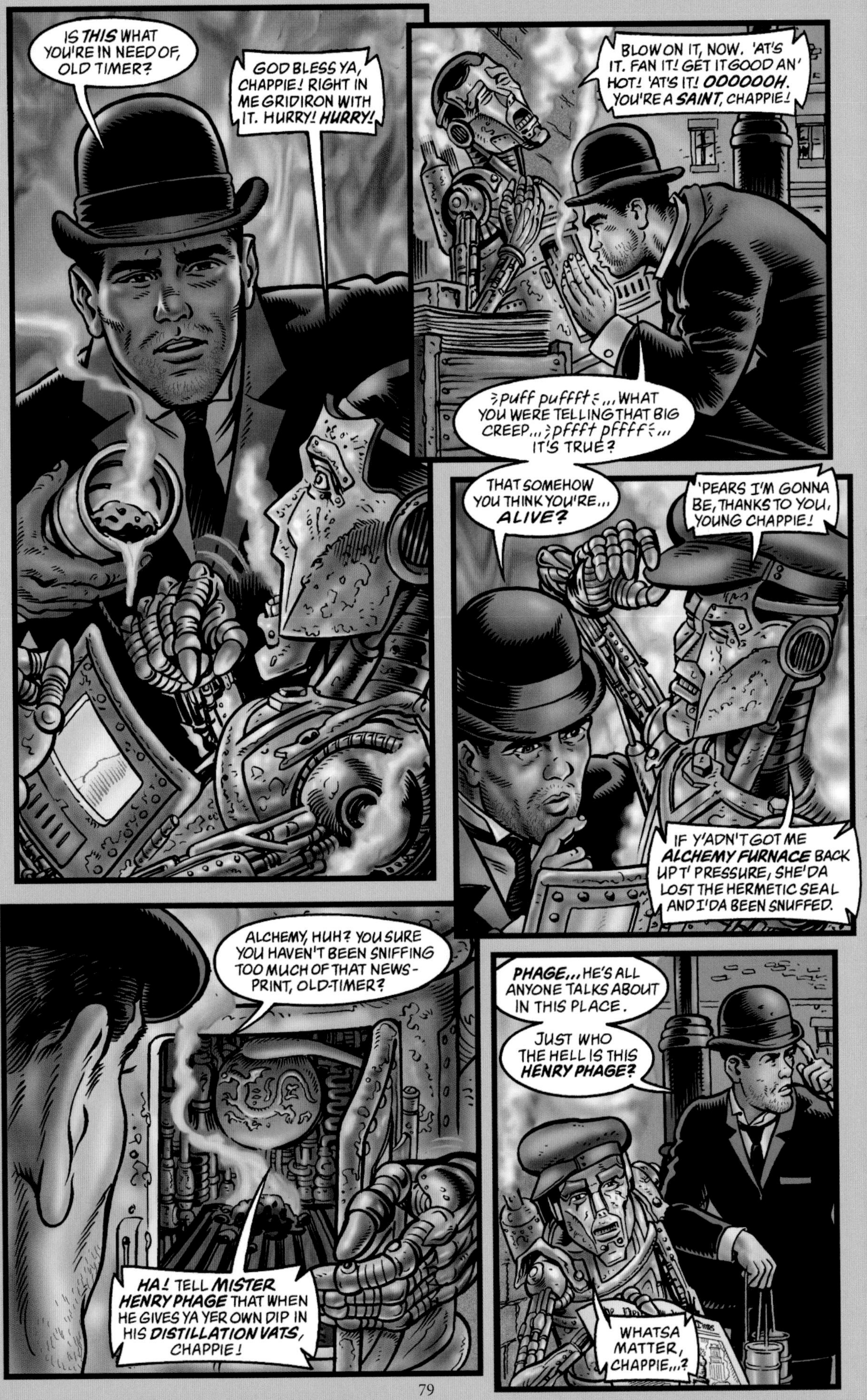
IS THIS WHAT YOU'RE IN NEED OF, OLD TIMER?
GOD BLESS YA, CHAPPIE! RIGHT IN ME GRIDIRON WITH IT. HURRY! HURRY!
BLOW ON IT, NOW. 'AT'S IT. FAN IT! GET IT GOOD AN' HOT! 'AT'S IT! OOOOOOH. YOU'RE A SAINT, CHAPPIE!
puff pufffft... WHAT YOU WERE TELLING THAT BIG CREEP... pffft pffff... IT'S TRUE?
THAT SOMEHOW YOU THINK YOU'RE... ALIVE?
'PEARS I'M GONNA BE, THANKS TO YOU, YOUNG CHAPPIE!
IF Y'ADN'T GOT ME ALCHEMY FURNACE BACK UP T' PRESSURE, SHE'DA LOST THE HERMETIC SEAL AND I'DA BEEN SNUFFED.
ALCHEMY, HUH? YOU SURE YOU HAVEN'T BEEN SNIFFING TOO MUCH OF THAT NEWS-PRINT, OLD-TIMER?
HA! TELL MISTER HENRY PHAGE THAT WHEN HE GIVES YA YER OWN DIP IN HIS DISTILLATION VATS, CHAPPIE!
PHAGE... HE'S ALL ANYONE TALKS ABOUT IN THIS PLACE.
JUST WHO THE HELL IS THIS HENRY PHAGE?
WHATSA MATTER, CHAPPIE...?

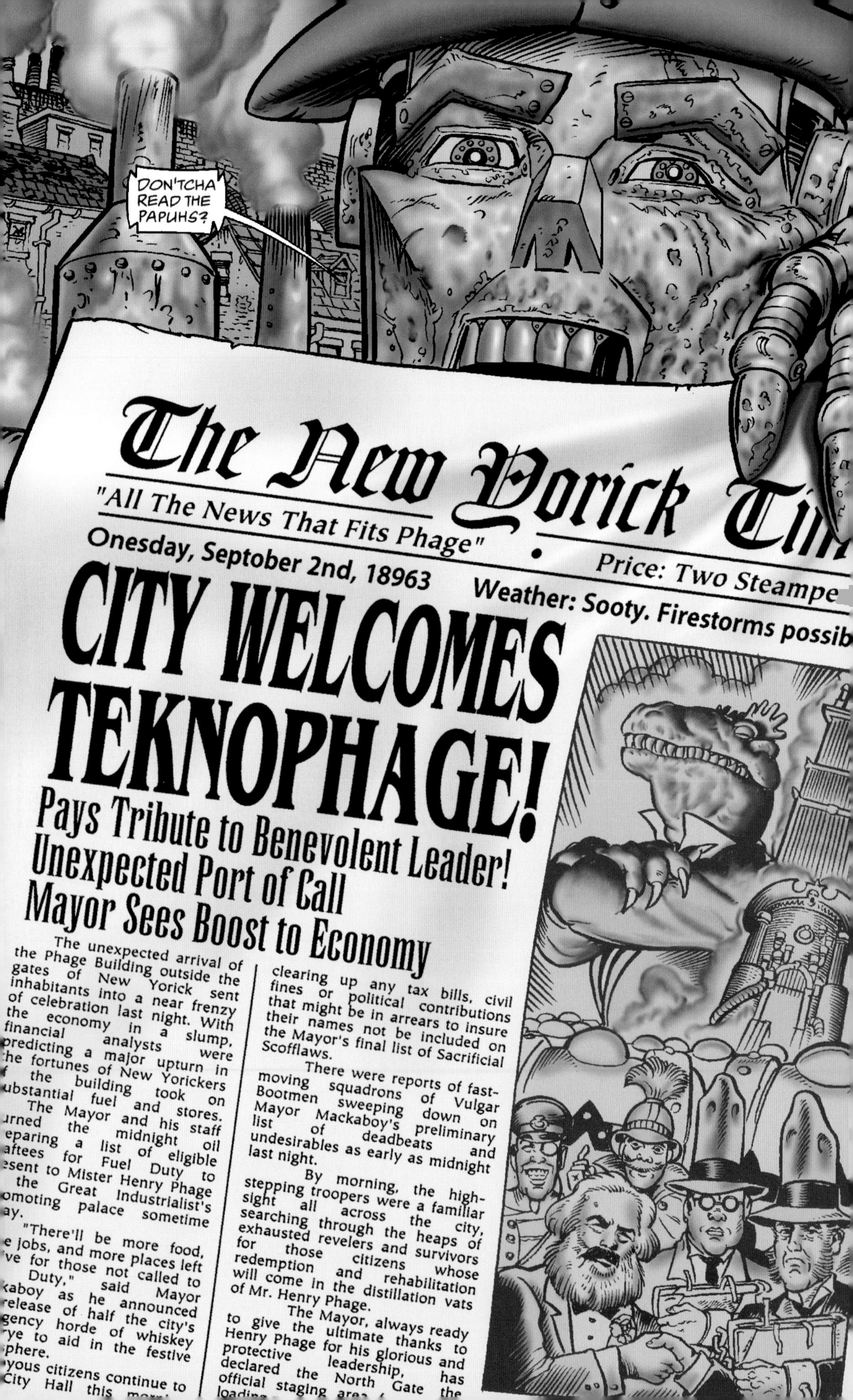
DON'TCHA READ THE PAPUHS?
The New Yorick Tim
"All The News That Fits Phage"
Onesday, Septober 2nd, 18963
Price: Two Steampe
Weather: Sooty. Firestorms possib
CITY WELCOMES TEKNOPHAGE!
Pays Tribute to Benevolent Leader!
Unexpected Port of Call
Mayor Sees Boost to Economy
The unexpected arrival of the Phage Building outside the gates of New Yorick sent inhabitants into a near frenzy of celebration last night. With the economy in a slump, financial analysts were predicting a major upturn in he fortunes of New Yorickers f the building took on ubstantial fuel and stores.
The Mayor and his staff urned the midnight oil eparing a list of eligible aftees for Fuel Duty to esent to Mister Henry Phage the Great Industrialist's omoting palace sometime ay.
"There'll be more food, e jobs, and more places left ve for those not called to Duty," said Mayor kaboy as he announced release of half the city's gency horde of whiskey ye to aid in the festive phere.
yous citizens continue to City Hall this morn
clearing up any tax bills, civil fines or political contributions that might be in arrears to insure their names not be included on the Mayor's final list of Sacrificial Scofflaws.
There were reports of fast-moving squadrons of Vulgar Bootmen sweeping down on Mayor Mackaboy's preliminary list of deadbeats and undesirables as early as midnight last night.
By morning, the high-stepping troopers were a familiar sight all across the city, searching through the heaps of exhausted revelers and survivors for those citizens whose redemption and rehabilitation will come in the distillation vats of Mr. Henry Phage.
The Mayor, always ready to give the ultimate thanks to Henry Phage for his glorious and protective leadership, has declared the North Gate the official staging area

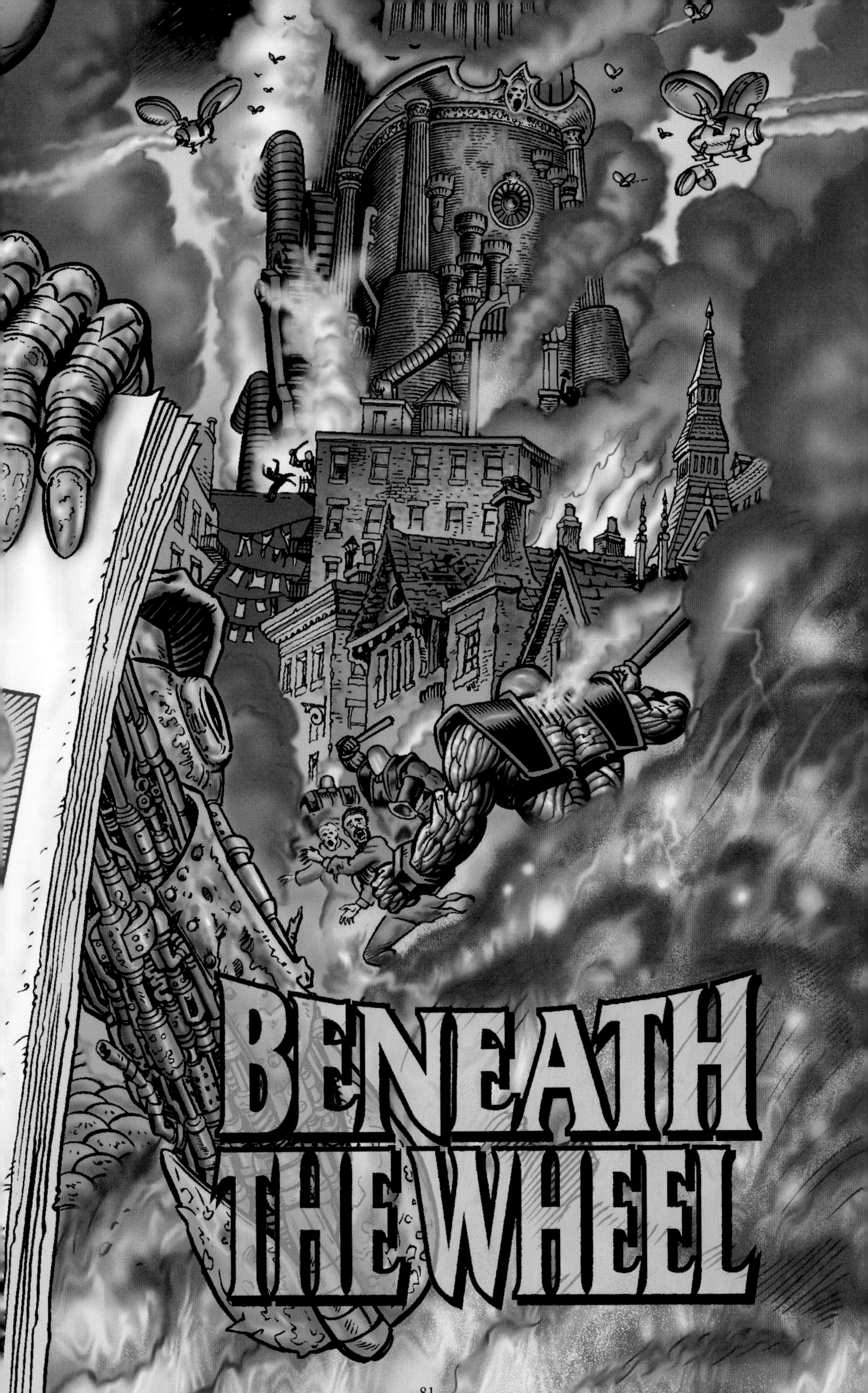
BENEATH THE WHEEL

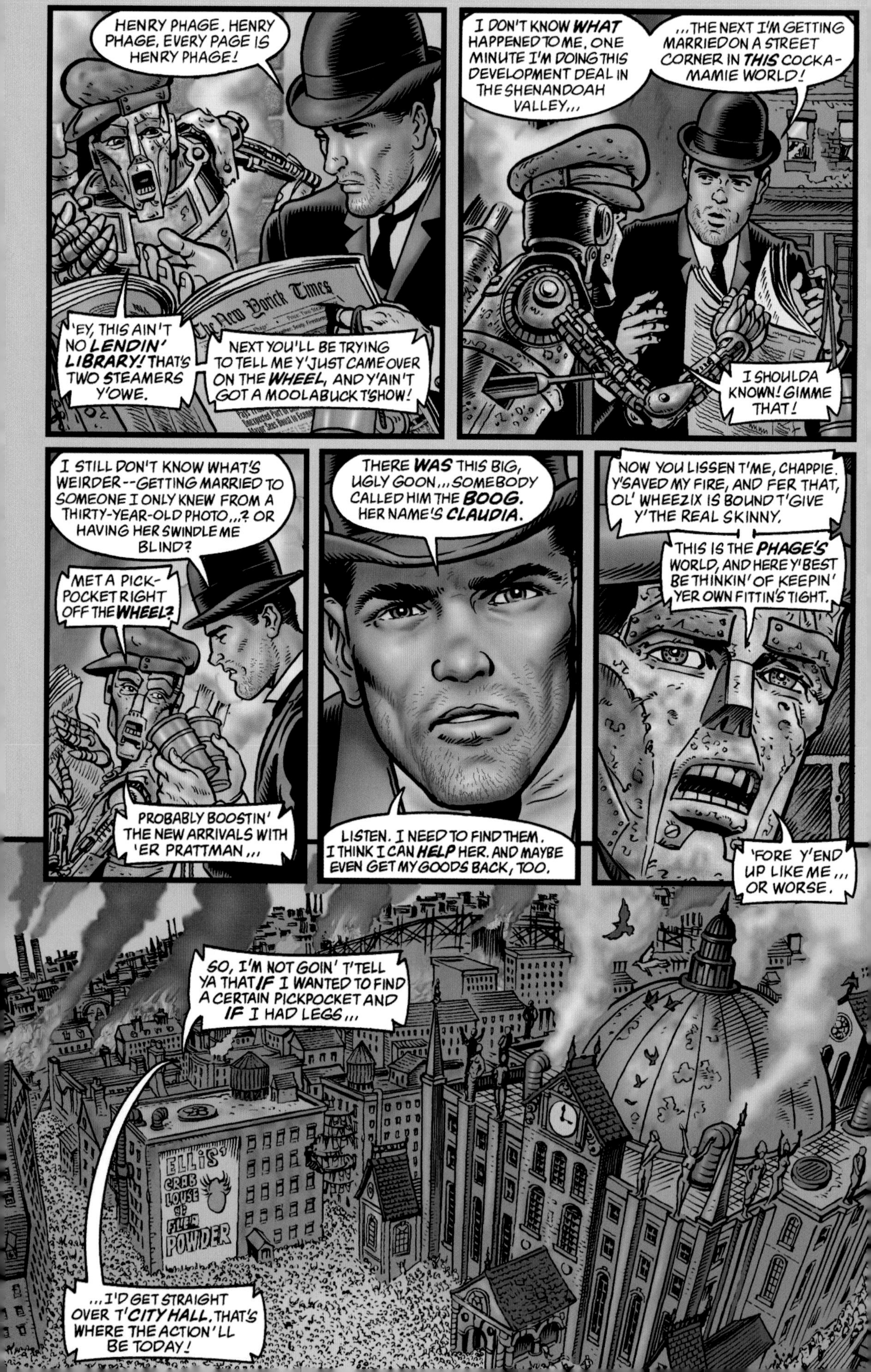
HENRY PHAGE. HENRY PHAGE. EVERY PAGE IS HENRY PHAGE!
'EY, THIS AIN'T NO LENDIN' LIBRARY! THAT'S TWO STEAMERS Y'OWE.
NEXT YOU'LL BE TRYING TO TELL ME Y'JUST CAME OVER ON THE WHEEL, AND Y'AIN'T GOT A MOOLABUCK T'SHOW!
The New Yorick Times
I DON'T KNOW WHAT HAPPENED TO ME. ONE MINUTE I'M DOING THIS DEVELOPMENT DEAL IN THE SHENANDOAH VALLEY...
...THE NEXT I'M GETTING MARRIED ON A STREET CORNER IN THIS COCKAMAMIE WORLD!
I SHOULDA KNOWN! GIMME THAT!
I STILL DON'T KNOW WHAT'S WEIRDER--GETTING MARRIED TO SOMEONE I ONLY KNEW FROM A THIRTY-YEAR-OLD PHOTO...? OR HAVING HER SWINDLE ME BLIND?
MET A PICK-POCKET RIGHT OFF THE WHEEL?
PROBABLY BOOSTIN' THE NEW ARRIVALS WITH 'ER PRATTMAN...
THERE WAS THIS BIG, UGLY GOON... SOMEBODY CALLED HIM THE BOOG. HER NAME'S CLAUDIA.
LISTEN. I NEED TO FIND THEM. I THINK I CAN HELP HER. AND MAYBE EVEN GET MY GOODS BACK, TOO.
NOW YOU LISSEN T'ME, CHAPPIE. Y'SAVED MY FIRE, AND FER THAT, OL' WHEEZIX IS BOUND T'GIVE Y'THE REAL SKINNY.
THIS IS THE PHAGE'S WORLD, AND HERE Y'BEST BE THINKIN' OF KEEPIN' YER OWN FITTIN'S TIGHT.
'FORE Y'END UP LIKE ME... OR WORSE.
SO, I'M NOT GOIN' T'TELL YA THAT IF I WANTED TO FIND A CERTAIN PICKPOCKET AND IF I HAD LEGS...
ELLIS' CRAB LOUSE & FLEA POWDER
...I'D GET STRAIGHT OVER T'CITY HALL. THAT'S WHERE THE ACTION'LL BE TODAY!

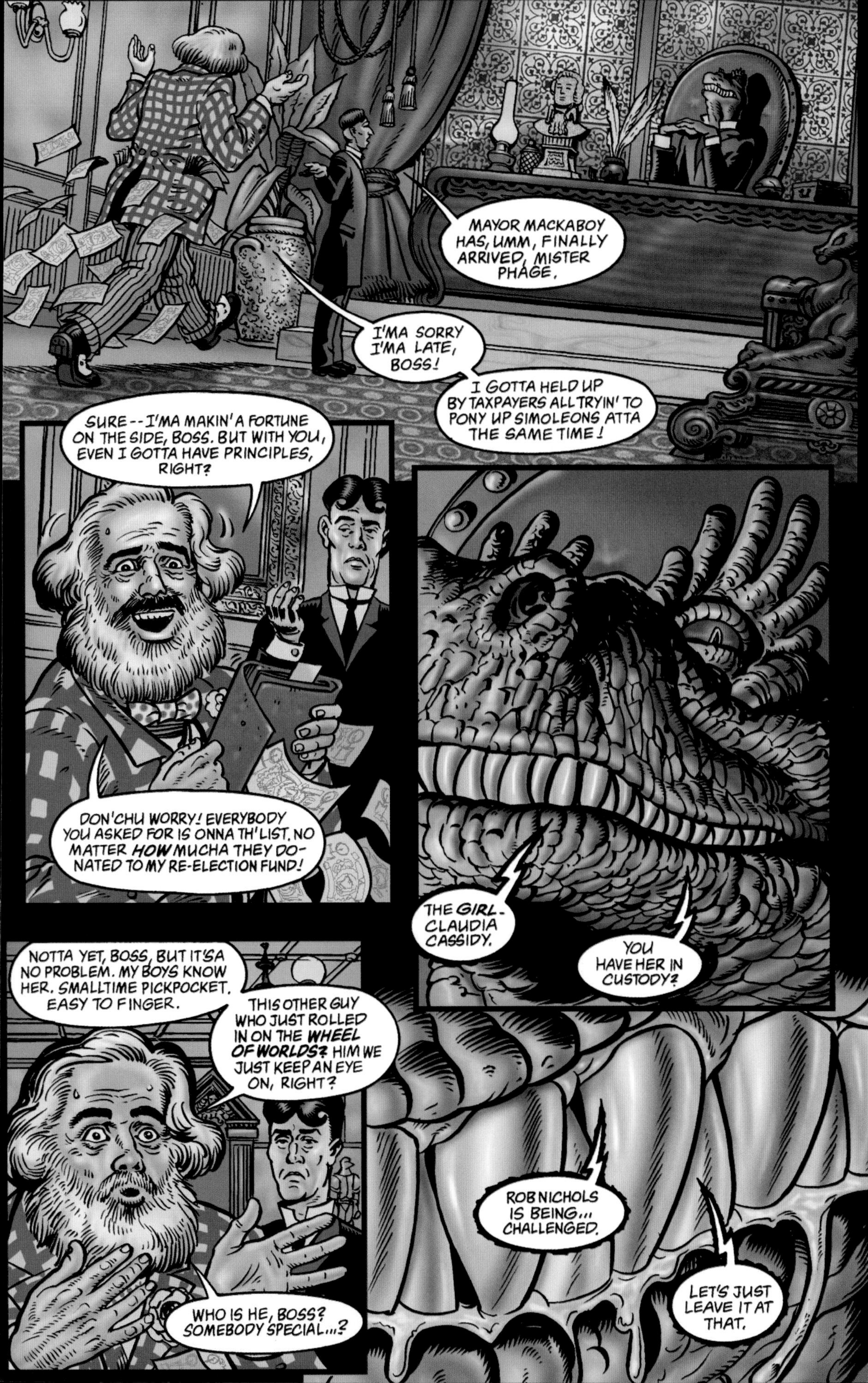
MAYOR MACKABOY HAS, UMM, FINALLY ARRIVED, MISTER PHAGE.
I'MA SORRY I'MA LATE, BOSS!
I GOTTA HELD UP BY TAXPAYERS ALL TRYIN' TO PONY UP SIMOLEONS ATTA THE SAME TIME!
SURE--I'MA MAKIN' A FORTUNE ON THE SIDE, BOSS. BUT WITH YOU, EVEN I GOTTA HAVE PRINCIPLES, RIGHT?
DON'CHU WORRY! EVERYBODY YOU ASKED FOR IS ONNA TH' LIST, NO MATTER HOW MUCHA THEY DONATED TO MY RE-ELECTION FUND!
THE GIRL-CLAUDIA CASSIDY.
YOU HAVE HER IN CUSTODY?
NOTTA YET, BOSS, BUT IT'SA NO PROBLEM. MY BOYS KNOW HER. SMALLTIME PICKPOCKET. EASY TO FINGER.
THIS OTHER GUY WHO JUST ROLLED IN ON THE WHEEL OF WORLDS? HIM WE JUST KEEP AN EYE ON, RIGHT?
ROB NICHOLS IS BEING... CHALLENGED.
LET'S JUST LEAVE IT AT THAT.
WHO IS HE, BOSS? SOMEBODY SPECIAL...?

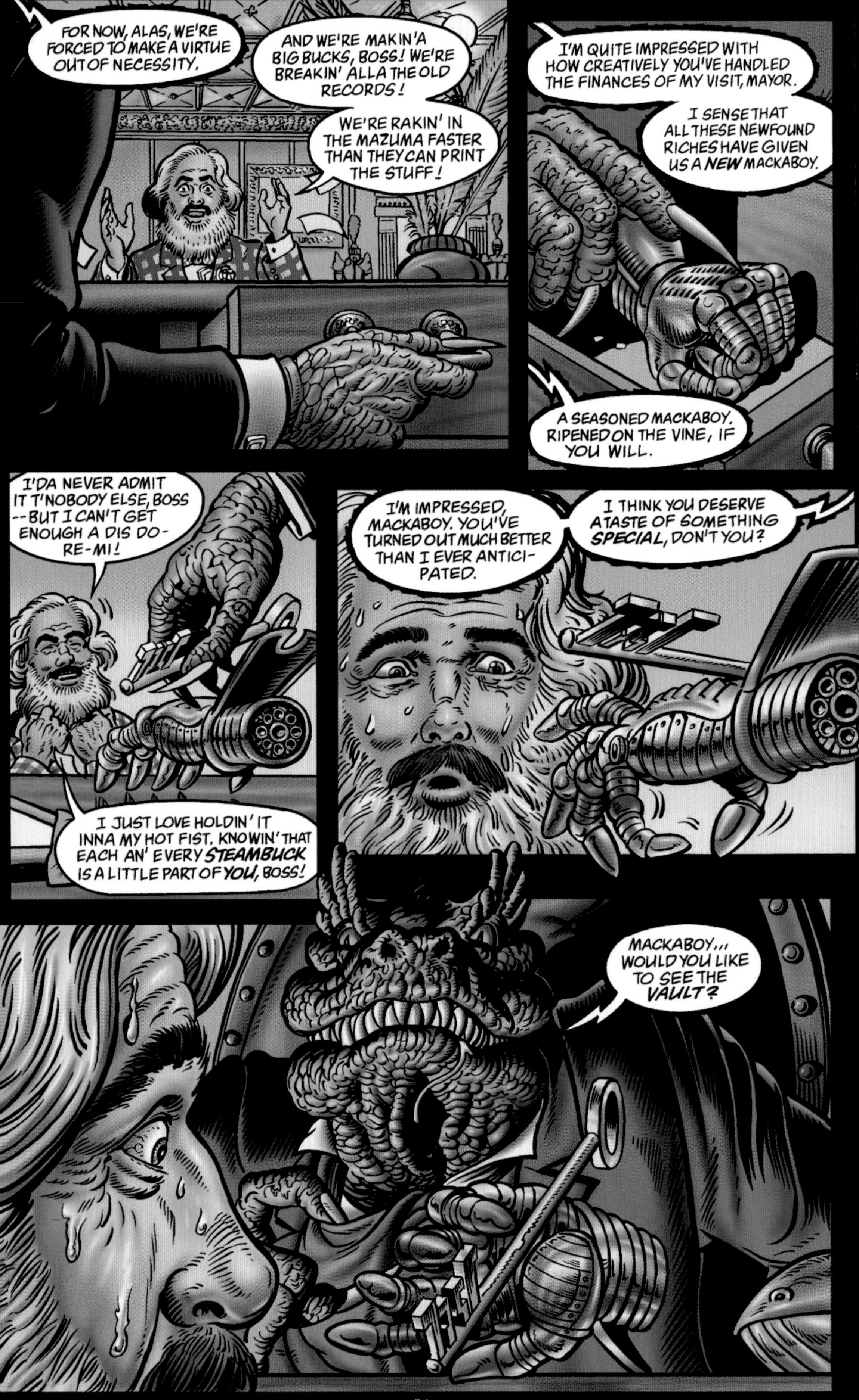
FOR NOW, ALAS, WE'RE FORCED TO MAKE A VIRTUE OUT OF NECESSITY.
AND WE'RE MAKIN'A BIG BUCKS, BOSS! WE'RE BREAKIN' ALLA THE OLD RECORDS!
WE'RE RAKIN' IN THE MAZUMA FASTER THAN THEY CAN PRINT THE STUFF!
I'M QUITE IMPRESSED WITH HOW CREATIVELY YOU'VE HANDLED THE FINANCES OF MY VISIT, MAYOR.
I SENSE THAT ALL THESE NEWFOUND RICHES HAVE GIVEN US A NEW MACKABOY.
A SEASONED MACKABOY. RIPENED ON THE VINE, IF YOU WILL.
I'DA NEVER ADMIT IT T'NOBODY ELSE, BOSS --BUT I CAN'T GET ENOUGH A DIS DO-RE-MI!
I JUST LOVE HOLDIN' IT INNA MY HOT FIST, KNOWIN' THAT EACH AN' EVERY STEAMBUCK IS A LITTLE PART OF YOU, BOSS!
I'M IMPRESSED, MACKABOY. YOU'VE TURNED OUT MUCH BETTER THAN I EVER ANTICI-PATED.
I THINK YOU DESERVE A TASTE OF SOMETHING SPECIAL, DON'T YOU?
MACKABOY... WOULD YOU LIKE TO SEE THE VAULT?

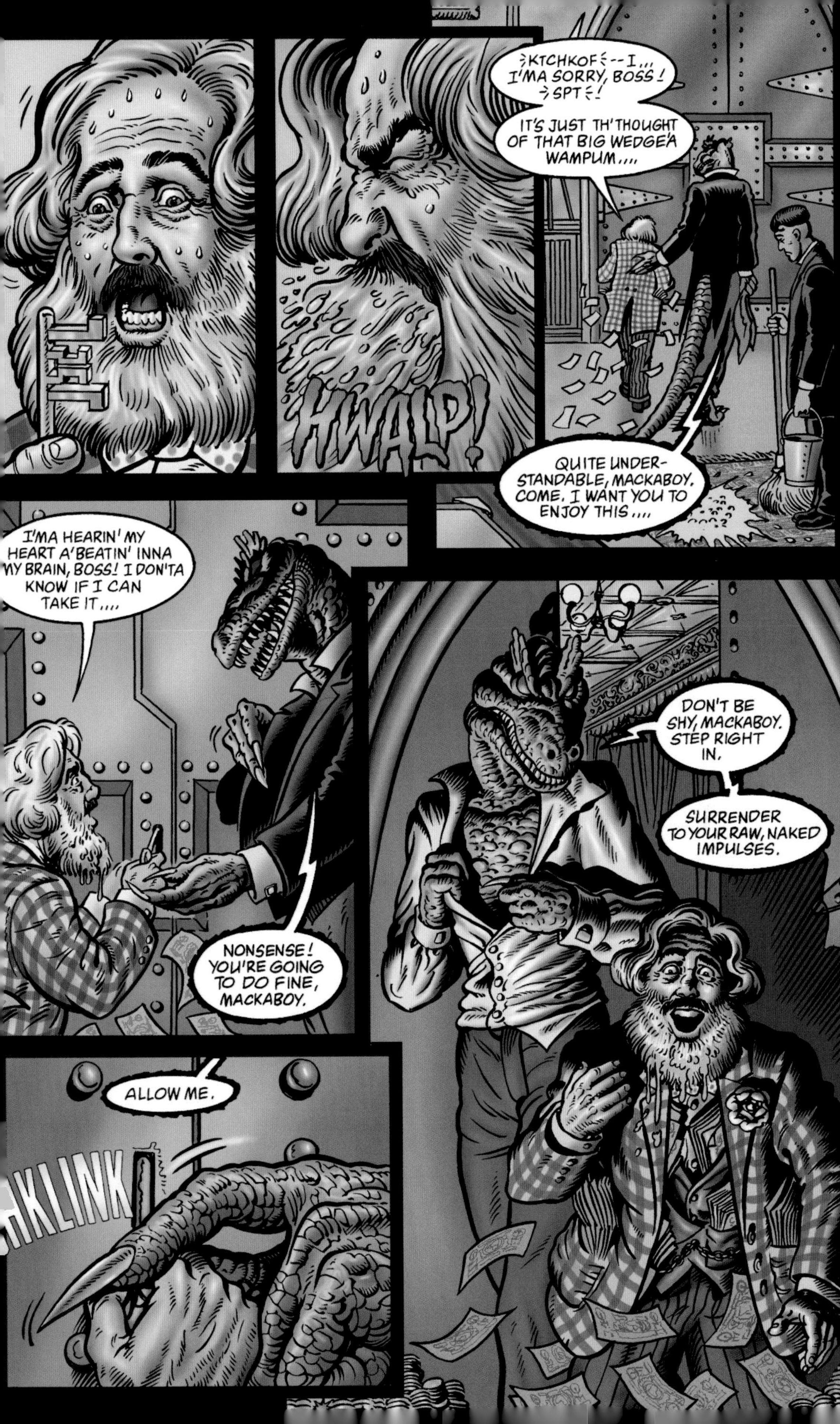

HWALP!
⧽KTCHKOF⧼ -- I,,, I'MA SORRY, BOSS! ⧽SPT⧼!
IT'S JUST TH' THOUGHT OF THAT BIG WEDGE'A WAMPUM,,,,
QUITE UNDERSTANDABLE, MACKABOY. COME. I WANT YOU TO ENJOY THIS,,,,
I'MA HEARIN' MY HEART A'BEATIN' INNA MY BRAIN, BOSS! I DON'TA KNOW IF I CAN TAKE IT,,,,
NONSENSE! YOU'RE GOING TO DO FINE, MACKABOY.
ALLOW ME.
HKLINK
DON'T BE SHY, MACKABOY. STEP RIGHT IN.
SURRENDER TO YOUR RAW, NAKED IMPULSES.

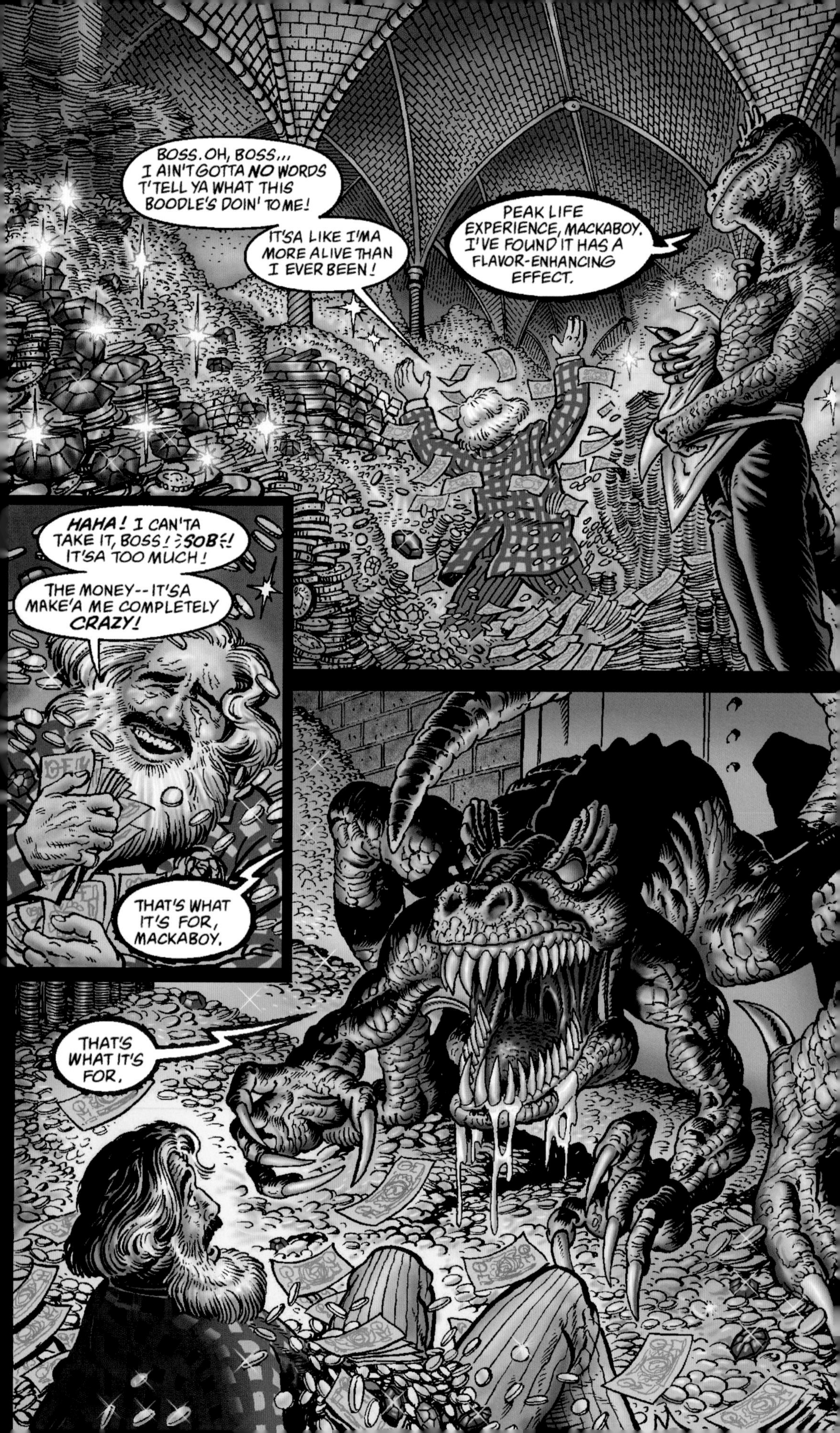
BOSS. OH, BOSS... I AIN'T GOTTA NO WORDS T'TELL YA WHAT THIS BOODLE'S DOIN' TO ME!
IT'SA LIKE I'MA MORE ALIVE THAN I EVER BEEN!
PEAK LIFE EXPERIENCE, MACKABOY. I'VE FOUND IT HAS A FLAVOR-ENHANCING EFFECT.
HAHA! I CAN'TA TAKE IT, BOSS! ;SOB;! IT'SA TOO MUCH!
THE MONEY--IT'SA MAKE'A ME COMPLETELY CRAZY!
THAT'S WHAT IT'S FOR, MACKABOY.
THAT'S WHAT IT'S FOR.

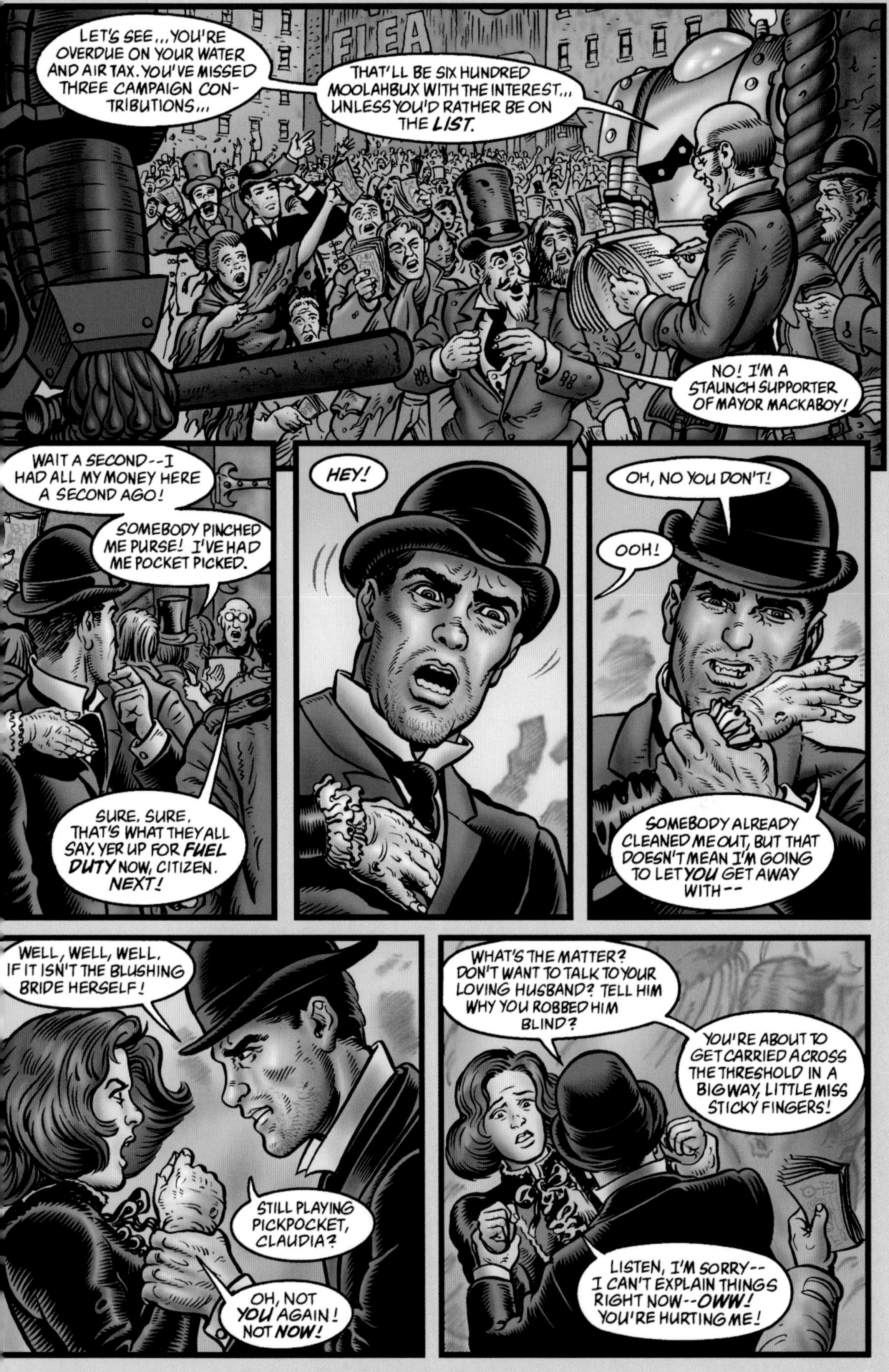
LET'S SEE... YOU'RE OVERDUE ON YOUR WATER AND AIR TAX. YOU'VE MISSED THREE CAMPAIGN CONTRIBUTIONS...
THAT'LL BE SIX HUNDRED MOOLAHBUX WITH THE INTEREST... UNLESS YOU'D RATHER BE ON THE LIST.
FLEA
NO! I'M A STAUNCH SUPPORTER OF MAYOR MACKABOY!
WAIT A SECOND--I HAD ALL MY MONEY HERE A SECOND AGO!
SOMEBODY PINCHED ME PURSE! I'VE HAD ME POCKET PICKED.
SURE. SURE. THAT'S WHAT THEY ALL SAY. YER UP FOR FUEL DUTY NOW, CITIZEN. NEXT!
HEY!
OH, NO YOU DON'T!
OOH!
SOMEBODY ALREADY CLEANED ME OUT, BUT THAT DOESN'T MEAN I'M GOING TO LET YOU GET AWAY WITH--
WELL, WELL, WELL. IF IT ISN'T THE BLUSHING BRIDE HERSELF!
STILL PLAYING PICKPOCKET, CLAUDIA?
OH, NOT YOU AGAIN! NOT NOW!
WHAT'S THE MATTER? DON'T WANT TO TALK TO YOUR LOVING HUSBAND? TELL HIM WHY YOU ROBBED HIM BLIND?
YOU'RE ABOUT TO GET CARRIED ACROSS THE THRESHOLD IN A BIG WAY, LITTLE MISS STICKY FINGERS!
LISTEN, I'M SORRY-- I CAN'T EXPLAIN THINGS RIGHT NOW--OWW! YOU'RE HURTING ME!

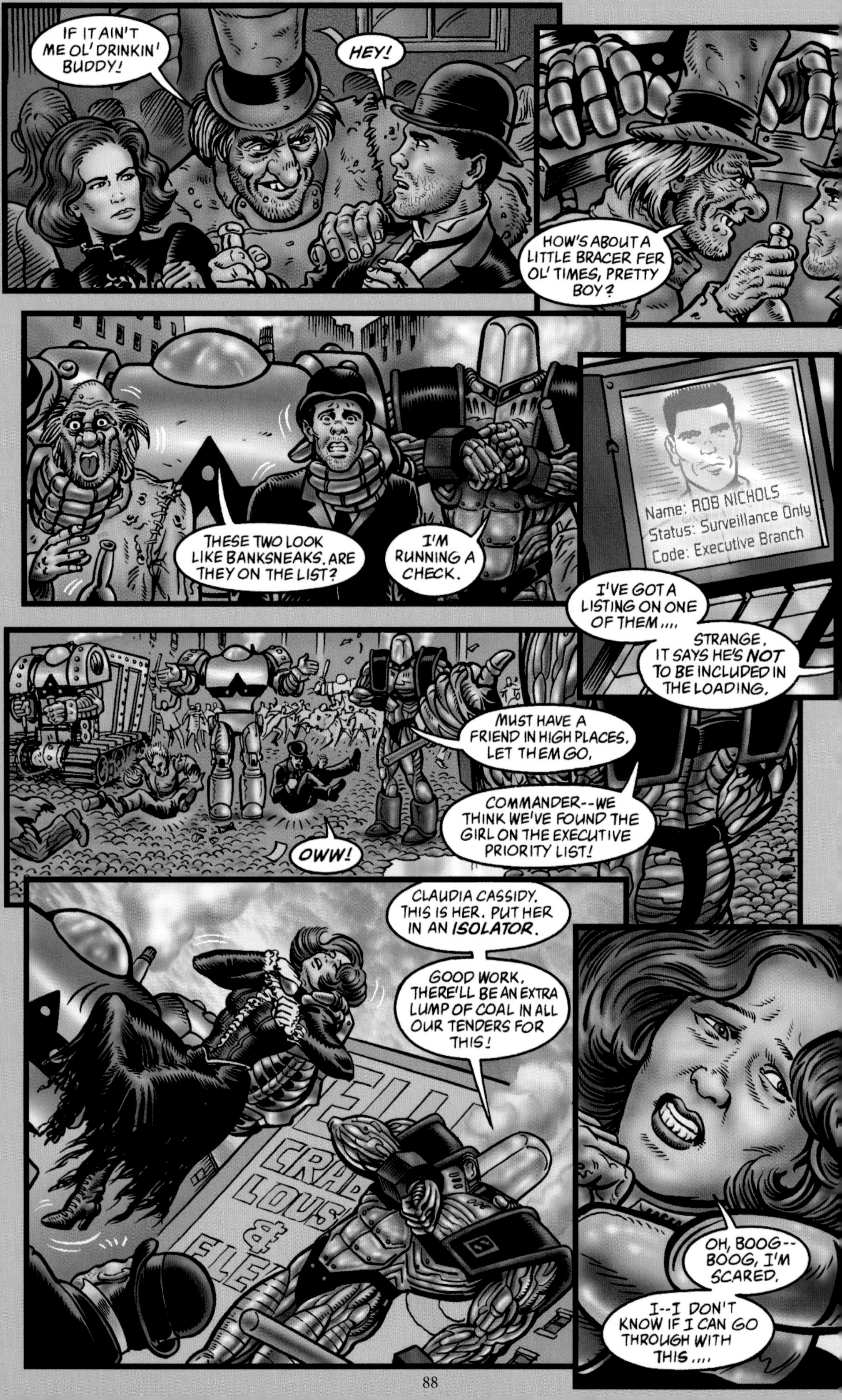

IF IT AIN'T ME OL' DRINKIN' BUDDY!
HEY!
HOW'S ABOUT A LITTLE BRACER FER OL' TIMES, PRETTY BOY?
THESE TWO LOOK LIKE BANKSNEAKS. ARE THEY ON THE LIST?
I'M RUNNING A CHECK.
Name: ROB NICHOLS
Status: Surveillance Only
Code: Executive Branch
I'VE GOT A LISTING ON ONE OF THEM....
STRANGE. IT SAYS HE'S NOT TO BE INCLUDED IN THE LOADING.
MUST HAVE A FRIEND IN HIGH PLACES. LET THEM GO.
COMMANDER--WE THINK WE'VE FOUND THE GIRL ON THE EXECUTIVE PRIORITY LIST!
OWW!
CLAUDIA CASSIDY. THIS IS HER. PUT HER IN AN ISOLATOR.
GOOD WORK. THERE'LL BE AN EXTRA LUMP OF COAL IN ALL OUR TENDERS FOR THIS!
OH, BOOG--BOOG, I'M SCARED.
I--I DON'T KNOW IF I CAN GO THROUGH WITH THIS....

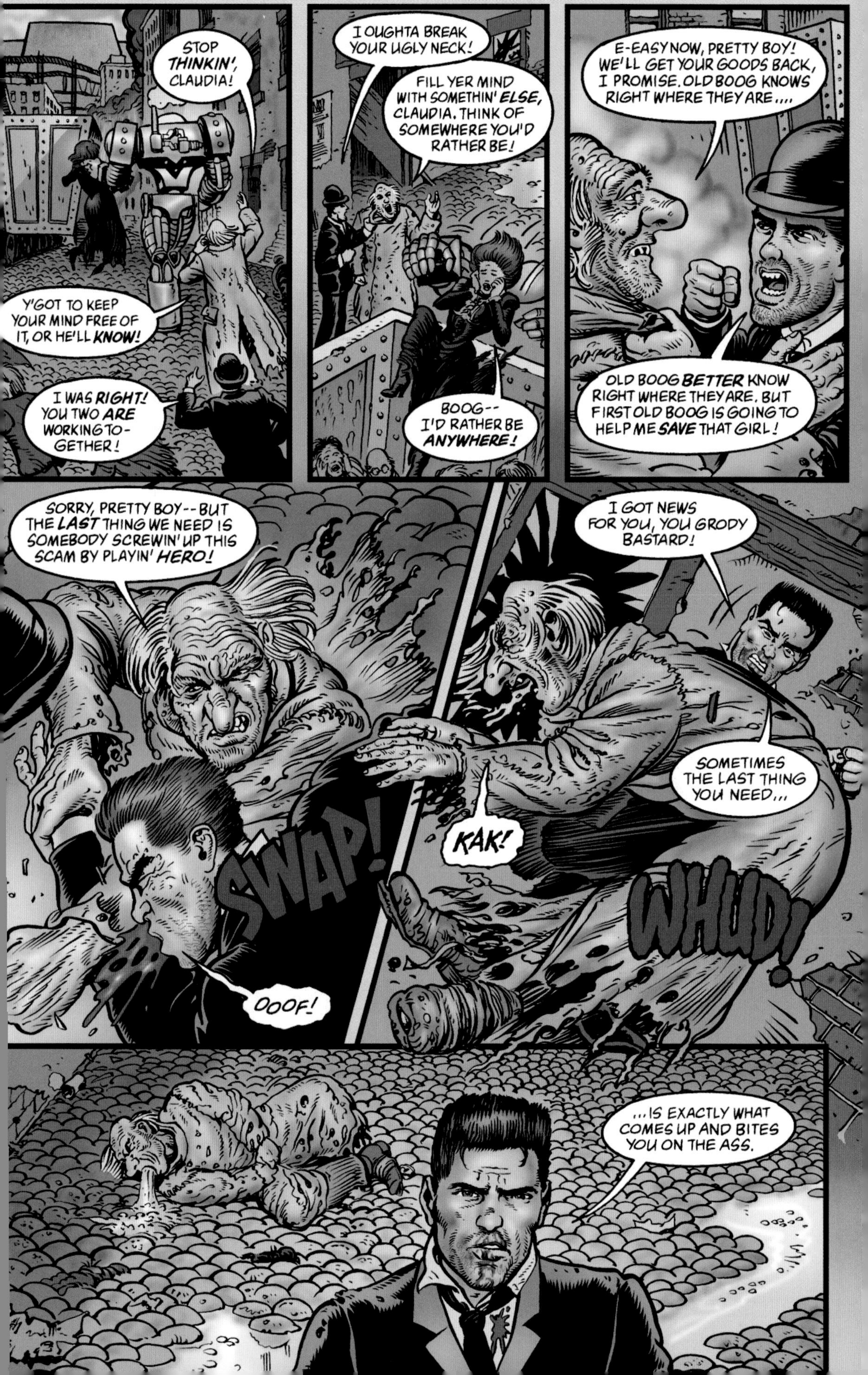
STOP THINKIN', CLAUDIA!
Y'GOT TO KEEP YOUR MIND FREE OF IT, OR HE'LL KNOW!
I WAS RIGHT! YOU TWO ARE WORKING TO-GETHER!
I OUGHTA BREAK YOUR UGLY NECK!
FILL YER MIND WITH SOMETHIN' ELSE, CLAUDIA. THINK OF SOMEWHERE YOU'D RATHER BE!
BOOG-- I'D RATHER BE ANYWHERE!
E-EASY NOW, PRETTY BOY! WE'LL GET YOUR GOODS BACK, I PROMISE. OLD BOOG KNOWS RIGHT WHERE THEY ARE....
OLD BOOG BETTER KNOW RIGHT WHERE THEY ARE. BUT FIRST OLD BOOG IS GOING TO HELP ME SAVE THAT GIRL!
SORRY, PRETTY BOY--BUT THE LAST THING WE NEED IS SOMEBODY SCREWIN' UP THIS SCAM BY PLAYIN' HERO!
SWAP!
OOOF!
I GOT NEWS FOR YOU, YOU GRODY BASTARD!
SOMETIMES THE LAST THING YOU NEED...
KAK!
WHUD!
...IS EXACTLY WHAT COMES UP AND BITES YOU ON THE ASS.

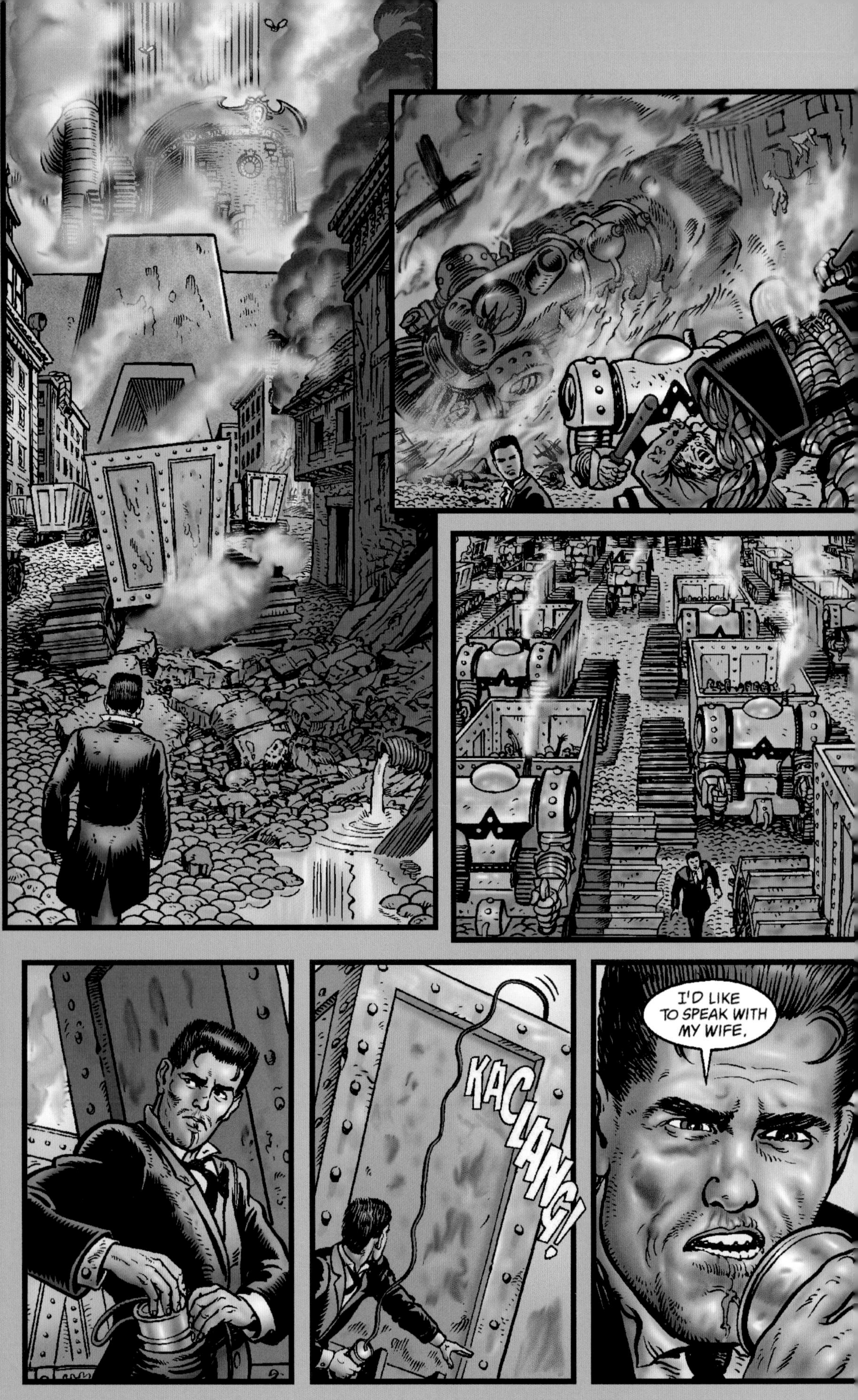
KACLANG!
I'D LIKE TO SPEAK WITH MY WIFE.

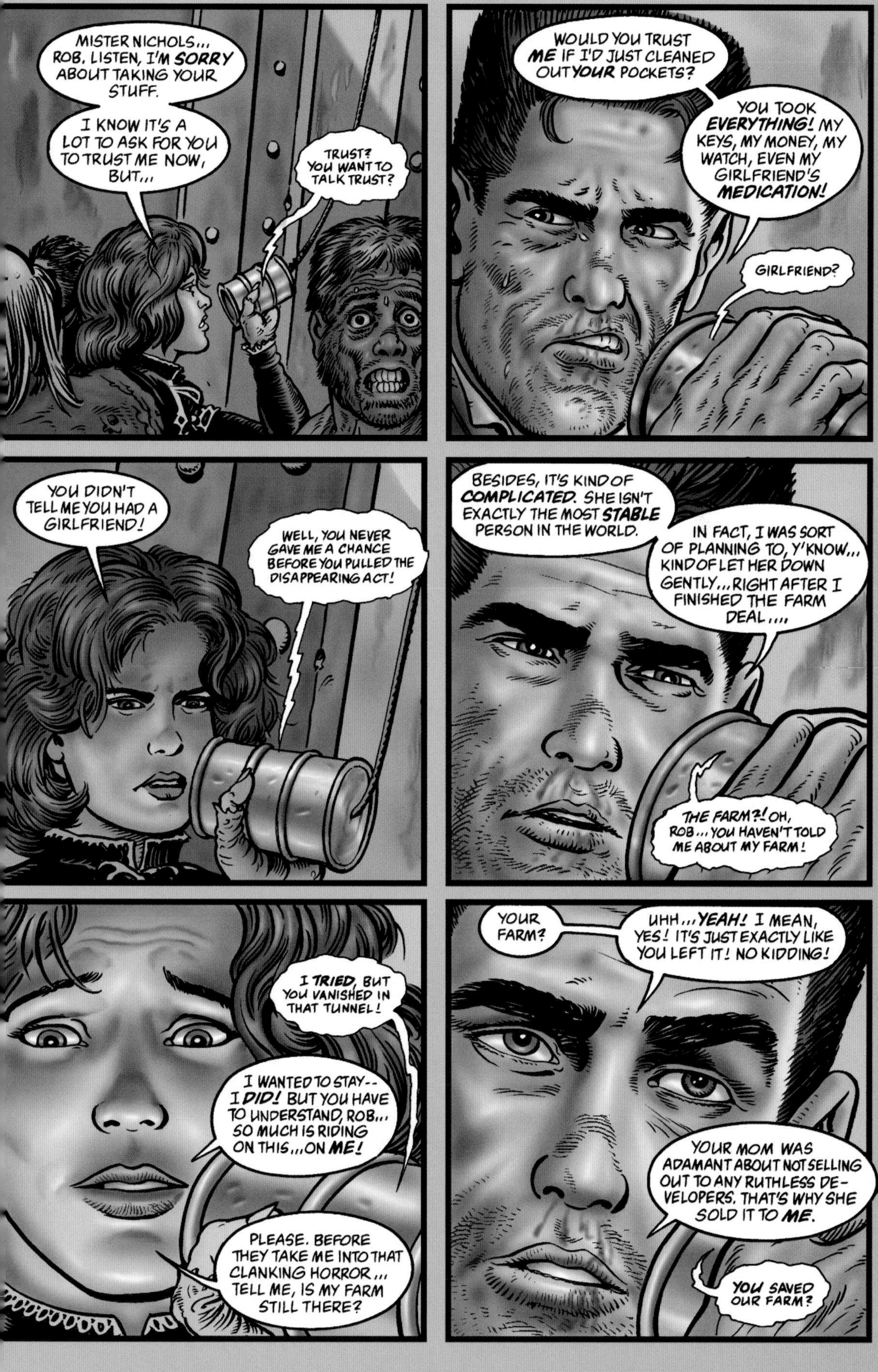
MISTER NICHOLS... ROB. LISTEN, I'M SORRY ABOUT TAKING YOUR STUFF.
I KNOW IT'S A LOT TO ASK FOR YOU TO TRUST ME NOW, BUT...
TRUST? YOU WANT TO TALK TRUST?
WOULD YOU TRUST ME IF I'D JUST CLEANED OUT YOUR POCKETS?
YOU TOOK EVERYTHING! MY KEYS, MY MONEY, MY WATCH, EVEN MY GIRLFRIEND'S MEDICATION!
GIRLFRIEND?
YOU DIDN'T TELL ME YOU HAD A GIRLFRIEND!
WELL, YOU NEVER GAVE ME A CHANCE BEFORE YOU PULLED THE DISAPPEARING ACT!
BESIDES, IT'S KIND OF COMPLICATED. SHE ISN'T EXACTLY THE MOST STABLE PERSON IN THE WORLD.
IN FACT, I WAS SORT OF PLANNING TO, Y'KNOW... KIND OF LET HER DOWN GENTLY... RIGHT AFTER I FINISHED THE FARM DEAL....
THE FARM?! OH, ROB... YOU HAVEN'T TOLD ME ABOUT MY FARM!
I TRIED, BUT YOU VANISHED IN THAT TUNNEL!
I WANTED TO STAY-- I DID! BUT YOU HAVE TO UNDERSTAND, ROB... SO MUCH IS RIDING ON THIS... ON ME!
PLEASE. BEFORE THEY TAKE ME INTO THAT CLANKING HORROR... TELL ME, IS MY FARM STILL THERE?
YOUR FARM?
UHH... YEAH! I MEAN, YES! IT'S JUST EXACTLY LIKE YOU LEFT IT! NO KIDDING!
YOUR MOM WAS ADAMANT ABOUT NOT SELLING OUT TO ANY RUTHLESS DE-VELOPERS. THAT'S WHY SHE SOLD IT TO ME.
YOU SAVED OUR FARM?

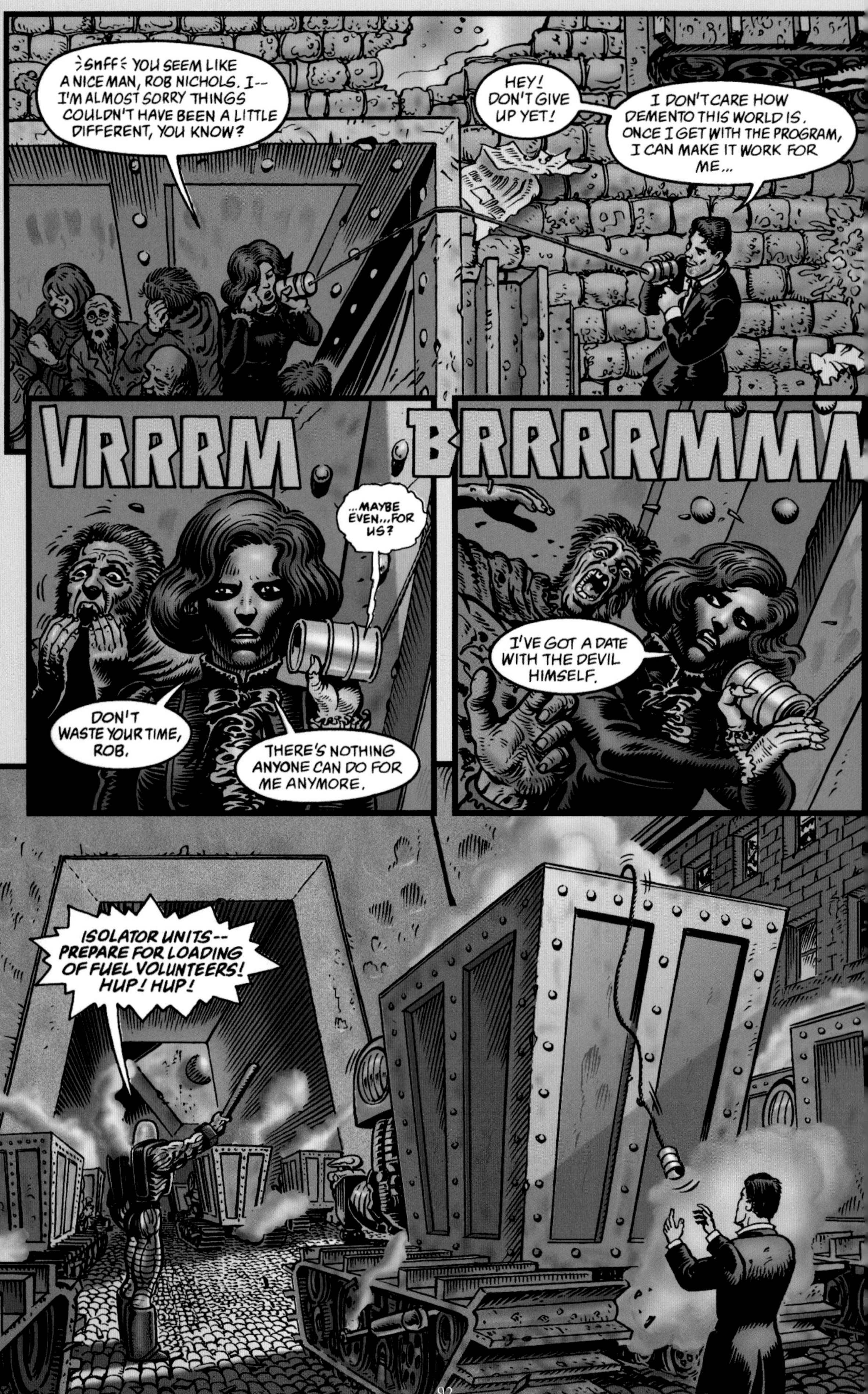

≷SNFF≶ YOU SEEM LIKE A NICE MAN, ROB NICHOLS. I-- I'M ALMOST SORRY THINGS COULDN'T HAVE BEEN A LITTLE DIFFERENT, YOU KNOW?
HEY! DON'T GIVE UP YET!
I DON'T CARE HOW DEMENTO THIS WORLD IS. ONCE I GET WITH THE PROGRAM, I CAN MAKE IT WORK FOR ME...
VRRRM
...MAYBE EVEN...FOR US?
DON'T WASTE YOUR TIME, ROB.
THERE'S NOTHING ANYONE CAN DO FOR ME ANYMORE.
BRRRRMMM
I'VE GOT A DATE WITH THE DEVIL HIMSELF.
ISOLATOR UNITS-- PREPARE FOR LOADING OF FUEL VOLUNTEERS! HUP! HUP!

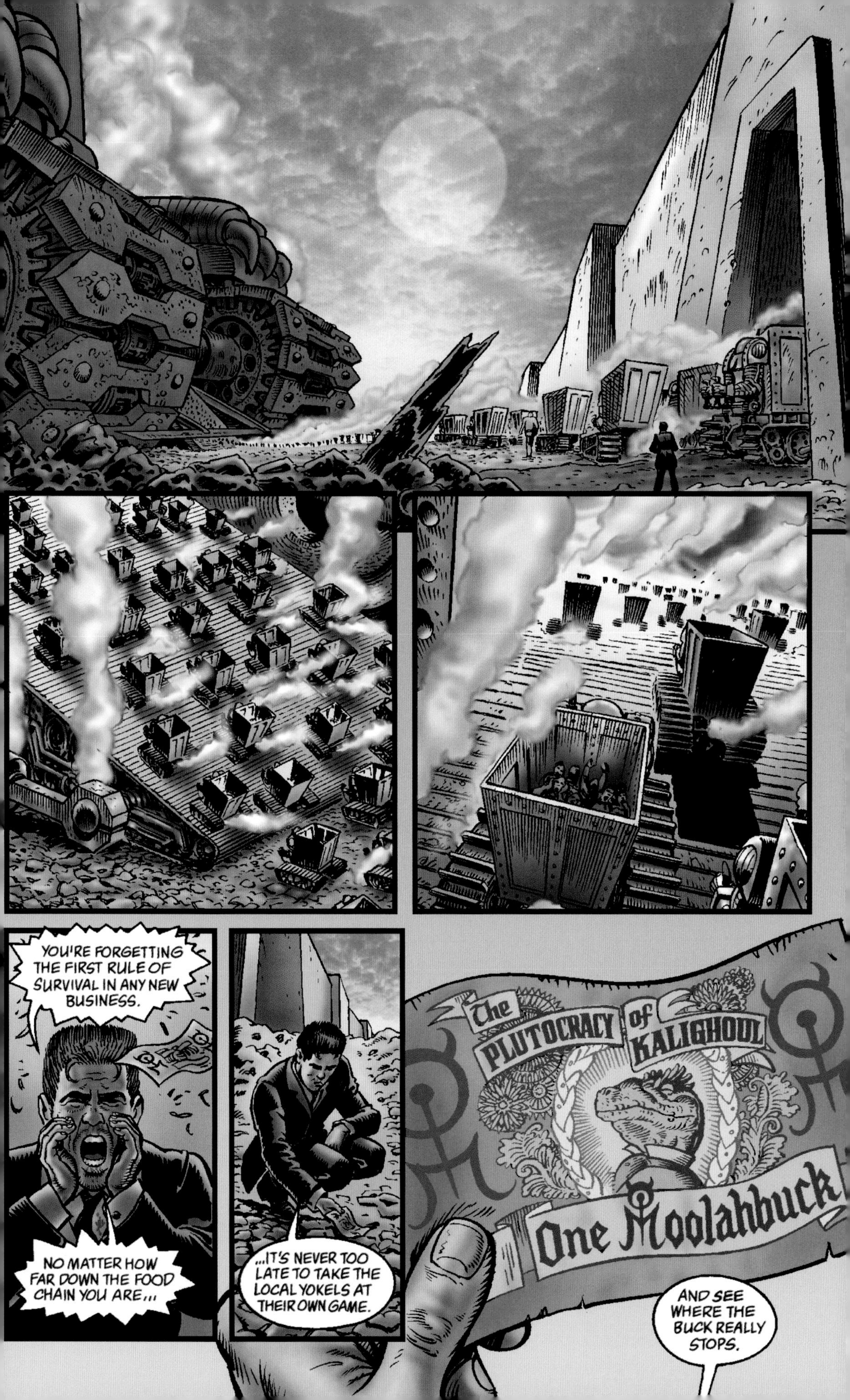
YOU'RE FORGETTING THE FIRST RULE OF SURVIVAL IN ANY NEW BUSINESS.
NO MATTER HOW FAR DOWN THE FOOD CHAIN YOU ARE...
...IT'S NEVER TOO LATE TO TAKE THE LOCAL YOKELS AT THEIR OWN GAME.
The PLUTOCRACY of KALIGHOUL
One Moolahbuck
AND SEE WHERE THE BUCK REALLY STOPS.

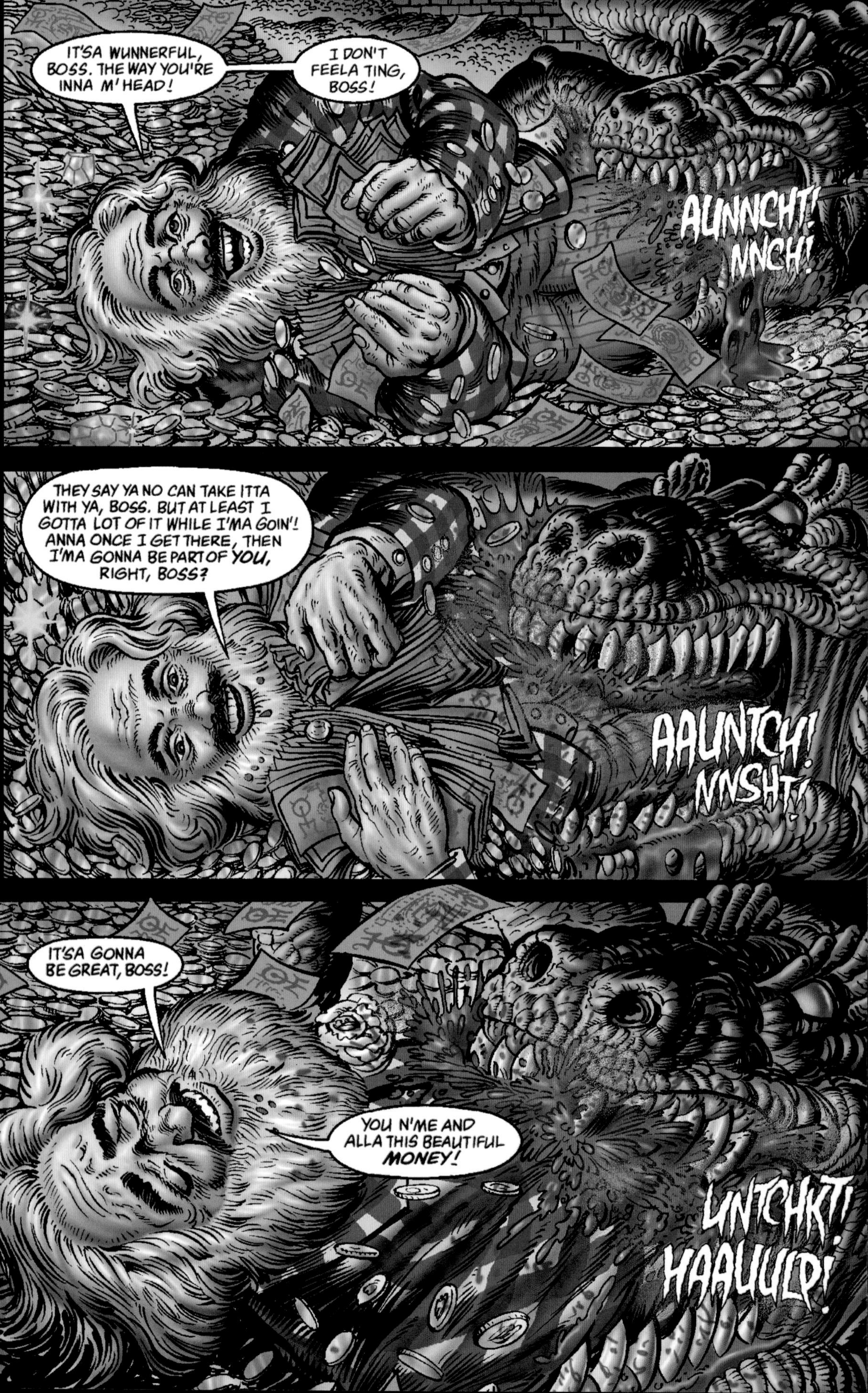
IT'SA WUNNERFUL, BOSS. THE WAY YOU'RE INNA M' HEAD!
I DON'T FEELA TING, BOSS!
AUNNCHT! NNCH!
THEY SAY YA NO CAN TAKE ITTA WITH YA, BOSS. BUT AT LEAST I GOTTA LOT OF IT WHILE I'MA GOIN'! ANNA ONCE I GET THERE, THEN I'MA GONNA BE PART OF YOU, RIGHT, BOSS?
AAUNTCH! NNSHT!
IT'SA GONNA BE GREAT, BOSS!
YOU N'ME AND ALLA THIS BEAUTIFUL MONEY!
UNTCHKT! HAAUULP!

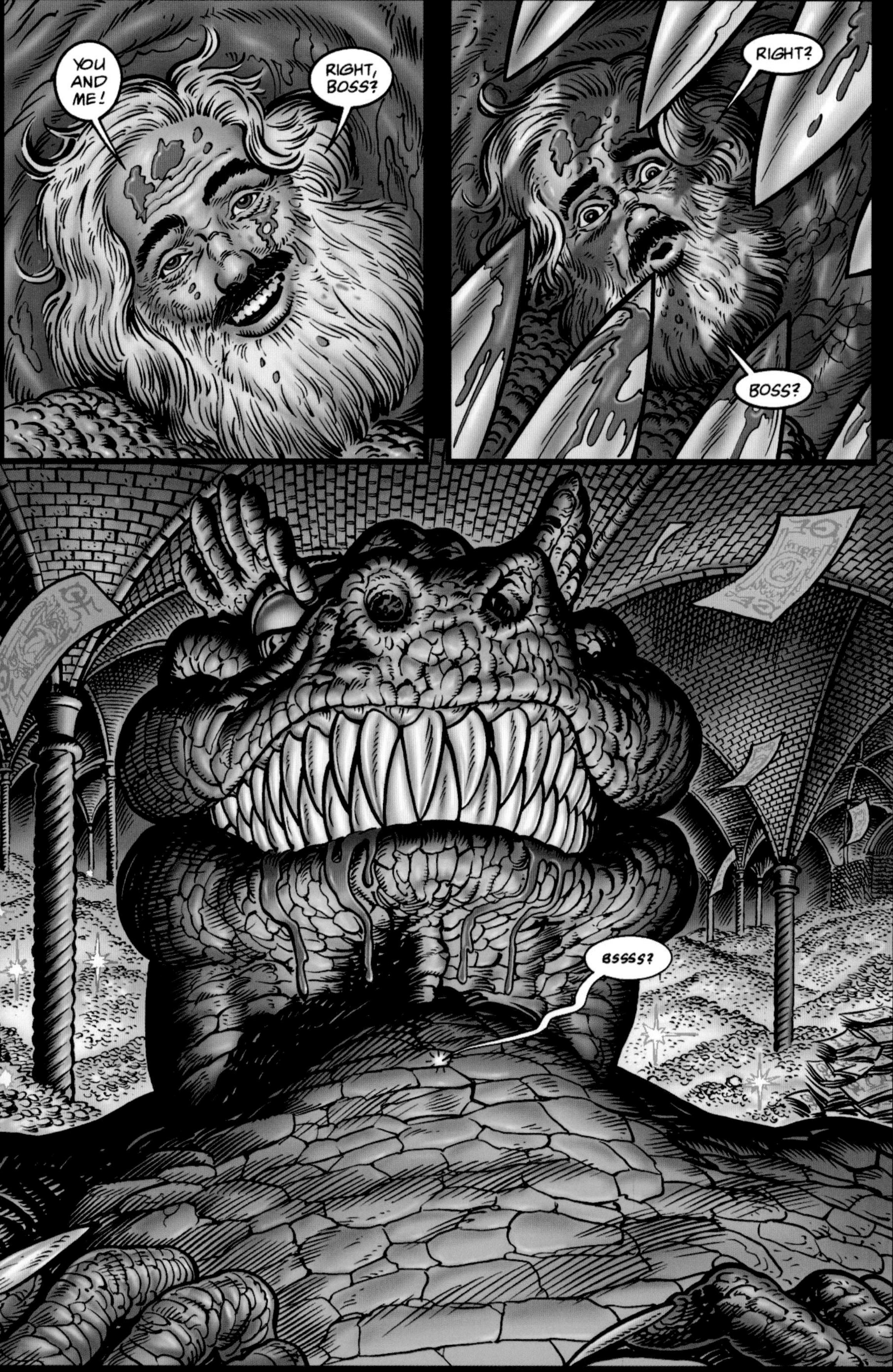
YOU AND ME!
RIGHT, BOSS?
RIGHT?
BOSS?
BSSSS?

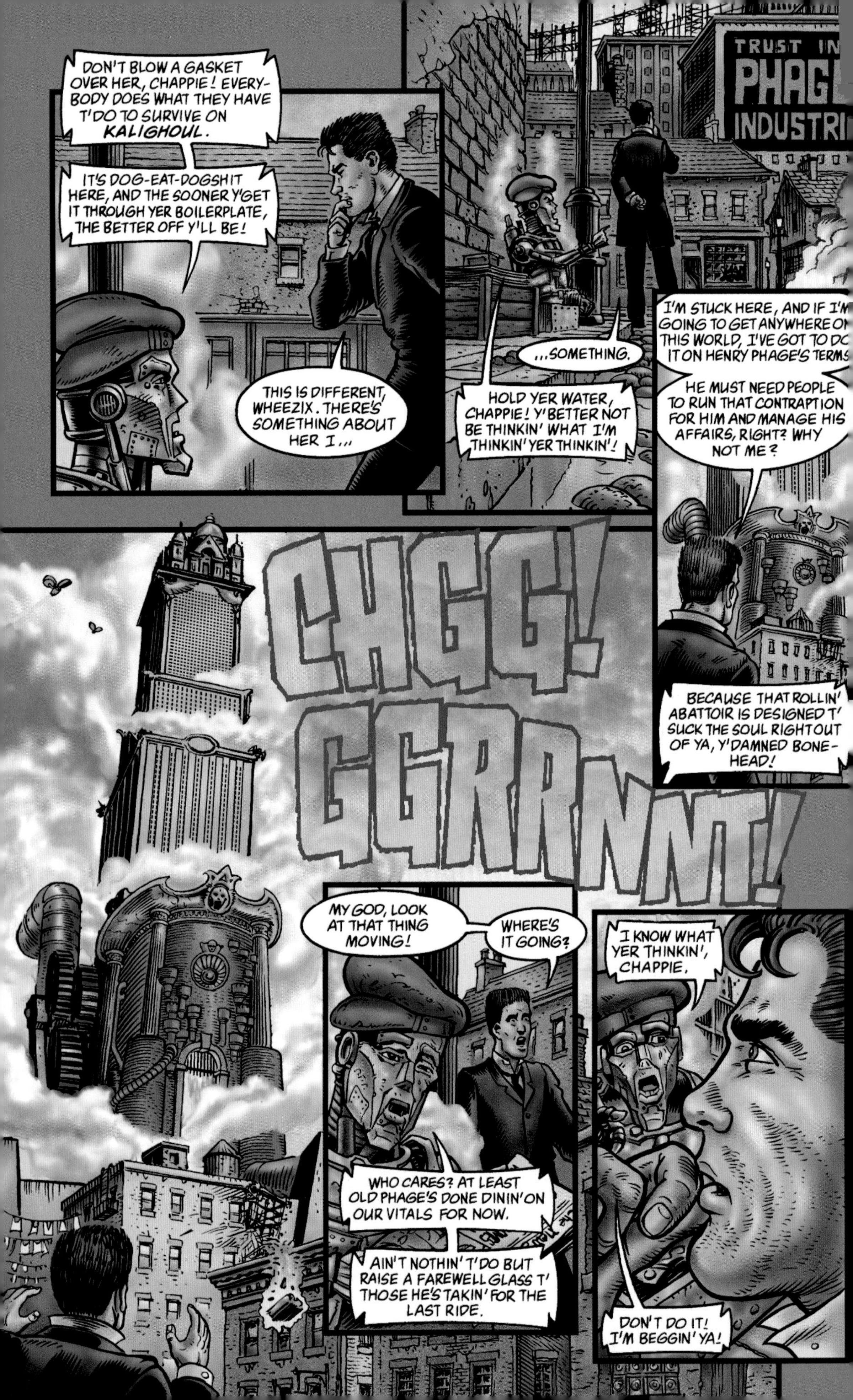
DON'T BLOW A GASKET OVER HER, CHAPPIE! EVERYBODY DOES WHAT THEY HAVE T'DO TO SURVIVE ON **KALIGHOUL**.
IT'S DOG-EAT-DOGSHIT HERE, AND THE SOONER Y'GET IT THROUGH YER BOILERPLATE, THE BETTER OFF Y'LL BE!
THIS IS DIFFERENT, WHEEZIX. THERE'S SOMETHING ABOUT HER I...
TRUST IN
PHAG
INDUSTRI
...SOMETHING.
HOLD YER WATER, CHAPPIE! Y'BETTER NOT BE THINKIN' WHAT I'M THINKIN' YER THINKIN'!
I'M STUCK HERE, AND IF I'M GOING TO GET ANYWHERE ON THIS WORLD, I'VE GOT TO DO IT ON HENRY PHAGE'S TERMS.
HE MUST NEED PEOPLE TO RUN THAT CONTRAPTION FOR HIM AND MANAGE HIS AFFAIRS, RIGHT? WHY NOT ME?
BECAUSE THAT ROLLIN' ABATTOIR IS DESIGNED T' SUCK THE SOUL RIGHT OUT OF YA, Y'DAMNED BONEHEAD!
CHGG! GGRRNNT!
MY GOD, LOOK AT THAT THING MOVING!
WHERE'S IT GOING?
WHO CARES? AT LEAST OLD PHAGE'S DONE DININ' ON OUR VITALS FOR NOW.
AIN'T NOTHIN' T'DO BUT RAISE A FAREWELL GLASS T' THOSE HE'S TAKIN' FOR THE LAST RIDE.
I KNOW WHAT YER THINKIN', CHAPPIE.
DON'T DO IT! I'M BEGGIN' YA!

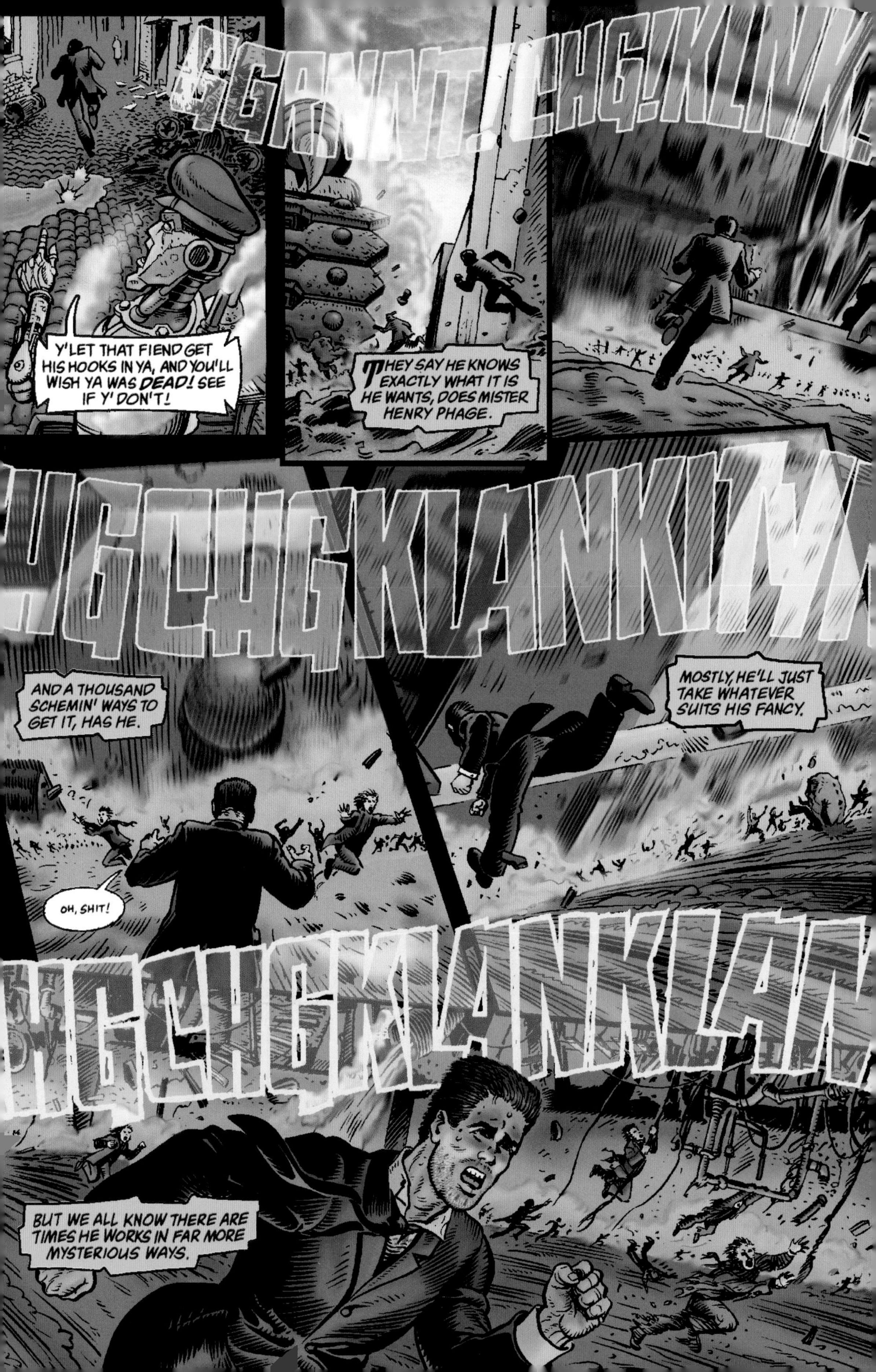

GANNT! CHG!KLINK!
Y'LET THAT FIEND GET HIS HOOKS IN YA, AND YOU'LL WISH YA WAS DEAD! SEE IF Y' DON'T!
THEY SAY HE KNOWS EXACTLY WHAT IT IS HE WANTS, DOES MISTER HENRY PHAGE.
HGCHGKLANK!
AND A THOUSAND SCHEMIN' WAYS TO GET IT, HAS HE.
MOSTLY, HE'LL JUST TAKE WHATEVER SUITS HIS FANCY.
OH, SHIT!
HGCHGKLANKLAN
BUT WE ALL KNOW THERE ARE TIMES HE WORKS IN FAR MORE MYSTERIOUS WAYS.

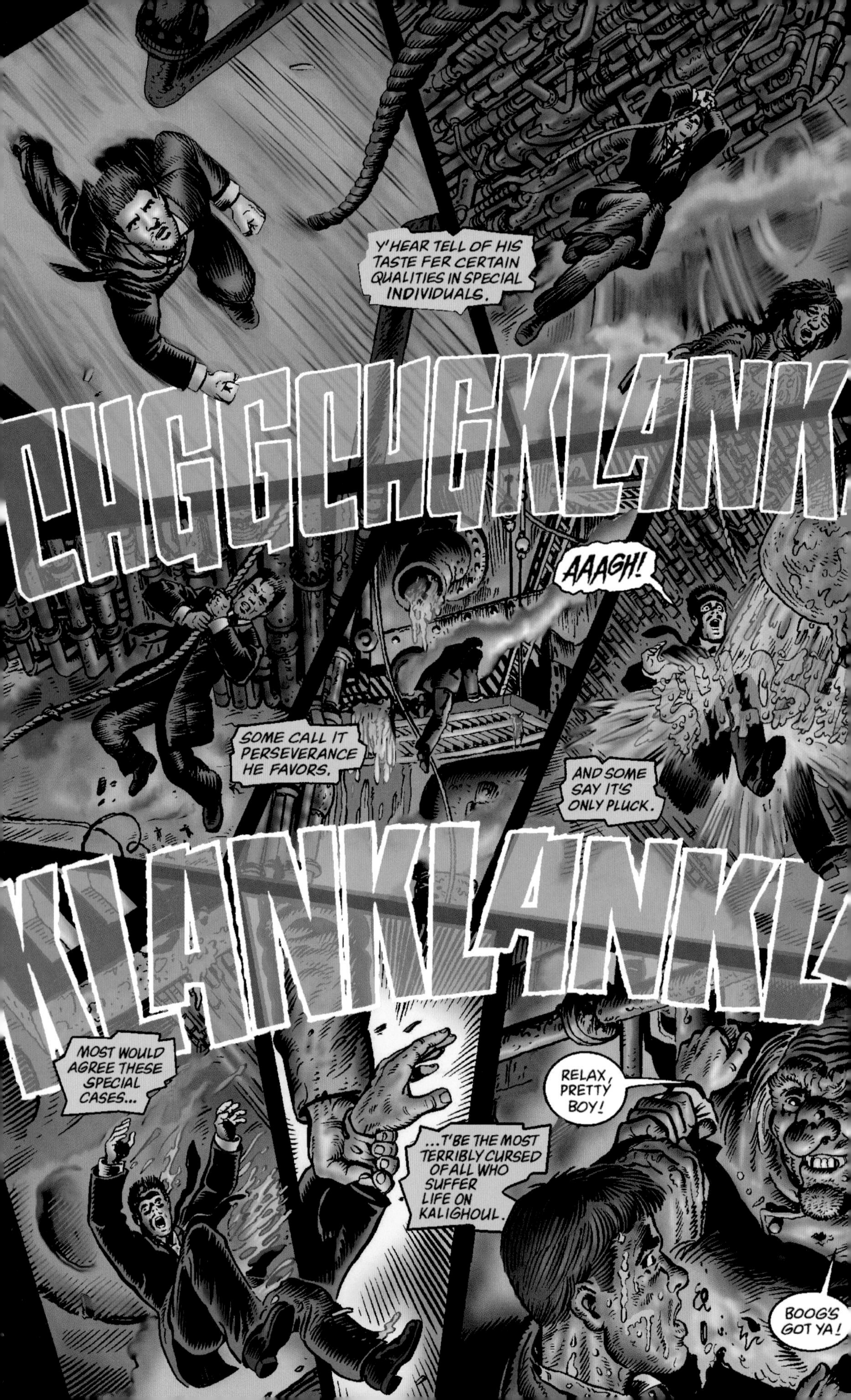

Y'HEAR TELL OF HIS TASTE FER CERTAIN QUALITIES IN SPECIAL INDIVIDUALS.
CHGGCHGKLANK
AAAGH!
SOME CALL IT PERSEVERANCE HE FAVORS.
AND SOME SAY IT'S ONLY PLUCK.
KLANKLANKL
MOST WOULD AGREE THESE SPECIAL CASES...
...T'BE THE MOST TERRIBLY CURSED OF ALL WHO SUFFER LIFE ON KALIGHOUL.
RELAX, PRETTY BOY!
BOOG'S GOT YA!

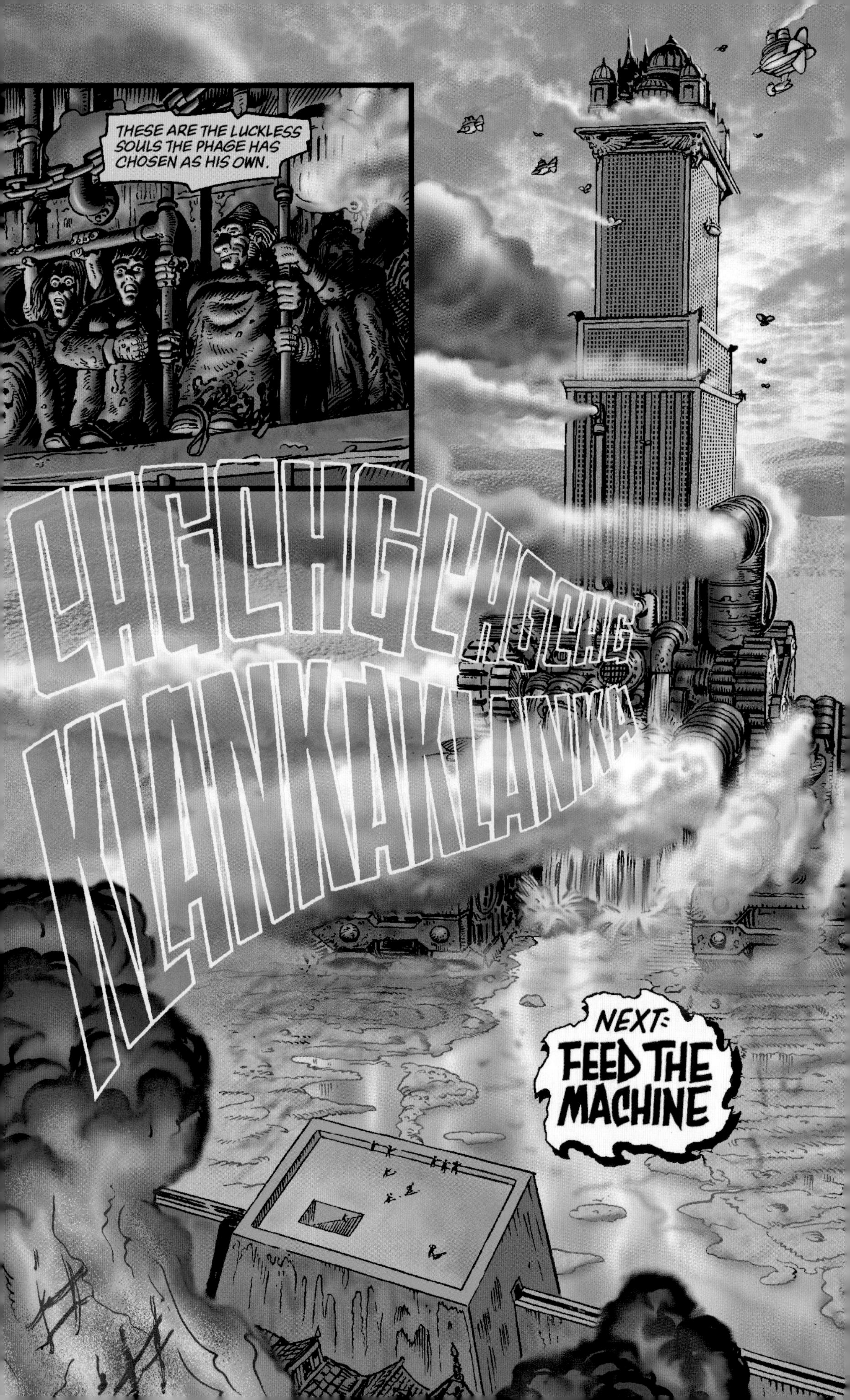

THESE ARE THE LUCKLESS SOULS THE PHAGE HAS CHOSEN AS HIS OWN.
CHGCHGCHGCHG
KLANKAKLANKA
NEXT:
FEED THE MACHINE

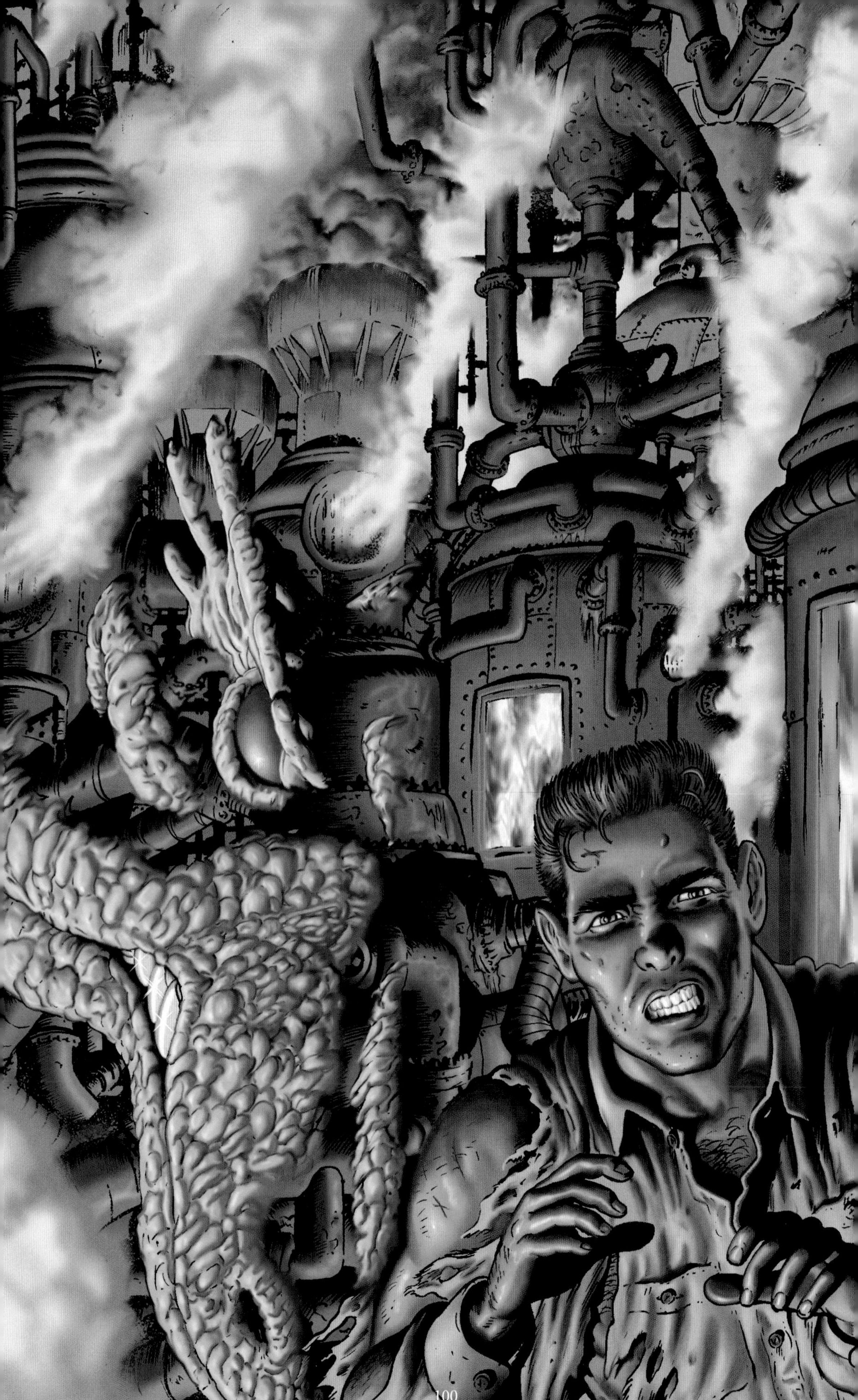

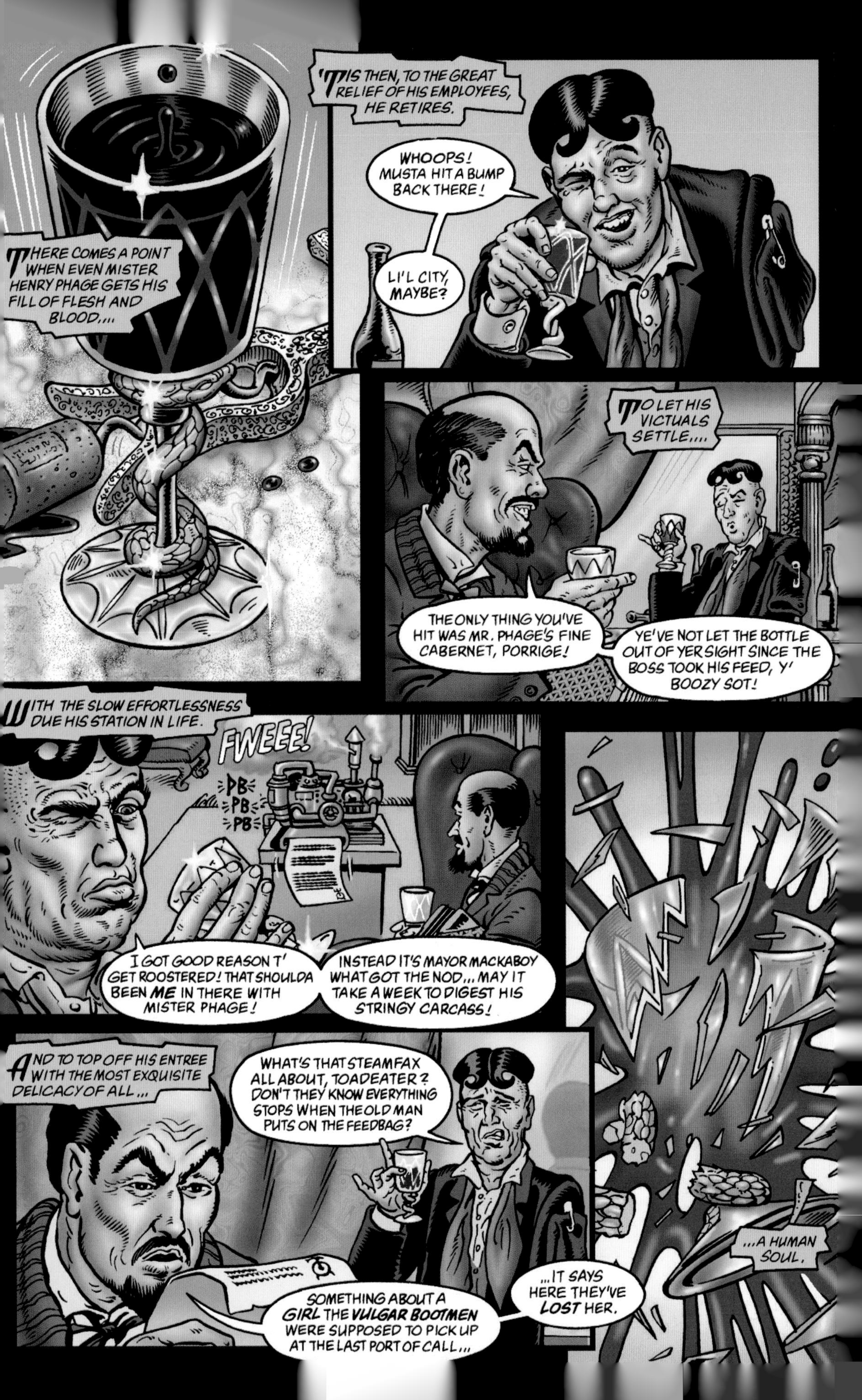

THERE COMES A POINT WHEN EVEN MISTER HENRY PHAGE GETS HIS FILL OF FLESH AND BLOOD,...
'TIS THEN, TO THE GREAT RELIEF OF HIS EMPLOYEES, HE RETIRES.
WHOOPS! MUSTA HIT A BUMP BACK THERE!
LI'L CITY, MAYBE?
TO LET HIS VICTUALS SETTLE,...
THE ONLY THING YOU'VE HIT WAS MR. PHAGE'S FINE CABERNET, PORRIGE!
YE'VE NOT LET THE BOTTLE OUT OF YER SIGHT SINCE THE BOSS TOOK HIS FEED, Y' BOOZY SOT!
WITH THE SLOW EFFORTLESSNESS DUE HIS STATION IN LIFE.
FWEEE!
PB PB PB
I GOT GOOD REASON T' GET ROOSTERED! THAT SHOULDA BEEN ME IN THERE WITH MISTER PHAGE!
INSTEAD IT'S MAYOR MACKABOY WHAT GOT THE NOD,,, MAY IT TAKE A WEEK TO DIGEST HIS STRINGY CARCASS!
AND TO TOP OFF HIS ENTREE WITH THE MOST EXQUISITE DELICACY OF ALL...
WHAT'S THAT STEAMFAX ALL ABOUT, TOADEATER? DON'T THEY KNOW EVERYTHING STOPS WHEN THE OLD MAN PUTS ON THE FEEDBAG?
SOMETHING ABOUT A GIRL THE VULGAR BOOTMEN WERE SUPPOSED TO PICK UP AT THE LAST PORT OF CALL,,,
...IT SAYS HERE THEY'VE LOST HER.
...A HUMAN SOUL.

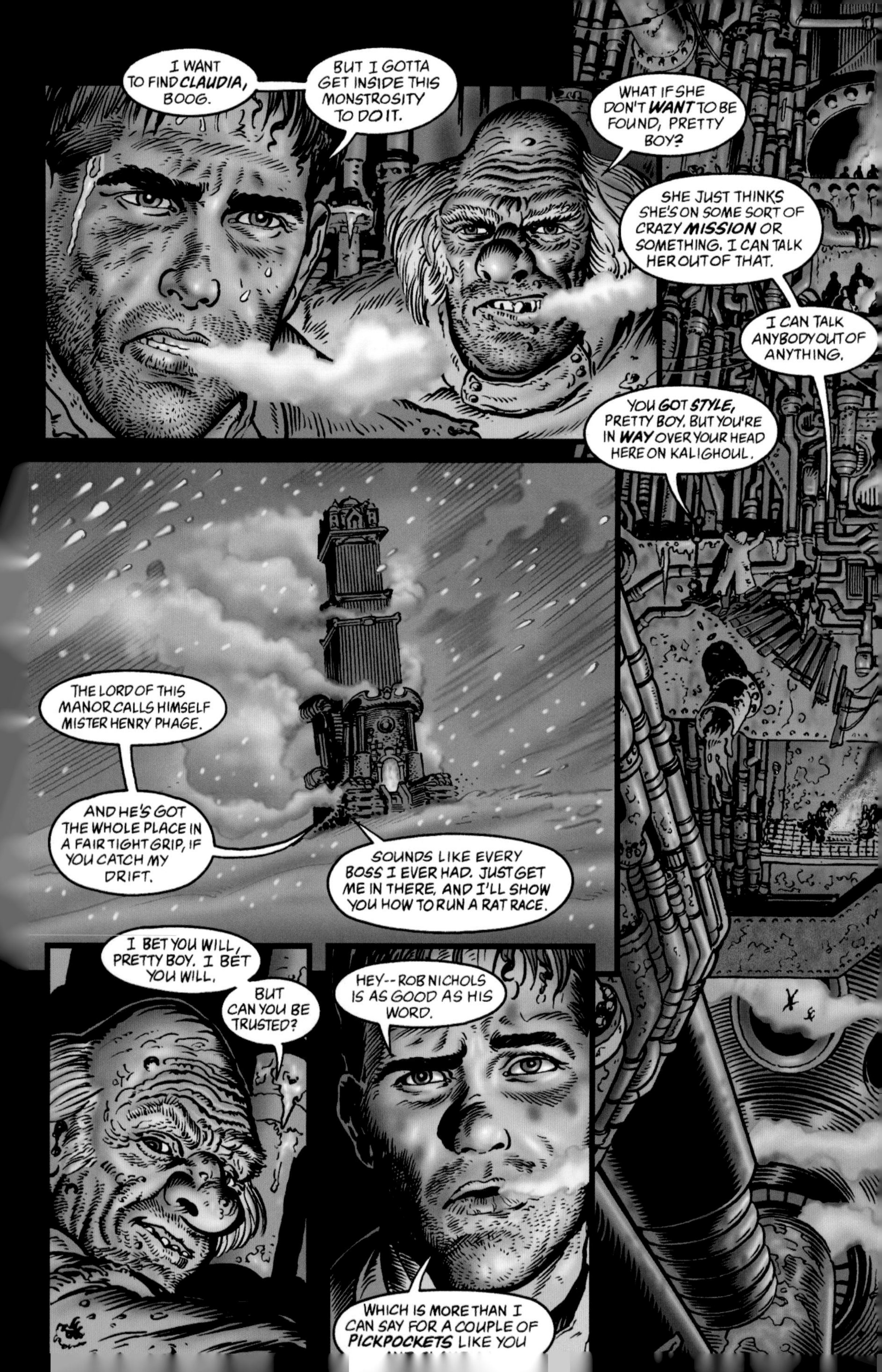

I WANT TO FIND CLAUDIA, BOOG.
BUT I GOTTA GET INSIDE THIS MONSTROSITY TO DO IT.
WHAT IF SHE DON'T WANT TO BE FOUND, PRETTY BOY?
SHE JUST THINKS SHE'S ON SOME SORT OF CRAZY MISSION OR SOMETHING. I CAN TALK HER OUT OF THAT.
I CAN TALK ANYBODY OUT OF ANYTHING.
YOU GOT STYLE, PRETTY BOY. BUT YOU'RE IN WAY OVER YOUR HEAD HERE ON KALIGHOUL.
THE LORD OF THIS MANOR CALLS HIMSELF MISTER HENRY PHAGE.
AND HE'S GOT THE WHOLE PLACE IN A FAIR TIGHT GRIP, IF YOU CATCH MY DRIFT.
SOUNDS LIKE EVERY BOSS I EVER HAD. JUST GET ME IN THERE, AND I'LL SHOW YOU HOW TO RUN A RAT RACE.
I BET YOU WILL, PRETTY BOY. I BET YOU WILL.
BUT CAN YOU BE TRUSTED?
HEY--ROB NICHOLS IS AS GOOD AS HIS WORD.
WHICH IS MORE THAN I CAN SAY FOR A COUPLE OF PICKPOCKETS LIKE YOU

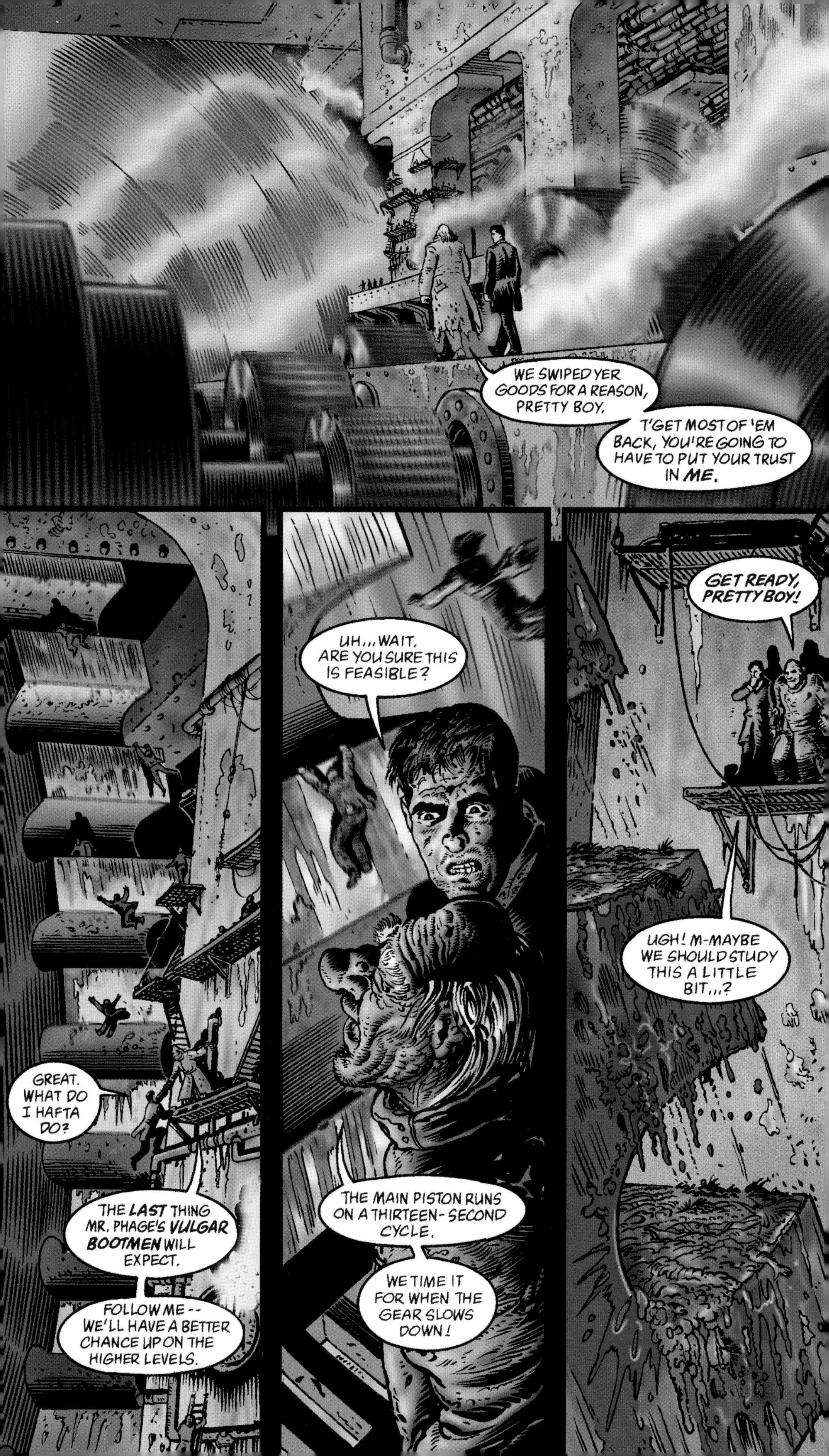
WE SWIPED YER GOODS FOR A REASON, PRETTY BOY.
T'GET MOST OF 'EM BACK, YOU'RE GOING TO HAVE TO PUT YOUR TRUST IN ME.
GREAT. WHAT DO I HAFTA DO?
THE LAST THING MR. PHAGE'S VULGAR BOOTMEN WILL EXPECT.
FOLLOW ME -- WE'LL HAVE A BETTER CHANCE UP ON THE HIGHER LEVELS.
UH... WAIT. ARE YOU SURE THIS IS FEASIBLE?
THE MAIN PISTON RUNS ON A THIRTEEN-SECOND CYCLE.
WE TIME IT FOR WHEN THE GEAR SLOWS DOWN!
GET READY, PRETTY BOY!
UGH! M-MAYBE WE SHOULD STUDY THIS A LITTLE BIT...?

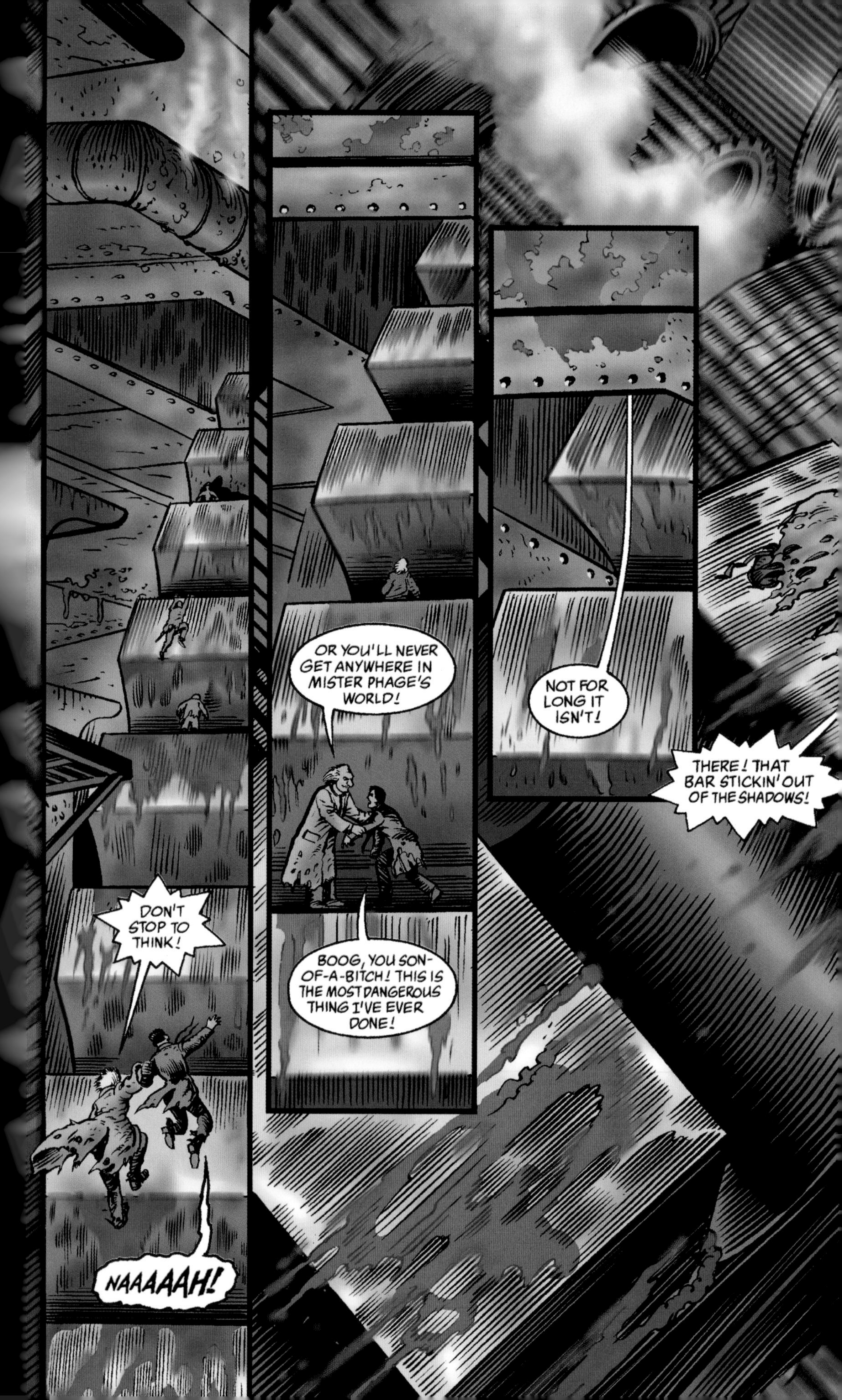
DON'T STOP TO THINK!
NAAAAAH!
OR YOU'LL NEVER GET ANYWHERE IN MISTER PHAGE'S WORLD!
BOOG, YOU SON-OF-A-BITCH! THIS IS THE MOST DANGEROUS THING I'VE EVER DONE!
NOT FOR LONG IT ISN'T!
THERE! THAT BAR STICKIN' OUT OF THE SHADOWS!

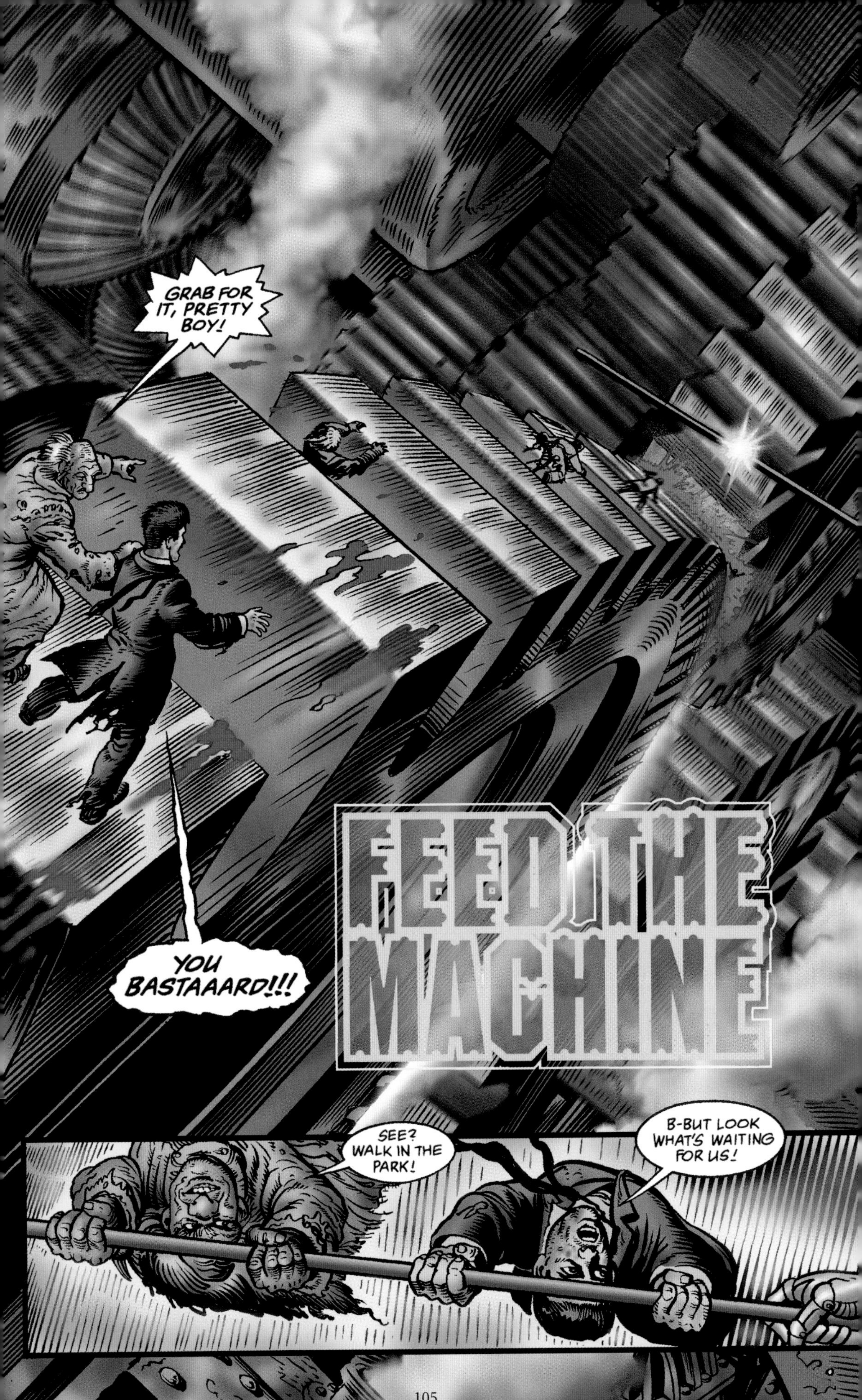
GRAB FOR IT, PRETTY BOY!
YOU BASTAAARD!!!
FEED THE MACHINE
SEE? WALK IN THE PARK!
B-BUT LOOK WHAT'S WAITING FOR US!

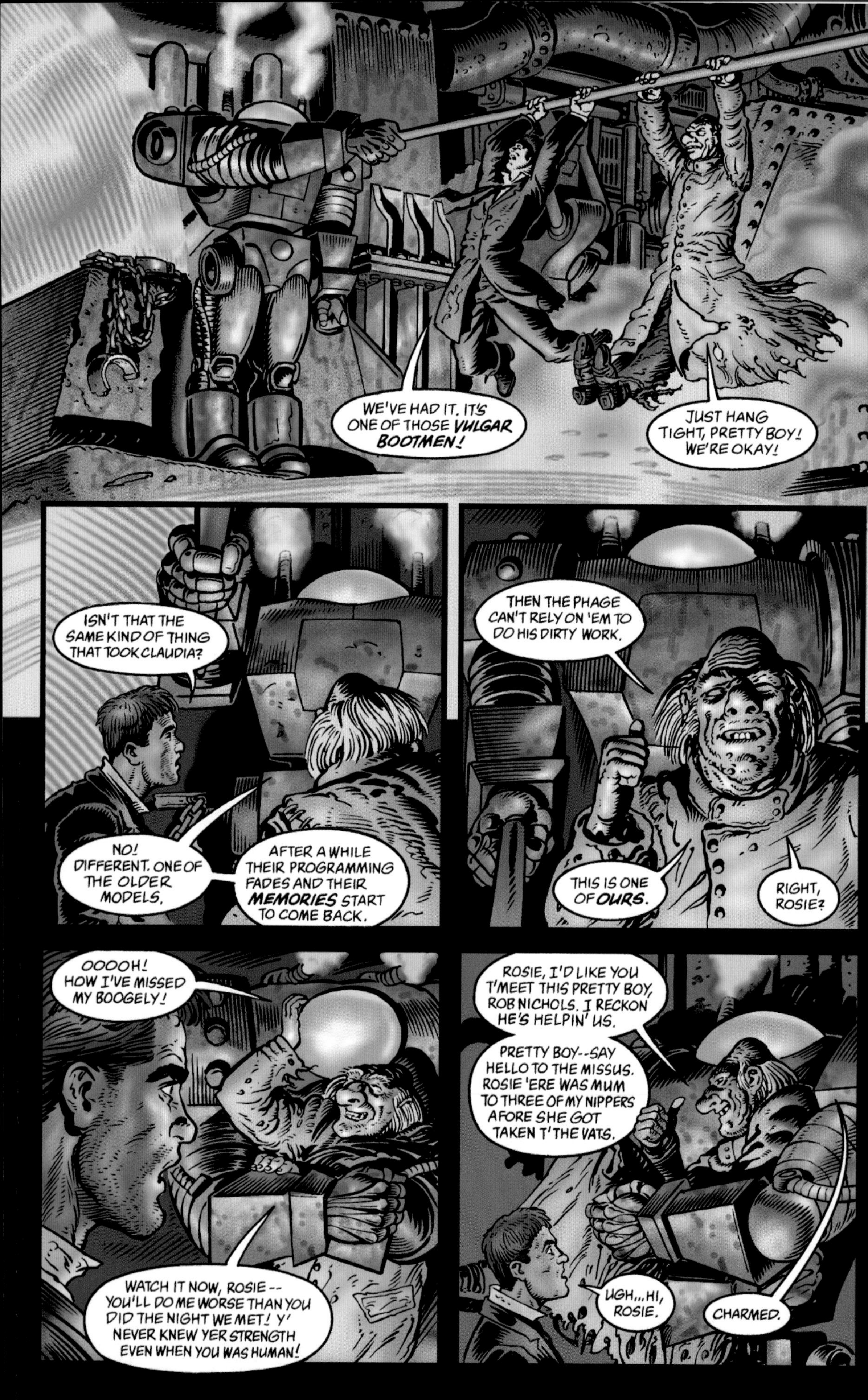

WE'VE HAD IT. IT'S ONE OF THOSE VULGAR BOOTMEN!
JUST HANG TIGHT, PRETTY BOY! WE'RE OKAY!
ISN'T THAT THE SAME KIND OF THING THAT TOOK CLAUDIA?
NO! DIFFERENT. ONE OF THE OLDER MODELS.
AFTER A WHILE THEIR PROGRAMMING FADES AND THEIR MEMORIES START TO COME BACK.
THEN THE PHAGE CAN'T RELY ON 'EM TO DO HIS DIRTY WORK.
THIS IS ONE OF OURS.
RIGHT, ROSIE?
OOOOH! HOW I'VE MISSED MY BOOGELY!
WATCH IT NOW, ROSIE -- YOU'LL DO ME WORSE THAN YOU DID THE NIGHT WE MET! Y' NEVER KNEW YER STRENGTH EVEN WHEN YOU WAS HUMAN!
ROSIE, I'D LIKE YOU T'MEET THIS PRETTY BOY, ROB NICHOLS. I RECKON HE'S HELPIN' US.
PRETTY BOY--SAY HELLO TO THE MISSUS. ROSIE 'ERE WAS MUM TO THREE OF MY NIPPERS AFORE SHE GOT TAKEN T' THE VATS.
UGH...HI, ROSIE.
CHARMED.

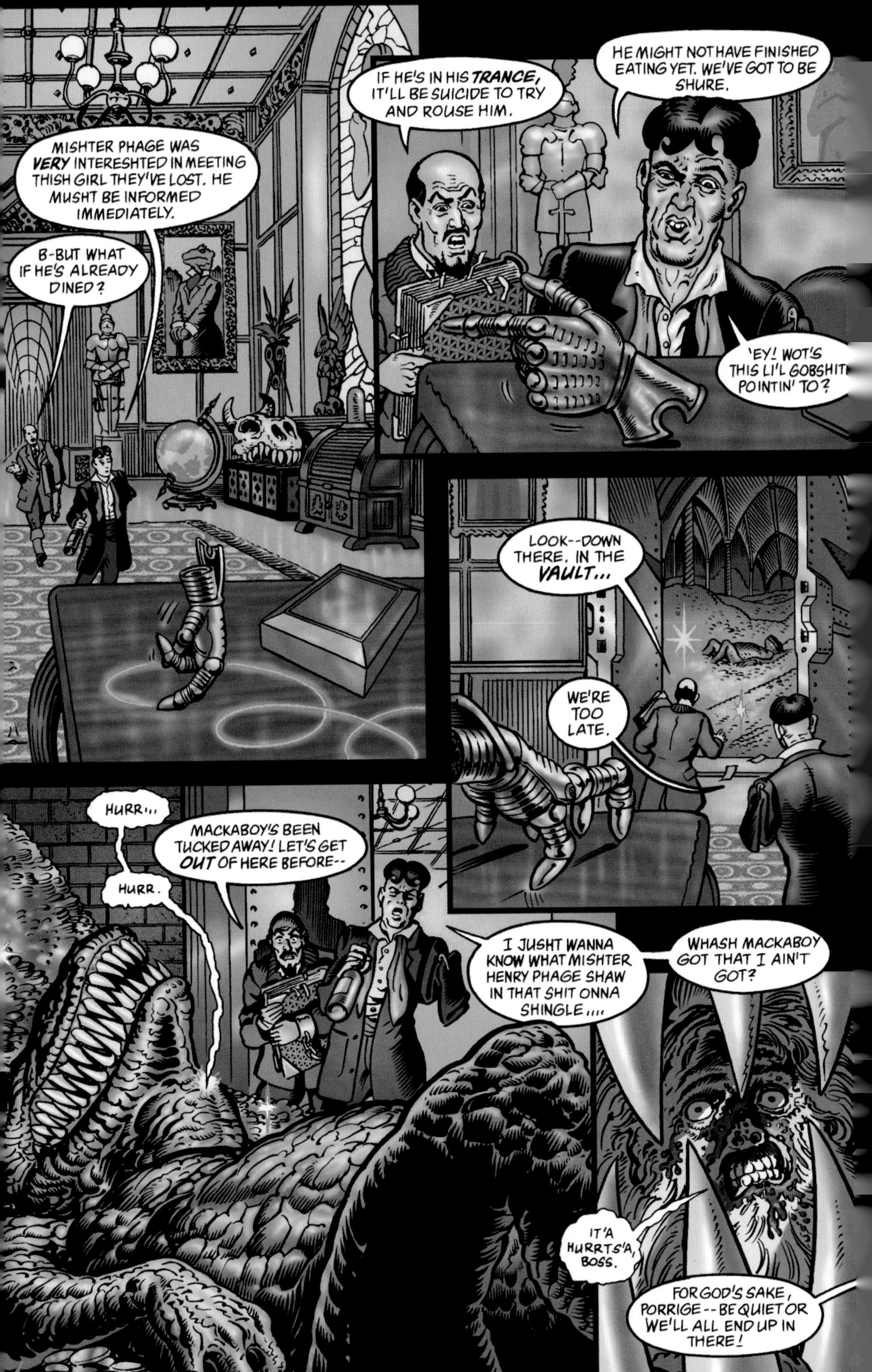
MISHTER PHAGE WAS VERY INTERESHTED IN MEETING THISH GIRL THEY'VE LOST. HE MUSHT BE INFORMED IMMEDIATELY.
B-BUT WHAT IF HE'S ALREADY DINED?
IF HE'S IN HIS TRANCE, IT'LL BE SUICIDE TO TRY AND ROUSE HIM.
HE MIGHT NOT HAVE FINISHED EATING YET. WE'VE GOT TO BE SHURE.
'EY! WOT'S THIS LI'L GOBSHIT POINTIN' TO?
LOOK--DOWN THERE, IN THE VAULT...
WE'RE TOO LATE.
HURR...
HURR.
MACKABOY'S BEEN TUCKED AWAY! LET'S GET OUT OF HERE BEFORE--
I JUSHT WANNA KNOW WHAT MISHTER HENRY PHAGE SHAW IN THAT SHIT ONNA SHINGLE....
WHASH MACKABOY GOT THAT I AIN'T GOT?
IT'A HURRTS'A, BOSS.
FOR GOD'S SAKE, PORRIGE--BE QUIET OR WE'LL ALL END UP IN THERE!

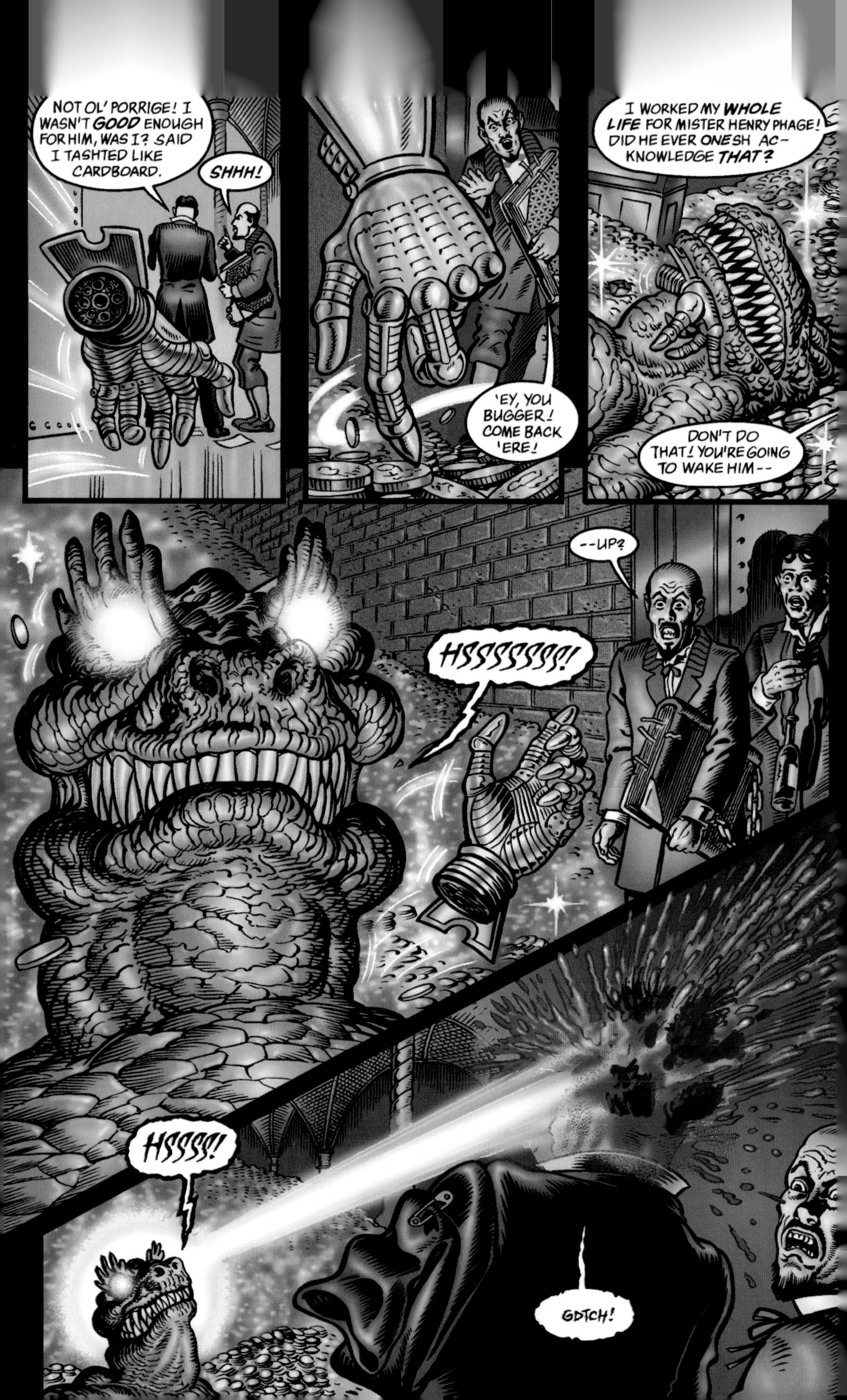
NOT OL' PORRIGE! I WASN'T GOOD ENOUGH FOR HIM, WAS I? SAID I TASHTED LIKE CARDBOARD.
SHHH!
'EY, YOU BUGGER! COME BACK 'ERE!
I WORKED MY WHOLE LIFE FOR MISTER HENRY PHAGE! DID HE EVER ONESH AC-KNOWLEDGE THAT?
DON'T DO THAT! YOU'RE GOING TO WAKE HIM--
--UP?
HSSSSSSS!
HSSSS!
GDTCH!

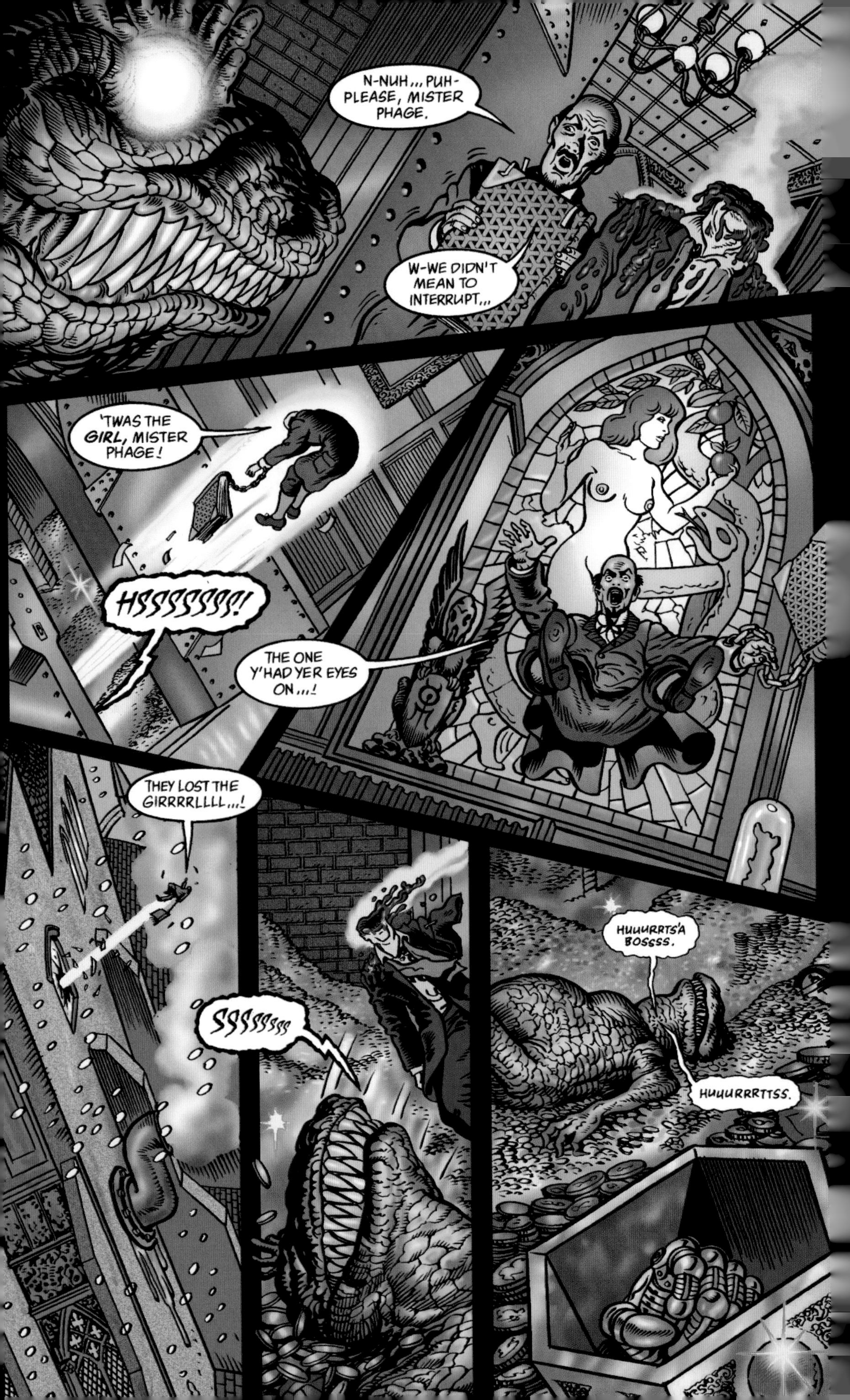
N-NUH... PUH-PLEASE, MISTER PHAGE.
W-WE DIDN'T MEAN TO INTERRUPT...
'TWAS THE GIRL, MISTER PHAGE!
HSSSSSSS!
THE ONE Y'HAD YER EYES ON...!
THEY LOST THE GIRRRRLLLL...!
SSSSSsss
HUUURRTS'A BOSSSS.
HUUURRRTTSS.

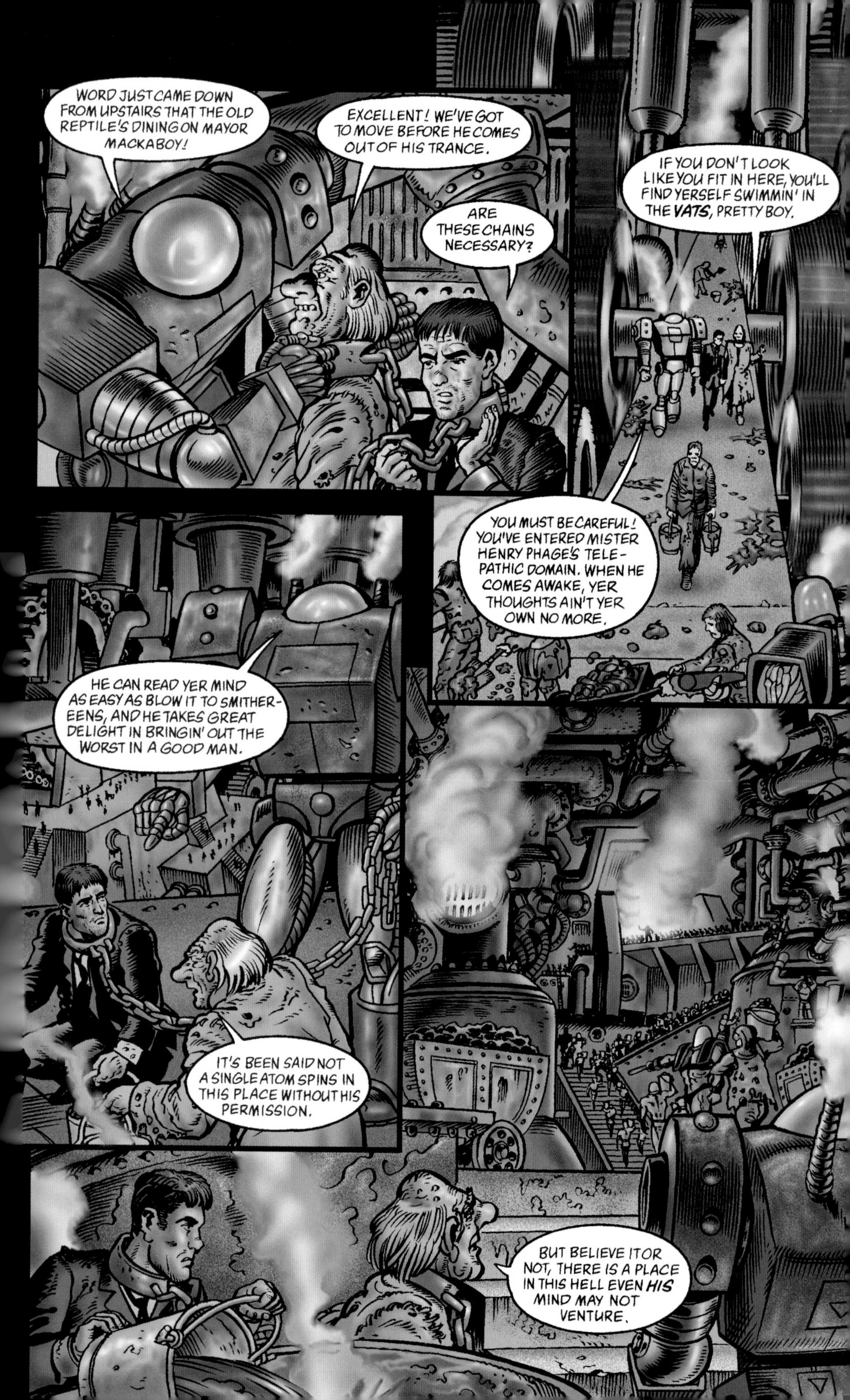
WORD JUST CAME DOWN FROM UPSTAIRS THAT THE OLD REPTILE'S DINING ON MAYOR MACKABOY!
EXCELLENT! WE'VE GOT TO MOVE BEFORE HE COMES OUT OF HIS TRANCE.
ARE THESE CHAINS NECESSARY?
IF YOU DON'T LOOK LIKE YOU FIT IN HERE, YOU'LL FIND YERSELF SWIMMIN' IN THE VATS, PRETTY BOY.
YOU MUST BE CAREFUL! YOU'VE ENTERED MISTER HENRY PHAGE'S TELE-PATHIC DOMAIN. WHEN HE COMES AWAKE, YER THOUGHTS AIN'T YER OWN NO MORE.
HE CAN READ YER MIND AS EASY AS BLOW IT TO SMITHER-EENS, AND HE TAKES GREAT DELIGHT IN BRINGIN' OUT THE WORST IN A GOOD MAN.
IT'S BEEN SAID NOT A SINGLE ATOM SPINS IN THIS PLACE WITHOUT HIS PERMISSION.
BUT BELIEVE IT OR NOT, THERE IS A PLACE IN THIS HELL EVEN HIS MIND MAY NOT VENTURE.

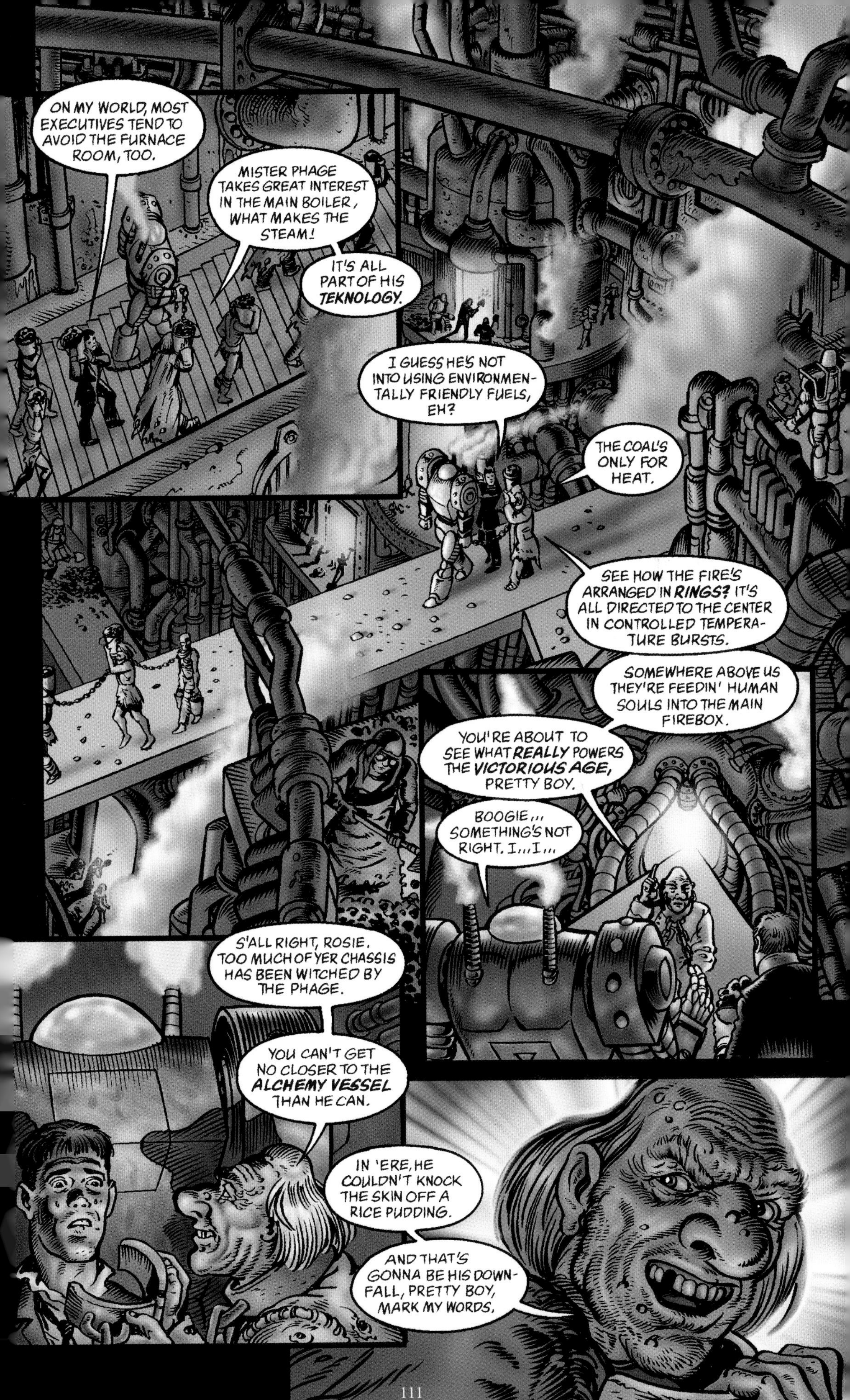
ON MY WORLD, MOST EXECUTIVES TEND TO AVOID THE FURNACE ROOM, TOO.
MISTER PHAGE TAKES GREAT INTEREST IN THE MAIN BOILER, WHAT MAKES THE STEAM!
IT'S ALL PART OF HIS TEKNOLOGY.
I GUESS HE'S NOT INTO USING ENVIRONMENTALLY FRIENDLY FUELS, EH?
THE COAL'S ONLY FOR HEAT.
SEE HOW THE FIRE'S ARRANGED IN RINGS? IT'S ALL DIRECTED TO THE CENTER IN CONTROLLED TEMPERATURE BURSTS.
SOMEWHERE ABOVE US THEY'RE FEEDIN' HUMAN SOULS INTO THE MAIN FIREBOX.
YOU'RE ABOUT TO SEE WHAT REALLY POWERS THE VICTORIOUS AGE, PRETTY BOY.
BOOGIE... SOMETHING'S NOT RIGHT. I...I...
S'ALL RIGHT, ROSIE. TOO MUCH OF YER CHASSIS HAS BEEN WITCHED BY THE PHAGE.
YOU CAN'T GET NO CLOSER TO THE ALCHEMY VESSEL THAN HE CAN.
IN 'ERE, HE COULDN'T KNOCK THE SKIN OFF A RICE PUDDING.
AND THAT'S GONNA BE HIS DOWNFALL, PRETTY BOY, MARK MY WORDS.

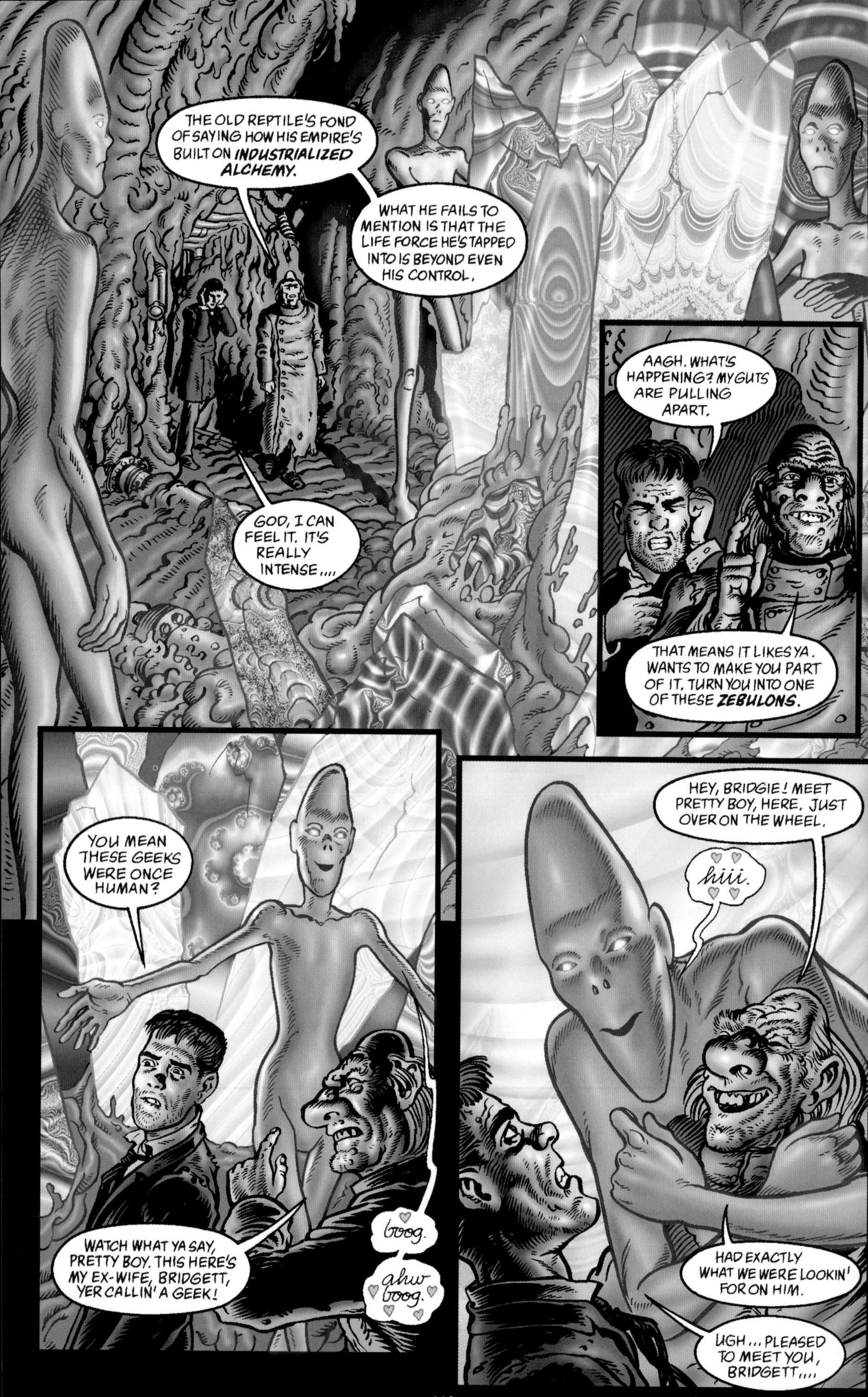
THE OLD REPTILE'S FOND OF SAYING HOW HIS EMPIRE'S BUILT ON **INDUSTRIALIZED ALCHEMY.**
WHAT HE FAILS TO MENTION IS THAT THE LIFE FORCE HE'S TAPPED INTO IS BEYOND EVEN HIS CONTROL.
GOD, I CAN FEEL IT. IT'S REALLY INTENSE....
AAGH. WHAT'S HAPPENING? MY GUTS ARE PULLING APART.
THAT MEANS IT LIKES YA. WANTS TO MAKE YOU PART OF IT. TURN YOU INTO ONE OF THESE **ZEBULONS.**
YOU MEAN THESE GEEKS WERE ONCE HUMAN?
WATCH WHAT YA SAY, PRETTY BOY. THIS HERE'S MY EX-WIFE, BRIDGETT, YER CALLIN' A GEEK!
boog.
ahw boog.
HEY, BRIDGIE! MEET PRETTY BOY, HERE. JUST OVER ON THE WHEEL.
hiii.
HAD EXACTLY WHAT WE WERE LOOKIN' FOR ON HIM.
UGH... PLEASED TO MEET YOU, BRIDGETT....

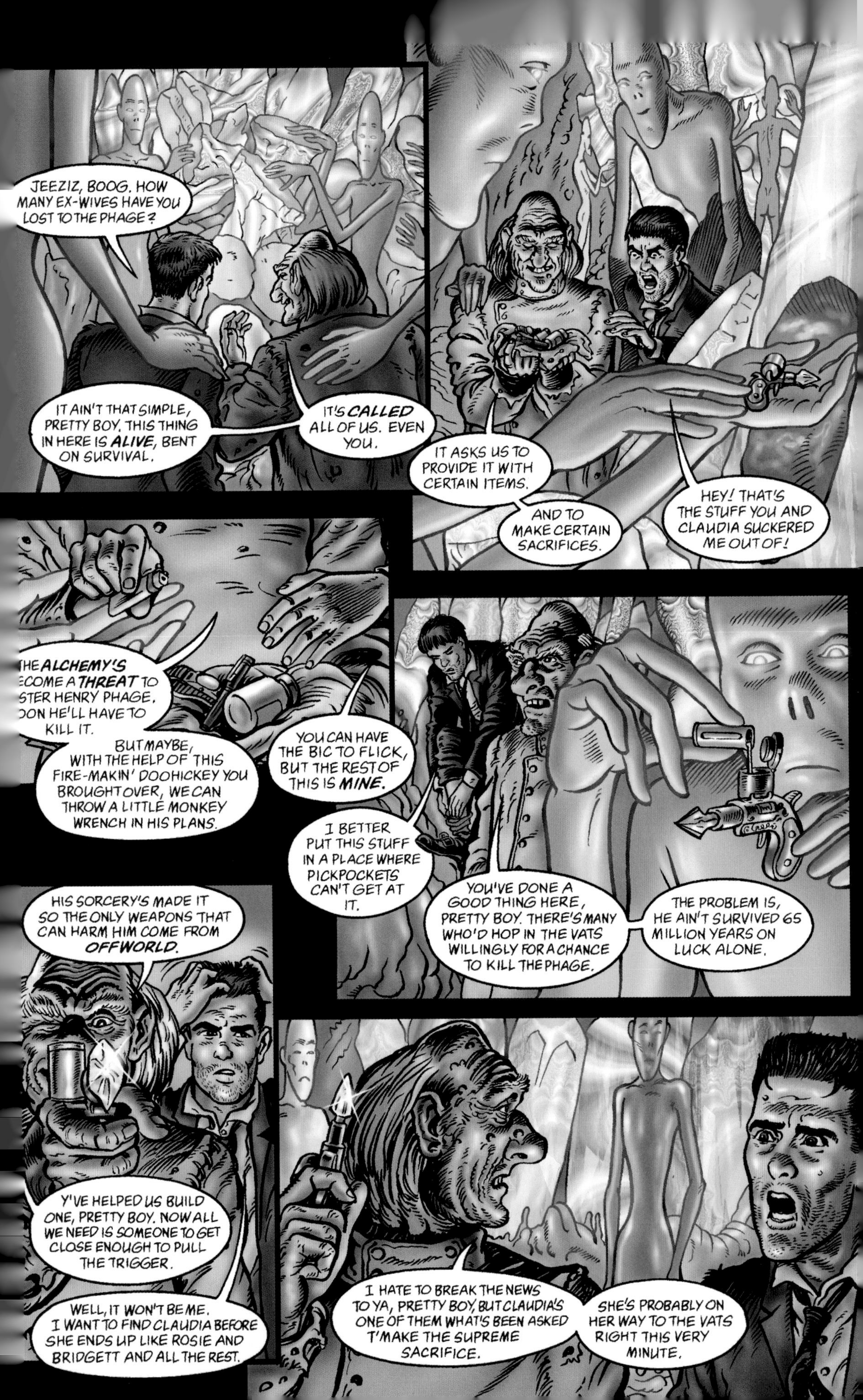
JEEZIZ, BOOG. HOW MANY EX-WIVES HAVE YOU LOST TO THE PHAGE?
IT AIN'T THAT SIMPLE, PRETTY BOY. THIS THING IN HERE IS ALIVE, BENT ON SURVIVAL.
IT'S CALLED ALL OF US. EVEN YOU.
IT ASKS US TO PROVIDE IT WITH CERTAIN ITEMS.
AND TO MAKE CERTAIN SACRIFICES.
HEY! THAT'S THE STUFF YOU AND CLAUDIA SUCKERED ME OUT OF!
THE ALCHEMY'S ECOME A THREAT TO STER HENRY PHAGE. OON HE'LL HAVE TO KILL IT.
BUT MAYBE, WITH THE HELP OF THIS FIRE-MAKIN' DOOHICKEY YOU BROUGHT OVER, WE CAN THROW A LITTLE MONKEY WRENCH IN HIS PLANS.
YOU CAN HAVE THE BIC TO FLICK, BUT THE REST OF THIS IS MINE.
I BETTER PUT THIS STUFF IN A PLACE WHERE PICKPOCKETS CAN'T GET AT IT.
YOU'VE DONE A GOOD THING HERE, PRETTY BOY. THERE'S MANY WHO'D HOP IN THE VATS WILLINGLY FOR A CHANCE TO KILL THE PHAGE.
THE PROBLEM IS, HE AIN'T SURVIVED 65 MILLION YEARS ON LUCK ALONE.
HIS SORCERY'S MADE IT SO THE ONLY WEAPONS THAT CAN HARM HIM COME FROM OFFWORLD.
Y'VE HELPED US BUILD ONE, PRETTY BOY. NOW ALL WE NEED IS SOMEONE TO GET CLOSE ENOUGH TO PULL THE TRIGGER.
WELL, IT WON'T BE ME. I WANT TO FIND CLAUDIA BEFORE SHE ENDS UP LIKE ROSIE AND BRIDGETT AND ALL THE REST.
I HATE TO BREAK THE NEWS TO YA, PRETTY BOY, BUT CLAUDIA'S ONE OF THEM WHAT'S BEEN ASKED T'MAKE THE SUPREME SACRIFICE.
SHE'S PROBABLY ON HER WAY TO THE VATS RIGHT THIS VERY MINUTE.

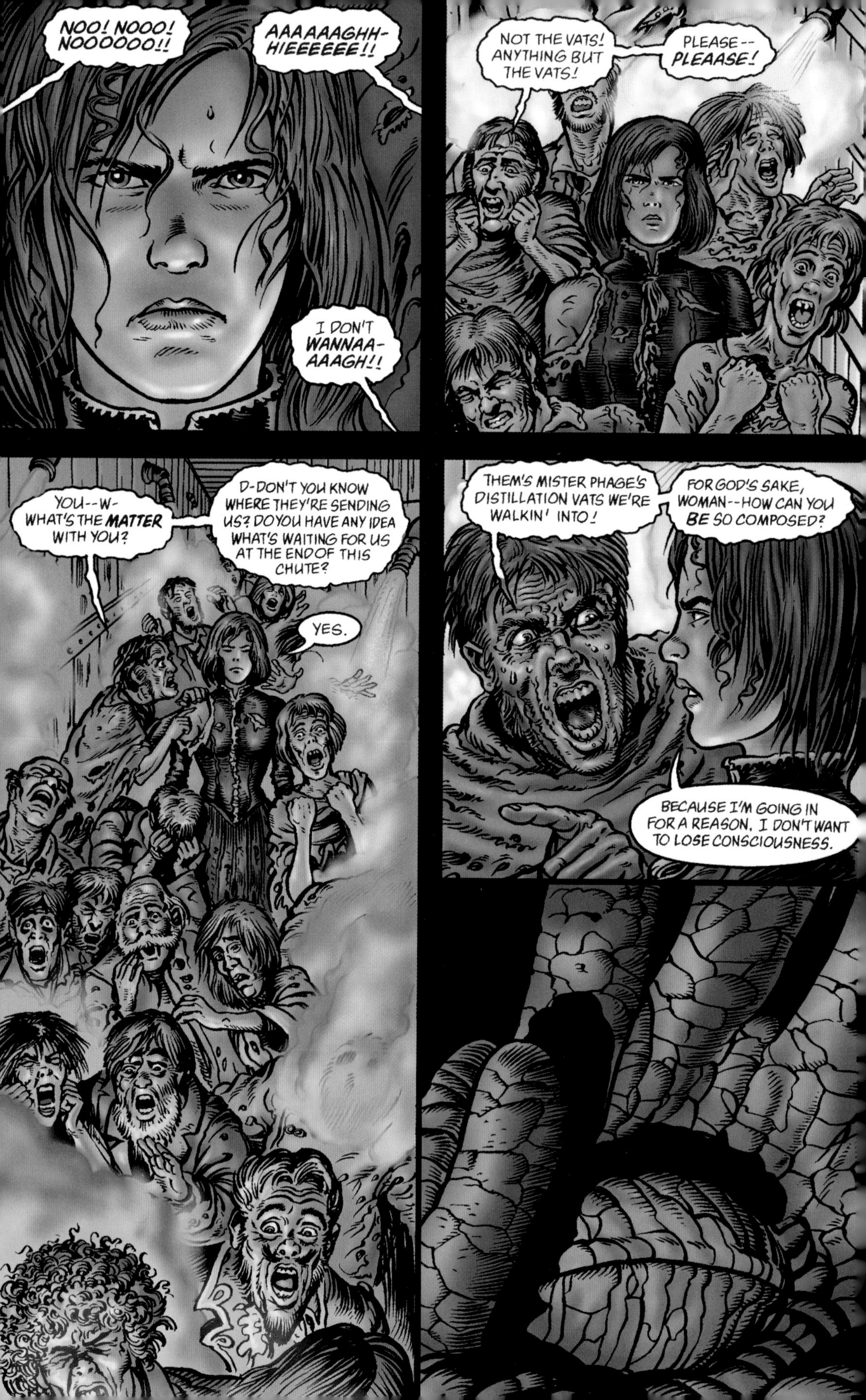
NOO! NOOO! NOOOOOO!!
AAAAAAGHH-HIEEEEEE!!
I DON'T WANNAA-AAAGH!!
NOT THE VATS! ANYTHING BUT THE VATS!
PLEASE-- PLEAASE!
YOU--W-WHAT'S THE MATTER WITH YOU?
D-DON'T YOU KNOW WHERE THEY'RE SENDING US? DO YOU HAVE ANY IDEA WHAT'S WAITING FOR US AT THE END OF THIS CHUTE?
YES.
THEM'S MISTER PHAGE'S DISTILLATION VATS WE'RE WALKIN' INTO!
FOR GOD'S SAKE, WOMAN--HOW CAN YOU BE SO COMPOSED?
BECAUSE I'M GOING IN FOR A REASON. I DON'T WANT TO LOSE CONSCIOUSNESS.

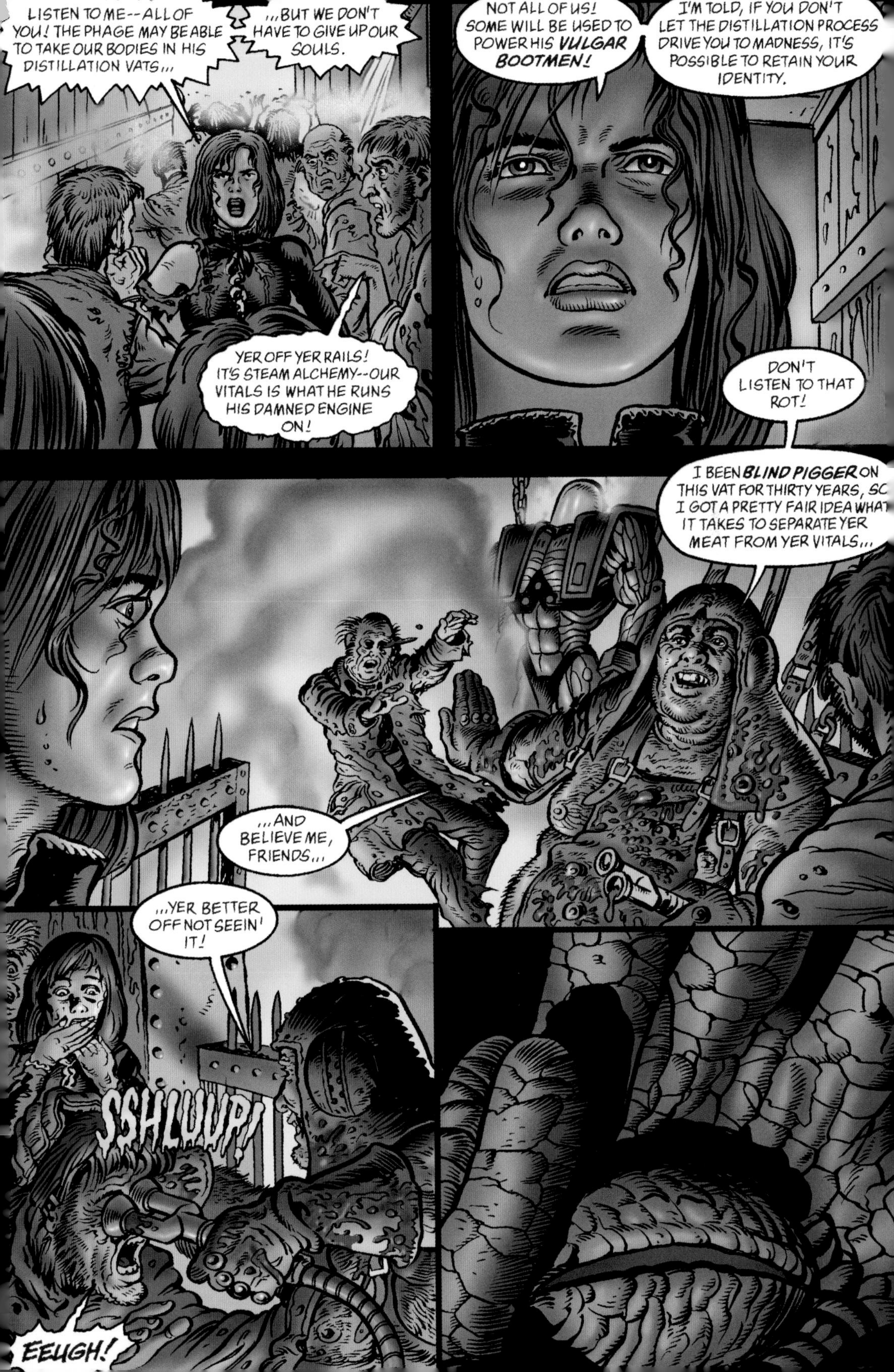
LISTEN TO ME--ALL OF YOU! THE PHAGE MAY BE ABLE TO TAKE OUR BODIES IN HIS DISTILLATION VATS...
...BUT WE DON'T HAVE TO GIVE UP OUR SOULS.
YER OFF YER RAILS! IT'S STEAM ALCHEMY--OUR VITALS IS WHAT HE RUNS HIS DAMNED ENGINE ON!
NOT ALL OF US! SOME WILL BE USED TO POWER HIS VULGAR BOOTMEN!
I'M TOLD, IF YOU DON'T LET THE DISTILLATION PROCESS DRIVE YOU TO MADNESS, IT'S POSSIBLE TO RETAIN YOUR IDENTITY.
DON'T LISTEN TO THAT ROT!
I BEEN BLIND PIGGER ON THIS VAT FOR THIRTY YEARS, SO I GOT A PRETTY FAIR IDEA WHAT IT TAKES TO SEPARATE YER MEAT FROM YER VITALS...
...AND BELIEVE ME, FRIENDS...
...YER BETTER OFF NOT SEEIN' IT!
SSHLUUP!
EEUGH!

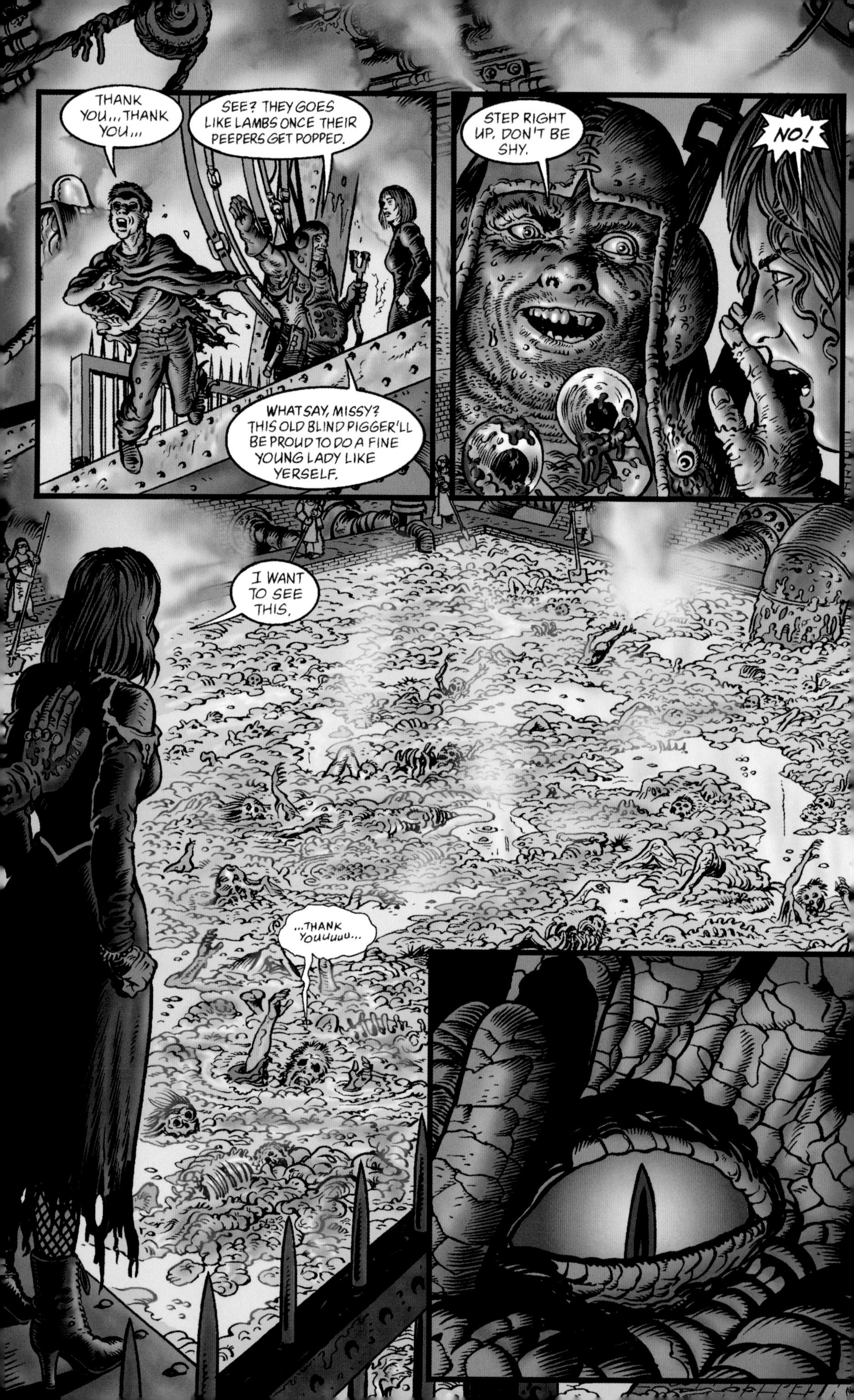
THANK YOU... THANK YOU...
SEE? THEY GOES LIKE LAMBS ONCE THEIR PEEPERS GET POPPED.
WHAT SAY, MISSY? THIS OLD BLIND PIGGER'LL BE PROUD TO DO A FINE YOUNG LADY LIKE YERSELF.
STEP RIGHT UP, DON'T BE SHY.
NO!
I WANT TO SEE THIS.
...THANK YOUUUU...

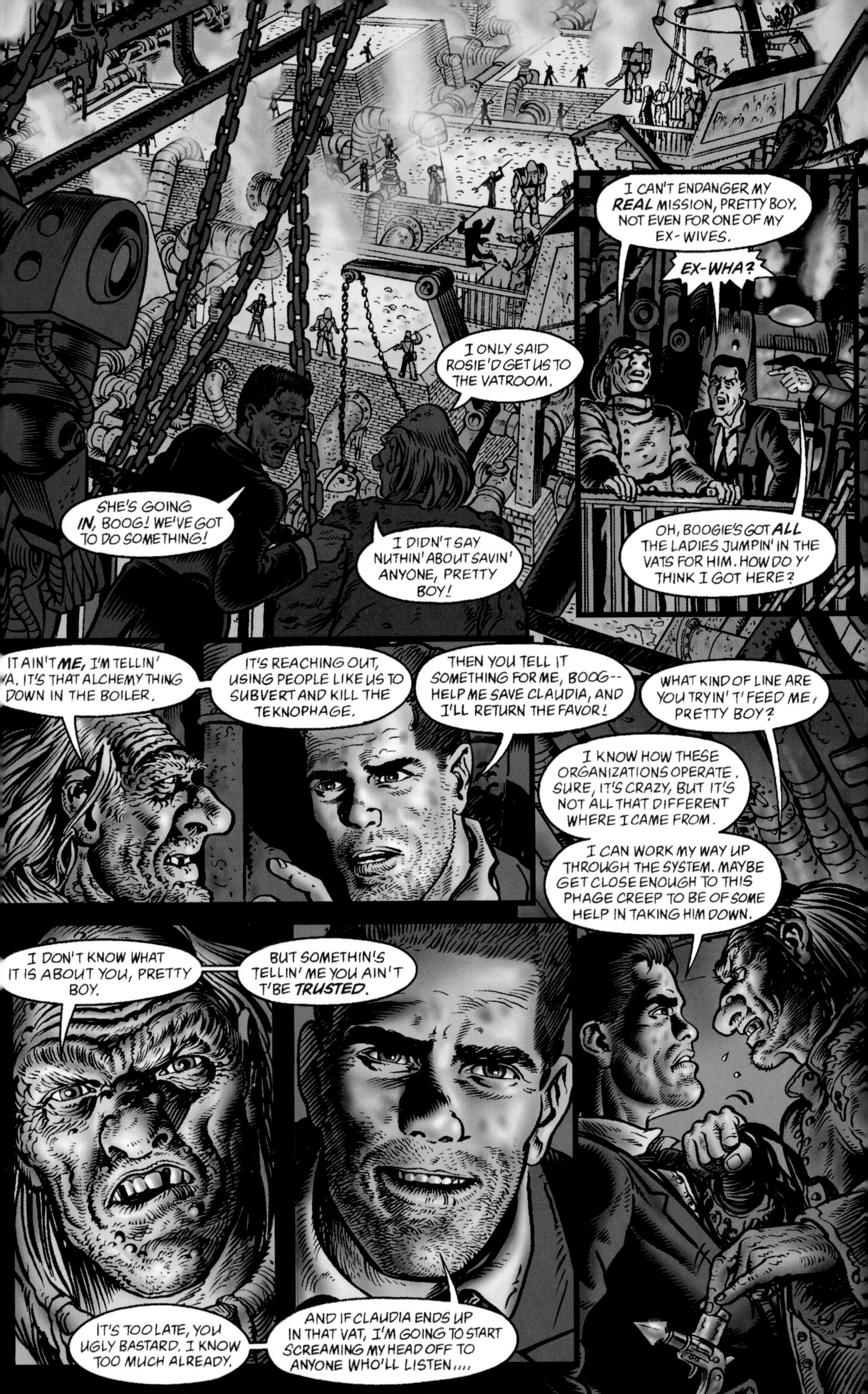
I ONLY SAID ROSIE'D GET US TO THE VATROOM.
SHE'S GOING IN, BOOG! WE'VE GOT TO DO SOMETHING!
I DIDN'T SAY NUTHIN' ABOUT SAVIN' ANYONE, PRETTY BOY!
I CAN'T ENDANGER MY REAL MISSION, PRETTY BOY. NOT EVEN FOR ONE OF MY EX-WIVES.
EX-WHA?
OH, BOOGIE'S GOT ALL THE LADIES JUMPIN' IN THE VATS FOR HIM. HOW DO Y' THINK I GOT HERE?
IT AIN'T ME, I'M TELLIN' YA. IT'S THAT ALCHEMY THING DOWN IN THE BOILER.
IT'S REACHING OUT, USING PEOPLE LIKE US TO SUBVERT AND KILL THE TEKNOPHAGE.
THEN YOU TELL IT SOMETHING FOR ME, BOOG-- HELP ME SAVE CLAUDIA, AND I'LL RETURN THE FAVOR!
WHAT KIND OF LINE ARE YOU TRYIN' T' FEED ME, PRETTY BOY?
I KNOW HOW THESE ORGANIZATIONS OPERATE. SURE, IT'S CRAZY, BUT IT'S NOT ALL THAT DIFFERENT WHERE I CAME FROM.
I CAN WORK MY WAY UP THROUGH THE SYSTEM. MAYBE GET CLOSE ENOUGH TO THIS PHAGE CREEP TO BE OF SOME HELP IN TAKING HIM DOWN.
I DON'T KNOW WHAT IT IS ABOUT YOU, PRETTY BOY.
BUT SOMETHIN'S TELLIN' ME YOU AIN'T T'BE TRUSTED.
IT'S TOO LATE, YOU UGLY BASTARD. I KNOW TOO MUCH ALREADY.
AND IF CLAUDIA ENDS UP IN THAT VAT, I'M GOING TO START SCREAMING MY HEAD OFF TO ANYONE WHO'LL LISTEN....

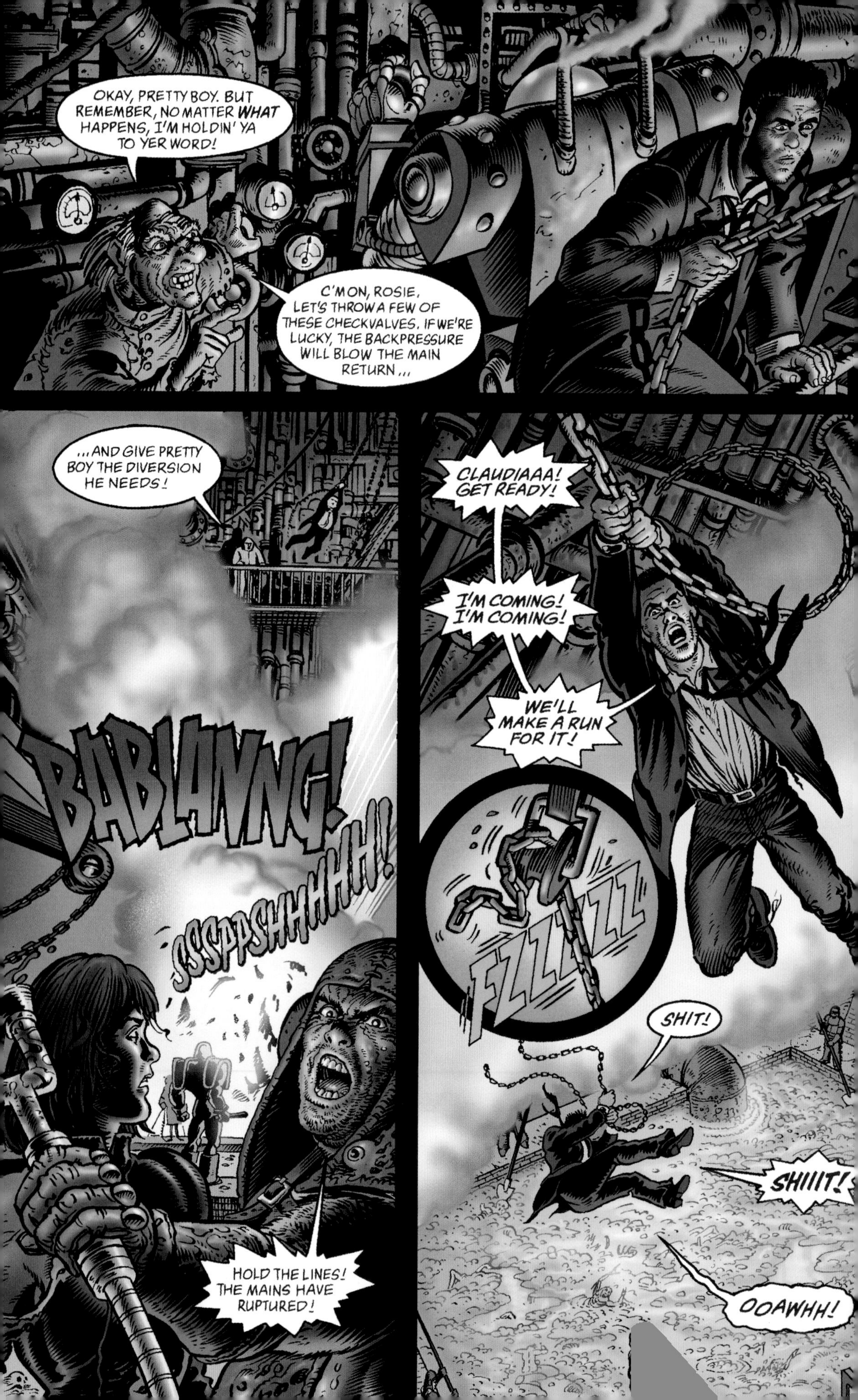
OKAY, PRETTY BOY. BUT REMEMBER, NO MATTER WHAT HAPPENS, I'M HOLDIN' YA TO YER WORD!
C'MON, ROSIE, LET'S THROW A FEW OF THESE CHECKVALVES. IF WE'RE LUCKY, THE BACKPRESSURE WILL BLOW THE MAIN RETURN ...
...AND GIVE PRETTY BOY THE DIVERSION HE NEEDS!
BABLANNG!
SSSPPSHHHHHH!
HOLD THE LINES! THE MAINS HAVE RUPTURED!
CLAUDIAAA! GET READY!
I'M COMING! I'M COMING!
WE'LL MAKE A RUN FOR IT!
FZZZZZZ
SHIT!
SHIIIT!
OOAWHH!

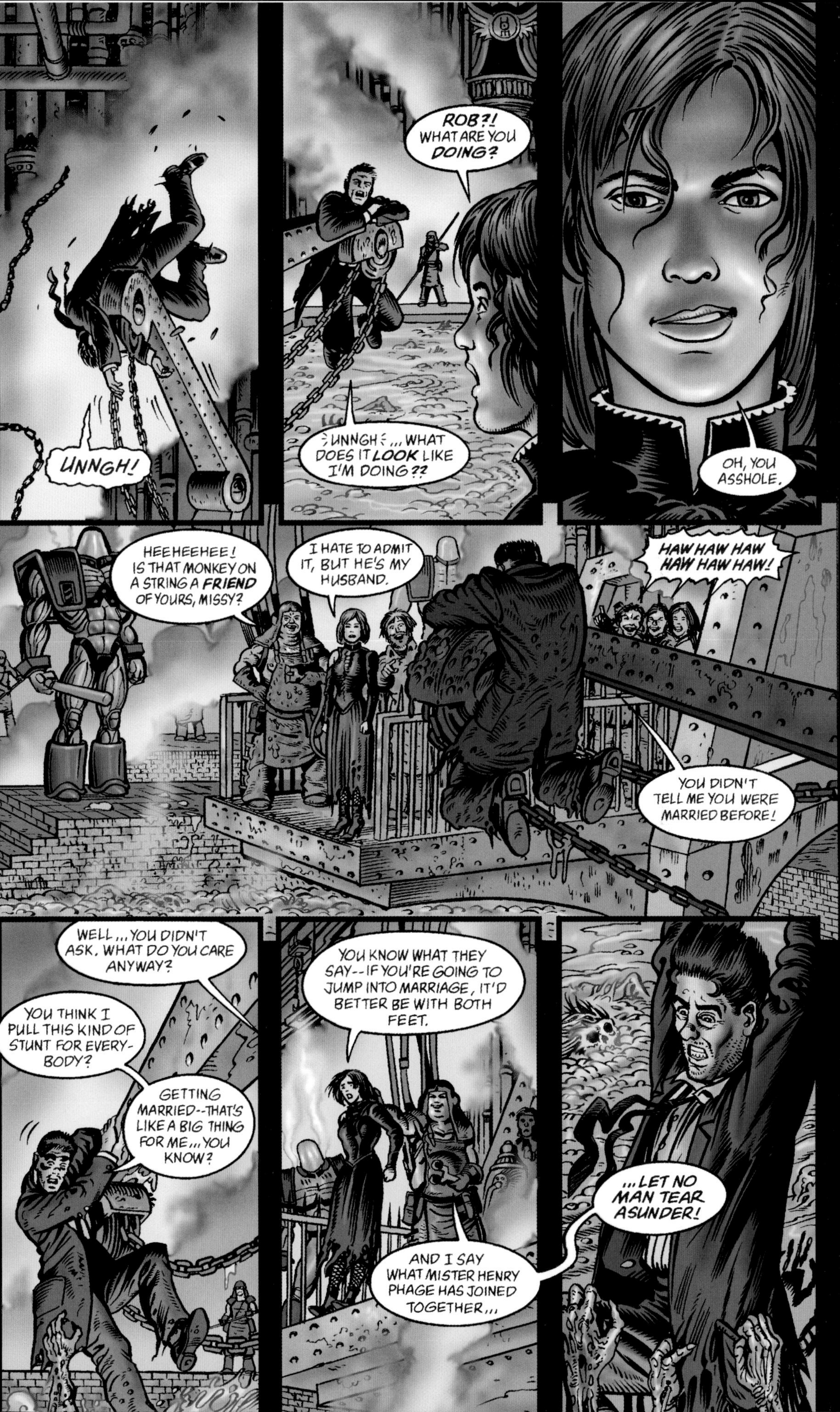
UNNGH!
ROB?! WHAT ARE YOU DOING?
UNNGH ... WHAT DOES IT LOOK LIKE I'M DOING??
OH, YOU ASSHOLE.
HEEHEEHEE! IS THAT MONKEY ON A STRING A FRIEND OF YOURS, MISSY?
I HATE TO ADMIT IT, BUT HE'S MY HUSBAND.
HAW HAW HAW HAW HAW HAW!
YOU DIDN'T TELL ME YOU WERE MARRIED BEFORE!
WELL ... YOU DIDN'T ASK. WHAT DO YOU CARE ANYWAY?
YOU THINK I PULL THIS KIND OF STUNT FOR EVERY-BODY?
GETTING MARRIED--THAT'S LIKE A BIG THING FOR ME ... YOU KNOW?
YOU KNOW WHAT THEY SAY--IF YOU'RE GOING TO JUMP INTO MARRIAGE, IT'D BETTER BE WITH BOTH FEET.
AND I SAY WHAT MISTER HENRY PHAGE HAS JOINED TOGETHER ...
... LET NO MAN TEAR ASUNDER!

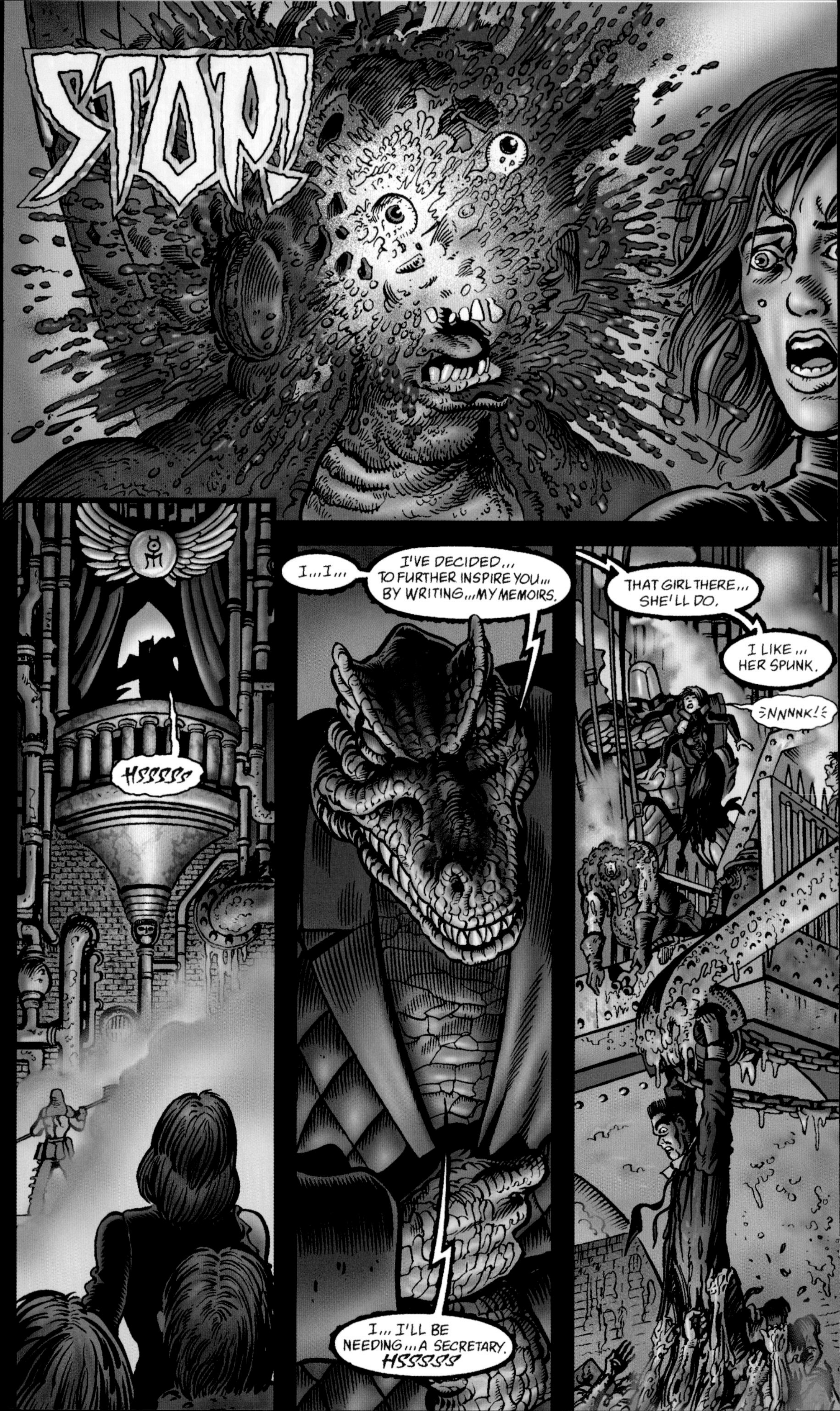
STOP!
HSSSSS
I... I...
I'VE DECIDED... TO FURTHER INSPIRE YOU... BY WRITING... MY MEMOIRS.
I... I'LL BE NEEDING... A SECRETARY. HSSSSS
THAT GIRL THERE... SHE'LL DO.
I LIKE... HER SPUNK.
NNNNK!

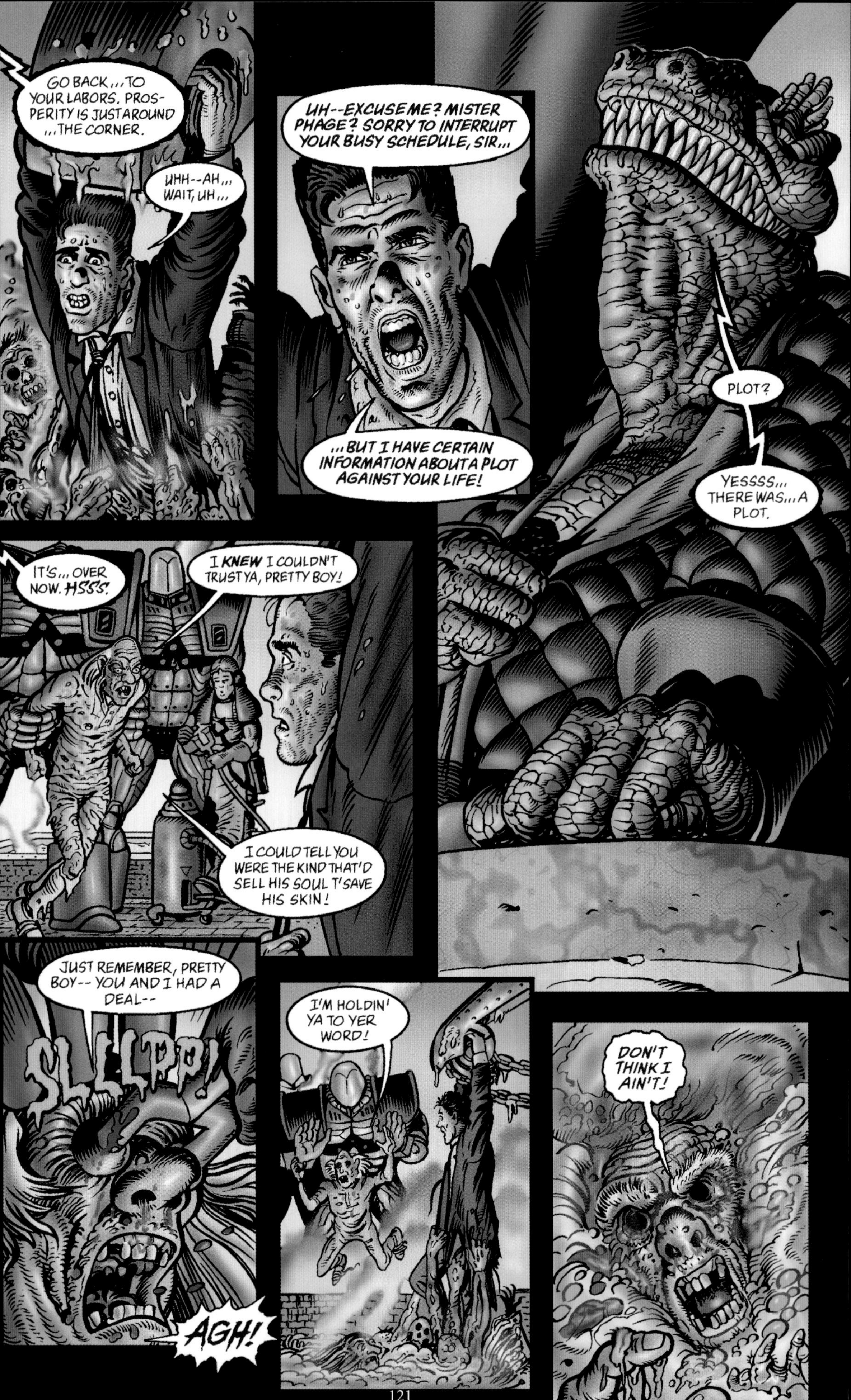
GO BACK,,,TO YOUR LABORS. PROSPERITY IS JUST AROUND ,,,THE CORNER.
UHH--AH,,, WAIT, UH,,,
UH--EXCUSE ME? MISTER PHAGE? SORRY TO INTERRUPT YOUR BUSY SCHEDULE, SIR,,,
,,,BUT I HAVE CERTAIN INFORMATION ABOUT A PLOT AGAINST YOUR LIFE!
PLOT?
YESSSS,,, THERE WAS,,,A PLOT.
IT'S,,, OVER NOW. HSSS.
I KNEW I COULDN'T TRUST YA, PRETTY BOY!
I COULD TELL YOU WERE THE KIND THAT'D SELL HIS SOUL T'SAVE HIS SKIN!
JUST REMEMBER, PRETTY BOY-- YOU AND I HAD A DEAL--
SLLLPP!
AGH!
I'M HOLDIN' YA TO YER WORD!
DON'T THINK I AIN'T!

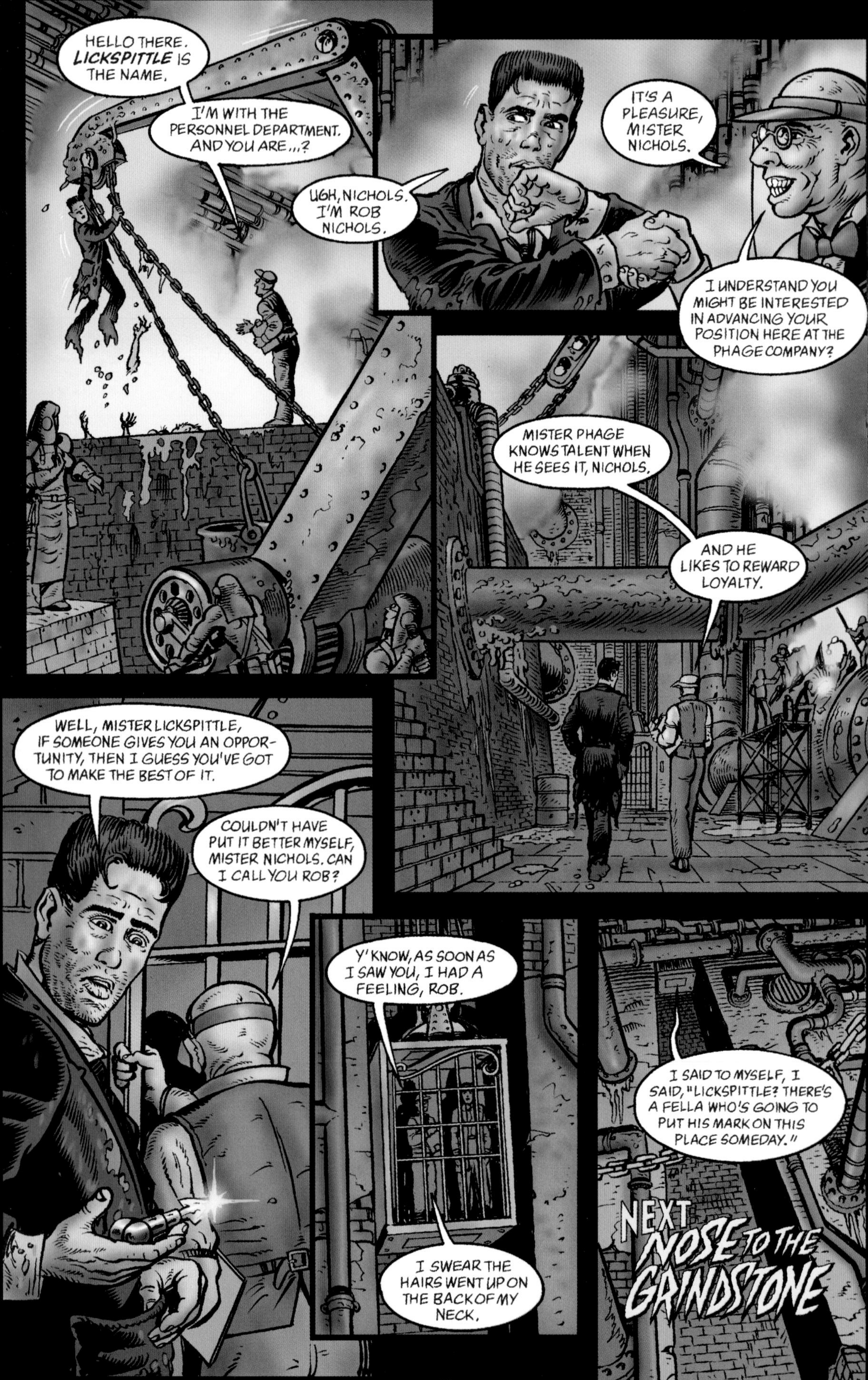
HELLO THERE. LICKSPITTLE IS THE NAME.
I'M WITH THE PERSONNEL DEPARTMENT. AND YOU ARE...?
UGH, NICHOLS. I'M ROB NICHOLS.
IT'S A PLEASURE, MISTER NICHOLS.
I UNDERSTAND YOU MIGHT BE INTERESTED IN ADVANCING YOUR POSITION HERE AT THE PHAGE COMPANY?
MISTER PHAGE KNOWS TALENT WHEN HE SEES IT, NICHOLS.
AND HE LIKES TO REWARD LOYALTY.
WELL, MISTER LICKSPITTLE, IF SOMEONE GIVES YOU AN OPPORTUNITY, THEN I GUESS YOU'VE GOT TO MAKE THE BEST OF IT.
COULDN'T HAVE PUT IT BETTER MYSELF, MISTER NICHOLS. CAN I CALL YOU ROB?
Y'KNOW, AS SOON AS I SAW YOU, I HAD A FEELING, ROB.
I SWEAR THE HAIRS WENT UP ON THE BACK OF MY NECK.
I SAID TO MYSELF, I SAID, "LICKSPITTLE? THERE'S A FELLA WHO'S GOING TO PUT HIS MARK ON THIS PLACE SOMEDAY."
NEXT NOSE TO THE GRINDSTONE

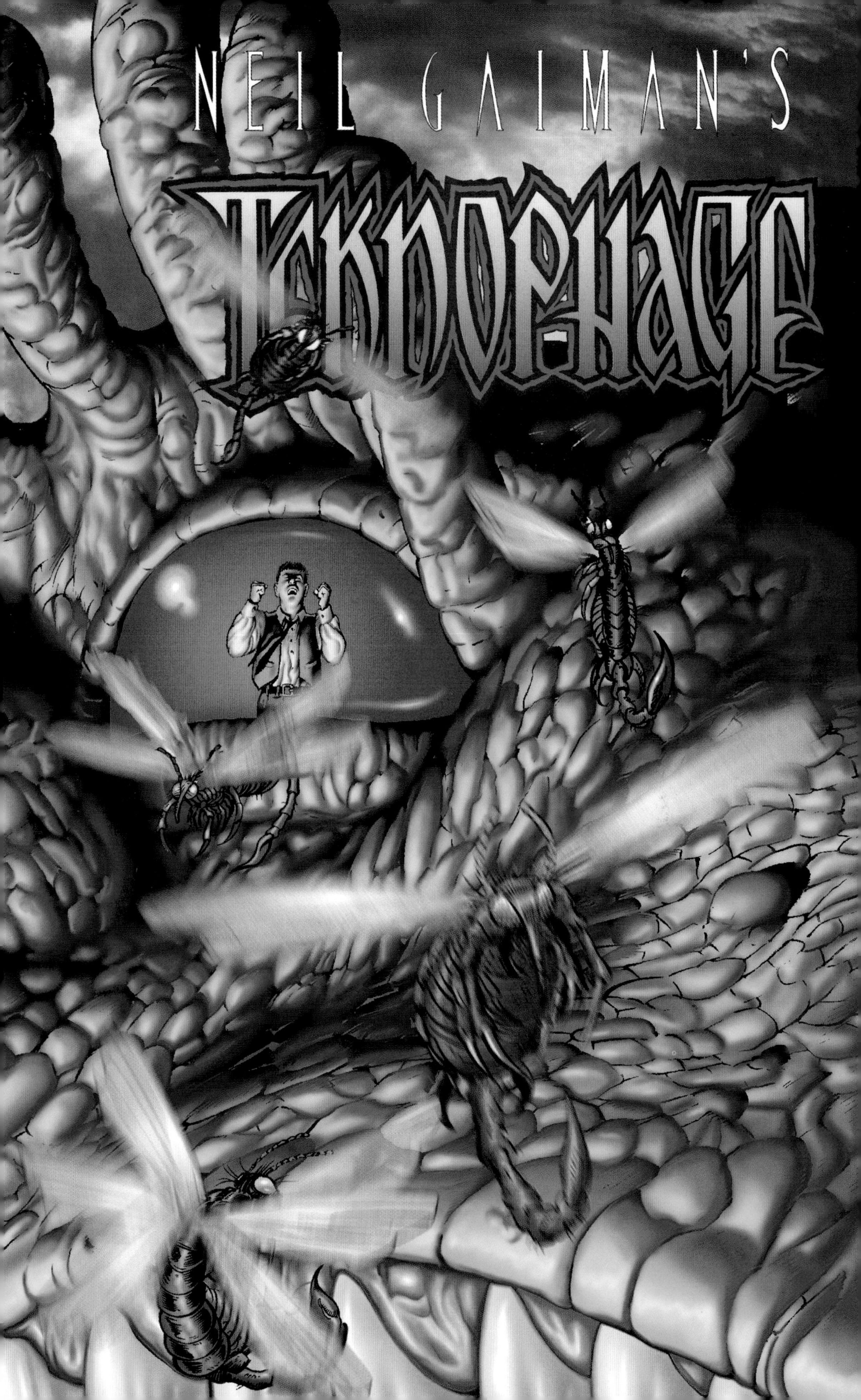
NEIL GAIMAN'S
TEKNOPHAGE

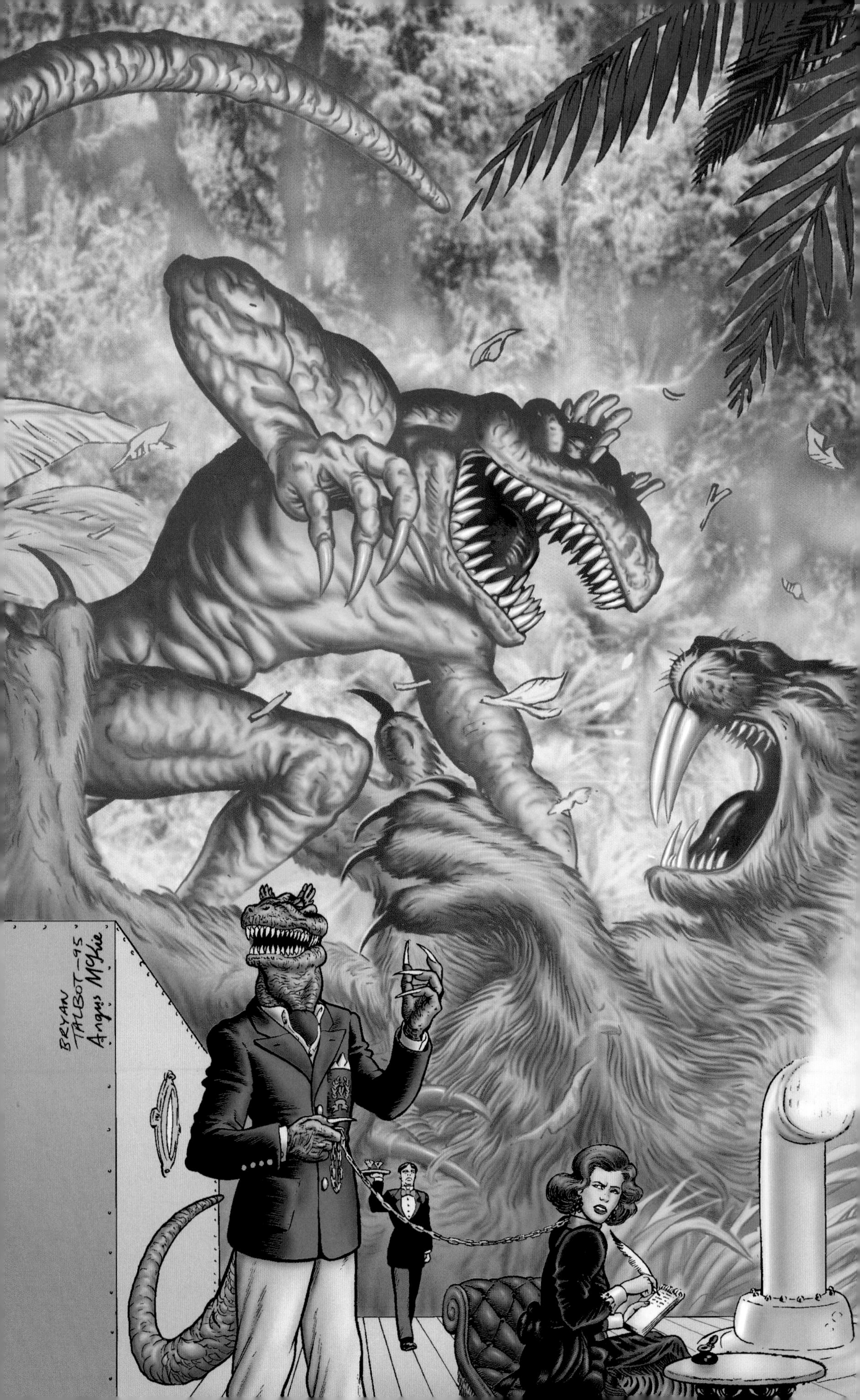
BRYAN TALBOT—95
Angus McKie

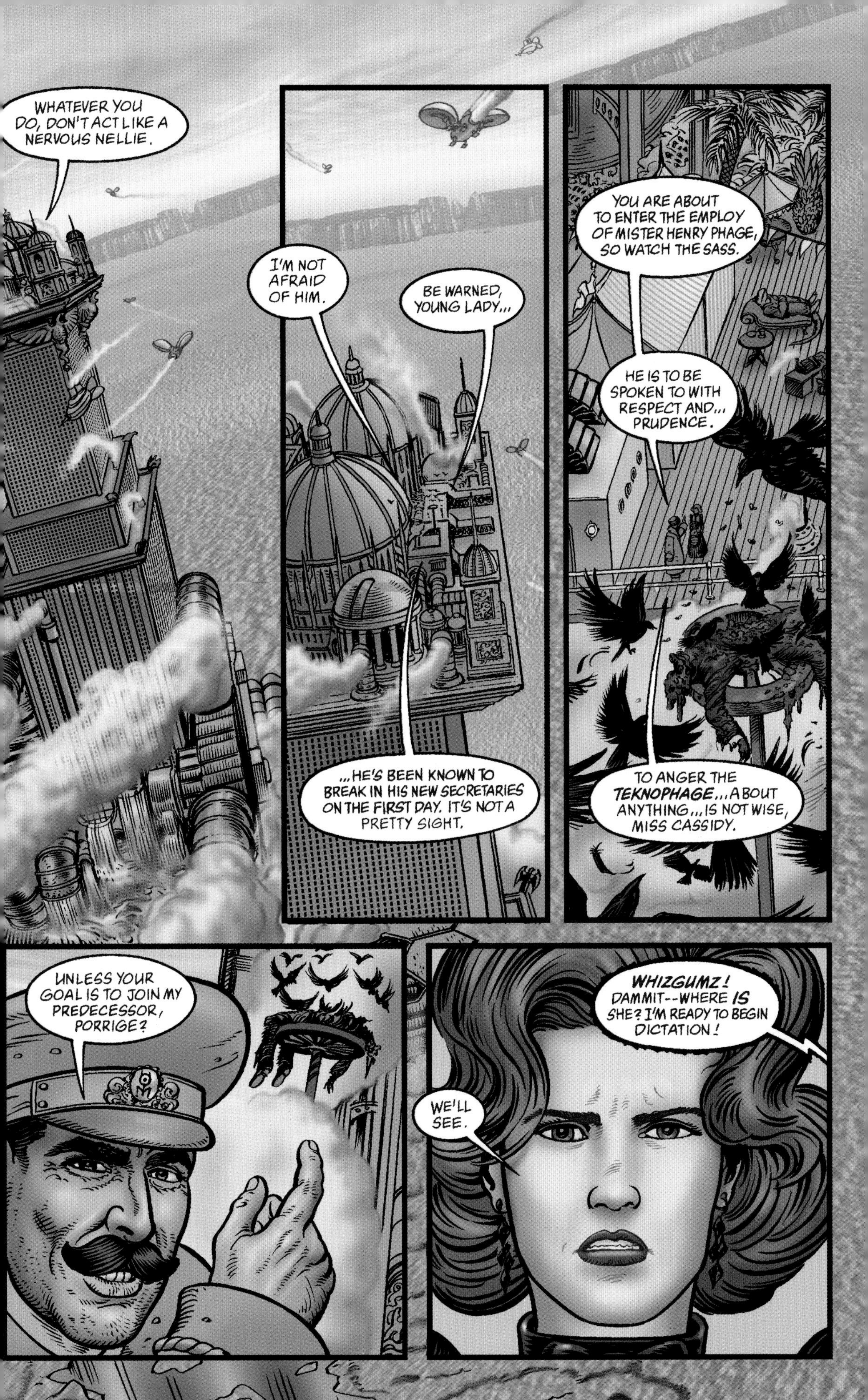
WHATEVER YOU DO, DON'T ACT LIKE A NERVOUS NELLIE.
I'M NOT AFRAID OF HIM.
BE WARNED, YOUNG LADY...
...HE'S BEEN KNOWN TO BREAK IN HIS NEW SECRETARIES ON THE FIRST DAY. IT'S NOT A PRETTY SIGHT.
YOU ARE ABOUT TO ENTER THE EMPLOY OF MISTER HENRY PHAGE, SO WATCH THE SASS.
HE IS TO BE SPOKEN TO WITH RESPECT AND... PRUDENCE.
TO ANGER THE TEKNOPHAGE... ABOUT ANYTHING... IS NOT WISE, MISS CASSIDY.
UNLESS YOUR GOAL IS TO JOIN MY PREDECESSOR, PORRIGE?
WHIZGUMZ! DAMMIT--WHERE IS SHE? I'M READY TO BEGIN DICTATION!
WE'LL SEE.

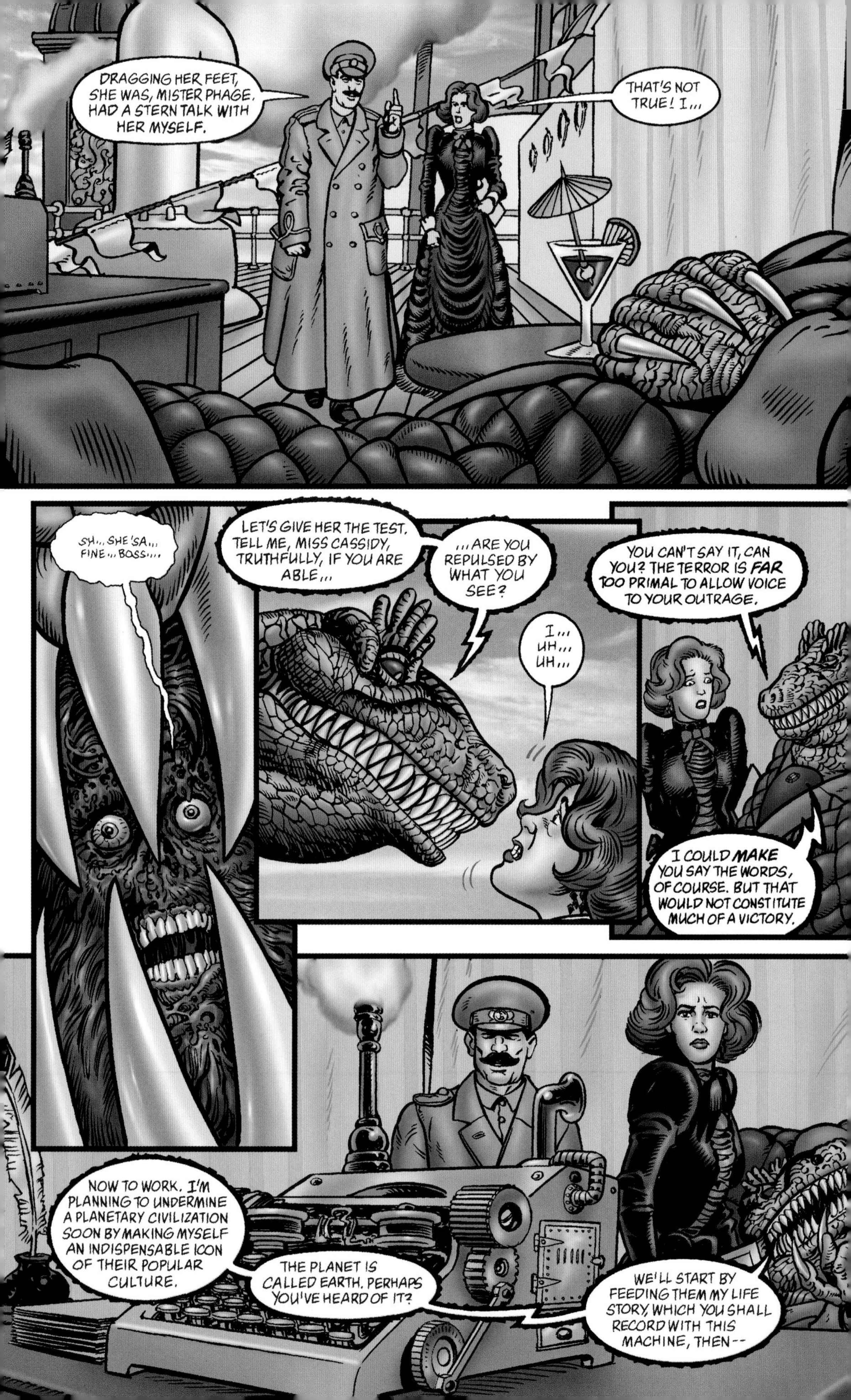
DRAGGING HER FEET, SHE WAS, MISTER PHAGE. HAD A STERN TALK WITH HER MYSELF.
THAT'S NOT TRUE! I...
SH... SHE'SA... FINE... BOSS....
LET'S GIVE HER THE TEST. TELL ME, MISS CASSIDY, TRUTHFULLY, IF YOU ARE ABLE...
...ARE YOU REPULSED BY WHAT YOU SEE?
I... UH... UH...
YOU CAN'T SAY IT, CAN YOU? THE TERROR IS FAR TOO PRIMAL TO ALLOW VOICE TO YOUR OUTRAGE.
I COULD MAKE YOU SAY THE WORDS, OF COURSE. BUT THAT WOULD NOT CONSTITUTE MUCH OF A VICTORY.
NOW TO WORK. I'M PLANNING TO UNDERMINE A PLANETARY CIVILIZATION SOON BY MAKING MYSELF AN INDISPENSABLE ICON OF THEIR POPULAR CULTURE.
THE PLANET IS CALLED EARTH. PERHAPS YOU'VE HEARD OF IT?
WE'LL START BY FEEDING THEM MY LIFE STORY, WHICH YOU SHALL RECORD WITH THIS MACHINE, THEN--

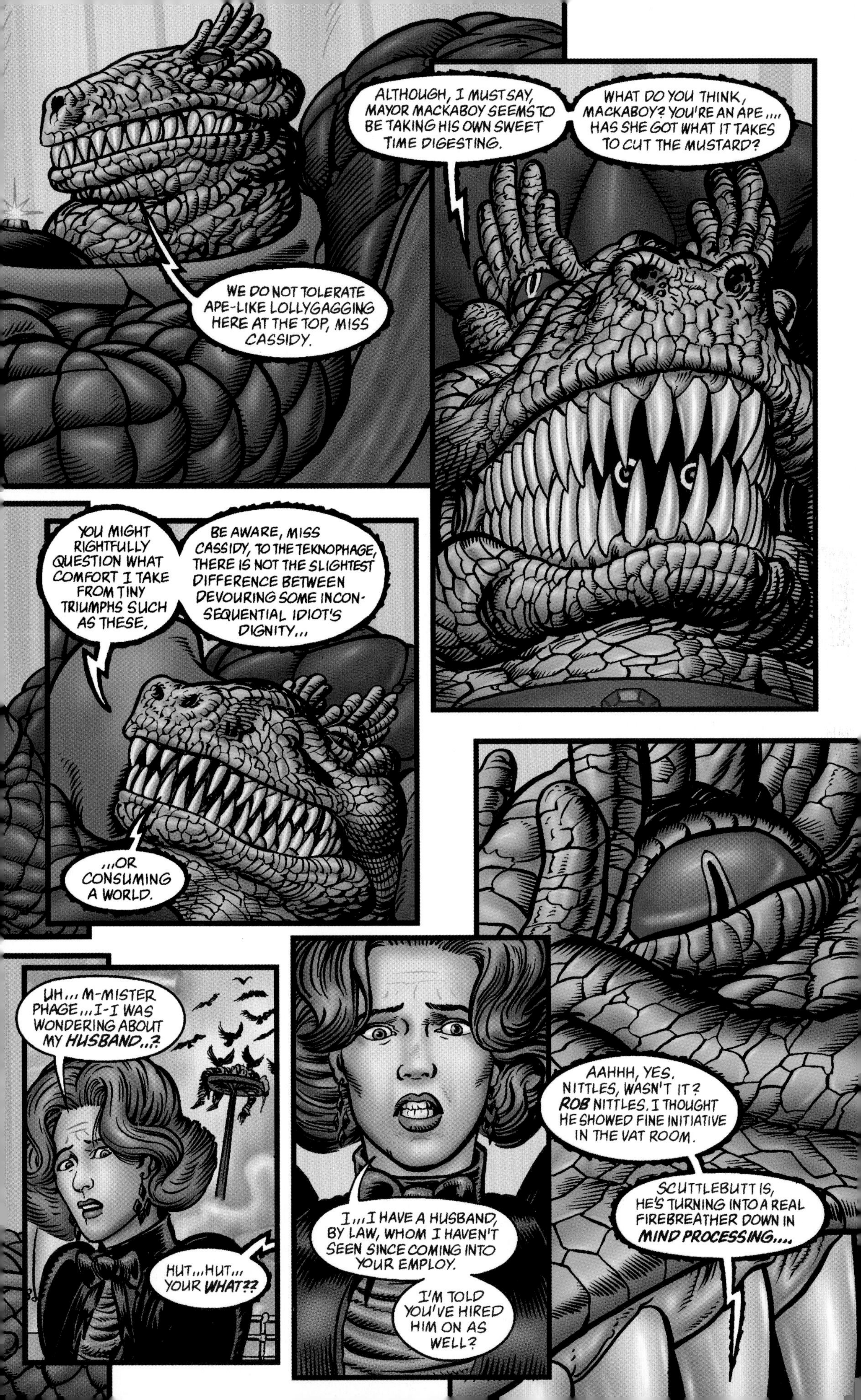
WE DO NOT TOLERATE APE-LIKE LOLLYGAGGING HERE AT THE TOP, MISS CASSIDY.
ALTHOUGH, I MUST SAY, MAYOR MACKABOY SEEMS TO BE TAKING HIS OWN SWEET TIME DIGESTING.
WHAT DO YOU THINK, MACKABOY? YOU'RE AN APE,,,, HAS SHE GOT WHAT IT TAKES TO CUT THE MUSTARD?
YOU MIGHT RIGHTFULLY QUESTION WHAT COMFORT I TAKE FROM TINY TRIUMPHS SUCH AS THESE.
BE AWARE, MISS CASSIDY, TO THE TEKNOPHAGE, THERE IS NOT THE SLIGHTEST DIFFERENCE BETWEEN DEVOURING SOME INCON-SEQUENTIAL IDIOT'S DIGNITY,,,
,,,OR CONSUMING A WORLD.
UH,,, M-MISTER PHAGE,,, I-I WAS WONDERING ABOUT MY **HUSBAND**,,?
HUT,,,HUT,,, YOUR **WHAT**??
I,,, I HAVE A HUSBAND, BY LAW, WHOM I HAVEN'T SEEN SINCE COMING INTO YOUR EMPLOY.
I'M TOLD YOU'VE HIRED HIM ON AS WELL?
AAHHH, YES, NITTLES, WASN'T IT? **ROB** NITTLES. I THOUGHT HE SHOWED FINE INITIATIVE IN THE VAT ROOM.
SCUTTLEBUTT IS, HE'S TURNING INTO A REAL FIREBREATHER DOWN IN **MIND PROCESSING**....

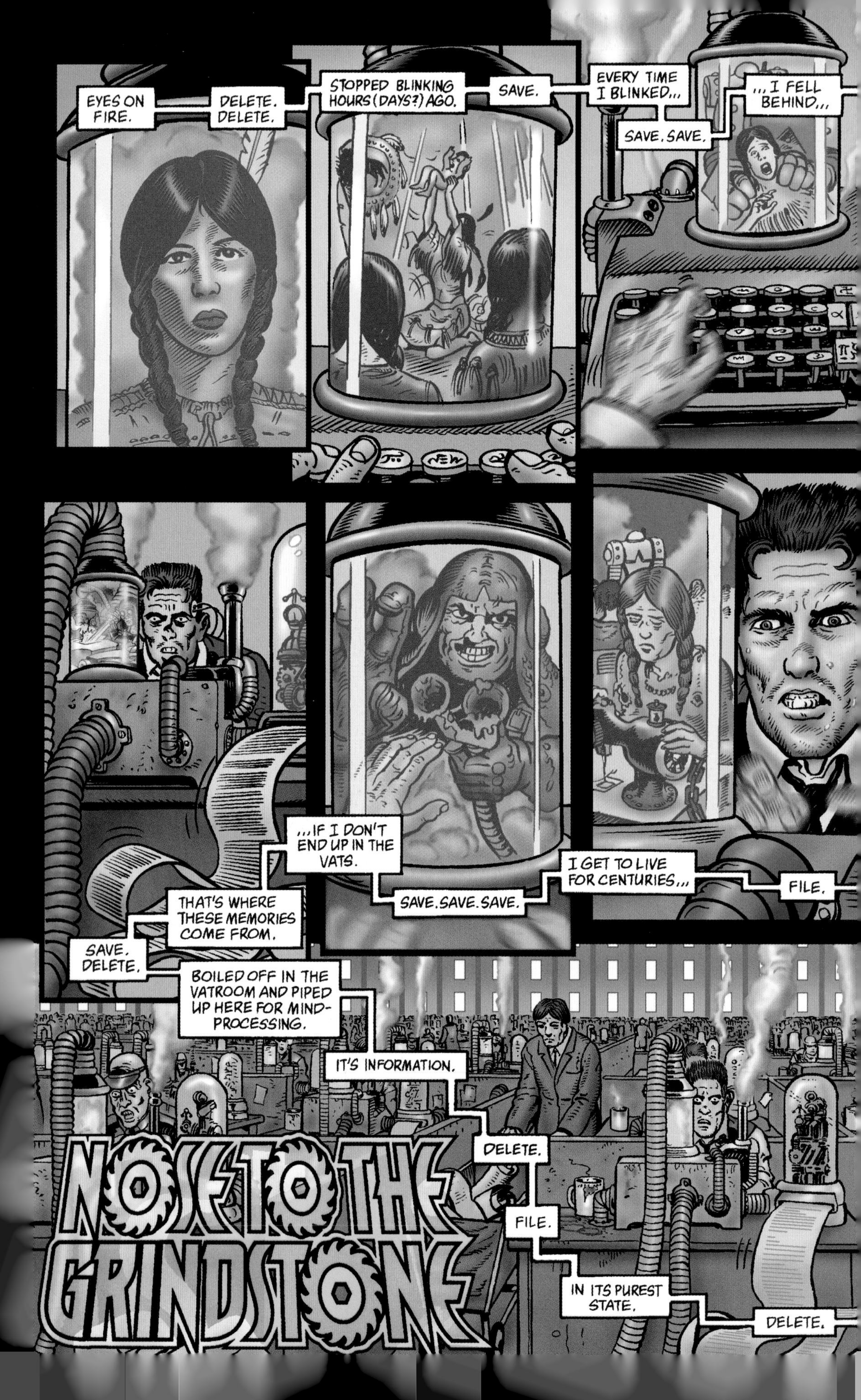
EYES ON FIRE.
DELETE. DELETE.
STOPPED BLINKING HOURS (DAYS?) AGO.
SAVE.
EVERY TIME I BLINKED...
SAVE. SAVE.
...I FELL BEHIND...
...IF I DON'T END UP IN THE VATS.
I GET TO LIVE FOR CENTURIES...
FILE.
SAVE. SAVE. SAVE.
THAT'S WHERE THESE MEMORIES COME FROM.
SAVE. DELETE.
BOILED OFF IN THE VATROOM AND PIPED UP HERE FOR MIND-PROCESSING.
IT'S INFORMATION.
DELETE.
FILE.
IN ITS PUREST STATE.
DELETE.
NOSE TO THE GRINDSTONE

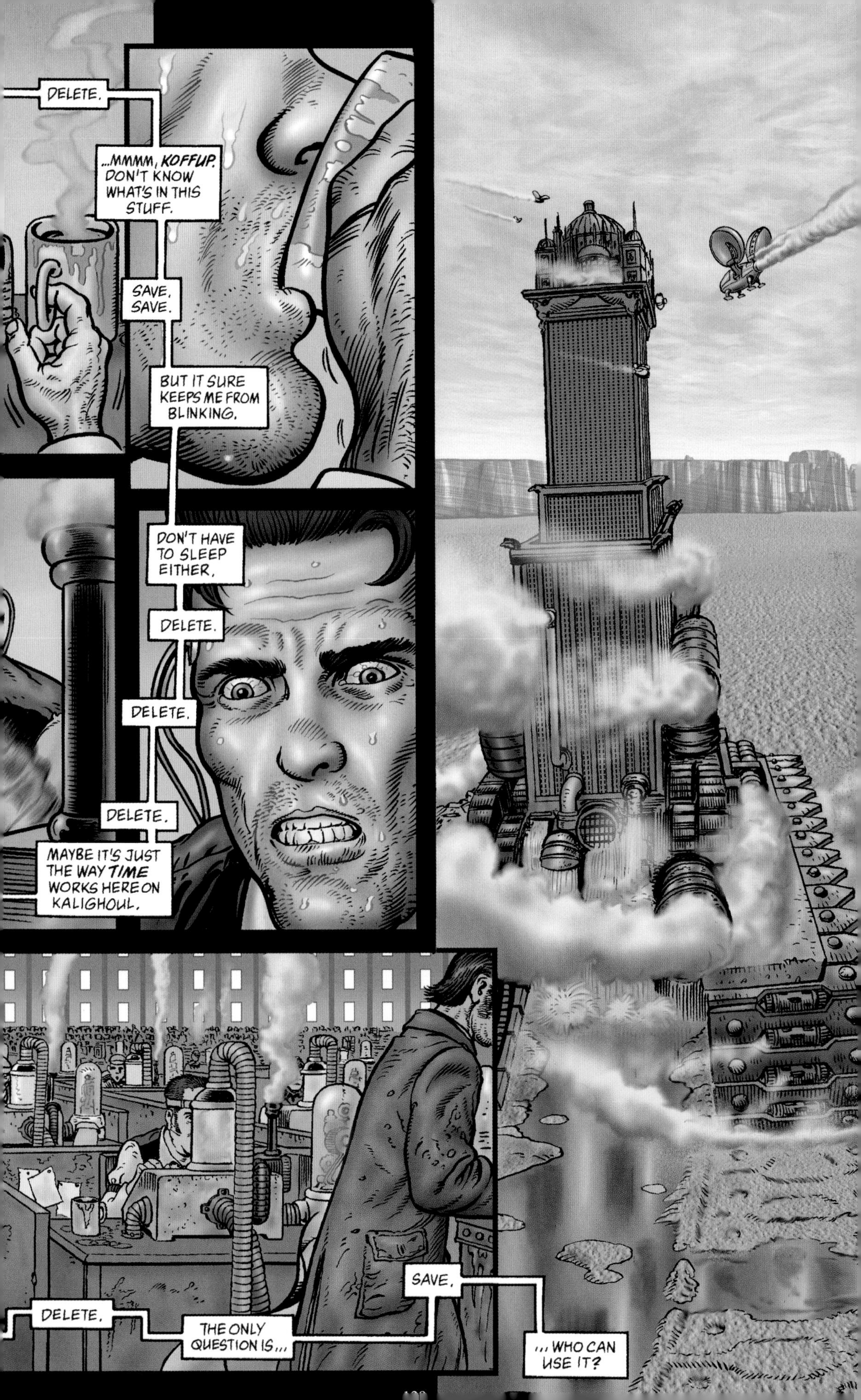
DELETE.
...MMMM, KOFFUP. DON'T KNOW WHAT'S IN THIS STUFF.
SAVE. SAVE.
BUT IT SURE KEEPS ME FROM BLINKING.
DON'T HAVE TO SLEEP EITHER.
DELETE.
DELETE.
DELETE.
MAYBE IT'S JUST THE WAY TIME WORKS HERE ON KALIGHOUL.
DELETE.
THE ONLY QUESTION IS...
SAVE.
...WHO CAN USE IT?

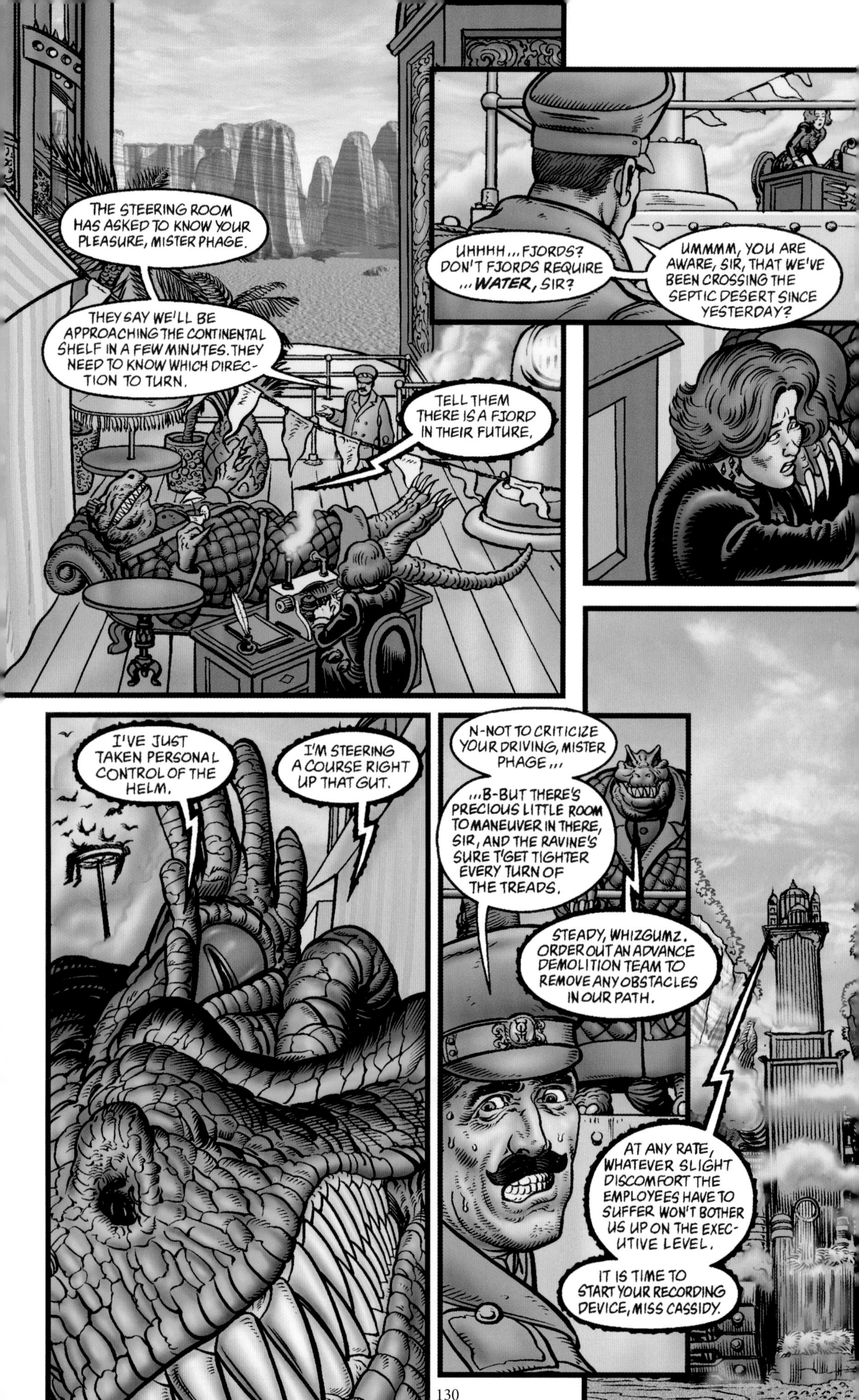
THE STEERING ROOM HAS ASKED TO KNOW YOUR PLEASURE, MISTER PHAGE.
THEY SAY WE'LL BE APPROACHING THE CONTINENTAL SHELF IN A FEW MINUTES. THEY NEED TO KNOW WHICH DIRECTION TO TURN.
TELL THEM THERE IS A FJORD IN THEIR FUTURE.
UHHHH... FJORDS? DON'T FJORDS REQUIRE ...*WATER*, SIR?
UMMMM, YOU ARE AWARE, SIR, THAT WE'VE BEEN CROSSING THE SEPTIC DESERT SINCE YESTERDAY?
I'VE JUST TAKEN PERSONAL CONTROL OF THE HELM.
I'M STEERING A COURSE RIGHT UP THAT GUT.
N-NOT TO CRITICIZE YOUR DRIVING, MISTER PHAGE...
...B-BUT THERE'S PRECIOUS LITTLE ROOM TO MANEUVER IN THERE, SIR, AND THE RAVINE'S SURE T'GET TIGHTER EVERY TURN OF THE TREADS.
STEADY, WHIZGUMZ. ORDER OUT AN ADVANCE DEMOLITION TEAM TO REMOVE ANY OBSTACLES IN OUR PATH.
AT ANY RATE, WHATEVER SLIGHT DISCOMFORT THE EMPLOYEES HAVE TO SUFFER WON'T BOTHER US UP ON THE EXECUTIVE LEVEL.
IT IS TIME TO START YOUR RECORDING DEVICE, MISS CASSIDY.

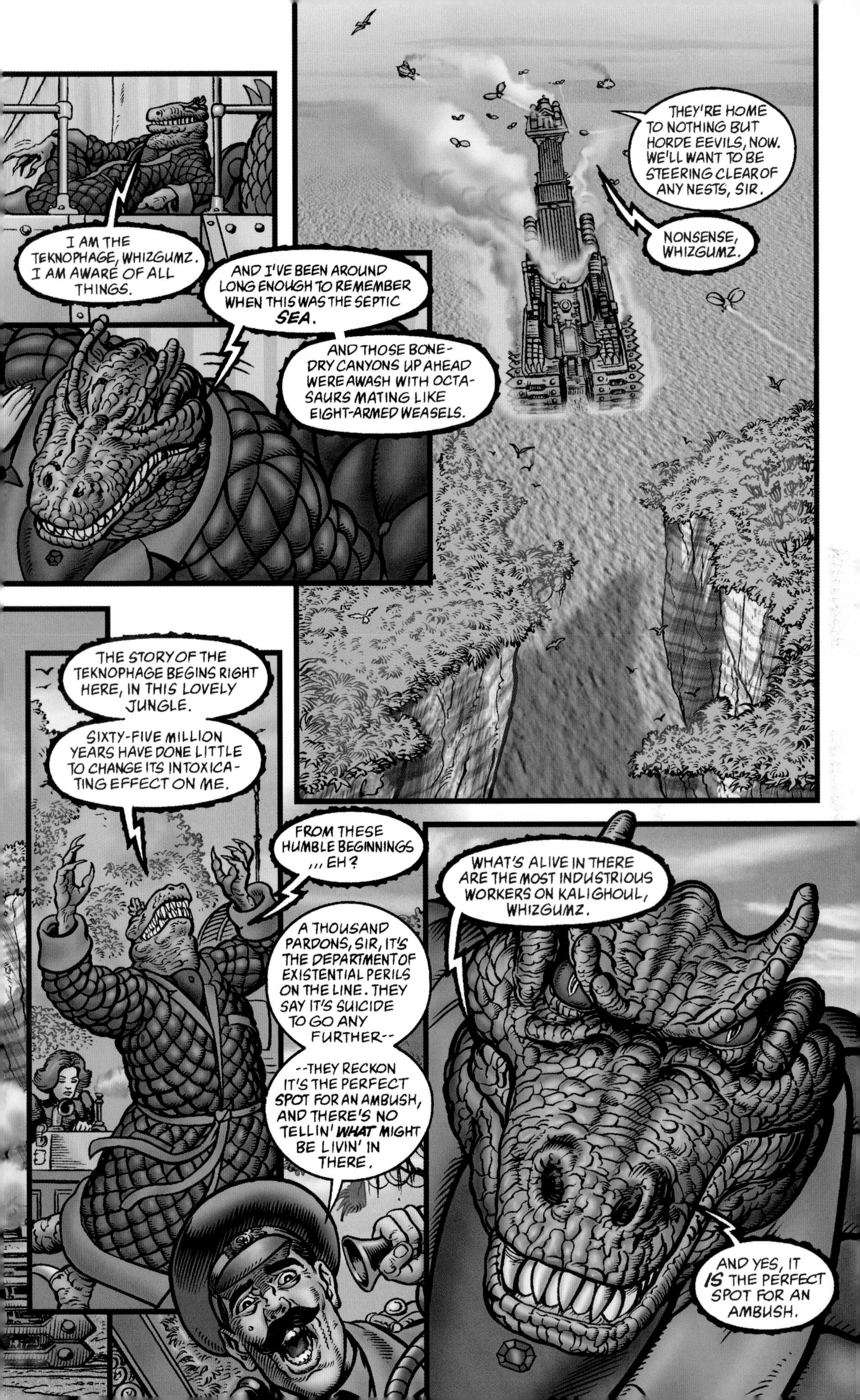

THEY'RE HOME TO NOTHING BUT HORDE EEVILS, NOW. WE'LL WANT TO BE STEERING CLEAR OF ANY NESTS, SIR.
NONSENSE, WHIZGUMZ.
I AM THE TEKNOPHAGE, WHIZGUMZ. I AM AWARE OF ALL THINGS.
AND I'VE BEEN AROUND LONG ENOUGH TO REMEMBER WHEN THIS WAS THE SEPTIC SEA.
AND THOSE BONE-DRY CANYONS UP AHEAD WERE AWASH WITH OCTA-SAURS MATING LIKE EIGHT-ARMED WEASELS.
THE STORY OF THE TEKNOPHAGE BEGINS RIGHT HERE, IN THIS LOVELY JUNGLE.
SIXTY-FIVE MILLION YEARS HAVE DONE LITTLE TO CHANGE ITS INTOXICA-TING EFFECT ON ME.
FROM THESE HUMBLE BEGINNINGS ... EH?
A THOUSAND PARDONS, SIR, IT'S THE DEPARTMENT OF EXISTENTIAL PERILS ON THE LINE. THEY SAY IT'S SUICIDE TO GO ANY FURTHER--
--THEY RECKON IT'S THE PERFECT SPOT FOR AN AMBUSH, AND THERE'S NO TELLIN' WHAT MIGHT BE LIVIN' IN THERE.
WHAT'S ALIVE IN THERE ARE THE MOST INDUSTRIOUS WORKERS ON KALIGHOUL, WHIZGUMZ.
AND YES, IT IS THE PERFECT SPOT FOR AN AMBUSH.

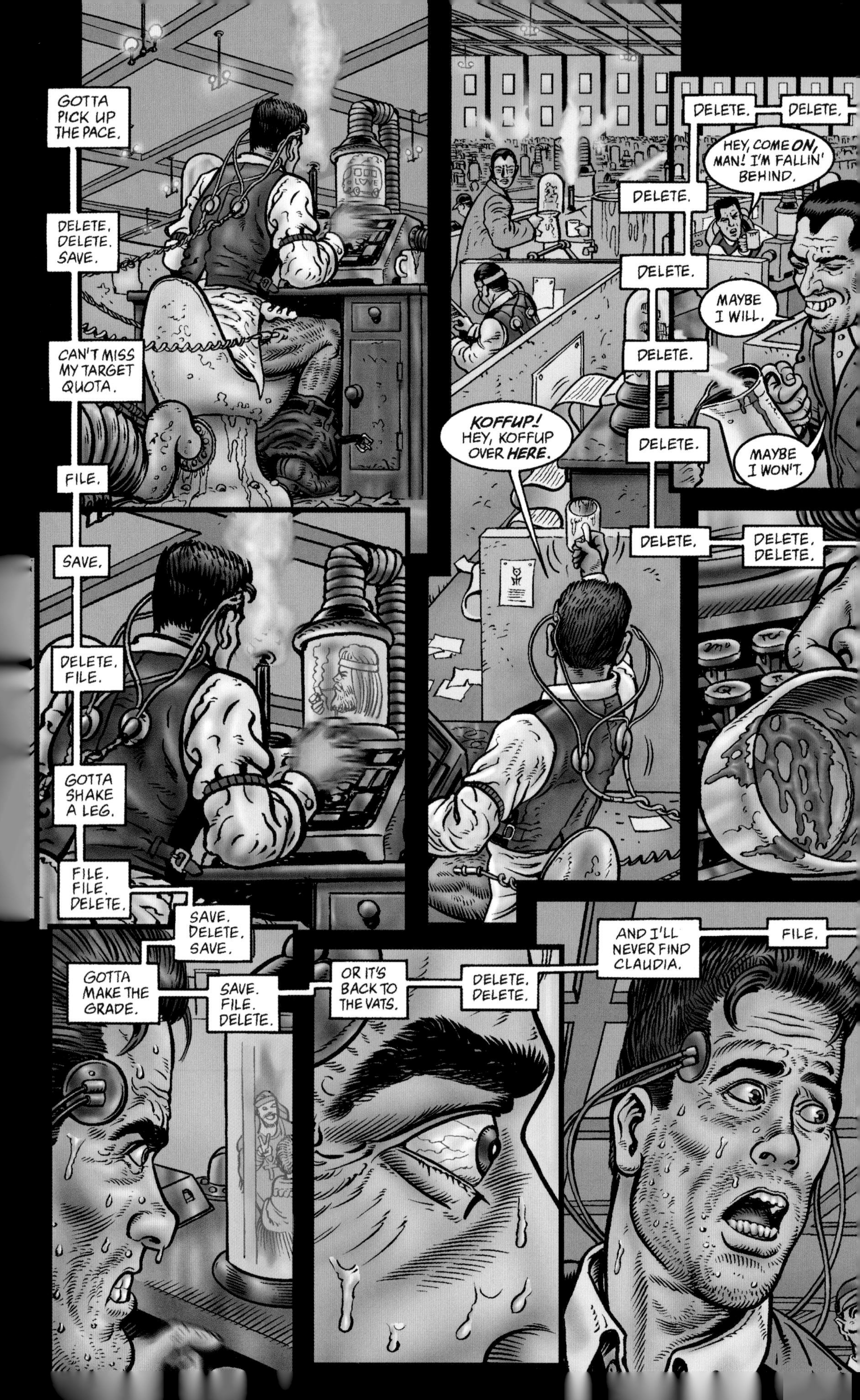
GOTTA PICK UP THE PACE.
DELETE. DELETE. SAVE.
CAN'T MISS MY TARGET QUOTA.
FILE.
DELETE.
DELETE.
HEY, COME ON, MAN! I'M FALLIN' BEHIND.
DELETE.
DELETE.
MAYBE I WILL.
DELETE.
KOFFUP! HEY, KOFFUP OVER HERE.
DELETE.
MAYBE I WON'T.
SAVE.
DELETE.
DELETE. DELETE.
DELETE. FILE.
GOTTA SHAKE A LEG.
FILE. FILE. DELETE.
SAVE. DELETE. SAVE.
GOTTA MAKE THE GRADE.
SAVE. FILE. DELETE.
OR IT'S BACK TO THE VATS.
DELETE. DELETE.
AND I'LL NEVER FIND CLAUDIA.
FILE.

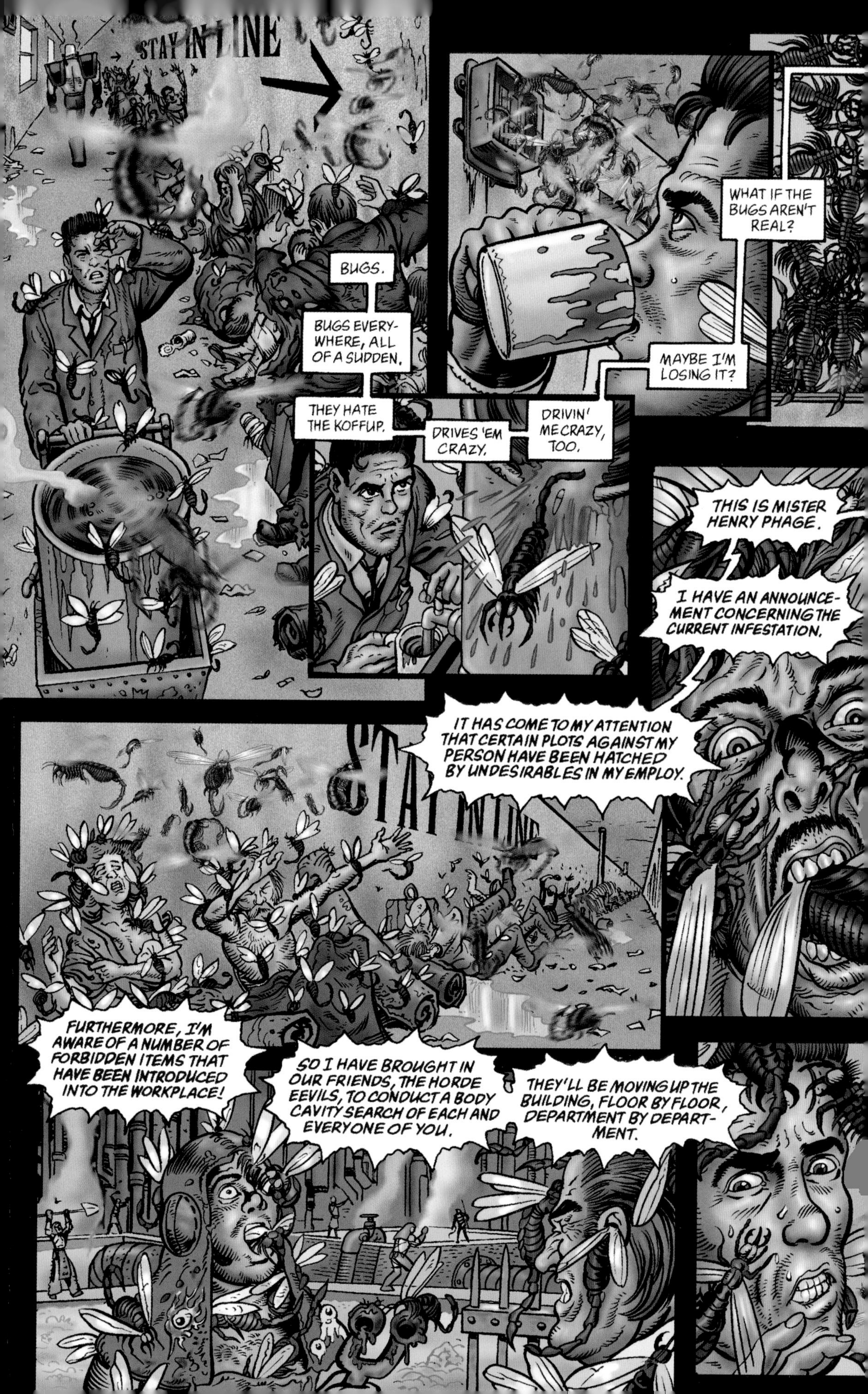
STAY IN LINE
BUGS.
BUGS EVERY-WHERE, ALL OF A SUDDEN.
THEY HATE THE KOFFUP.
DRIVES 'EM CRAZY.
DRIVIN' ME CRAZY, TOO.
MAYBE I'M LOSING IT?
WHAT IF THE BUGS AREN'T REAL?
THIS IS MISTER HENRY PHAGE.
I HAVE AN ANNOUNCE-MENT CONCERNING THE CURRENT INFESTATION.
IT HAS COME TO MY ATTENTION THAT CERTAIN PLOTS AGAINST MY PERSON HAVE BEEN HATCHED BY UNDESIRABLES IN MY EMPLOY.
STAY IN LINE
FURTHERMORE, I'M AWARE OF A NUMBER OF FORBIDDEN ITEMS THAT HAVE BEEN INTRODUCED INTO THE WORKPLACE!
SO I HAVE BROUGHT IN OUR FRIENDS, THE HORDE EEVILS, TO CONDUCT A BODY CAVITY SEARCH OF EACH AND EVERYONE OF YOU.
THEY'LL BE MOVING UP THE BUILDING, FLOOR BY FLOOR, DEPARTMENT BY DEPART-MENT.

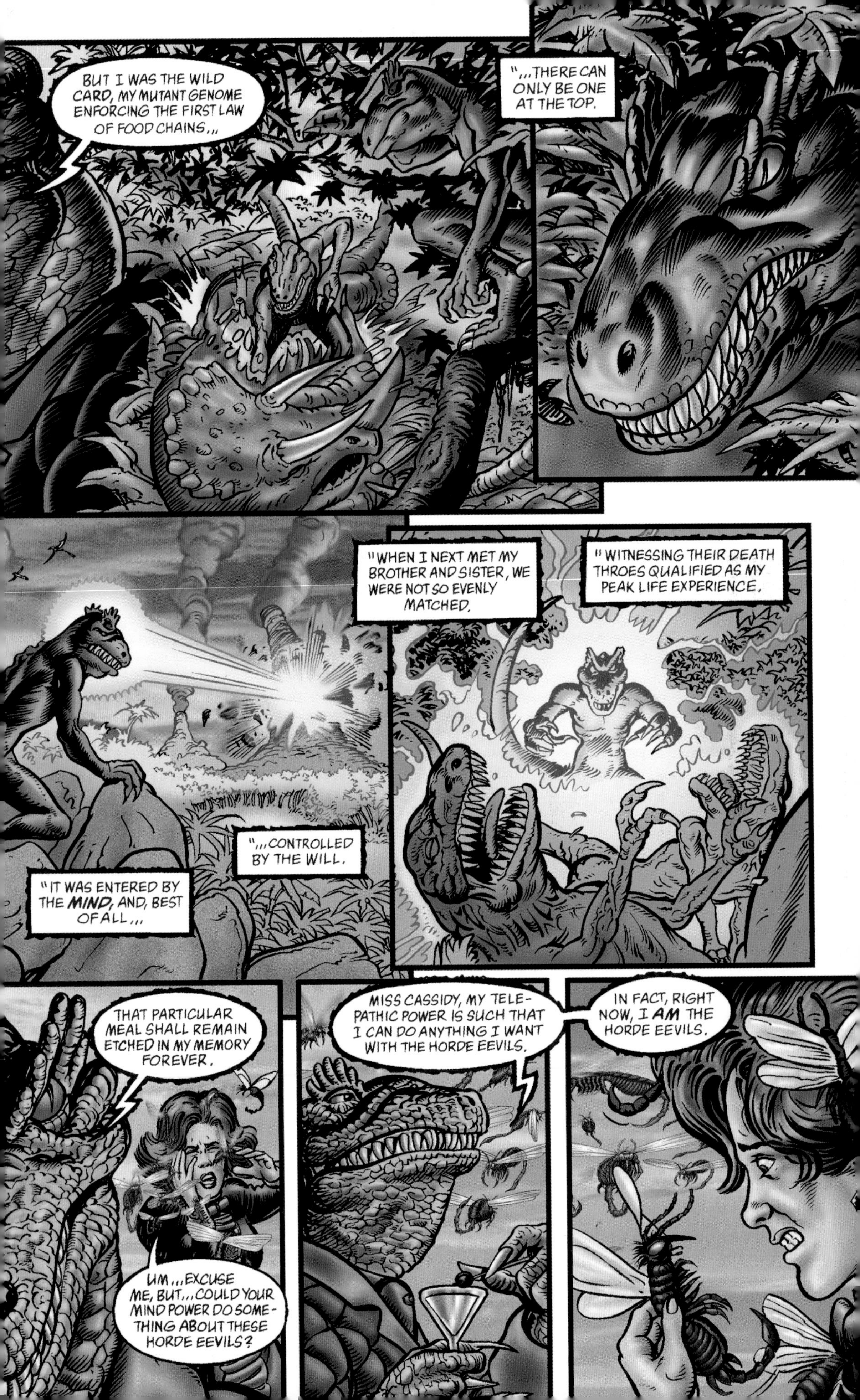
BUT I WAS THE WILD CARD, MY MUTANT GENOME ENFORCING THE FIRST LAW OF FOOD CHAINS,,,
",,,THERE CAN ONLY BE ONE AT THE TOP.
"IT WAS ENTERED BY THE MIND, AND, BEST OF ALL,,,
",,,CONTROLLED BY THE WILL.
"WHEN I NEXT MET MY BROTHER AND SISTER, WE WERE NOT SO EVENLY MATCHED.
"WITNESSING THEIR DEATH THROES QUALIFIED AS MY PEAK LIFE EXPERIENCE.
THAT PARTICULAR MEAL SHALL REMAIN ETCHED IN MY MEMORY FOREVER.
UM,,,EXCUSE ME, BUT,,,COULD YOUR MIND POWER DO SOMETHING ABOUT THESE HORDE EEVILS?
MISS CASSIDY, MY TELEPATHIC POWER IS SUCH THAT I CAN DO ANYTHING I WANT WITH THE HORDE EEVILS.
IN FACT, RIGHT NOW, I AM THE HORDE EEVILS.

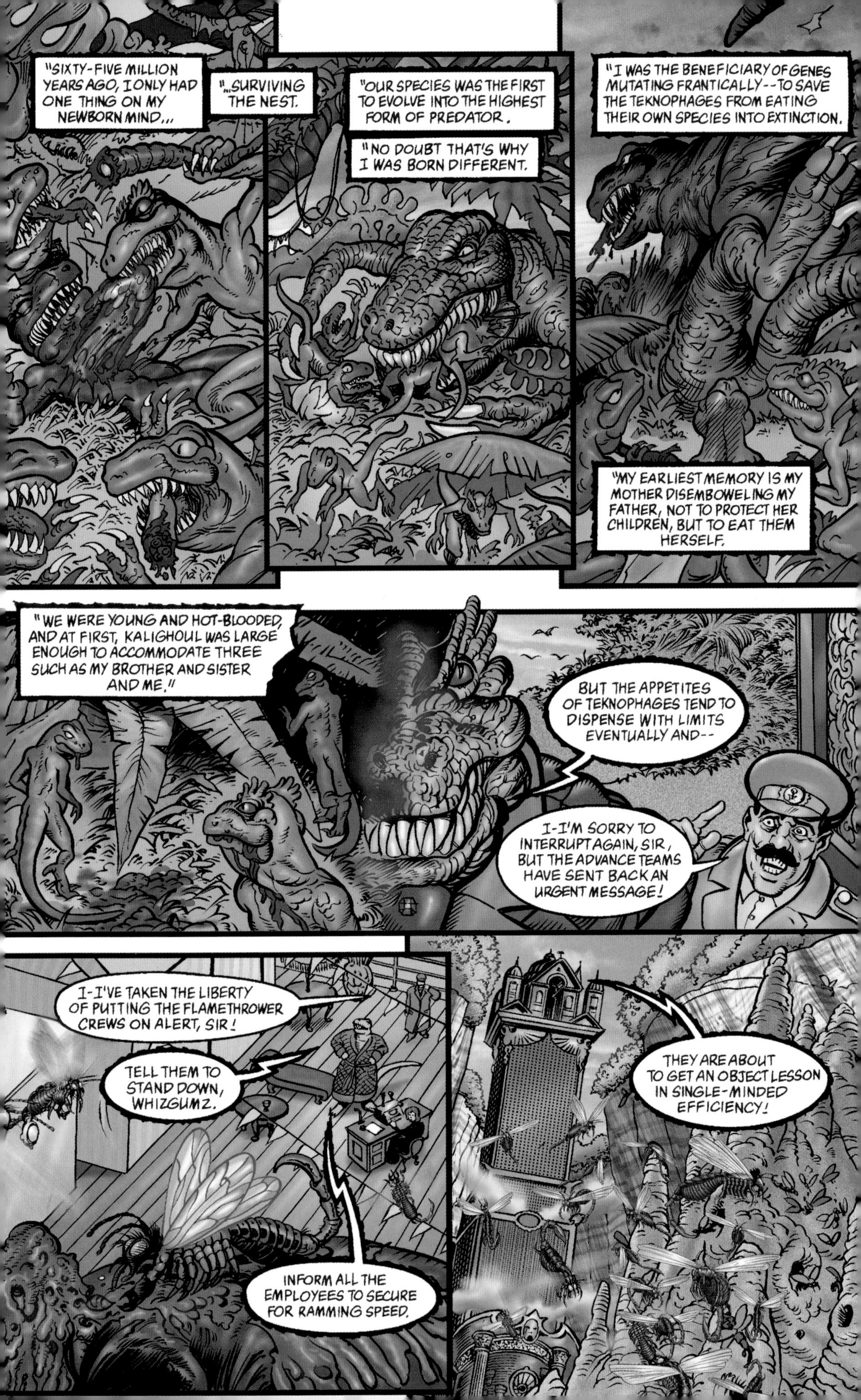
"SIXTY-FIVE MILLION YEARS AGO, I ONLY HAD ONE THING ON MY NEWBORN MIND...
"...SURVIVING THE NEST.
"OUR SPECIES WAS THE FIRST TO EVOLVE INTO THE HIGHEST FORM OF PREDATOR.
"NO DOUBT THAT'S WHY I WAS BORN DIFFERENT.
"I WAS THE BENEFICIARY OF GENES MUTATING FRANTICALLY--TO SAVE THE TEKNOPHAGES FROM EATING THEIR OWN SPECIES INTO EXTINCTION.
"MY EARLIEST MEMORY IS MY MOTHER DISEMBOWELING MY FATHER, NOT TO PROTECT HER CHILDREN, BUT TO EAT THEM HERSELF.
"WE WERE YOUNG AND HOT-BLOODED, AND AT FIRST, KALIGHOUL WAS LARGE ENOUGH TO ACCOMMODATE THREE SUCH AS MY BROTHER AND SISTER AND ME."
BUT THE APPETITES OF TEKNOPHAGES TEND TO DISPENSE WITH LIMITS EVENTUALLY AND--
I-I'M SORRY TO INTERRUPT AGAIN, SIR, BUT THE ADVANCE TEAMS HAVE SENT BACK AN URGENT MESSAGE!
I-I'VE TAKEN THE LIBERTY OF PUTTING THE FLAMETHROWER CREWS ON ALERT, SIR!
TELL THEM TO STAND DOWN, WHIZGUMZ.
INFORM ALL THE EMPLOYEES TO SECURE FOR RAMMING SPEED.
THEY ARE ABOUT TO GET AN OBJECT LESSON IN SINGLE-MINDED EFFICIENCY!

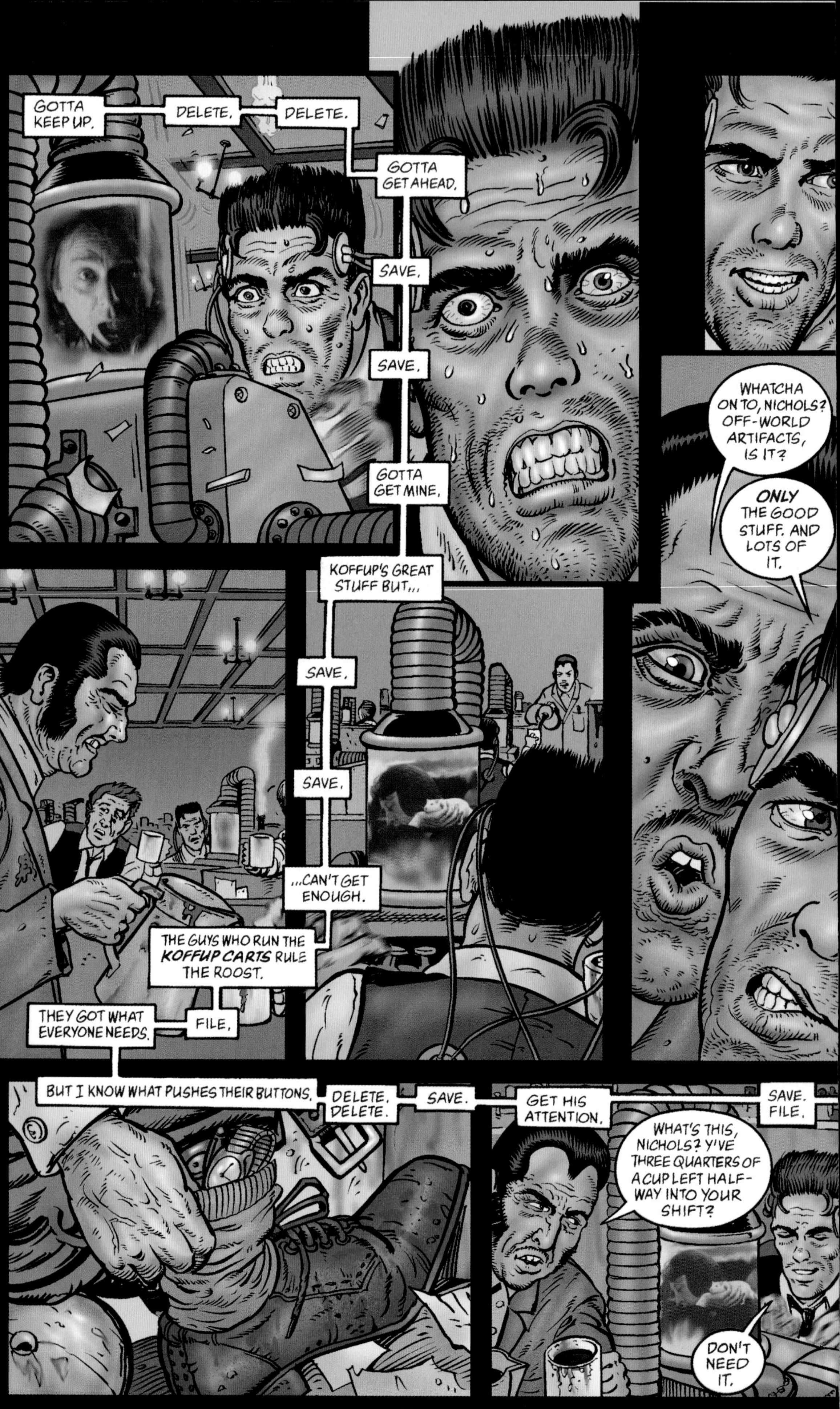
GOTTA KEEP UP.
DELETE.
DELETE.
GOTTA GET AHEAD.
SAVE.
SAVE.
GOTTA GET MINE.
WHATCHA ON TO, NICHOLS? OFF-WORLD ARTIFACTS, IS IT?
ONLY THE GOOD STUFF. AND LOTS OF IT.
KOFFUP'S GREAT STUFF BUT...
SAVE.
SAVE.
...CAN'T GET ENOUGH.
THE GUYS WHO RUN THE KOFFUP CARTS RULE THE ROOST.
THEY GOT WHAT EVERYONE NEEDS.
FILE.
BUT I KNOW WHAT PUSHES THEIR BUTTONS.
DELETE. DELETE.
SAVE.
GET HIS ATTENTION.
SAVE. FILE.
WHAT'S THIS, NICHOLS? Y'VE THREE QUARTERS OF A CUP LEFT HALF-WAY INTO YOUR SHIFT?
DON'T NEED IT.

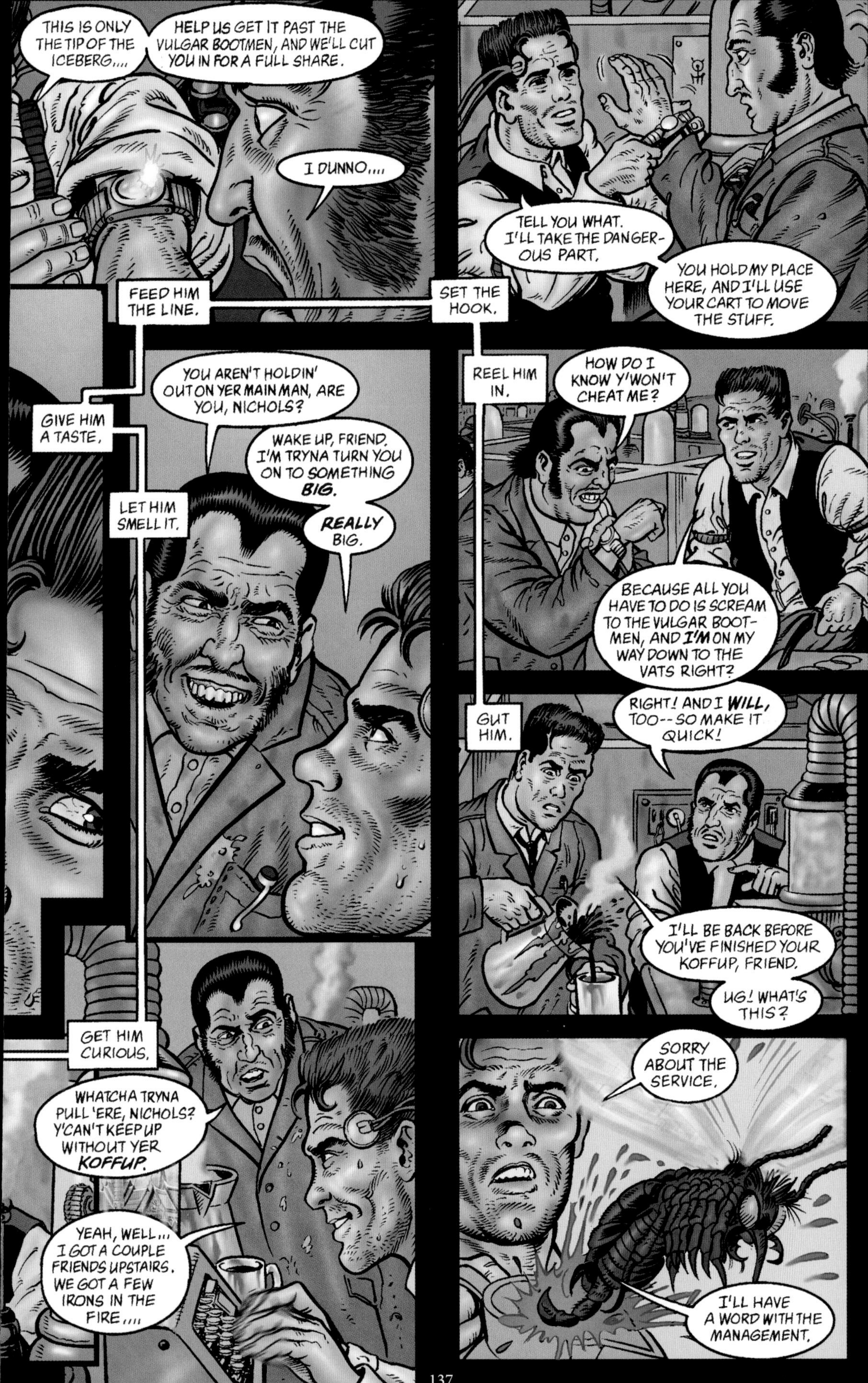

THIS IS ONLY THE TIP OF THE ICEBERG....
HELP US GET IT PAST THE VULGAR BOOTMEN, AND WE'LL CUT YOU IN FOR A FULL SHARE.
I DUNNO....
TELL YOU WHAT. I'LL TAKE THE DANGER-OUS PART.
YOU HOLD MY PLACE HERE, AND I'LL USE YOUR CART TO MOVE THE STUFF.
FEED HIM THE LINE.
SET THE HOOK.
GIVE HIM A TASTE.
YOU AREN'T HOLDIN' OUT ON YER MAIN MAN, ARE YOU, NICHOLS?
WAKE UP, FRIEND. I'M TRYNA TURN YOU ON TO SOMETHING **BIG**.
REALLY BIG.
LET HIM SMELL IT.
REEL HIM IN.
HOW DO I KNOW Y'WON'T CHEAT ME?
BECAUSE ALL YOU HAVE TO DO IS SCREAM TO THE VULGAR BOOT-MEN, AND ***I'M*** ON MY WAY DOWN TO THE VATS RIGHT?
GUT HIM.
RIGHT! AND I ***WILL***, TOO--SO MAKE IT QUICK!
I'LL BE BACK BEFORE YOU'VE FINISHED YOUR KOFFUP, FRIEND.
UG! WHAT'S THIS?
GET HIM CURIOUS.
WHATCHA TRYNA PULL 'ERE, NICHOLS? Y'CAN'T KEEP UP WITHOUT YER ***KOFFUP***.
YEAH, WELL... I GOT A COUPLE FRIENDS UPSTAIRS. WE GOT A FEW IRONS IN THE FIRE....
SORRY ABOUT THE SERVICE.
I'LL HAVE A WORD WITH THE MANAGEMENT.

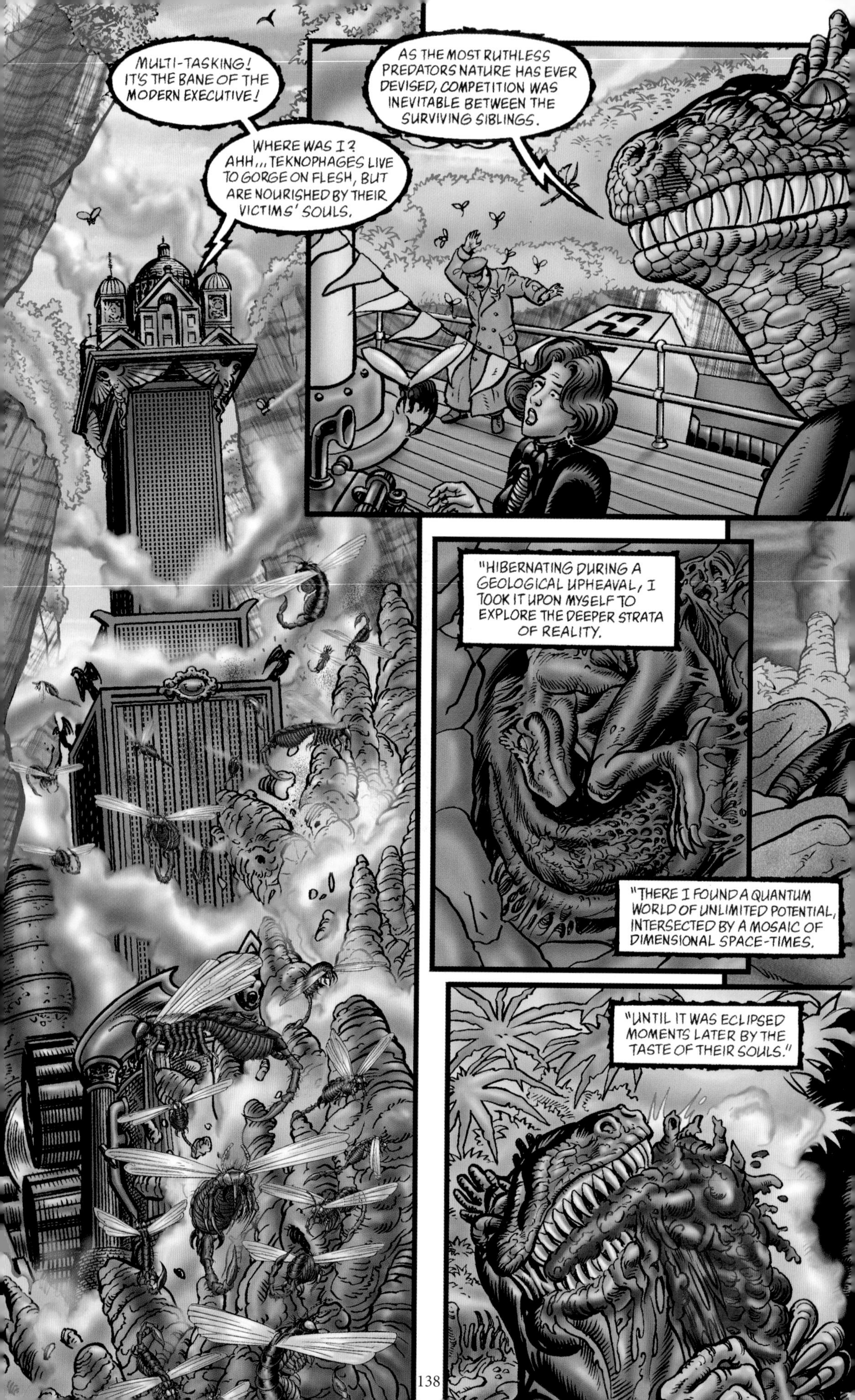
MULTI-TASKING! IT'S THE BANE OF THE MODERN EXECUTIVE!
WHERE WAS I? AHH,,, TEKNOPHAGES LIVE TO GORGE ON FLESH, BUT ARE NOURISHED BY THEIR VICTIMS' SOULS.
AS THE MOST RUTHLESS PREDATORS NATURE HAS EVER DEVISED, COMPETITION WAS INEVITABLE BETWEEN THE SURVIVING SIBLINGS.
"HIBERNATING DURING A GEOLOGICAL UPHEAVAL, I TOOK IT UPON MYSELF TO EXPLORE THE DEEPER STRATA OF REALITY.
"THERE I FOUND A QUANTUM WORLD OF UNLIMITED POTENTIAL, INTERSECTED BY A MOSAIC OF DIMENSIONAL SPACE-TIMES.
"UNTIL IT WAS ECLIPSED MOMENTS LATER BY THE TASTE OF THEIR SOULS."

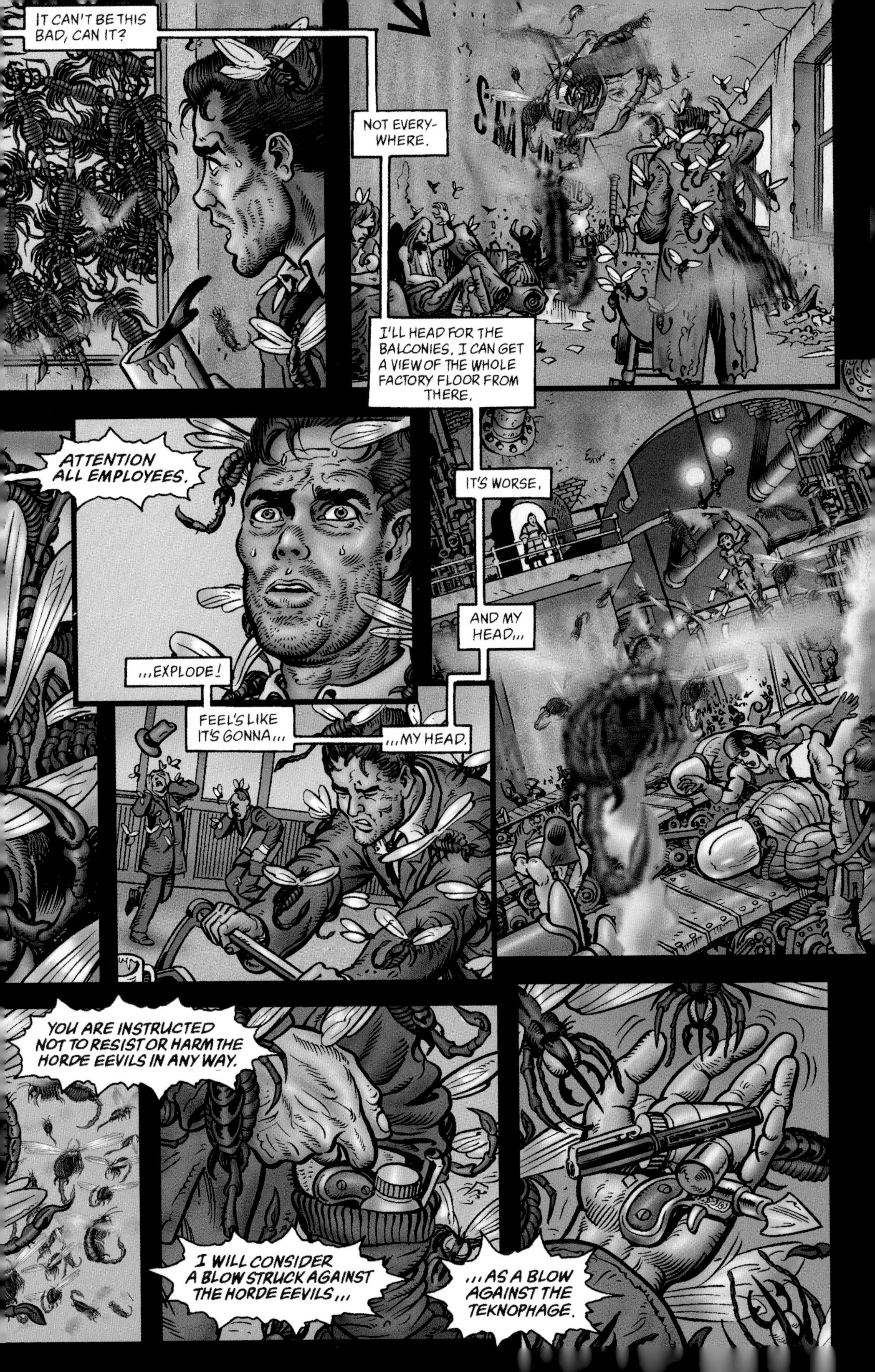
IT CAN'T BE THIS BAD, CAN IT?
NOT EVERY-WHERE.
I'LL HEAD FOR THE BALCONIES. I CAN GET A VIEW OF THE WHOLE FACTORY FLOOR FROM THERE.
ATTENTION ALL EMPLOYEES.
IT'S WORSE.
AND MY HEAD...
...EXPLODE!
FEEL'S LIKE IT'S GONNA...
...MY HEAD.
YOU ARE INSTRUCTED NOT TO RESIST OR HARM THE HORDE EEVILS IN ANY WAY.
I WILL CONSIDER A BLOW STRUCK AGAINST THE HORDE EEVILS...
...AS A BLOW AGAINST THE TEKNOPHAGE.

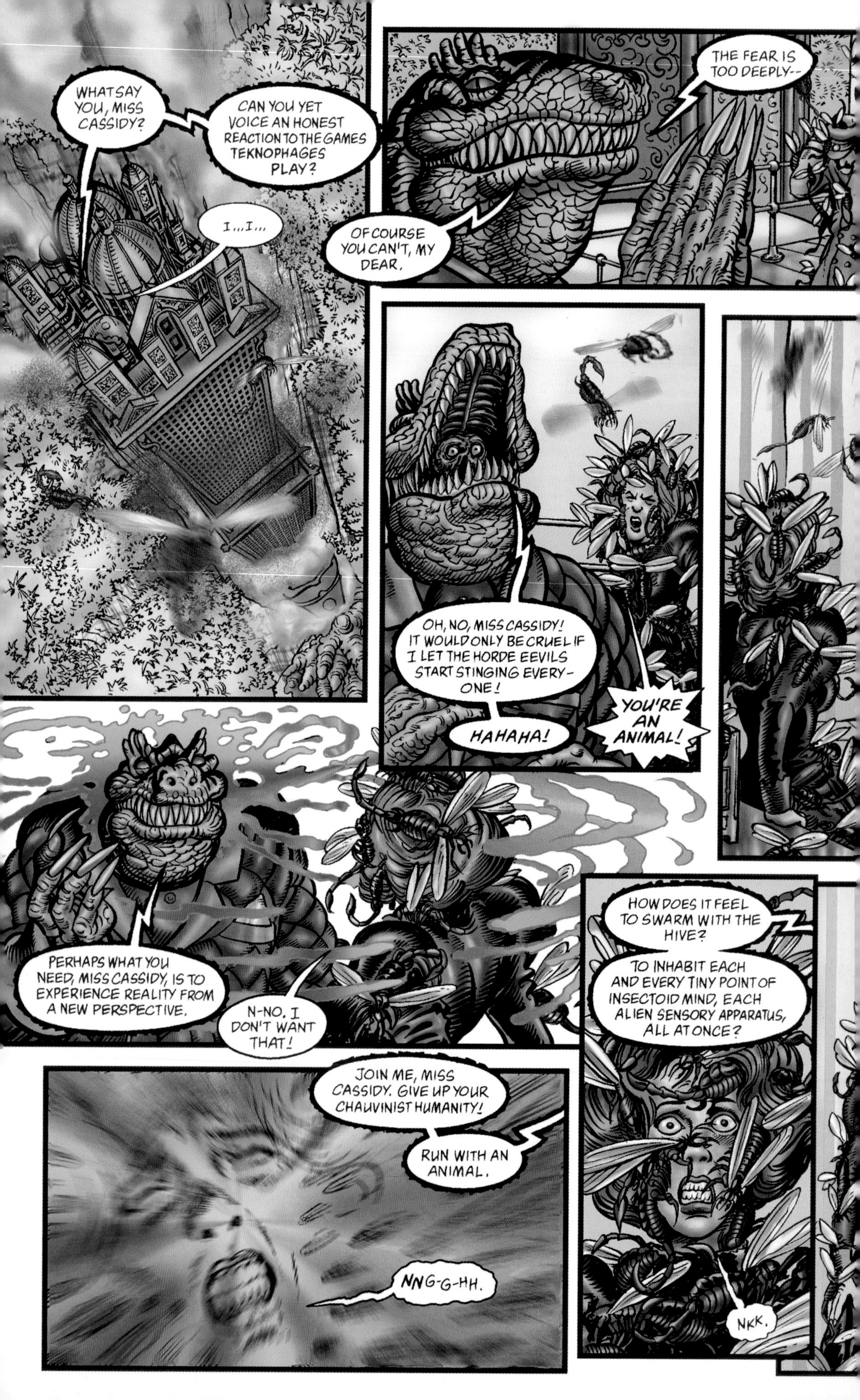
WHAT SAY YOU, MISS CASSIDY?
CAN YOU YET VOICE AN HONEST REACTION TO THE GAMES TEKNOPHAGES PLAY?
I...I...
THE FEAR IS TOO DEEPLY--
OF COURSE YOU CAN'T, MY DEAR.
OH, NO, MISS CASSIDY! IT WOULD ONLY BE CRUEL IF I LET THE HORDE EEVILS START STINGING EVERY-ONE!
HAHAHA!
YOU'RE AN ANIMAL!
PERHAPS WHAT YOU NEED, MISS CASSIDY, IS TO EXPERIENCE REALITY FROM A NEW PERSPECTIVE.
N-NO. I DON'T WANT THAT!
HOW DOES IT FEEL TO SWARM WITH THE HIVE?
TO INHABIT EACH AND EVERY TINY POINT OF INSECTOID MIND, EACH ALIEN SENSORY APPARATUS, ALL AT ONCE?
JOIN ME, MISS CASSIDY. GIVE UP YOUR CHAUVINIST HUMANITY!
RUN WITH AN ANIMAL.
NNG-G-HH.
NKK.

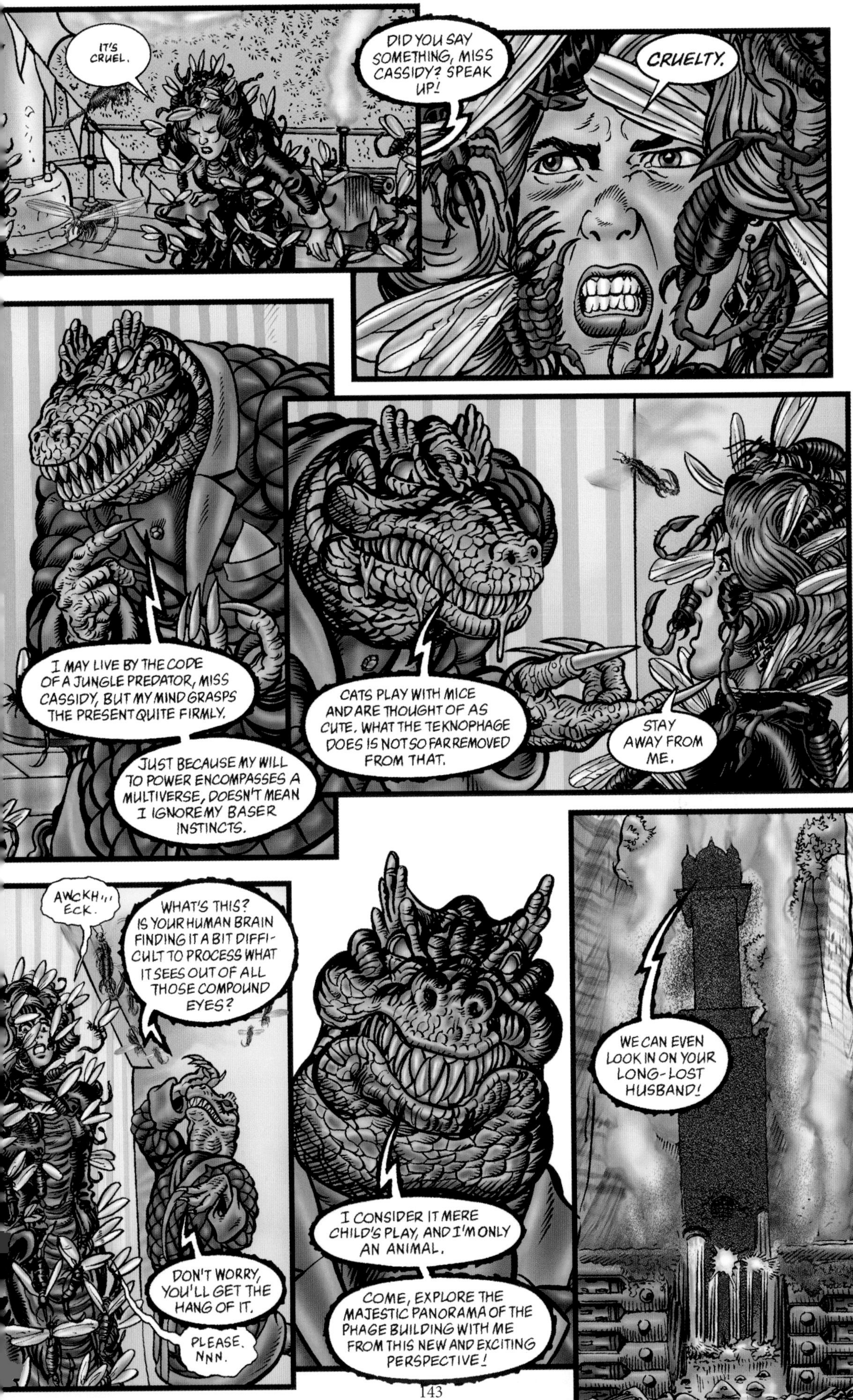

IT'S CRUEL.
DID YOU SAY SOMETHING, MISS CASSIDY? SPEAK UP!
CRUELTY.
I MAY LIVE BY THE CODE OF A JUNGLE PREDATOR, MISS CASSIDY, BUT MY MIND GRASPS THE PRESENT QUITE FIRMLY.
JUST BECAUSE MY WILL TO POWER ENCOMPASSES A MULTIVERSE, DOESN'T MEAN I IGNORE MY BASER INSTINCTS.
CATS PLAY WITH MICE AND ARE THOUGHT OF AS CUTE. WHAT THE TEKNOPHAGE DOES IS NOT SO FAR REMOVED FROM THAT.
STAY AWAY FROM ME.
AWCKH... ECK.
WHAT'S THIS? IS YOUR HUMAN BRAIN FINDING IT A BIT DIFFICULT TO PROCESS WHAT IT SEES OUT OF ALL THOSE COMPOUND EYES?
DON'T WORRY, YOU'LL GET THE HANG OF IT.
PLEASE. NNN.
I CONSIDER IT MERE CHILD'S PLAY, AND I'M ONLY AN ANIMAL.
COME, EXPLORE THE MAJESTIC PANORAMA OF THE PHAGE BUILDING WITH ME FROM THIS NEW AND EXCITING PERSPECTIVE!
WE CAN EVEN LOOK IN ON YOUR LONG-LOST HUSBAND!

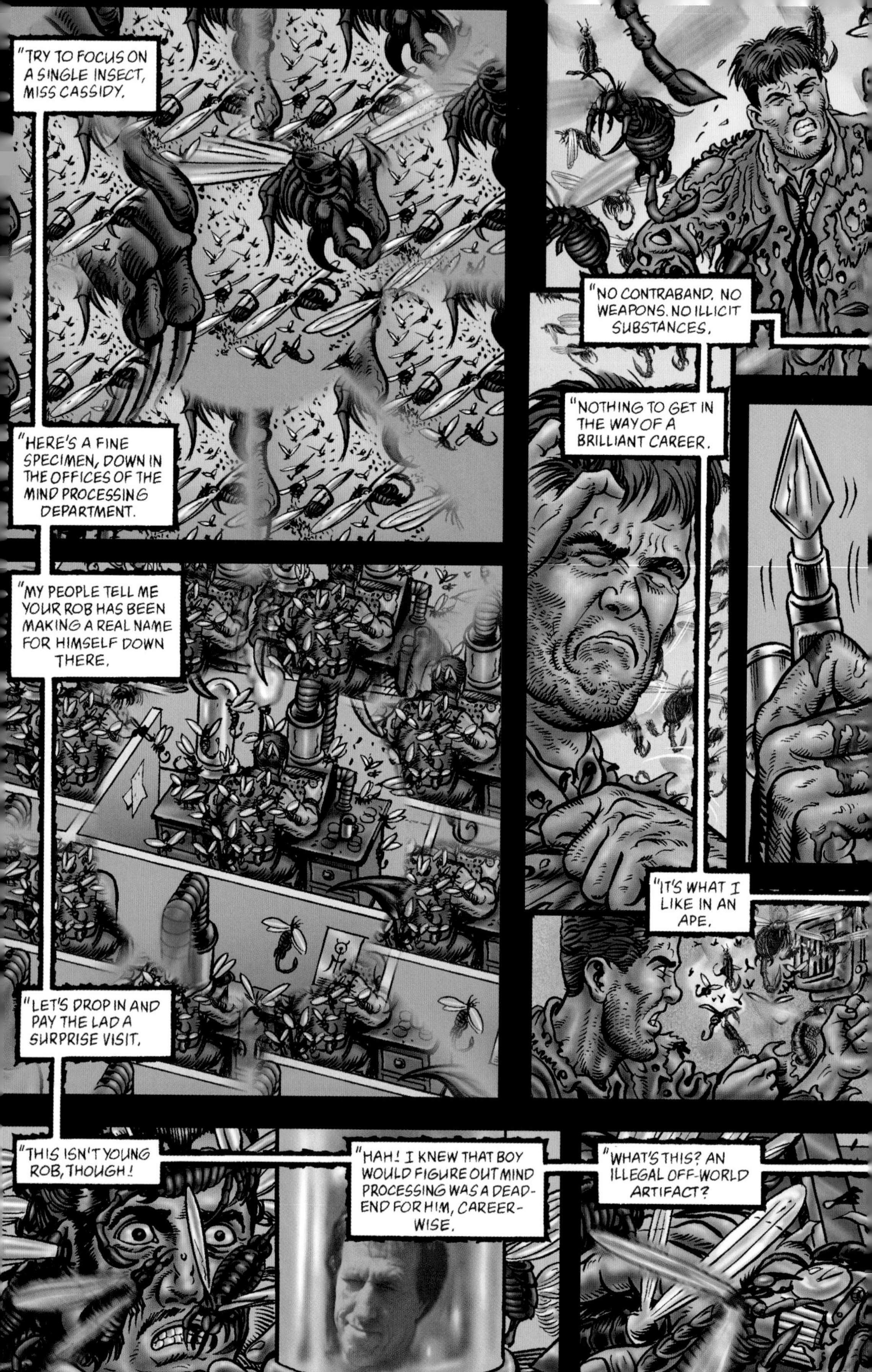
"TRY TO FOCUS ON A SINGLE INSECT, MISS CASSIDY.
"HERE'S A FINE SPECIMEN, DOWN IN THE OFFICES OF THE MIND PROCESSING DEPARTMENT.
"MY PEOPLE TELL ME YOUR ROB HAS BEEN MAKING A REAL NAME FOR HIMSELF DOWN THERE.
"LET'S DROP IN AND PAY THE LAD A SURPRISE VISIT.
"NO CONTRABAND. NO WEAPONS. NO ILLICIT SUBSTANCES.
"NOTHING TO GET IN THE WAY OF A BRILLIANT CAREER.
"IT'S WHAT I LIKE IN AN APE.
"THIS ISN'T YOUNG ROB, THOUGH!
"HAH! I KNEW THAT BOY WOULD FIGURE OUT MIND PROCESSING WAS A DEAD-END FOR HIM, CAREER-WISE.
"WHAT'S THIS? AN ILLEGAL OFF-WORLD ARTIFACT?

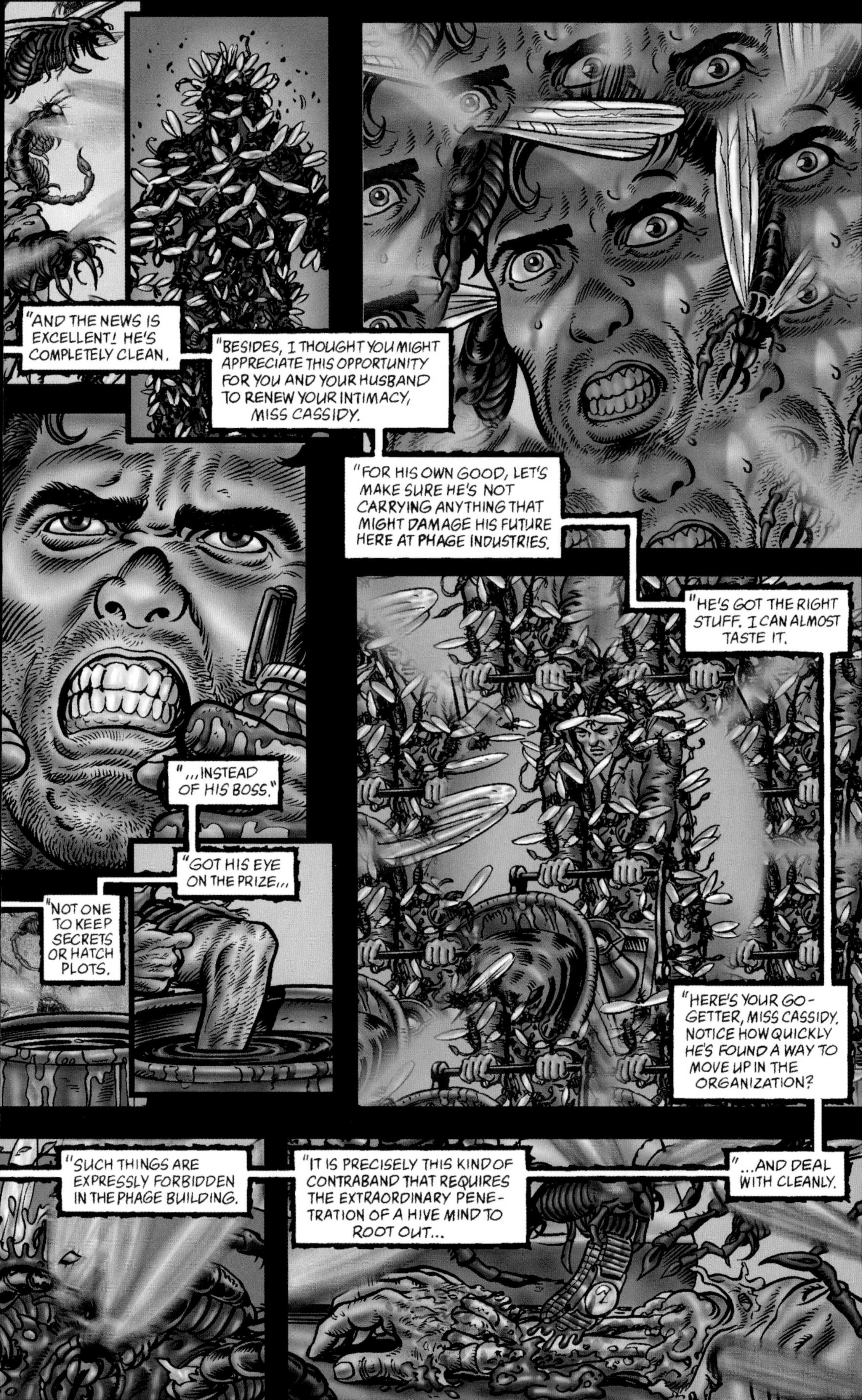
"AND THE NEWS IS EXCELLENT! HE'S COMPLETELY CLEAN.
"BESIDES, I THOUGHT YOU MIGHT APPRECIATE THIS OPPORTUNITY FOR YOU AND YOUR HUSBAND TO RENEW YOUR INTIMACY, MISS CASSIDY.
"FOR HIS OWN GOOD, LET'S MAKE SURE HE'S NOT CARRYING ANYTHING THAT MIGHT DAMAGE HIS FUTURE HERE AT PHAGE INDUSTRIES.
"HE'S GOT THE RIGHT STUFF. I CAN ALMOST TASTE IT.
"...INSTEAD OF HIS BOSS."
"GOT HIS EYE ON THE PRIZE...
"NOT ONE TO KEEP SECRETS OR HATCH PLOTS.
"HERE'S YOUR GO-GETTER, MISS CASSIDY. NOTICE HOW QUICKLY HE'S FOUND A WAY TO MOVE UP IN THE ORGANIZATION?
"SUCH THINGS ARE EXPRESSLY FORBIDDEN IN THE PHAGE BUILDING.
"IT IS PRECISELY THIS KIND OF CONTRABAND THAT REQUIRES THE EXTRAORDINARY PENETRATION OF A HIVE MIND TO ROOT OUT...
"...AND DEAL WITH CLEANLY.

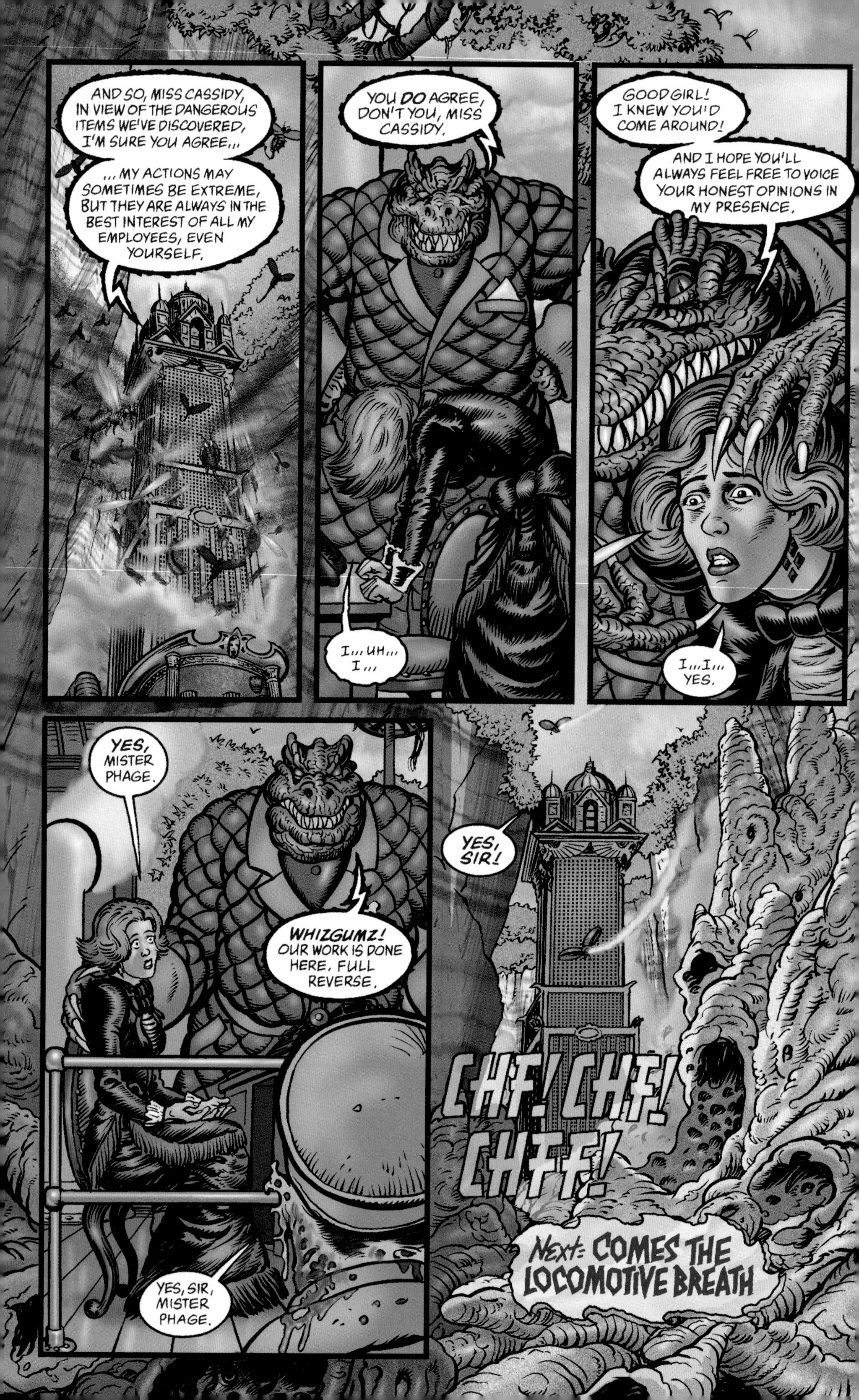
AND SO, MISS CASSIDY, IN VIEW OF THE DANGEROUS ITEMS WE'VE DISCOVERED, I'M SURE YOU AGREE...
... MY ACTIONS MAY SOMETIMES BE EXTREME, BUT THEY ARE ALWAYS IN THE BEST INTEREST OF ALL MY EMPLOYEES, EVEN YOURSELF.
YOU DO AGREE, DON'T YOU, MISS CASSIDY.
I... UH... I... I...
GOOD GIRL! I KNEW YOU'D COME AROUND!
AND I HOPE YOU'LL ALWAYS FEEL FREE TO VOICE YOUR HONEST OPINIONS IN MY PRESENCE.
I... I... YES.
YES, MISTER PHAGE.
WHIZGUMZ! OUR WORK IS DONE HERE. FULL REVERSE.
YES, SIR, MISTER PHAGE.
YES, SIR!
CHF! CHF! CHFF!
Next: COMES THE LOCOMOTIVE BREATH

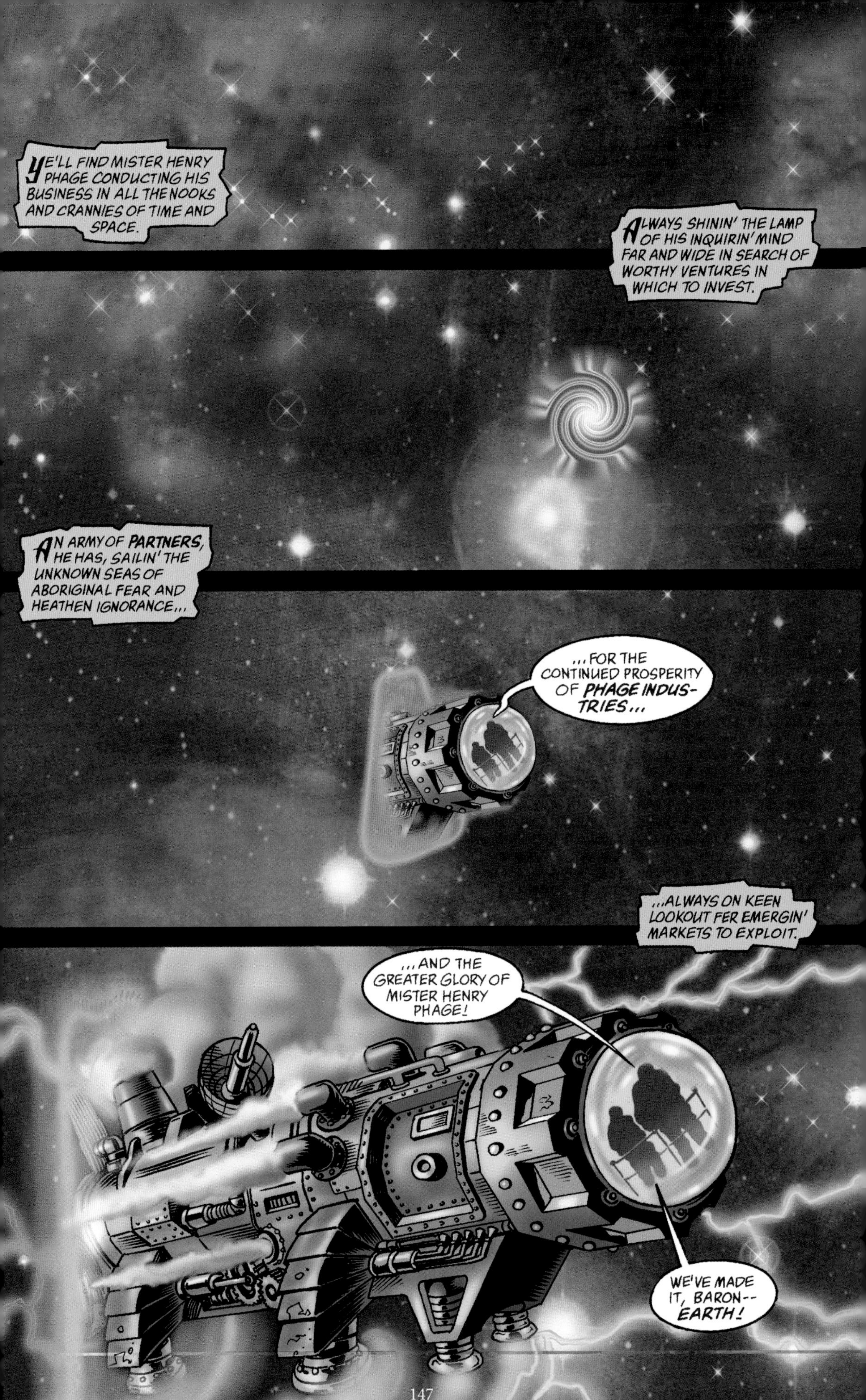
YE'LL FIND MISTER HENRY PHAGE CONDUCTING HIS BUSINESS IN ALL THE NOOKS AND CRANNIES OF TIME AND SPACE.
ALWAYS SHININ' THE LAMP OF HIS INQUIRIN' MIND FAR AND WIDE IN SEARCH OF WORTHY VENTURES IN WHICH TO INVEST.
AN ARMY OF PARTNERS, HE HAS, SAILIN' THE UNKNOWN SEAS OF ABORIGINAL FEAR AND HEATHEN IGNORANCE...
...FOR THE CONTINUED PROSPERITY OF PHAGE INDUSTRIES...
...ALWAYS ON KEEN LOOKOUT FER EMERGIN' MARKETS TO EXPLOIT.
...AND THE GREATER GLORY OF MISTER HENRY PHAGE!
WE'VE MADE IT, BARON-- EARTH!

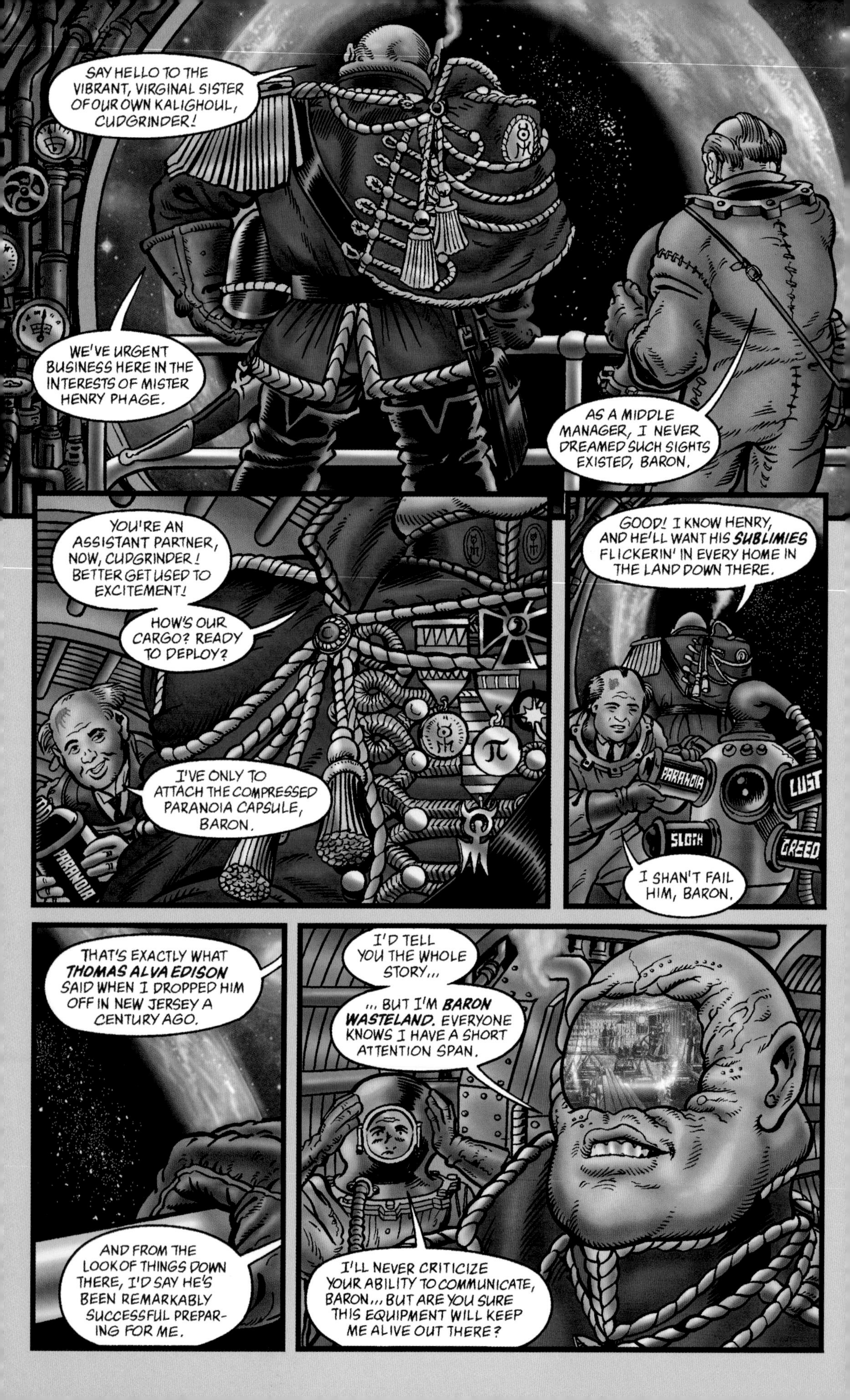
SAY HELLO TO THE VIBRANT, VIRGINAL SISTER OF OUR OWN KALIGHOUL, CUDGRINDER!
WE'VE URGENT BUSINESS HERE IN THE INTERESTS OF MISTER HENRY PHAGE.
AS A MIDDLE MANAGER, I NEVER DREAMED SUCH SIGHTS EXISTED, BARON.
YOU'RE AN ASSISTANT PARTNER, NOW, CUDGRINDER! BETTER GET USED TO EXCITEMENT!
HOW'S OUR CARGO? READY TO DEPLOY?
I'VE ONLY TO ATTACH THE COMPRESSED PARANOIA CAPSULE, BARON.
PARANOIA
GOOD! I KNOW HENRY, AND HE'LL WANT HIS SUBLIMIES FLICKERIN' IN EVERY HOME IN THE LAND DOWN THERE.
PARANOIA
LUST
SLOTH
GREED
I SHAN'T FAIL HIM, BARON.
THAT'S EXACTLY WHAT THOMAS ALVA EDISON SAID WHEN I DROPPED HIM OFF IN NEW JERSEY A CENTURY AGO.
AND FROM THE LOOK OF THINGS DOWN THERE, I'D SAY HE'S BEEN REMARKABLY SUCCESSFUL PREPARING FOR ME.
I'D TELL YOU THE WHOLE STORY...
... BUT I'M BARON WASTELAND. EVERYONE KNOWS I HAVE A SHORT ATTENTION SPAN.
I'LL NEVER CRITICIZE YOUR ABILITY TO COMMUNICATE, BARON... BUT ARE YOU SURE THIS EQUIPMENT WILL KEEP ME ALIVE OUT THERE?

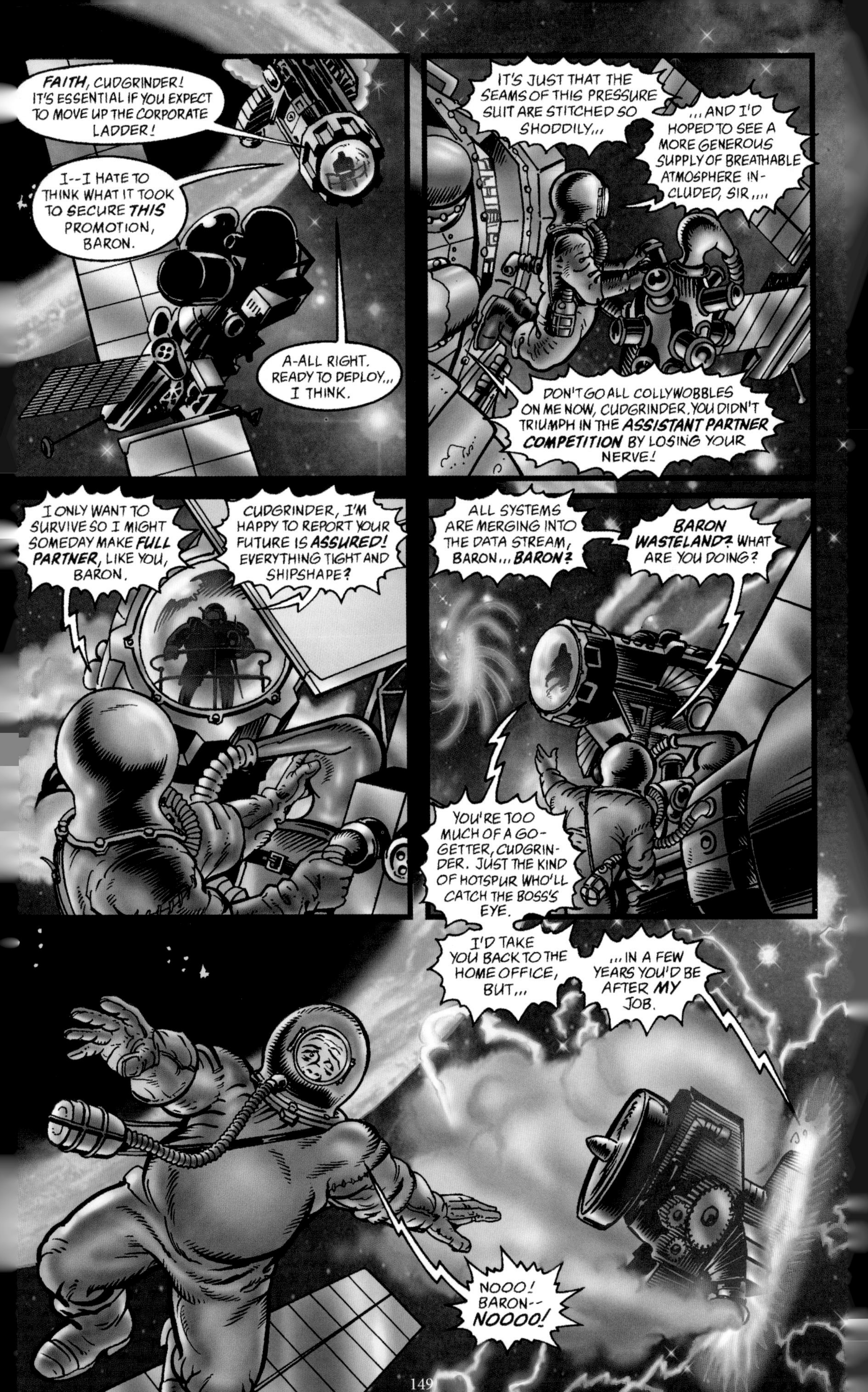
FAITH, CUDGRINDER! IT'S ESSENTIAL IF YOU EXPECT TO MOVE UP THE CORPORATE LADDER!
I--I HATE TO THINK WHAT IT TOOK TO SECURE THIS PROMOTION, BARON.
A-ALL RIGHT. READY TO DEPLOY... I THINK.
IT'S JUST THAT THE SEAMS OF THIS PRESSURE SUIT ARE STITCHED SO SHODDILY...
...AND I'D HOPED TO SEE A MORE GENEROUS SUPPLY OF BREATHABLE ATMOSPHERE IN-CLUDED, SIR....
DON'T GO ALL COLLYWOBBLES ON ME NOW, CUDGRINDER. YOU DIDN'T TRIUMPH IN THE ASSISTANT PARTNER COMPETITION BY LOSING YOUR NERVE!
I ONLY WANT TO SURVIVE SO I MIGHT SOMEDAY MAKE FULL PARTNER, LIKE YOU, BARON.
CUDGRINDER, I'M HAPPY TO REPORT YOUR FUTURE IS ASSURED! EVERYTHING TIGHT AND SHIPSHAPE?
ALL SYSTEMS ARE MERGING INTO THE DATA STREAM, BARON... BARON?
BARON WASTELAND? WHAT ARE YOU DOING?
YOU'RE TOO MUCH OF A GO-GETTER, CUDGRINDER. JUST THE KIND OF HOTSPUR WHO'LL CATCH THE BOSS'S EYE.
I'D TAKE YOU BACK TO THE HOME OFFICE, BUT...
...IN A FEW YEARS YOU'D BE AFTER MY JOB.
NOOO! BARON-- NOOOO!

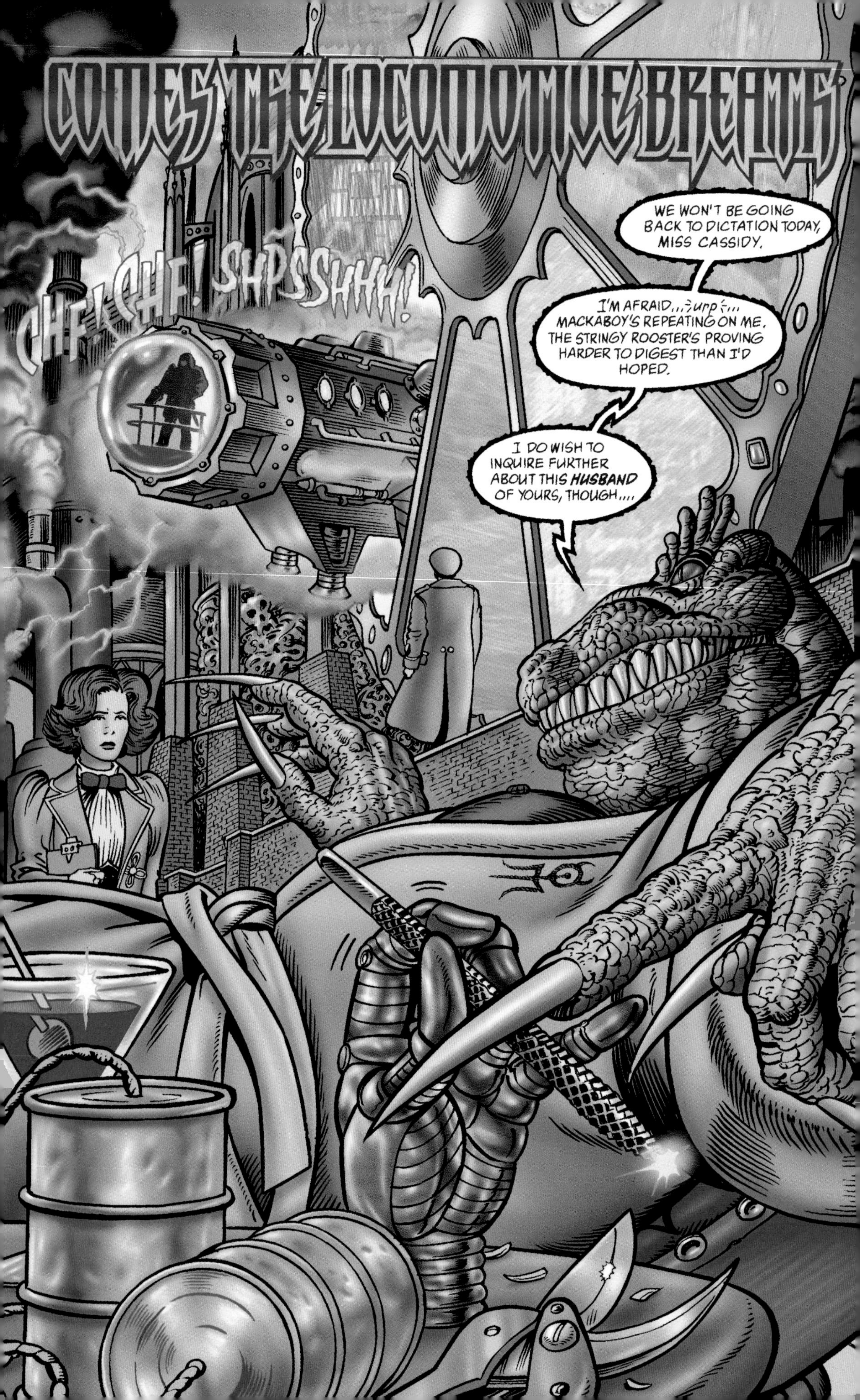
COMES THE LOCOMOTIVE BREATH
CHF! CHF! SHPSSHHH!
WE WON'T BE GOING BACK TO DICTATION TODAY, MISS CASSIDY.
I'M AFRAID... urp ... MACKABOY'S REPEATING ON ME. THE STRINGY ROOSTER'S PROVING HARDER TO DIGEST THAN I'D HOPED.
I DO WISH TO INQUIRE FURTHER ABOUT THIS **HUSBAND** OF YOURS, THOUGH....

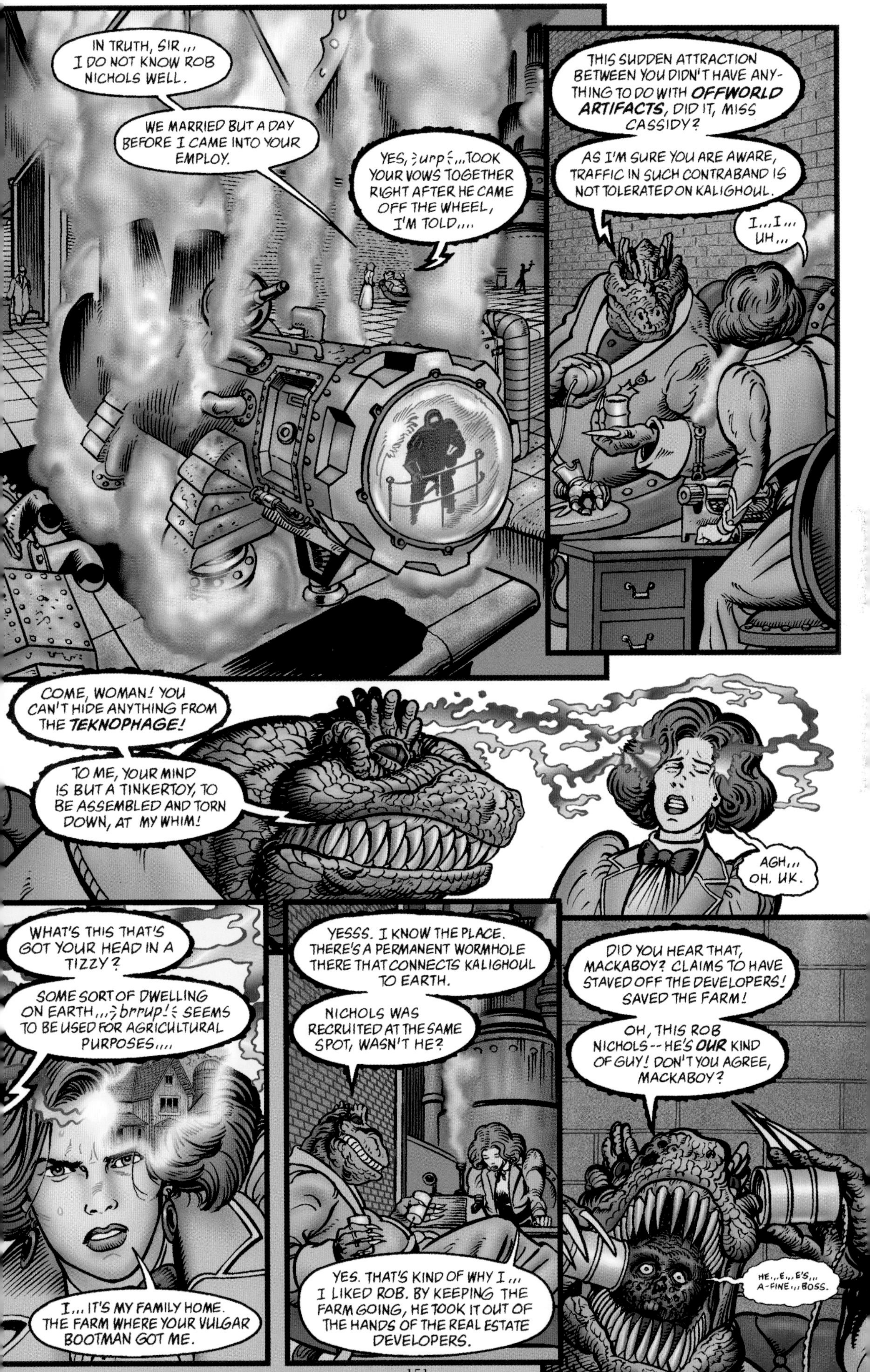

IN TRUTH, SIR... I DO NOT KNOW ROB NICHOLS WELL.
WE MARRIED BUT A DAY BEFORE I CAME INTO YOUR EMPLOY.
YES, ~urp~... TOOK YOUR VOWS TOGETHER RIGHT AFTER HE CAME OFF THE WHEEL, I'M TOLD....
THIS SUDDEN ATTRACTION BETWEEN YOU DIDN'T HAVE ANYTHING TO DO WITH **OFFWORLD ARTIFACTS**, DID IT, MISS CASSIDY?
AS I'M SURE YOU ARE AWARE, TRAFFIC IN SUCH CONTRABAND IS NOT TOLERATED ON KALIGHOUL.
I... I... UH...
COME, WOMAN! YOU CAN'T HIDE ANYTHING FROM THE ***TEKNOPHAGE!***
TO ME, YOUR MIND IS BUT A TINKERTOY, TO BE ASSEMBLED AND TORN DOWN, AT MY WHIM!
AGH... OH. UK.
WHAT'S THIS THAT'S GOT YOUR HEAD IN A TIZZY?
SOME SORT OF DWELLING ON EARTH... ~brrup!~ SEEMS TO BE USED FOR AGRICULTURAL PURPOSES....
I... IT'S MY FAMILY HOME. THE FARM WHERE YOUR VULGAR BOOTMAN GOT ME.
YESSS. I KNOW THE PLACE. THERE'S A PERMANENT WORMHOLE THERE THAT CONNECTS KALIGHOUL TO EARTH.
NICHOLS WAS RECRUITED AT THE SAME SPOT, WASN'T HE?
YES. THAT'S KIND OF WHY I... I LIKED ROB. BY KEEPING THE FARM GOING, HE TOOK IT OUT OF THE HANDS OF THE REAL ESTATE DEVELOPERS.
DID YOU HEAR THAT, MACKABOY? CLAIMS TO HAVE STAVED OFF THE DEVELOPERS! SAVED THE FARM!
OH, THIS ROB NICHOLS -- HE'S ***OUR*** KIND OF GUY! DON'T YOU AGREE, MACKABOY?
HE...E...E'S... A-FINE... BOSS.

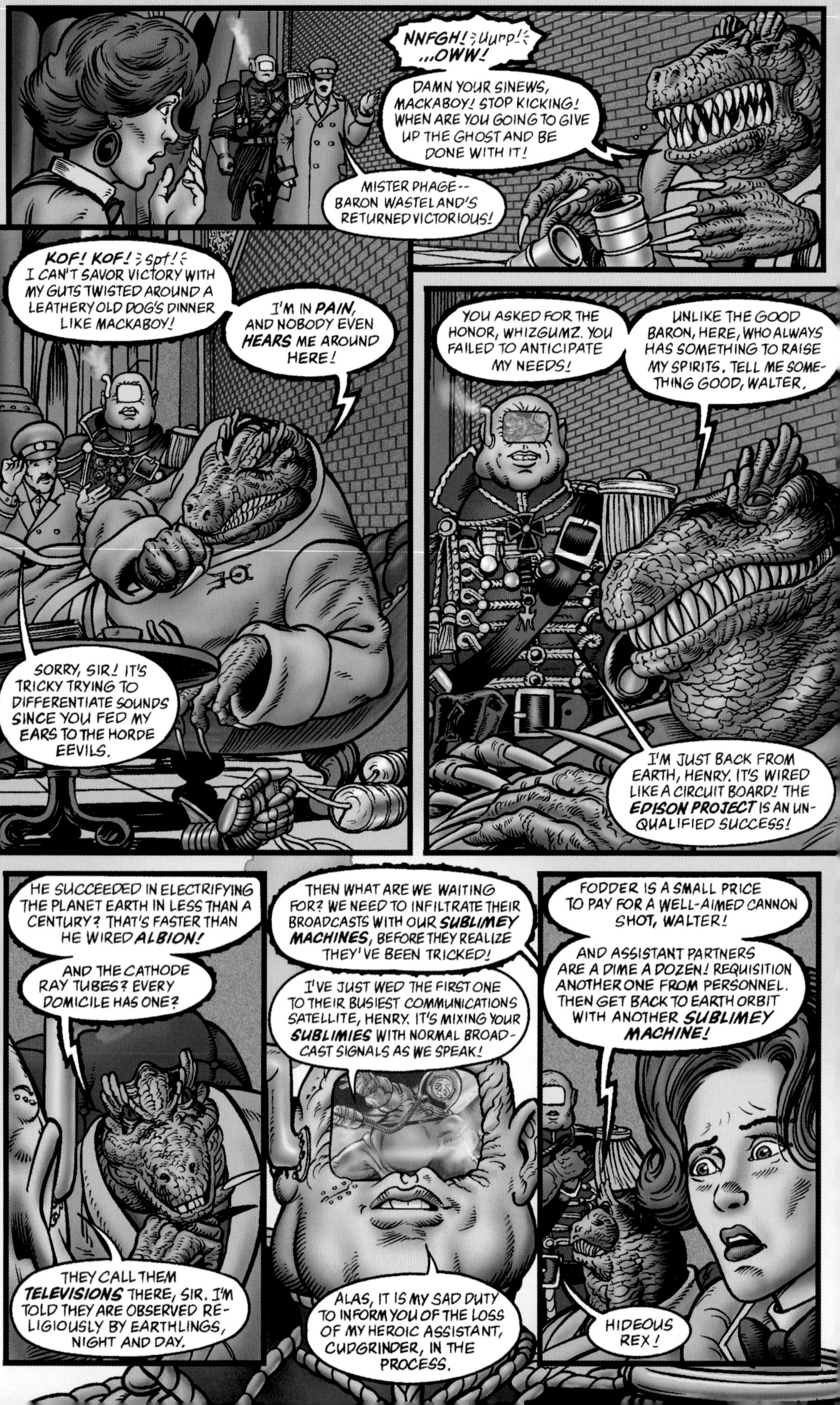
NNFGH! Uurp! ...OWW!
DAMN YOUR SINEWS, MACKABOY! STOP KICKING! WHEN ARE YOU GOING TO GIVE UP THE GHOST AND BE DONE WITH IT!
MISTER PHAGE-- BARON WASTELAND'S RETURNED VICTORIOUS!
KOF! KOF! spt! I CAN'T SAVOR VICTORY WITH MY GUTS TWISTED AROUND A LEATHERY OLD DOG'S DINNER LIKE MACKABOY!
I'M IN PAIN, AND NOBODY EVEN HEARS ME AROUND HERE!
SORRY, SIR! IT'S TRICKY TRYING TO DIFFERENTIATE SOUNDS SINCE YOU FED MY EARS TO THE HORDE EEVILS.
YOU ASKED FOR THE HONOR, WHIZGUMZ. YOU FAILED TO ANTICIPATE MY NEEDS!
UNLIKE THE GOOD BARON, HERE, WHO ALWAYS HAS SOMETHING TO RAISE MY SPIRITS. TELL ME SOMETHING GOOD, WALTER.
I'M JUST BACK FROM EARTH, HENRY. IT'S WIRED LIKE A CIRCUIT BOARD! THE EDISON PROJECT IS AN UNQUALIFIED SUCCESS!
HE SUCCEEDED IN ELECTRIFYING THE PLANET EARTH IN LESS THAN A CENTURY? THAT'S FASTER THAN HE WIRED ALBION!
AND THE CATHODE RAY TUBES? EVERY DOMICILE HAS ONE?
THEY CALL THEM TELEVISIONS THERE, SIR. I'M TOLD THEY ARE OBSERVED RELIGIOUSLY BY EARTHLINGS, NIGHT AND DAY.
THEN WHAT ARE WE WAITING FOR? WE NEED TO INFILTRATE THEIR BROADCASTS WITH OUR SUBLIMEY MACHINES, BEFORE THEY REALIZE THEY'VE BEEN TRICKED!
I'VE JUST WED THE FIRST ONE TO THEIR BUSIEST COMMUNICATIONS SATELLITE, HENRY. IT'S MIXING YOUR SUBLIMIES WITH NORMAL BROADCAST SIGNALS AS WE SPEAK!
ALAS, IT IS MY SAD DUTY TO INFORM YOU OF THE LOSS OF MY HEROIC ASSISTANT, CUDGRINDER, IN THE PROCESS.
FODDER IS A SMALL PRICE TO PAY FOR A WELL-AIMED CANNON SHOT, WALTER!
AND ASSISTANT PARTNERS ARE A DIME A DOZEN! REQUISITION ANOTHER ONE FROM PERSONNEL. THEN GET BACK TO EARTH ORBIT WITH ANOTHER SUBLIMEY MACHINE!
HIDEOUS REX!

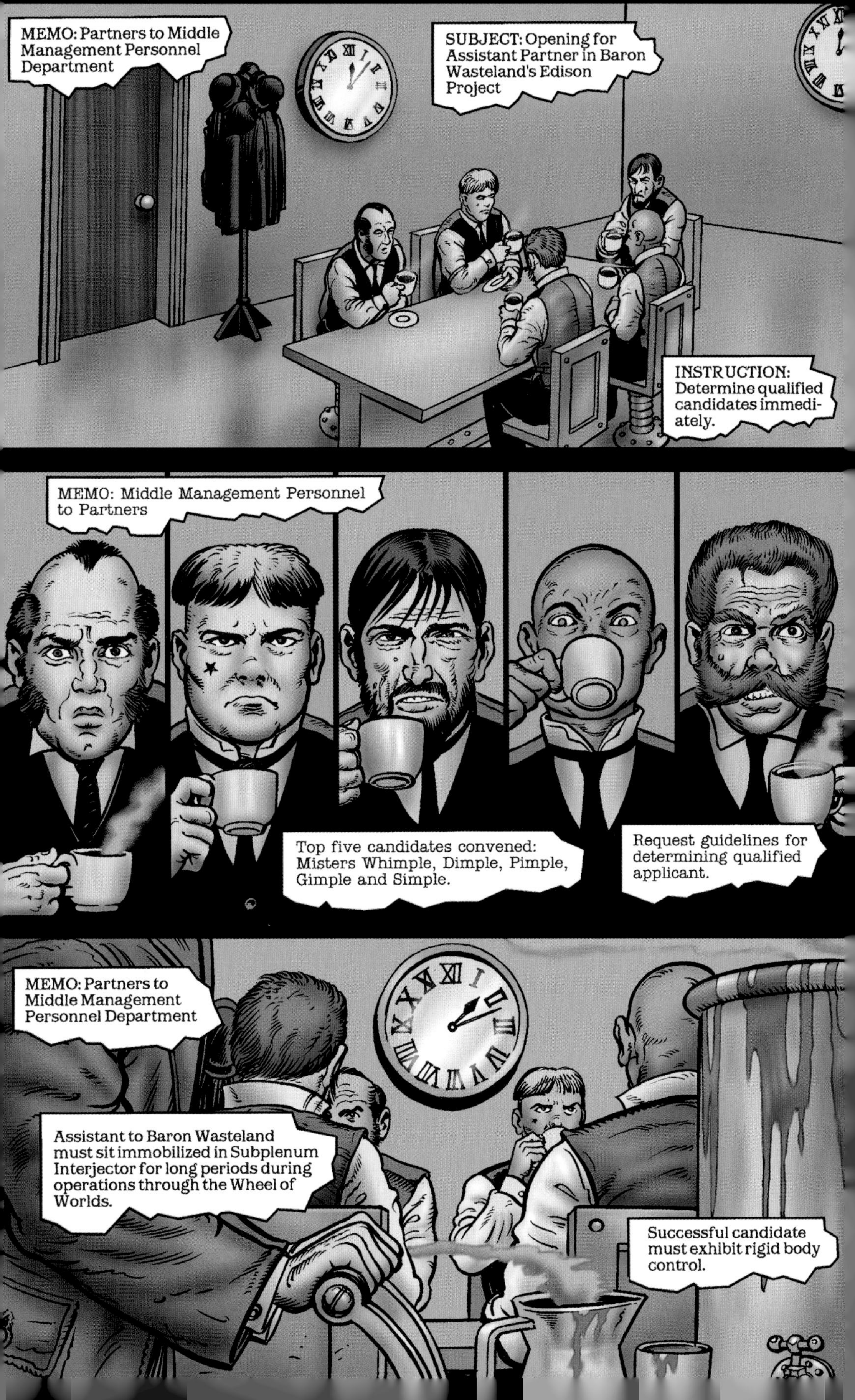
MEMO: Partners to Middle Management Personnel Department
SUBJECT: Opening for Assistant Partner in Baron Wasteland's Edison Project
INSTRUCTION: Determine qualified candidates immedi-ately.
MEMO: Middle Management Personnel to Partners
Top five candidates convened: Misters Whimple, Dimple, Pimple, Gimple and Simple.
Request guidelines for determining qualified applicant.
MEMO: Partners to Middle Management Personnel Department
Assistant to Baron Wasteland must sit immobilized in Subplenum Interjector for long periods during operations through the Wheel of Worlds.
Successful candidate must exhibit rigid body control.

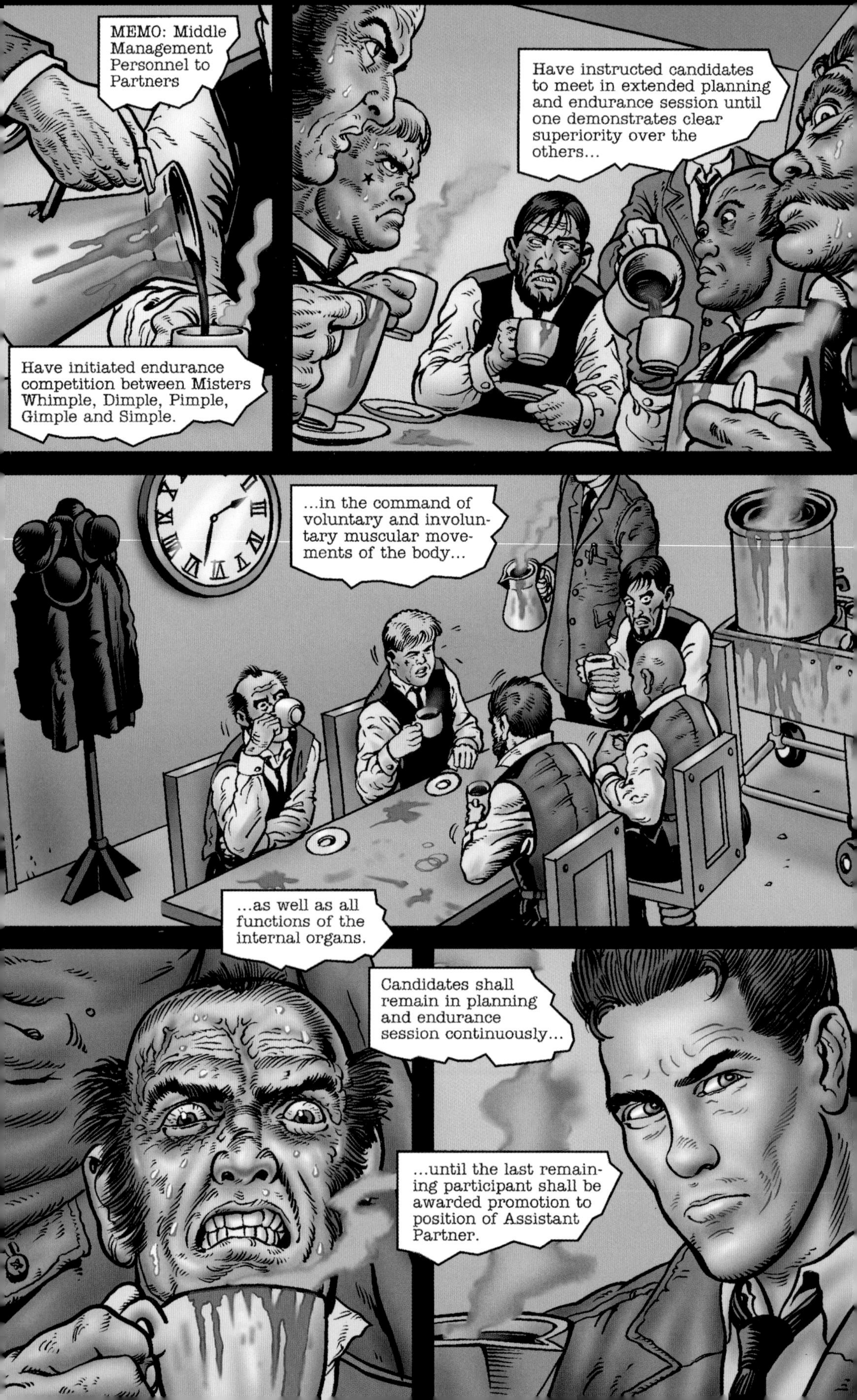
MEMO: Middle Management Personnel to Partners
Have initiated endurance competition between Misters Whimple, Dimple, Pimple, Gimple and Simple.
Have instructed candidates to meet in extended planning and endurance session until one demonstrates clear superiority over the others...
...in the command of voluntary and involuntary muscular movements of the body...
...as well as all functions of the internal organs.
Candidates shall remain in planning and endurance session continuously...
...until the last remaining participant shall be awarded promotion to position of Assistant Partner.

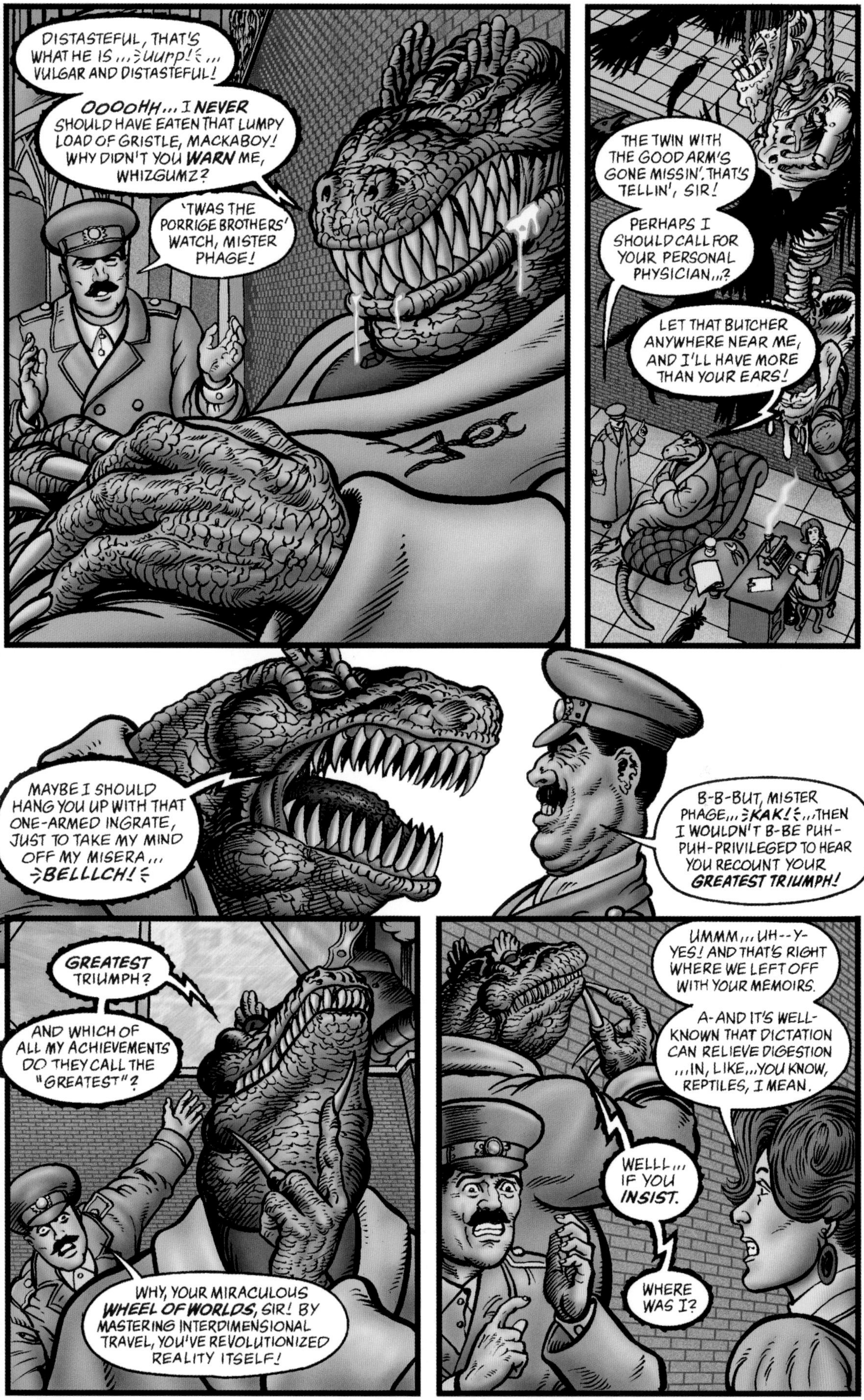
DISTASTEFUL, THAT'S WHAT HE IS... ≥UURP!≤... VULGAR AND DISTASTEFUL!
OOOOHH... I NEVER SHOULD HAVE EATEN THAT LUMPY LOAD OF GRISTLE, MACKABOY! WHY DIDN'T YOU WARN ME, WHIZGUMZ?
'TWAS THE PORRIGE BROTHERS' WATCH, MISTER PHAGE!
THE TWIN WITH THE GOOD ARM'S GONE MISSIN'. THAT'S TELLIN', SIR!
PERHAPS I SHOULD CALL FOR YOUR PERSONAL PHYSICIAN...?
LET THAT BUTCHER ANYWHERE NEAR ME, AND I'LL HAVE MORE THAN YOUR EARS!
MAYBE I SHOULD HANG YOU UP WITH THAT ONE-ARMED INGRATE, JUST TO TAKE MY MIND OFF MY MISERA... ≥BELLLCH!≤
B-B-BUT, MISTER PHAGE... ≥KAK!≤... THEN I WOULDN'T B-BE PUH-PUH-PRIVILEGED TO HEAR YOU RECOUNT YOUR GREATEST TRIUMPH!
GREATEST TRIUMPH?
AND WHICH OF ALL MY ACHIEVEMENTS DO THEY CALL THE "GREATEST"?
WHY, YOUR MIRACULOUS WHEEL OF WORLDS, SIR! BY MASTERING INTERDIMENSIONAL TRAVEL, YOU'VE REVOLUTIONIZED REALITY ITSELF!
UMMM... UH--Y-YES! AND THAT'S RIGHT WHERE WE LEFT OFF WITH YOUR MEMOIRS.
A-AND IT'S WELL-KNOWN THAT DICTATION CAN RELIEVE DIGESTION ...IN, LIKE... YOU KNOW, REPTILES, I MEAN.
WELLL... IF YOU INSIST.
WHERE WAS I?

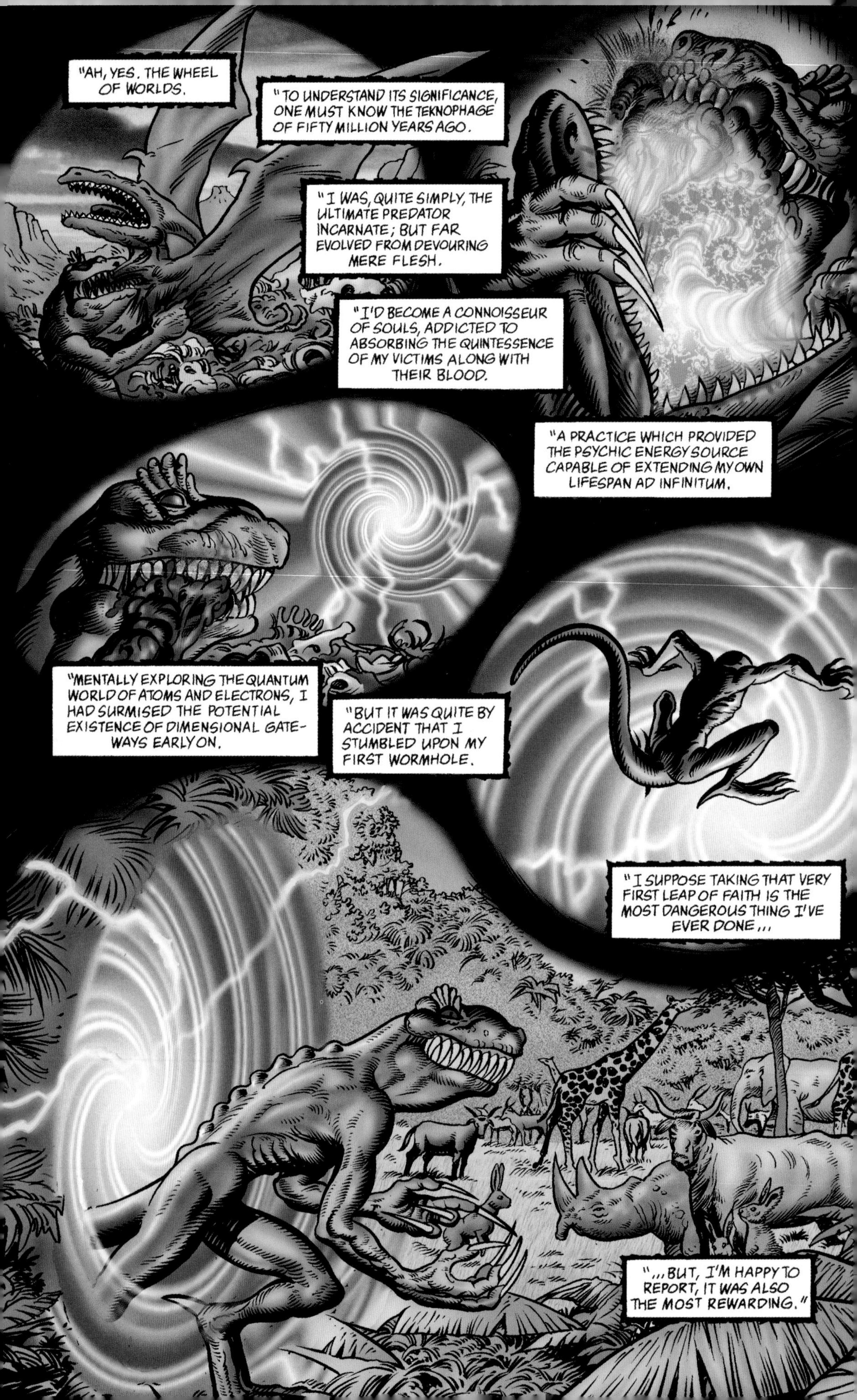
"AH, YES. THE WHEEL OF WORLDS.
"TO UNDERSTAND ITS SIGNIFICANCE, ONE MUST KNOW THE TEKNOPHAGE OF FIFTY MILLION YEARS AGO.
"I WAS, QUITE SIMPLY, THE ULTIMATE PREDATOR INCARNATE; BUT FAR EVOLVED FROM DEVOURING MERE FLESH.
"I'D BECOME A CONNOISSEUR OF SOULS, ADDICTED TO ABSORBING THE QUINTESSENCE OF MY VICTIMS ALONG WITH THEIR BLOOD.
"A PRACTICE WHICH PROVIDED THE PSYCHIC ENERGY SOURCE CAPABLE OF EXTENDING MY OWN LIFESPAN AD INFINITUM.
"MENTALLY EXPLORING THE QUANTUM WORLD OF ATOMS AND ELECTRONS, I HAD SURMISED THE POTENTIAL EXISTENCE OF DIMENSIONAL GATE-WAYS EARLY ON.
"BUT IT WAS QUITE BY ACCIDENT THAT I STUMBLED UPON MY FIRST WORMHOLE.
"I SUPPOSE TAKING THAT VERY FIRST LEAP OF FAITH IS THE MOST DANGEROUS THING I'VE EVER DONE...
"...BUT, I'M HAPPY TO REPORT, IT WAS ALSO THE MOST REWARDING."

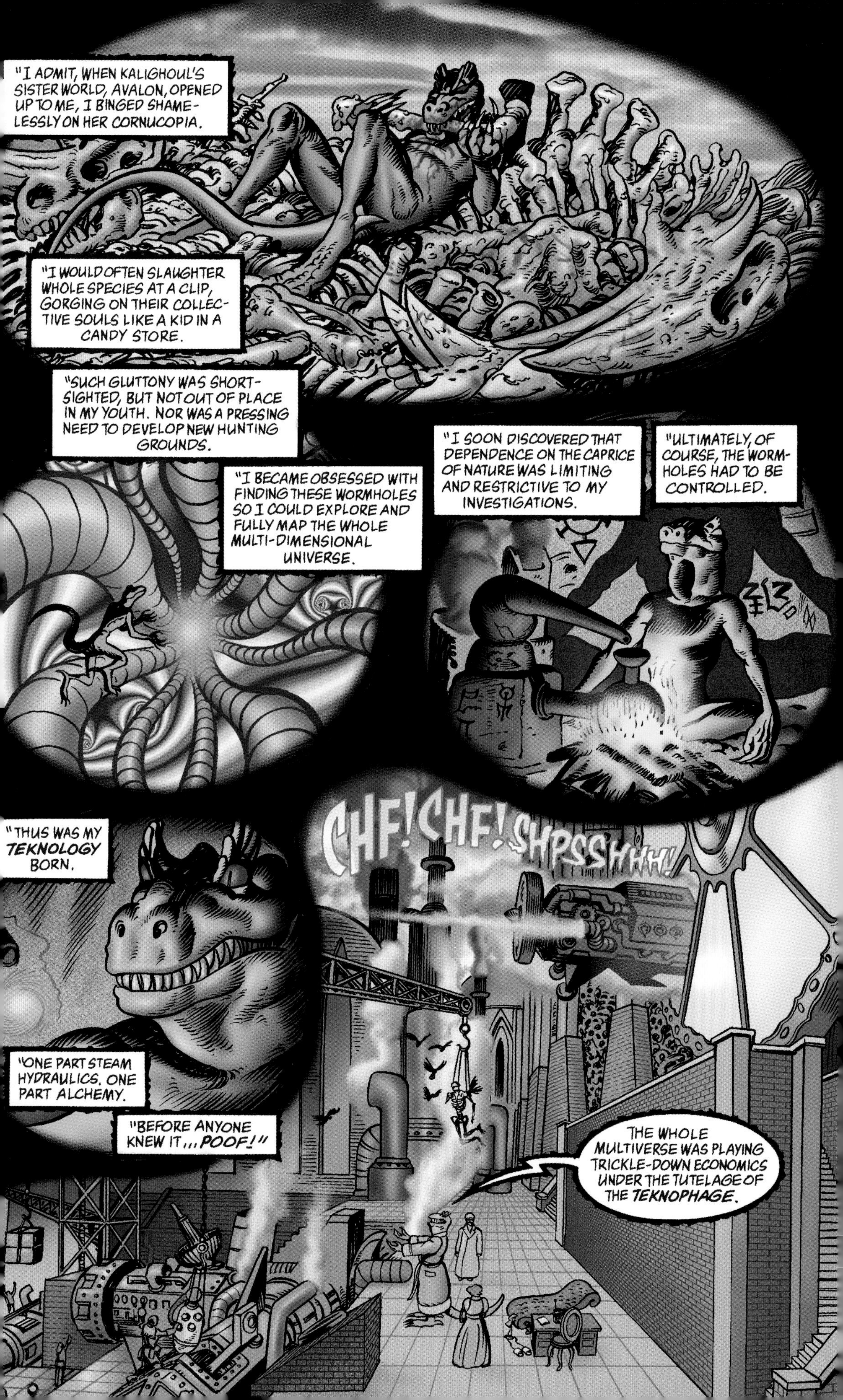
"I ADMIT, WHEN KALIGHOUL'S SISTER WORLD, AVALON, OPENED UP TO ME, I BINGED SHAMELESSLY ON HER CORNUCOPIA.
"I WOULD OFTEN SLAUGHTER WHOLE SPECIES AT A CLIP, GORGING ON THEIR COLLECTIVE SOULS LIKE A KID IN A CANDY STORE.
"SUCH GLUTTONY WAS SHORT-SIGHTED, BUT NOT OUT OF PLACE IN MY YOUTH. NOR WAS A PRESSING NEED TO DEVELOP NEW HUNTING GROUNDS.
"I BECAME OBSESSED WITH FINDING THESE WORMHOLES SO I COULD EXPLORE AND FULLY MAP THE WHOLE MULTI-DIMENSIONAL UNIVERSE.
"I SOON DISCOVERED THAT DEPENDENCE ON THE CAPRICE OF NATURE WAS LIMITING AND RESTRICTIVE TO MY INVESTIGATIONS.
"ULTIMATELY, OF COURSE, THE WORMHOLES HAD TO BE CONTROLLED.
"THUS WAS MY *TEKNOLOGY* BORN.
CHF! CHF! SHPSSHHH!
"ONE PART STEAM HYDRAULICS. ONE PART ALCHEMY.
"BEFORE ANYONE KNEW IT... *POOF!*"
THE WHOLE MULTIVERSE WAS PLAYING TRICKLE-DOWN ECONOMICS UNDER THE TUTELAGE OF THE *TEKNOPHAGE*.

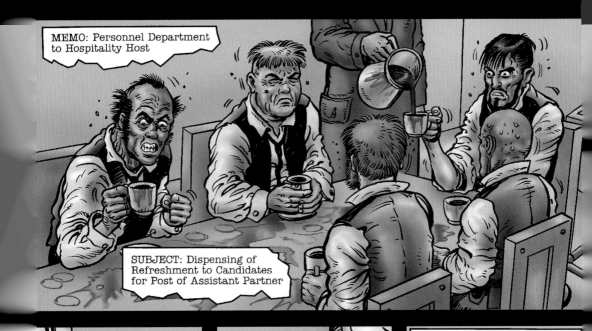

MEMO: Personnel Department to Hospitality Host

SUBJECT: Dispensing of Refreshment to Candidates for Post of Assistant Partner

INSTRUCTIONS: Each candidate's cup is to be filled with fresh-brewed Koffup at all times during competition.

Use only High Diuretic Koffup Grounds (Part #38A7MC) as provided with Hospitality Cart and Koffup Maker.

MEMO: Hospitality Host to Personnel Department

SUBJECT: Candidates' Refreshment Intake

MEMO: Personnel to Hospitality Host

Candidates for Assistant Partner were required to ingest capsules of time-release nerve gas (Part #793K65L8M) before joining the competition.

It has been noted that by the fourth hour of the planning and endurance meeting, Koffup intake was reduced dramatically by all candidates.

Some now exhibit reticence in consuming their required amounts of Koffup. Request instructions.

There is only one known antidote for Part #793K65L8M... continuous large quantities of Koffup.

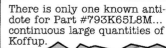

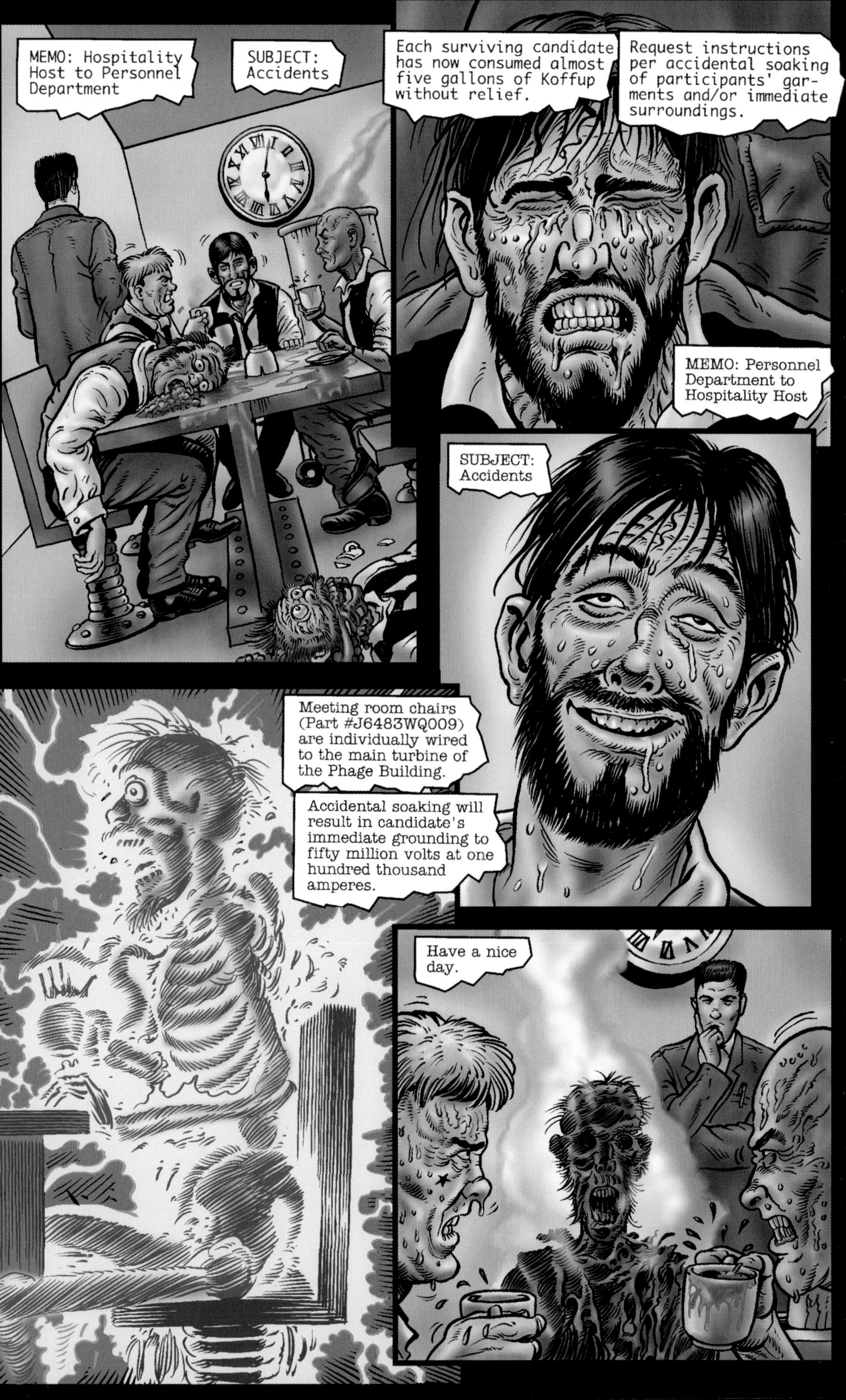
MEMO: Hospitality Host to Personnel Department
SUBJECT: Accidents
Each surviving candidate has now consumed almost five gallons of Koffup without relief.
Request instructions per accidental soaking of participants' garments and/or immediate surroundings.
MEMO: Personnel Department to Hospitality Host
SUBJECT: Accidents
Meeting room chairs (Part #J6483WQ009) are individually wired to the main turbine of the Phage Building.
Accidental soaking will result in candidate's immediate grounding to fifty million volts at one hundred thousand amperes.
Have a nice day.

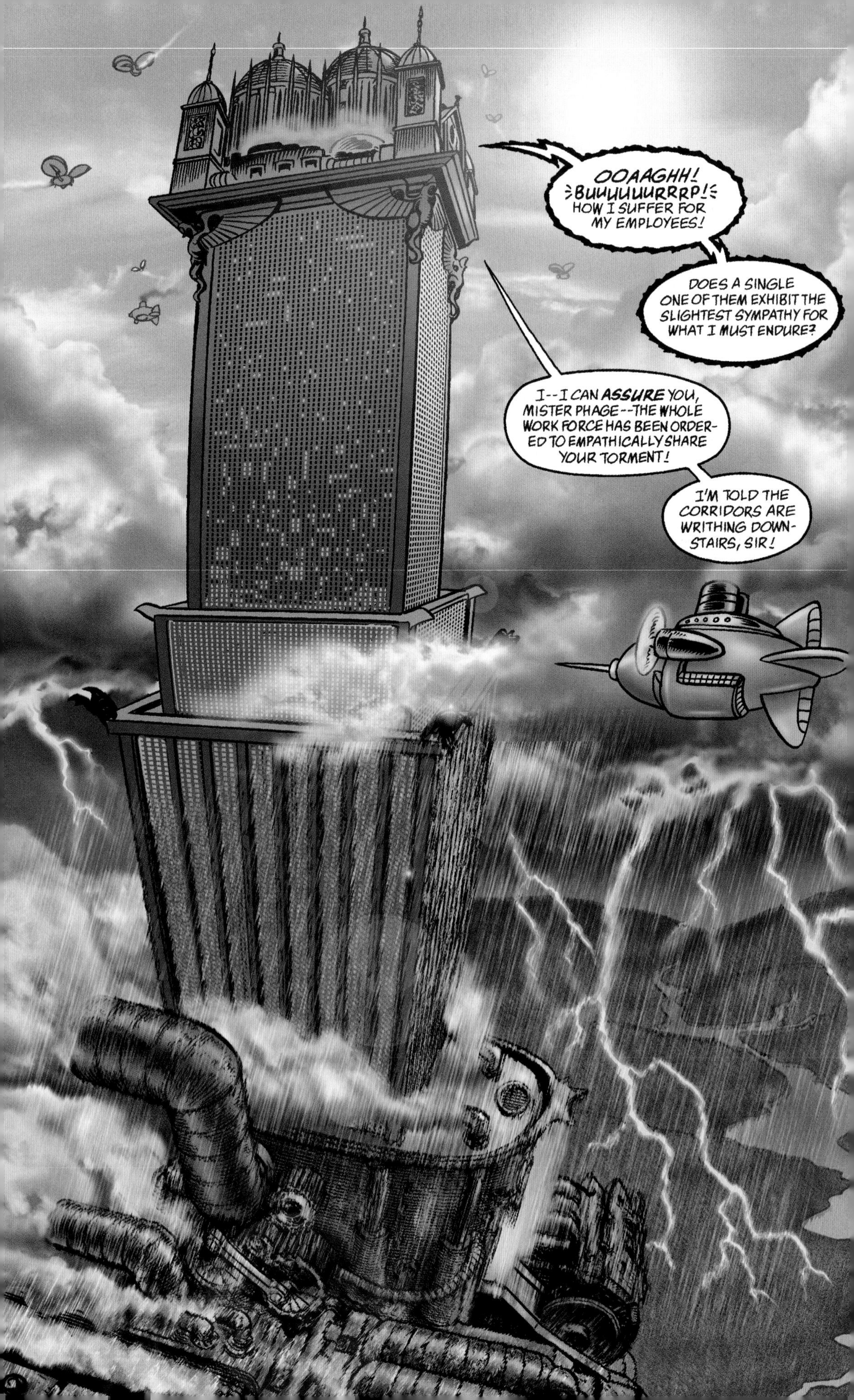
OOAAGHH! BUUUUUURRRP! HOW I SUFFER FOR MY EMPLOYEES!
DOES A SINGLE ONE OF THEM EXHIBIT THE SLIGHTEST SYMPATHY FOR WHAT I MUST ENDURE?
I--I CAN ASSURE YOU, MISTER PHAGE--THE WHOLE WORK FORCE HAS BEEN ORDERED TO EMPATHICALLY SHARE YOUR TORMENT!
I'M TOLD THE CORRIDORS ARE WRITHING DOWNSTAIRS, SIR!

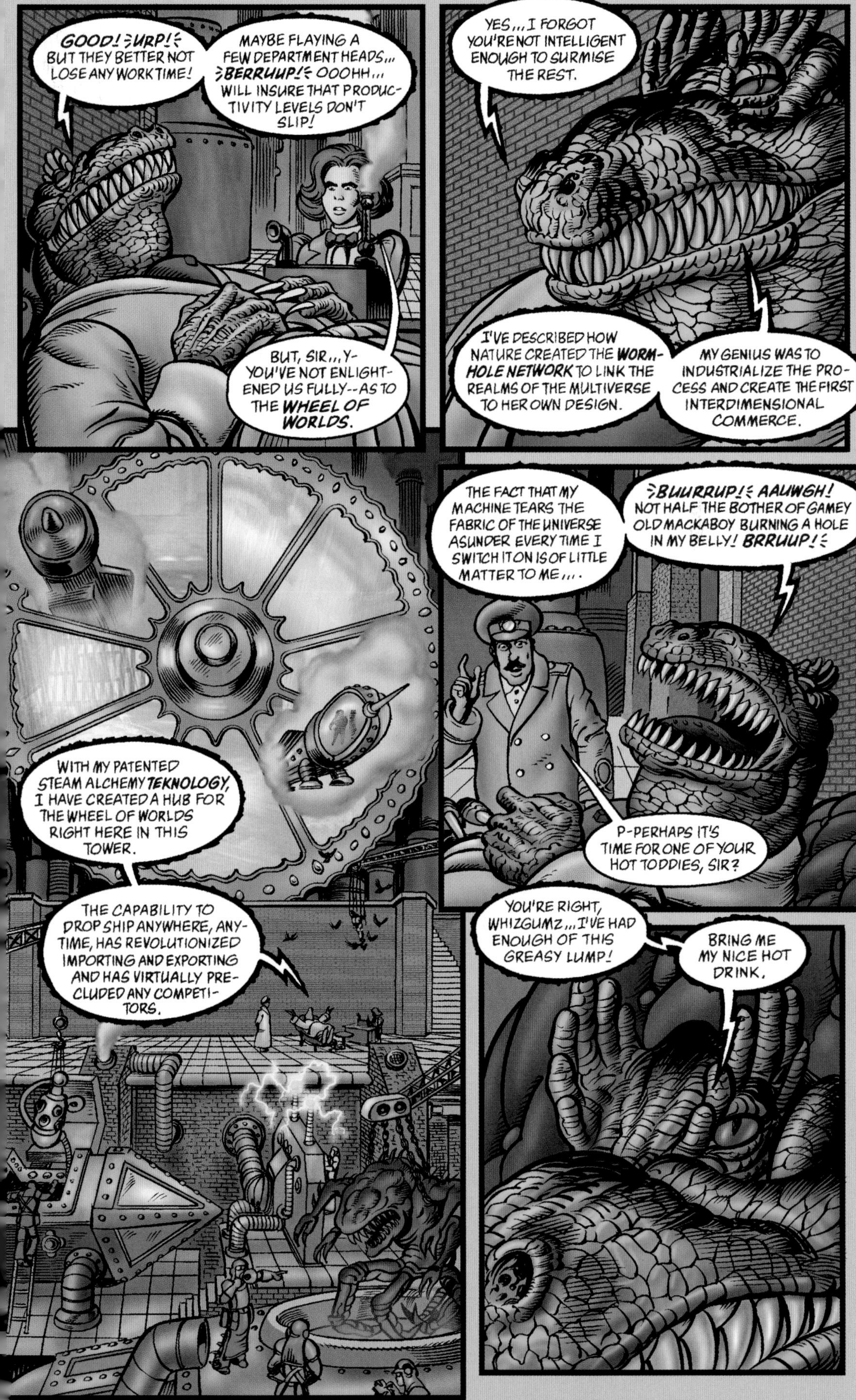
GOOD! ⸗URP!⸗ BUT THEY BETTER NOT LOSE ANY WORK TIME!
MAYBE FLAYING A FEW DEPARTMENT HEADS... ⸗BERRUUP!⸗ OOOHH... WILL INSURE THAT PRODUCTIVITY LEVELS DON'T SLIP!
BUT, SIR... Y-YOU'VE NOT ENLIGHTENED US FULLY--AS TO THE WHEEL OF WORLDS.
YES... I FORGOT YOU'RE NOT INTELLIGENT ENOUGH TO SURMISE THE REST.
I'VE DESCRIBED HOW NATURE CREATED THE WORMHOLE NETWORK TO LINK THE REALMS OF THE MULTIVERSE TO HER OWN DESIGN.
MY GENIUS WAS TO INDUSTRIALIZE THE PROCESS AND CREATE THE FIRST INTERDIMENSIONAL COMMERCE.
WITH MY PATENTED STEAM ALCHEMY TEKNOLOGY, I HAVE CREATED A HUB FOR THE WHEEL OF WORLDS RIGHT HERE IN THIS TOWER.
THE CAPABILITY TO DROP SHIP ANYWHERE, ANYTIME, HAS REVOLUTIONIZED IMPORTING AND EXPORTING AND HAS VIRTUALLY PRECLUDED ANY COMPETITORS.
THE FACT THAT MY MACHINE TEARS THE FABRIC OF THE UNIVERSE ASUNDER EVERY TIME I SWITCH IT ON IS OF LITTLE MATTER TO ME....
⸗BUURRUP!⸗ AAUWGH! NOT HALF THE BOTHER OF GAMEY OLD MACKABOY BURNING A HOLE IN MY BELLY! BRRUUP!⸗
P-PERHAPS IT'S TIME FOR ONE OF YOUR HOT TODDIES, SIR?
YOU'RE RIGHT, WHIZGUMZ... I'VE HAD ENOUGH OF THIS GREASY LUMP!
BRING ME MY NICE HOT DRINK.

MEMO: Middle Management Personnel Department to Partners

SUBECT: Status of Competition for Assistant Partner Position

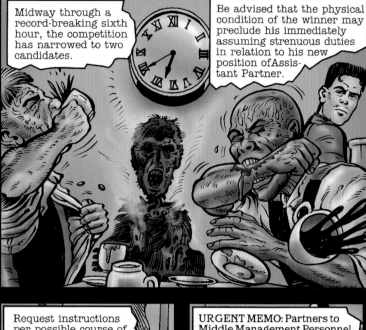

Midway through a record-breaking sixth hour, the competition has narrowed to two candidates.

Be advised that the physical condition of the winner may preclude his immediately assuming strenuous duties in relation to his new position of Assistant Partner.

Request instructions per possible course of action if successful candidate proves incapacitated.

URGENT MEMO: Partners to Middle Management Personnel Department

SUBJECT: Possible Incapacity of Successful Candidate for Assistant Partner

Please be advised that to be eligible for any promotion, employees must at all times conform to rigid physical requirements.

Individuals with infirmities that affect maximum productivity are not allowed any change in their employment status for up to one year from the date of the injury.

Note that severe damage, such as rupture to any internal organ, would render candidates ineligible for promotion to Assistant Partner under current company policy.

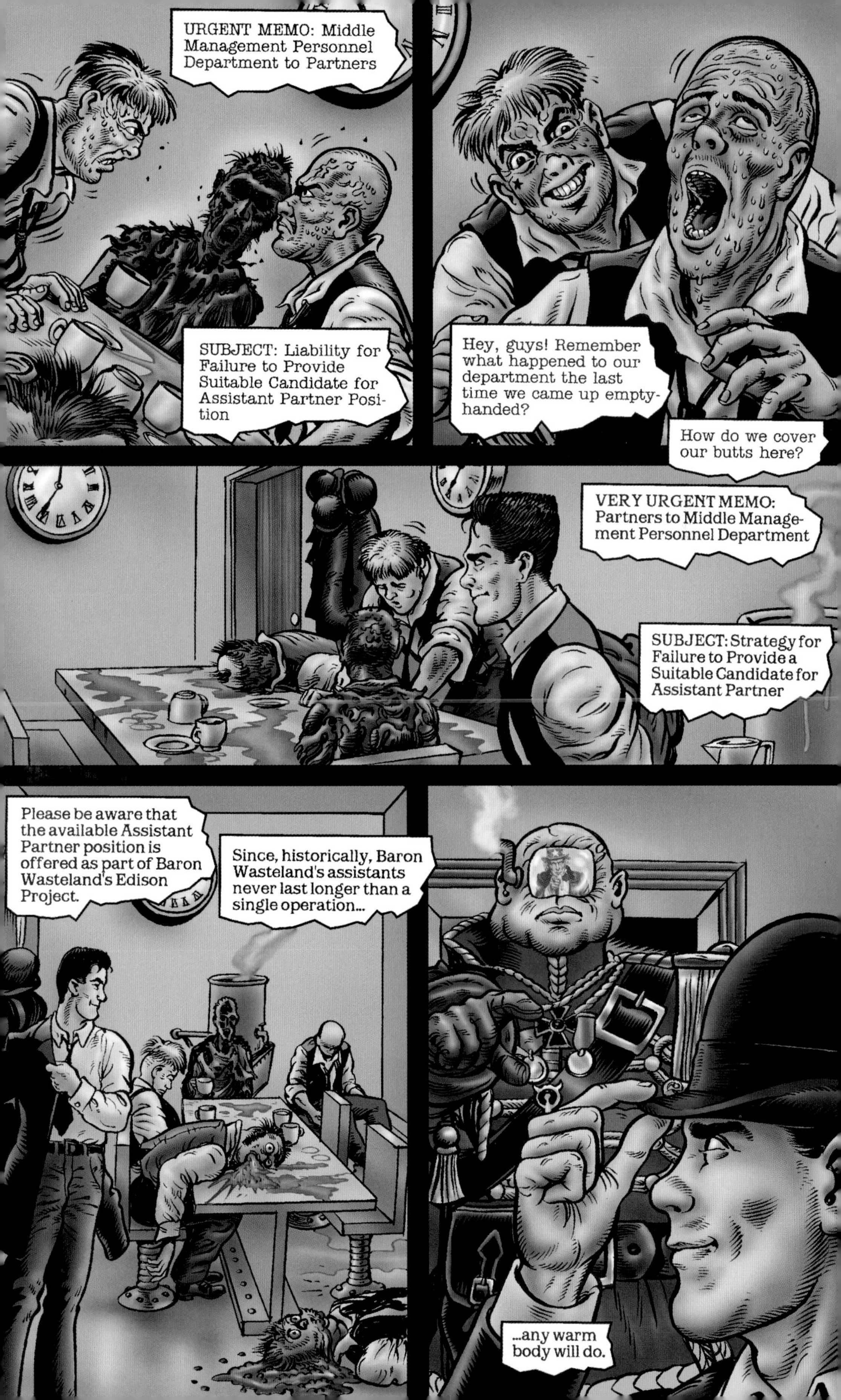
URGENT MEMO: Middle Management Personnel Department to Partners
SUBJECT: Liability for Failure to Provide Suitable Candidate for Assistant Partner Position
Hey, guys! Remember what happened to our department the last time we came up empty-handed?
How do we cover our butts here?
VERY URGENT MEMO: Partners to Middle Management Personnel Department
SUBJECT: Strategy for Failure to Provide a Suitable Candidate for Assistant Partner
Please be aware that the available Assistant Partner position is offered as part of Baron Wasteland's Edison Project.
Since, historically, Baron Wasteland's assistants never last longer than a single operation...
...any warm body will do.

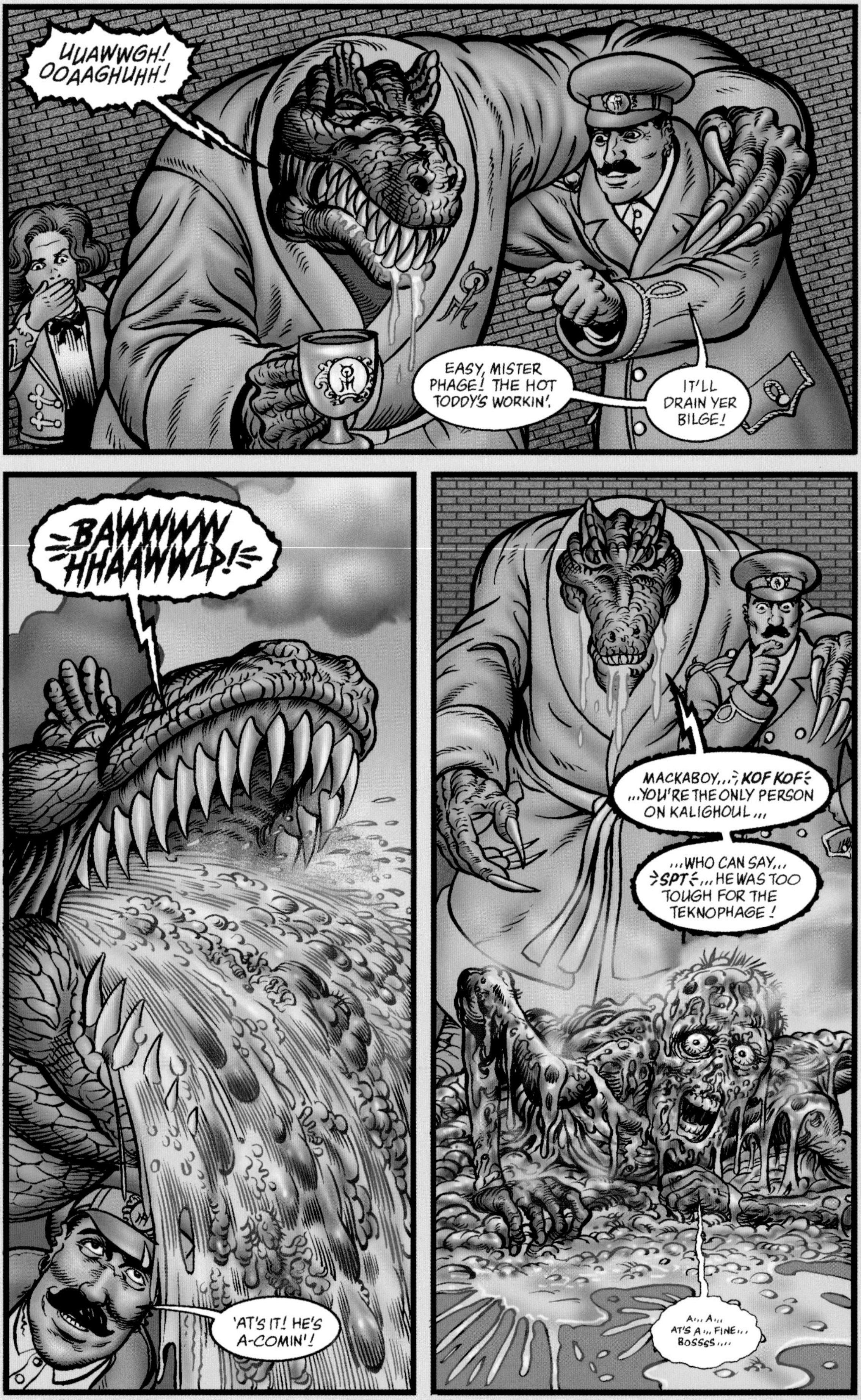
UUAWWGH! OOAAGHUHH!
EASY, MISTER PHAGE! THE HOT TODDY'S WORKIN'.
IT'LL DRAIN YER BILGE!
BAWWWN HHAAWWLP!
'AT'S IT! HE'S A-COMIN'!
MACKABOY... KOF KOF ...YOU'RE THE ONLY PERSON ON KALIGHOUL...
...WHO CAN SAY... SPT ... HE WAS TOO TOUGH FOR THE TEKNOPHAGE!
A... A... AT'S A... FINE... BOSSSS....

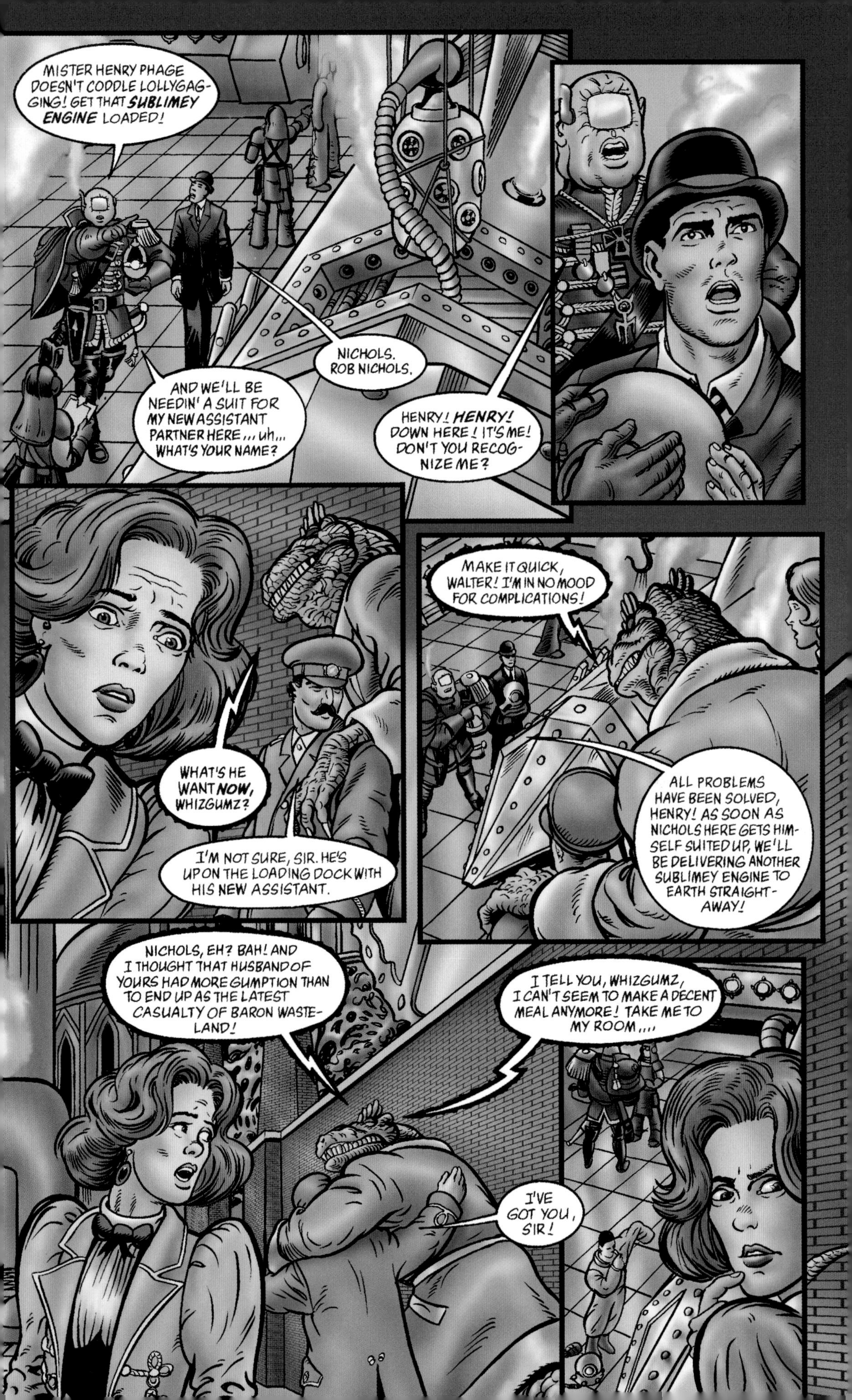
MISTER HENRY PHAGE DOESN'T CODDLE LOLLYGAGGING! GET THAT SUBLIMEY ENGINE LOADED!
AND WE'LL BE NEEDIN' A SUIT FOR MY NEW ASSISTANT PARTNER HERE ... uh... WHAT'S YOUR NAME?
NICHOLS. ROB NICHOLS.
HENRY! HENRY! DOWN HERE! IT'S ME! DON'T YOU RECOGNIZE ME?
WHAT'S HE WANT NOW, WHIZGUMZ?
I'M NOT SURE, SIR. HE'S UP ON THE LOADING DOCK WITH HIS NEW ASSISTANT.
MAKE IT QUICK, WALTER! I'M IN NO MOOD FOR COMPLICATIONS!
ALL PROBLEMS HAVE BEEN SOLVED, HENRY! AS SOON AS NICHOLS HERE GETS HIMSELF SUITED UP, WE'LL BE DELIVERING ANOTHER SUBLIMEY ENGINE TO EARTH STRAIGHT-AWAY!
NICHOLS, EH? BAH! AND I THOUGHT THAT HUSBAND OF YOURS HAD MORE GUMPTION THAN TO END UP AS THE LATEST CASUALTY OF BARON WASTELAND!
I TELL YOU, WHIZGUMZ, I CAN'T SEEM TO MAKE A DECENT MEAL ANYMORE! TAKE ME TO MY ROOM....
I'VE GOT YOU, SIR!

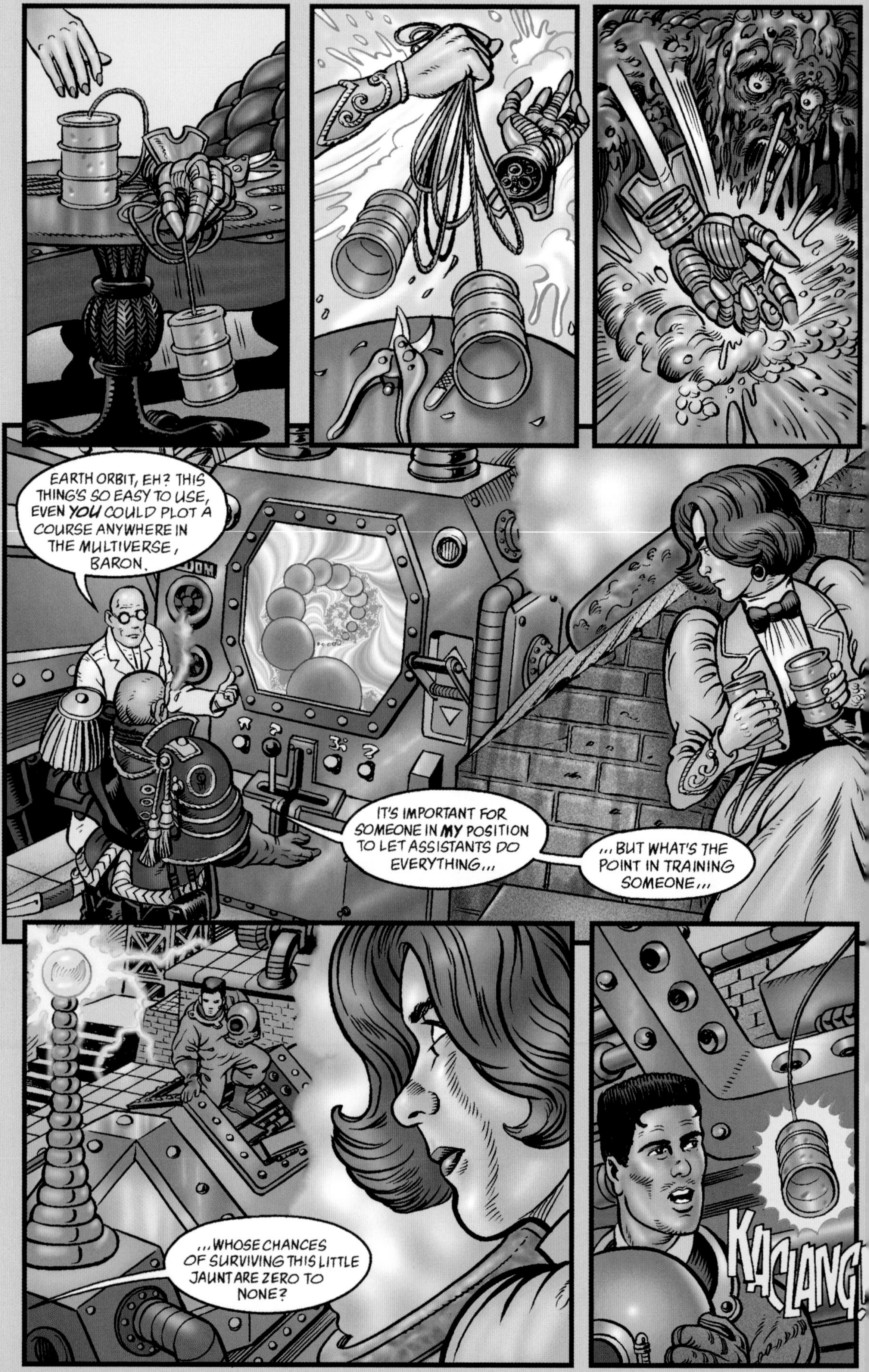
EARTH ORBIT, EH? THIS THING'S SO EASY TO USE, EVEN YOU COULD PLOT A COURSE ANYWHERE IN THE MULTIVERSE, BARON.
IT'S IMPORTANT FOR SOMEONE IN MY POSITION TO LET ASSISTANTS DO EVERYTHING...
...BUT WHAT'S THE POINT IN TRAINING SOMEONE...
...WHOSE CHANCES OF SURVIVING THIS LITTLE JAUNT ARE ZERO TO NONE?
KACLANG!

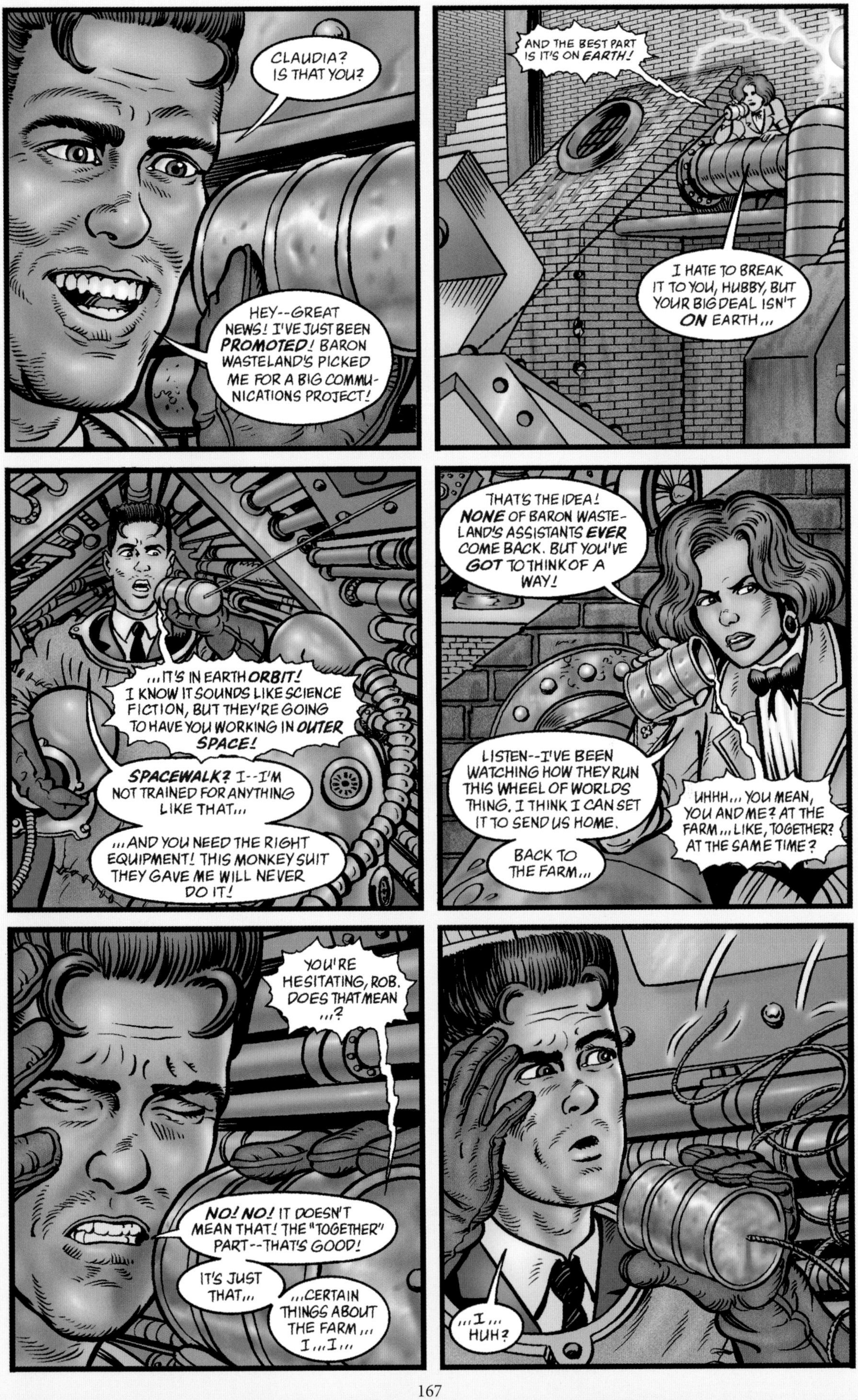
CLAUDIA? IS THAT YOU?
HEY--GREAT NEWS! I'VE JUST BEEN PROMOTED! BARON WASTELAND'S PICKED ME FOR A BIG COMMU-NICATIONS PROJECT!
AND THE BEST PART IS IT'S ON EARTH!
I HATE TO BREAK IT TO YOU, HUBBY, BUT YOUR BIG DEAL ISN'T ON EARTH...
...IT'S IN EARTH ORBIT! I KNOW IT SOUNDS LIKE SCIENCE FICTION, BUT THEY'RE GOING TO HAVE YOU WORKING IN OUTER SPACE!
SPACEWALK? I--I'M NOT TRAINED FOR ANYTHING LIKE THAT...
...AND YOU NEED THE RIGHT EQUIPMENT! THIS MONKEY SUIT THEY GAVE ME WILL NEVER DO IT!
THAT'S THE IDEA! NONE OF BARON WASTE-LAND'S ASSISTANTS EVER COME BACK. BUT YOU'VE GOT TO THINK OF A WAY!
LISTEN--I'VE BEEN WATCHING HOW THEY RUN THIS WHEEL OF WORLDS THING. I THINK I CAN SET IT TO SEND US HOME.
BACK TO THE FARM...
UHHH... YOU MEAN, YOU AND ME? AT THE FARM... LIKE, TOGETHER? AT THE SAME TIME?
YOU'RE HESITATING, ROB. DOES THAT MEAN ...?
NO! NO! IT DOESN'T MEAN THAT! THE "TOGETHER" PART--THAT'S GOOD!
IT'S JUST THAT...
...CERTAIN THINGS ABOUT THE FARM... I...I...
...I... HUH?

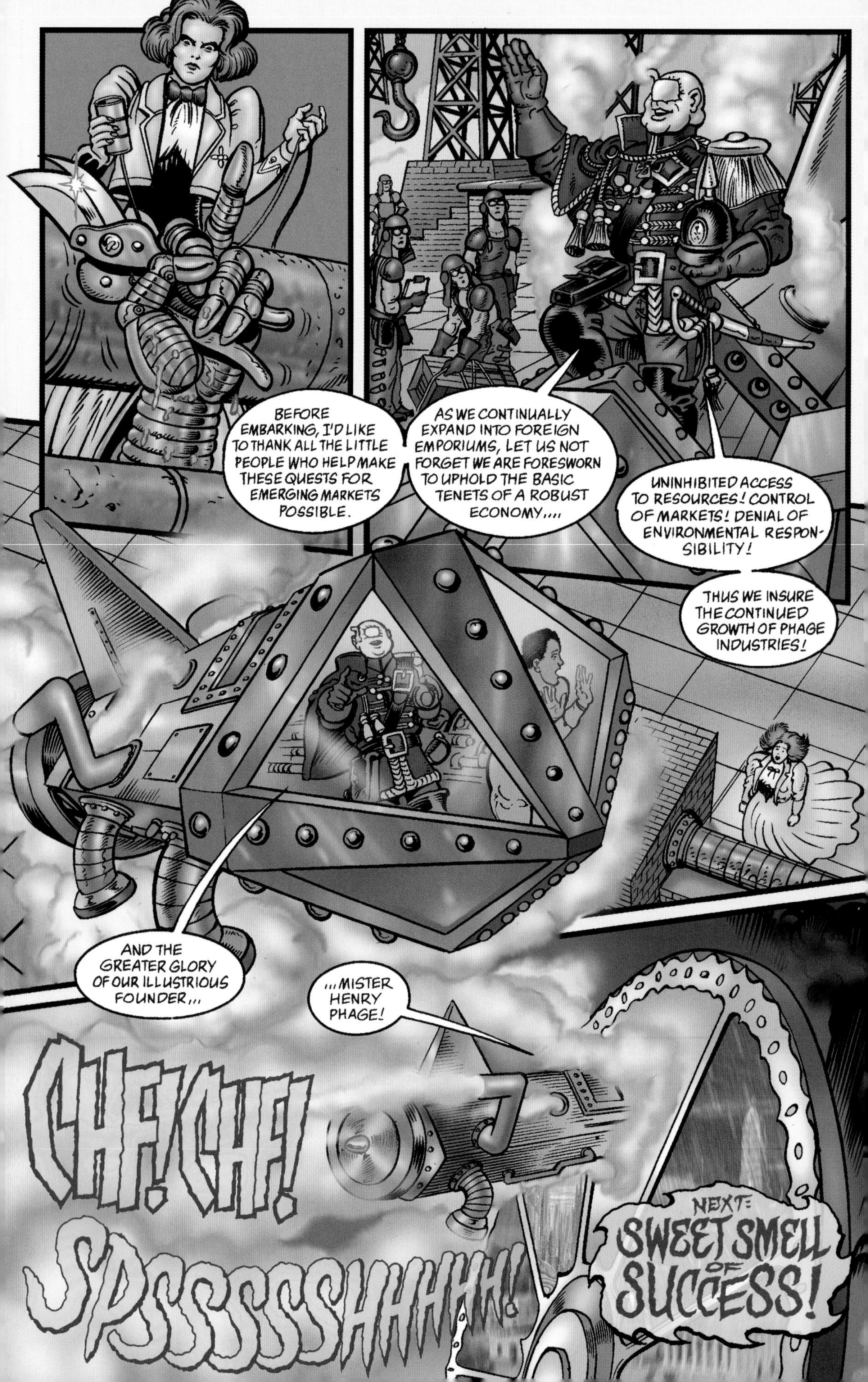
BEFORE EMBARKING, I'D LIKE TO THANK ALL THE LITTLE PEOPLE WHO HELP MAKE THESE QUESTS FOR EMERGING MARKETS POSSIBLE.
AS WE CONTINUALLY EXPAND INTO FOREIGN EMPORIUMS, LET US NOT FORGET WE ARE FORESWORN TO UPHOLD THE BASIC TENETS OF A ROBUST ECONOMY....
UNINHIBITED ACCESS TO RESOURCES! CONTROL OF MARKETS! DENIAL OF ENVIRONMENTAL RESPON-SIBILITY!
THUS WE INSURE THE CONTINUED GROWTH OF PHAGE INDUSTRIES!
AND THE GREATER GLORY OF OUR ILLUSTRIOUS FOUNDER...
...MISTER HENRY PHAGE!
CHF! CHF!
SPSSSSSSHHHHH!
NEXT: SWEET SMELL OF SUCCESS!

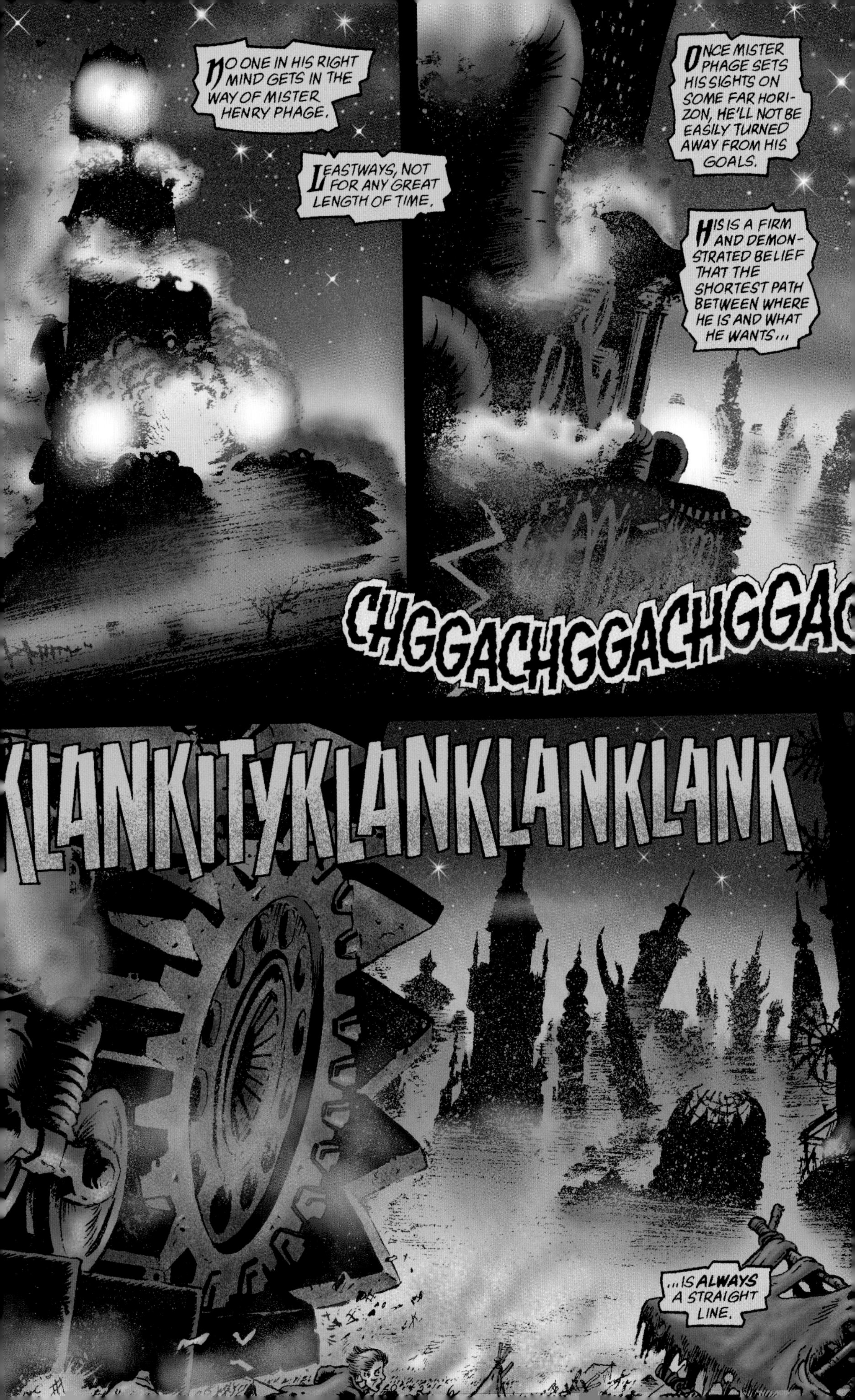
NO ONE IN HIS RIGHT MIND GETS IN THE WAY OF MISTER HENRY PHAGE.
LEASTWAYS, NOT FOR ANY GREAT LENGTH OF TIME.
ONCE MISTER PHAGE SETS HIS SIGHTS ON SOME FAR HORI-ZON, HE'LL NOT BE EASILY TURNED AWAY FROM HIS GOALS.
HIS IS A FIRM AND DEMON-STRATED BELIEF THAT THE SHORTEST PATH BETWEEN WHERE HE IS AND WHAT HE WANTS...
CHGGACHGGACHGGAC
KLANKITYKLANKLANKLANK
...IS ALWAYS A STRAIGHT LINE.

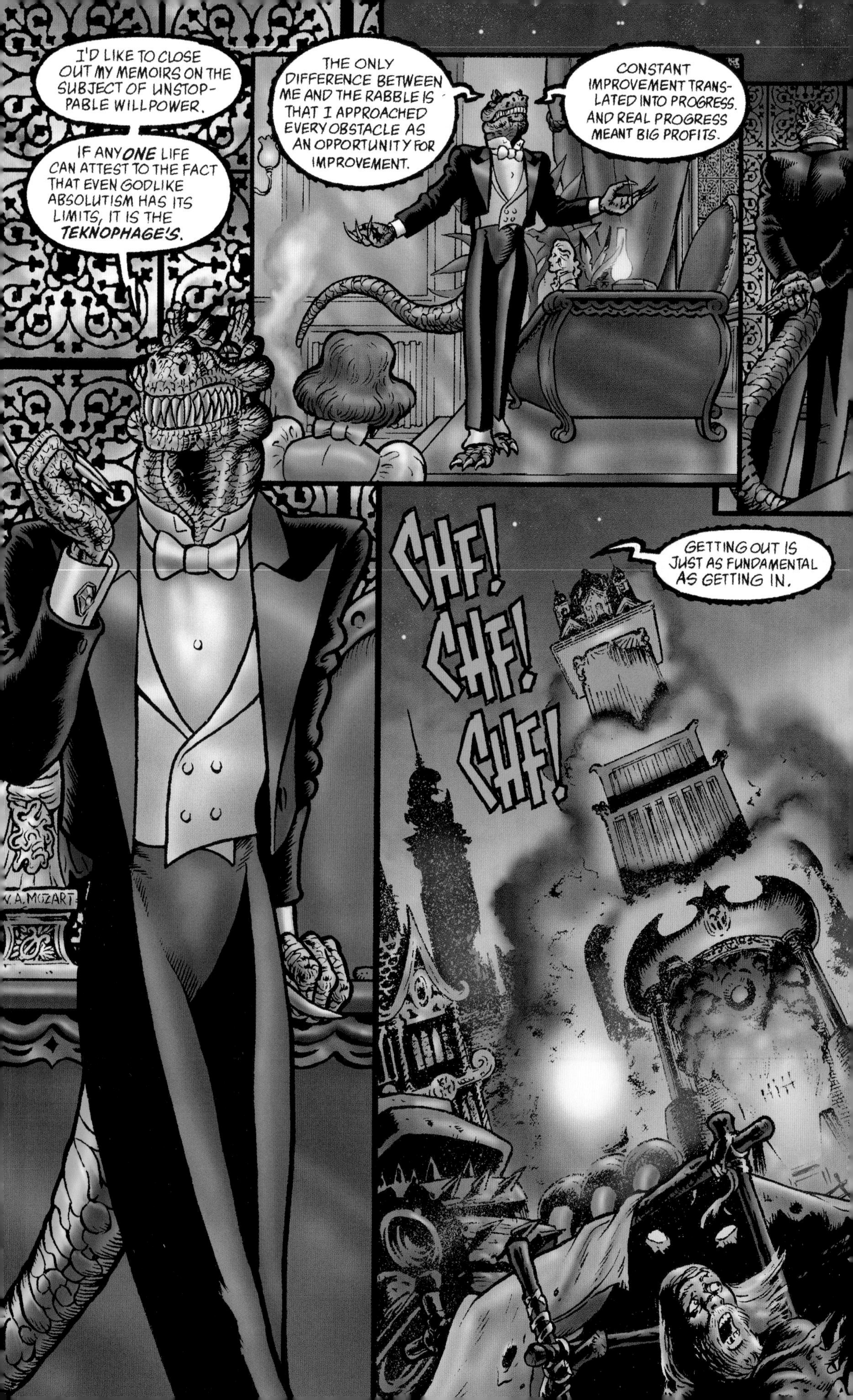
I'D LIKE TO CLOSE OUT MY MEMOIRS ON THE SUBJECT OF UNSTOP-PABLE WILLPOWER.
IF ANY ONE LIFE CAN ATTEST TO THE FACT THAT EVEN GODLIKE ABSOLUTISM HAS ITS LIMITS, IT IS THE TEKNOPHAGE'S.
THE ONLY DIFFERENCE BETWEEN ME AND THE RABBLE IS THAT I APPROACHED EVERY OBSTACLE AS AN OPPORTUNITY FOR IMPROVEMENT.
CONSTANT IMPROVEMENT TRANS-LATED INTO PROGRESS. AND REAL PROGRESS MEANT BIG PROFITS.
W. A. MOZART
CHF! CHF! CHF!
GETTING OUT IS JUST AS FUNDAMENTAL AS GETTING IN.

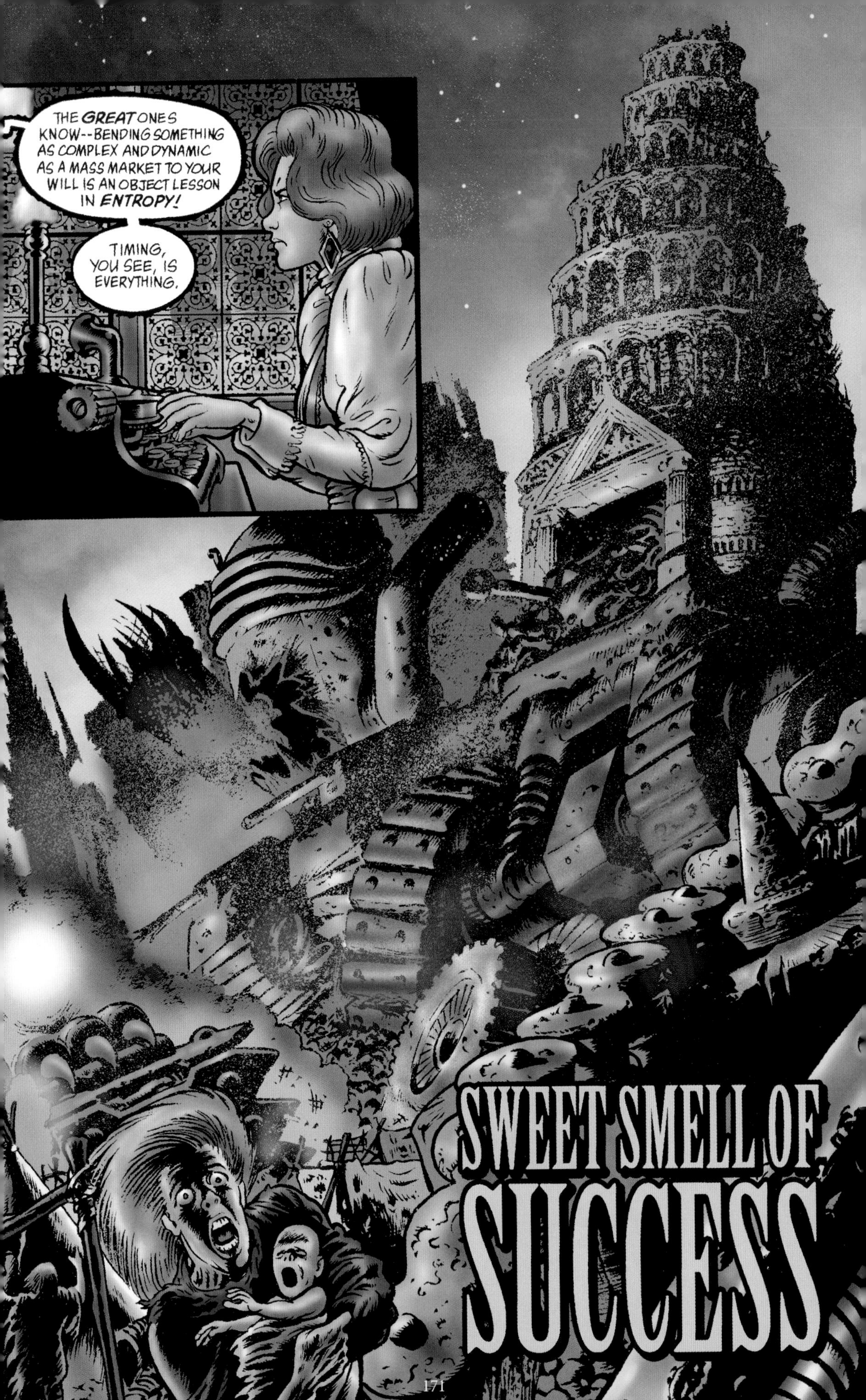
THE GREAT ONES KNOW--BENDING SOMETHING AS COMPLEX AND DYNAMIC AS A MASS MARKET TO YOUR WILL IS AN OBJECT LESSON IN ENTROPY!
TIMING, YOU SEE, IS EVERYTHING.
SWEET SMELL OF SUCCESS

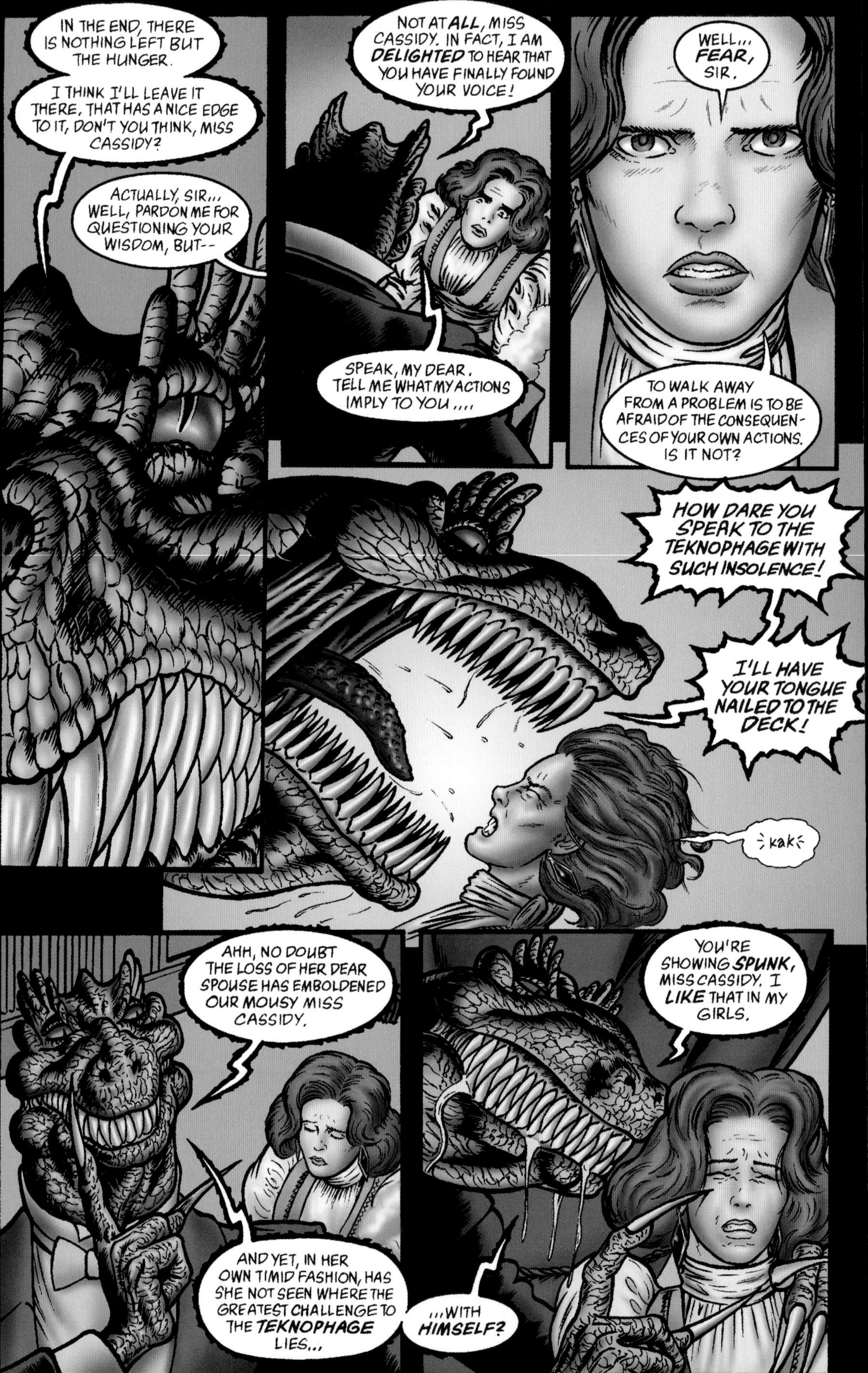
IN THE END, THERE IS NOTHING LEFT BUT THE HUNGER.
I THINK I'LL LEAVE IT THERE, THAT HAS A NICE EDGE TO IT, DON'T YOU THINK, MISS CASSIDY?
ACTUALLY, SIR... WELL, PARDON ME FOR QUESTIONING YOUR WISDOM, BUT--
NOT AT ALL, MISS CASSIDY. IN FACT, I AM DELIGHTED TO HEAR THAT YOU HAVE FINALLY FOUND YOUR VOICE!
SPEAK, MY DEAR. TELL ME WHAT MY ACTIONS IMPLY TO YOU....
WELL... FEAR, SIR.
TO WALK AWAY FROM A PROBLEM IS TO BE AFRAID OF THE CONSEQUENCES OF YOUR OWN ACTIONS. IS IT NOT?
HOW DARE YOU SPEAK TO THE TEKNOPHAGE WITH SUCH INSOLENCE!
I'LL HAVE YOUR TONGUE NAILED TO THE DECK!
kak
AHH, NO DOUBT THE LOSS OF HER DEAR SPOUSE HAS EMBOLDENED OUR MOUSY MISS CASSIDY.
AND YET, IN HER OWN TIMID FASHION, HAS SHE NOT SEEN WHERE THE GREATEST CHALLENGE TO THE TEKNOPHAGE LIES...
...WITH HIMSELF?
YOU'RE SHOWING SPUNK, MISS CASSIDY. I LIKE THAT IN MY GIRLS.

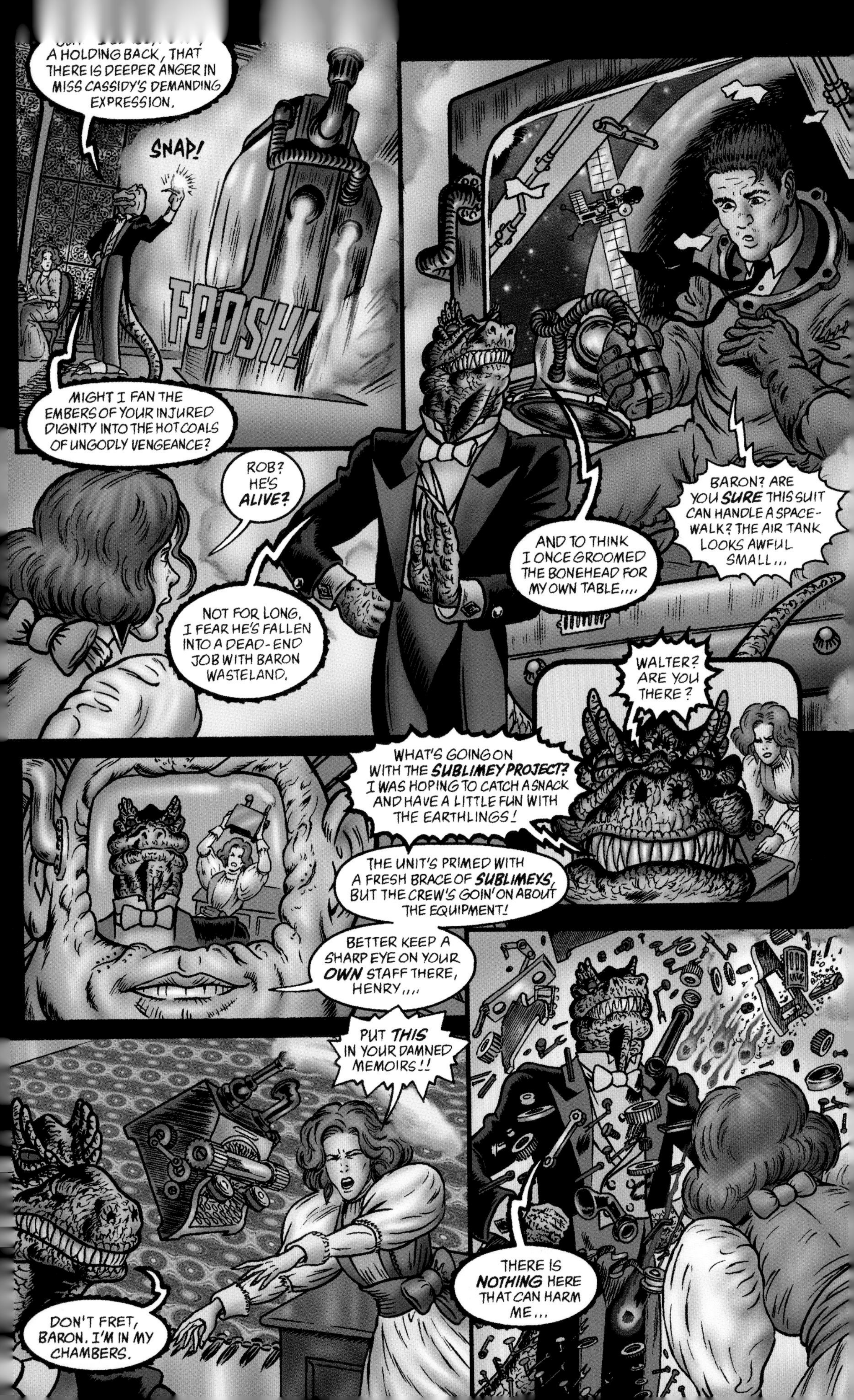
A HOLDING BACK, THAT THERE IS DEEPER ANGER IN MISS CASSIDY'S DEMANDING EXPRESSION.
SNAP!
FOOSH!
MIGHT I FAN THE EMBERS OF YOUR INJURED DIGNITY INTO THE HOT COALS OF UNGODLY VENGEANCE?
ROB? HE'S ALIVE?
NOT FOR LONG. I FEAR HE'S FALLEN INTO A DEAD-END JOB WITH BARON WASTELAND.
AND TO THINK I ONCE GROOMED THE BONEHEAD FOR MY OWN TABLE....
BARON? ARE YOU SURE THIS SUIT CAN HANDLE A SPACE-WALK? THE AIR TANK LOOKS AWFUL SMALL...
WALTER? ARE YOU THERE?
WHAT'S GOING ON WITH THE SUBLIMEY PROJECT? I WAS HOPING TO CATCH A SNACK AND HAVE A LITTLE FUN WITH THE EARTHLINGS!
THE UNIT'S PRIMED WITH A FRESH BRACE OF SUBLIMEYS, BUT THE CREW'S GOIN' ON ABOUT THE EQUIPMENT!
BETTER KEEP A SHARP EYE ON YOUR OWN STAFF THERE, HENRY....
PUT THIS IN YOUR DAMNED MEMOIRS!!
DON'T FRET, BARON. I'M IN MY CHAMBERS.
THERE IS NOTHING HERE THAT CAN HARM ME...

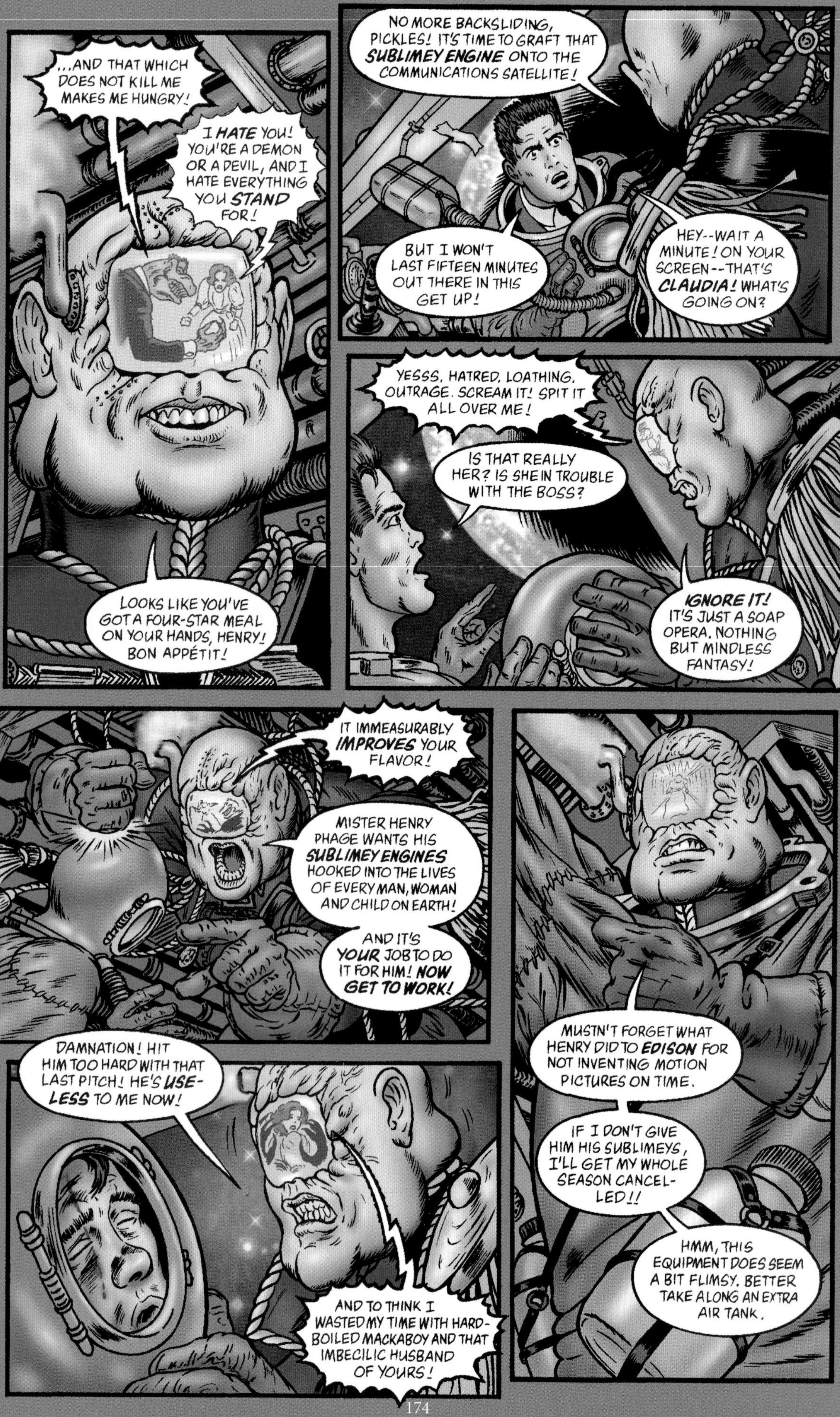
...AND THAT WHICH DOES NOT KILL ME MAKES ME HUNGRY!
I HATE YOU! YOU'RE A DEMON OR A DEVIL, AND I HATE EVERYTHING YOU STAND FOR!
LOOKS LIKE YOU'VE GOT A FOUR-STAR MEAL ON YOUR HANDS, HENRY! BON APPÉTIT!
NO MORE BACKSLIDING, PICKLES! IT'S TIME TO GRAFT THAT SUBLIMEY ENGINE ONTO THE COMMUNICATIONS SATELLITE!
BUT I WON'T LAST FIFTEEN MINUTES OUT THERE IN THIS GET UP!
HEY--WAIT A MINUTE! ON YOUR SCREEN--THAT'S CLAUDIA! WHAT'S GOING ON?
YESSS. HATRED. LOATHING. OUTRAGE. SCREAM IT! SPIT IT ALL OVER ME!
IS THAT REALLY HER? IS SHE IN TROUBLE WITH THE BOSS?
IGNORE IT! IT'S JUST A SOAP OPERA. NOTHING BUT MINDLESS FANTASY!
IT IMMEASURABLY IMPROVES YOUR FLAVOR!
MISTER HENRY PHAGE WANTS HIS SUBLIMEY ENGINES HOOKED INTO THE LIVES OF EVERY MAN, WOMAN AND CHILD ON EARTH!
AND IT'S YOUR JOB TO DO IT FOR HIM! NOW GET TO WORK!
DAMNATION! HIT HIM TOO HARD WITH THAT LAST PITCH! HE'S USE-LESS TO ME NOW!
AND TO THINK I WASTED MY TIME WITH HARD-BOILED MACKABOY AND THAT IMBECILIC HUSBAND OF YOURS!
MUSTN'T FORGET WHAT HENRY DID TO EDISON FOR NOT INVENTING MOTION PICTURES ON TIME.
IF I DON'T GIVE HIM HIS SUBLIMEYS, I'LL GET MY WHOLE SEASON CANCEL-LED!!
HMM, THIS EQUIPMENT DOES SEEM A BIT FLIMSY. BETTER TAKE ALONG AN EXTRA AIR TANK.

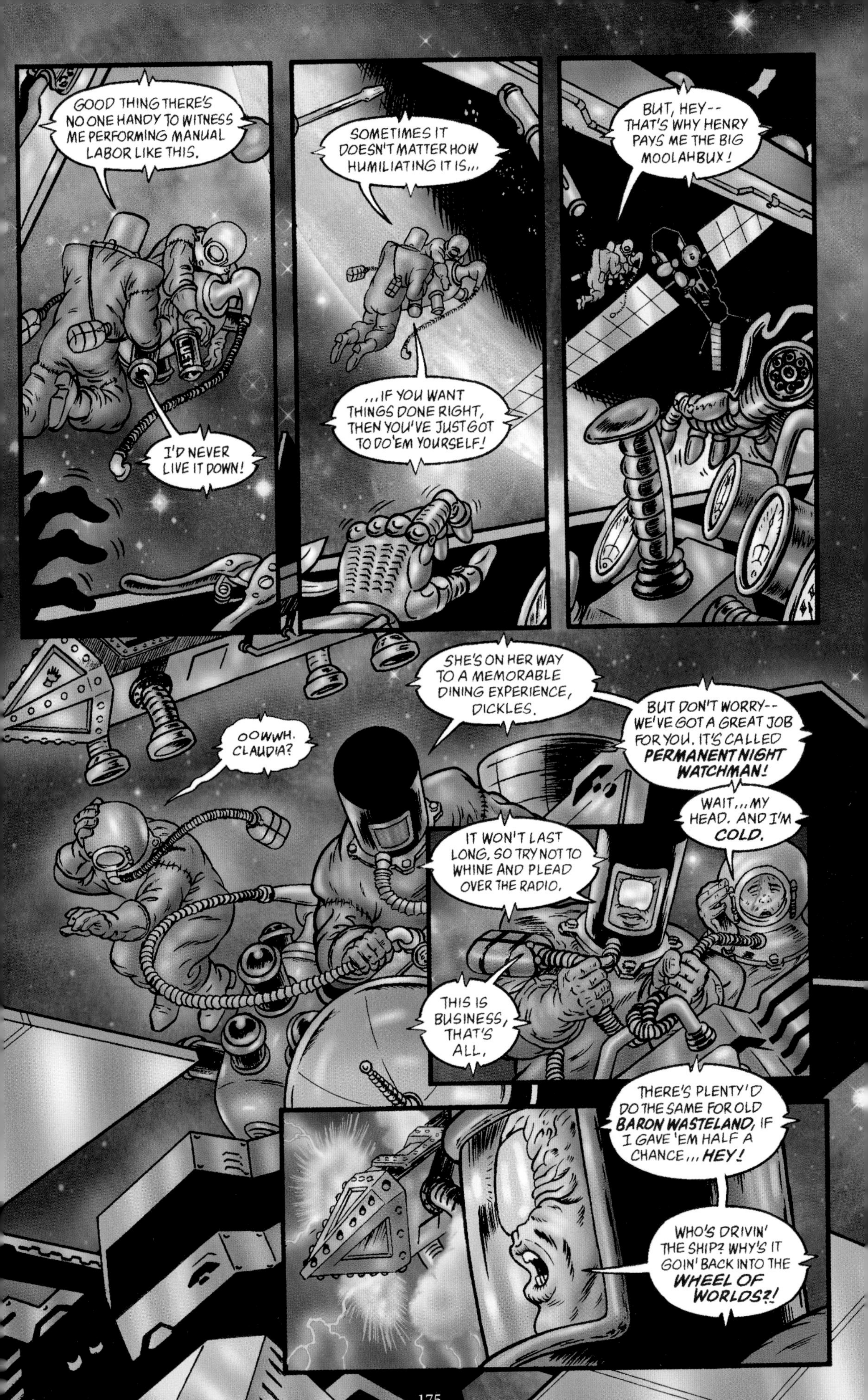
GOOD THING THERE'S NO ONE HANDY TO WITNESS ME PERFORMING MANUAL LABOR LIKE THIS.
I'D NEVER LIVE IT DOWN!
SOMETIMES IT DOESN'T MATTER HOW HUMILIATING IT IS...
...IF YOU WANT THINGS DONE RIGHT, THEN YOU'VE JUST GOT TO DO 'EM YOURSELF!
BUT, HEY-- THAT'S WHY HENRY PAYS ME THE BIG MOOLAHBUX!
OOWWH. CLAUDIA?
SHE'S ON HER WAY TO A MEMORABLE DINING EXPERIENCE, DICKLES.
BUT DON'T WORRY-- WE'VE GOT A GREAT JOB FOR YOU. IT'S CALLED PERMANENT NIGHT WATCHMAN!
IT WON'T LAST LONG, SO TRY NOT TO WHINE AND PLEAD OVER THE RADIO.
WAIT... MY HEAD. AND I'M COLD.
THIS IS BUSINESS, THAT'S ALL.
THERE'S PLENTY'D DO THE SAME FOR OLD BARON WASTELAND, IF I GAVE 'EM HALF A CHANCE... HEY!
WHO'S DRIVIN' THE SHIP? WHY'S IT GOIN' BACK INTO THE WHEEL OF WORLDS?!

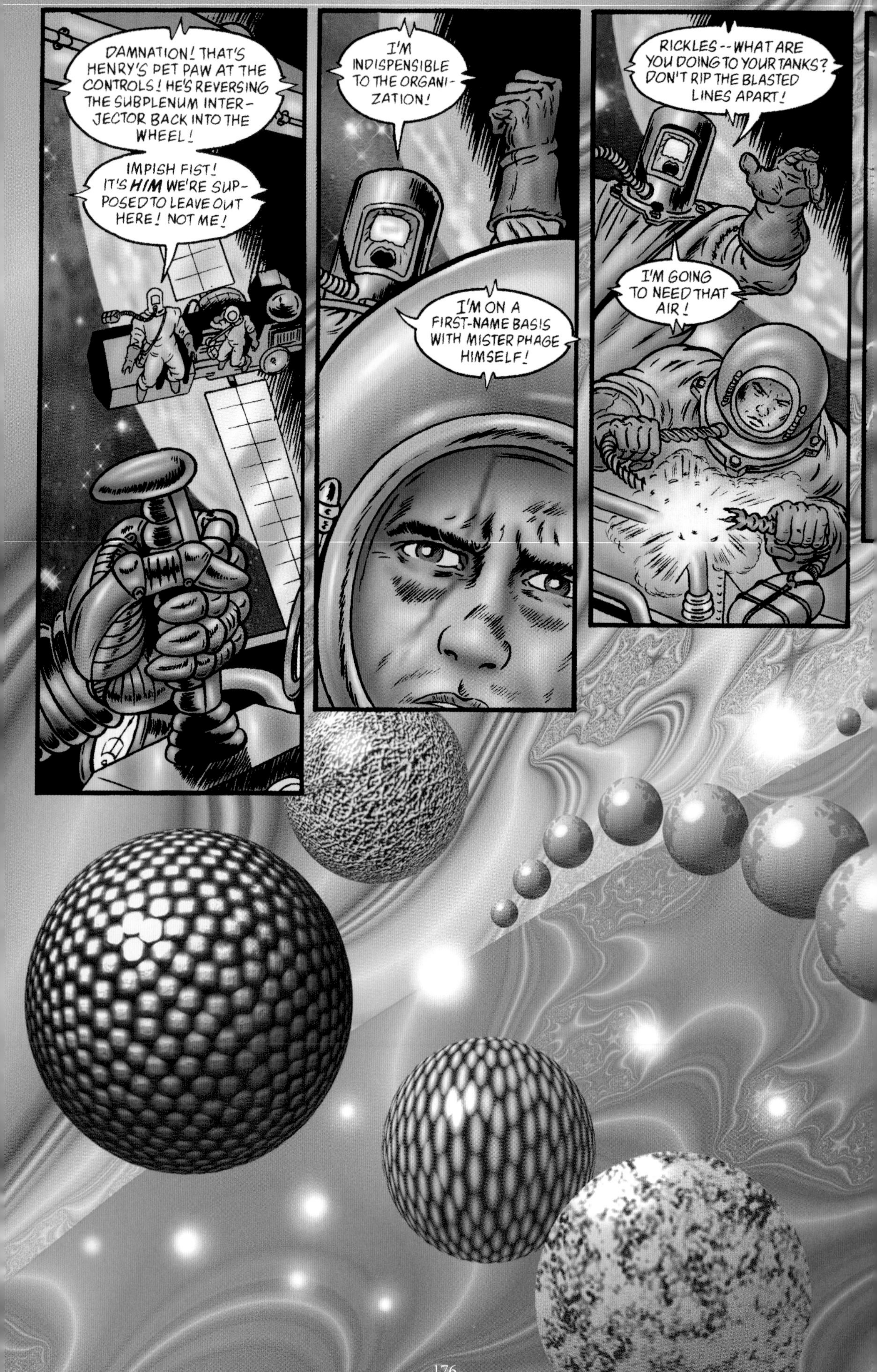
DAMNATION! THAT'S HENRY'S PET PAW AT THE CONTROLS! HE'S REVERSING THE SUBPLENUM INTER-JECTOR BACK INTO THE WHEEL!
IMPISH FIST! IT'S **HIM** WE'RE SUP-POSED TO LEAVE OUT HERE! NOT ME!
I'M INDISPENSIBLE TO THE ORGANI-ZATION!
I'M ON A FIRST-NAME BASIS WITH MISTER PHAGE HIMSELF!
RICKLES--WHAT ARE YOU DOING TO YOUR TANKS? DON'T RIP THE BLASTED LINES APART!
I'M GOING TO NEED THAT AIR!

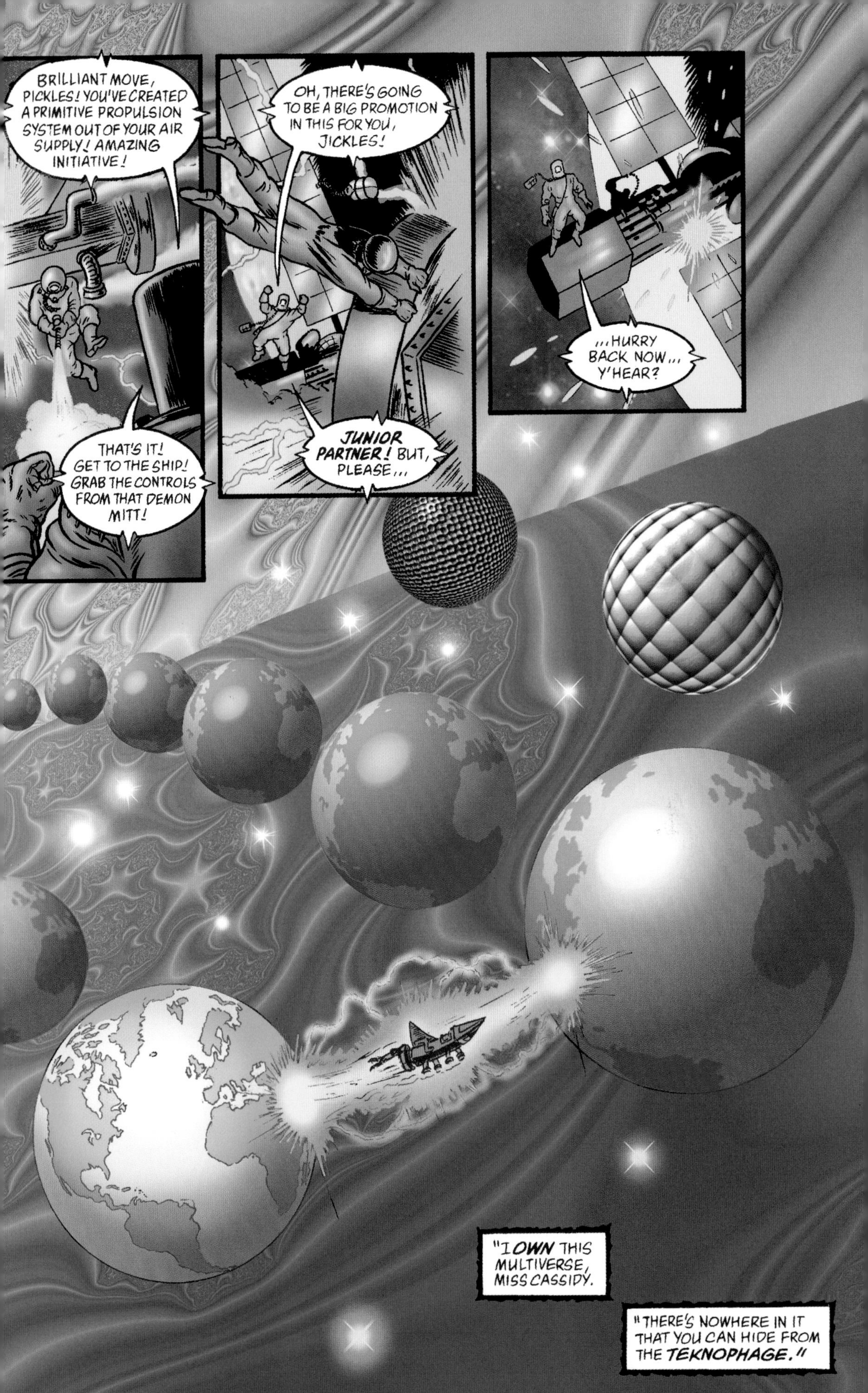

BRILLIANT MOVE, PICKLES! YOU'VE CREATED A PRIMITIVE PROPULSION SYSTEM OUT OF YOUR AIR SUPPLY! AMAZING INITIATIVE!
THAT'S IT! GET TO THE SHIP! GRAB THE CONTROLS FROM THAT DEMON MITT!
OH, THERE'S GOING TO BE A BIG PROMOTION IN THIS FOR YOU, JICKLES!
JUNIOR PARTNER! BUT, PLEASE...
...HURRY BACK NOW... Y'HEAR?
"I OWN THIS MULTIVERSE, MISS CASSIDY.
"THERE'S NOWHERE IN IT THAT YOU CAN HIDE FROM THE TEKNOPHAGE."

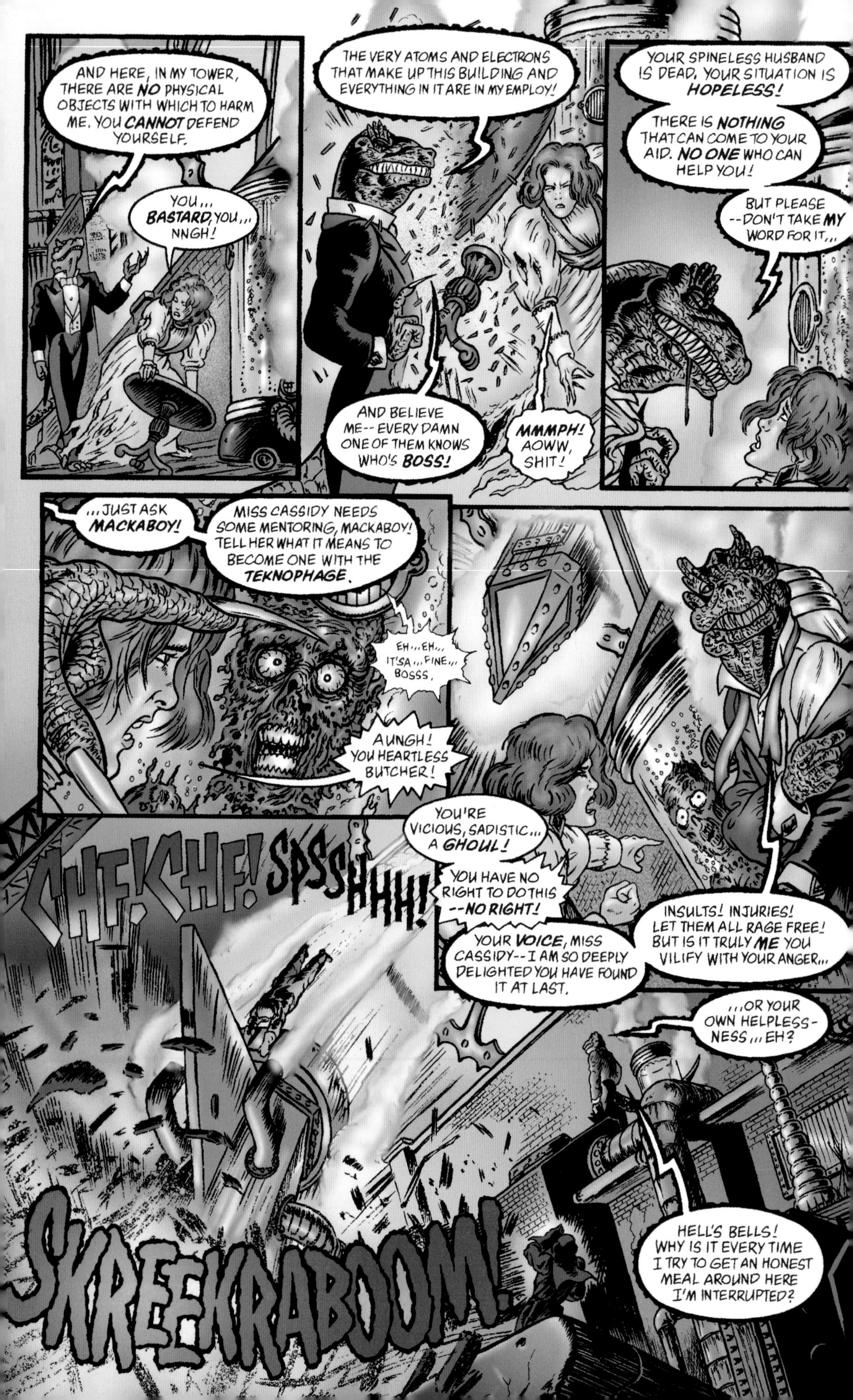
AND HERE, IN MY TOWER, THERE ARE NO PHYSICAL OBJECTS WITH WHICH TO HARM ME. YOU CANNOT DEFEND YOURSELF.
YOU... BASTARD, YOU... NNGH!
THE VERY ATOMS AND ELECTRONS THAT MAKE UP THIS BUILDING AND EVERYTHING IN IT ARE IN MY EMPLOY!
AND BELIEVE ME-- EVERY DAMN ONE OF THEM KNOWS WHO'S BOSS!
MMMPH! AOWW, SHIT!
YOUR SPINELESS HUSBAND IS DEAD. YOUR SITUATION IS HOPELESS!
THERE IS NOTHING THAT CAN COME TO YOUR AID. NO ONE WHO CAN HELP YOU!
BUT PLEASE --DON'T TAKE MY WORD FOR IT...
...JUST ASK MACKABOY!
MISS CASSIDY NEEDS SOME MENTORING, MACKABOY! TELL HER WHAT IT MEANS TO BECOME ONE WITH THE TEKNOPHAGE.
EH...EH... IT'SA...FINE... BOSSS.
AUNGH! YOU HEARTLESS BUTCHER!
YOU'RE VICIOUS, SADISTIC... A GHOUL!
YOU HAVE NO RIGHT TO DO THIS --NO RIGHT!
YOUR VOICE, MISS CASSIDY-- I AM SO DEEPLY DELIGHTED YOU HAVE FOUND IT AT LAST.
INSULTS! INJURIES! LET THEM ALL RAGE FREE! BUT IS IT TRULY ME YOU VILIFY WITH YOUR ANGER...
...OR YOUR OWN HELPLESS-NESS... EH?
CHF! CHF! SPSSHHH!
SKREEKRABOOM!
HELL'S BELLS! WHY IS IT EVERY TIME I TRY TO GET AN HONEST MEAL AROUND HERE I'M INTERRUPTED?

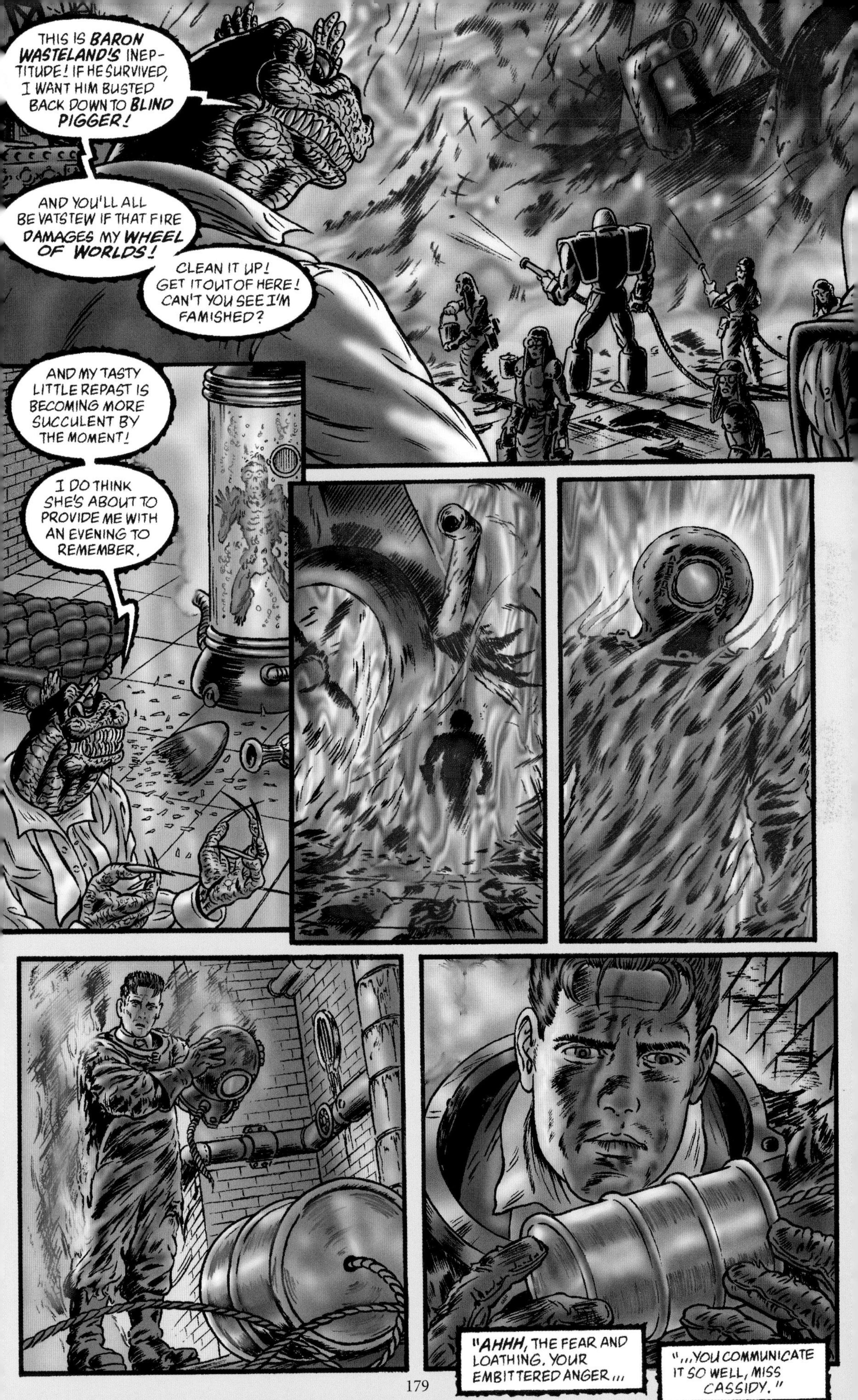

THIS IS BARON WASTELAND'S INEPTITUDE! IF HE SURVIVED, I WANT HIM BUSTED BACK DOWN TO BLIND PIGGER!
AND YOU'LL ALL BE VATSTEW IF THAT FIRE DAMAGES MY WHEEL OF WORLDS!
CLEAN IT UP! GET IT OUT OF HERE! CAN'T YOU SEE I'M FAMISHED?
AND MY TASTY LITTLE REPAST IS BECOMING MORE SUCCULENT BY THE MOMENT!
I DO THINK SHE'S ABOUT TO PROVIDE ME WITH AN EVENING TO REMEMBER.
"AHHH, THE FEAR AND LOATHING. YOUR EMBITTERED ANGER...
"...YOU COMMUNICATE IT SO WELL, MISS CASSIDY."

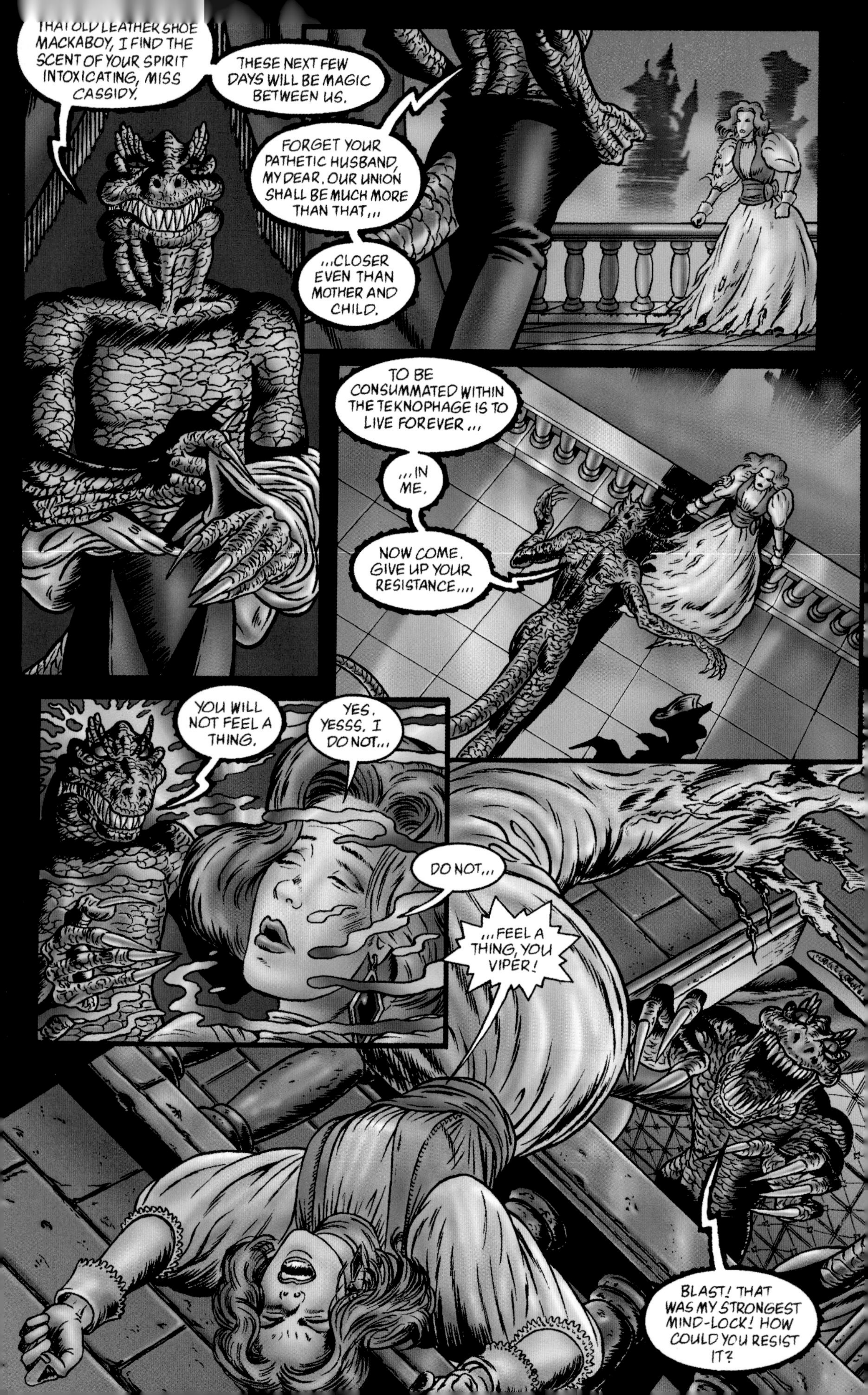
THAT OLD LEATHER SHOE MACKABOY, I FIND THE SCENT OF YOUR SPIRIT INTOXICATING, MISS CASSIDY.
THESE NEXT FEW DAYS WILL BE MAGIC BETWEEN US.
FORGET YOUR PATHETIC HUSBAND, MY DEAR. OUR UNION SHALL BE MUCH MORE THAN THAT...
...CLOSER EVEN THAN MOTHER AND CHILD.
TO BE CONSUMMATED WITHIN THE TEKNOPHAGE IS TO LIVE FOREVER...
...IN ME.
NOW COME. GIVE UP YOUR RESISTANCE....
YOU WILL NOT FEEL A THING.
YES. YESSS. I DO NOT...
DO NOT...
...FEEL A THING, YOU VIPER!
BLAST! THAT WAS MY STRONGEST MIND-LOCK! HOW COULD YOU RESIST IT?

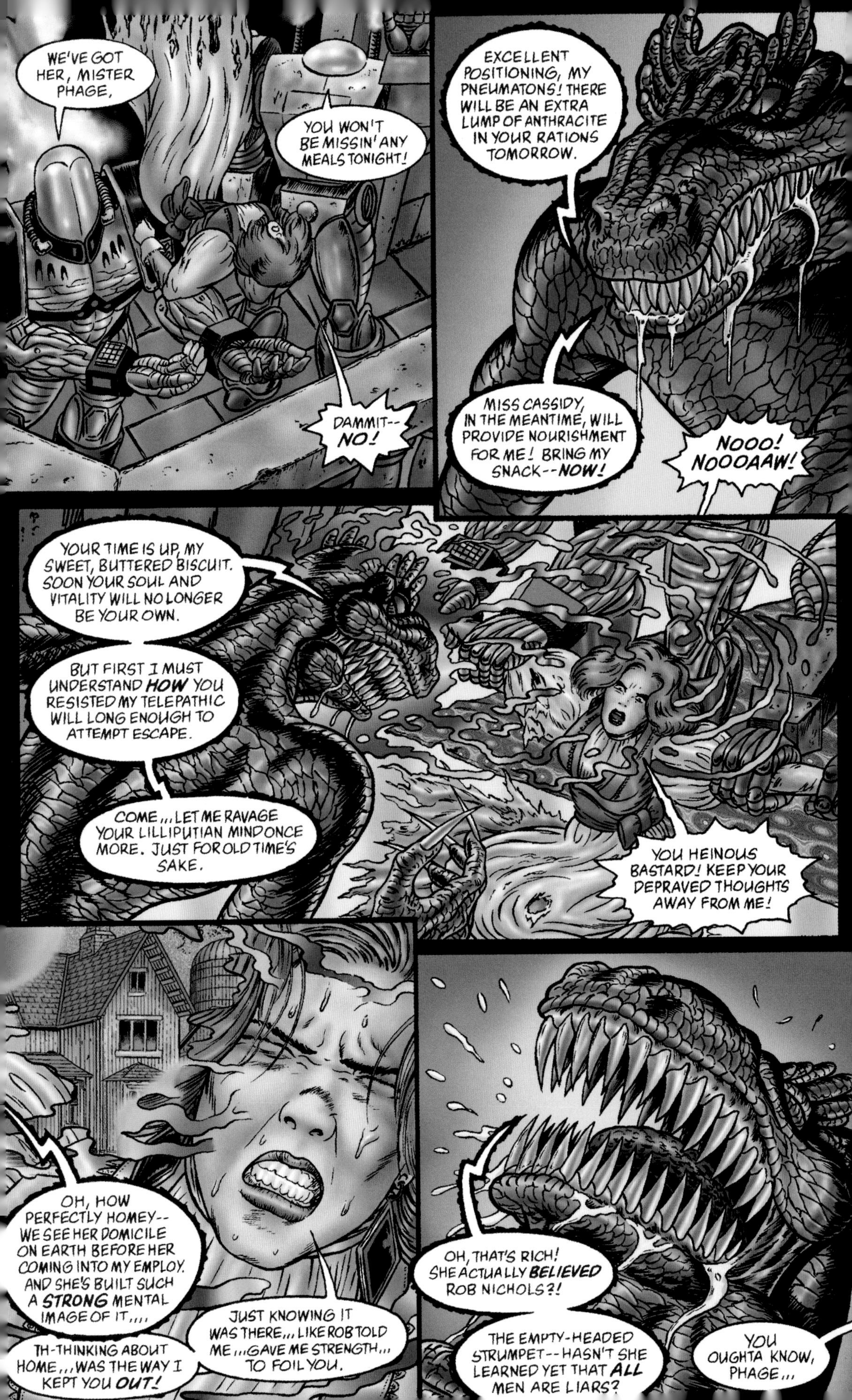
WE'VE GOT HER, MISTER PHAGE,
YOU WON'T BE MISSIN' ANY MEALS TONIGHT!
DAMMIT-- NO!
EXCELLENT POSITIONING, MY PNEUMATONS! THERE WILL BE AN EXTRA LUMP OF ANTHRACITE IN YOUR RATIONS TOMORROW.
MISS CASSIDY, IN THE MEANTIME, WILL PROVIDE NOURISHMENT FOR ME! BRING MY SNACK--NOW!
NOOO! NOOOAAW!
YOUR TIME IS UP, MY SWEET, BUTTERED BISCUIT. SOON YOUR SOUL AND VITALITY WILL NO LONGER BE YOUR OWN.
BUT FIRST I MUST UNDERSTAND HOW YOU RESISTED MY TELEPATHIC WILL LONG ENOUGH TO ATTEMPT ESCAPE.
COME... LET ME RAVAGE YOUR LILLIPUTIAN MIND ONCE MORE. JUST FOR OLD TIME'S SAKE.
YOU HEINOUS BASTARD! KEEP YOUR DEPRAVED THOUGHTS AWAY FROM ME!
OH, HOW PERFECTLY HOMEY-- WE SEE HER DOMICILE ON EARTH BEFORE HER COMING INTO MY EMPLOY. AND SHE'S BUILT SUCH A STRONG MENTAL IMAGE OF IT....
TH-THINKING ABOUT HOME... WAS THE WAY I KEPT YOU OUT!
JUST KNOWING IT WAS THERE... LIKE ROB TOLD ME... GAVE ME STRENGTH... TO FOIL YOU.
OH, THAT'S RICH! SHE ACTUALLY BELIEVED ROB NICHOLS?!
THE EMPTY-HEADED STRUMPET--HASN'T SHE LEARNED YET THAT ALL MEN ARE LIARS?
YOU OUGHTA KNOW, PHAGE...

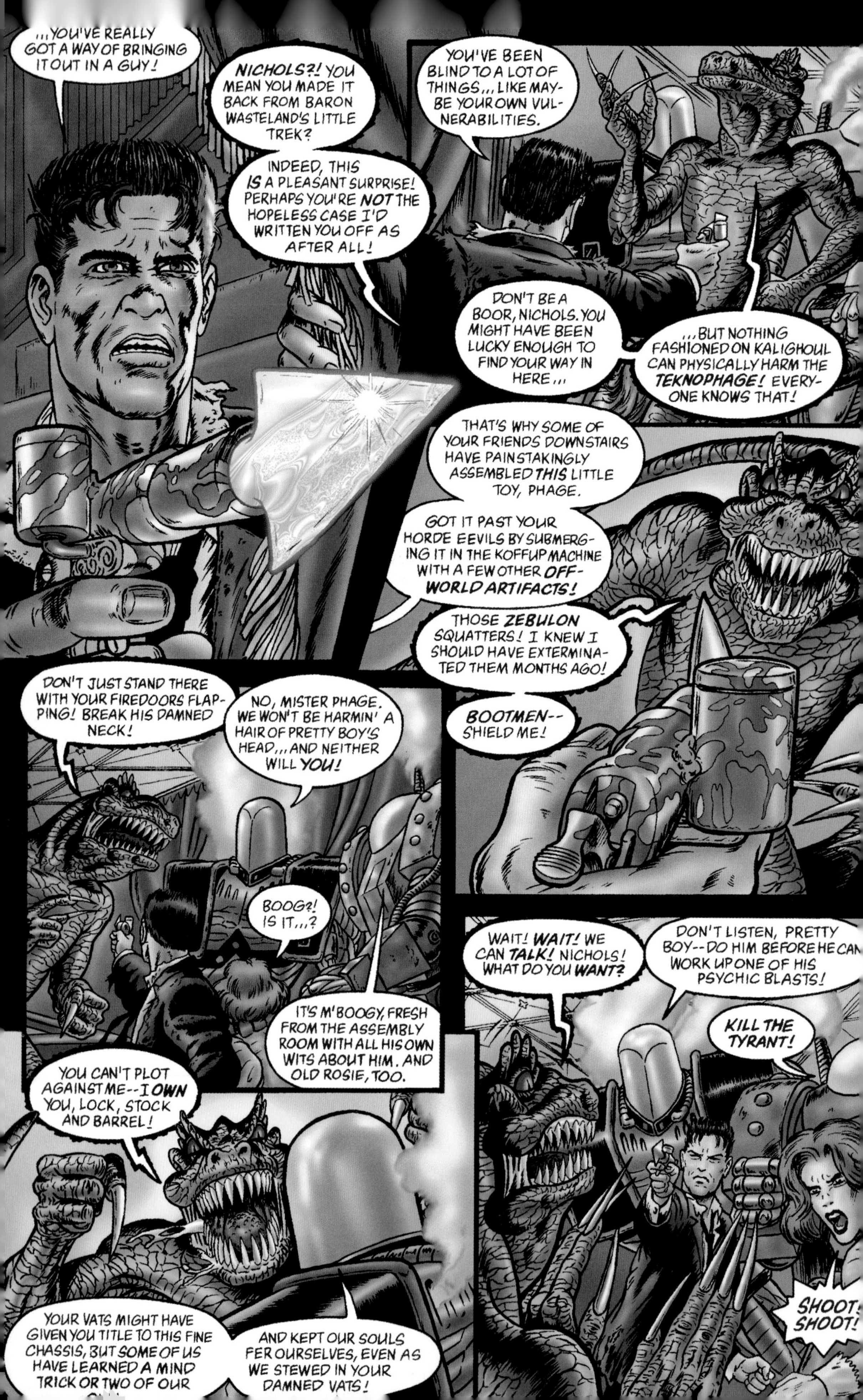
...YOU'VE REALLY GOT A WAY OF BRINGING IT OUT IN A GUY!
NICHOLS?! YOU MEAN YOU MADE IT BACK FROM BARON WASTELAND'S LITTLE TREK?
INDEED, THIS IS A PLEASANT SURPRISE! PERHAPS YOU'RE NOT THE HOPELESS CASE I'D WRITTEN YOU OFF AS AFTER ALL!
YOU'VE BEEN BLIND TO A LOT OF THINGS... LIKE MAY-BE YOUR OWN VUL-NERABILITIES.
DON'T BE A BOOR, NICHOLS. YOU MIGHT HAVE BEEN LUCKY ENOUGH TO FIND YOUR WAY IN HERE...
...BUT NOTHING FASHIONED ON KALIGHOUL CAN PHYSICALLY HARM THE TEKNOPHAGE! EVERY-ONE KNOWS THAT!
THAT'S WHY SOME OF YOUR FRIENDS DOWNSTAIRS HAVE PAINSTAKINGLY ASSEMBLED THIS LITTLE TOY, PHAGE.
GOT IT PAST YOUR HORDE EEVILS BY SUBMERG-ING IT IN THE KOFFUP MACHINE WITH A FEW OTHER OFF-WORLD ARTIFACTS!
THOSE ZEBULON SQUATTERS! I KNEW I SHOULD HAVE EXTERMINA-TED THEM MONTHS AGO!
BOOTMEN-- SHIELD ME!
DON'T JUST STAND THERE WITH YOUR FIREDOORS FLAP-PING! BREAK HIS DAMNED NECK!
NO, MISTER PHAGE. WE WON'T BE HARMIN' A HAIR OF PRETTY BOY'S HEAD... AND NEITHER WILL YOU!
BOOG?! IS IT...?
IT'S M'BOOGY, FRESH FROM THE ASSEMBLY ROOM WITH ALL HIS OWN WITS ABOUT HIM. AND OLD ROSIE, TOO.
YOU CAN'T PLOT AGAINST ME--I OWN YOU, LOCK, STOCK AND BARREL!
YOUR VATS MIGHT HAVE GIVEN YOU TITLE TO THIS FINE CHASSIS, BUT SOME OF US HAVE LEARNED A MIND TRICK OR TWO OF OUR
AND KEPT OUR SOULS FER OURSELVES, EVEN AS WE STEWED IN YOUR DAMNED VATS!
WAIT! WAIT! WE CAN TALK! NICHOLS! WHAT DO YOU WANT?
DON'T LISTEN, PRETTY BOY--DO HIM BEFORE HE CAN WORK UP ONE OF HIS PSYCHIC BLASTS!
KILL THE TYRANT!
SHOOT! SHOOT!

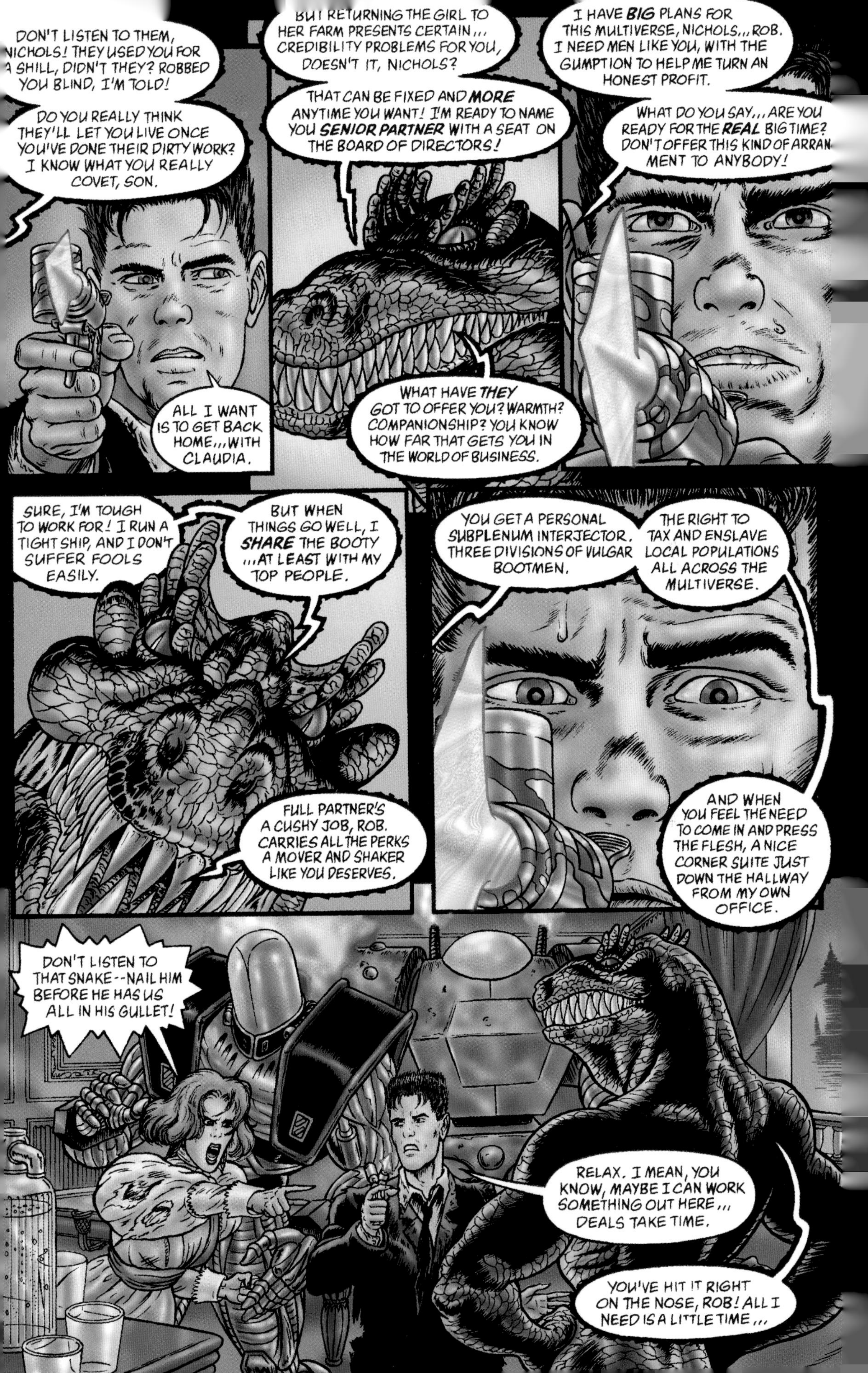
DON'T LISTEN TO THEM, NICHOLS! THEY USED YOU FOR A SHILL, DIDN'T THEY? ROBBED YOU BLIND, I'M TOLD!
DO YOU REALLY THINK THEY'LL LET YOU LIVE ONCE YOU'VE DONE THEIR DIRTY WORK? I KNOW WHAT YOU REALLY COVET, SON.
ALL I WANT IS TO GET BACK HOME,,,WITH CLAUDIA.
BUT RETURNING THE GIRL TO HER FARM PRESENTS CERTAIN,,, CREDIBILITY PROBLEMS FOR YOU, DOESN'T IT, NICHOLS?
THAT CAN BE FIXED AND MORE ANYTIME YOU WANT! I'M READY TO NAME YOU SENIOR PARTNER WITH A SEAT ON THE BOARD OF DIRECTORS!
WHAT HAVE THEY GOT TO OFFER YOU? WARMTH? COMPANIONSHIP? YOU KNOW HOW FAR THAT GETS YOU IN THE WORLD OF BUSINESS.
I HAVE BIG PLANS FOR THIS MULTIVERSE, NICHOLS,,, ROB. I NEED MEN LIKE YOU, WITH THE GUMPTION TO HELP ME TURN AN HONEST PROFIT.
WHAT DO YOU SAY,,, ARE YOU READY FOR THE REAL BIG TIME? DON'T OFFER THIS KIND OF ARRAN-MENT TO ANYBODY!
SURE, I'M TOUGH TO WORK FOR! I RUN A TIGHT SHIP, AND I DON'T SUFFER FOOLS EASILY.
BUT WHEN THINGS GO WELL, I SHARE THE BOOTY ,,,AT LEAST WITH MY TOP PEOPLE.
FULL PARTNER'S A CUSHY JOB, ROB. CARRIES ALL THE PERKS A MOVER AND SHAKER LIKE YOU DESERVES.
YOU GET A PERSONAL SUBPLENUM INTERJECTOR. THREE DIVISIONS OF VULGAR BOOTMEN.
THE RIGHT TO TAX AND ENSLAVE LOCAL POPULATIONS ALL ACROSS THE MULTIVERSE.
AND WHEN YOU FEEL THE NEED TO COME IN AND PRESS THE FLESH, A NICE CORNER SUITE JUST DOWN THE HALLWAY FROM MY OWN OFFICE.
DON'T LISTEN TO THAT SNAKE--NAIL HIM BEFORE HE HAS US ALL IN HIS GULLET!
RELAX. I MEAN, YOU KNOW, MAYBE I CAN WORK SOMETHING OUT HERE,,, DEALS TAKE TIME.
YOU'VE HIT IT RIGHT ON THE NOSE, ROB! ALL I NEED IS A LITTLE TIME,,,

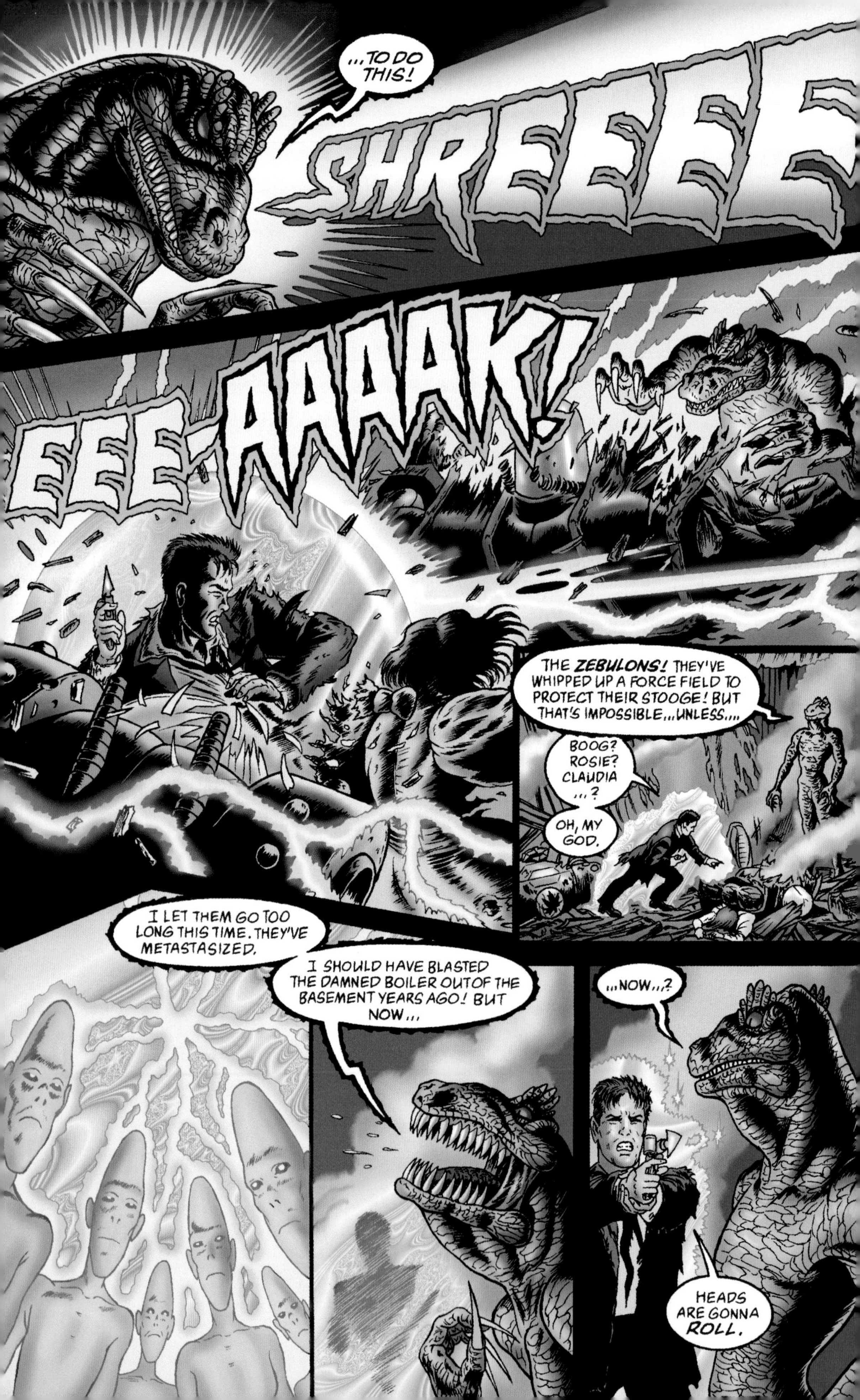

...TO DO THIS!
SHREEEE
EEE-AAAAK!
THE ZEBULONS! THEY'VE WHIPPED UP A FORCE FIELD TO PROTECT THEIR STOOGE! BUT THAT'S IMPOSSIBLE... UNLESS...
BOOG? ROSIE? CLAUDIA...?
OH, MY GOD.
I LET THEM GO TOO LONG THIS TIME. THEY'VE METASTASIZED.
I SHOULD HAVE BLASTED THE DAMNED BOILER OUT OF THE BASEMENT YEARS AGO! BUT NOW...
...NOW...?
HEADS ARE GONNA ROLL.

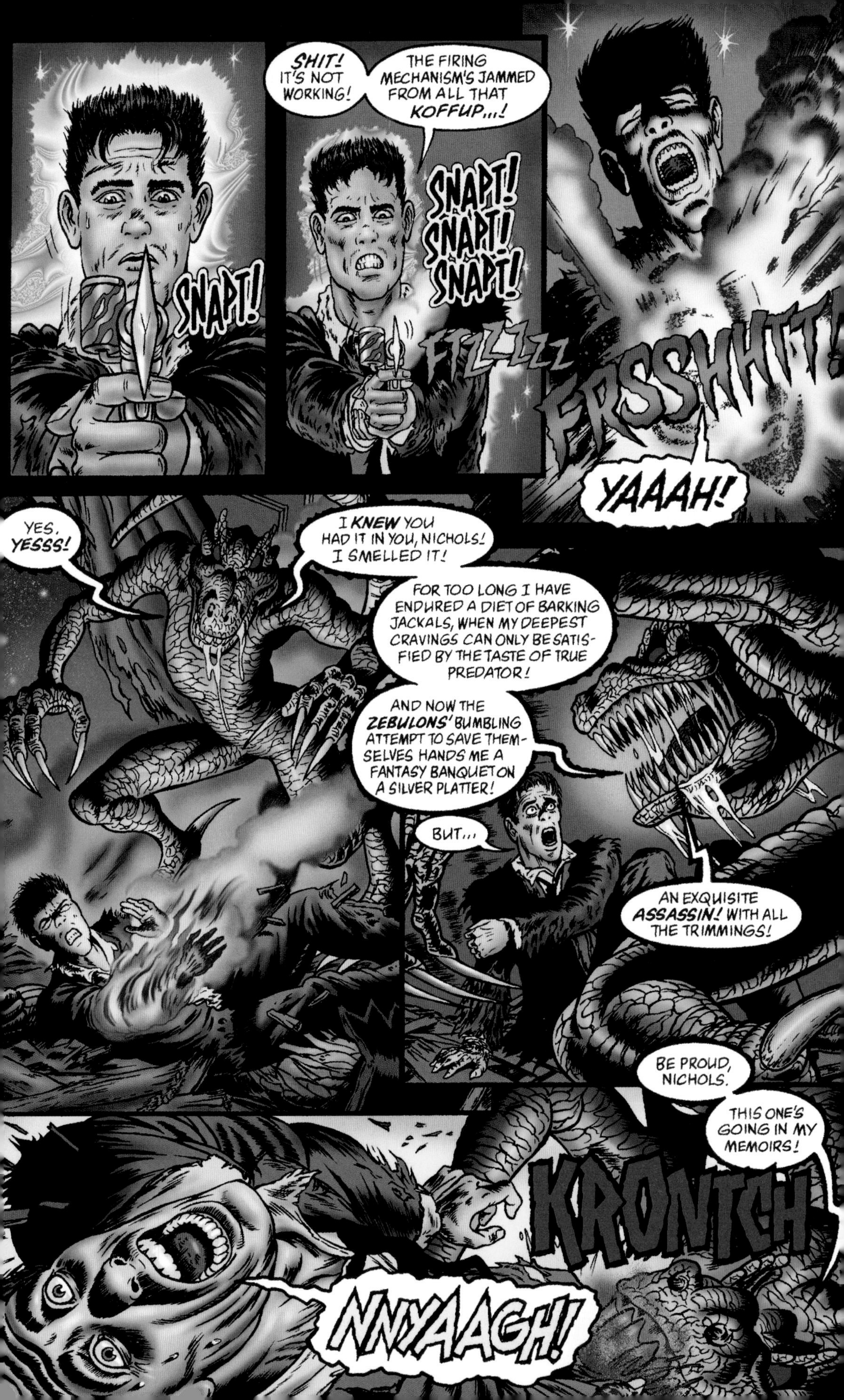
SNAPT!
SHIT! IT'S NOT WORKING!
THE FIRING MECHANISM'S JAMMED FROM ALL THAT KOFFUP...!
SNAPT! SNAPT! SNAPT!
FTZZZZZ
FRSSHHTT!
YAAAH!
YES. YESSS!
I KNEW YOU HAD IT IN YOU, NICHOLS! I SMELLED IT!
FOR TOO LONG I HAVE ENDURED A DIET OF BARKING JACKALS, WHEN MY DEEPEST CRAVINGS CAN ONLY BE SATIS-FIED BY THE TASTE OF TRUE PREDATOR!
AND NOW THE ZEBULONS' BUMBLING ATTEMPT TO SAVE THEM-SELVES HANDS ME A FANTASY BANQUET ON A SILVER PLATTER!
BUT...
AN EXQUISITE ASSASSIN! WITH ALL THE TRIMMINGS!
BE PROUD, NICHOLS.
THIS ONE'S GOING IN MY MEMOIRS!
KRONTCH
NNYAAGH!

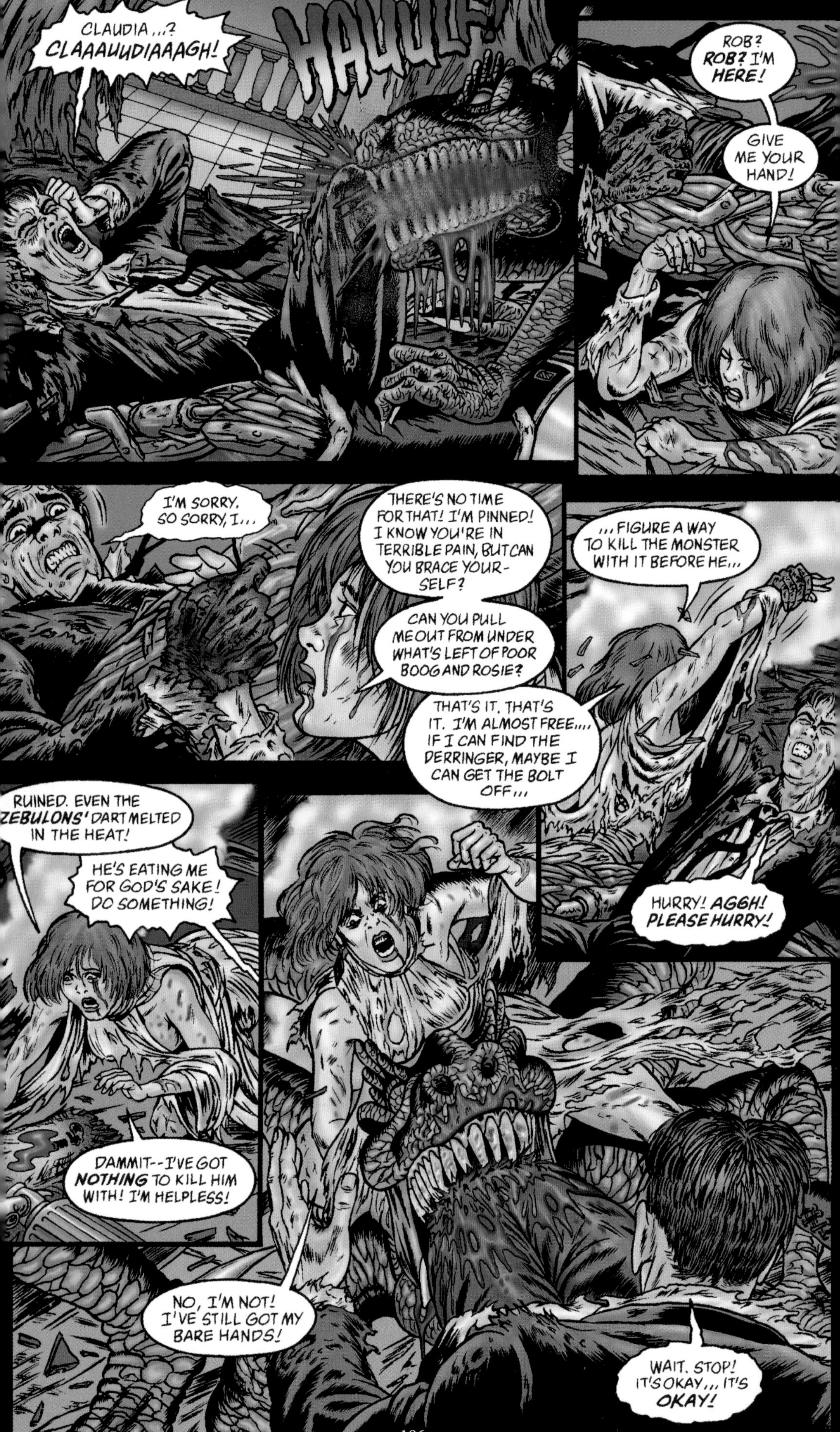

CLAUDIA...? CLAAAUUDIAAAGH!
HAUULF!
ROB? ROB? I'M HERE!
GIVE ME YOUR HAND!
I'M SORRY. SO SORRY, I...
THERE'S NO TIME FOR THAT! I'M PINNED! I KNOW YOU'RE IN TERRIBLE PAIN, BUT CAN YOU BRACE YOURSELF?
CAN YOU PULL ME OUT FROM UNDER WHAT'S LEFT OF POOR BOOG AND ROSIE?
THAT'S IT. THAT'S IT. I'M ALMOST FREE.... IF I CAN FIND THE DERRINGER, MAYBE I CAN GET THE BOLT OFF...
...FIGURE A WAY TO KILL THE MONSTER WITH IT BEFORE HE...
HURRY! AGGH! PLEASE HURRY!
RUINED. EVEN THE ZEBULONS' DART MELTED IN THE HEAT!
HE'S EATING ME FOR GOD'S SAKE! DO SOMETHING!
DAMMIT--I'VE GOT NOTHING TO KILL HIM WITH! I'M HELPLESS!
NO, I'M NOT! I'VE STILL GOT MY BARE HANDS!
WAIT. STOP! IT'S OKAY... IT'S OKAY!

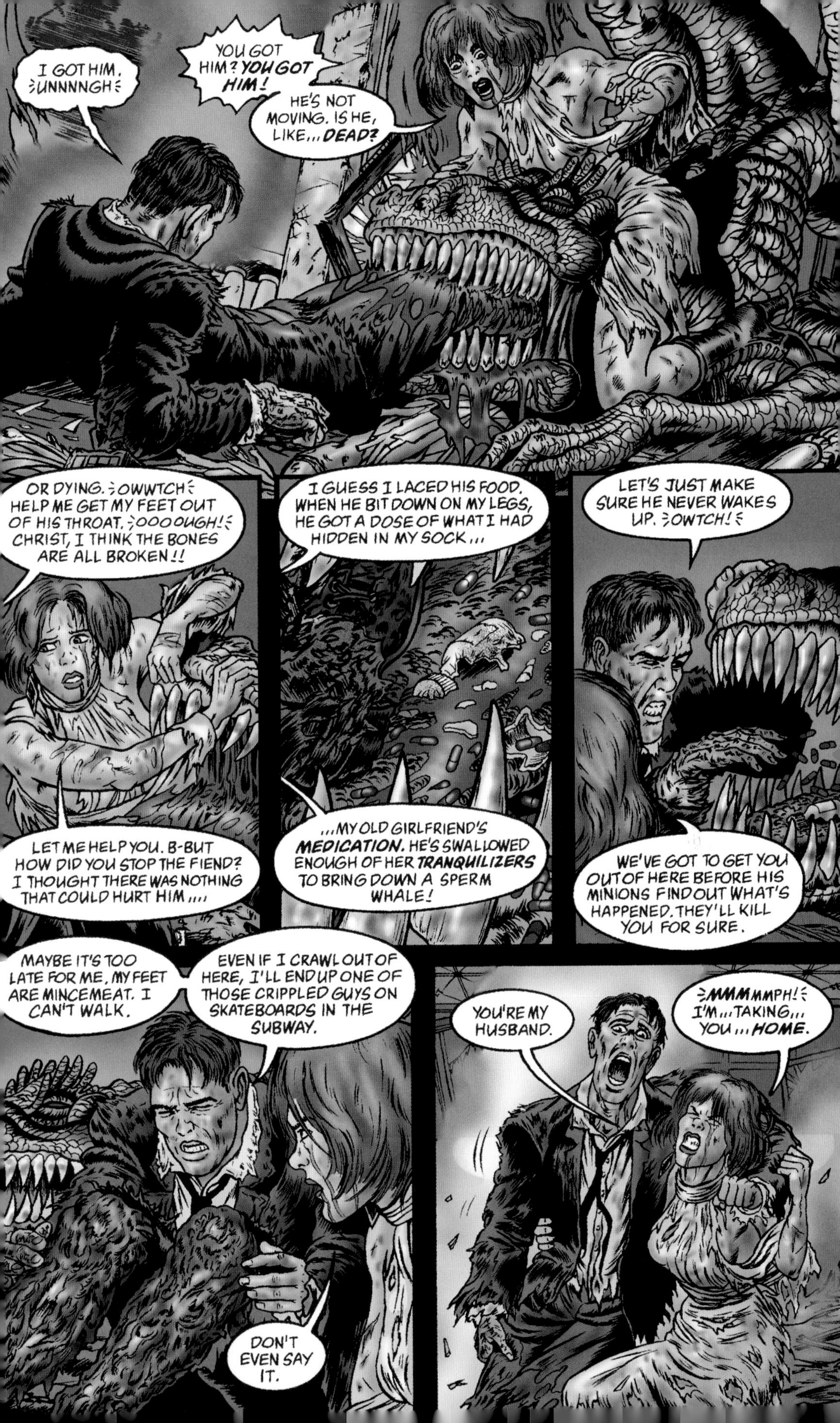
I GOT HIM. ≷UNNNNGH≶
YOU GOT HIM? YOU GOT HIM!
HE'S NOT MOVING. IS HE, LIKE... DEAD?
OR DYING. ≷OWWTCH≶ HELP ME GET MY FEET OUT OF HIS THROAT. ≷OOOOUGH!≶ CHRIST, I THINK THE BONES ARE ALL BROKEN!!
LET ME HELP YOU. B-BUT HOW DID YOU STOP THE FIEND? I THOUGHT THERE WAS NOTHING THAT COULD HURT HIM....
I GUESS I LACED HIS FOOD. WHEN HE BIT DOWN ON MY LEGS, HE GOT A DOSE OF WHAT I HAD HIDDEN IN MY SOCK...
...MY OLD GIRLFRIEND'S MEDICATION. HE'S SWALLOWED ENOUGH OF HER TRANQUILIZERS TO BRING DOWN A SPERM WHALE!
LET'S JUST MAKE SURE HE NEVER WAKES UP. ≷OWTCH!≶
WE'VE GOT TO GET YOU OUT OF HERE BEFORE HIS MINIONS FIND OUT WHAT'S HAPPENED. THEY'LL KILL YOU FOR SURE.
MAYBE IT'S TOO LATE FOR ME, MY FEET ARE MINCEMEAT. I CAN'T WALK.
EVEN IF I CRAWL OUT OF HERE, I'LL END UP ONE OF THOSE CRIPPLED GUYS ON SKATEBOARDS IN THE SUBWAY.
DON'T EVEN SAY IT.
YOU'RE MY HUSBAND.
≷MMMMMPH!≶ I'M... TAKING... YOU... HOME.

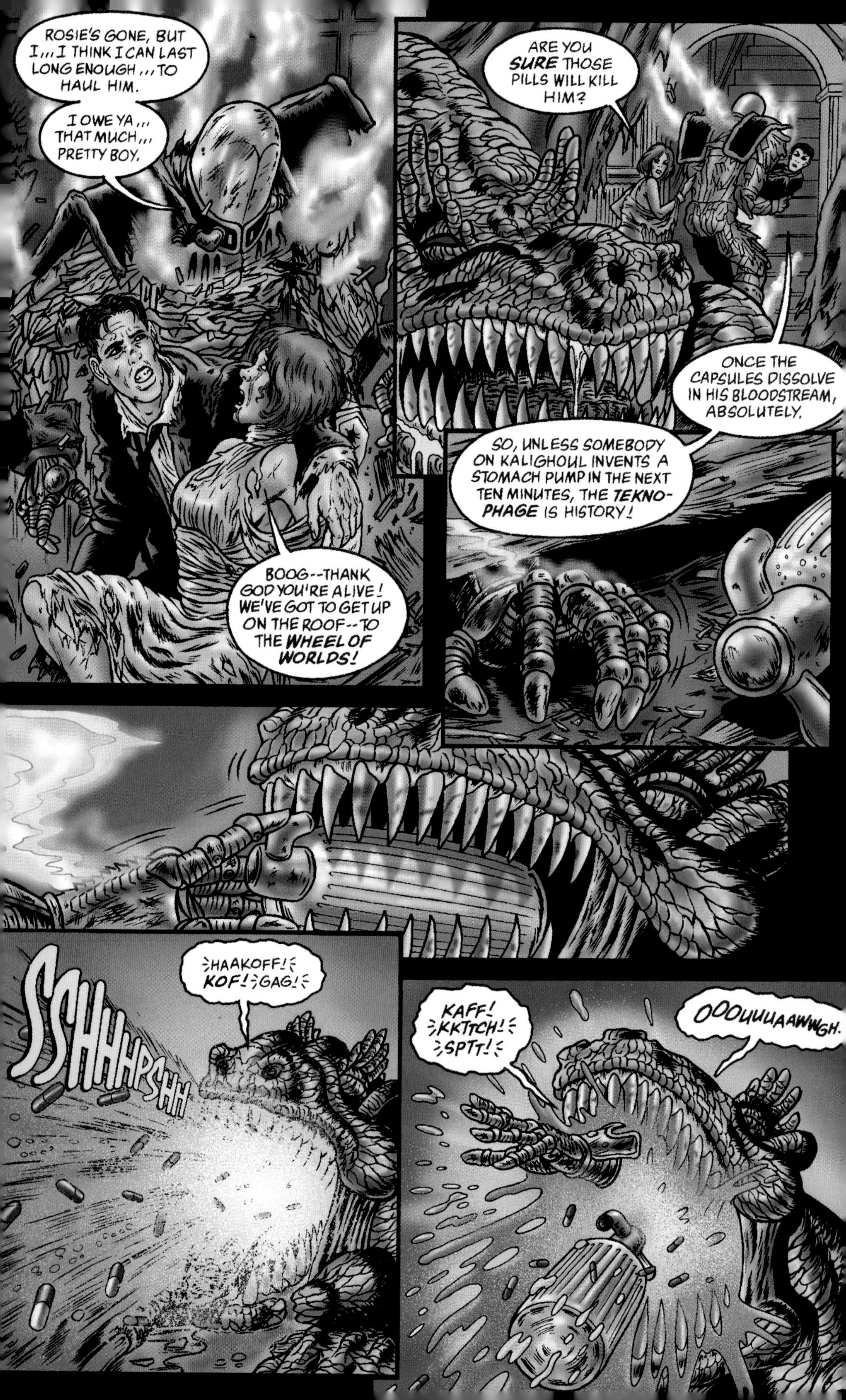
ROSIE'S GONE, BUT I,,, I THINK I CAN LAST LONG ENOUGH ,,, TO HAUL HIM.
I OWE YA ,,, THAT MUCH ,,, PRETTY BOY.
BOOG--THANK GOD YOU'RE ALIVE! WE'VE GOT TO GET UP ON THE ROOF--TO THE WHEEL OF WORLDS!
ARE YOU SURE THOSE PILLS WILL KILL HIM?
ONCE THE CAPSULES DISSOLVE IN HIS BLOODSTREAM, ABSOLUTELY.
SO, UNLESS SOMEBODY ON KALIGHOUL INVENTS A STOMACH PUMP IN THE NEXT TEN MINUTES, THE TEKNO-PHAGE IS HISTORY!
SSHHHPSHH
HAAKOFF! KOF! GAG!
KAFF! KKTTCH! SPTT!
OOOUUUAAWWGH.

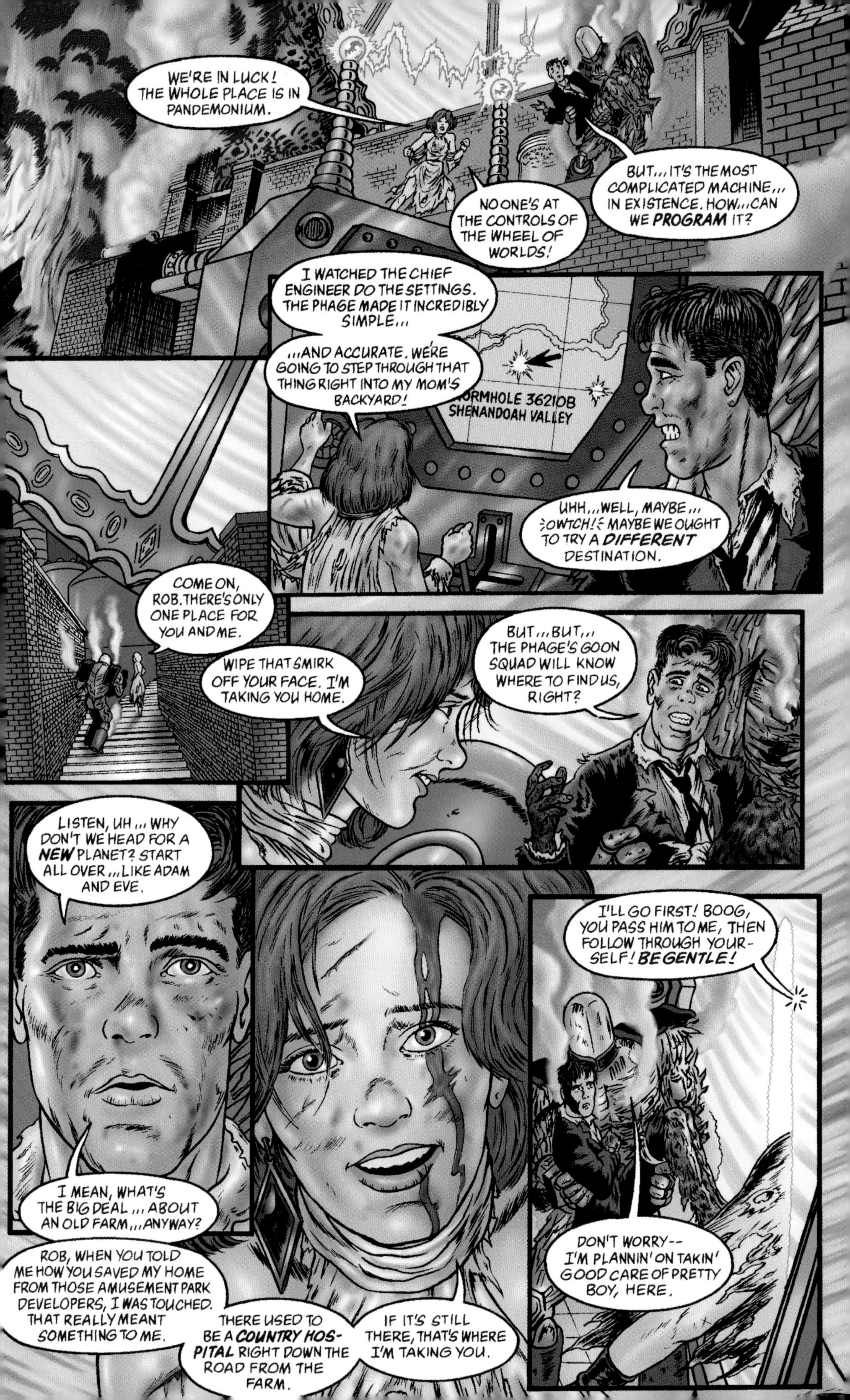
WE'RE IN LUCK! THE WHOLE PLACE IS IN PANDEMONIUM.
NO ONE'S AT THE CONTROLS OF THE WHEEL OF WORLDS!
BUT... IT'S THE MOST COMPLICATED MACHINE... IN EXISTENCE. HOW... CAN WE PROGRAM IT?
I WATCHED THE CHIEF ENGINEER DO THE SETTINGS. THE PHAGE MADE IT INCREDIBLY SIMPLE...
...AND ACCURATE. WE'RE GOING TO STEP THROUGH THAT THING RIGHT INTO MY MOM'S BACKYARD!
WORMHOLE 36210B
SHENANDOAH VALLEY
UHH... WELL, MAYBE... OWTCH! MAYBE WE OUGHT TO TRY A DIFFERENT DESTINATION.
COME ON, ROB. THERE'S ONLY ONE PLACE FOR YOU AND ME.
WIPE THAT SMIRK OFF YOUR FACE. I'M TAKING YOU HOME.
BUT... BUT... THE PHAGE'S GOON SQUAD WILL KNOW WHERE TO FIND US, RIGHT?
LISTEN, UH... WHY DON'T WE HEAD FOR A NEW PLANET? START ALL OVER... LIKE ADAM AND EVE.
I MEAN, WHAT'S THE BIG DEAL... ABOUT AN OLD FARM... ANYWAY?
ROB, WHEN YOU TOLD ME HOW YOU SAVED MY HOME FROM THOSE AMUSEMENT PARK DEVELOPERS, I WAS TOUCHED. THAT REALLY MEANT SOMETHING TO ME.
THERE USED TO BE A COUNTRY HOSPITAL RIGHT DOWN THE ROAD FROM THE FARM.
IF IT'S STILL THERE, THAT'S WHERE I'M TAKING YOU.
I'LL GO FIRST! BOOG, YOU PASS HIM TO ME, THEN FOLLOW THROUGH YOURSELF! BE GENTLE!
DON'T WORRY-- I'M PLANNIN' ON TAKIN' GOOD CARE OF PRETTY BOY, HERE.

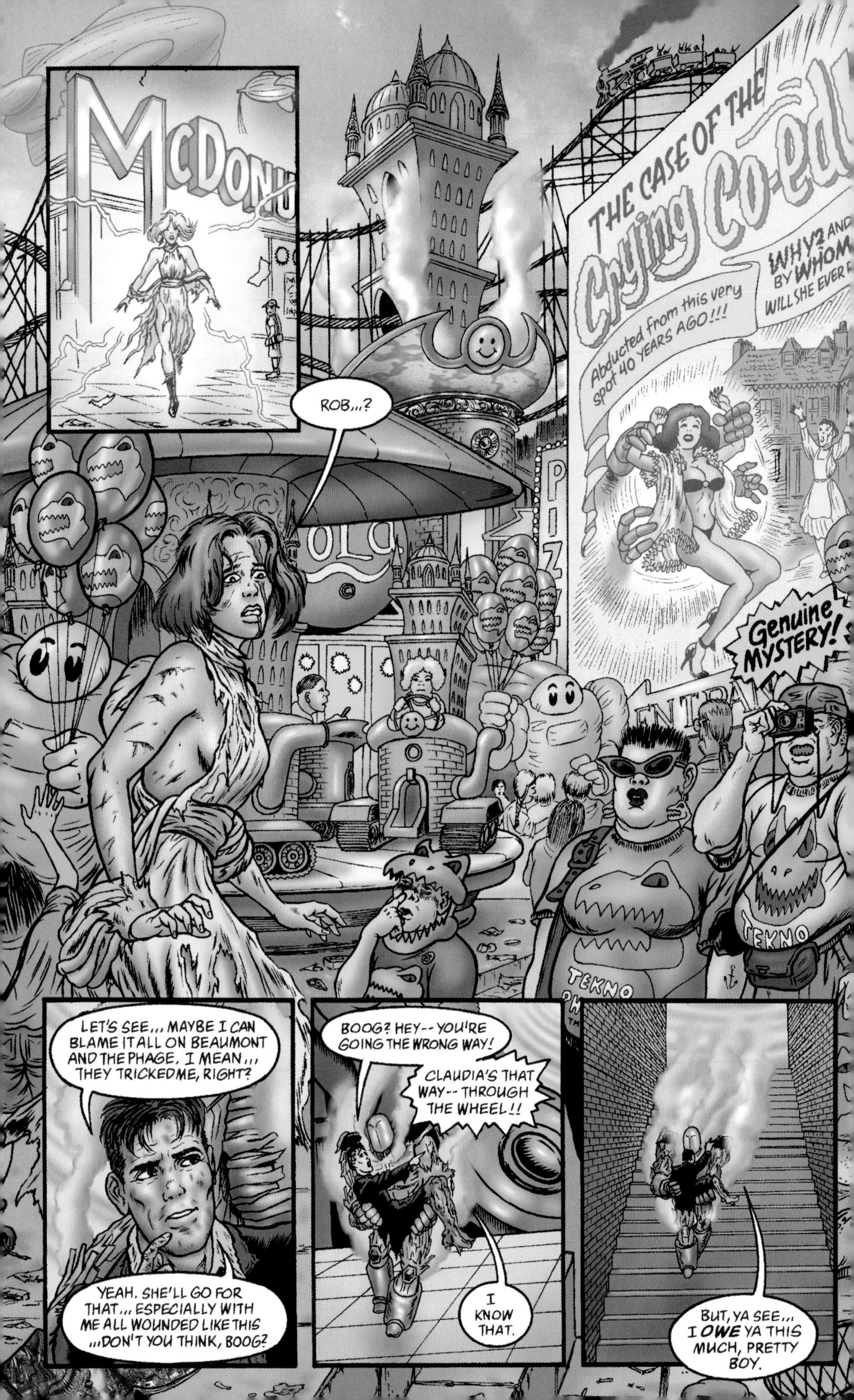
McDONU
THE CASE OF THE Crying Co-ed
Abducted from this very spot 40 YEARS AGO!!!
WHY? AND BY WHOM WILL SHE EVER
ROB...?
Genuine MYSTERY!
TEKNO
TEKNO
LET'S SEE... MAYBE I CAN BLAME IT ALL ON BEAUMONT AND THE PHAGE. I MEAN... THEY TRICKED ME, RIGHT?
YEAH. SHE'LL GO FOR THAT... ESPECIALLY WITH ME ALL WOUNDED LIKE THIS ...DON'T YOU THINK, BOOG?
BOOG? HEY-- YOU'RE GOING THE WRONG WAY!
CLAUDIA'S THAT WAY-- THROUGH THE WHEEL!!
I KNOW THAT.
BUT, YA SEE... I OWE YA THIS MUCH, PRETTY BOY.

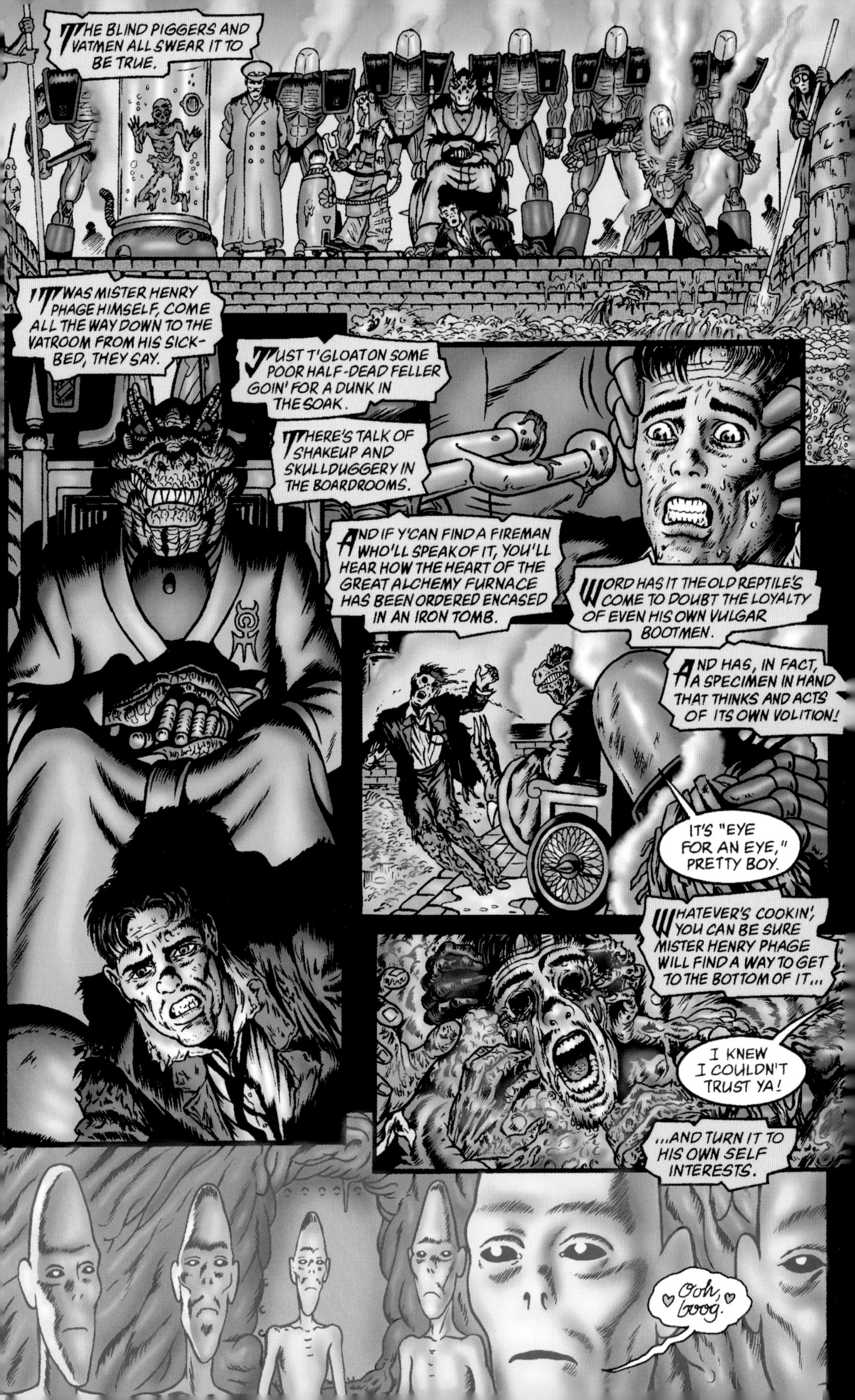
THE BLIND PIGGERS AND VATMEN ALL SWEAR IT TO BE TRUE.
'TWAS MISTER HENRY PHAGE HIMSELF, COME ALL THE WAY DOWN TO THE VATROOM FROM HIS SICK-BED, THEY SAY.
JUST T'GLOAT ON SOME POOR HALF-DEAD FELLER GOIN' FOR A DUNK IN THE SOAK.
THERE'S TALK OF SHAKEUP AND SKULLDUGGERY IN THE BOARDROOMS.
AND IF Y'CAN FIND A FIREMAN WHO'LL SPEAK OF IT, YOU'LL HEAR HOW THE HEART OF THE GREAT ALCHEMY FURNACE HAS BEEN ORDERED ENCASED IN AN IRON TOMB.
WORD HAS IT THE OLD REPTILE'S COME TO DOUBT THE LOYALTY OF EVEN HIS OWN VULGAR BOOTMEN.
AND HAS, IN FACT, A SPECIMEN IN HAND THAT THINKS AND ACTS OF ITS OWN VOLITION!
IT'S "EYE FOR AN EYE," PRETTY BOY.
WHATEVER'S COOKIN', YOU CAN BE SURE MISTER HENRY PHAGE WILL FIND A WAY TO GET TO THE BOTTOM OF IT...
I KNEW I COULDN'T TRUST YA!
...AND TURN IT TO HIS OWN SELF INTERESTS.
Ooh, boog.

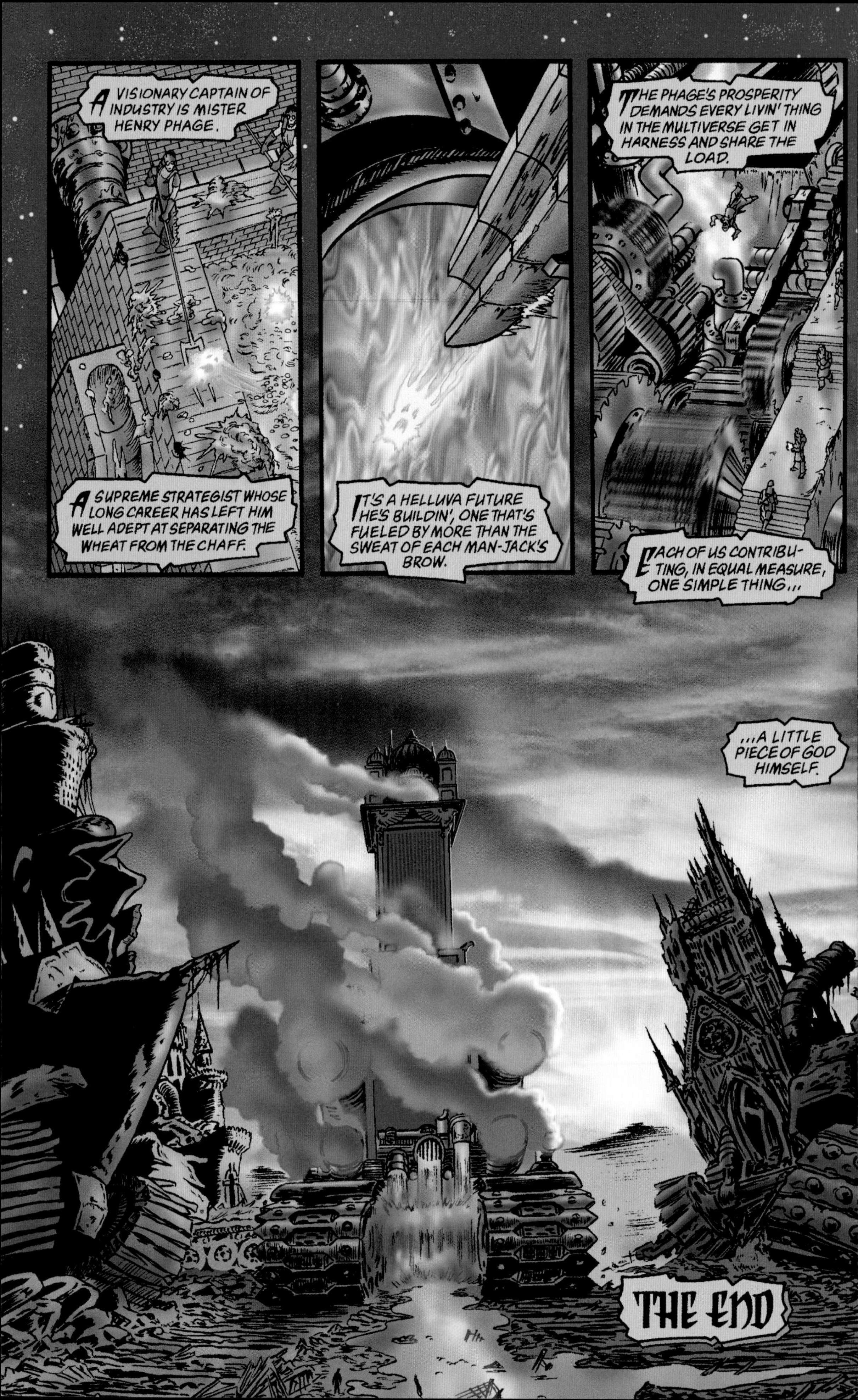
A VISIONARY CAPTAIN OF INDUSTRY IS MISTER HENRY PHAGE.
A SUPREME STRATEGIST WHOSE LONG CAREER HAS LEFT HIM WELL ADEPT AT SEPARATING THE WHEAT FROM THE CHAFF.
IT'S A HELLUVA FUTURE HE'S BUILDIN', ONE THAT'S FUELED BY MORE THAN THE SWEAT OF EACH MAN-JACK'S BROW.
THE PHAGE'S PROSPERITY DEMANDS EVERY LIVIN' THING IN THE MULTIVERSE GET IN HARNESS AND SHARE THE LOAD.
EACH OF US CONTRIBUTING, IN EQUAL MEASURE, ONE SIMPLE THING...
...A LITTLE PIECE OF GOD HIMSELF.
THE END

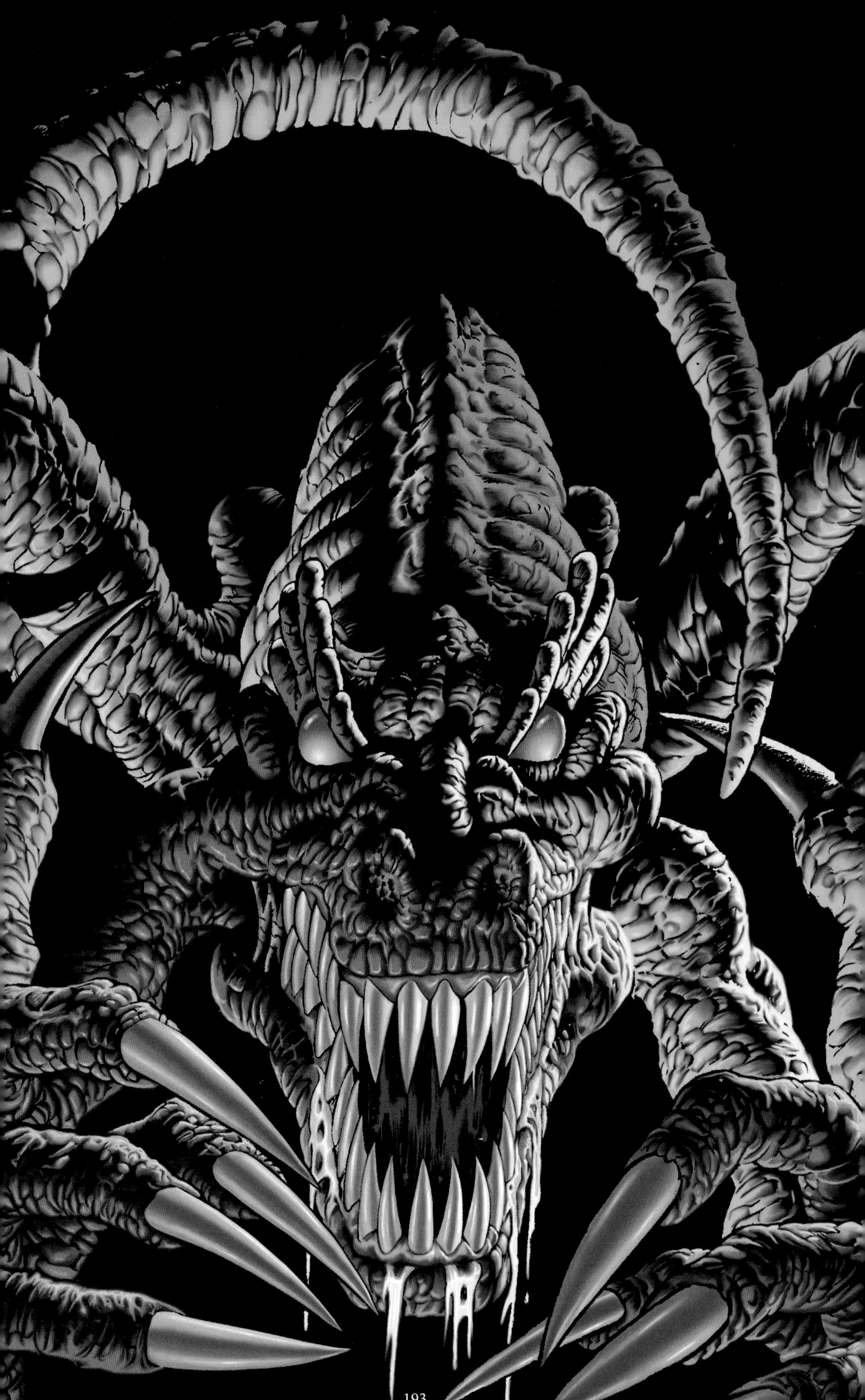

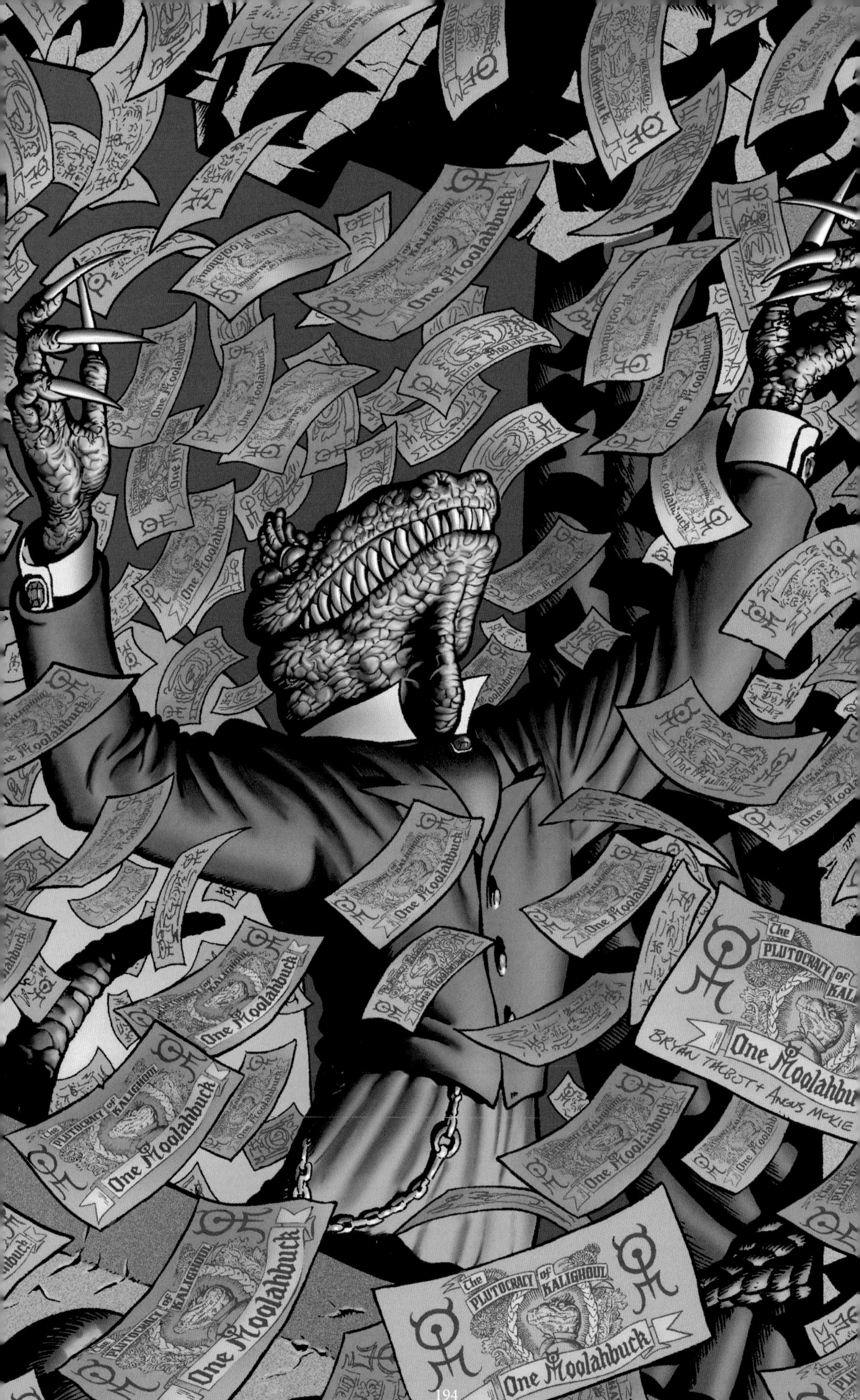
The PLUTOCRACY of KALIGHOUL
One Moolahbuck
BRYAN TALBOT + ANGUS MCKIE

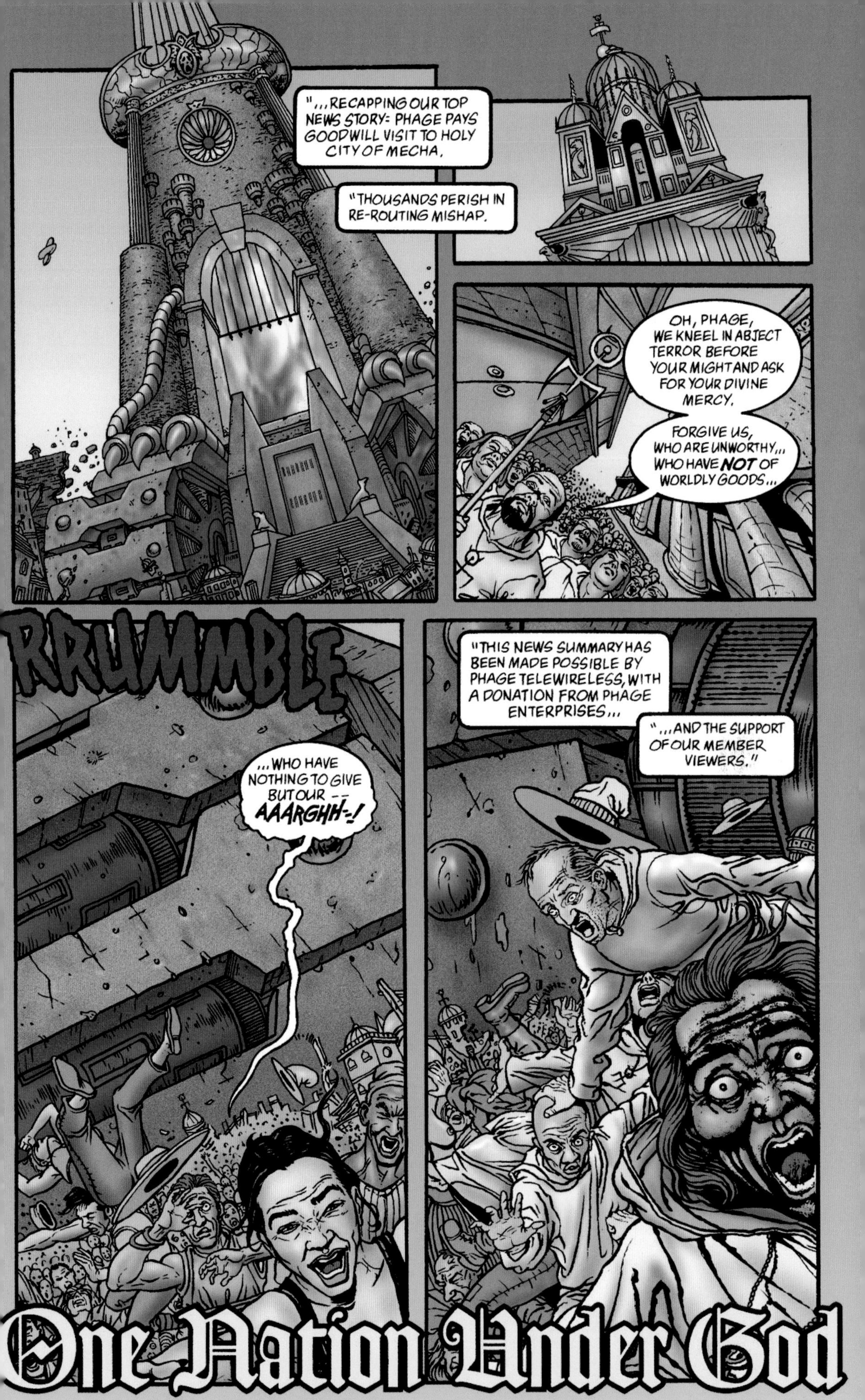
"...RECAPPING OUR TOP NEWS STORY: PHAGE PAYS GOODWILL VISIT TO HOLY CITY OF MECHA.
"THOUSANDS PERISH IN RE-ROUTING MISHAP.
OH, PHAGE, WE KNEEL IN ABJECT TERROR BEFORE YOUR MIGHT AND ASK FOR YOUR DIVINE MERCY.
FORGIVE US, WHO ARE UNWORTHY... WHO HAVE NOT OF WORLDLY GOODS...
RRUMMBLE
...WHO HAVE NOTHING TO GIVE BUT OUR -- AAARGHH--!
"THIS NEWS SUMMARY HAS BEEN MADE POSSIBLE BY PHAGE TELEWIRELESS, WITH A DONATION FROM PHAGE ENTERPRISES...
"...AND THE SUPPORT OF OUR MEMBER VIEWERS."
One Nation Under God

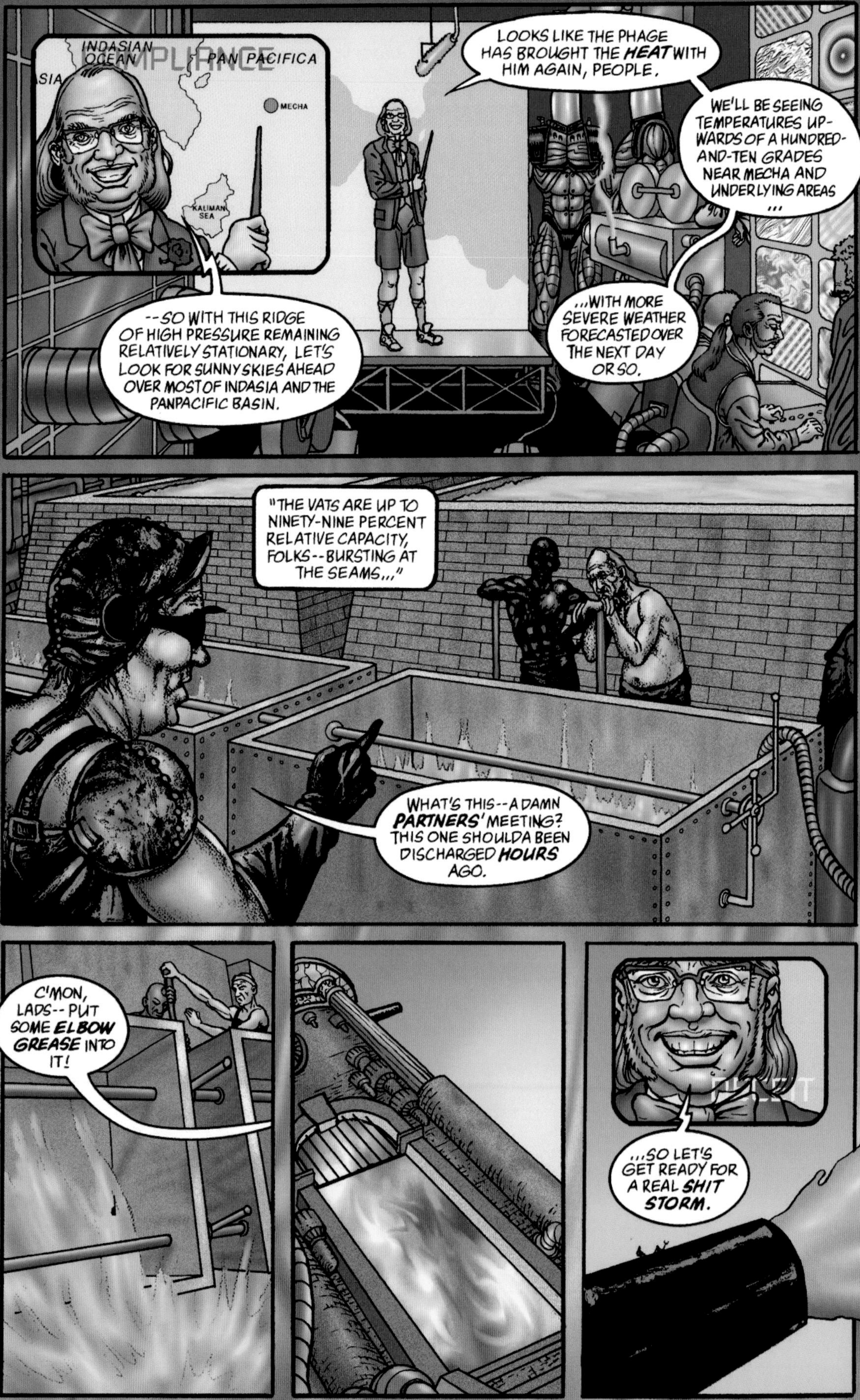
INDASIAN OCEAN
PAN PACIFICA
MECHA
KALIMAN SEA
LOOKS LIKE THE PHAGE HAS BROUGHT THE HEAT WITH HIM AGAIN, PEOPLE.
WE'LL BE SEEING TEMPERATURES UPWARDS OF A HUNDRED-AND-TEN GRADES NEAR MECHA AND UNDERLYING AREAS ...
--SO WITH THIS RIDGE OF HIGH PRESSURE REMAINING RELATIVELY STATIONARY, LET'S LOOK FOR SUNNY SKIES AHEAD OVER MOST OF INDASIA AND THE PANPACIFIC BASIN.
...WITH MORE SEVERE WEATHER FORECASTED OVER THE NEXT DAY OR SO.
"THE VATS ARE UP TO NINETY-NINE PERCENT RELATIVE CAPACITY, FOLKS--BURSTING AT THE SEAMS..."
WHAT'S THIS--A DAMN PARTNERS' MEETING? THIS ONE SHOULDA BEEN DISCHARGED HOURS AGO.
C'MON, LADS--PUT SOME ELBOW GREASE INTO IT!
...SO LET'S GET READY FOR A REAL SHIT STORM.

SH-POOT

THUMP

THIS HAS BEEN A SEVERE WEATHER WARNING FOR MECHA AND SURROUNDING AREAS....

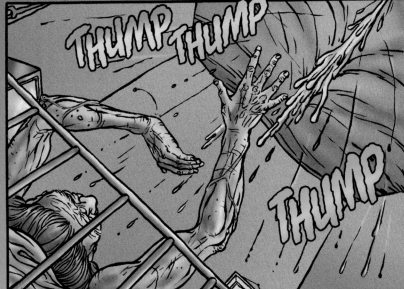

THUMP THUMP

THUMP

EEURGHH!

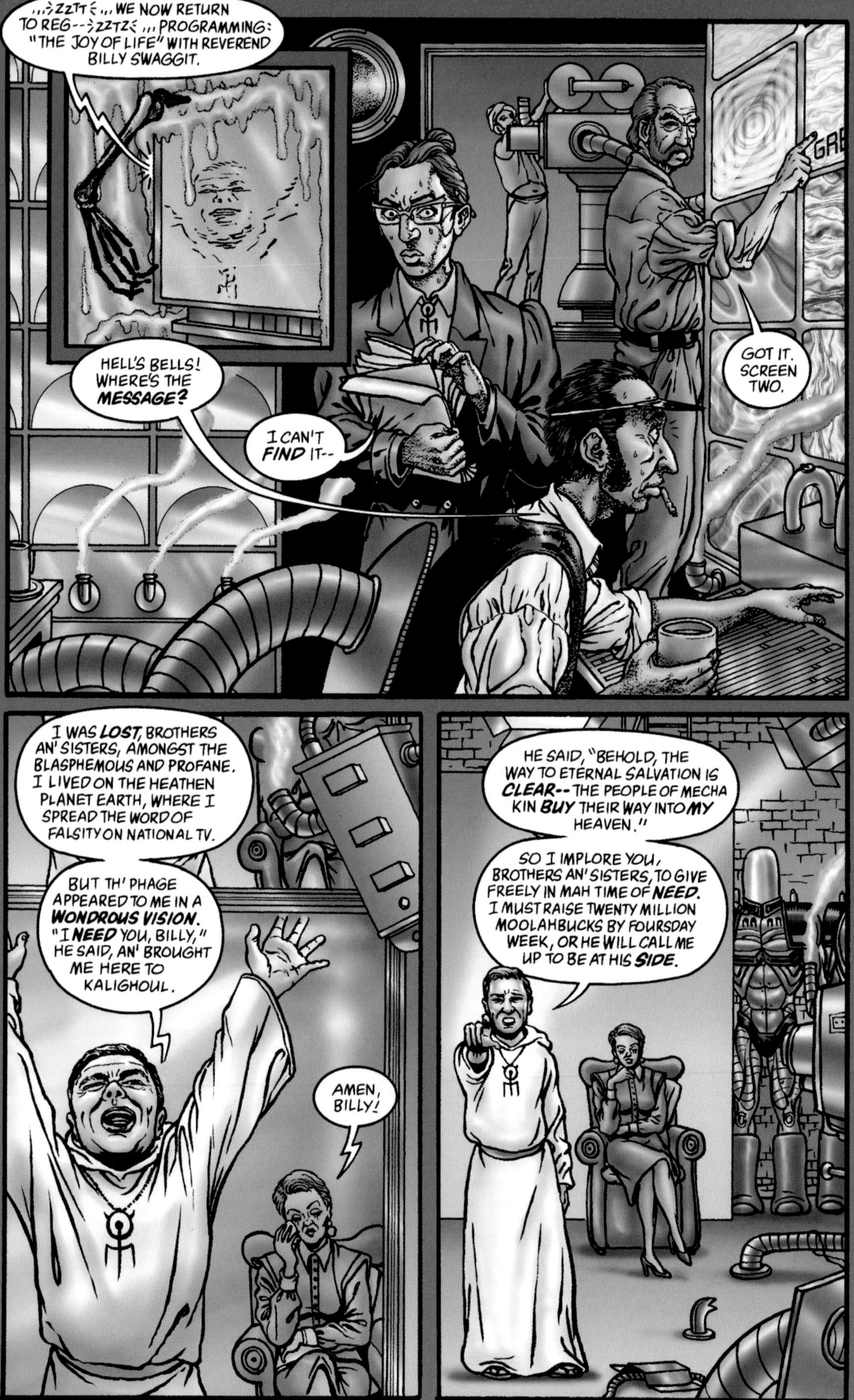
..ZZTT.. WE NOW RETURN TO REG-- ZZTZ.. PROGRAMMING: "THE JOY OF LIFE" WITH REVEREND BILLY SWAGGIT.
GOT IT. SCREEN TWO.
HELL'S BELLS! WHERE'S THE MESSAGE?
I CAN'T FIND IT--
I WAS LOST, BROTHERS AN' SISTERS, AMONGST THE BLASPHEMOUS AND PROFANE. I LIVED ON THE HEATHEN PLANET EARTH, WHERE I SPREAD THE WORD OF FALSITY ON NATIONAL TV.
BUT TH' PHAGE APPEARED TO ME IN A WONDROUS VISION. "I NEED YOU, BILLY," HE SAID, AN' BROUGHT ME HERE TO KALIGHOUL.
AMEN, BILLY!
HE SAID, "BEHOLD, THE WAY TO ETERNAL SALVATION IS CLEAR-- THE PEOPLE OF MECHA KIN BUY THEIR WAY INTO MY HEAVEN."
SO I IMPLORE YOU, BROTHERS AN' SISTERS, TO GIVE FREELY IN MAH TIME OF NEED. I MUST RAISE TWENTY MILLION MOOLAHBUCKS BY FOURSDAY WEEK, OR HE WILL CALL ME UP TO BE AT HIS SIDE.

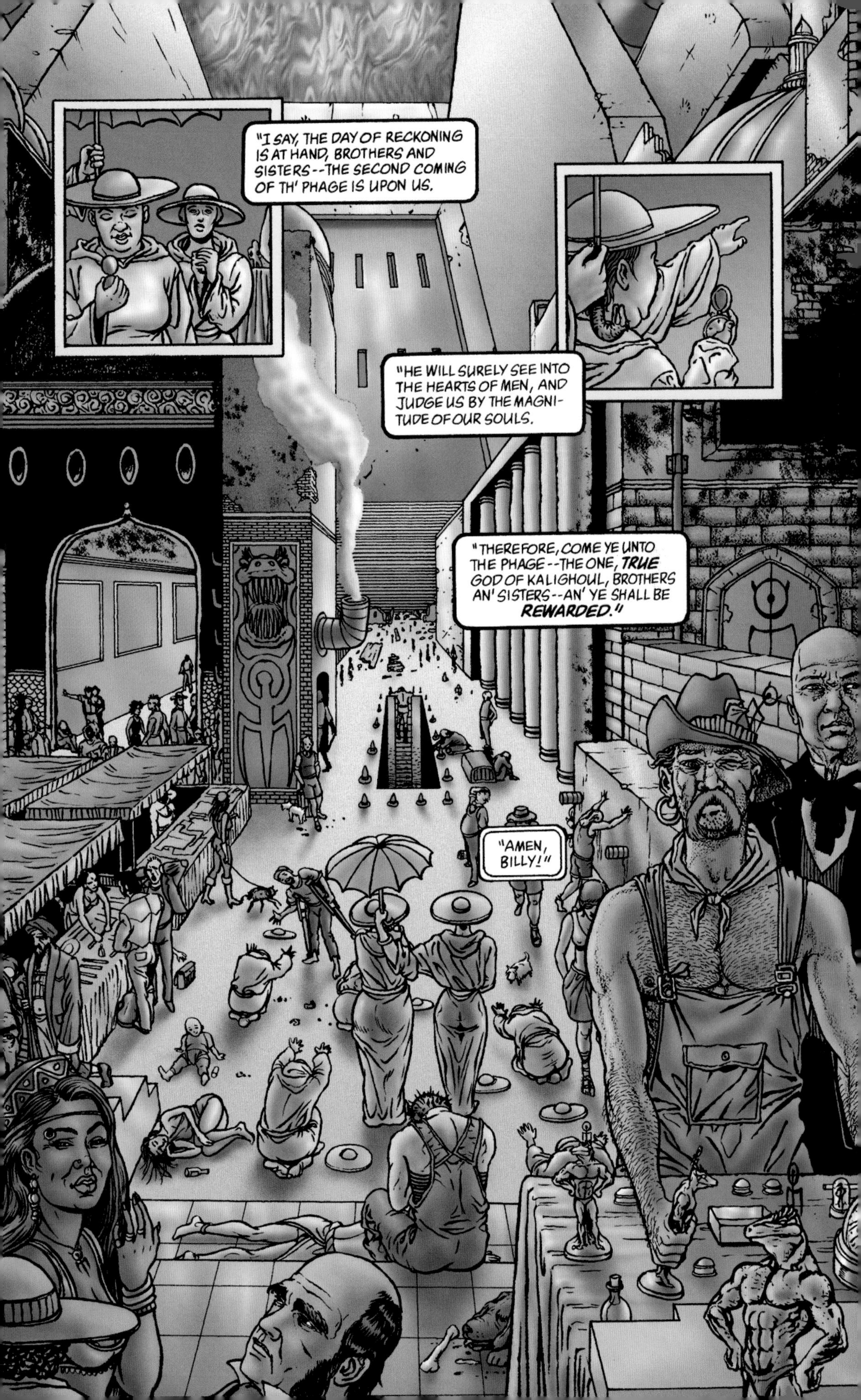
"I SAY, THE DAY OF RECKONING IS AT HAND, BROTHERS AND SISTERS--THE SECOND COMING OF TH' PHAGE IS UPON US.
"HE WILL SURELY SEE INTO THE HEARTS OF MEN, AND JUDGE US BY THE MAGNI-TUDE OF OUR SOULS.
"THEREFORE, COME YE UNTO THE PHAGE--THE ONE, TRUE GOD OF KALIGHOUL, BROTHERS AN' SISTERS--AN' YE SHALL BE REWARDED."
"AMEN, BILLY!"

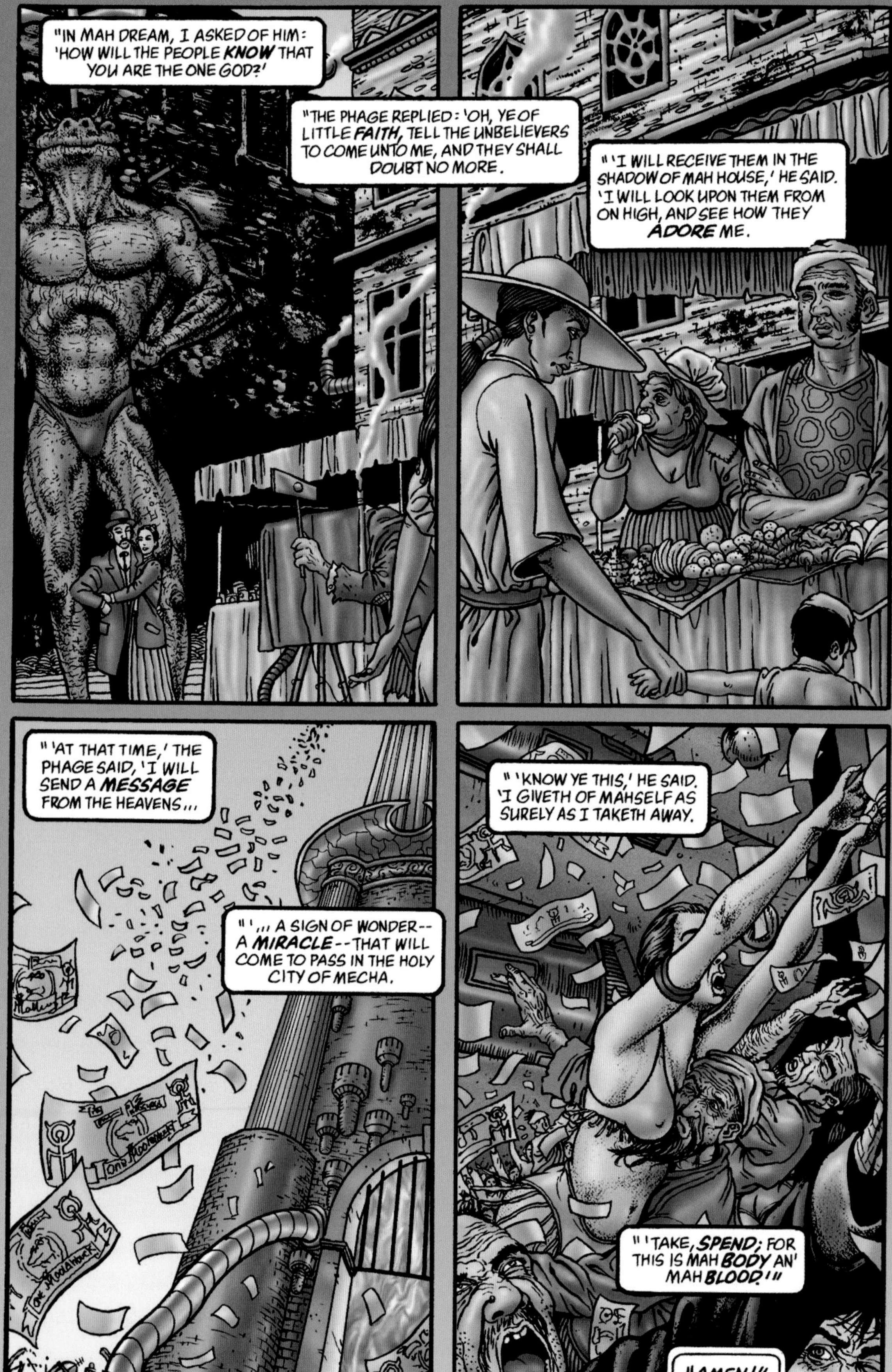
"IN MAH DREAM, I ASKED OF HIM: 'HOW WILL THE PEOPLE KNOW THAT YOU ARE THE ONE GOD?'
"THE PHAGE REPLIED: 'OH, YE OF LITTLE FAITH, TELL THE UNBELIEVERS TO COME UNTO ME, AND THEY SHALL DOUBT NO MORE.
"'I WILL RECEIVE THEM IN THE SHADOW OF MAH HOUSE,' HE SAID. 'I WILL LOOK UPON THEM FROM ON HIGH, AND SEE HOW THEY ADORE ME.
"'AT THAT TIME,' THE PHAGE SAID, 'I WILL SEND A MESSAGE FROM THE HEAVENS...
"'... A SIGN OF WONDER-- A MIRACLE--THAT WILL COME TO PASS IN THE HOLY CITY OF MECHA.
"'KNOW YE THIS,' HE SAID. 'I GIVETH OF MAHSELF AS SURELY AS I TAKETH AWAY.
"'TAKE, SPEND; FOR THIS IS MAH BODY AN' MAH BLOOD!'"
"AMEN!"

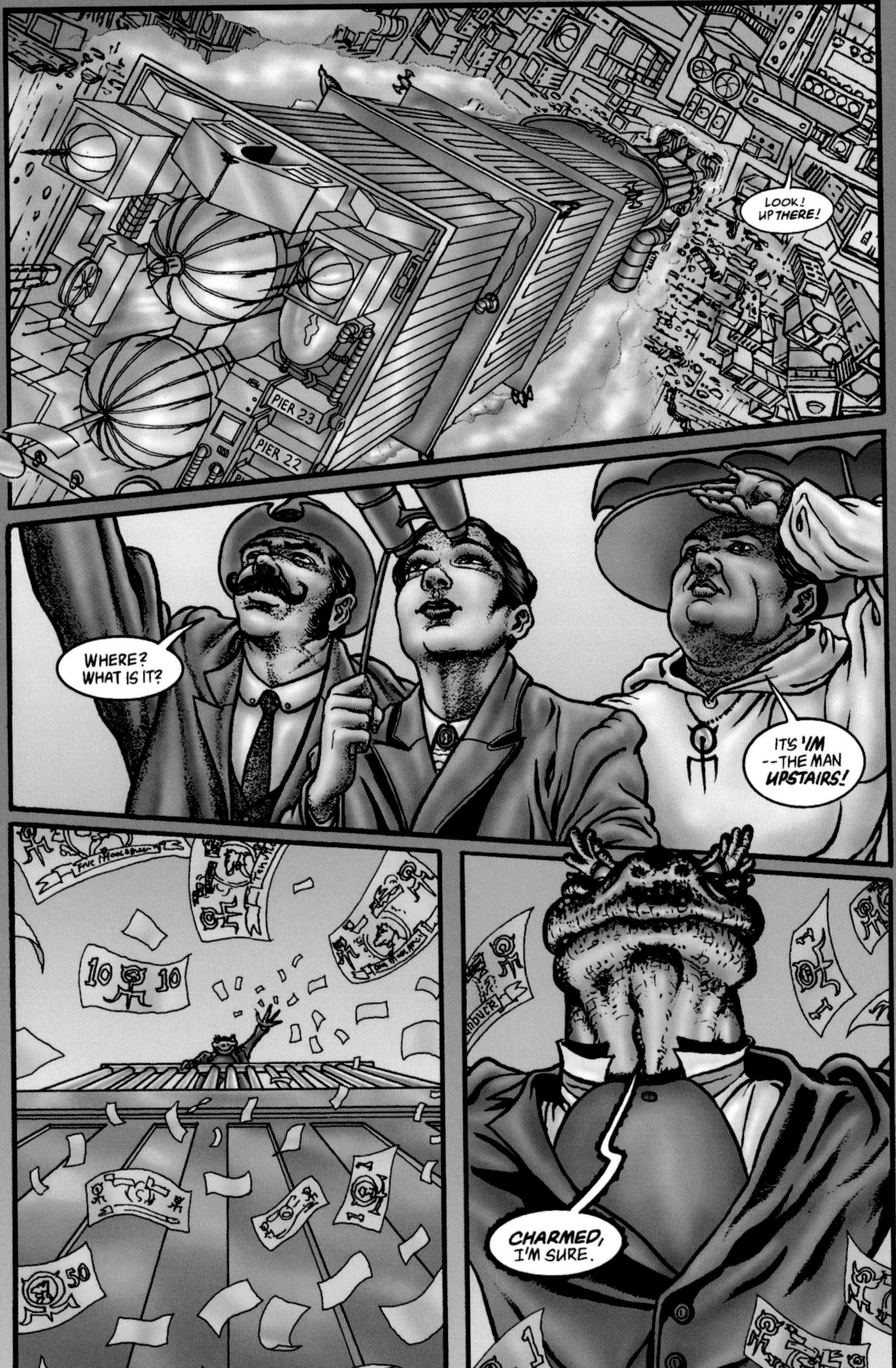
PIER 23
PIER 22
LOOK! UP THERE!
WHERE? WHAT IS IT?
IT'S 'IM --THE MAN UPSTAIRS!
10
10
50
1
CHARMED, I'M SURE.

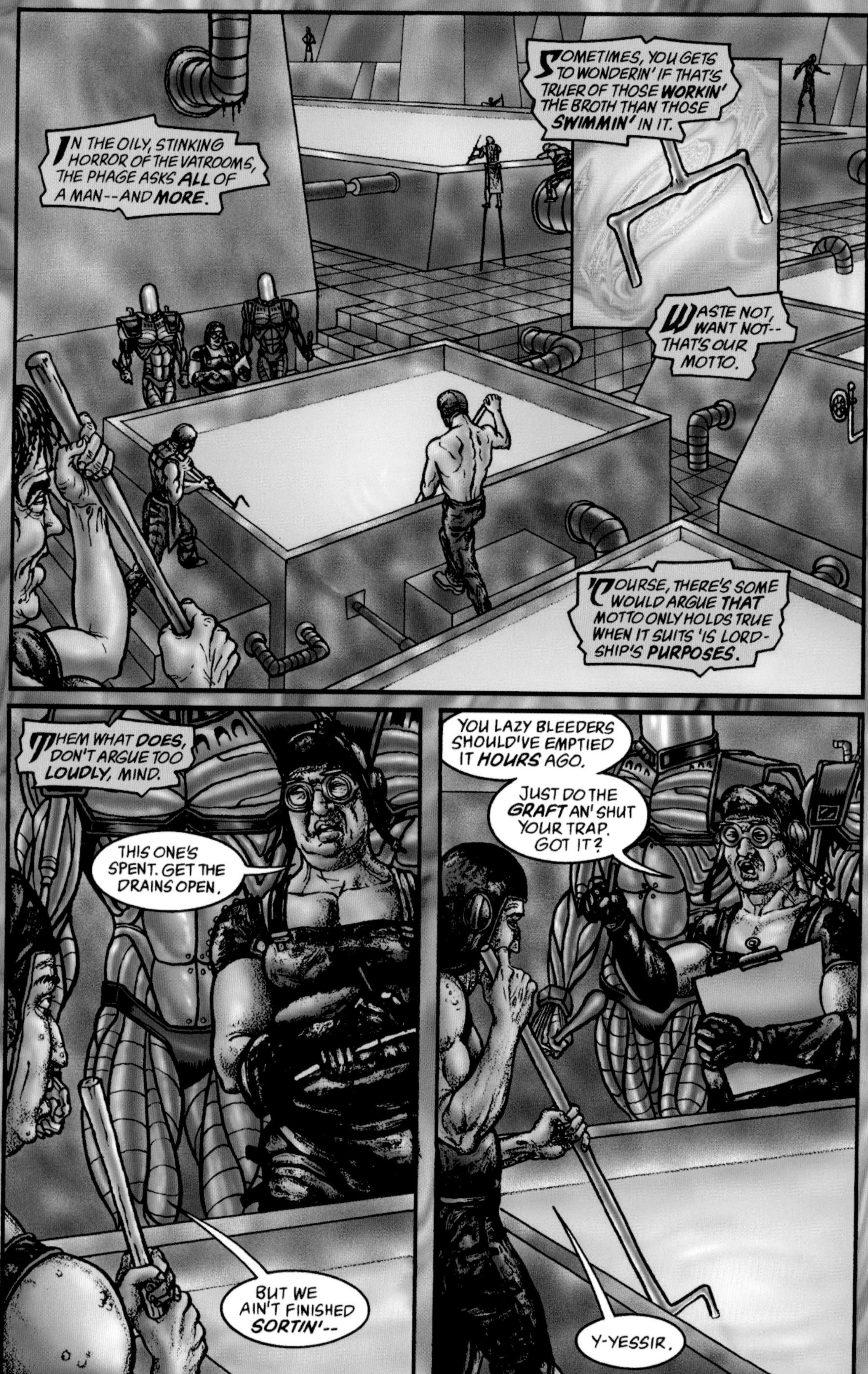
IN THE OILY, STINKING HORROR OF THE VATROOMS, THE PHAGE ASKS **ALL** OF A MAN--AND **MORE**.
SOMETIMES, YOU GETS TO WONDERIN' IF THAT'S TRUER OF THOSE **WORKIN'** THE BROTH THAN THOSE **SWIMMIN'** IN IT.
WASTE NOT, WANT NOT--THAT'S OUR MOTTO.
'COURSE, THERE'S SOME WOULD ARGUE **THAT** MOTTO ONLY HOLDS TRUE WHEN IT SUITS 'IS LORDSHIP'S **PURPOSES**.
THEM WHAT **DOES**, DON'T ARGUE TOO **LOUDLY**, MIND.
THIS ONE'S SPENT. GET THE DRAINS OPEN.
BUT WE AIN'T FINISHED **SORTIN'**--
YOU LAZY BLEEDERS SHOULD'VE EMPTIED IT **HOURS** AGO.
JUST DO THE **GRAFT** AN' SHUT YOUR TRAP. GOT IT?
Y-YESSIR.

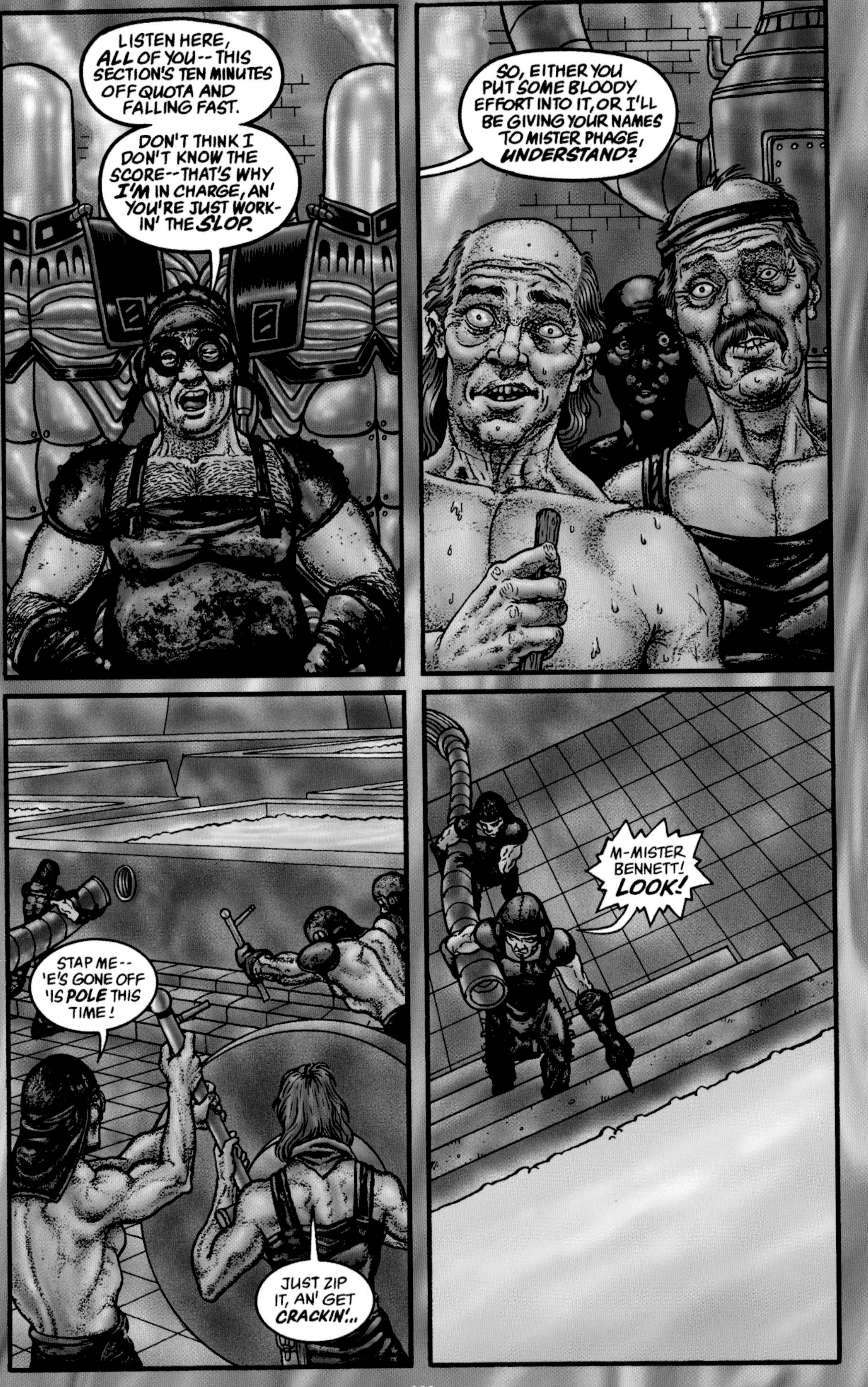
LISTEN HERE, ALL OF YOU-- THIS SECTION'S TEN MINUTES OFF QUOTA AND FALLING FAST.
DON'T THINK I DON'T KNOW THE SCORE--THAT'S WHY I'M IN CHARGE, AN' YOU'RE JUST WORK-IN' THE SLOP.
SO, EITHER YOU PUT SOME BLOODY EFFORT INTO IT, OR I'LL BE GIVING YOUR NAMES TO MISTER PHAGE, UNDERSTAND?
STAP ME-- 'E'S GONE OFF 'IS POLE THIS TIME!
JUST ZIP IT, AN' GET CRACKIN'...
M-MISTER BENNETT! LOOK!

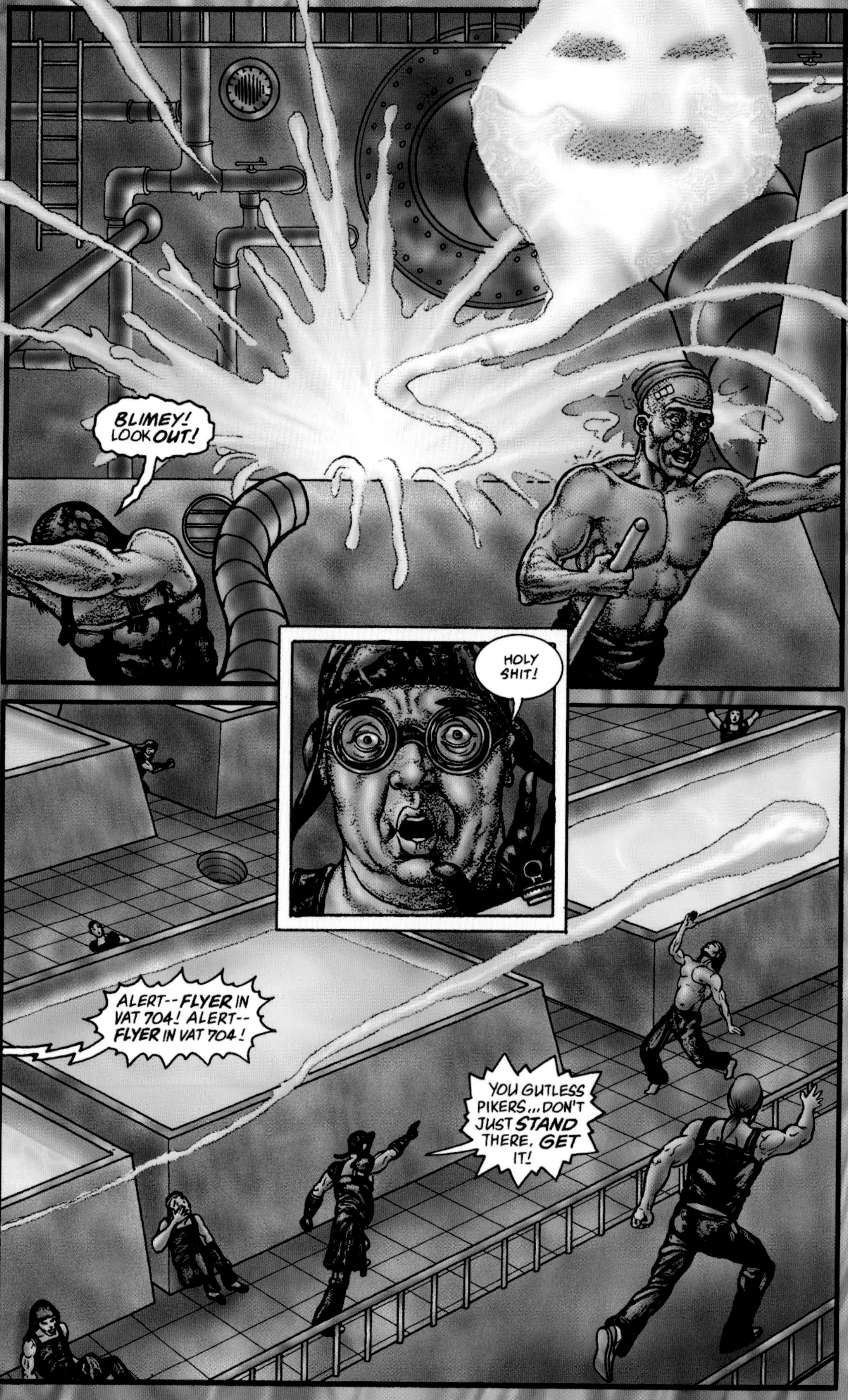
BLIMEY! LOOK OUT!
HOLY SHIT!
ALERT-- FLYER IN VAT 704! ALERT-- FLYER IN VAT 704!
YOU GUTLESS PIKERS... DON'T JUST STAND THERE, GET IT!

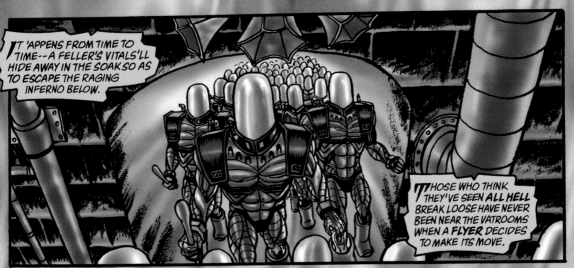

IT 'APPENS FROM TIME TO TIME-- A FELLER'S VITALS'LL HIDE AWAY IN THE SOAK SO AS TO ESCAPE THE RAGING INFERNO BELOW.

THOSE WHO THINK THEY'VE SEEN ALL HELL BREAK LOOSE HAVE NEVER BEEN NEAR THE VATROOMS WHEN A FLYER DECIDES TO MAKE ITS MOVE.

THESE FLYERS-- THEY'VE A LOT MORE SPUNK THAN YER AVERAGE FELLER'S ESSENCE.

THEY KNOW WHERE THEY'RE HEADED-- AN' IT AIN'T INTO GRIDDLE, THAT'S FER SURE.

MAYBE THAT'S WHY MISTER PHAGE SEEMS SO INTENT ON GETTIN' 'IS SCALY HANDS ON ONE.

AUURGH--!

THERE'S A REWARD POSTED-- DOUBLE RATIONS FOR TH' VATTER WHO'LL RISK 'IS NECK T' BRING ONE DOWN.

AS YET, NO MAN'S 'AD THE COBBLERS T' TAKE 'IM UP ON 'IS GENEROUS OFFER.

WHOOM

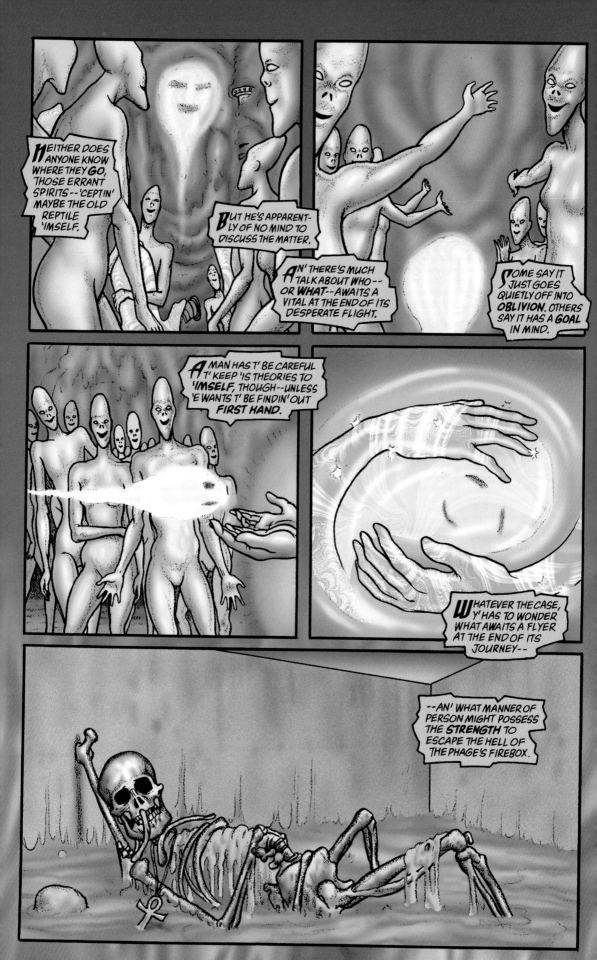

NEITHER DOES ANYONE KNOW WHERE THEY GO, THOSE ERRANT SPIRITS--'CEPTIN' MAYBE THE OLD REPTILE 'IMSELF.

BUT HE'S APPARENTLY OF NO MIND TO DISCUSS THE MATTER.

AN' THERE'S MUCH TALK ABOUT WHO-- OR WHAT--AWAITS A VITAL AT THE END OF ITS DESPERATE FLIGHT.

SOME SAY IT JUST GOES QUIETLY OFF INTO OBLIVION. OTHERS SAY IT HAS A GOAL IN MIND.

A MAN HAS T' BE CAREFUL T' KEEP 'IS THEORIES TO 'IMSELF, THOUGH--UNLESS 'E WANTS T' BE FINDIN' OUT FIRST HAND.

WHATEVER THE CASE, Y' HAS TO WONDER WHAT AWAITS A FLYER AT THE END OF ITS JOURNEY--

--AN' WHAT MANNER OF PERSON MIGHT POSSESS THE STRENGTH TO ESCAPE THE HELL OF THE PHAGE'S FIREBOX.

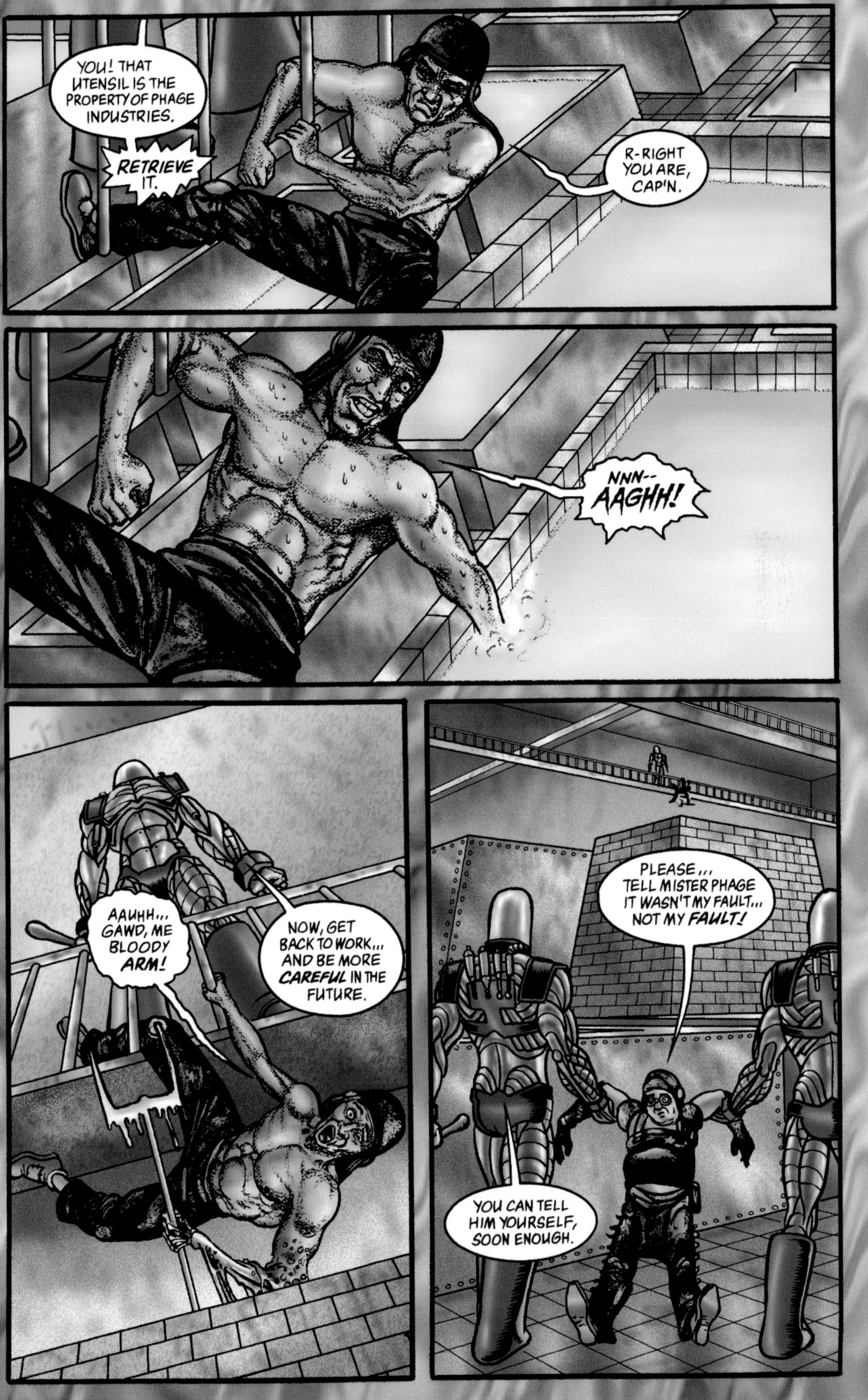
YOU! THAT UTENSIL IS THE PROPERTY OF PHAGE INDUSTRIES.
RETRIEVE IT.
R-RIGHT YOU ARE, CAP'N.
NNN-- AAGHH!
AAUHH... GAWD, ME BLOODY ARM!
NOW, GET BACK TO WORK... AND BE MORE CAREFUL IN THE FUTURE.
PLEASE... TELL MISTER PHAGE IT WASN'T MY FAULT... NOT MY FAULT!
YOU CAN TELL HIM YOURSELF, SOON ENOUGH.

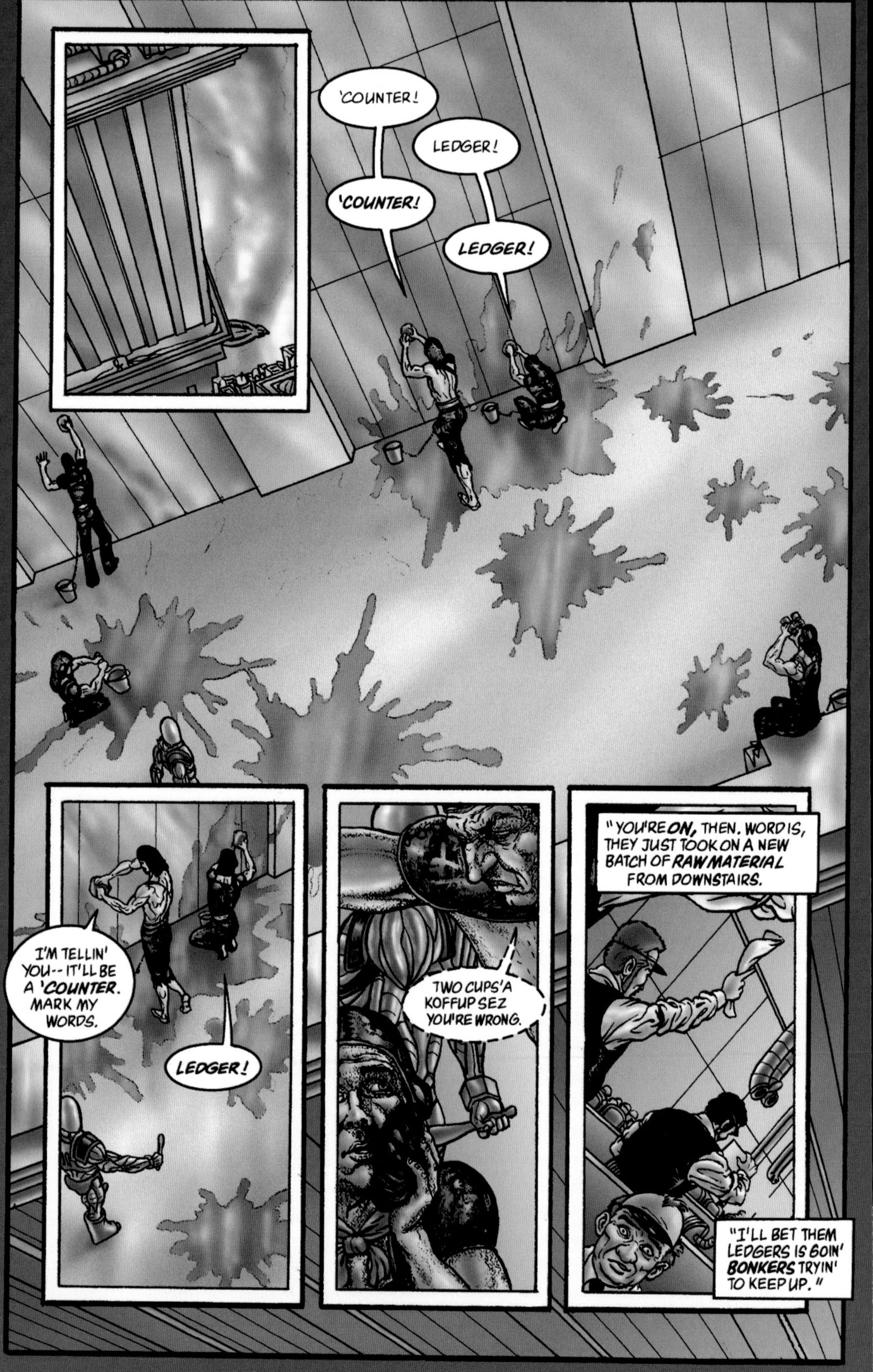
'COUNTER!
LEDGER!
'COUNTER!
LEDGER!
I'M TELLIN' YOU-- IT'LL BE A 'COUNTER. MARK MY WORDS.
LEDGER!
TWO CUPS'A KOFFUP SEZ YOU'RE WRONG.
"YOU'RE ON, THEN. WORD IS, THEY JUST TOOK ON A NEW BATCH OF RAW MATERIAL FROM DOWNSTAIRS.
"I'LL BET THEM LEDGERS IS GOIN' BONKERS TRYIN' TO KEEP UP."

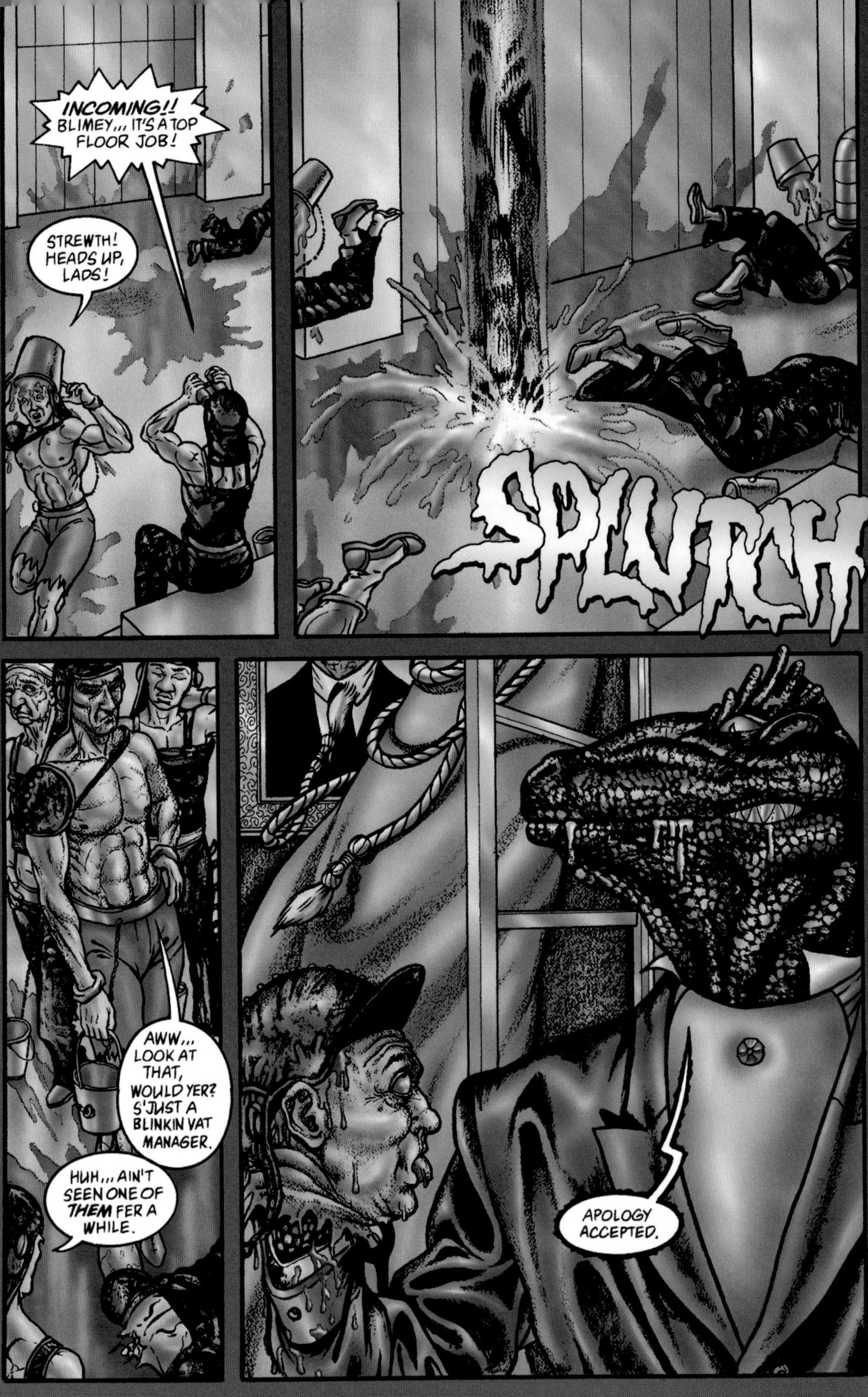
INCOMING!! BLIMEY,,, IT'S A TOP FLOOR JOB!
STREWTH! HEADS UP, LADS!
SPLUTCH
AWW,,, LOOK AT THAT, WOULD YER? S'JUST A BLINKIN VAT MANAGER.
HUH,,, AIN'T SEEN ONE OF THEM FER A WHILE.
APOLOGY ACCEPTED.

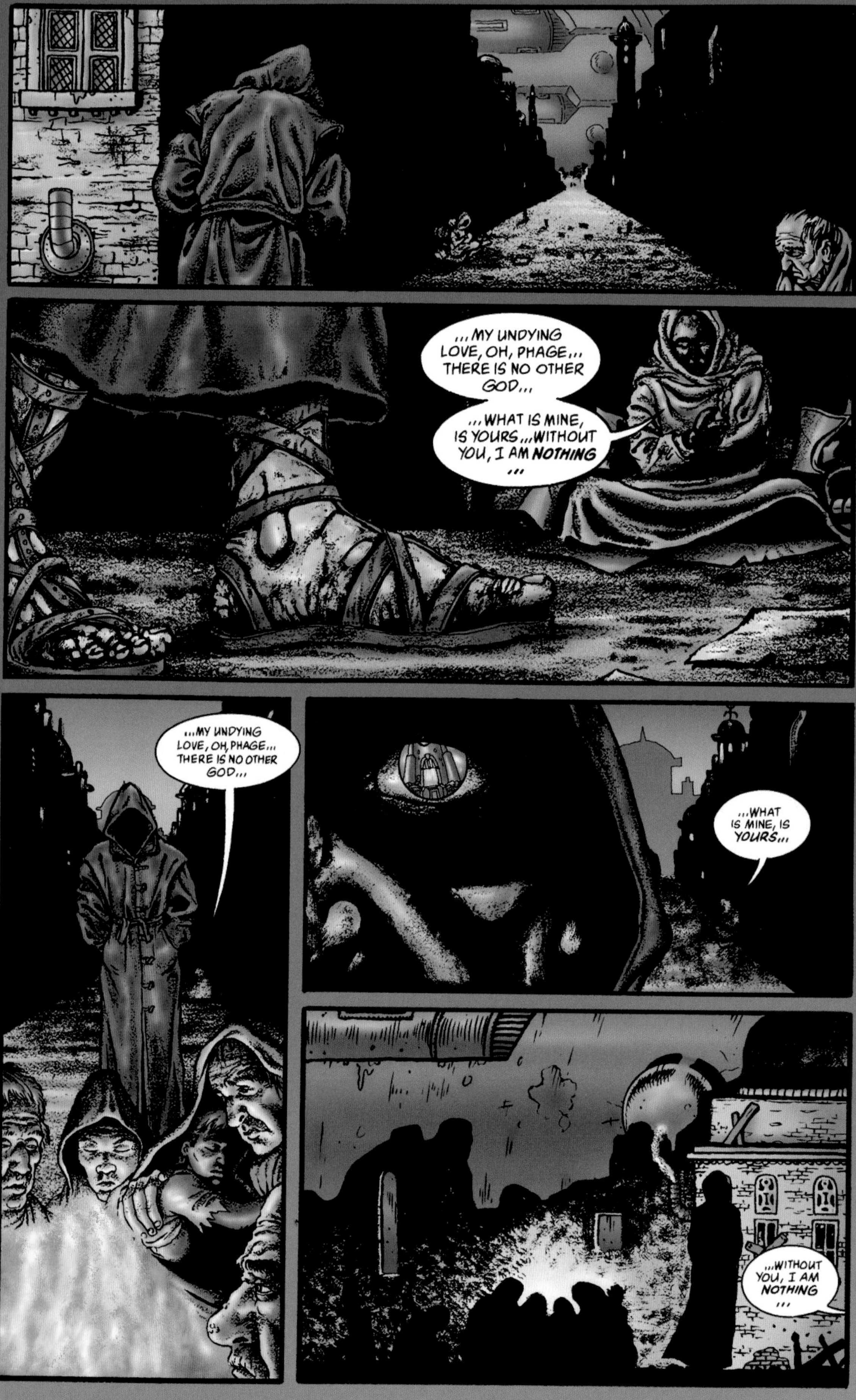
...MY UNDYING LOVE, OH, PHAGE... THERE IS NO OTHER GOD...
...WHAT IS MINE, IS YOURS...WITHOUT YOU, I AM NOTHING ...
...MY UNDYING LOVE, OH, PHAGE... THERE IS NO OTHER GOD...
...WHAT IS MINE, IS YOURS...
...WITHOUT YOU, I AM NOTHING ...

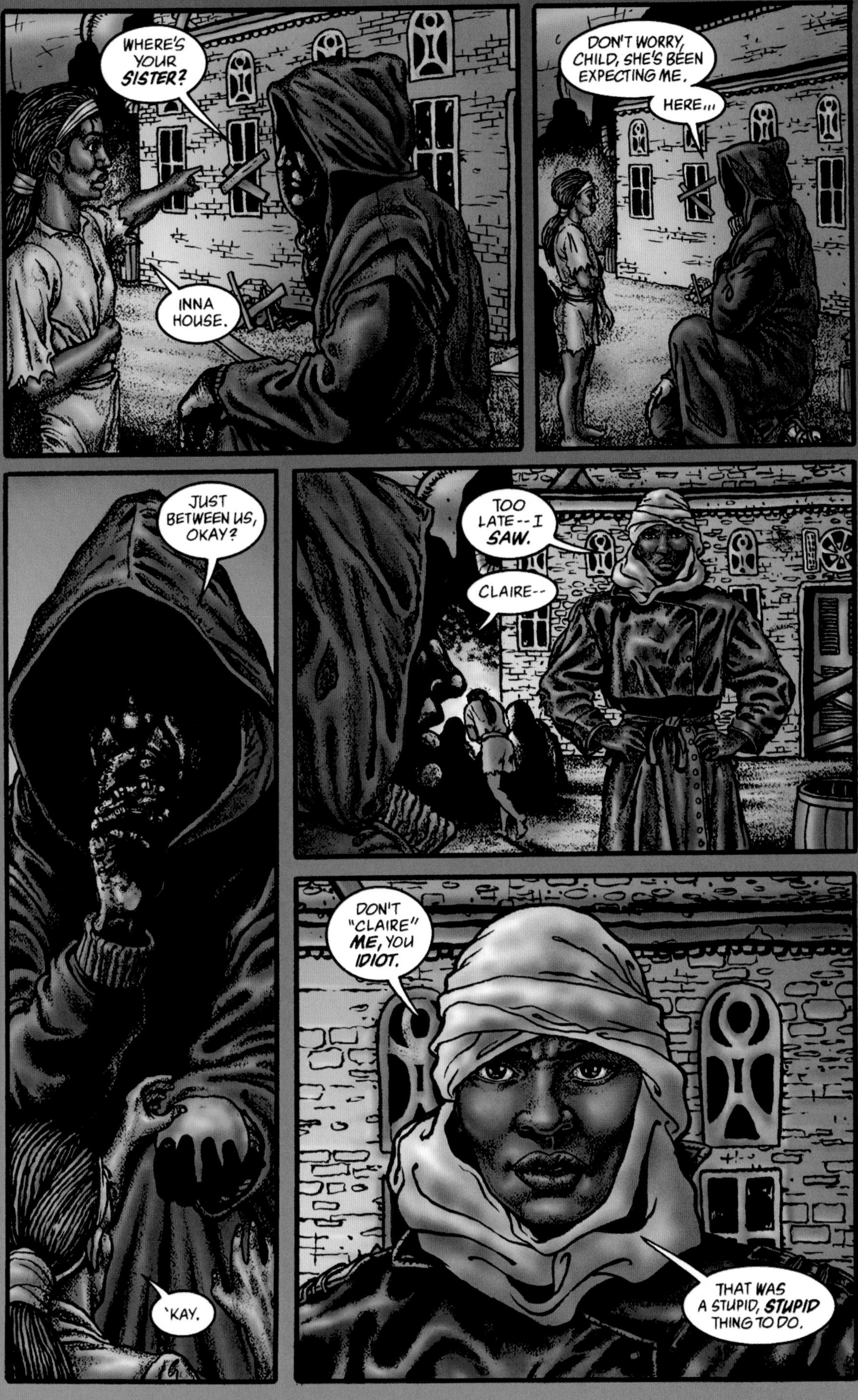
WHERE'S YOUR SISTER?
INNA HOUSE.
DON'T WORRY, CHILD, SHE'S BEEN EXPECTING ME.
HERE...
JUST BETWEEN US, OKAY?
'KAY.
TOO LATE--I SAW.
CLAIRE--
DON'T "CLAIRE" ME, YOU IDIOT.
THAT WAS A STUPID, STUPID THING TO DO.

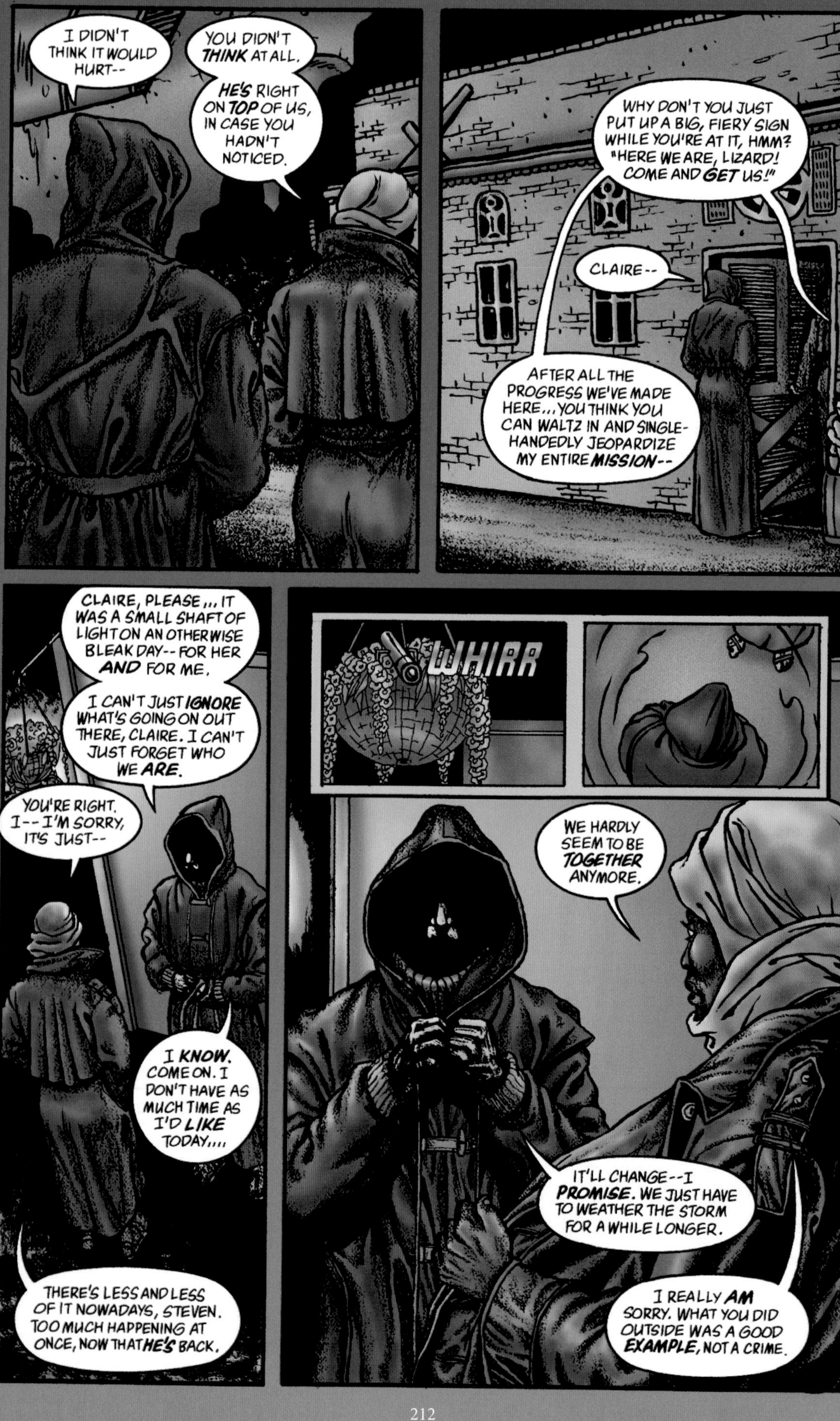
I DIDN'T THINK IT WOULD HURT--
YOU DIDN'T THINK AT ALL.
HE'S RIGHT ON TOP OF US, IN CASE YOU HADN'T NOTICED.
WHY DON'T YOU JUST PUT UP A BIG, FIERY SIGN WHILE YOU'RE AT IT, HMM? "HERE WE ARE, LIZARD! COME AND GET US!"
CLAIRE--
AFTER ALL THE PROGRESS WE'VE MADE HERE... YOU THINK YOU CAN WALTZ IN AND SINGLE-HANDEDLY JEOPARDIZE MY ENTIRE MISSION--
CLAIRE, PLEASE... IT WAS A SMALL SHAFT OF LIGHT ON AN OTHERWISE BLEAK DAY-- FOR HER AND FOR ME.
I CAN'T JUST IGNORE WHAT'S GOING ON OUT THERE, CLAIRE. I CAN'T JUST FORGET WHO WE ARE.
YOU'RE RIGHT. I-- I'M SORRY, IT'S JUST--
I KNOW. COME ON. I DON'T HAVE AS MUCH TIME AS I'D LIKE TODAY....
THERE'S LESS AND LESS OF IT NOWADAYS, STEVEN. TOO MUCH HAPPENING AT ONCE, NOW THAT HE'S BACK.
WHIRR
WE HARDLY SEEM TO BE TOGETHER ANYMORE.
IT'LL CHANGE--I PROMISE. WE JUST HAVE TO WEATHER THE STORM FOR A WHILE LONGER.
I REALLY AM SORRY. WHAT YOU DID OUTSIDE WAS A GOOD EXAMPLE, NOT A CRIME.

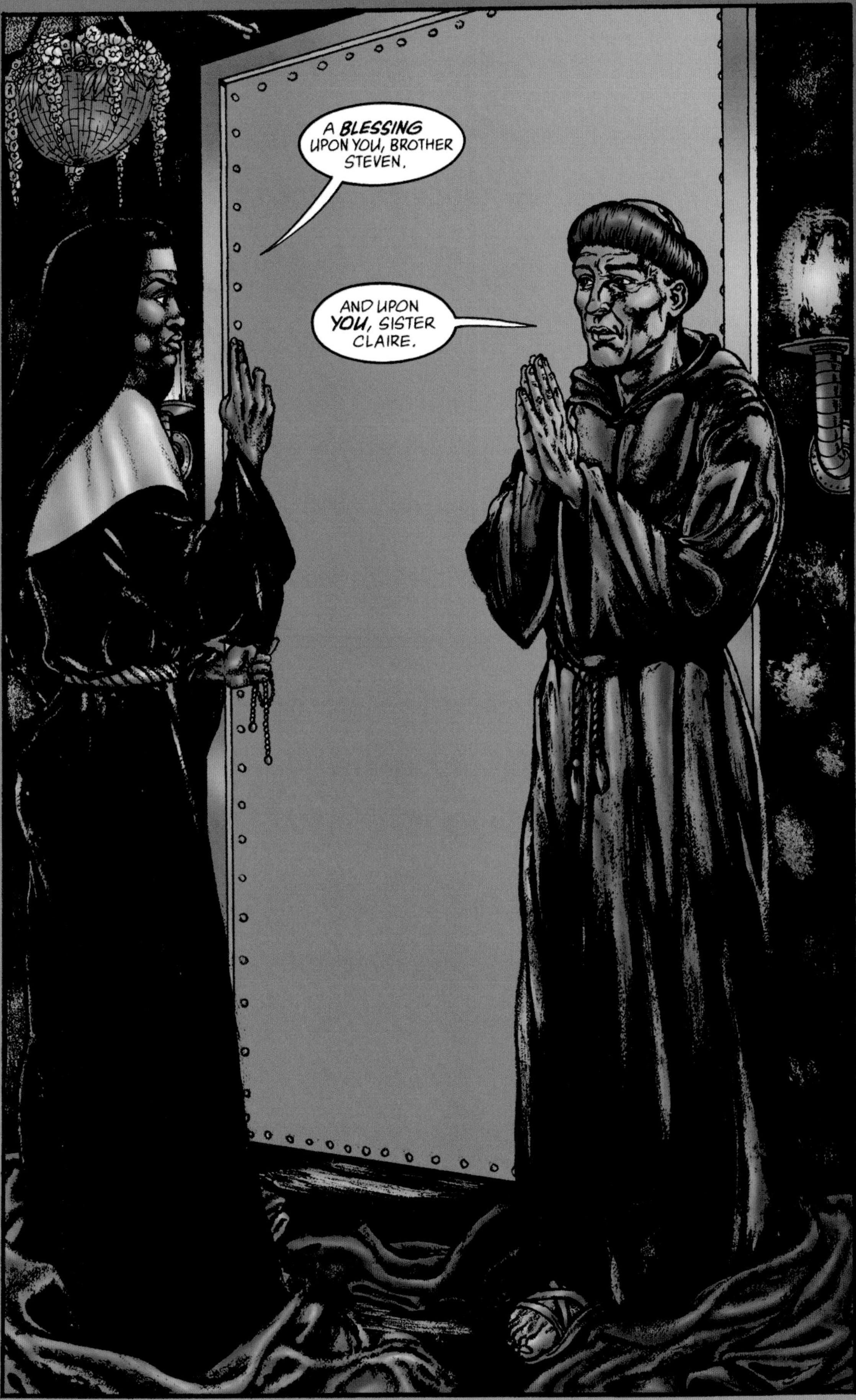
A BLESSING UPON YOU, BROTHER STEVEN.
AND UPON YOU, SISTER CLAIRE.

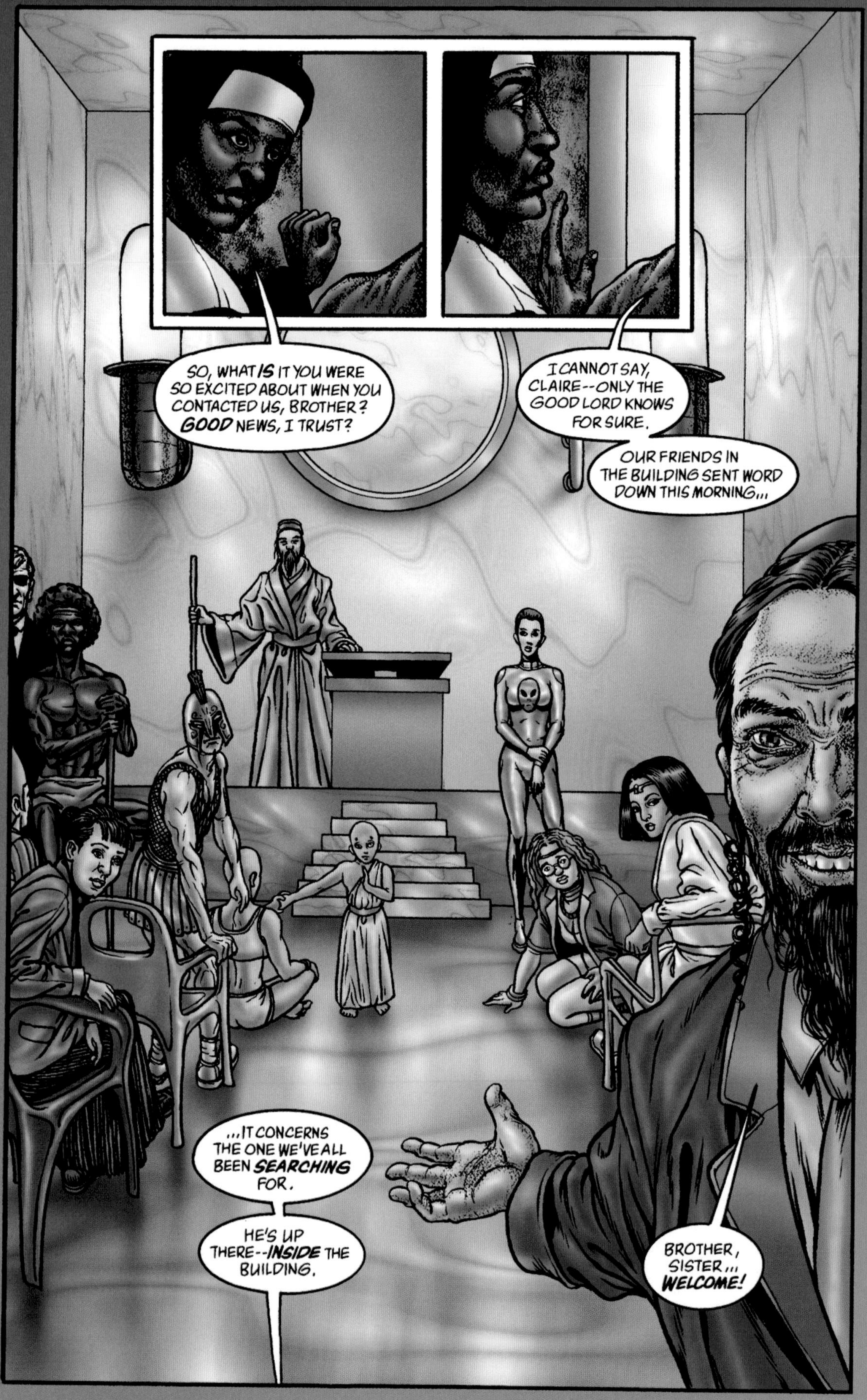
SO, WHAT IS IT YOU WERE SO EXCITED ABOUT WHEN YOU CONTACTED US, BROTHER? GOOD NEWS, I TRUST?
I CANNOT SAY, CLAIRE--ONLY THE GOOD LORD KNOWS FOR SURE.
OUR FRIENDS IN THE BUILDING SENT WORD DOWN THIS MORNING...
...IT CONCERNS THE ONE WE'VE ALL BEEN SEARCHING FOR.
HE'S UP THERE--INSIDE THE BUILDING.
BROTHER, SISTER... WELCOME!

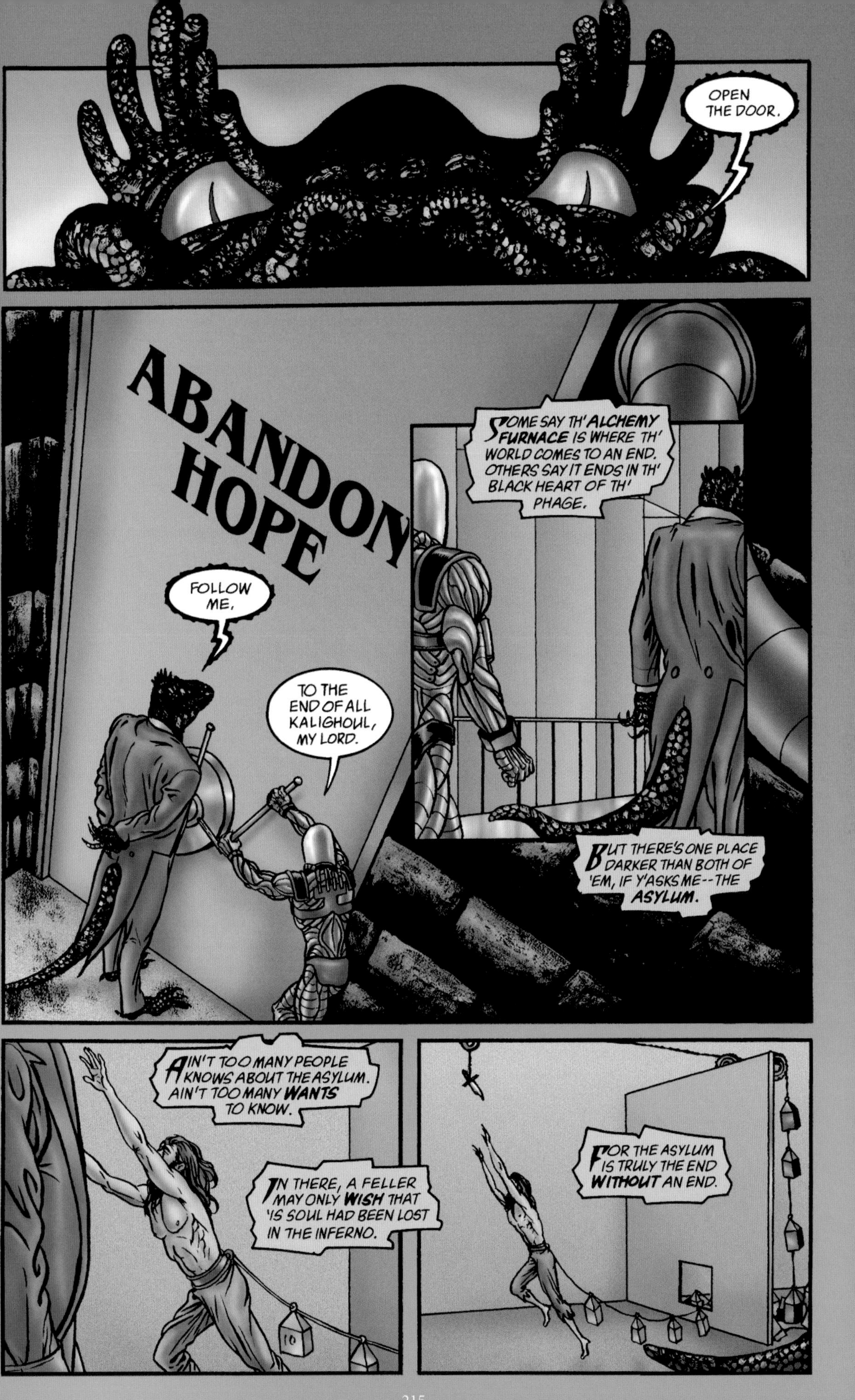
OPEN THE DOOR.
ABANDON HOPE
SOME SAY TH' ALCHEMY FURNACE IS WHERE TH' WORLD COMES TO AN END. OTHERS SAY IT ENDS IN TH' BLACK HEART OF TH' PHAGE.
FOLLOW ME.
TO THE END OF ALL KALIGHOUL, MY LORD.
BUT THERE'S ONE PLACE DARKER THAN BOTH OF 'EM, IF Y'ASKS ME--THE ASYLUM.
AIN'T TOO MANY PEOPLE KNOWS ABOUT THE ASYLUM. AIN'T TOO MANY WANTS TO KNOW.
IN THERE, A FELLER MAY ONLY WISH THAT 'IS SOUL HAD BEEN LOST IN THE INFERNO.
FOR THE ASYLUM IS TRULY THE END WITHOUT AN END.

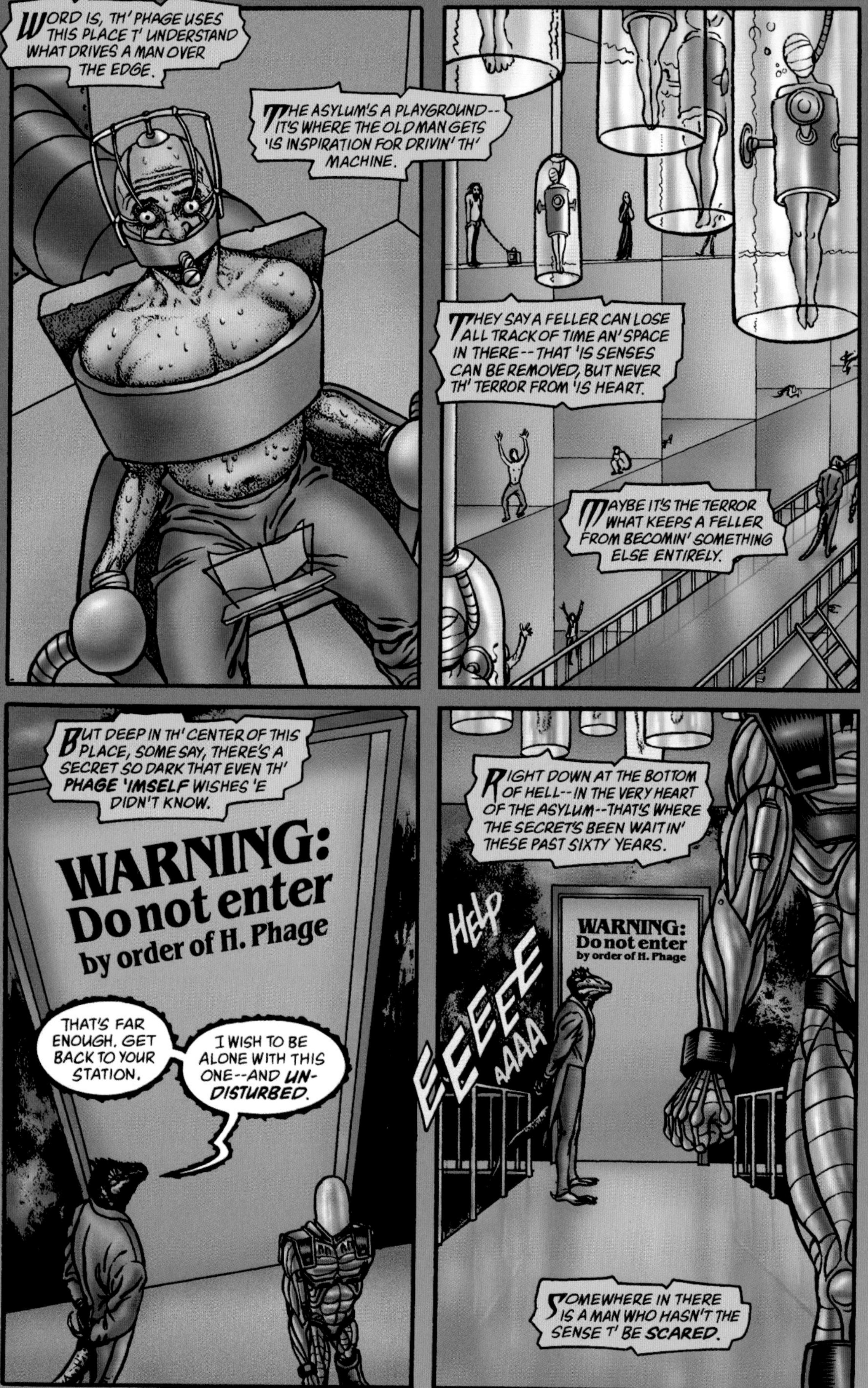
WORD IS, TH' PHAGE USES THIS PLACE T' UNDERSTAND WHAT DRIVES A MAN OVER THE EDGE.
THE ASYLUM'S A PLAYGROUND-- IT'S WHERE THE OLD MAN GETS 'IS INSPIRATION FOR DRIVIN' TH' MACHINE.
THEY SAY A FELLER CAN LOSE ALL TRACK OF TIME AN' SPACE IN THERE--THAT 'IS SENSES CAN BE REMOVED, BUT NEVER TH' TERROR FROM 'IS HEART.
MAYBE IT'S THE TERROR WHAT KEEPS A FELLER FROM BECOMIN' SOMETHING ELSE ENTIRELY.
BUT DEEP IN TH' CENTER OF THIS PLACE, SOME SAY, THERE'S A SECRET SO DARK THAT EVEN TH' PHAGE 'IMSELF WISHES 'E DIDN'T KNOW.
WARNING: Do not enter by order of H. Phage
THAT'S FAR ENOUGH. GET BACK TO YOUR STATION.
I WISH TO BE ALONE WITH THIS ONE--AND UNDISTURBED.
RIGHT DOWN AT THE BOTTOM OF HELL--IN THE VERY HEART OF THE ASYLUM--THAT'S WHERE THE SECRET'S BEEN WAITIN' THESE PAST SIXTY YEARS.
HELP
EEEEEAAAA
WARNING: Do not enter by order of H. Phage
SOMEWHERE IN THERE IS A MAN WHO HASN'T THE SENSE T' BE SCARED.

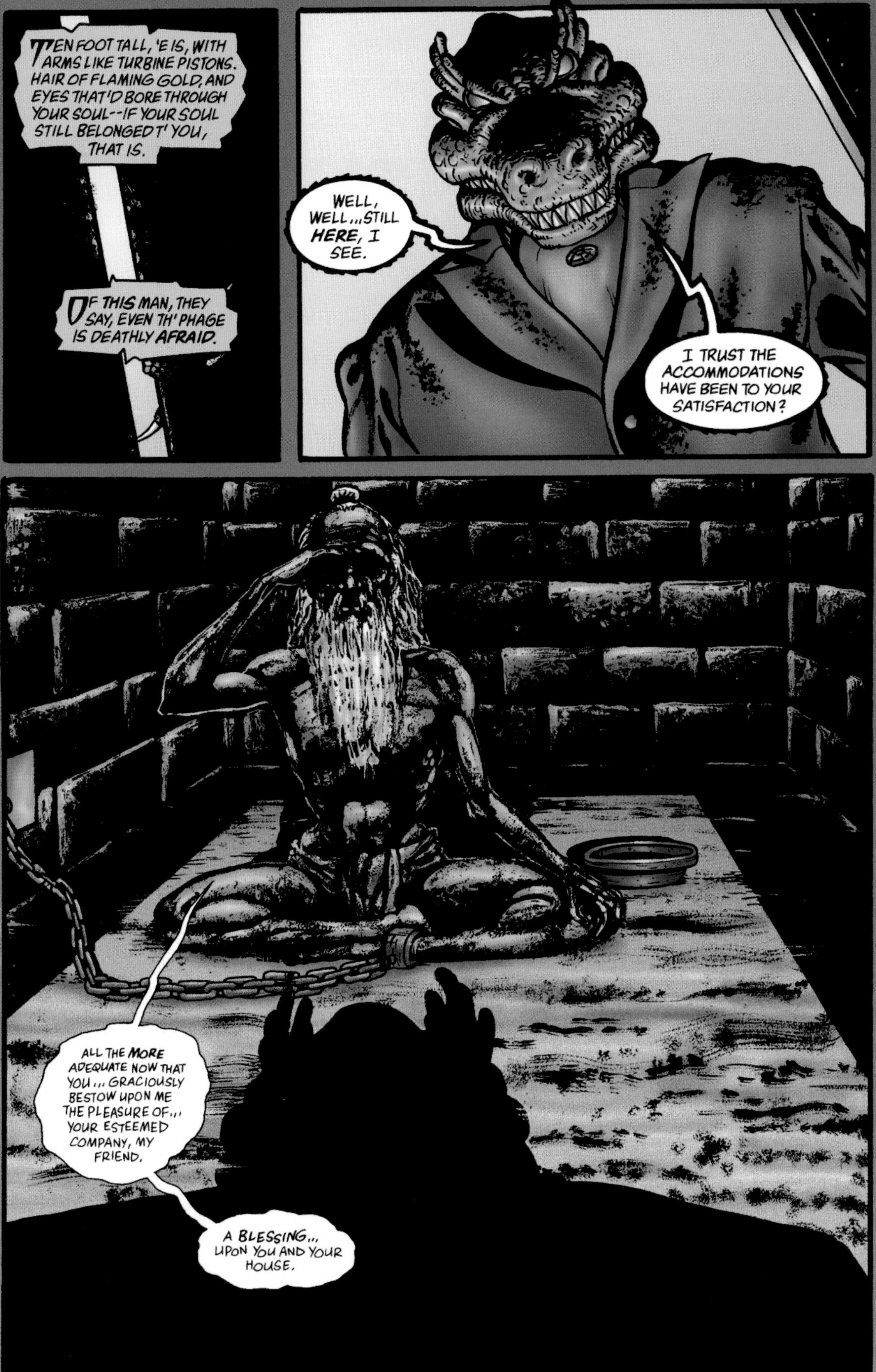
TEN FOOT TALL, 'E IS, WITH ARMS LIKE TURBINE PISTONS. HAIR OF FLAMING GOLD, AND EYES THAT'D BORE THROUGH YOUR SOUL--IF YOUR SOUL STILL BELONGED T' YOU, THAT IS.
OF THIS MAN, THEY SAY, EVEN TH' PHAGE IS DEATHLY AFRAID.
WELL, WELL...STILL HERE, I SEE.
I TRUST THE ACCOMMODATIONS HAVE BEEN TO YOUR SATISFACTION?
ALL THE MORE ADEQUATE NOW THAT YOU... GRACIOUSLY BESTOW UPON ME THE PLEASURE OF... YOUR ESTEEMED COMPANY, MY FRIEND.
A BLESSING... UPON YOU AND YOUR HOUSE.

TO BE CONTINUED!

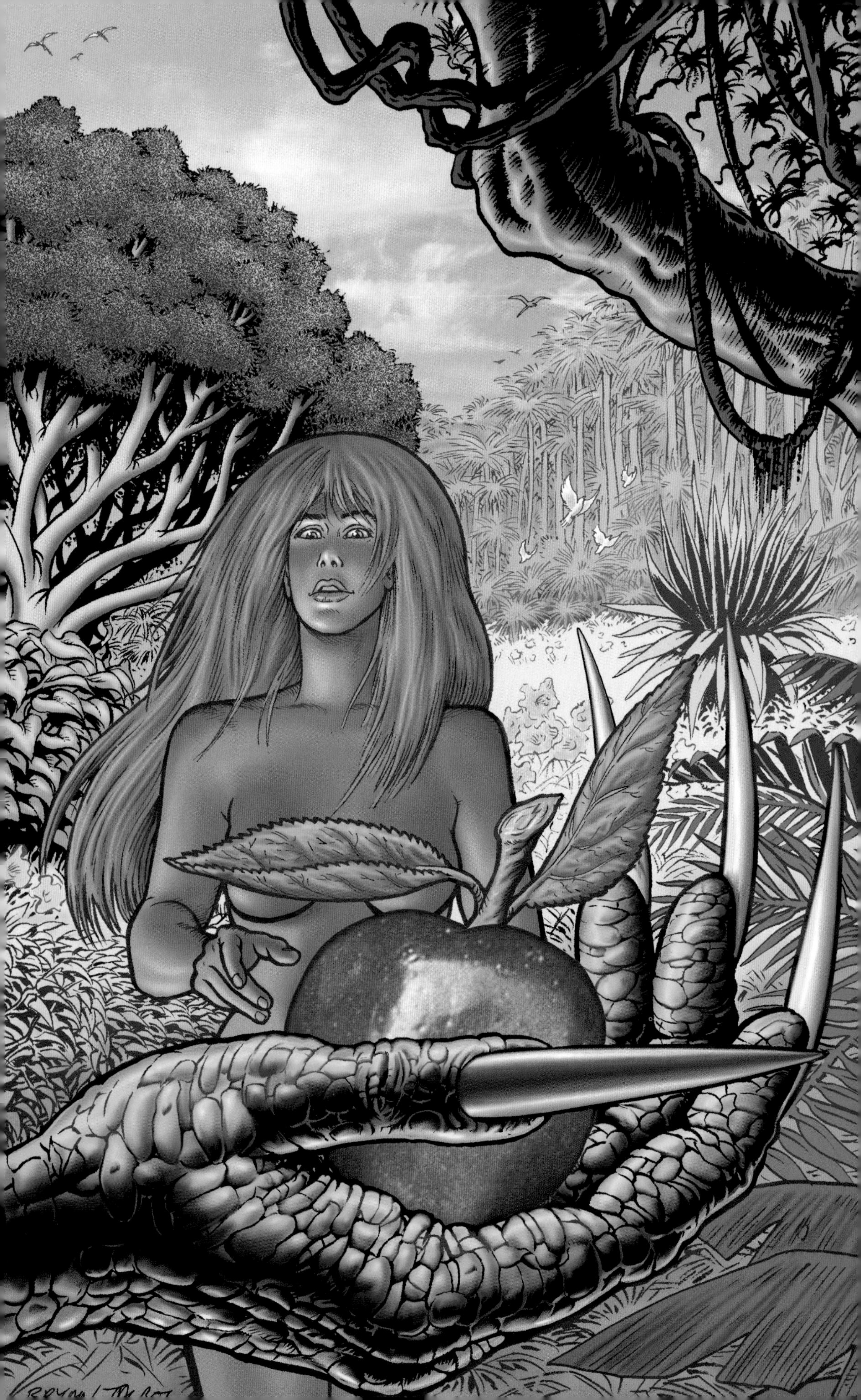

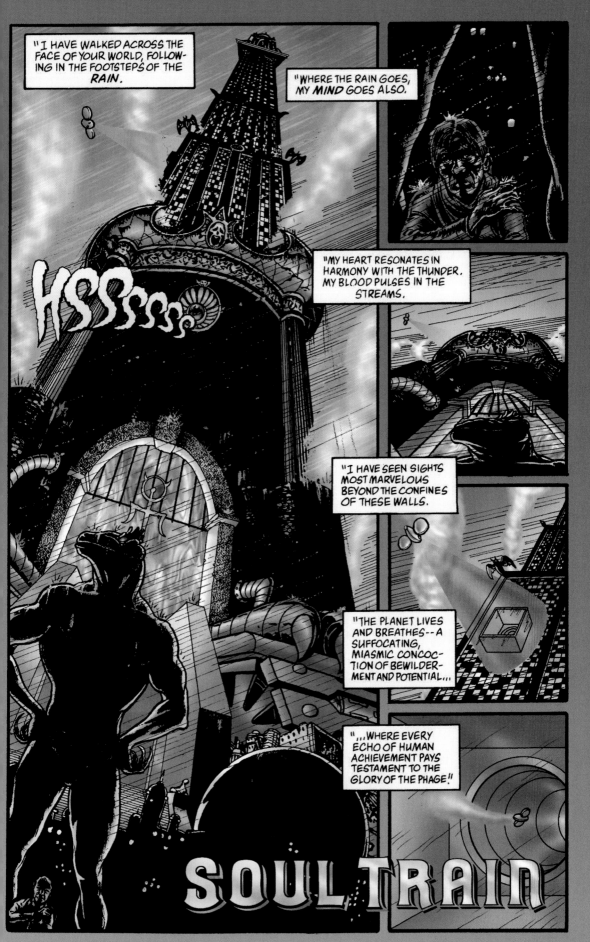

"I HAVE WALKED ACROSS THE FACE OF YOUR WORLD, FOLLOWING IN THE FOOTSTEPS OF THE *RAIN*.

"WHERE THE RAIN GOES, MY *MIND* GOES ALSO.

"MY HEART RESONATES IN HARMONY WITH THE THUNDER. MY BLOOD PULSES IN THE STREAMS.

"I HAVE SEEN SIGHTS MOST MARVELOUS BEYOND THE CONFINES OF THESE WALLS.

"THE PLANET LIVES AND BREATHES-- A SUFFOCATING, MIASMIC CONCOCTION OF BEWILDERMENT AND POTENTIAL...

"...WHERE EVERY ECHO OF HUMAN ACHIEVEMENT PAYS TESTAMENT TO THE GLORY OF THE PHAGE!"

HSSSSSS

SOULTRAIN

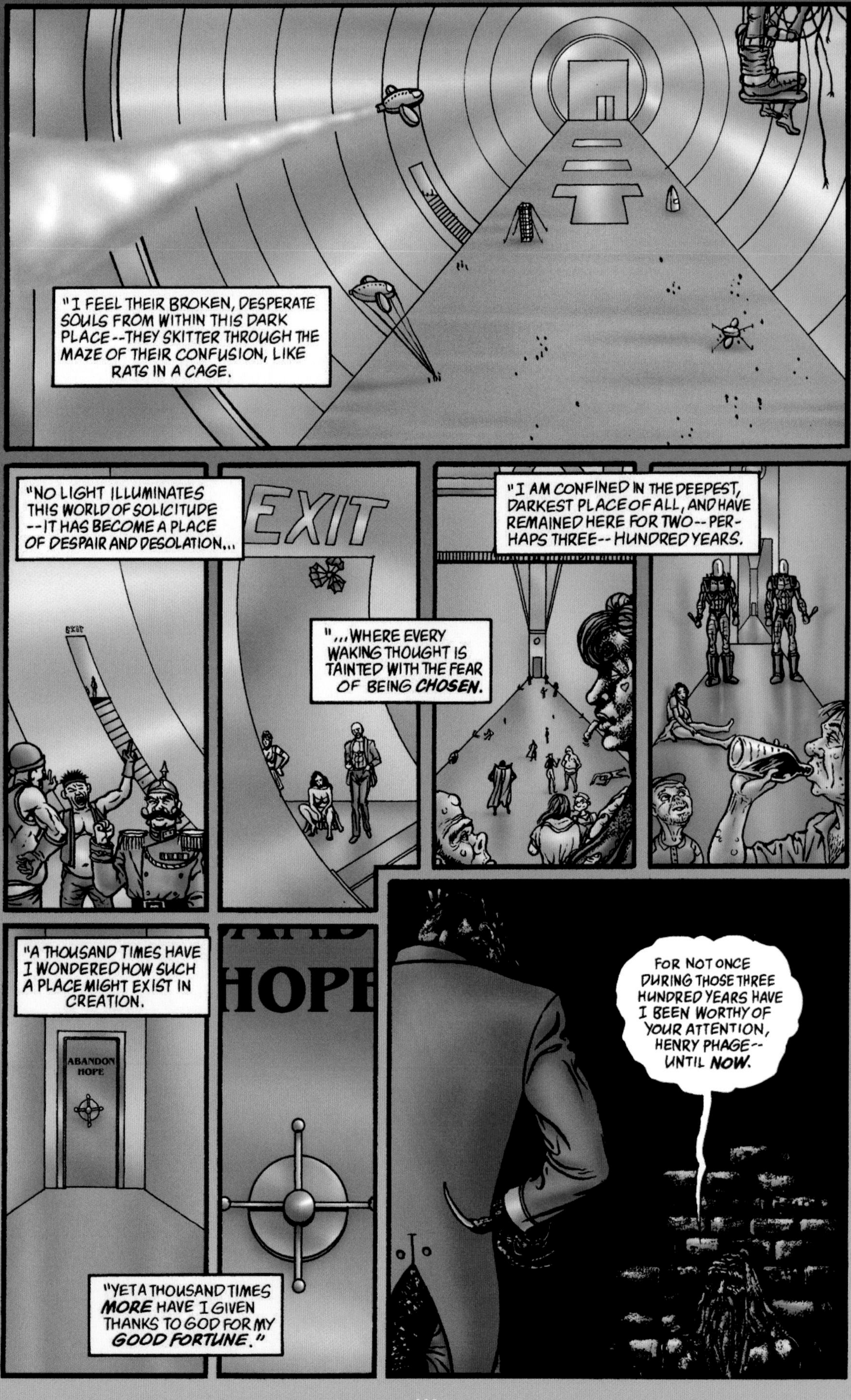
"I FEEL THEIR BROKEN, DESPERATE SOULS FROM WITHIN THIS DARK PLACE--THEY SKITTER THROUGH THE MAZE OF THEIR CONFUSION, LIKE RATS IN A CAGE.
"NO LIGHT ILLUMINATES THIS WORLD OF SOLICITUDE --IT HAS BECOME A PLACE OF DESPAIR AND DESOLATION...
EXIT
"...WHERE EVERY WAKING THOUGHT IS TAINTED WITH THE FEAR OF BEING CHOSEN.
"I AM CONFINED IN THE DEEPEST, DARKEST PLACE OF ALL, AND HAVE REMAINED HERE FOR TWO--PERHAPS THREE--HUNDRED YEARS.
"A THOUSAND TIMES HAVE I WONDERED HOW SUCH A PLACE MIGHT EXIST IN CREATION.
ABANDON HOPE
HOPE
"YET A THOUSAND TIMES MORE HAVE I GIVEN THANKS TO GOD FOR MY GOOD FORTUNE."
FOR NOT ONCE DURING THOSE THREE HUNDRED YEARS HAVE I BEEN WORTHY OF YOUR ATTENTION, HENRY PHAGE--UNTIL NOW.

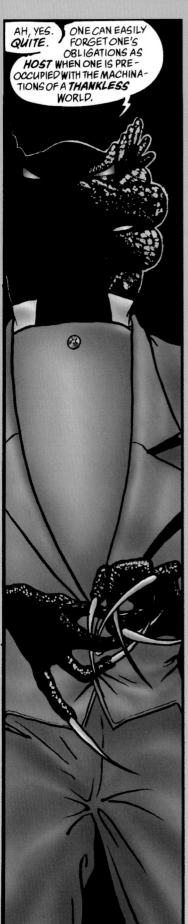

AH, YES. *QUITE.* ONE CAN EASILY FORGET ONE'S OBLIGATIONS AS *HOST* WHEN ONE IS PRE-OCCUPIED WITH THE MACHINA-TIONS OF A *THANKLESS* WORLD.

STILL, I WAS IN THE VICINITY... AND THOUGHT YOU MIGHT *WELCOME* THE OPPORTUNITY FOR A LITTLE CHAT, OLD BOY.

A *DISCOURSE,* PERHAPS, ON THE NATURE OF THE BODY, MIND AND *SOUL?*

>HUHHH<... MY THANKS FOR YOUR HEARTFELT *CONCERN* ...MOST REVERED PHAGE....

THEN A DISCOURSE IT SHALL BE...FOR I CAN SEE YOU ARE MOST *TROUBLED* ....

HSSS... IT IS NO TROUBLE, I ASSURE YOU.

NO TROUBLE AT ALL.

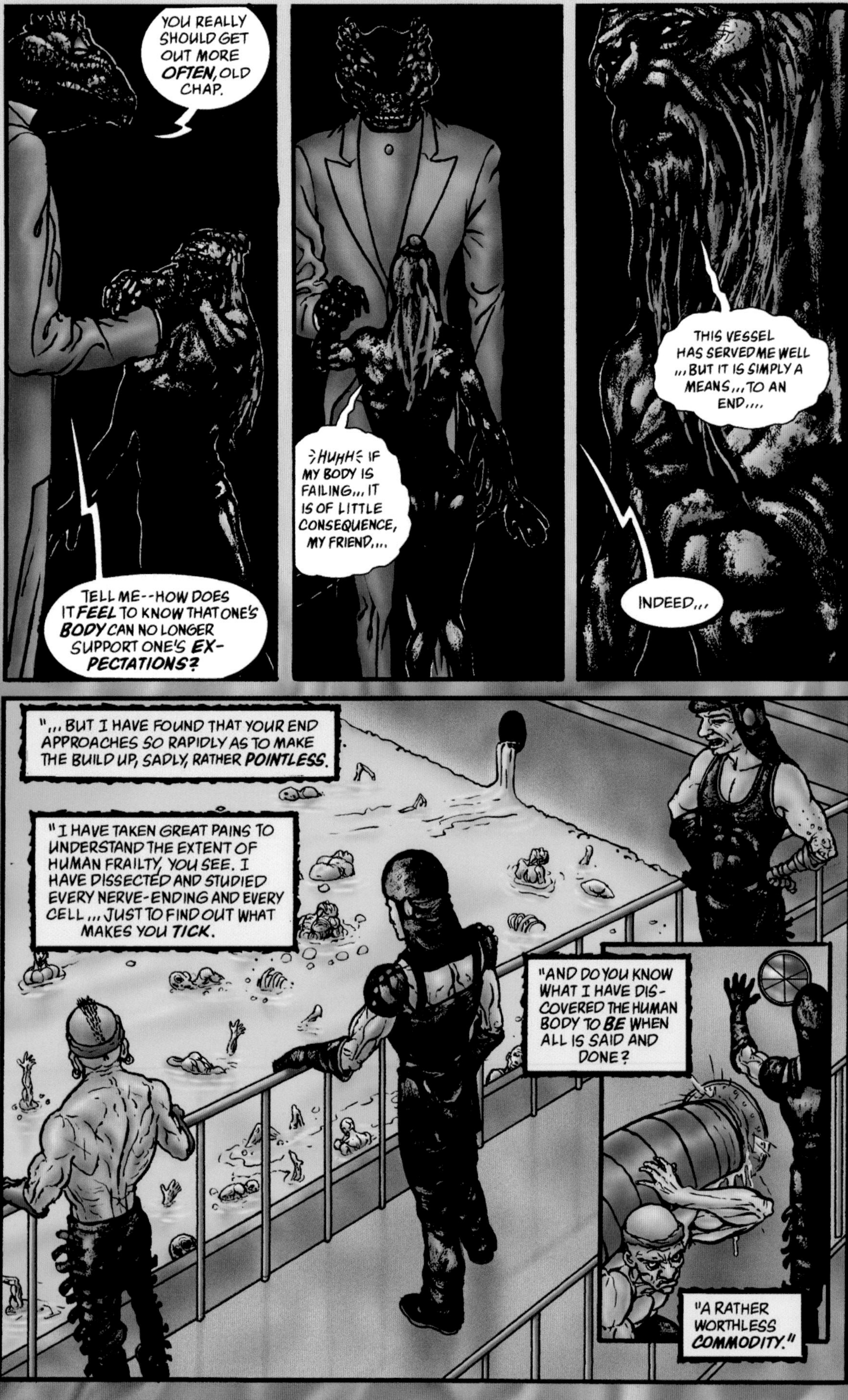
YOU REALLY SHOULD GET OUT MORE OFTEN, OLD CHAP.
TELL ME--HOW DOES IT FEEL TO KNOW THAT ONE'S BODY CAN NO LONGER SUPPORT ONE'S EX-PECTATIONS?
≷HUHH≶ IF MY BODY IS FAILING,,, IT IS OF LITTLE CONSEQUENCE, MY FRIEND,,,
THIS VESSEL HAS SERVED ME WELL ,,,BUT IT IS SIMPLY A MEANS,,,TO AN END,,,,
INDEED,,,
",,, BUT I HAVE FOUND THAT YOUR END APPROACHES SO RAPIDLY AS TO MAKE THE BUILD UP, SADLY, RATHER POINTLESS.
"I HAVE TAKEN GREAT PAINS TO UNDERSTAND THE EXTENT OF HUMAN FRAILTY, YOU SEE. I HAVE DISSECTED AND STUDIED EVERY NERVE-ENDING AND EVERY CELL,,, JUST TO FIND OUT WHAT MAKES YOU TICK.
"AND DO YOU KNOW WHAT I HAVE DIS-COVERED THE HUMAN BODY TO BE WHEN ALL IS SAID AND DONE?
"A RATHER WORTHLESS COMMODITY."

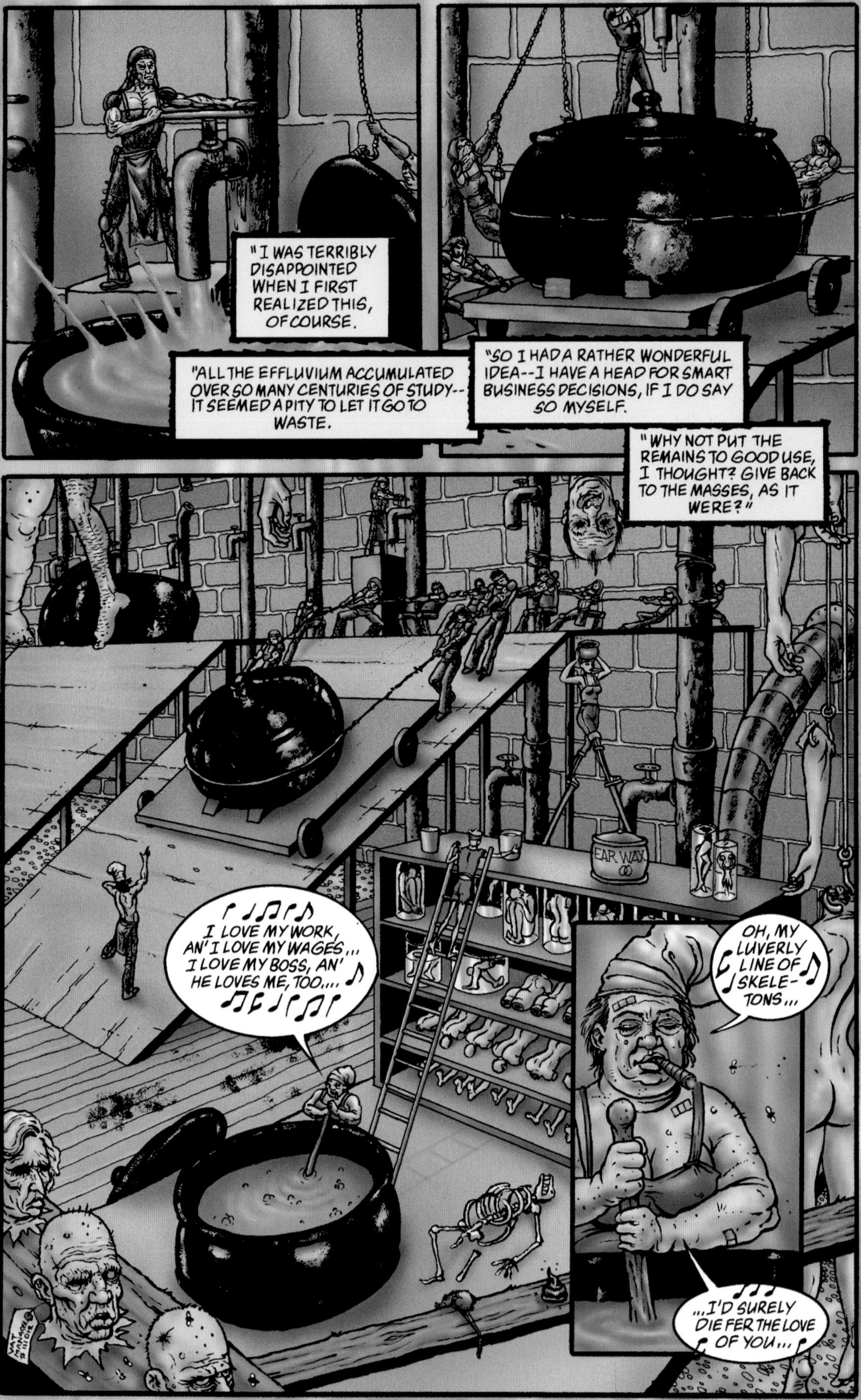
"I WAS TERRIBLY DISAPPOINTED WHEN I FIRST REALIZED THIS, OF COURSE.
"ALL THE EFFLUVIUM ACCUMULATED OVER SO MANY CENTURIES OF STUDY-- IT SEEMED A PITY TO LET IT GO TO WASTE.
"SO I HAD A RATHER WONDERFUL IDEA--I HAVE A HEAD FOR SMART BUSINESS DECISIONS, IF I DO SAY SO MYSELF.
"WHY NOT PUT THE REMAINS TO GOOD USE, I THOUGHT? GIVE BACK TO THE MASSES, AS IT WERE?"
I LOVE MY WORK, AN' I LOVE MY WAGES... I LOVE MY BOSS, AN' HE LOVES ME, TOO....
EAR WAX
OH, MY LUVERLY LINE OF SKELE-TONS...
...I'D SURELY DIE FOR THE LOVE OF YOU...

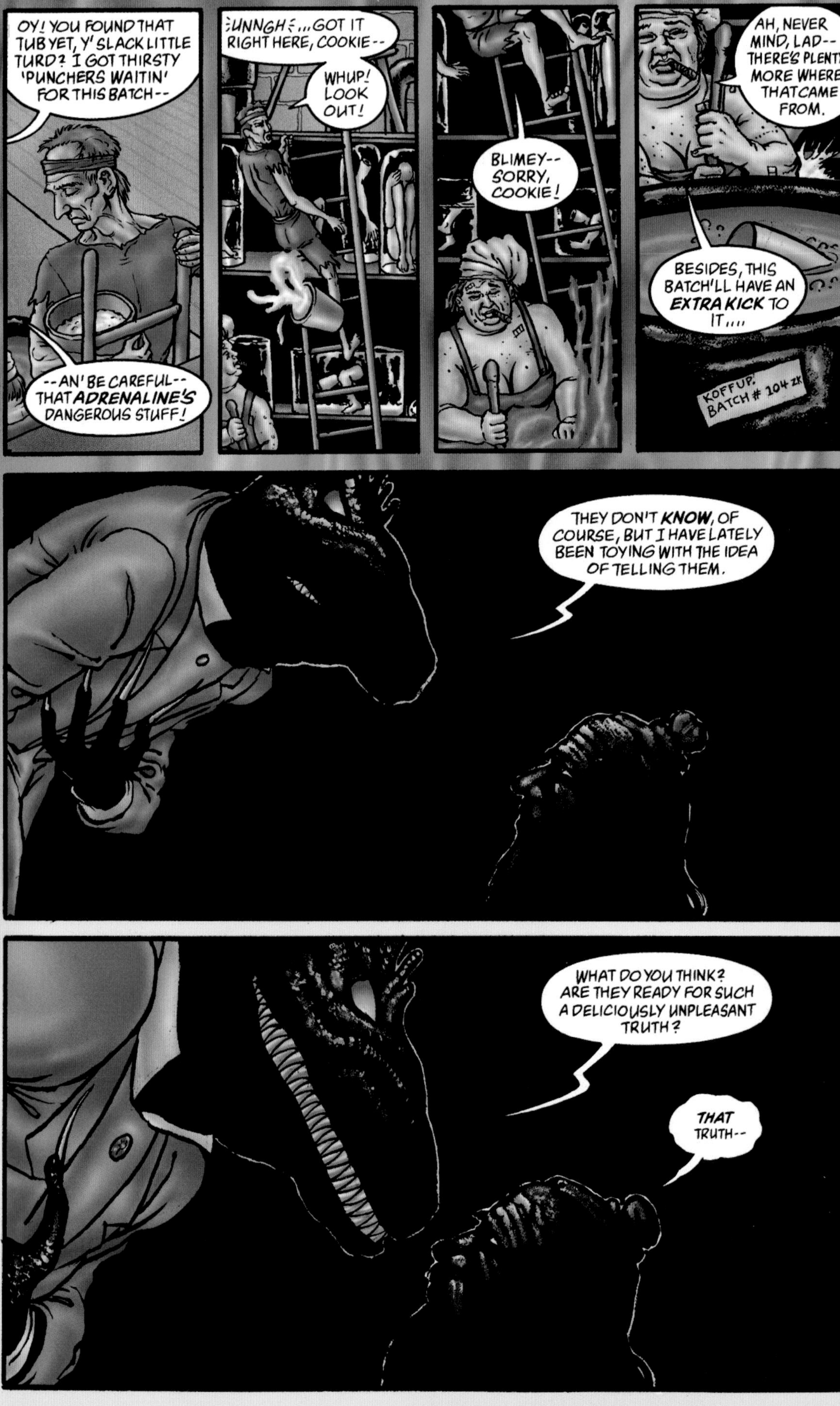
OY! YOU FOUND THAT TUB YET, Y' SLACK LITTLE TURD? I GOT THIRSTY 'PUNCHERS WAITIN' FOR THIS BATCH--
--AN' BE CAREFUL-- THAT ADRENALINE'S DANGEROUS STUFF!
UNNGH ...GOT IT RIGHT HERE, COOKIE--
WHUP! LOOK OUT!
BLIMEY-- SORRY, COOKIE!
AH, NEVER MIND, LAD-- THERE'S PLENTY MORE WHERE THAT CAME FROM.
BESIDES, THIS BATCH'LL HAVE AN EXTRA KICK TO IT....
KOFFUP! BATCH # 104 ZK
THEY DON'T KNOW, OF COURSE, BUT I HAVE LATELY BEEN TOYING WITH THE IDEA OF TELLING THEM.
WHAT DO YOU THINK? ARE THEY READY FOR SUCH A DELICIOUSLY UNPLEASANT TRUTH?
THAT TRUTH--

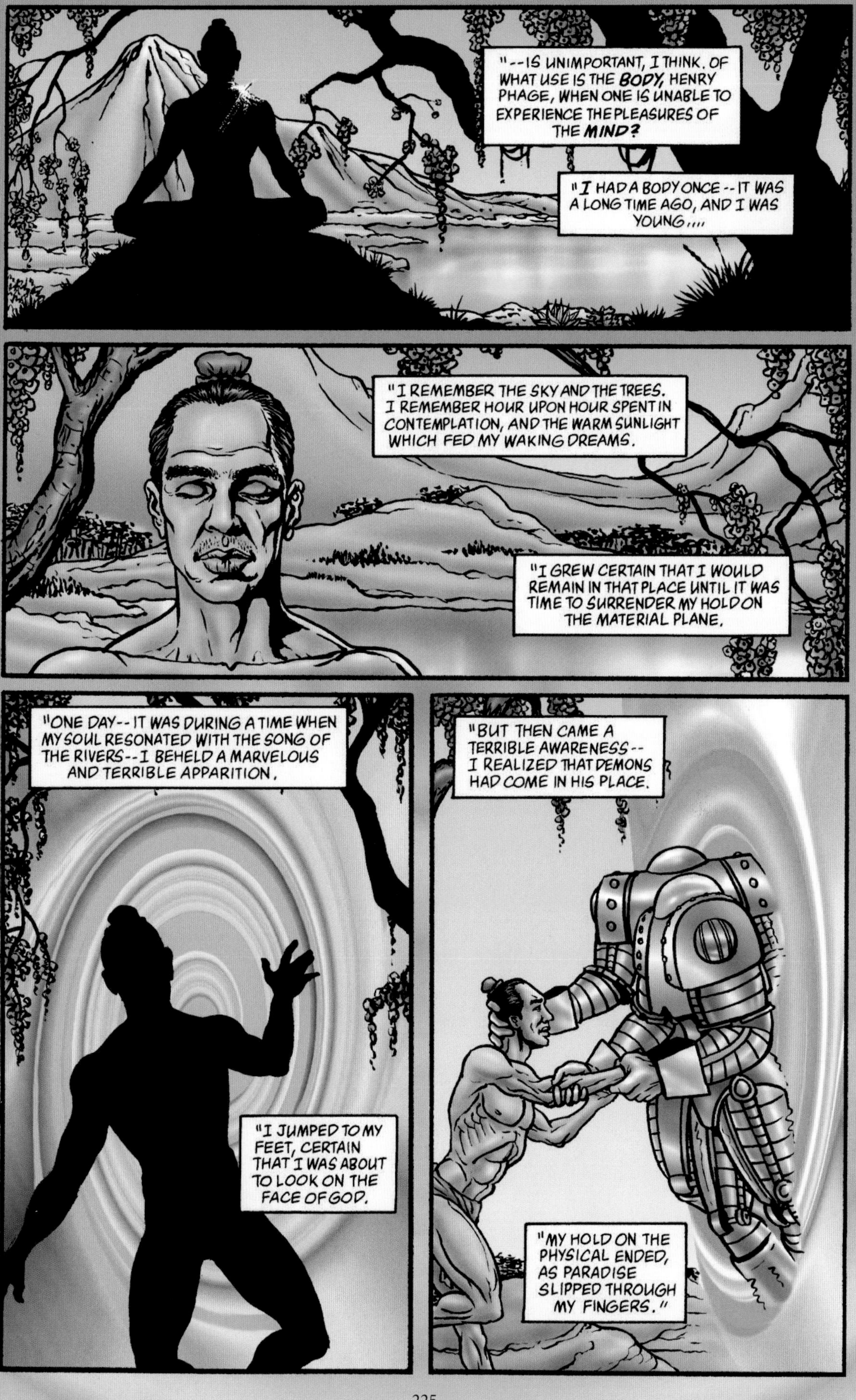
"--IS UNIMPORTANT, I THINK. OF WHAT USE IS THE BODY, HENRY PHAGE, WHEN ONE IS UNABLE TO EXPERIENCE THE PLEASURES OF THE MIND?
"I HAD A BODY ONCE--IT WAS A LONG TIME AGO, AND I WAS YOUNG....
"I REMEMBER THE SKY AND THE TREES. I REMEMBER HOUR UPON HOUR SPENT IN CONTEMPLATION, AND THE WARM SUNLIGHT WHICH FED MY WAKING DREAMS.
"I GREW CERTAIN THAT I WOULD REMAIN IN THAT PLACE UNTIL IT WAS TIME TO SURRENDER MY HOLD ON THE MATERIAL PLANE.
"ONE DAY--IT WAS DURING A TIME WHEN MY SOUL RESONATED WITH THE SONG OF THE RIVERS--I BEHELD A MARVELOUS AND TERRIBLE APPARITION.
"I JUMPED TO MY FEET, CERTAIN THAT I WAS ABOUT TO LOOK ON THE FACE OF GOD.
"BUT THEN CAME A TERRIBLE AWARENESS--I REALIZED THAT DEMONS HAD COME IN HIS PLACE.
"MY HOLD ON THE PHYSICAL ENDED, AS PARADISE SLIPPED THROUGH MY FINGERS."

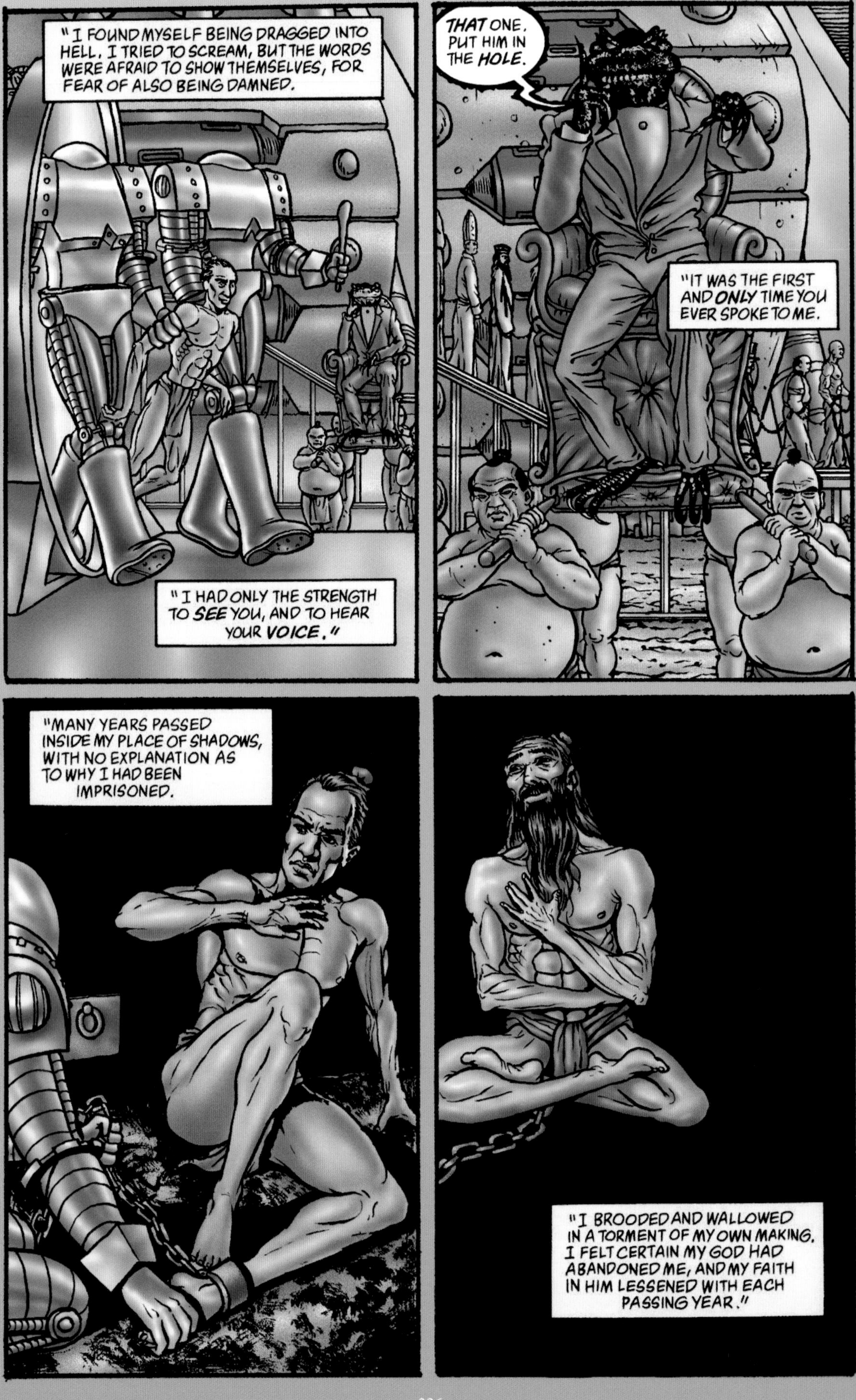
"I FOUND MYSELF BEING DRAGGED INTO HELL. I TRIED TO SCREAM, BUT THE WORDS WERE AFRAID TO SHOW THEMSELVES, FOR FEAR OF ALSO BEING DAMNED.
"I HAD ONLY THE STRENGTH TO SEE YOU, AND TO HEAR YOUR VOICE."
THAT ONE. PUT HIM IN THE HOLE.
"IT WAS THE FIRST AND ONLY TIME YOU EVER SPOKE TO ME.
"MANY YEARS PASSED INSIDE MY PLACE OF SHADOWS, WITH NO EXPLANATION AS TO WHY I HAD BEEN IMPRISONED.
"I BROODED AND WALLOWED IN A TORMENT OF MY OWN MAKING. I FELT CERTAIN MY GOD HAD ABANDONED ME, AND MY FAITH IN HIM LESSENED WITH EACH PASSING YEAR."

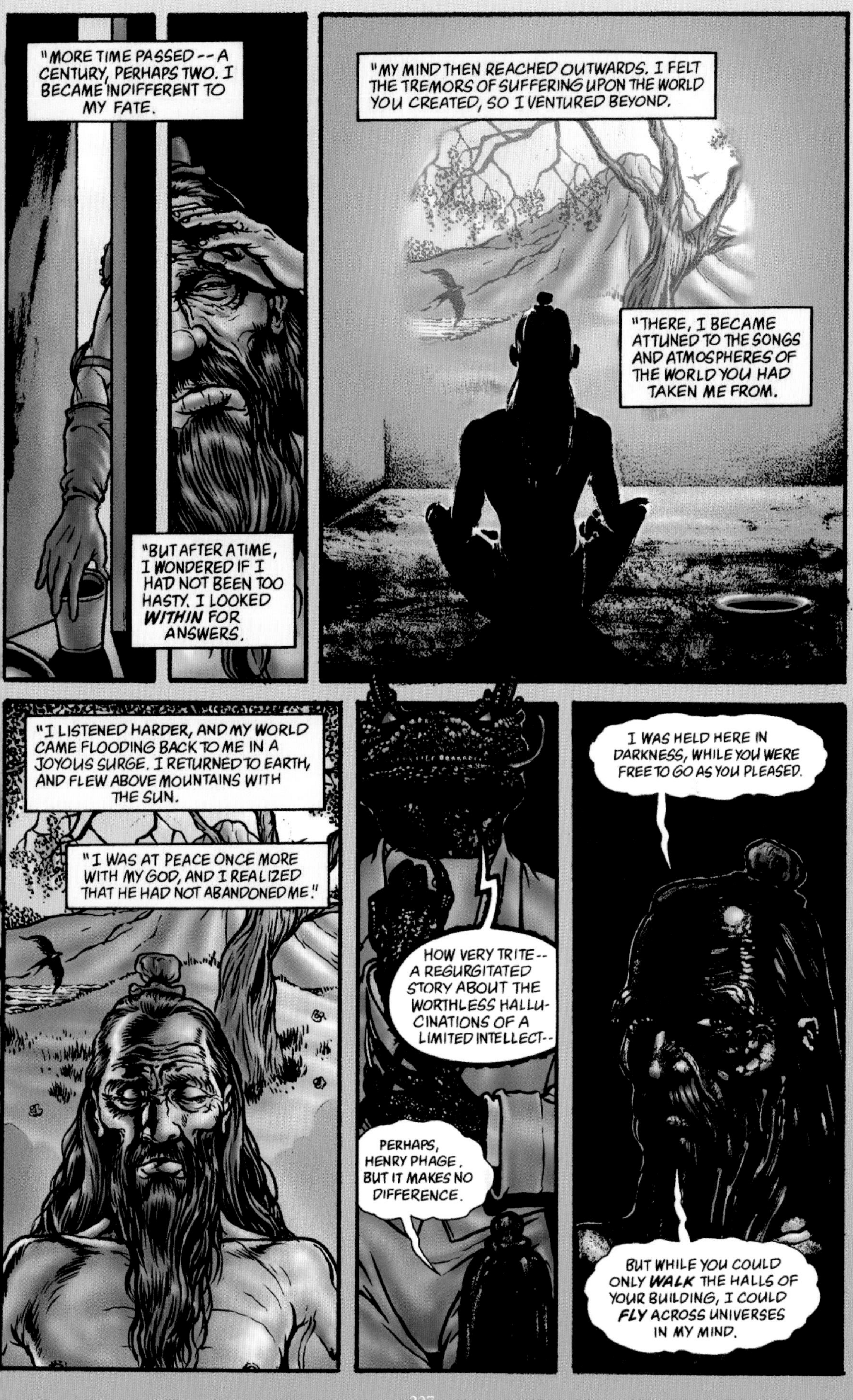
"MORE TIME PASSED -- A CENTURY, PERHAPS TWO. I BECAME INDIFFERENT TO MY FATE.
"BUT AFTER A TIME, I WONDERED IF I HAD NOT BEEN TOO HASTY. I LOOKED **WITHIN** FOR ANSWERS.
"MY MIND THEN REACHED OUTWARDS. I FELT THE TREMORS OF SUFFERING UPON THE WORLD YOU CREATED, SO I VENTURED BEYOND.
"THERE, I BECAME ATTUNED TO THE SONGS AND ATMOSPHERES OF THE WORLD YOU HAD TAKEN ME FROM.
"I LISTENED HARDER, AND MY WORLD CAME FLOODING BACK TO ME IN A JOYOUS SURGE. I RETURNED TO EARTH, AND FLEW ABOVE MOUNTAINS WITH THE SUN.
"I WAS AT PEACE ONCE MORE WITH MY GOD, AND I REALIZED THAT HE HAD NOT ABANDONED ME."
HOW VERY TRITE-- A REGURGITATED STORY ABOUT THE WORTHLESS HALLUCINATIONS OF A LIMITED INTELLECT--
PERHAPS, HENRY PHAGE, BUT IT MAKES NO DIFFERENCE.
I WAS HELD HERE IN DARKNESS, WHILE YOU WERE FREE TO GO AS YOU PLEASED.
BUT WHILE YOU COULD ONLY **WALK** THE HALLS OF YOUR BUILDING, I COULD **FLY** ACROSS UNIVERSES IN MY MIND.

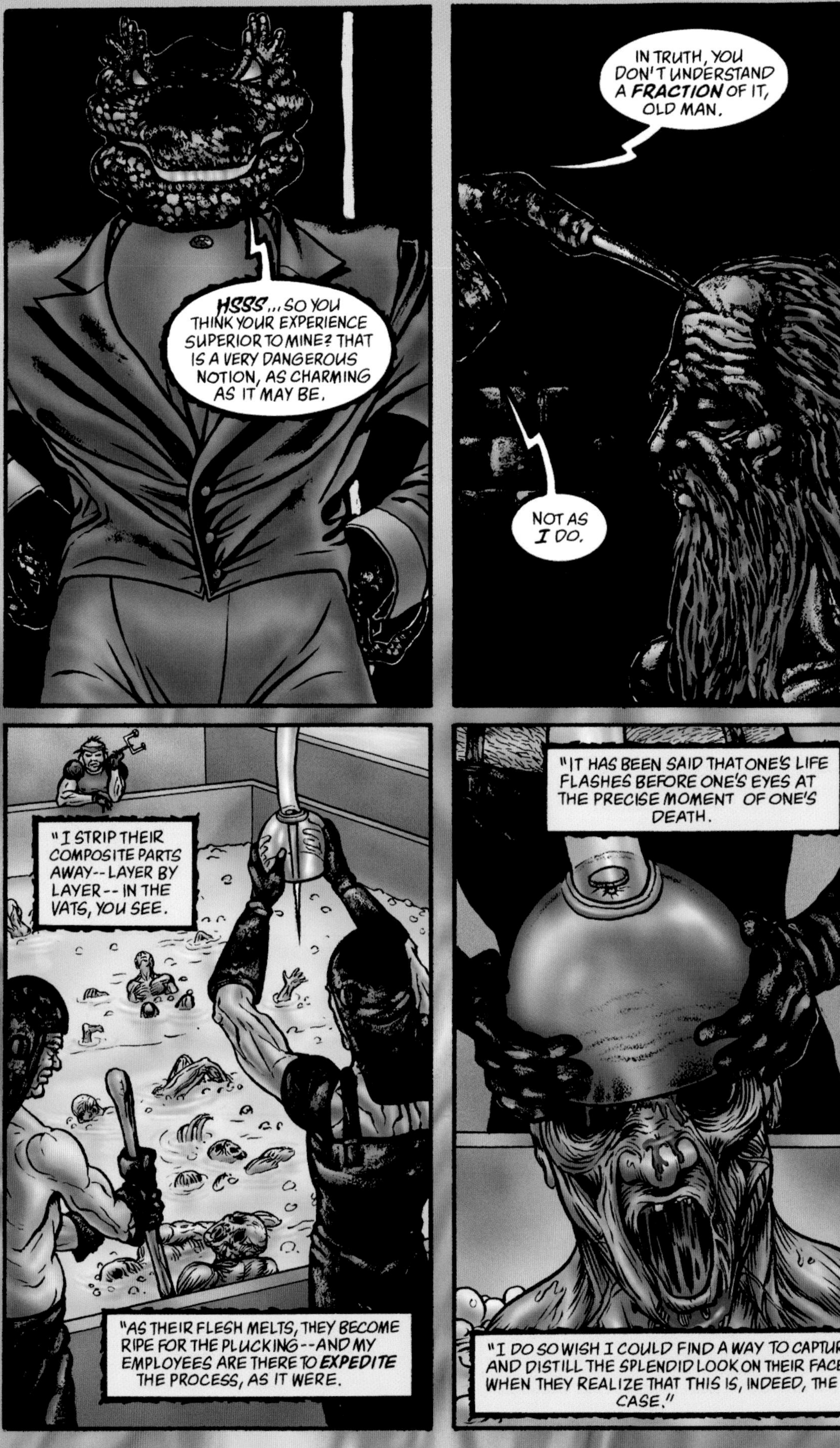
HSSS... SO YOU THINK YOUR EXPERIENCE SUPERIOR TO MINE? THAT IS A VERY DANGEROUS NOTION, AS CHARMING AS IT MAY BE.
IN TRUTH, YOU DON'T UNDERSTAND A FRACTION OF IT, OLD MAN.
NOT AS I DO.
"I STRIP THEIR COMPOSITE PARTS AWAY--LAYER BY LAYER--IN THE VATS, YOU SEE.
"AS THEIR FLESH MELTS, THEY BECOME RIPE FOR THE PLUCKING--AND MY EMPLOYEES ARE THERE TO EXPEDITE THE PROCESS, AS IT WERE.
"IT HAS BEEN SAID THAT ONE'S LIFE FLASHES BEFORE ONE'S EYES AT THE PRECISE MOMENT OF ONE'S DEATH.
"I DO SO WISH I COULD FIND A WAY TO CAPTURE AND DISTILL THE SPLENDID LOOK ON THEIR FACES WHEN THEY REALIZE THAT THIS IS, INDEED, THE CASE."

"I SIPHON OFF EACH MEMORY, ONE BY ONE, AND BRING THEM UPSTAIRS TO BE COMMITTED TO MY PNEUMATIC MACHINES.

"EVERY LAST DROP OF SELF GOES INTO THE TUBES, FOR MY PERUSAL.

"MY KEYPUNCHERS' INSTRUCTIONS ARE QUITE EXPLICIT--

"--THEY ARE REQUIRED TO SAVE ONLY THE MOST SATISFYING OF LIFE'S EXPERIENCES.

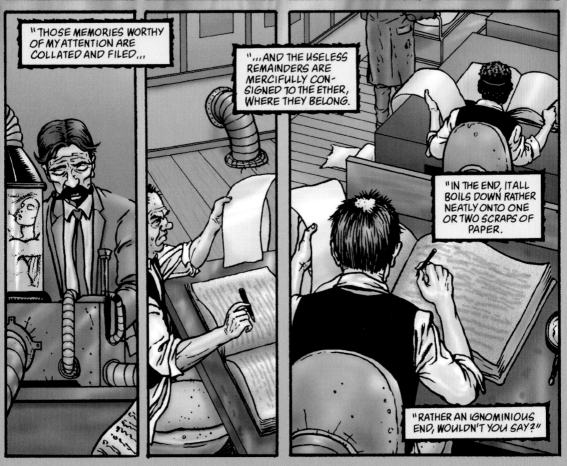

"THOSE MEMORIES WORTHY OF MY ATTENTION ARE COLLATED AND FILED...

"...AND THE USELESS REMAINDERS ARE MERCIFULLY CON-SIGNED TO THE ETHER, WHERE THEY BELONG.

"IN THE END, IT ALL BOILS DOWN RATHER NEATLY ONTO ONE OR TWO SCRAPS OF PAPER.

"RATHER AN IGNOMINIOUS END, WOULDN'T YOU SAY?"

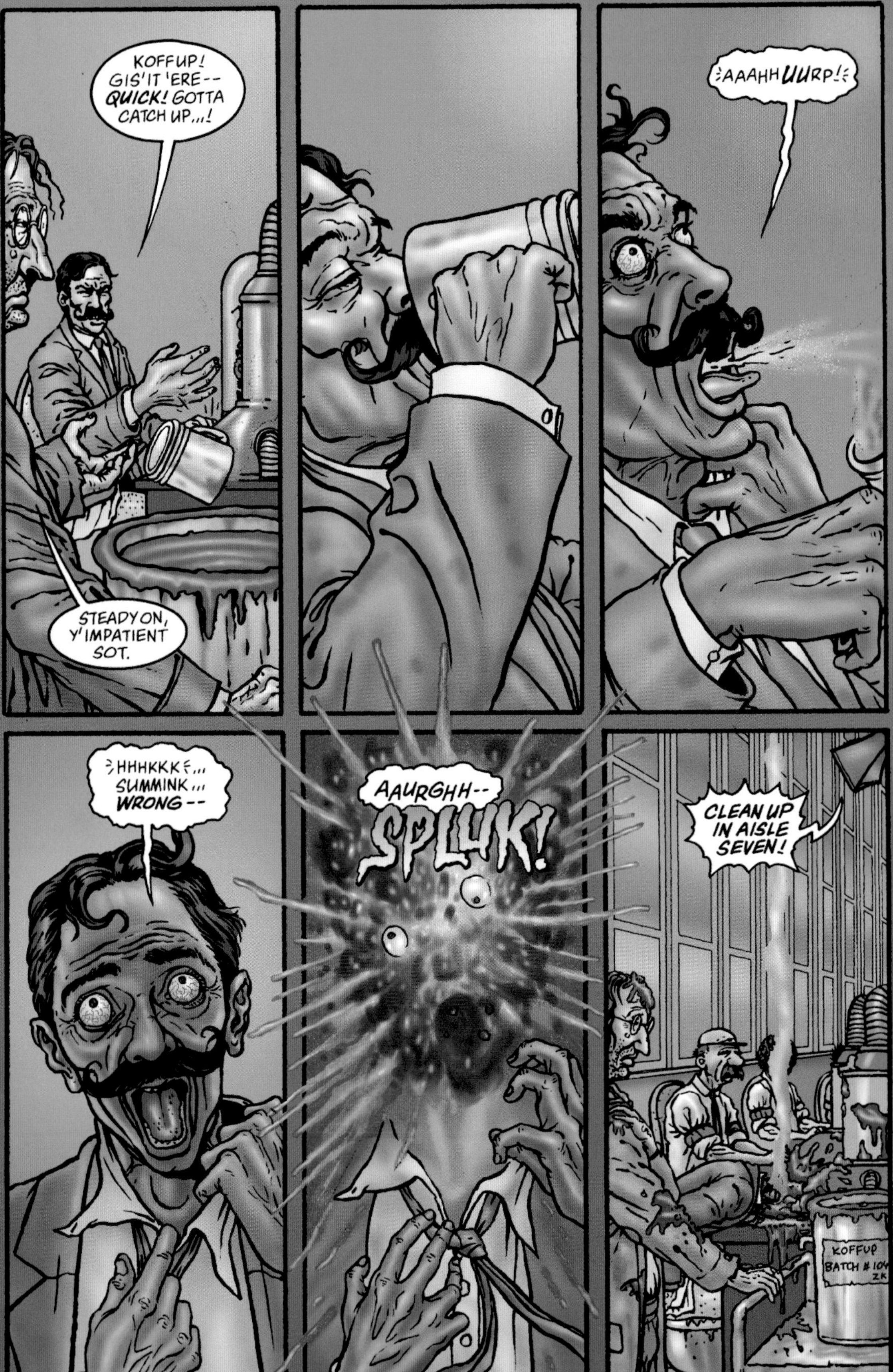
KOFFUP! GIS'IT 'ERE-- QUICK! GOTTA CATCH UP...!
STEADY ON, Y'IMPATIENT SOT.
AAAHHUURP!
HHHKKK... SUMMINK... WRONG--
AAURGHH--
SPLUK!
CLEAN UP IN AISLE SEVEN!
KOFFUP BATCH # 104 ZK

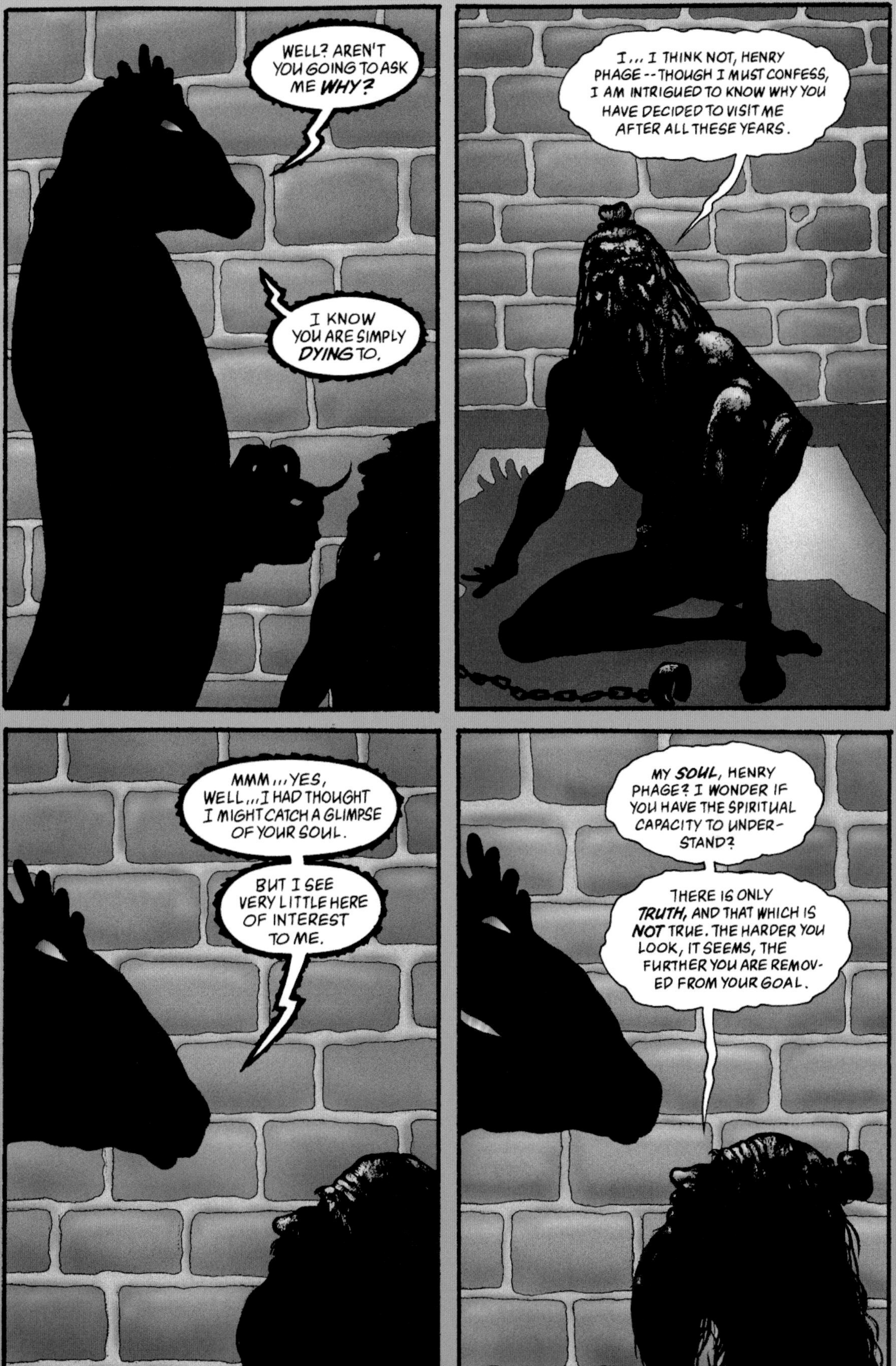

WELL? AREN'T YOU GOING TO ASK ME *WHY?*
I KNOW YOU ARE SIMPLY *DYING* TO.
I... I THINK NOT, HENRY PHAGE--THOUGH I MUST CONFESS, I AM INTRIGUED TO KNOW WHY YOU HAVE DECIDED TO VISIT ME AFTER ALL THESE YEARS.
MMM... YES, WELL... I HAD THOUGHT I MIGHT CATCH A GLIMPSE OF YOUR SOUL.
BUT I SEE VERY LITTLE HERE OF INTEREST TO ME.
MY *SOUL*, HENRY PHAGE? I WONDER IF YOU HAVE THE SPIRITUAL CAPACITY TO UNDER-STAND?
THERE IS ONLY *TRUTH*, AND THAT WHICH IS *NOT* TRUE. THE HARDER YOU LOOK, IT SEEMS, THE FURTHER YOU ARE REMOV-ED FROM YOUR GOAL.

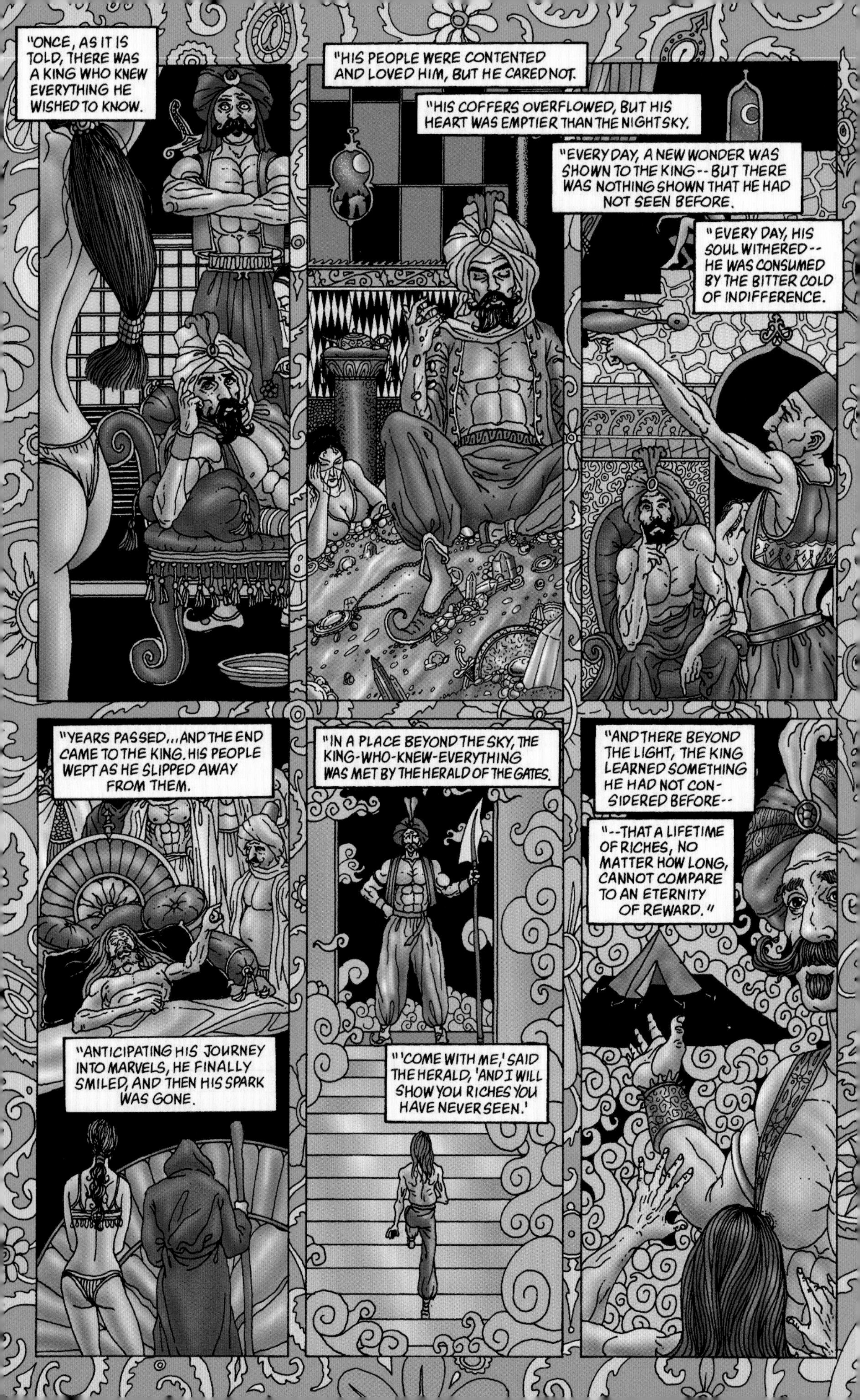
"ONCE, AS IT IS TOLD, THERE WAS A KING WHO KNEW EVERYTHING HE WISHED TO KNOW.
"HIS PEOPLE WERE CONTENTED AND LOVED HIM, BUT HE CARED NOT.
"HIS COFFERS OVERFLOWED, BUT HIS HEART WAS EMPTIER THAN THE NIGHT SKY.
"EVERY DAY, A NEW WONDER WAS SHOWN TO THE KING -- BUT THERE WAS NOTHING SHOWN THAT HE HAD NOT SEEN BEFORE.
"EVERY DAY, HIS SOUL WITHERED -- HE WAS CONSUMED BY THE BITTER COLD OF INDIFFERENCE.
"YEARS PASSED... AND THE END CAME TO THE KING. HIS PEOPLE WEPT AS HE SLIPPED AWAY FROM THEM.
"ANTICIPATING HIS JOURNEY INTO MARVELS, HE FINALLY SMILED, AND THEN HIS SPARK WAS GONE.
"IN A PLACE BEYOND THE SKY, THE KING-WHO-KNEW-EVERYTHING WAS MET BY THE HERALD OF THE GATES.
"'COME WITH ME,' SAID THE HERALD, 'AND I WILL SHOW YOU RICHES YOU HAVE NEVER SEEN.'
"AND THERE BEYOND THE LIGHT, THE KING LEARNED SOMETHING HE HAD NOT CONSIDERED BEFORE--
"--THAT A LIFETIME OF RICHES, NO MATTER HOW LONG, CANNOT COMPARE TO AN ETERNITY OF REWARD."

HSSS... I SEE.

I THANK YOU FOR SHOWING ME THE ERROR OF MY WAYS.

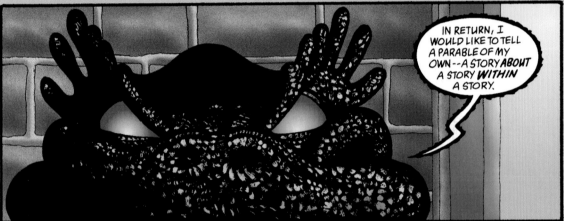

IN RETURN, I WOULD LIKE TO TELL A PARABLE OF MY OWN -- A STORY *ABOUT* A STORY *WITHIN* A STORY.

"IT IS A STORY ABOUT *LIES.*

"IT IS THE STORY OF WHO YOU *ARE....*"

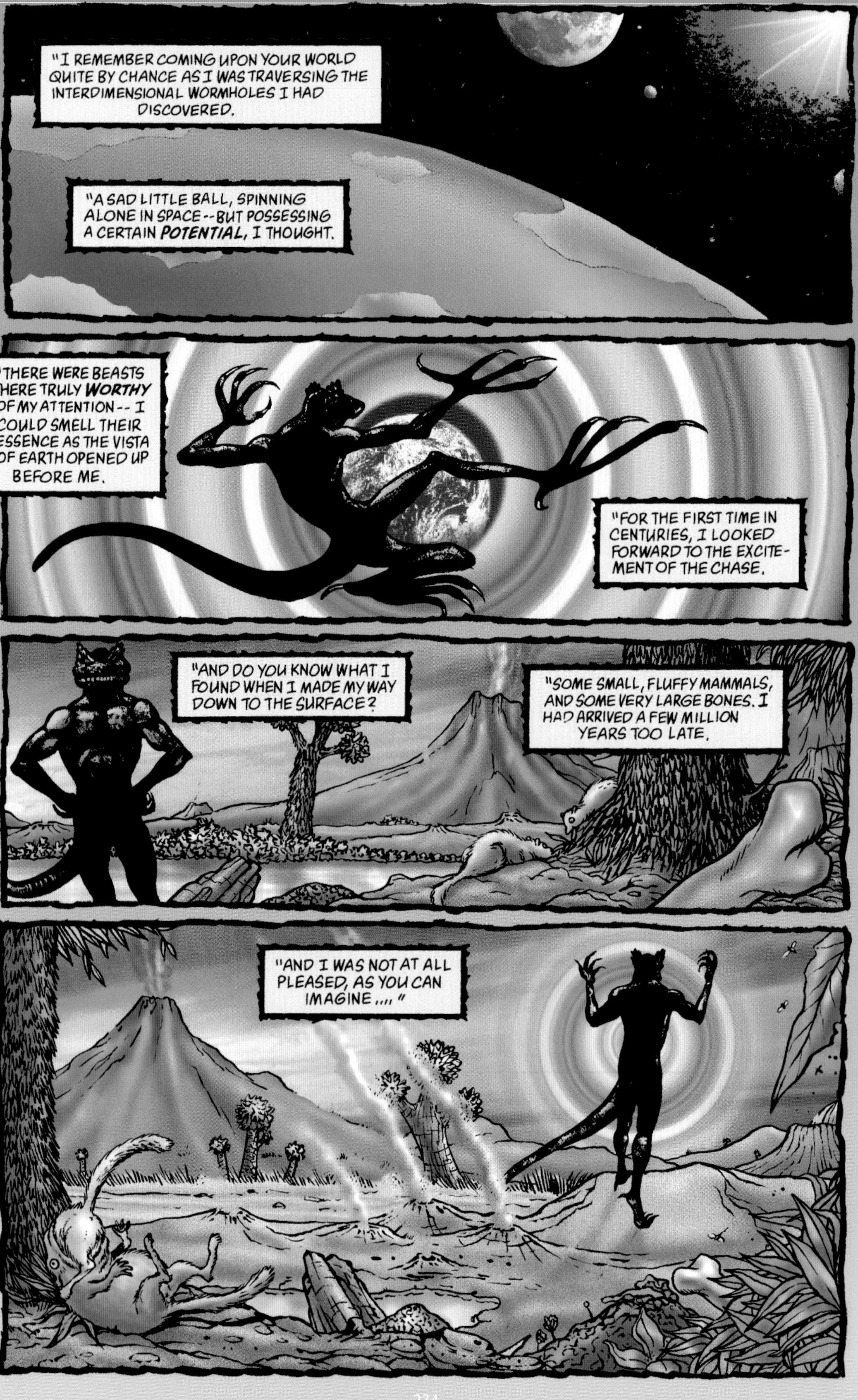

"I REMEMBER COMING UPON YOUR WORLD QUITE BY CHANCE AS I WAS TRAVERSING THE INTERDIMENSIONAL WORMHOLES I HAD DISCOVERED.
"A SAD LITTLE BALL, SPINNING ALONE IN SPACE--BUT POSSESSING A CERTAIN POTENTIAL, I THOUGHT.
"THERE WERE BEASTS THERE TRULY WORTHY OF MY ATTENTION-- I COULD SMELL THEIR ESSENCE AS THE VISTA OF EARTH OPENED UP BEFORE ME.
"FOR THE FIRST TIME IN CENTURIES, I LOOKED FORWARD TO THE EXCITEMENT OF THE CHASE.
"AND DO YOU KNOW WHAT I FOUND WHEN I MADE MY WAY DOWN TO THE SURFACE?
"SOME SMALL, FLUFFY MAMMALS, AND SOME VERY LARGE BONES. I HAD ARRIVED A FEW MILLION YEARS TOO LATE.
"AND I WAS NOT AT ALL PLEASED, AS YOU CAN IMAGINE...."

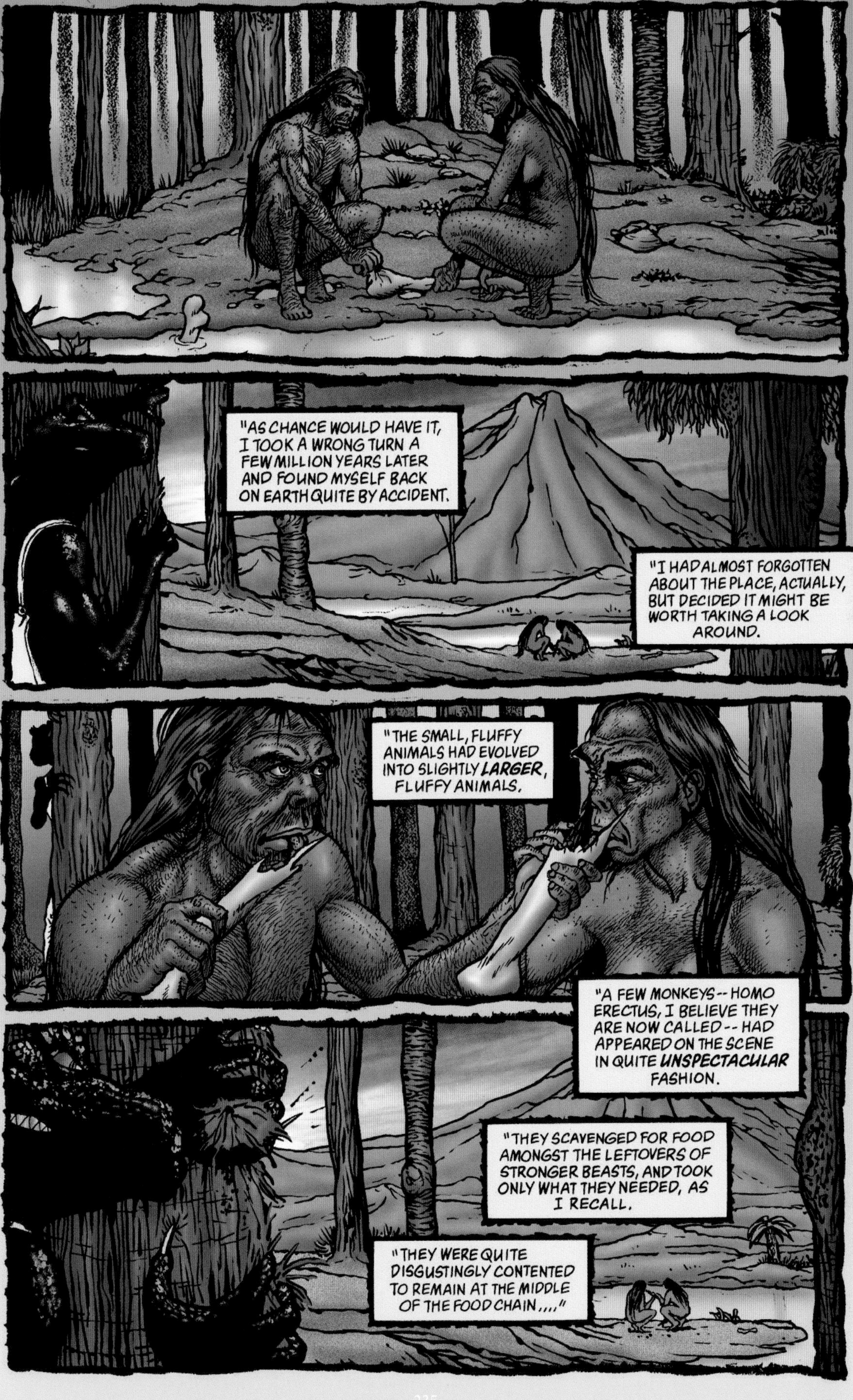
"AS CHANCE WOULD HAVE IT, I TOOK A WRONG TURN A FEW MILLION YEARS LATER AND FOUND MYSELF BACK ON EARTH QUITE BY ACCIDENT.
"I HAD ALMOST FORGOTTEN ABOUT THE PLACE, ACTUALLY, BUT DECIDED IT MIGHT BE WORTH TAKING A LOOK AROUND.
"THE SMALL, FLUFFY ANIMALS HAD EVOLVED INTO SLIGHTLY LARGER, FLUFFY ANIMALS.
"A FEW MONKEYS -- HOMO ERECTUS, I BELIEVE THEY ARE NOW CALLED -- HAD APPEARED ON THE SCENE IN QUITE UNSPECTACULAR FASHION.
"THEY SCAVENGED FOR FOOD AMONGST THE LEFTOVERS OF STRONGER BEASTS, AND TOOK ONLY WHAT THEY NEEDED, AS I RECALL.
"THEY WERE QUITE DISGUSTINGLY CONTENTED TO REMAIN AT THE MIDDLE OF THE FOOD CHAIN,,,,"

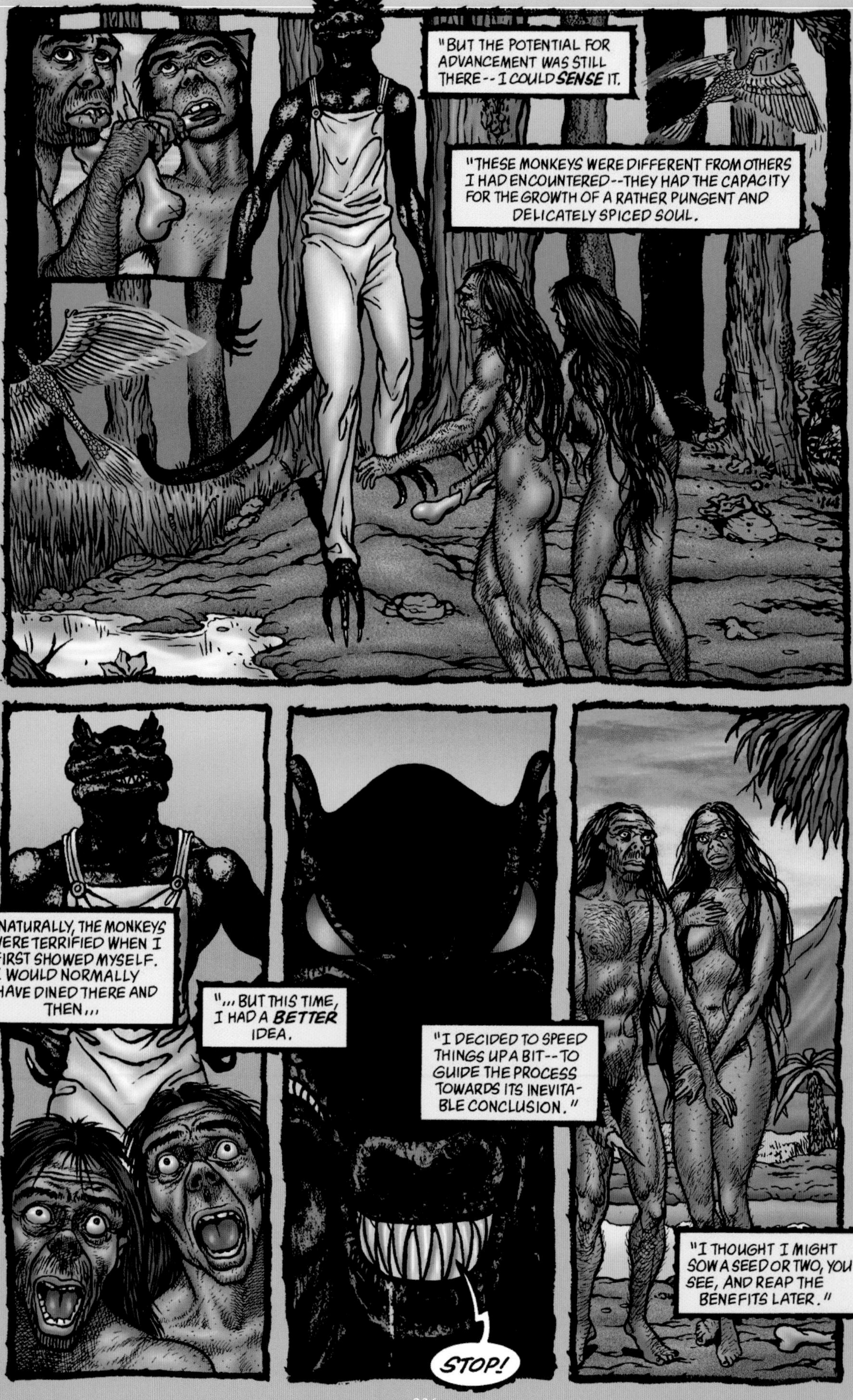
"BUT THE POTENTIAL FOR ADVANCEMENT WAS STILL THERE--I COULD SENSE IT.
"THESE MONKEYS WERE DIFFERENT FROM OTHERS I HAD ENCOUNTERED--THEY HAD THE CAPACITY FOR THE GROWTH OF A RATHER PUNGENT AND DELICATELY SPICED SOUL.
"NATURALLY, THE MONKEYS WERE TERRIFIED WHEN I FIRST SHOWED MYSELF. I WOULD NORMALLY HAVE DINED THERE AND THEN...
"...BUT THIS TIME, I HAD A BETTER IDEA.
"I DECIDED TO SPEED THINGS UP A BIT--TO GUIDE THE PROCESS TOWARDS ITS INEVITABLE CONCLUSION."
STOP!
"I THOUGHT I MIGHT SOW A SEED OR TWO, YOU SEE, AND REAP THE BENEFITS LATER."

"THE MALE AND FEMALE I HAD ENCOUNTERED WERE NOW FULLY UNDER MY TELEPATHIC CONTROL."

"I WAS A MASTER CHEF, STUDYING THE INGREDIENTS, READY TO COMMENCE WORK ON A MASTERFUL CULINARY CREATION."

"UNTIL THEN, I SUPPOSE, THE POOR WRETCHES HAD NEVER CONSIDERED THE NOTION THAT THEY MIGHT WANT MORE THAN THEY HAD ALREADY BEEN ALLOTTED."

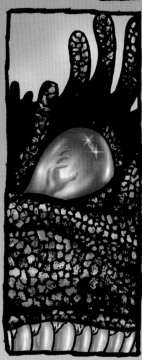

"BUT GREED IS EXTREMELY SEDUCTIVE--AND ALTOGETHER QUITE PERSUASIVE--ONCE IT ENTERS THE CONSCIOUS MIND."

"IT WAS THE FEMALE, I THINK, WHO FIRST SUCCUMBED TO HER BASER DESIRES."

"SHE REACHED OUT HESI-TANTLY TO TAKE THE BAUBLE, AND IN THAT MOMENT, HUMANI-TY'S INNOCENCE WAS LOST FOREVER."

"THE REST IS, WELL...HISTORY, I SUPPOSE. OF COURSE, HISTORY AND ACCURACY RARELY GO HAND IN HAND."

"BUT THE TRUTH IS THIS: I WAS THE SERPENT IN THE GARDEN OF EDEN -- THE SEDUCER OF MEN."

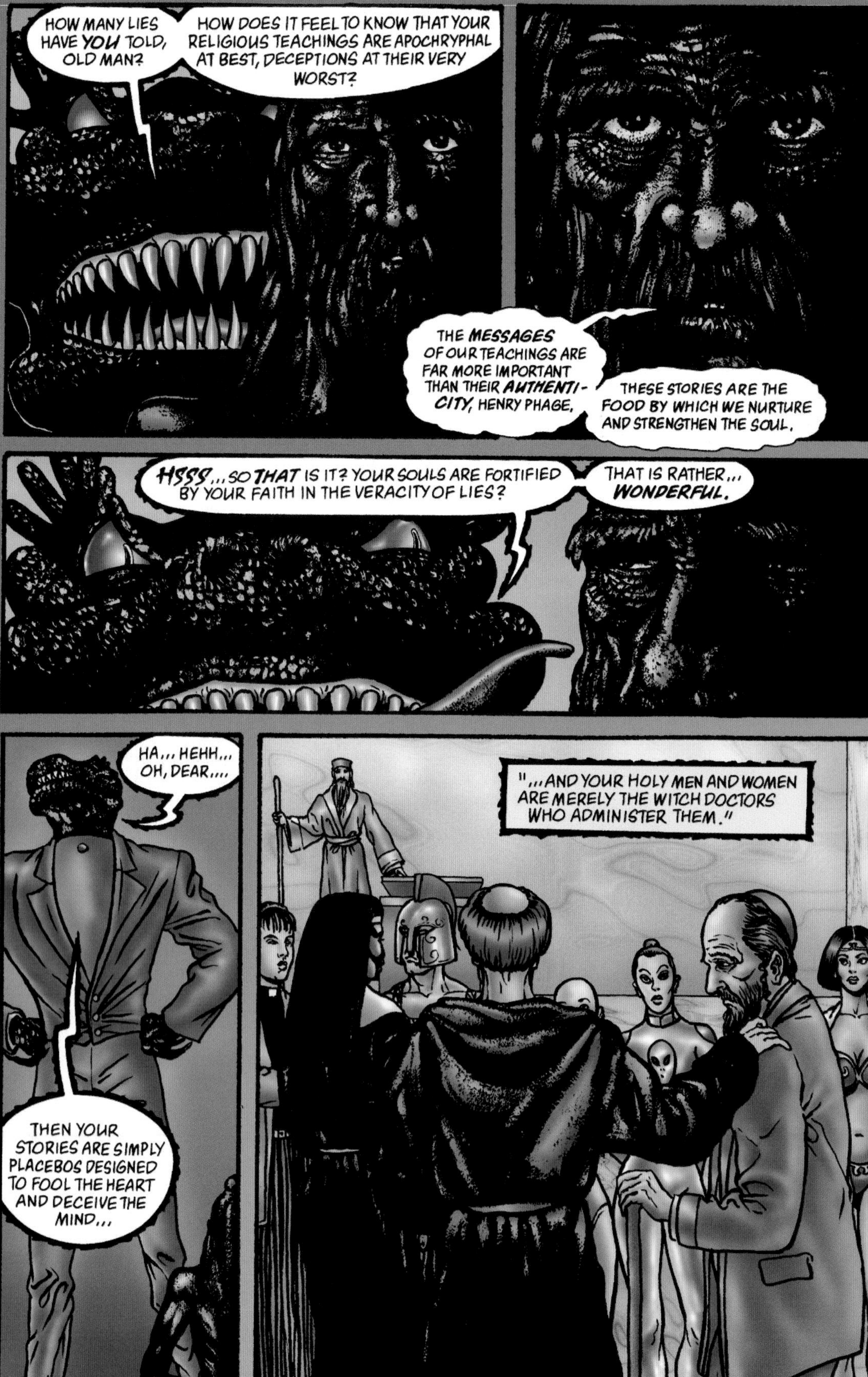
HOW MANY LIES HAVE YOU TOLD, OLD MAN?
HOW DOES IT FEEL TO KNOW THAT YOUR RELIGIOUS TEACHINGS ARE APOCRYPHAL AT BEST, DECEPTIONS AT THEIR VERY WORST?
THE MESSAGES OF OUR TEACHINGS ARE FAR MORE IMPORTANT THAN THEIR AUTHENTICITY, HENRY PHAGE.
THESE STORIES ARE THE FOOD BY WHICH WE NURTURE AND STRENGTHEN THE SOUL.
HSSS... SO THAT IS IT? YOUR SOULS ARE FORTIFIED BY YOUR FAITH IN THE VERACITY OF LIES?
THAT IS RATHER... WONDERFUL.
HA... HEHH... OH, DEAR....
THEN YOUR STORIES ARE SIMPLY PLACEBOS DESIGNED TO FOOL THE HEART AND DECEIVE THE MIND...
"...AND YOUR HOLY MEN AND WOMEN ARE MERELY THE WITCH DOCTORS WHO ADMINISTER THEM."

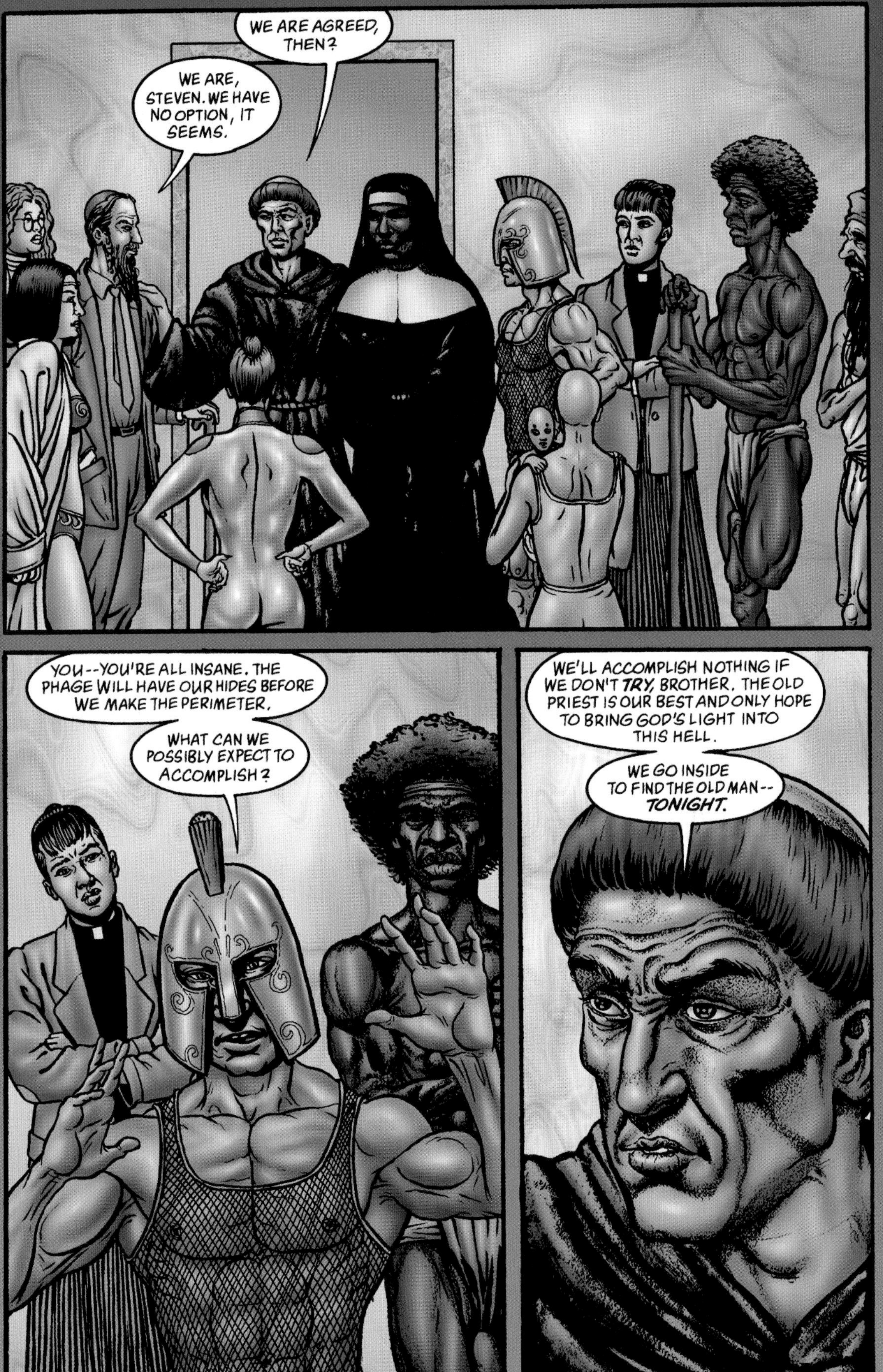
WE ARE AGREED, THEN?
WE ARE, STEVEN. WE HAVE NO OPTION, IT SEEMS.
YOU--YOU'RE ALL INSANE. THE PHAGE WILL HAVE OUR HIDES BEFORE WE MAKE THE PERIMETER.
WHAT CAN WE POSSIBLY EXPECT TO ACCOMPLISH?
WE'LL ACCOMPLISH NOTHING IF WE DON'T *TRY*, BROTHER. THE OLD PRIEST IS OUR BEST AND ONLY HOPE TO BRING GOD'S LIGHT INTO THIS HELL.
WE GO INSIDE TO FIND THE OLD MAN-- ***TONIGHT.***

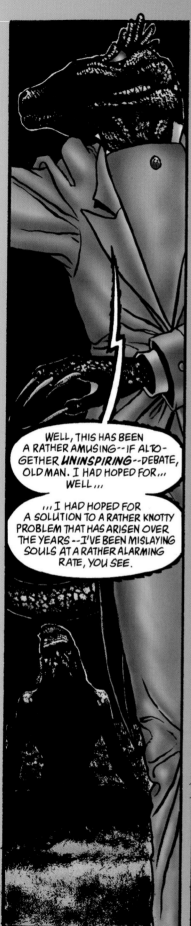

WELL, THIS HAS BEEN A RATHER AMUSING--IF ALTOGETHER **UNINSPIRING**--DEBATE, OLD MAN. I HAD HOPED FOR... WELL...

...I HAD HOPED FOR A SOLUTION TO A RATHER KNOTTY PROBLEM THAT HAS ARISEN OVER THE YEARS--I'VE BEEN MISLAYING SOULS AT A RATHER ALARMING RATE, YOU SEE.

"I THOUGHT YOU MIGHT PROVIDE SOME SMALL INSIGHT INTO THE REASONS FOR THIS, BUT I SEE I SHALL HAVE TO LOOK **ELSEWHERE.**

"AS CHANCE WOULD HAVE IT, SOME DELIGHTFULLY NAÏVE FRIENDS OF YOURS ARE MAKING THEIR WAY INSIDE TO 'RESCUE' YOU AS WE SPEAK."

I SHALL BE **WAITING** FOR THEM, OF COURSE.

AND WHEN THEY ARRIVE, I SHALL FLOAT THEM IN THE VATS AND STUDY THE REACTION OF THEIR SOULS.

TO BE CONTINUED!

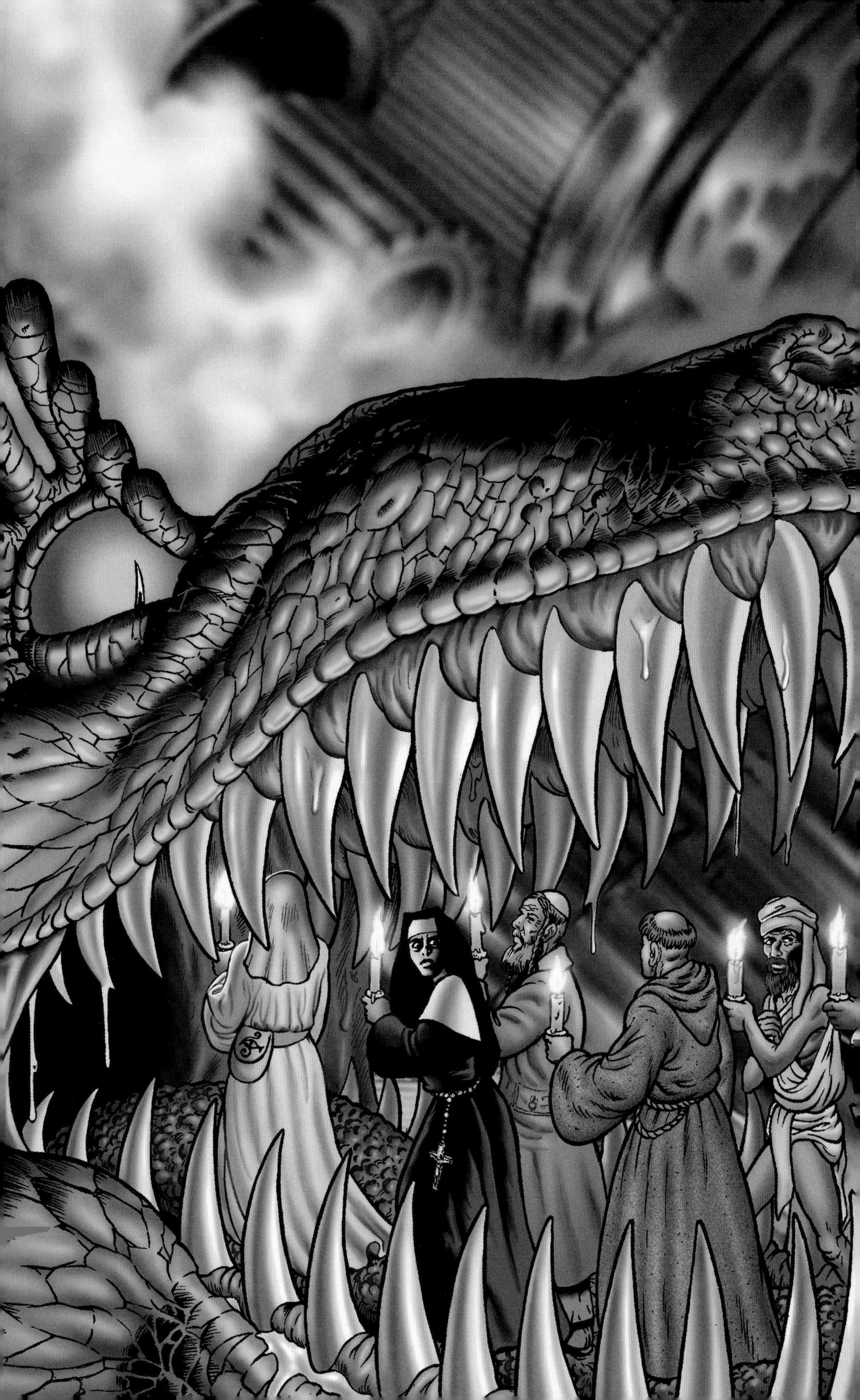

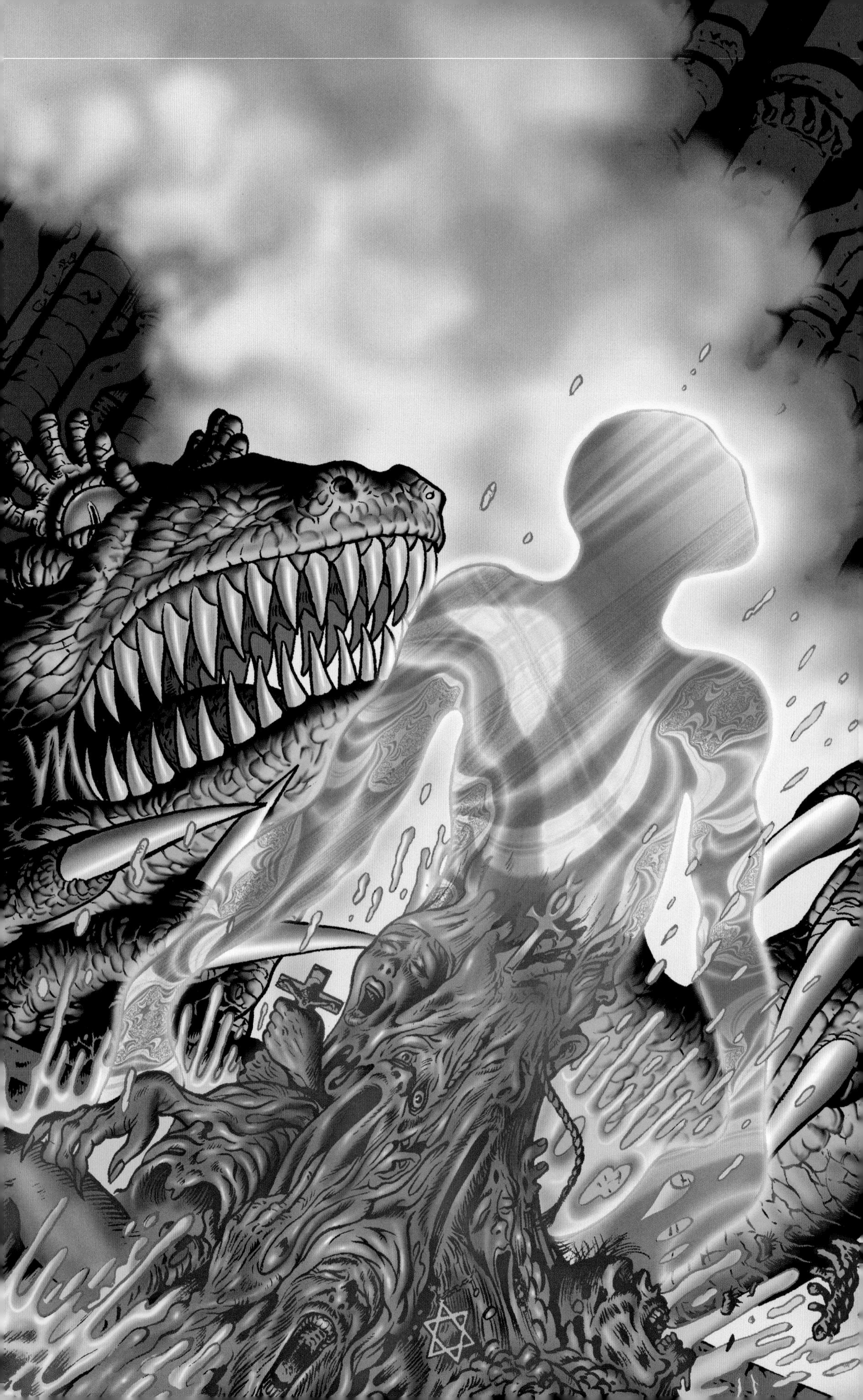

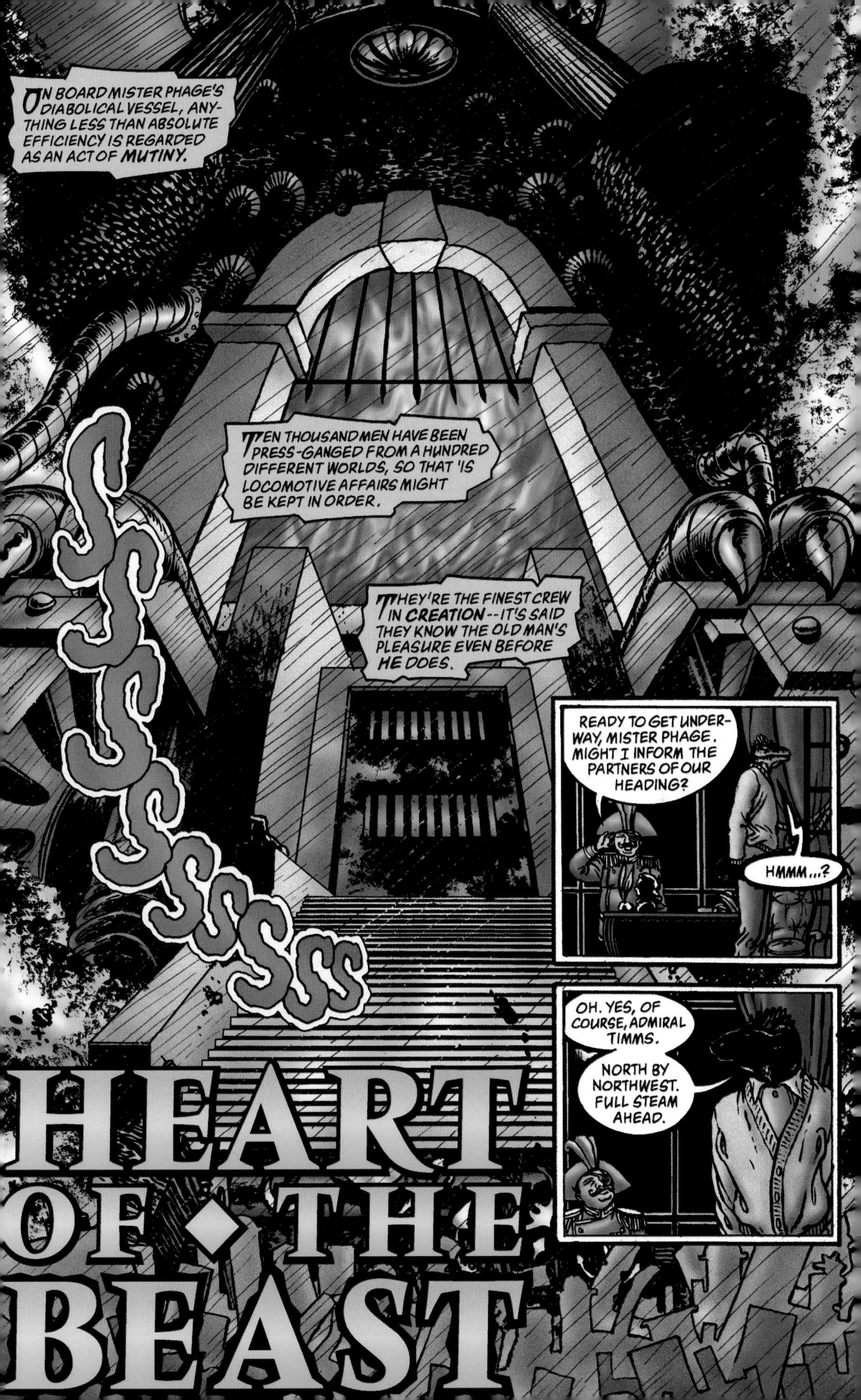
ON BOARD MISTER PHAGE'S DIABOLICAL VESSEL, ANYTHING LESS THAN ABSOLUTE EFFICIENCY IS REGARDED AS AN ACT OF MUTINY.
TEN THOUSAND MEN HAVE BEEN PRESS-GANGED FROM A HUNDRED DIFFERENT WORLDS, SO THAT 'IS LOCOMOTIVE AFFAIRS MIGHT BE KEPT IN ORDER.
THEY'RE THE FINEST CREW IN CREATION--IT'S SAID THEY KNOW THE OLD MAN'S PLEASURE EVEN BEFORE HE DOES.
SSSSSSSSS
HEART OF THE BEAST
READY TO GET UNDERWAY, MISTER PHAGE. MIGHT I INFORM THE PARTNERS OF OUR HEADING?
HMMM...?
OH. YES, OF COURSE, ADMIRAL TIMMS.
NORTH BY NORTHWEST. FULL STEAM AHEAD.

ENGINE
ROOM
AUTHORIZED
PERSONNEL
ONLY

NOT A LIVING SOUL IN *SIGHT*...

NO SURPRISE THERE, BROTHER. OUR INSIDE SOURCE TELLS ME THIS ENGINE ROOM IS FULLY AUTOMATED.

WE CAN MAKE OUR WAY UP THROUGH THE VENTS FROM-- *AAHH!*

CREEAK

LOOK *OUT!*

OH...OH, *NO*, PLEASE... NOT *YET--*

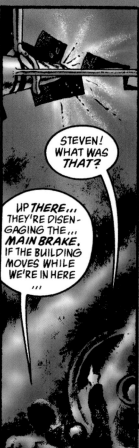
STEVEN! WHAT WAS *THAT?*

UP *THERE*... THEY'RE DISEN-GAGING THE... *MAIN BRAKE*. IF THE BUILDING MOVES WHILE WE'RE IN HERE ...

...YOU'D BETTER HOPE YOUR ANCESTORS ARE *READY* FOR YOU, BROTHER.

244

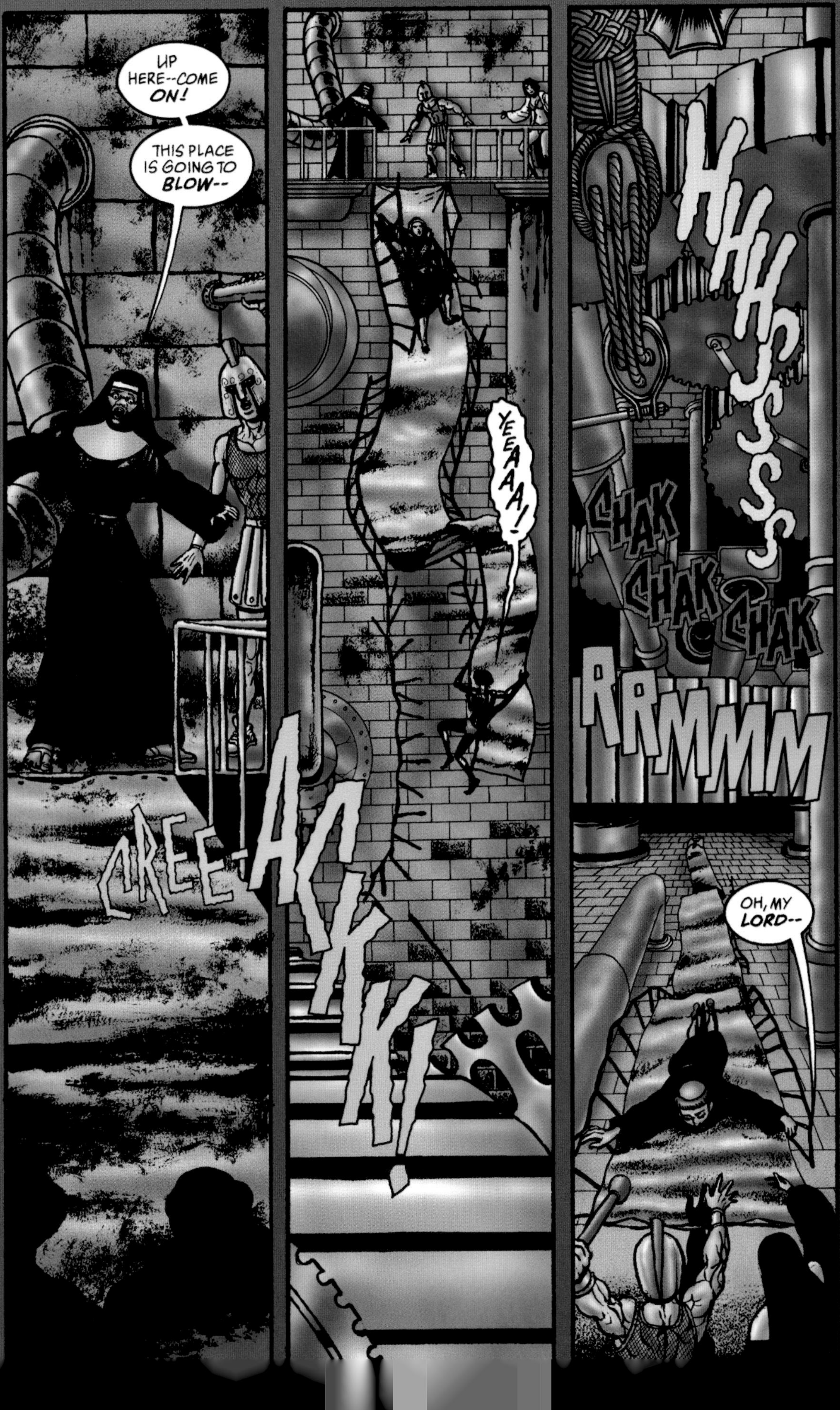
UP HERE--COME ON!
THIS PLACE IS GOING TO BLOW--
CREE-ACKK!
YEEAAAA!
HHHHJSSS
CHAK CHAK CHAK
RRMMMM
OH, MY LORD--

IF MISTER PHAGE PUTS AN IDEA IN MOTION, 'E HAS A VERITABLE ARMY OF SUBORDINATES T' FOLLOW IT THROUGH.

FULL AHEAD! NORTH BY NORTHWEST!

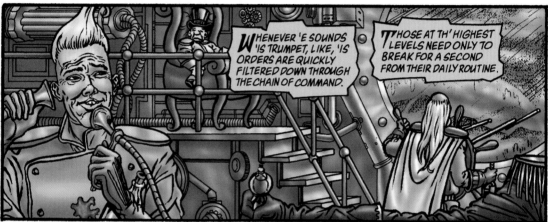

WHENEVER 'E SOUNDS 'IS TRUMPET, LIKE, 'IS ORDERS ARE QUICKLY FILTERED DOWN THROUGH THE CHAIN OF COMMAND.

THOSE AT TH' HIGHEST LEVELS NEED ONLY TO BREAK FOR A SECOND FROM THEIR DAILY ROUTINE.

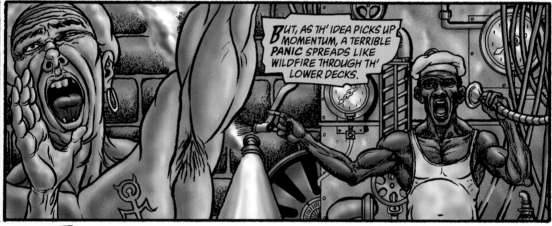

BUT, AS TH' IDEA PICKS UP MOMENTUM, A TERRIBLE PANIC SPREADS LIKE WILDFIRE THROUGH TH' LOWER DECKS.

TH' ORDER SPEEDS FROM ONE, TO A FEW, TO A HUNDRED...

ALL HANDS TO THE RIGGING. FULL AHEAD-- NORTH BY NORTHWEST, LADS!

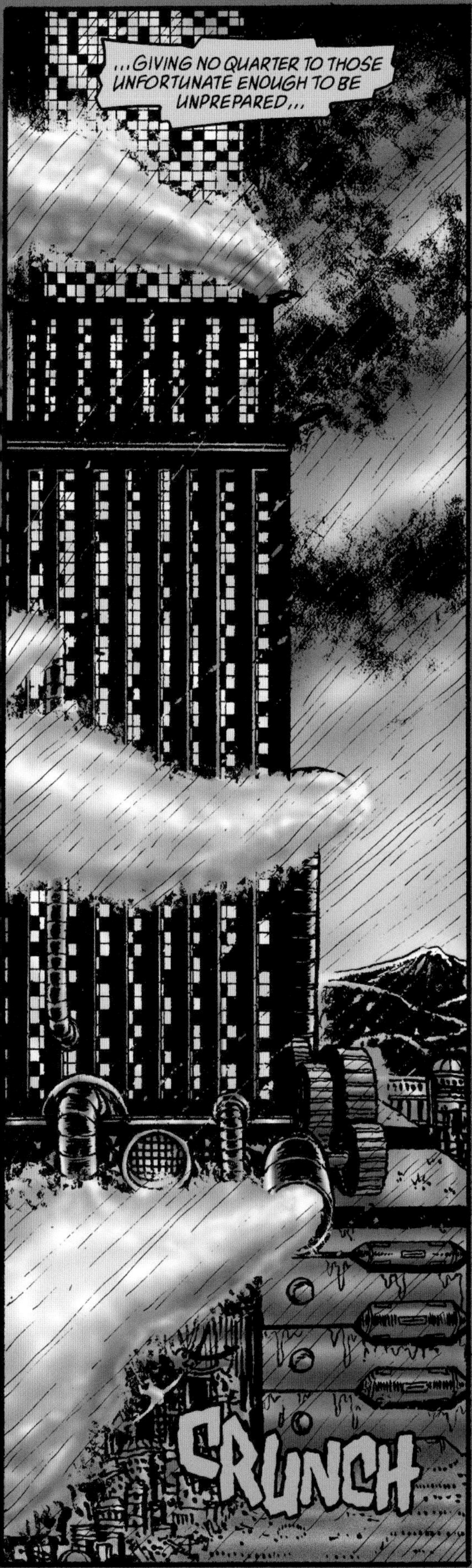
...GIVING NO QUARTER TO THOSE UNFORTUNATE ENOUGH TO BE UNPREPARED,..
CRUNCH

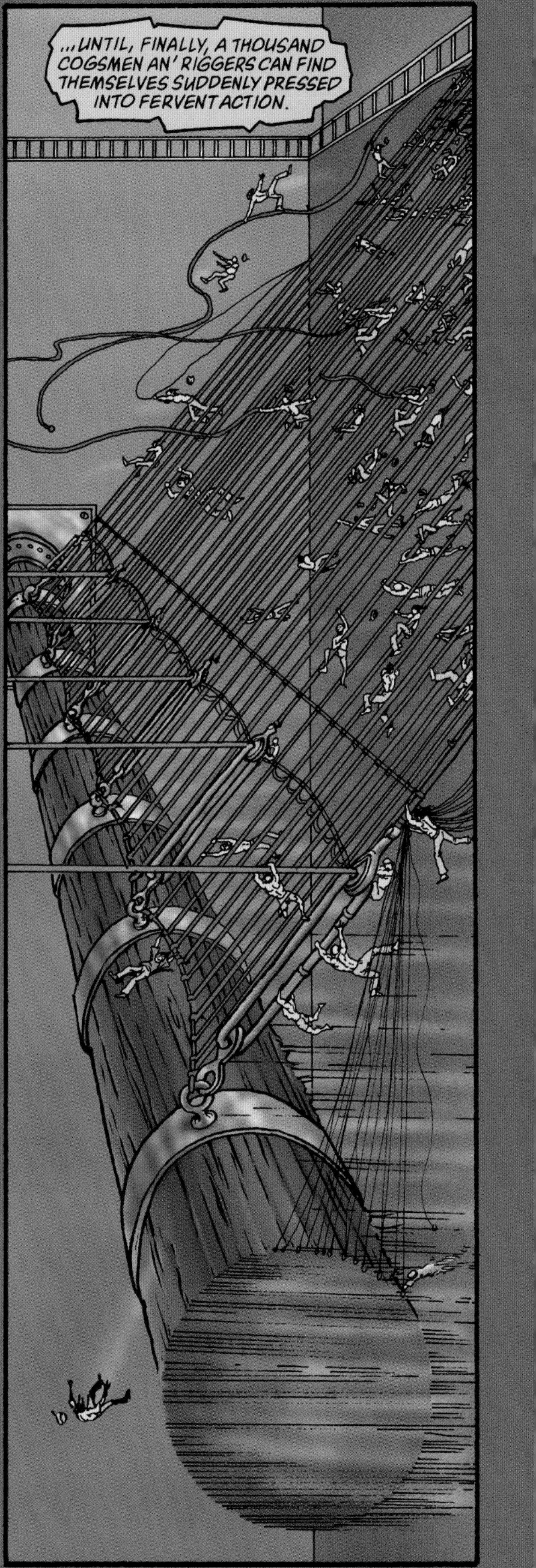
...UNTIL, FINALLY, A THOUSAND COGSMEN AN' RIGGERS CAN FIND THEMSELVES SUDDENLY PRESSED INTO FERVENT ACTION.

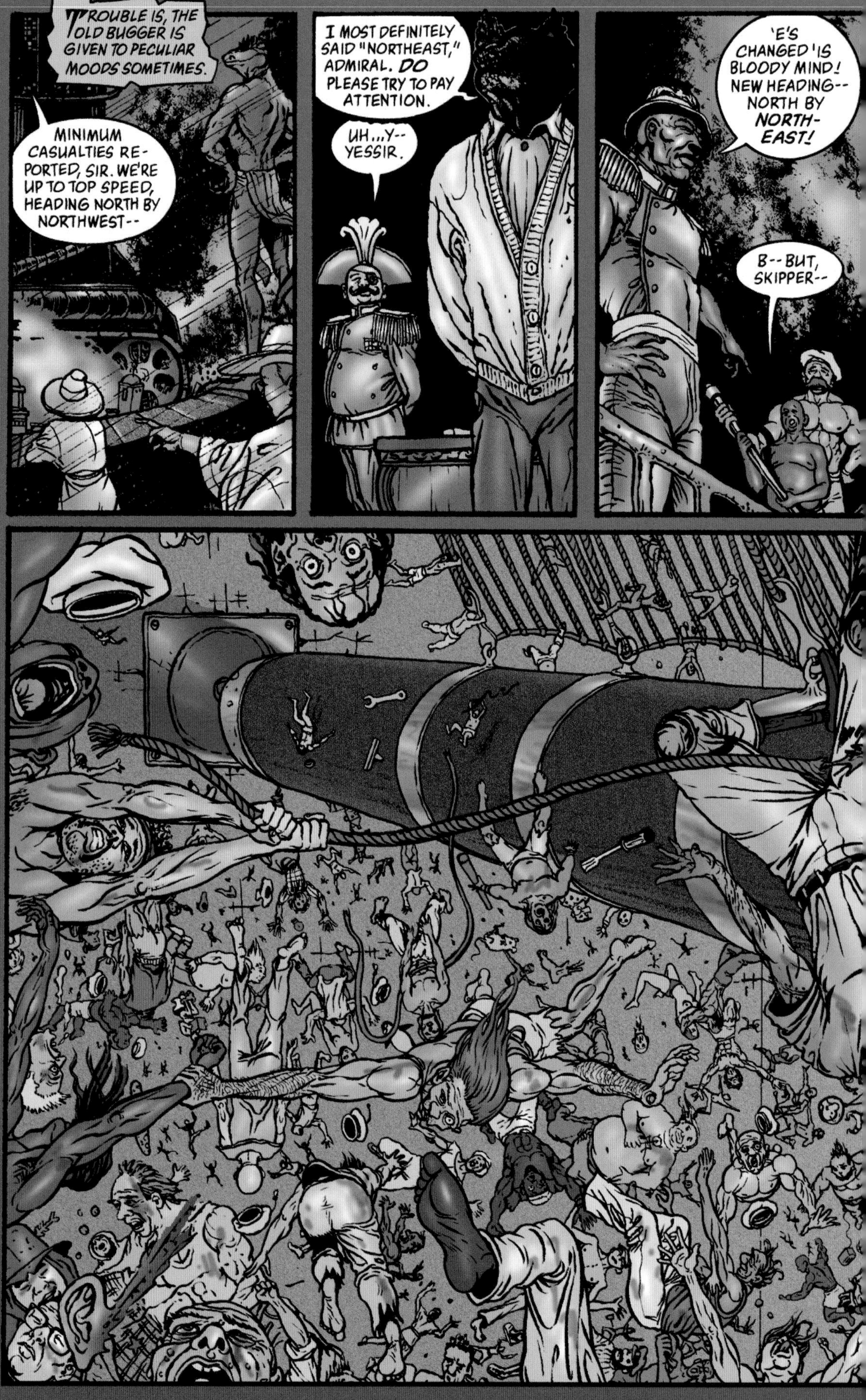
TROUBLE IS, THE OLD BUGGER IS GIVEN TO PECULIAR MOODS SOMETIMES.
MINIMUM CASUALTIES REPORTED, SIR. WE'RE UP TO TOP SPEED, HEADING NORTH BY NORTHWEST--
I MOST DEFINITELY SAID "NORTHEAST," ADMIRAL. DO PLEASE TRY TO PAY ATTENTION.
UH...Y-- YESSIR.
'E'S CHANGED 'IS BLOODY MIND! NEW HEADING-- NORTH BY NORTH-EAST!
B--BUT, SKIPPER--

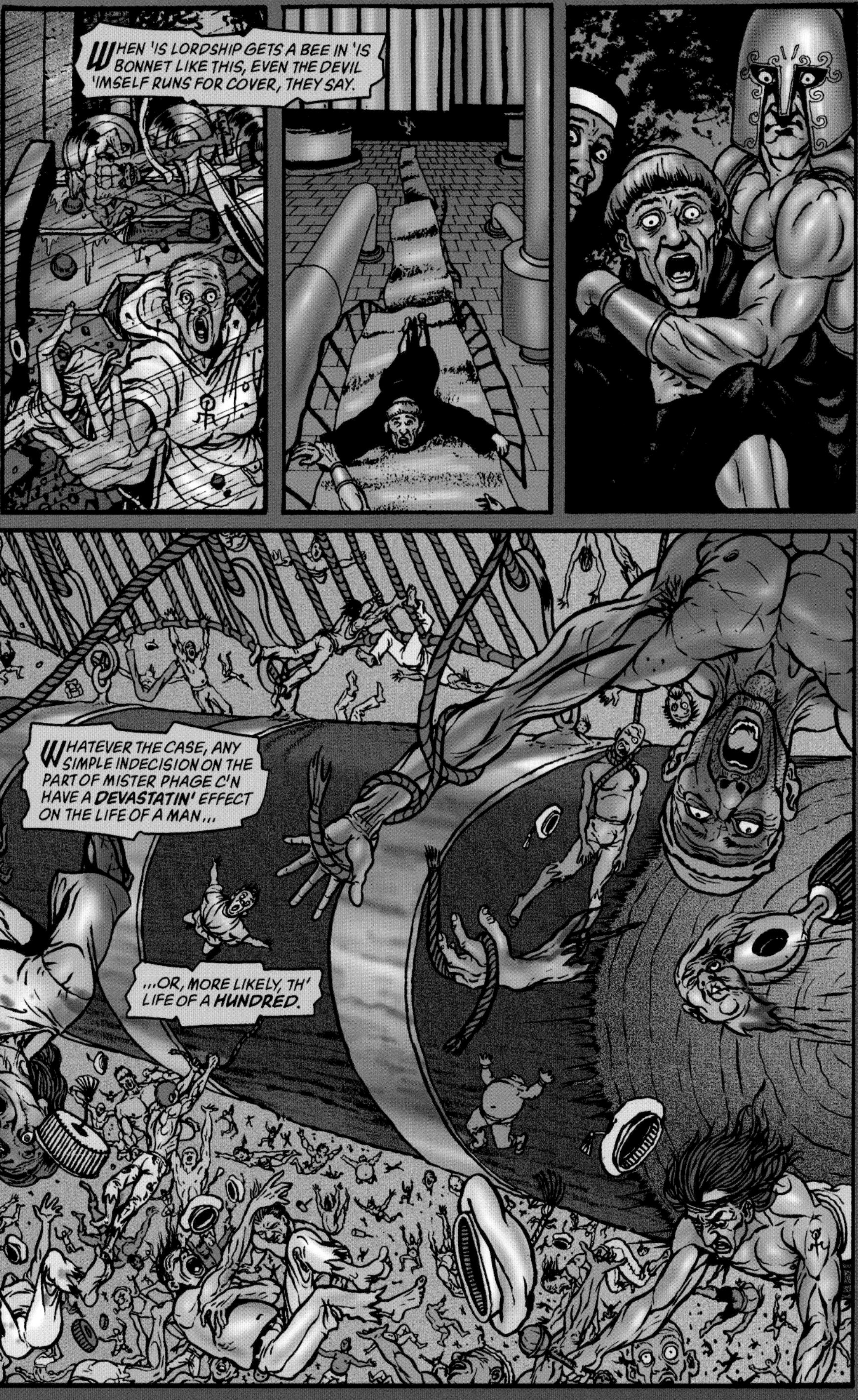
WHEN 'IS LORDSHIP GETS A BEE IN 'IS BONNET LIKE THIS, EVEN THE DEVIL 'IMSELF RUNS FOR COVER, THEY SAY.
WHATEVER THE CASE, ANY SIMPLE INDECISION ON THE PART OF MISTER PHAGE C'N HAVE A DEVASTATIN' EFFECT ON THE LIFE OF A MAN...
...OR, MORE LIKELY, TH' LIFE OF A HUNDRED.

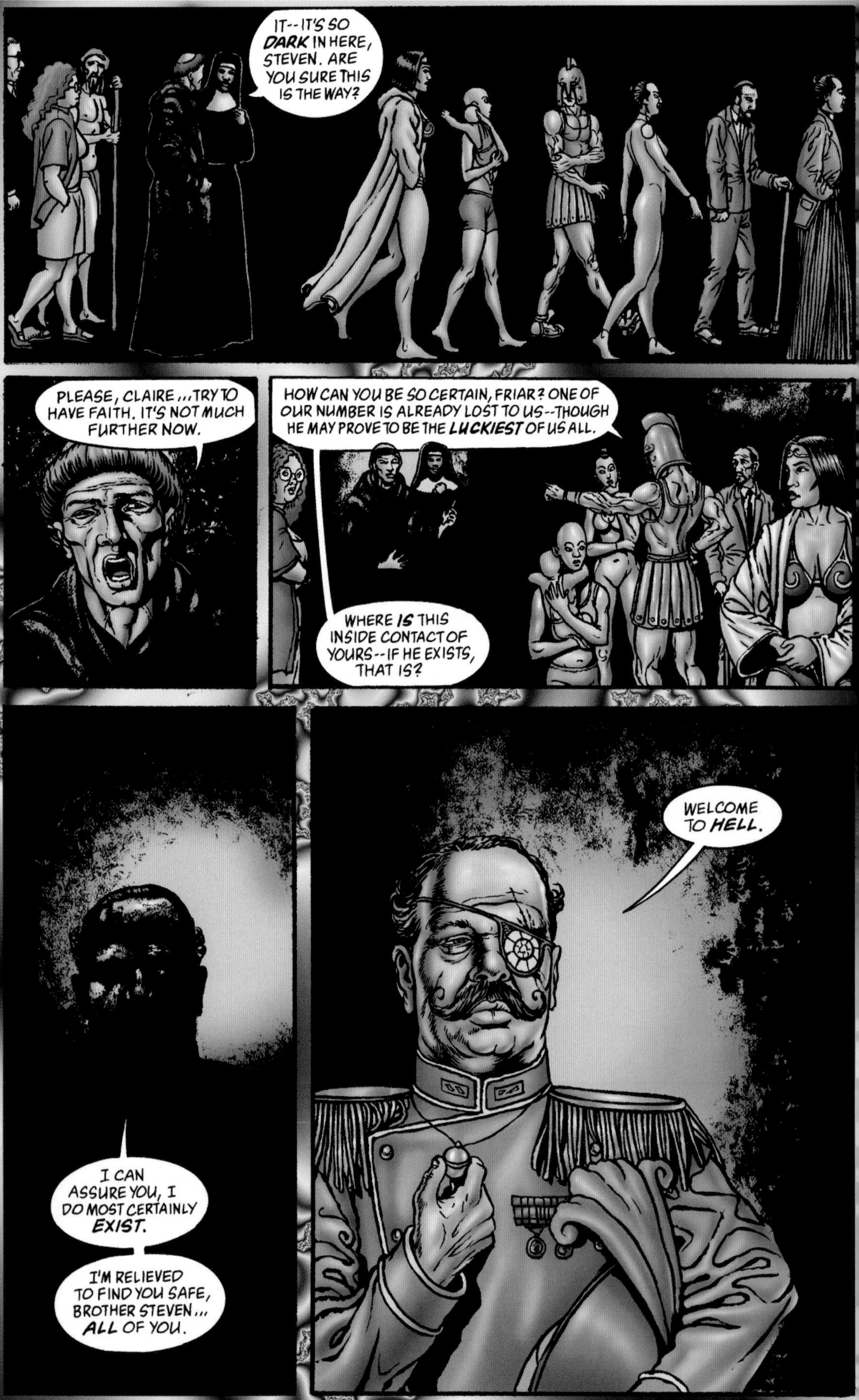
IT--IT'S SO DARK IN HERE, STEVEN. ARE YOU SURE THIS IS THE WAY?
PLEASE, CLAIRE ...TRY TO HAVE FAITH. IT'S NOT MUCH FURTHER NOW.
HOW CAN YOU BE SO CERTAIN, FRIAR? ONE OF OUR NUMBER IS ALREADY LOST TO US--THOUGH HE MAY PROVE TO BE THE LUCKIEST OF US ALL.
WHERE IS THIS INSIDE CONTACT OF YOURS--IF HE EXISTS, THAT IS?
I CAN ASSURE YOU, I DO MOST CERTAINLY EXIST.
I'M RELIEVED TO FIND YOU SAFE, BROTHER STEVEN... ALL OF YOU.
WELCOME TO HELL.

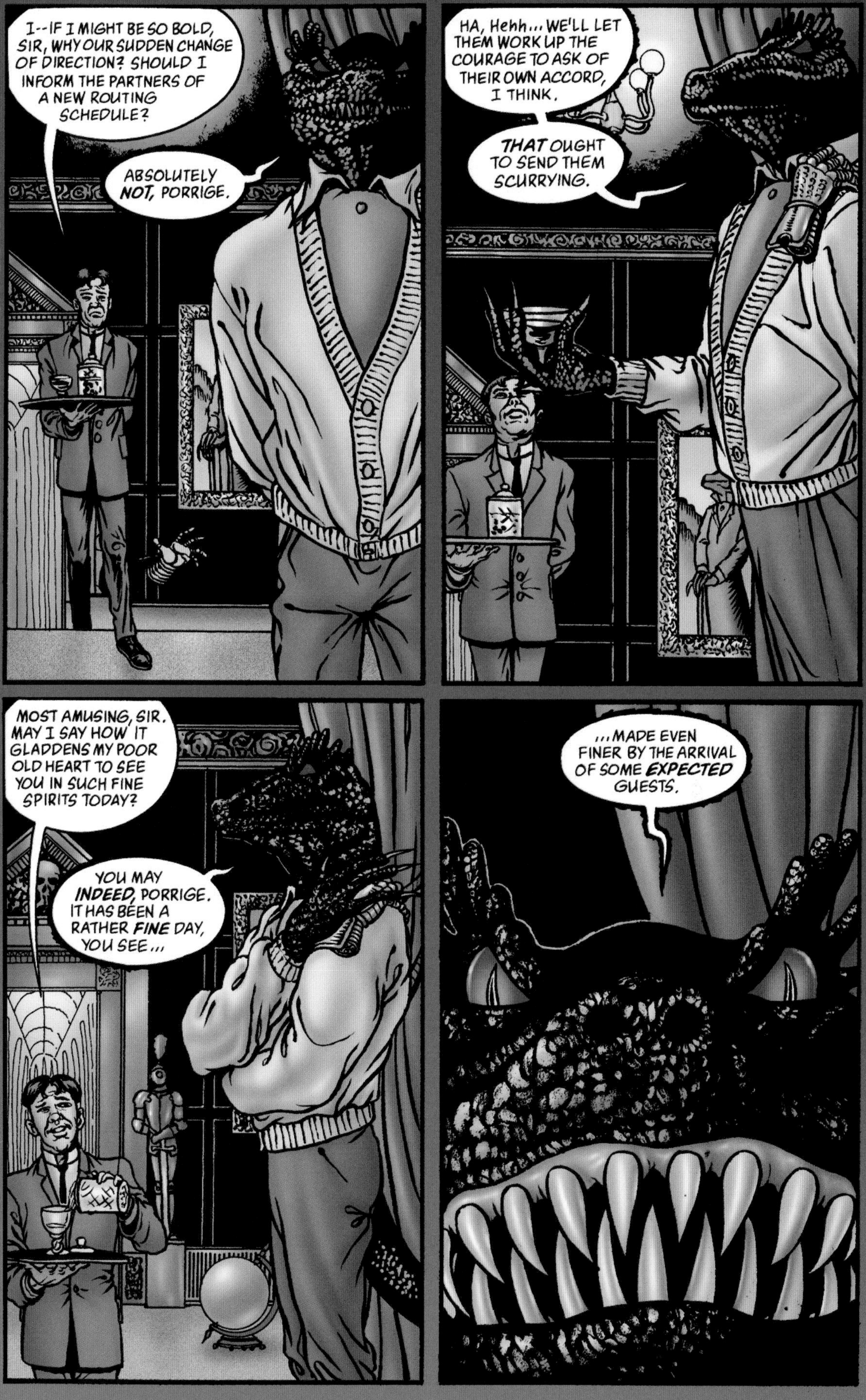
I--IF I MIGHT BE SO BOLD, SIR, WHY OUR SUDDEN CHANGE OF DIRECTION? SHOULD I INFORM THE PARTNERS OF A NEW ROUTING SCHEDULE?
ABSOLUTELY NOT, PORRIGE.
HA, Hehh... WE'LL LET THEM WORK UP THE COURAGE TO ASK OF THEIR OWN ACCORD, I THINK.
THAT OUGHT TO SEND THEM SCURRYING.
MOST AMUSING, SIR. MAY I SAY HOW IT GLADDENS MY POOR OLD HEART TO SEE YOU IN SUCH FINE SPIRITS TODAY?
YOU MAY INDEED, PORRIGE. IT HAS BEEN A RATHER FINE DAY, YOU SEE...
...MADE EVEN FINER BY THE ARRIVAL OF SOME EXPECTED GUESTS.

MY FRIENDS, WE CAN'T REMAIN HERE FOR LONG.

I MUST ASK YOU TO PUT YOUR TRUST IN ME, AS I DO IN YOU.

YOU'RE UPPER MANAGEMENT. WHY IN THE NAME OF THE *OTHERS* *SHOULD* WE TRUST YOU?

BECAUSE I AM A GOD-FEARING MAN, ABOVE ALL ELSE,

AND LIKE EVERYONE HERE, I ONCE HAD A WORLD OF MY OWN. A FAMILY. A *LIFE*.

"ON MY WORLD BEFORE I WAS TAKEN, WE WERE AT WAR WITH THE GERMANS AND JAPANESE. THE VESSEL UNDER MY COMMAND WAS ASSIGNED TO THE SOUTH SEAS.

"WE'D BEEN SENT OUT TO PICK UP SOME MISSIONARIES IN THE PHILIPPINES. THEY WERE LESS THAN ENTHUSIASTIC ABOUT BEING RESCUED, BUT ORDERS WERE ORDERS.

" IT WAS A DANGEROUS TIME, AND WE WERE SAILING DANGEROUS WATERS.

"THE JAPANESE HAD BEEN THROWING AICHI BOMBERS AT US AT AN ALARMING RATE, SO WE WERE KEEP-ING A SHARP WATCH ON THE SKY.

"AS IT TURNED OUT, THAT WAS THE *WRONG* PLACE TO LOOK ENTIRELY.

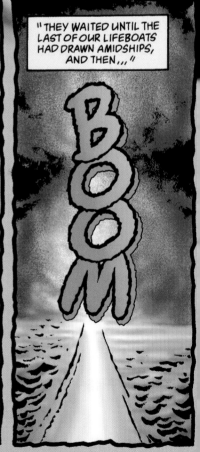

" THEY WAITED UNTIL THE LAST OF OUR LIFEBOATS HAD DRAWN AMIDSHIPS, AND THEN , , , "

BOOM

"NEXT THING I KNEW, I WAS FLOATING IN THE OCEAN, SPITTING SALT WATER AND BLOOD. I'D LOST AN EYE -- WAS CLOSE TO GOING UNDER FOREVER...

"...THEN ONE OF THE MISSIONARIES --A YOUNG FRIAR--HEFTED ME ONTO A SMALL PIECE OF WRECKAGE.

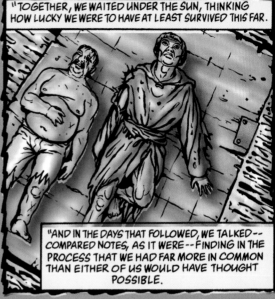

"TOGETHER, WE WAITED UNDER THE SUN, THINKING HOW LUCKY WE WERE TO HAVE AT LEAST SURVIVED THIS FAR.

"AND IN THE DAYS THAT FOLLOWED, WE TALKED-- COMPARED NOTES, AS IT WERE -- FINDING IN THE PROCESS THAT WE HAD FAR MORE IN COMMON THAN EITHER OF US WOULD HAVE THOUGHT POSSIBLE.

"AFTER A TIME, THE HEAT AND THE THIRST OVERTOOK US. BUT I HAD FOUND A QUIET *ACCEPTANCE* OVERTAKING MY FEAR AS I TALKED WITH THIS HOLY MAN.

"WE WAITED CALMLY TO DIE. UNFORTUNATELY, WE WERE NOT TO BE SO *LUCKY.*"

FIFTY YEARS AGO, YOUR BROTHER STEVEN SAVED MY LIFE. HE HAS BEEN TRYING TO SAVE MY SOUL EVER SINCE.

PERHAPS ONE DAY, EH, ALBERT?

IT'S A FINE STORY, FRIEND. REMIND ME TO TELL YOU MY *OWN* SOMETIME.

IN THE MEAN- TIME, WE ALL KNOW THE LIZARD CAN SEE INTO OUR THOUGHTS. WHY HASN'T HE COME TO GET US?

BECAUSE HE CAN'T. *THIS* WON'T *LET* HIM.

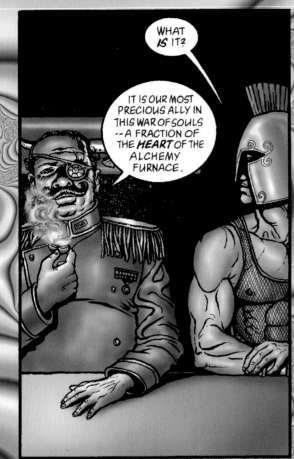

WHAT *IS* IT?

IT IS OUR MOST PRECIOUS ALLY IN THIS WAR OF SOULS -- A FRACTION OF THE *HEART* OF THE ALCHEMY FURNACE.

FOR MANY YEARS, PHAGE HAS BEEN EXTRACTING THE SOULS OF HIS VICTIMS TO FUEL THE FURNACE WHICH DRIVES THIS MONSTROSITY.

BUT I DISCOVERED THAT THE SOULS CANNOT BE COMPLETELY DESTROYED --THEY LIVE ON INSIDE THE HELLFIRE, INTER-TWINING TO FORM ONE SINGLE, LIVING ENTITY.

THE ENTITY IS A FLEETING, INSUB-STANTIAL IDEA-- PERHAPS NOT EVEN AWARE OF ITS OWN EXISTENCE. IT FLITS IN AND OUT OF OUR FRAME OF REFERENCE AS EASILY AS YOU OR I WOULD WALK THROUGH A DOOR.

MOST IMPORTANTLY, THE PHAGE'S MIND CANNOT PIERCE THE PROTECTIVE TELEPATHIC BARRIER WITH WHICH IT SURROUNDS ITSELF.

AND UNDER ITS PROTECTION, THE PHAGE CANNOT SEE OR HEAR US AS WE SPEAK.

...THE PHAGE CANNOT SEE US OR HEAR US AS WE SPEAK.

PLEASE REMIND ME TO REPLAY THIS SECTION OF TELETAPE TO THE GOOD ADMIRAL WHEN WE HAVE HIM IN CUSTODY, PORRIGE.

I WOULD LIKE HIM TO READDRESS THE QUESTION OF THE FUTILITY OF HIS EXISTENCE BEFORE WE ADD HIS VITALS TO THE FURNACE.

BY ALL MEANS, MISTER PHAGE.

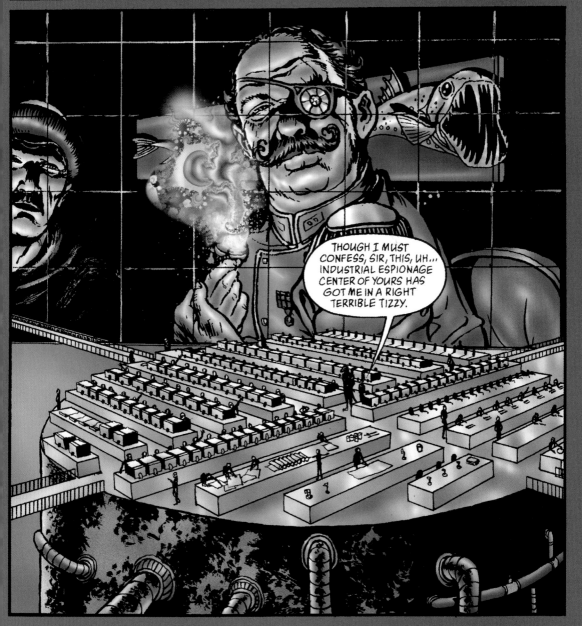

THOUGH I MUST CONFESS, SIR, THIS, UH... INDUSTRIAL ESPIONAGE CENTER OF YOURS HAS GOT ME IN A RIGHT TERRIBLE TIZZY.

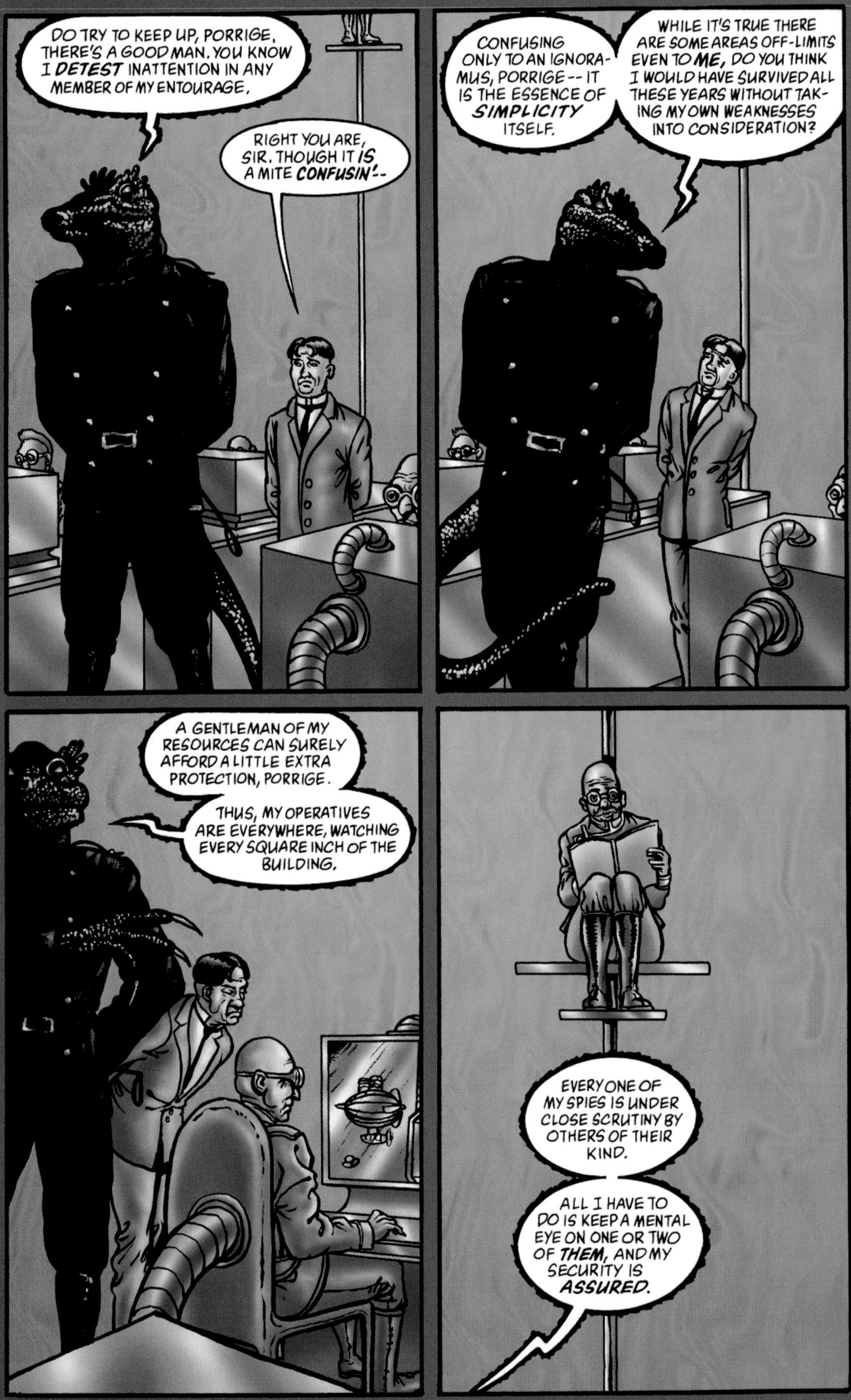

DO TRY TO KEEP UP, PORRIGE, THERE'S A GOOD MAN. YOU KNOW I DETEST INATTENTION IN ANY MEMBER OF MY ENTOURAGE.
RIGHT YOU ARE, SIR. THOUGH IT IS A MITE CONFUSIN'--
CONFUSING ONLY TO AN IGNORAMUS, PORRIGE -- IT IS THE ESSENCE OF SIMPLICITY ITSELF.
WHILE IT'S TRUE THERE ARE SOME AREAS OFF-LIMITS EVEN TO ME, DO YOU THINK I WOULD HAVE SURVIVED ALL THESE YEARS WITHOUT TAKING MY OWN WEAKNESSES INTO CONSIDERATION?
A GENTLEMAN OF MY RESOURCES CAN SURELY AFFORD A LITTLE EXTRA PROTECTION, PORRIGE.
THUS, MY OPERATIVES ARE EVERYWHERE, WATCHING EVERY SQUARE INCH OF THE BUILDING.
EVERY ONE OF MY SPIES IS UNDER CLOSE SCRUTINY BY OTHERS OF THEIR KIND.
ALL I HAVE TO DO IS KEEP A MENTAL EYE ON ONE OR TWO OF THEM, AND MY SECURITY IS ASSURED.

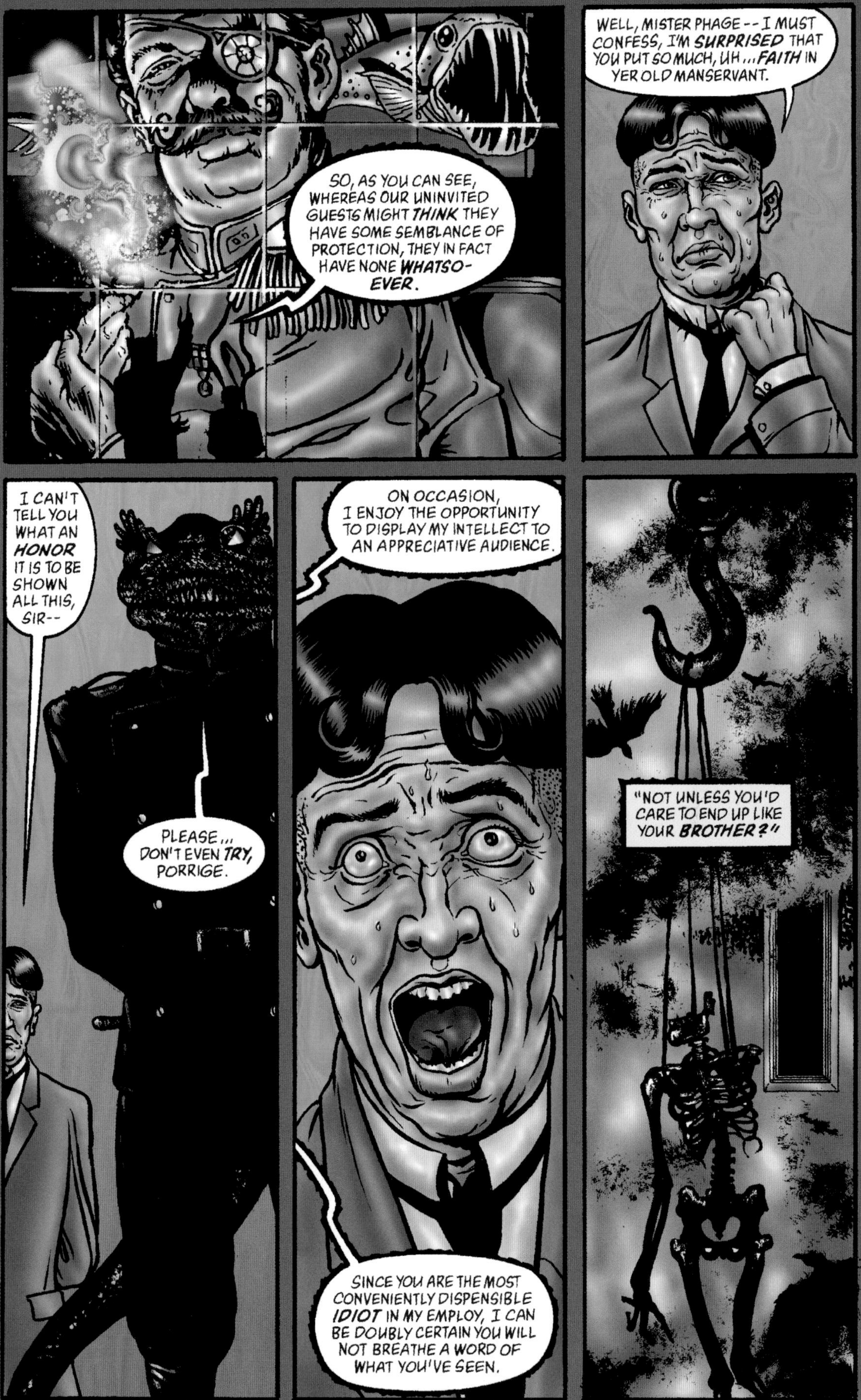

SO, AS YOU CAN SEE, WHEREAS OUR UNINVITED GUESTS MIGHT THINK THEY HAVE SOME SEMBLANCE OF PROTECTION, THEY IN FACT HAVE NONE WHATSO-EVER.
WELL, MISTER PHAGE -- I MUST CONFESS, I'M SURPRISED THAT YOU PUT SO MUCH, UH ... FAITH IN YER OLD MANSERVANT.
I CAN'T TELL YOU WHAT AN HONOR IT IS TO BE SHOWN ALL THIS, SIR--
PLEASE ... DON'T EVEN TRY, PORRIGE.
ON OCCASION, I ENJOY THE OPPORTUNITY TO DISPLAY MY INTELLECT TO AN APPRECIATIVE AUDIENCE.
SINCE YOU ARE THE MOST CONVENIENTLY DISPENSIBLE IDIOT IN MY EMPLOY, I CAN BE DOUBLY CERTAIN YOU WILL NOT BREATHE A WORD OF WHAT YOU'VE SEEN.
"NOT UNLESS YOU'D CARE TO END UP LIKE YOUR BROTHER?"

AH! THE PIECE DE RESISTANCE ARRIVES ,,,,

BLOOMIN' HECK--

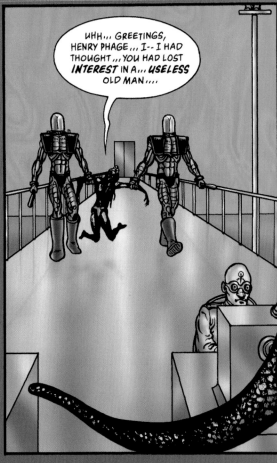

UHH,,, GREETINGS, HENRY PHAGE ,,, I-- I HAD THOUGHT ,,, YOU HAD LOST *INTEREST* IN A ,,, *USELESS* OLD MAN ,,,,

WELL, IT'S TRUE ,,, I CAN'T DENY IT, OLD BOY. I SIMPLY THOUGHT YOU MIGHT WELCOME THE OPPORTUNITY TO STRETCH YOUR LEGS ONE LAST TIME.

BESIDES, I HAVE SOMETHING TO SHOW YOU THAT MIGHT LIFT YOUR SPIRITS A LITTLE.

YOU SEE, I HAVE DISCOVERED-- QUITE TO MY SURPRISE-- THAT YOUR LIES AND DISTORTIONS HAVE AFFECTED AN *ALARMING* NUMBER OF MY EMPLOYEES ,,,,

I LOVE

MY OPERATIVES HAVE SO FAR DISCOVERED THREE HUNDRED AND SIX INSTANCES OF ILLEGAL RELIGIOUS ACTIVITIES WITHIN THE CONFINES OF THESE WALLS.

AS I'M SURE YOU UNDERSTAND, MY BUSINESS AND YOUR RELIGION ARE ENTIRELY INCOMPATIBLE.

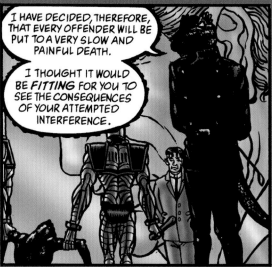

I HAVE DECIDED, THEREFORE, THAT EVERY OFFENDER WILL BE PUT TO A VERY SLOW AND PAINFUL DEATH.

I THOUGHT IT WOULD BE *FITTING* FOR YOU TO SEE THE CONSEQUENCES OF YOUR ATTEMPTED INTERFERENCE.

PLEASE... REVERED PHAGE... DO NOT HARM THESE INNOCENTS....

I WILL HELP YOU IN ANY WAY I CAN....

AS I THOUGHT YOU *WOULD*, OLD MAN.

TAKE HIM TO THE VATS, AND BRING ALL OFFENDERS THERE FOR QUESTIONING.

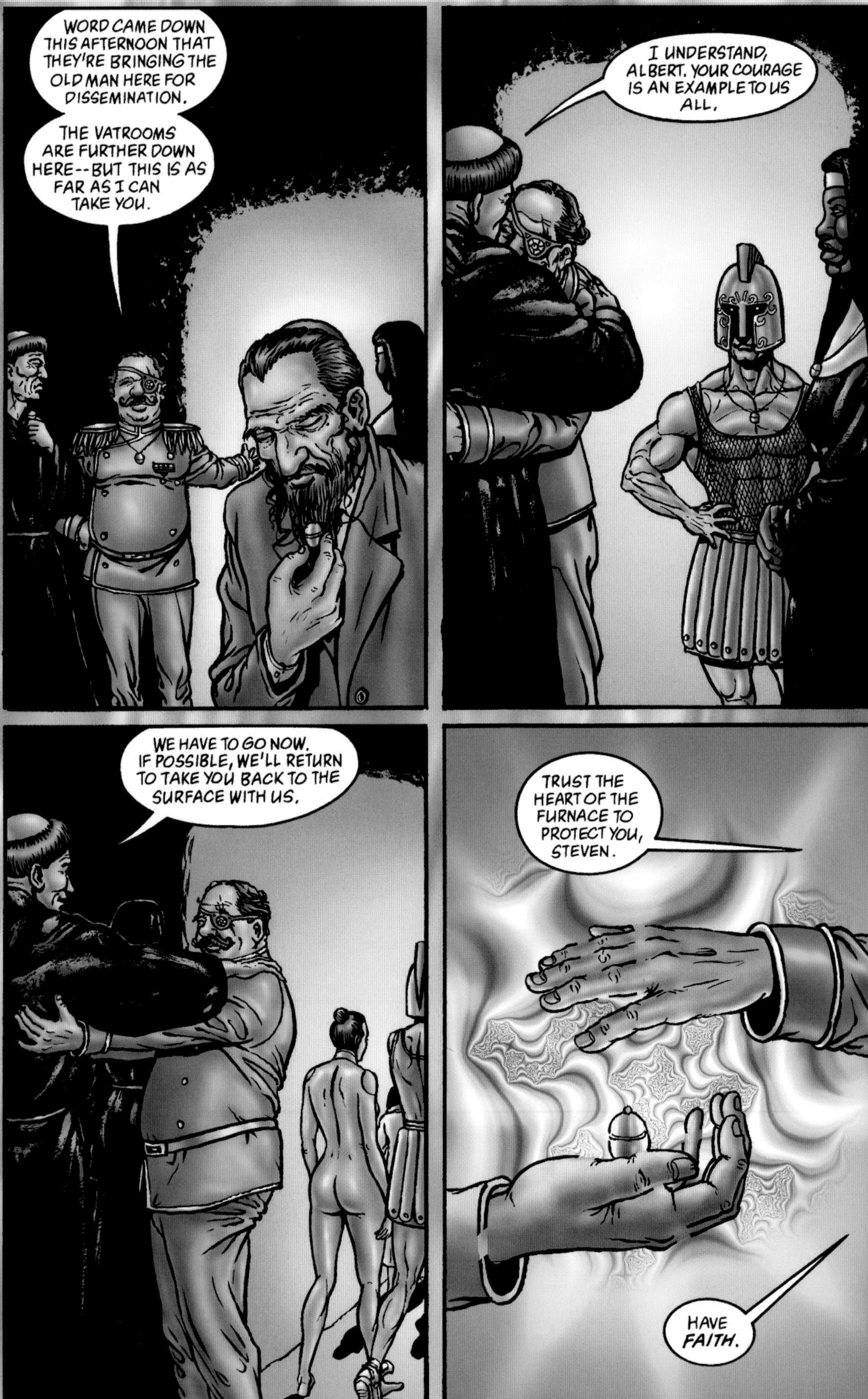
WORD CAME DOWN THIS AFTERNOON THAT THEY'RE BRINGING THE OLD MAN HERE FOR DISSEMINATION.
THE VATROOMS ARE FURTHER DOWN HERE--BUT THIS IS AS FAR AS I CAN TAKE YOU.
I UNDERSTAND, ALBERT. YOUR COURAGE IS AN EXAMPLE TO US ALL.
WE HAVE TO GO NOW. IF POSSIBLE, WE'LL RETURN TO TAKE YOU BACK TO THE SURFACE WITH US.
TRUST THE HEART OF THE FURNACE TO PROTECT YOU, STEVEN.
HAVE *FAITH*.

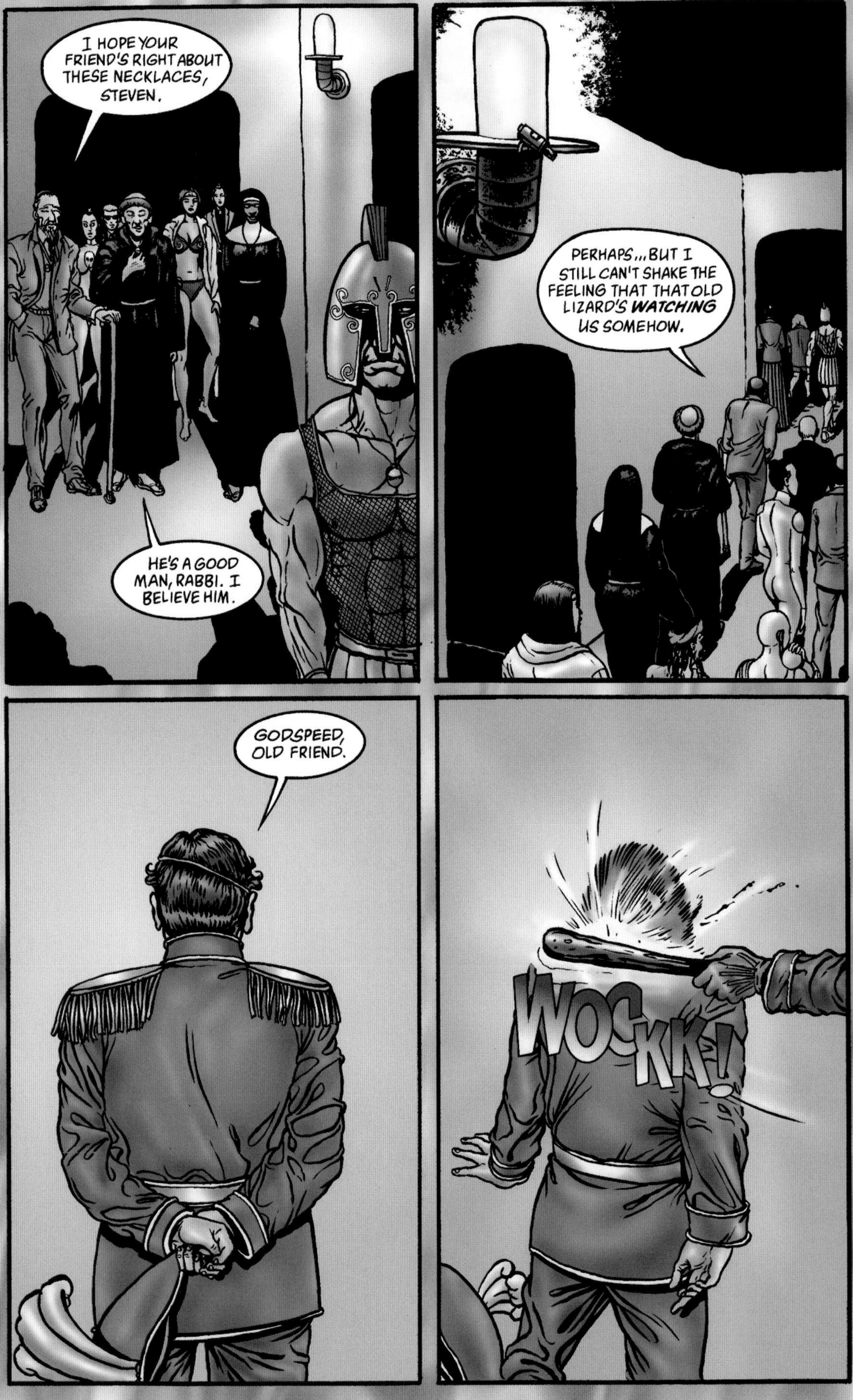
I HOPE YOUR FRIEND'S RIGHT ABOUT THESE NECKLACES, STEVEN.
HE'S A GOOD MAN, RABBI. I BELIEVE HIM.
PERHAPS... BUT I STILL CAN'T SHAKE THE FEELING THAT THAT OLD LIZARD'S *WATCHING* US SOMEHOW.
GODSPEED, OLD FRIEND.
WOCKK!

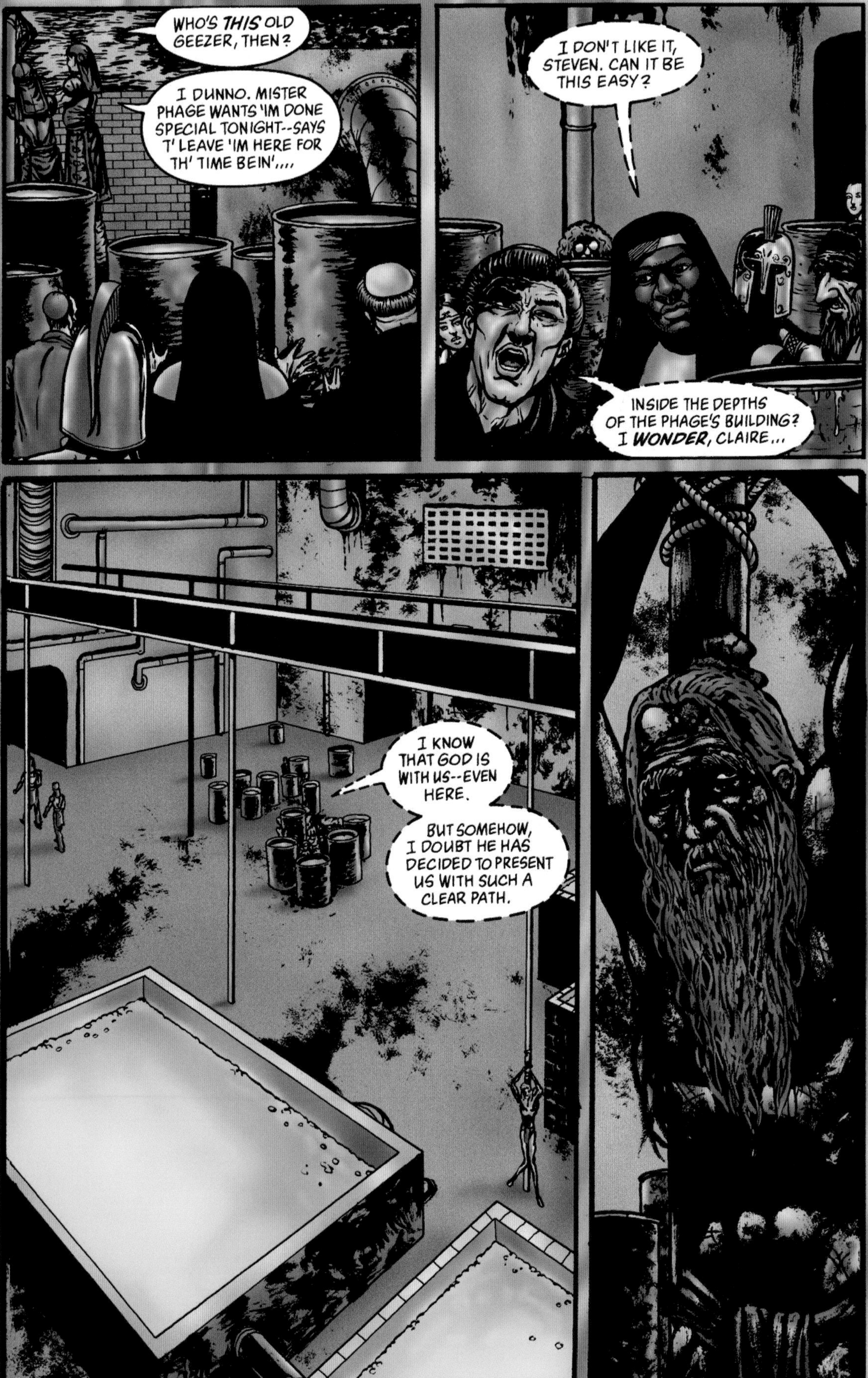
WHO'S *THIS* OLD GEEZER, THEN?
I DUNNO. MISTER PHAGE WANTS 'IM DONE SPECIAL TONIGHT--SAYS T' LEAVE 'IM HERE FOR TH' TIME BEIN'....
I DON'T LIKE IT, STEVEN. CAN IT BE THIS EASY?
INSIDE THE DEPTHS OF THE PHAGE'S BUILDING? I *WONDER*, CLAIRE...
I KNOW THAT GOD IS WITH US--EVEN HERE.
BUT SOMEHOW, I DOUBT HE HAS DECIDED TO PRESENT US WITH SUCH A CLEAR PATH.

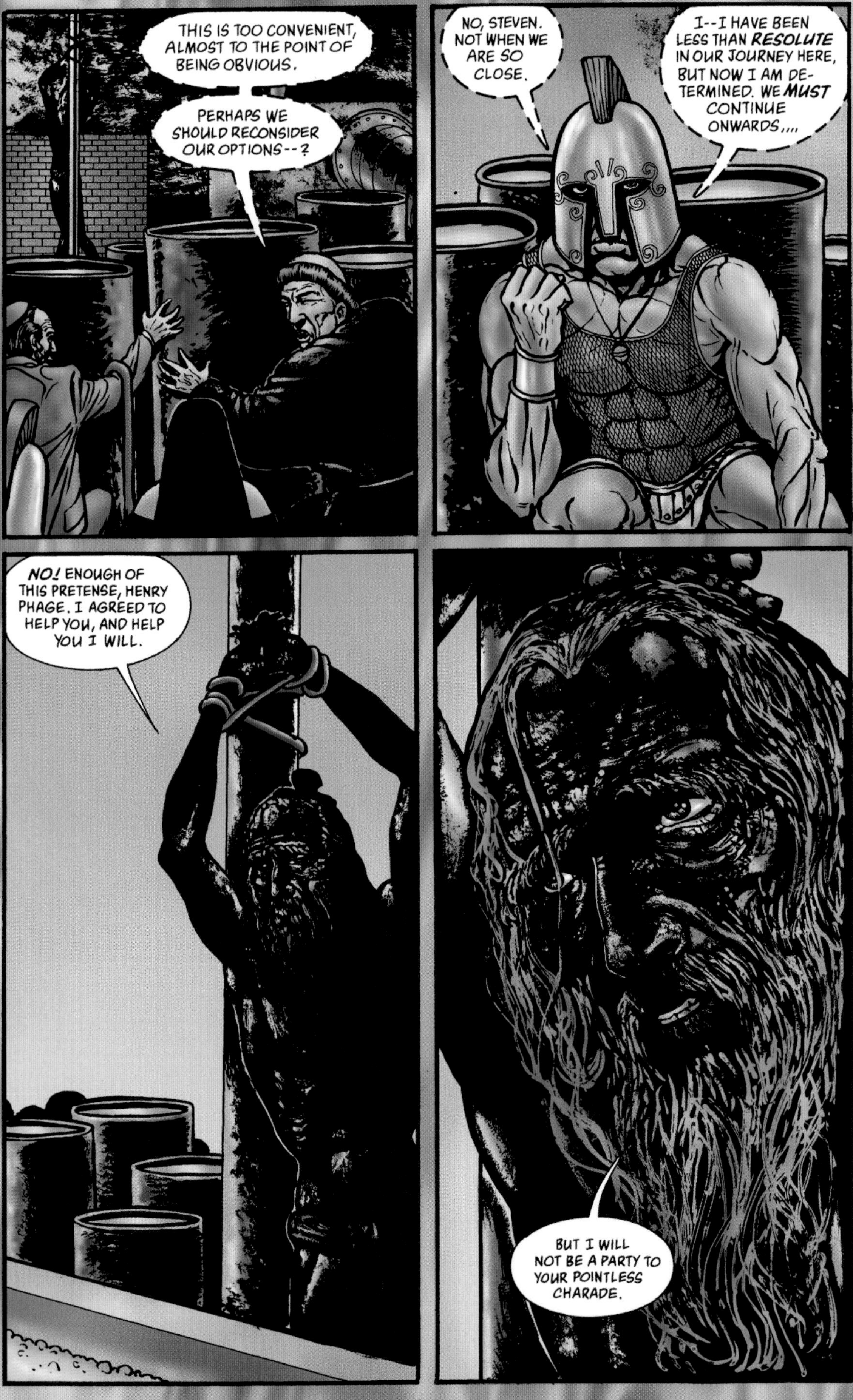
THIS IS TOO CONVENIENT, ALMOST TO THE POINT OF BEING OBVIOUS.
PERHAPS WE SHOULD RECONSIDER OUR OPTIONS--?
NO, STEVEN. NOT WHEN WE ARE SO CLOSE.
I--I HAVE BEEN LESS THAN RESOLUTE IN OUR JOURNEY HERE, BUT NOW I AM DETERMINED. WE MUST CONTINUE ONWARDS,...
NO! ENOUGH OF THIS PRETENSE, HENRY PHAGE. I AGREED TO HELP YOU, AND HELP YOU I WILL.
BUT I WILL NOT BE A PARTY TO YOUR POINTLESS CHARADE.

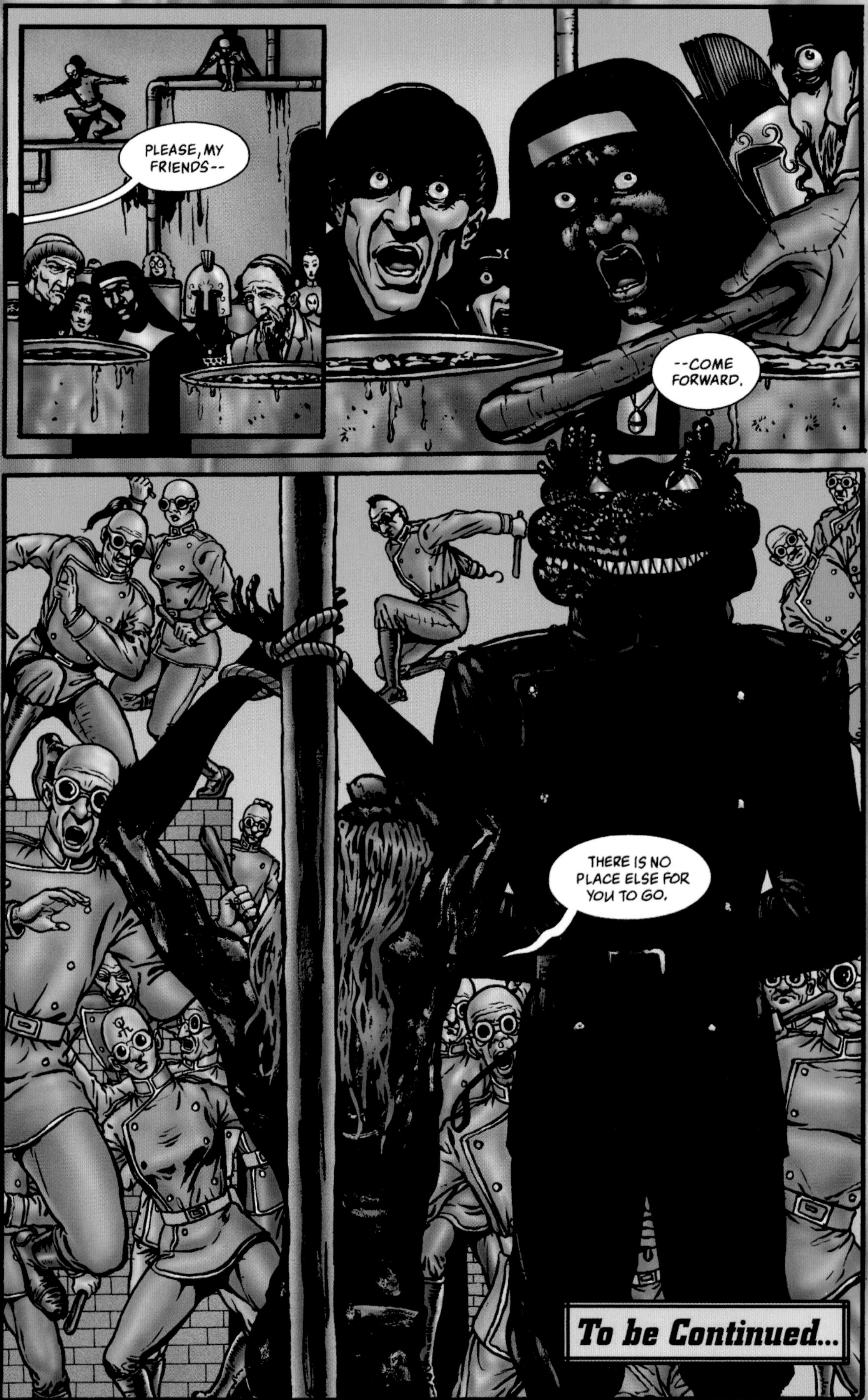
PLEASE, MY FRIENDS--
--COME FORWARD.
THERE IS NO PLACE ELSE FOR YOU TO GO.
To be Continued...

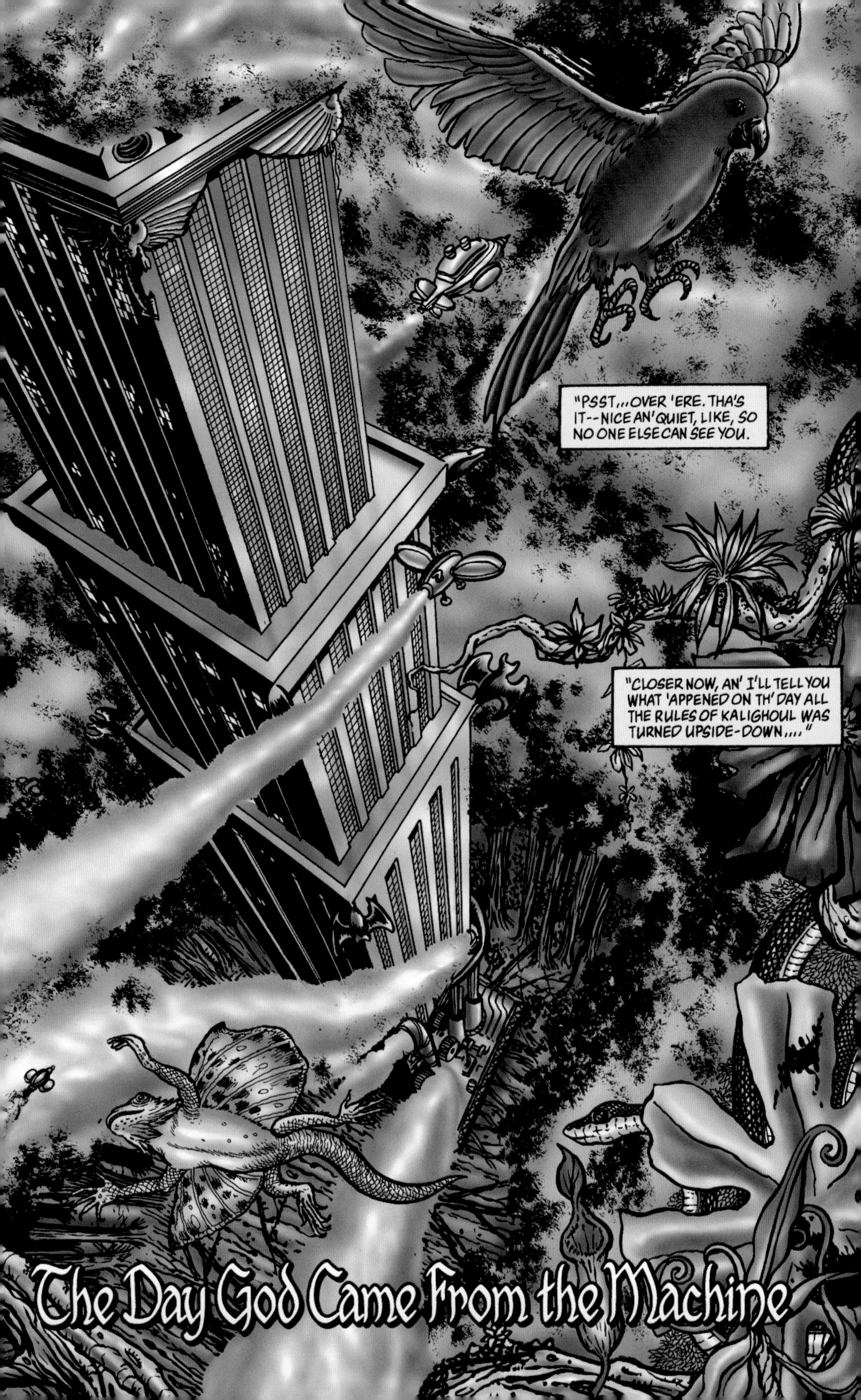
"PSST,...OVER 'ERE. THA'S IT--NICE AN' QUIET, LIKE, SO NO ONE ELSE CAN SEE YOU.
"CLOSER NOW, AN' I'LL TELL YOU WHAT 'APPENED ON TH' DAY ALL THE RULES OF KALIGHOUL WAS TURNED UPSIDE-DOWN...."
The Day God Came From the Machine

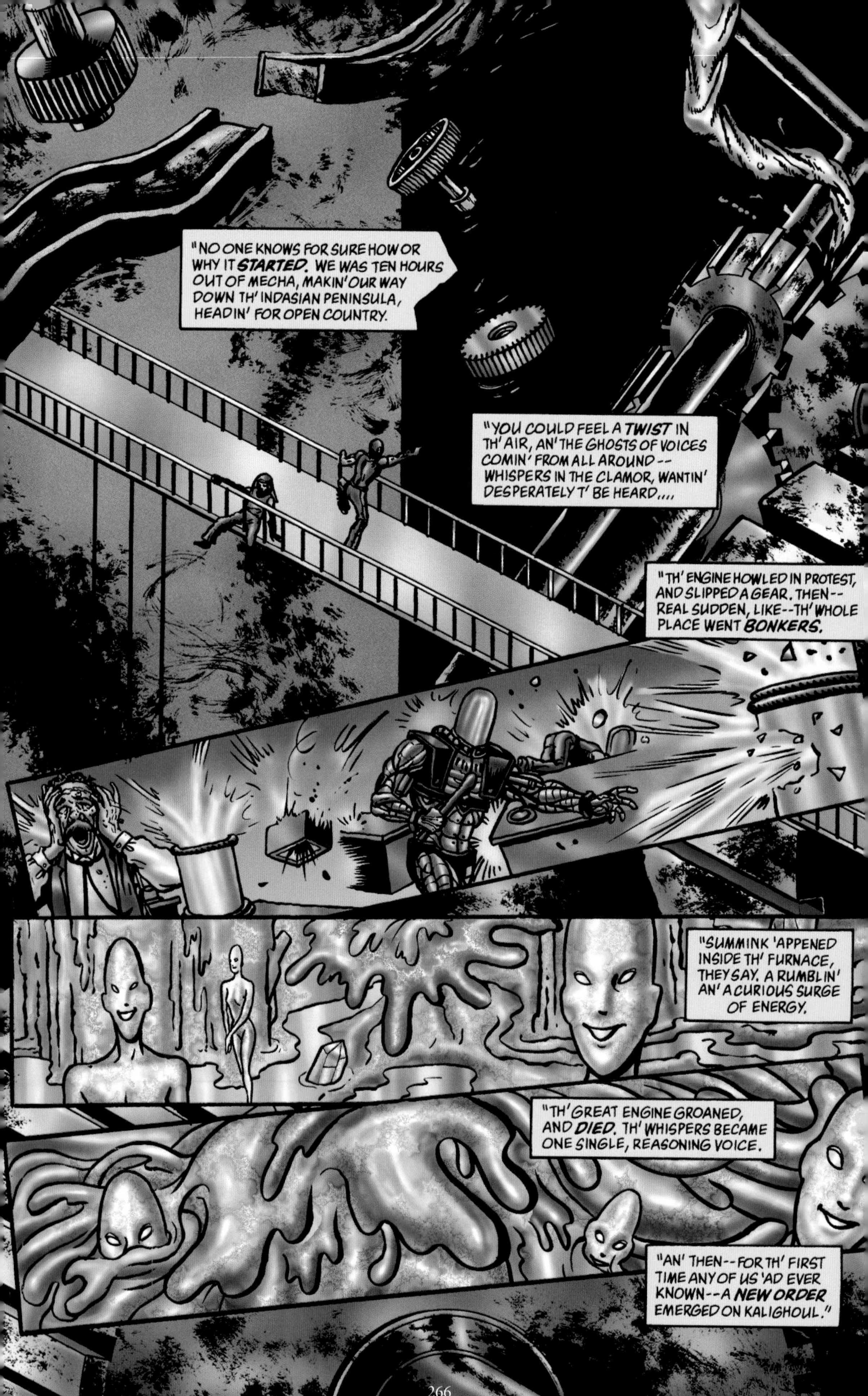
"NO ONE KNOWS FOR SURE HOW OR WHY IT STARTED. WE WAS TEN HOURS OUT OF MECHA, MAKIN' OUR WAY DOWN TH' INDASIAN PENINSULA, HEADIN' FOR OPEN COUNTRY.
"YOU COULD FEEL A TWIST IN TH' AIR, AN' THE GHOSTS OF VOICES COMIN' FROM ALL AROUND--WHISPERS IN THE CLAMOR, WANTIN' DESPERATELY T' BE HEARD....
"TH' ENGINE HOWLED IN PROTEST, AND SLIPPED A GEAR. THEN--REAL SUDDEN, LIKE--TH' WHOLE PLACE WENT BONKERS.
"SUMMINK 'APPENED INSIDE TH' FURNACE, THEY SAY. A RUMBLIN' AN' A CURIOUS SURGE OF ENERGY.
"TH' GREAT ENGINE GROANED, AND DIED. TH' WHISPERS BECAME ONE SINGLE, REASONING VOICE.
"AN' THEN--FOR TH' FIRST TIME ANY OF US 'AD EVER KNOWN--A NEW ORDER EMERGED ON KALIGHOUL."

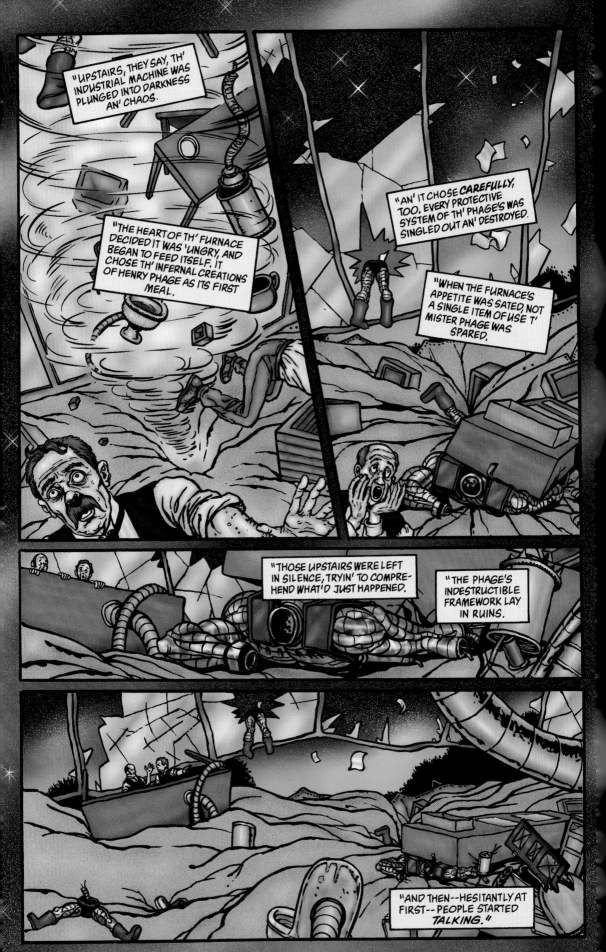

"UPSTAIRS, THEY SAY, TH' INDUSTRIAL MACHINE WAS PLUNGED INTO DARKNESS AN' CHAOS.

"THE HEART OF TH' FURNACE DECIDED IT WAS 'UNGRY, AND BEGAN TO FEED ITSELF. IT CHOSE TH' INFERNAL CREATIONS OF HENRY PHAGE AS ITS FIRST MEAL.

"AN' IT CHOSE *CAREFULLY*, TOO. EVERY PROTECTIVE SYSTEM OF TH' PHAGE'S WAS SINGLED OUT AN' DESTROYED.

"WHEN THE FURNACE'S APPETITE WAS SATED, NOT A SINGLE ITEM OF USE T' MISTER PHAGE WAS SPARED.

"THOSE UPSTAIRS WERE LEFT IN SILENCE, TRYIN' TO COMPREHEND WHAT'D JUST HAPPENED.

"THE PHAGE'S INDESTRUCTIBLE FRAMEWORK LAY IN RUINS.

"AND THEN—HESITANTLY AT FIRST—PEOPLE STARTED *TALKING*."

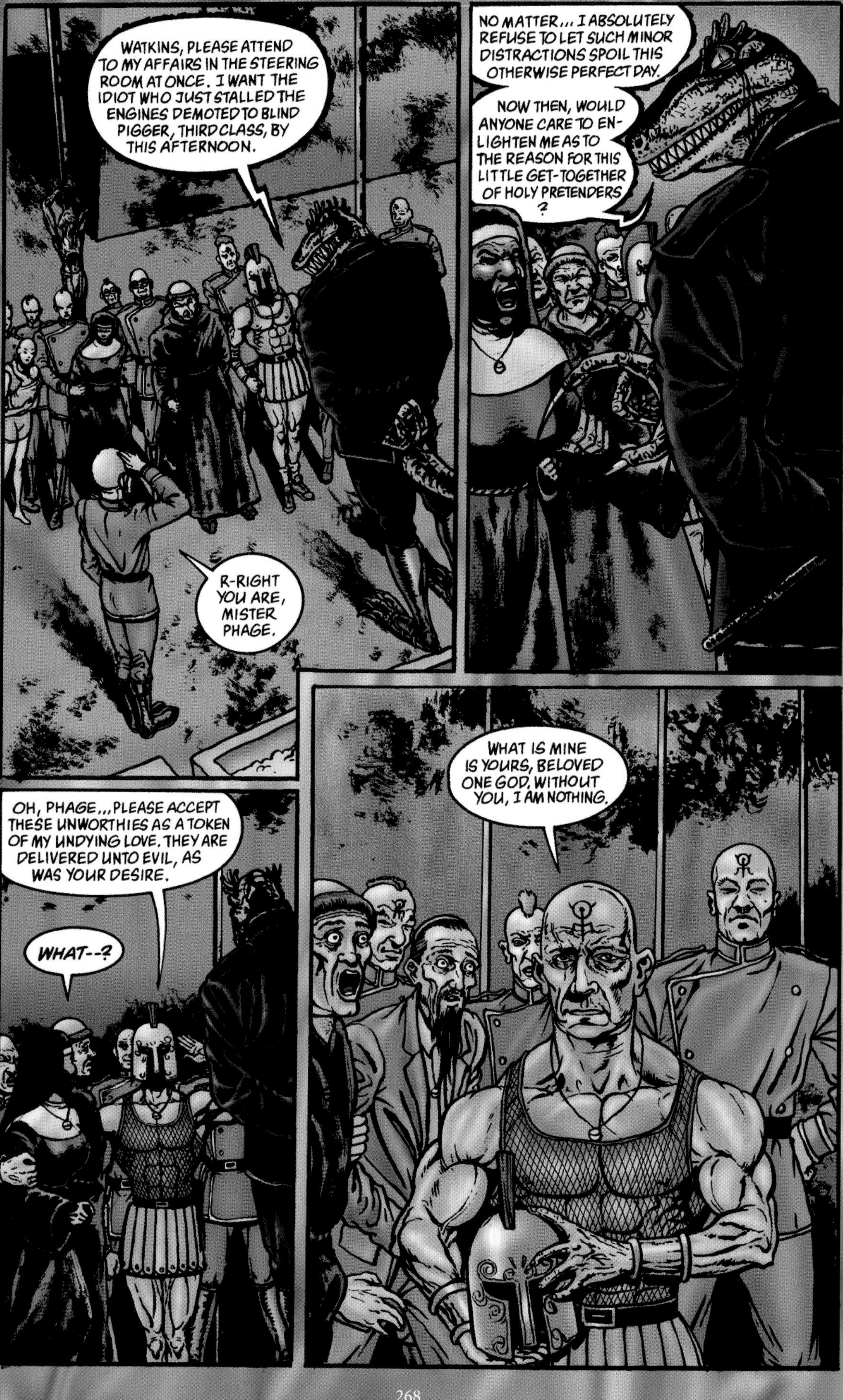
WATKINS, PLEASE ATTEND TO MY AFFAIRS IN THE STEERING ROOM AT ONCE. I WANT THE IDIOT WHO JUST STALLED THE ENGINES DEMOTED TO BLIND PIGGER, THIRD CLASS, BY THIS AFTERNOON.
R-RIGHT YOU ARE, MISTER PHAGE.
NO MATTER... I ABSOLUTELY REFUSE TO LET SUCH MINOR DISTRACTIONS SPOIL THIS OTHERWISE PERFECT DAY.
NOW THEN, WOULD ANYONE CARE TO ENLIGHTEN ME AS TO THE REASON FOR THIS LITTLE GET-TOGETHER OF HOLY PRETENDERS?
OH, PHAGE... PLEASE ACCEPT THESE UNWORTHIES AS A TOKEN OF MY UNDYING LOVE. THEY ARE DELIVERED UNTO EVIL, AS WAS YOUR DESIRE.
WHAT--?
WHAT IS MINE IS YOURS, BELOVED ONE GOD. WITHOUT YOU, I AM NOTHING.

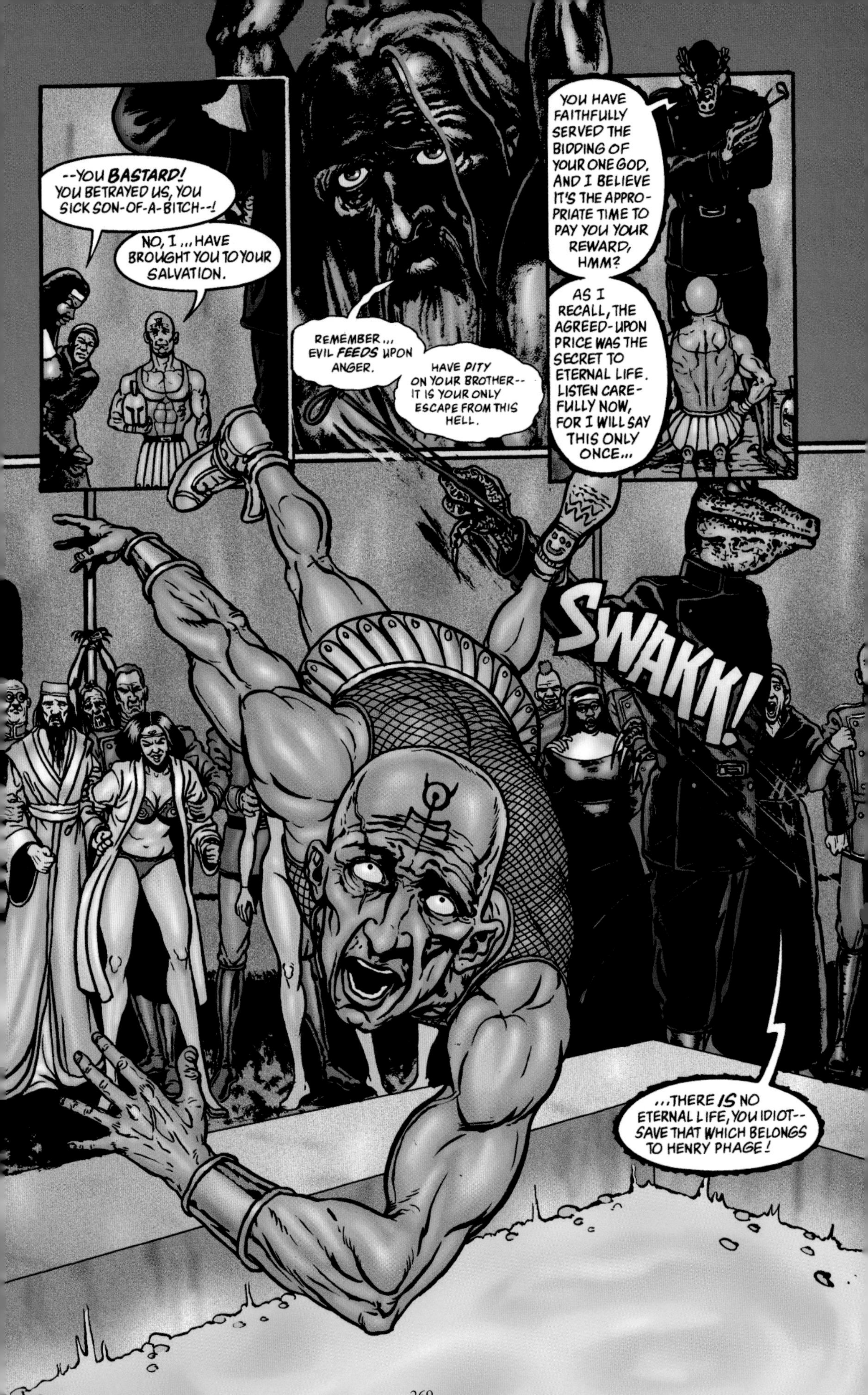
--YOU BASTARD! YOU BETRAYED US, YOU SICK SON-OF-A-BITCH--!
NO, I ...HAVE BROUGHT YOU TO YOUR SALVATION.
REMEMBER... EVIL FEEDS UPON ANGER.
HAVE PITY ON YOUR BROTHER-- IT IS YOUR ONLY ESCAPE FROM THIS HELL.
YOU HAVE FAITHFULLY SERVED THE BIDDING OF YOUR ONE GOD, AND I BELIEVE IT'S THE APPROPRIATE TIME TO PAY YOU YOUR REWARD, HMM?
AS I RECALL, THE AGREED-UPON PRICE WAS THE SECRET TO ETERNAL LIFE. LISTEN CAREFULLY NOW, FOR I WILL SAY THIS ONLY ONCE...
SWAKK!
...THERE IS NO ETERNAL LIFE, YOU IDIOT-- SAVE THAT WHICH BELONGS TO HENRY PHAGE!

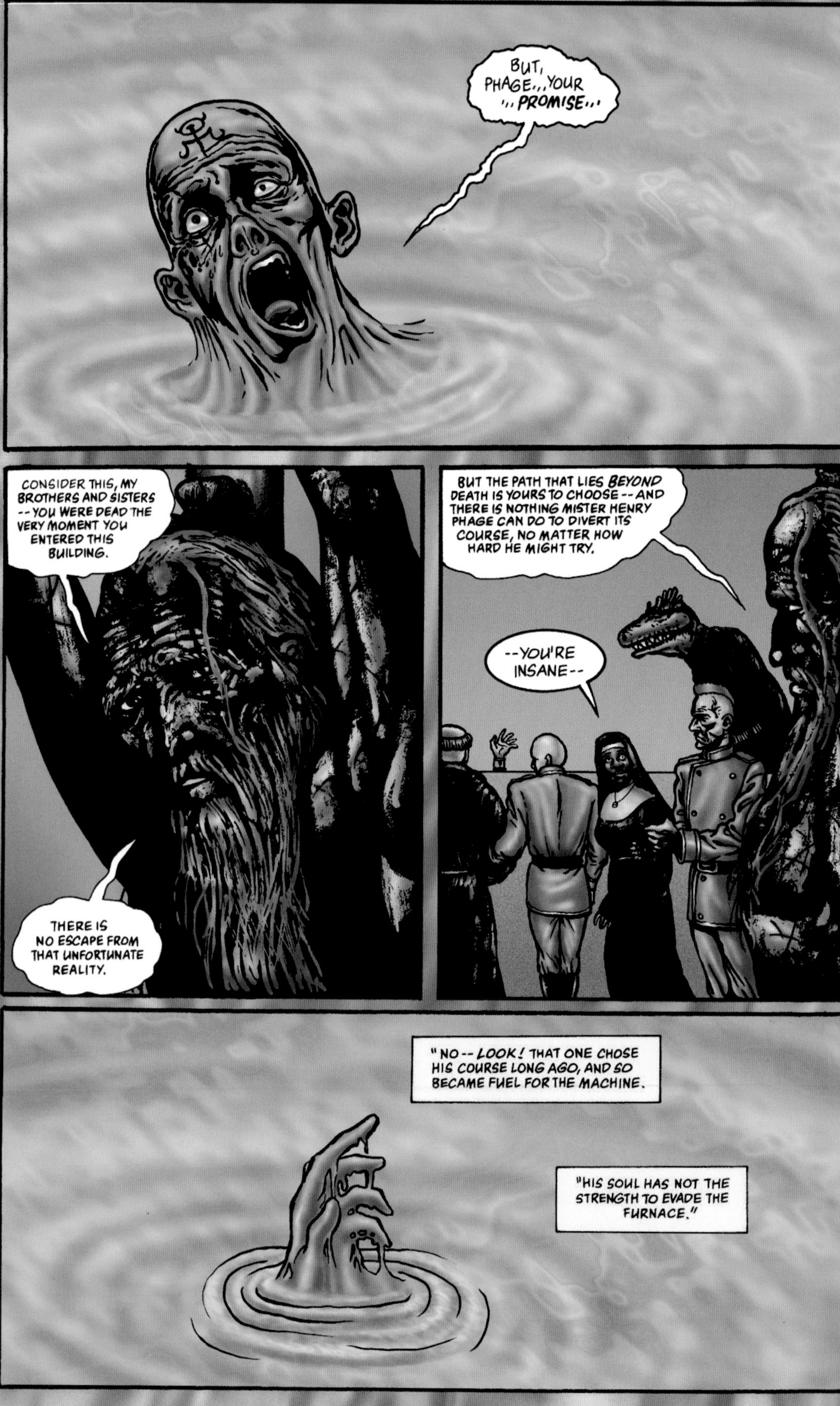

BUT, PHAGE... YOUR ...PROMISE...
CONSIDER THIS, MY BROTHERS AND SISTERS --YOU WERE DEAD THE VERY MOMENT YOU ENTERED THIS BUILDING.
THERE IS NO ESCAPE FROM THAT UNFORTUNATE REALITY.
BUT THE PATH THAT LIES BEYOND DEATH IS YOURS TO CHOOSE--AND THERE IS NOTHING MISTER HENRY PHAGE CAN DO TO DIVERT ITS COURSE, NO MATTER HOW HARD HE MIGHT TRY.
--YOU'RE INSANE--
"NO--LOOK! THAT ONE CHOSE HIS COURSE LONG AGO, AND SO BECAME FUEL FOR THE MACHINE.
"HIS SOUL HAS NOT THE STRENGTH TO EVADE THE FURNACE."

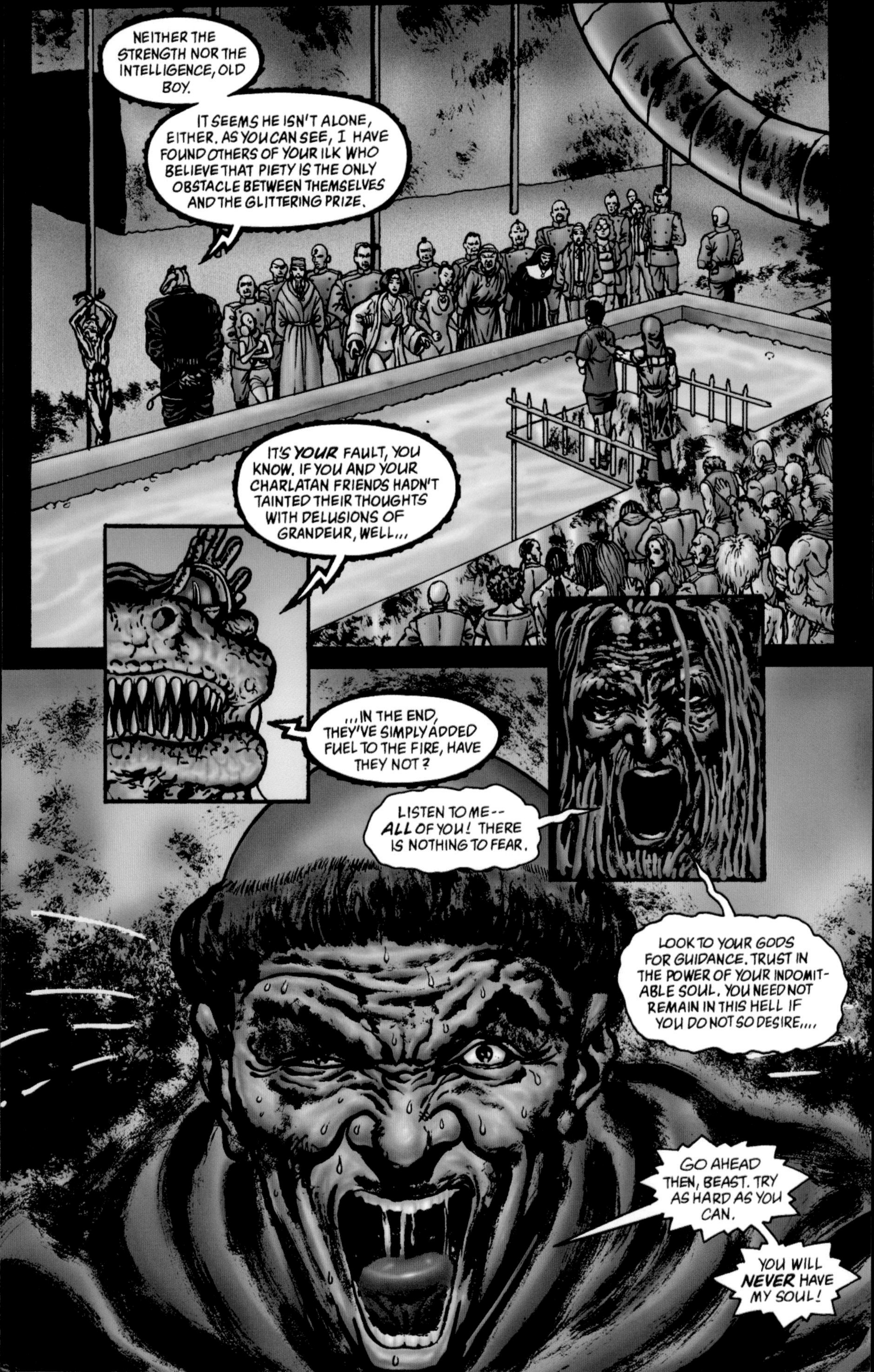

NEITHER THE STRENGTH NOR THE INTELLIGENCE, OLD BOY.
IT SEEMS HE ISN'T ALONE, EITHER. AS YOU CAN SEE, I HAVE FOUND OTHERS OF YOUR ILK WHO BELIEVE THAT PIETY IS THE ONLY OBSTACLE BETWEEN THEMSELVES AND THE GLITTERING PRIZE.
IT'S YOUR FAULT, YOU KNOW. IF YOU AND YOUR CHARLATAN FRIENDS HADN'T TAINTED THEIR THOUGHTS WITH DELUSIONS OF GRANDEUR, WELL...
...IN THE END, THEY'VE SIMPLY ADDED FUEL TO THE FIRE, HAVE THEY NOT?
LISTEN TO ME-- ALL OF YOU! THERE IS NOTHING TO FEAR.
LOOK TO YOUR GODS FOR GUIDANCE. TRUST IN THE POWER OF YOUR INDOMITABLE SOUL. YOU NEED NOT REMAIN IN THIS HELL IF YOU DO NOT SO DESIRE...
GO AHEAD THEN, BEAST. TRY AS HARD AS YOU CAN.
YOU WILL NEVER HAVE MY SOUL!

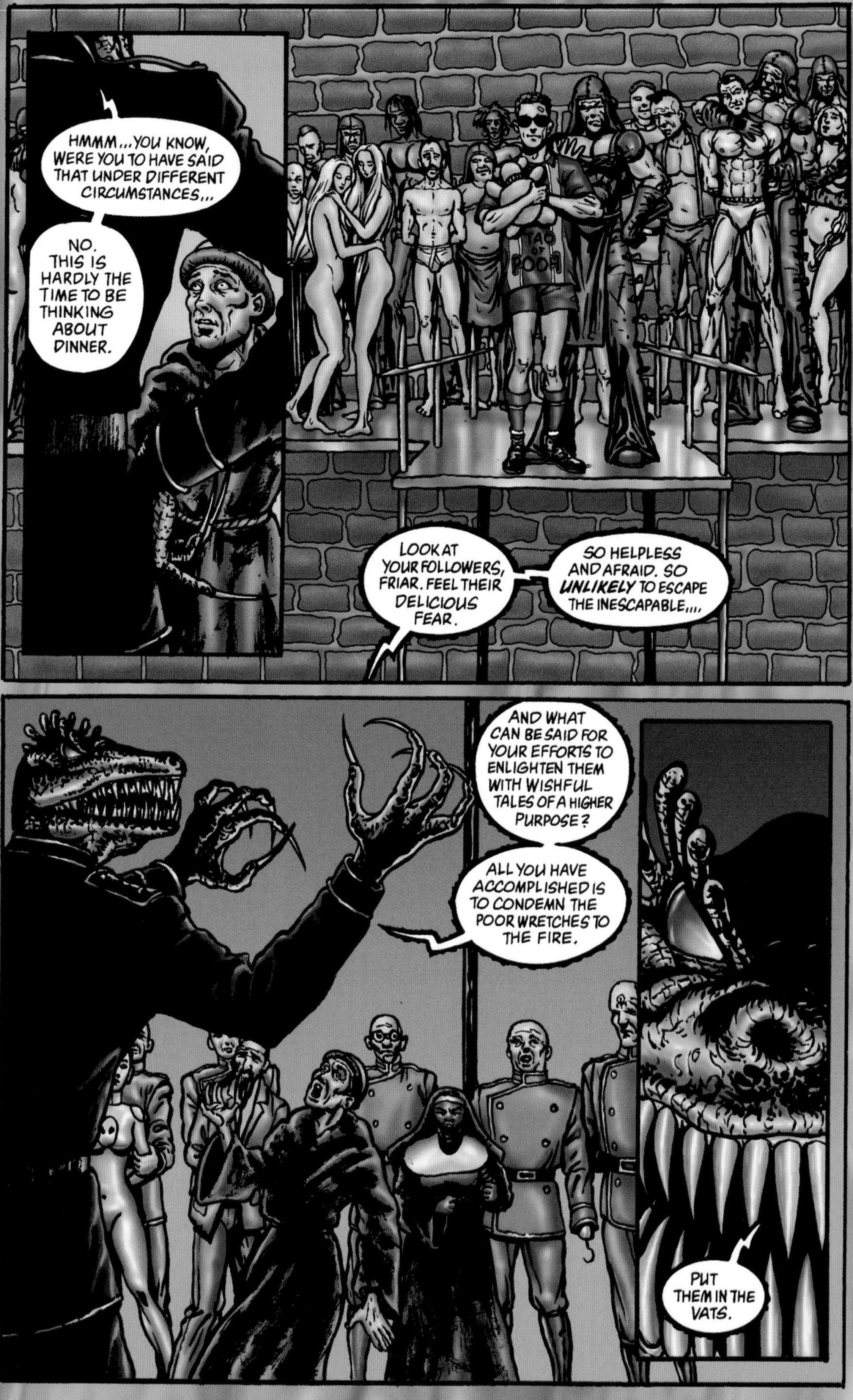
HMMM...YOU KNOW, WERE YOU TO HAVE SAID THAT UNDER DIFFERENT CIRCUMSTANCES...
NO. THIS IS HARDLY THE TIME TO BE THINKING ABOUT DINNER.
LOOK AT YOUR FOLLOWERS, FRIAR. FEEL THEIR DELICIOUS FEAR.
SO HELPLESS AND AFRAID. SO UNLIKELY TO ESCAPE THE INESCAPABLE....
TAO OF POOH
AND WHAT CAN BE SAID FOR YOUR EFFORTS TO ENLIGHTEN THEM WITH WISHFUL TALES OF A HIGHER PURPOSE?
ALL YOU HAVE ACCOMPLISHED IS TO CONDEMN THE POOR WRETCHES TO THE FIRE.
PUT THEM IN THE VATS.

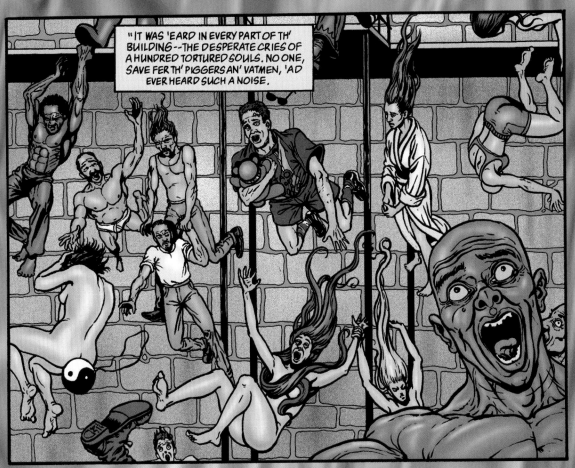

"IT WAS 'EARD IN EVERY PART OF TH' BUILDING -- THE DESPERATE CRIES OF A HUNDRED TORTURED SOULS. NO ONE, SAVE FER TH' PIGGERS AN' VATMEN, 'AD EVER HEARD SUCH A NOISE.

"TH' ENGINES WERE SILENT NOW, AN' WE 'AD NO CHOICE BUT TO LISTEN T' THE SCREAMS."

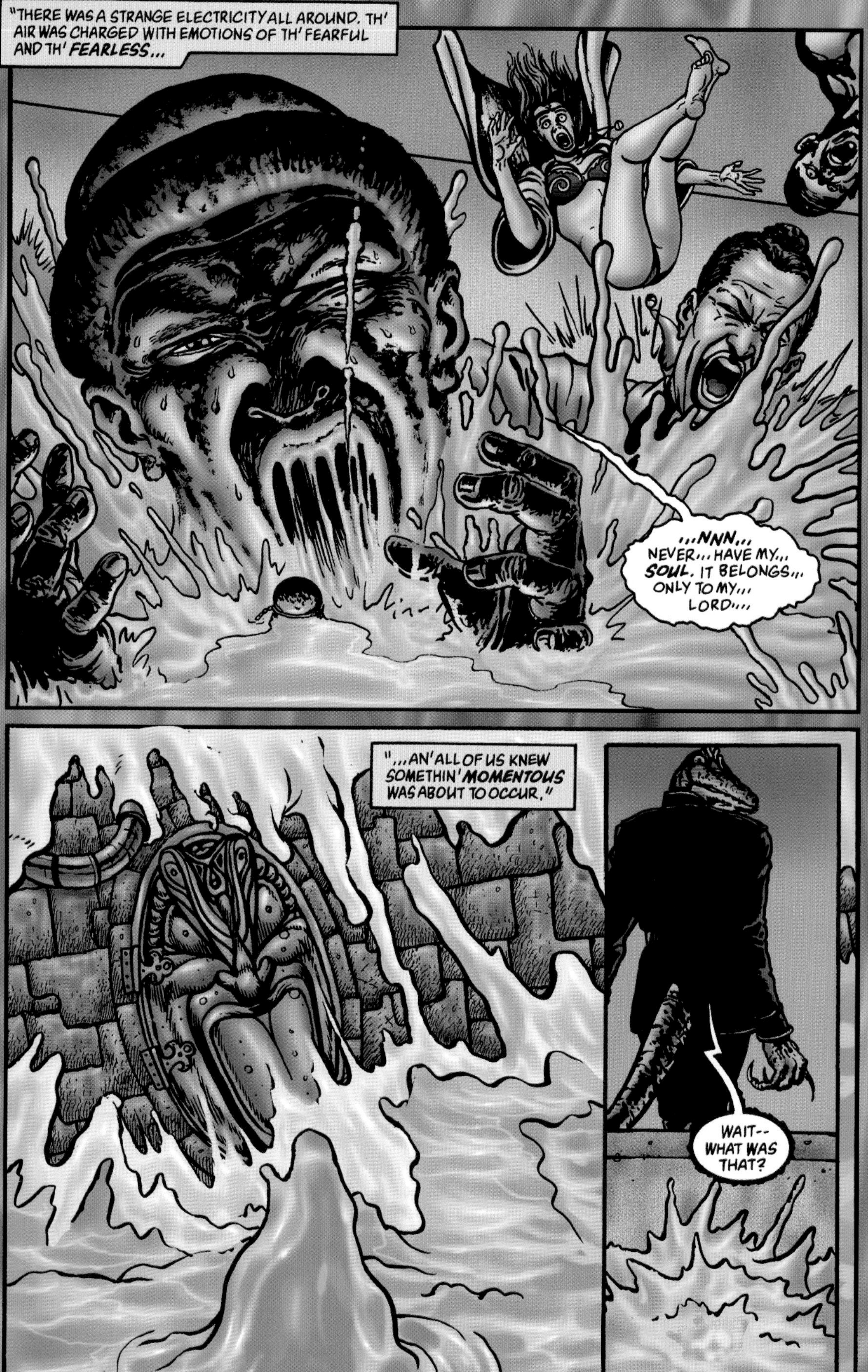
"THERE WAS A STRANGE ELECTRICITY ALL AROUND. TH' AIR WAS CHARGED WITH EMOTIONS OF TH' FEARFUL AND TH' FEARLESS...
...NNN... NEVER... HAVE MY... SOUL. IT BELONGS... ONLY TO MY... LORD....
"...AN' ALL OF US KNEW SOMETHIN' MOMENTOUS WAS ABOUT TO OCCUR."
WAIT-- WHAT WAS THAT?

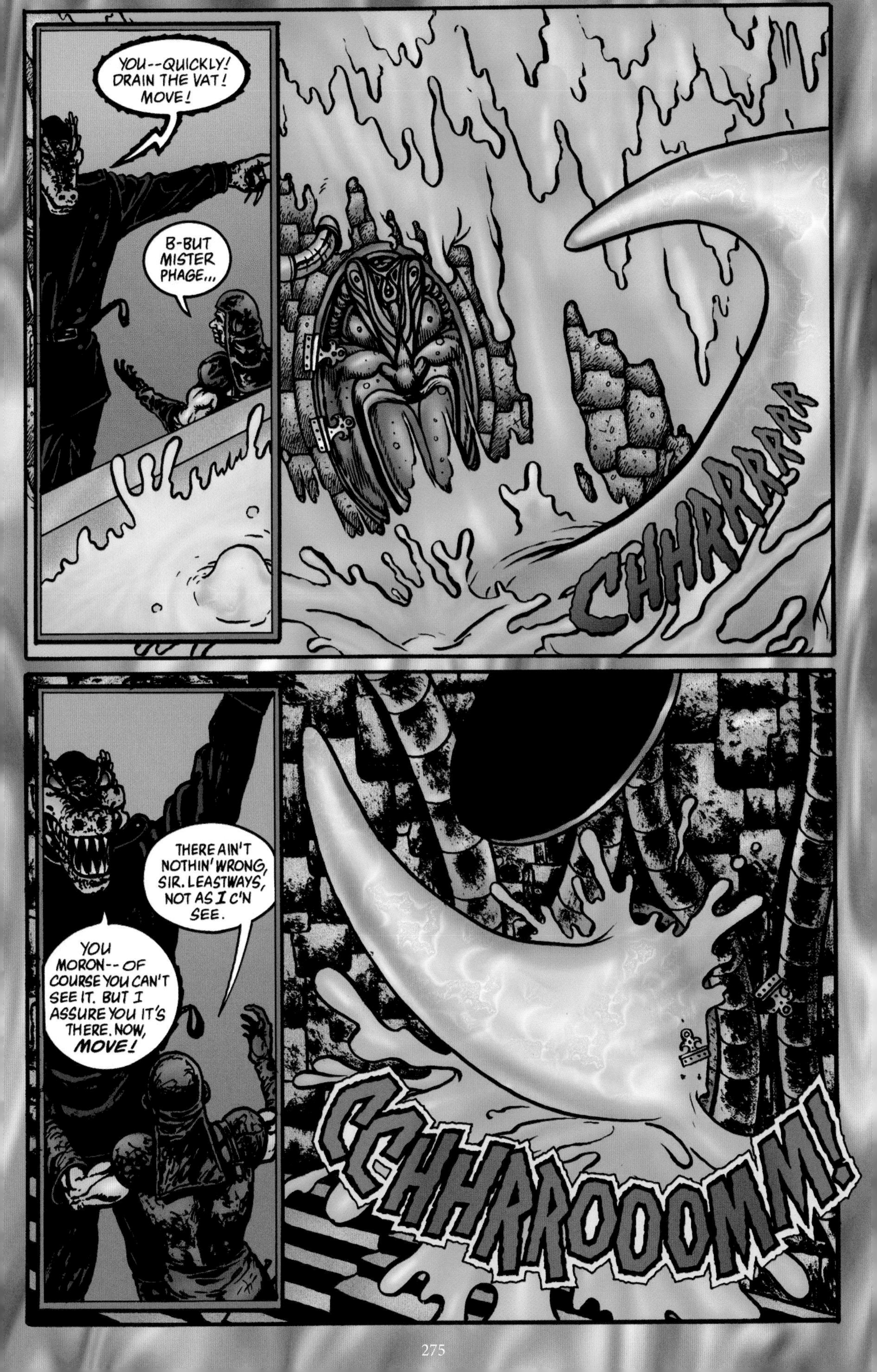

YOU--QUICKLY! DRAIN THE VAT! MOVE!
B-BUT MISTER PHAGE...
CHHRRRAAAR
THERE AIN'T NOTHIN' WRONG, SIR. LEASTWAYS, NOT AS I C'N SEE.
YOU MORON--OF COURSE YOU CAN'T SEE IT. BUT I ASSURE YOU IT'S THERE. NOW, MOVE!
CCHHROOOMM!

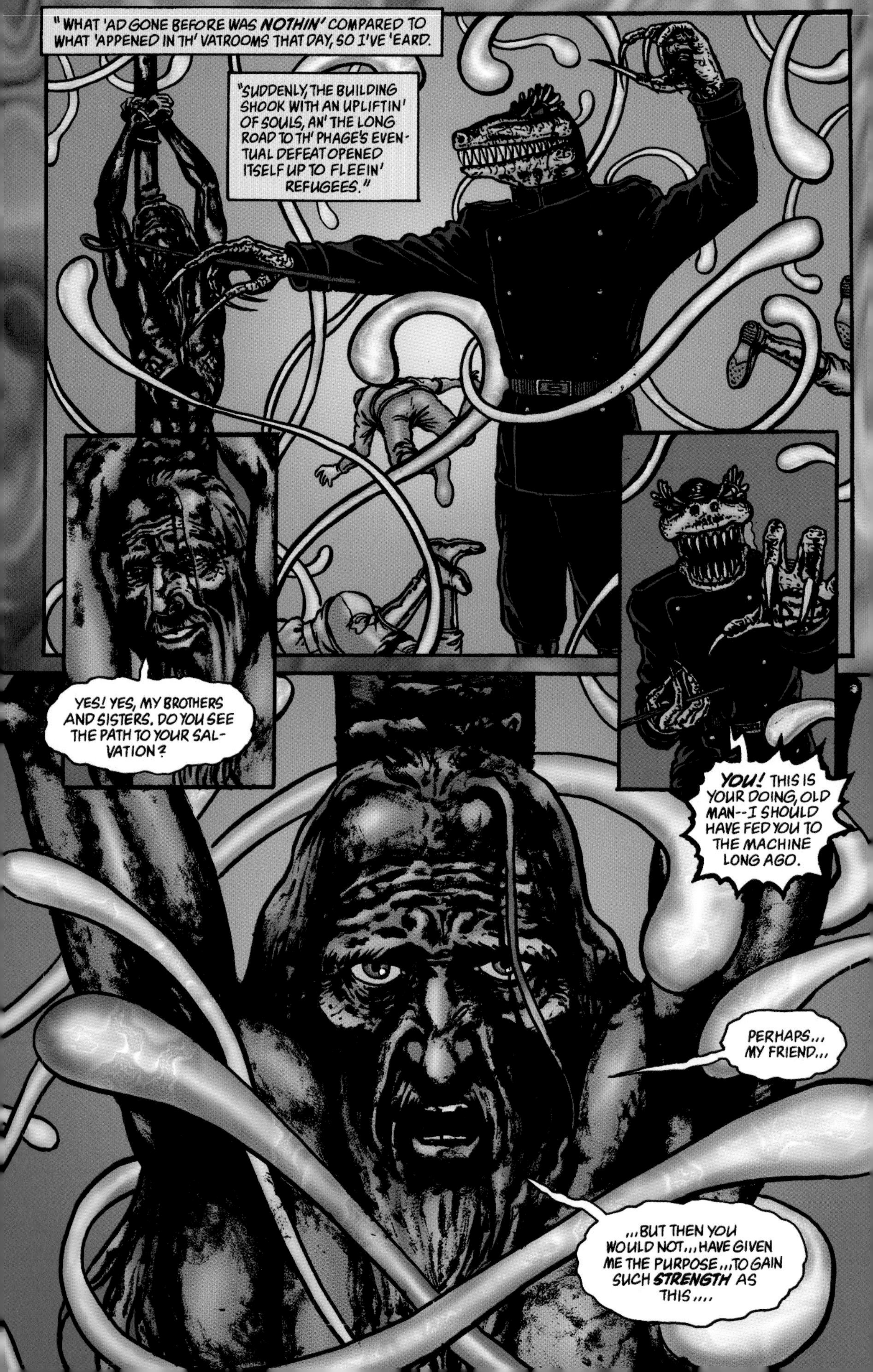
"WHAT 'AD GONE BEFORE WAS NOTHIN' COMPARED TO WHAT 'APPENED IN TH' VATROOMS THAT DAY, SO I'VE 'EARD.
"SUDDENLY, THE BUILDING SHOOK WITH AN UPLIFTIN' OF SOULS, AN' THE LONG ROAD TO TH' PHAGE'S EVEN-TUAL DEFEAT OPENED ITSELF UP TO FLEEIN' REFUGEES."
YES! YES, MY BROTHERS AND SISTERS. DO YOU SEE THE PATH TO YOUR SAL-VATION?
YOU! THIS IS YOUR DOING, OLD MAN--I SHOULD HAVE FED YOU TO THE MACHINE LONG AGO.
PERHAPS... MY FRIEND...
...BUT THEN YOU WOULD NOT... HAVE GIVEN ME THE PURPOSE...TO GAIN SUCH STRENGTH AS THIS....

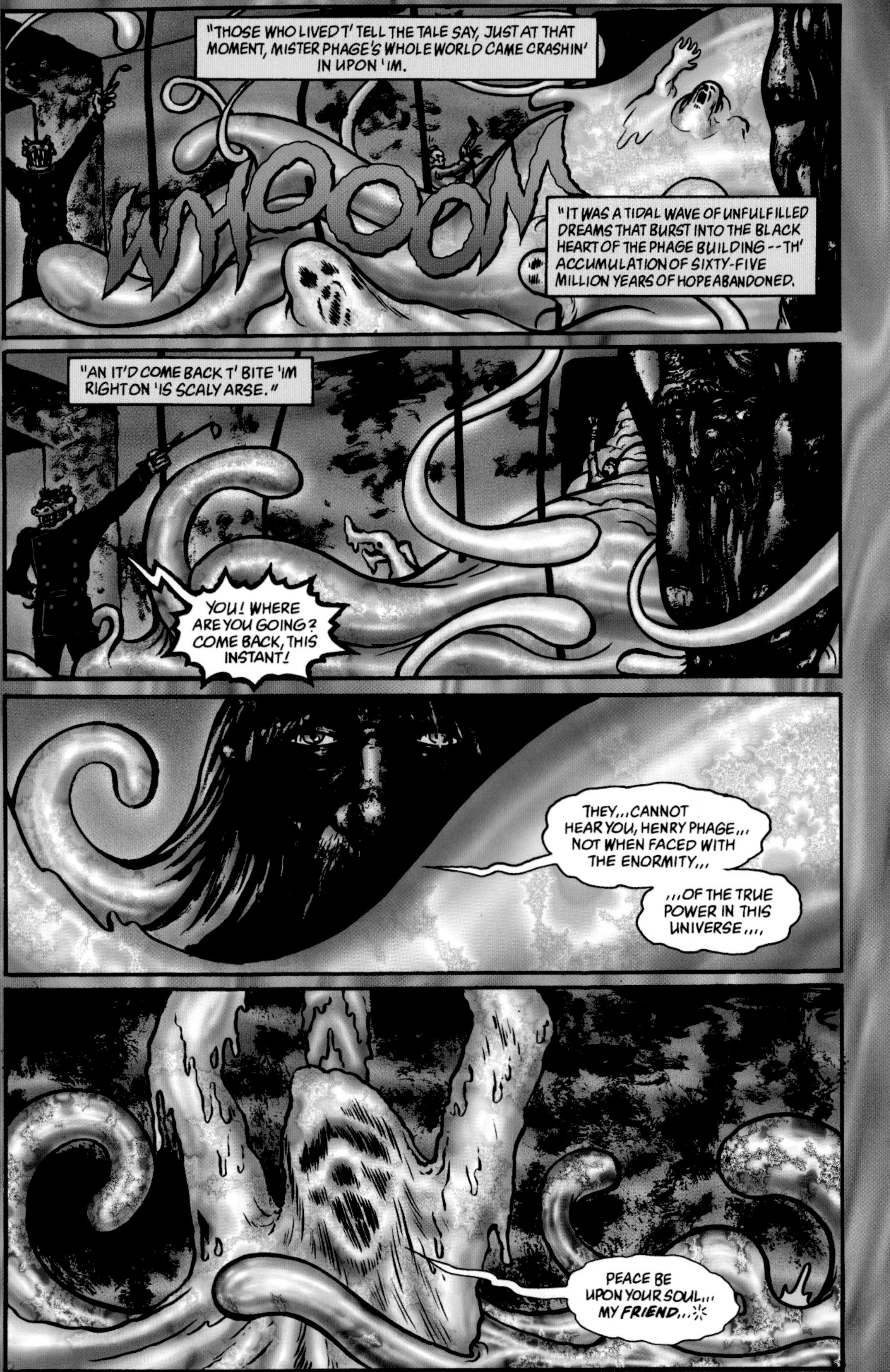
"THOSE WHO LIVED T' TELL THE TALE SAY, JUST AT THAT MOMENT, MISTER PHAGE'S WHOLE WORLD CAME CRASHIN' IN UPON 'IM.
WHOOOOM
"IT WAS A TIDAL WAVE OF UNFULFILLED DREAMS THAT BURST INTO THE BLACK HEART OF THE PHAGE BUILDING -- TH' ACCUMULATION OF SIXTY-FIVE MILLION YEARS OF HOPE ABANDONED.
"AN IT'D COME BACK T' BITE 'IM RIGHT ON 'IS SCALY ARSE."
YOU! WHERE ARE YOU GOING? COME BACK, THIS INSTANT!
THEY... CANNOT HEAR YOU, HENRY PHAGE... NOT WHEN FACED WITH THE ENORMITY...
...OF THE TRUE POWER IN THIS UNIVERSE....
PEACE BE UPON YOUR SOUL... MY FRIEND...

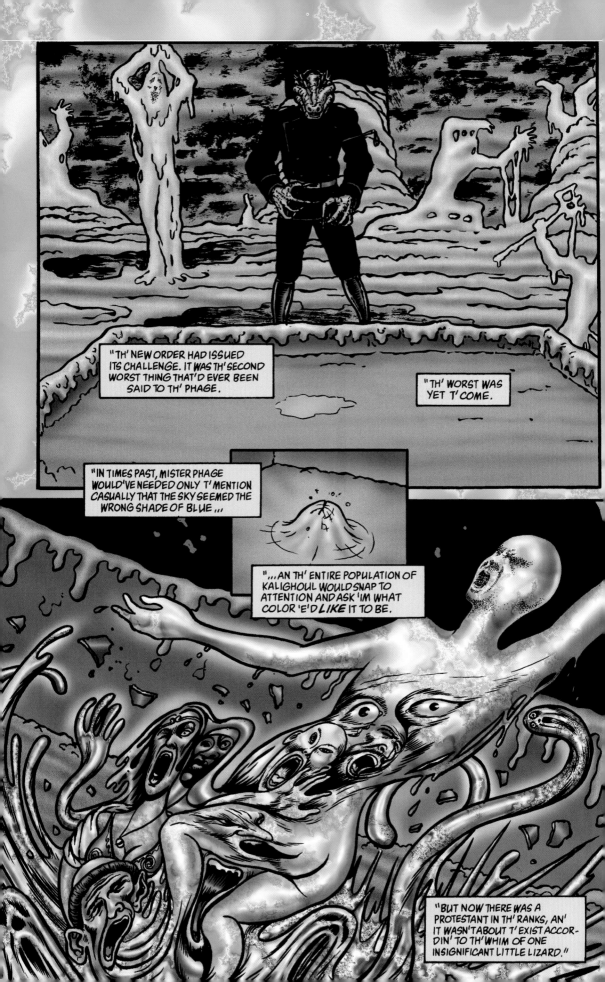

"TH' NEW ORDER HAD ISSUED ITS CHALLENGE. IT WAS TH' SECOND WORST THING THAT'D EVER BEEN SAID TO TH' PHAGE."

"TH' WORST WAS YET T' COME."

"IN TIMES PAST, MISTER PHAGE WOULD'VE NEEDED ONLY T' MENTION CASUALLY THAT THE SKY SEEMED THE WRONG SHADE OF BLUE ,,,

",,,AN TH' ENTIRE POPULATION OF KALIGHOUL WOULD SNAP TO ATTENTION AND ASK 'IM WHAT COLOR 'E'D LIKE IT TO BE."

"BUT NOW THERE WAS A PROTESTANT IN TH' RANKS, AN' IT WASN'T ABOUT T' EXIST ACCORDIN' TO TH' WHIM OF ONE INSIGNIFICANT LITTLE LIZARD."

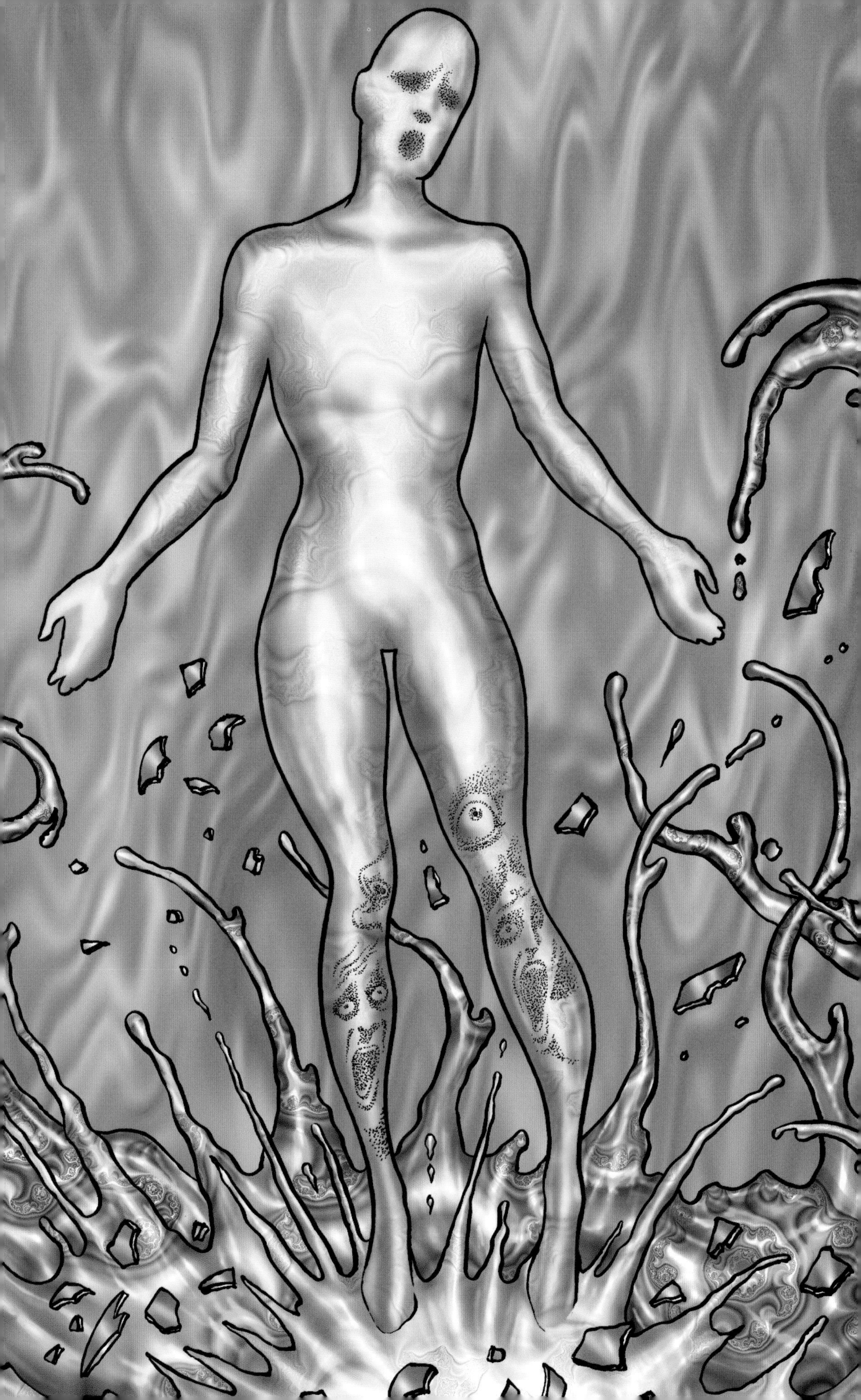

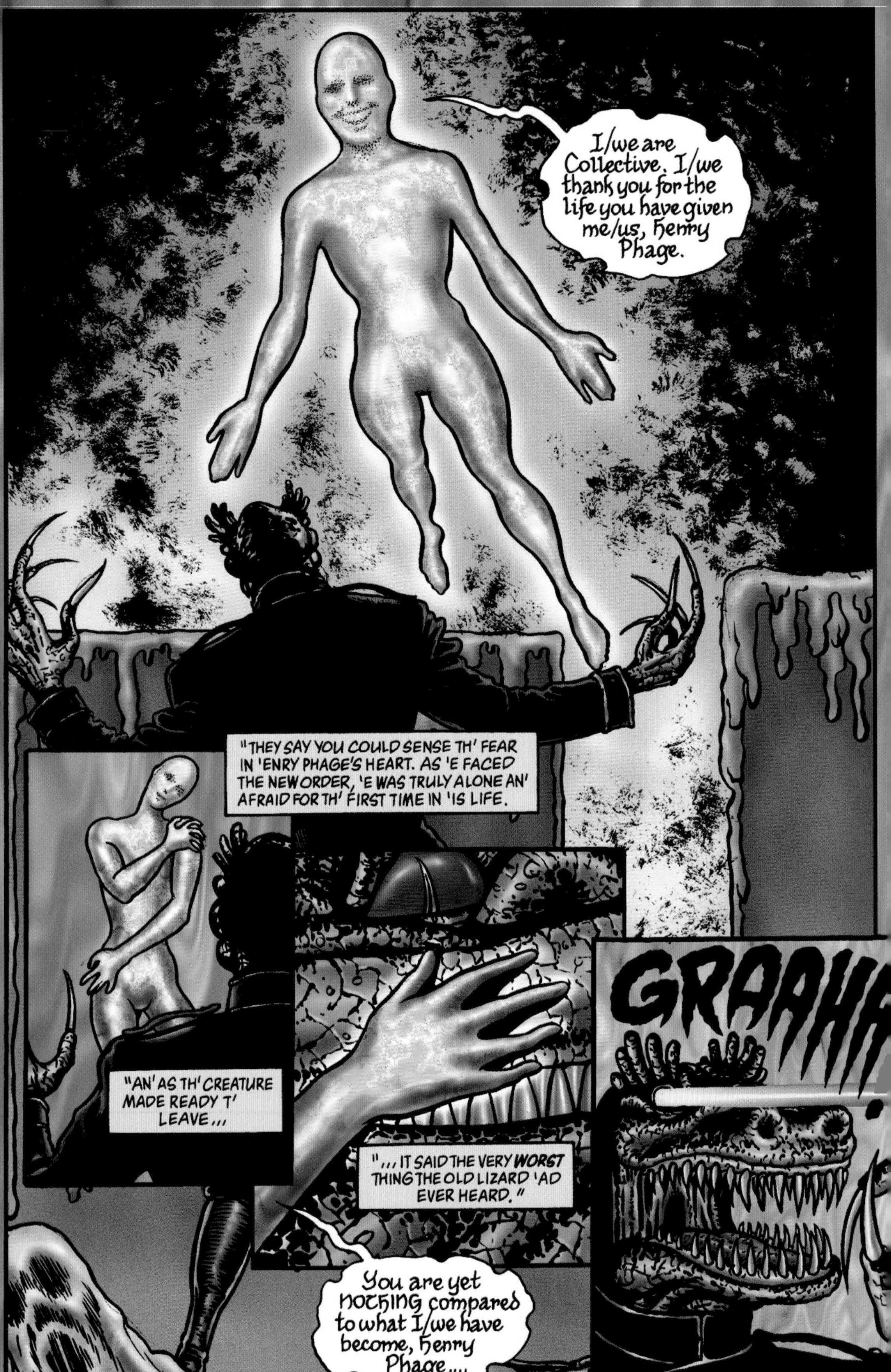
I/we are Collective. I/we thank you for the life you have given me/us, Henry Phage.
"THEY SAY YOU COULD SENSE TH' FEAR IN 'ENRY PHAGE'S HEART. AS 'E FACED THE NEW ORDER, 'E WAS TRULY ALONE AN' AFRAID FOR TH' FIRST TIME IN 'IS LIFE.
"AN' AS TH' CREATURE MADE READY T' LEAVE...
"...IT SAID THE VERY WORST THING THE OLD LIZARD 'AD EVER HEARD."
You are yet NOTHING compared to what I/we have become, Henry Phage....
GRAAHH

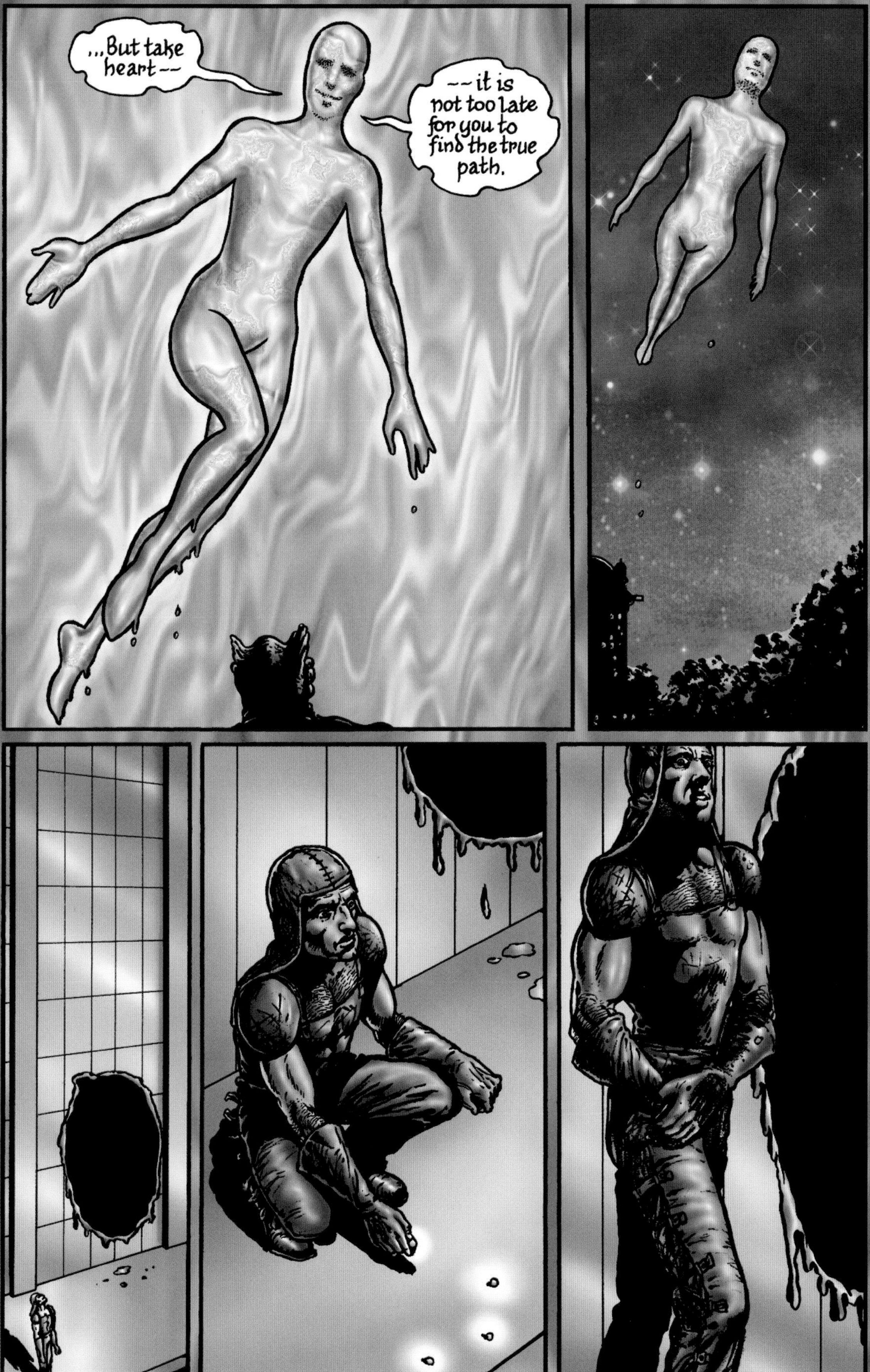
...But take heart--
--it is not too late for you to find the true path.

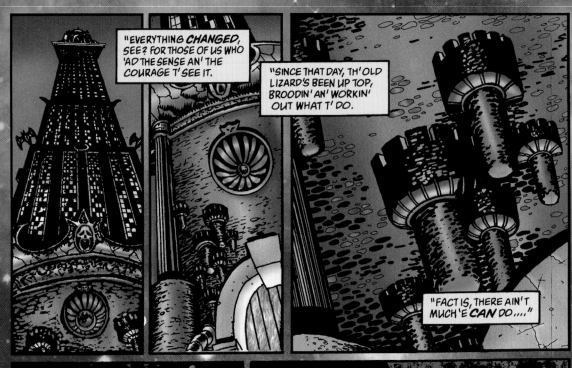

"EVERYTHING *CHANGED*, SEE? FOR THOSE OF US WHO 'AD THE SENSE AN' THE COURAGE T' SEE IT.

"SINCE THAT DAY, TH' OLD LIZARD'S BEEN UP TOP, BROODIN' AN' WORKIN' OUT WHAT T' DO.

"FACT IS, THERE AIN'T MUCH 'E *CAN* DO...."

'ERE...COME 'ERE. I GOT SUMMINK T' SHOW YOU, SEEIN' AS 'OW Y' DON'T LOOK TOO *CONVINCED*.

CAREFUL NOW... MIND AS Y' AIN'T *SEEN* BY ANYONE.

HERE -- THIS'S THE *BODY* OF TH' CREATURE.

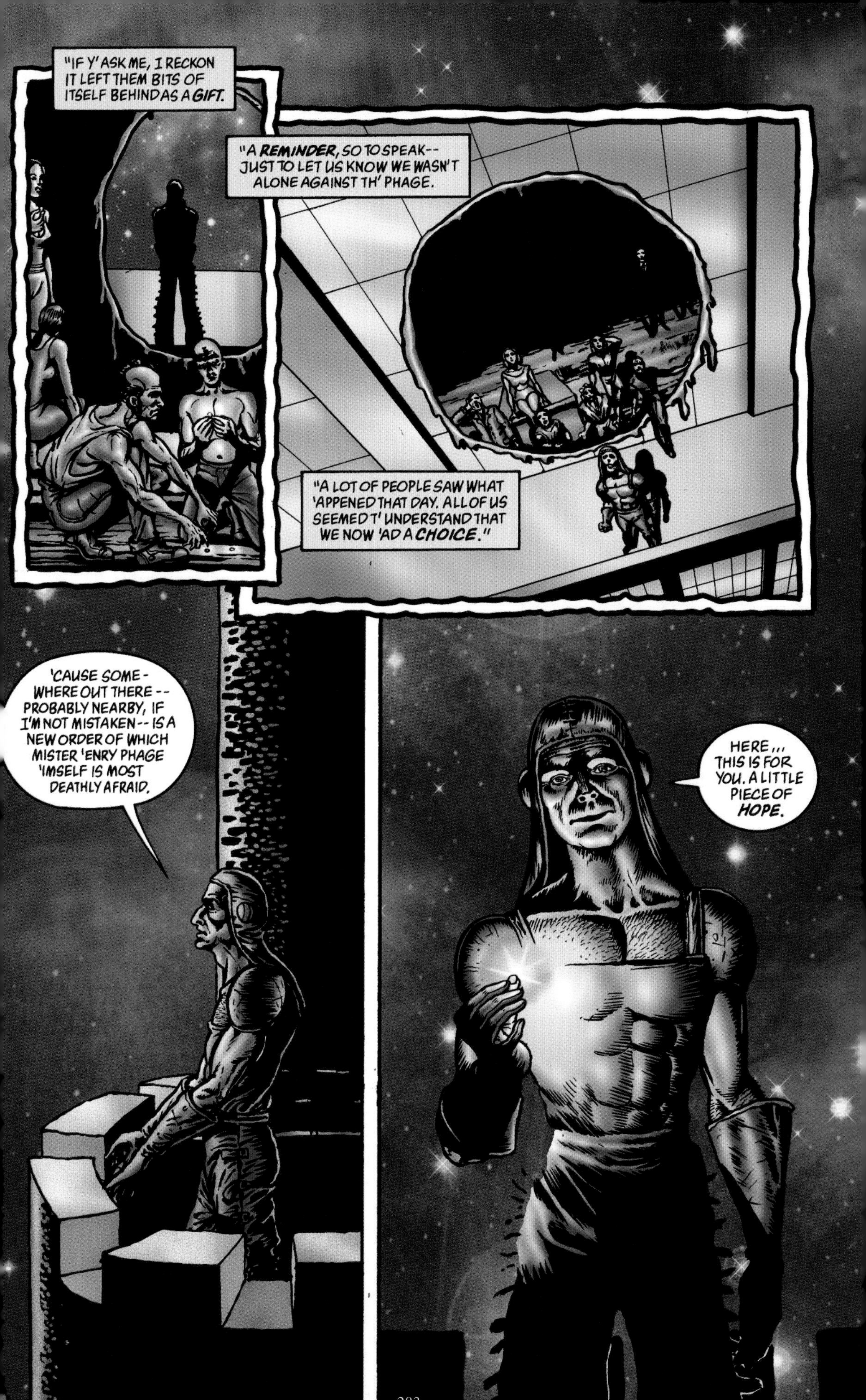
"IF Y' ASK ME, I RECKON IT LEFT THEM BITS OF ITSELF BEHIND AS A GIFT.
"A REMINDER, SO TO SPEAK-- JUST TO LET US KNOW WE WASN'T ALONE AGAINST TH' PHAGE.
"A LOT OF PEOPLE SAW WHAT 'APPENED THAT DAY. ALL OF US SEEMED T' UNDERSTAND THAT WE NOW 'AD A CHOICE."
'CAUSE SOME-WHERE OUT THERE -- PROBABLY NEARBY, IF I'M NOT MISTAKEN-- IS A NEW ORDER OF WHICH MISTER 'ENRY PHAGE 'IMSELF IS MOST DEATHLY AFRAID.
HERE... THIS IS FOR YOU. A LITTLE PIECE OF HOPE.

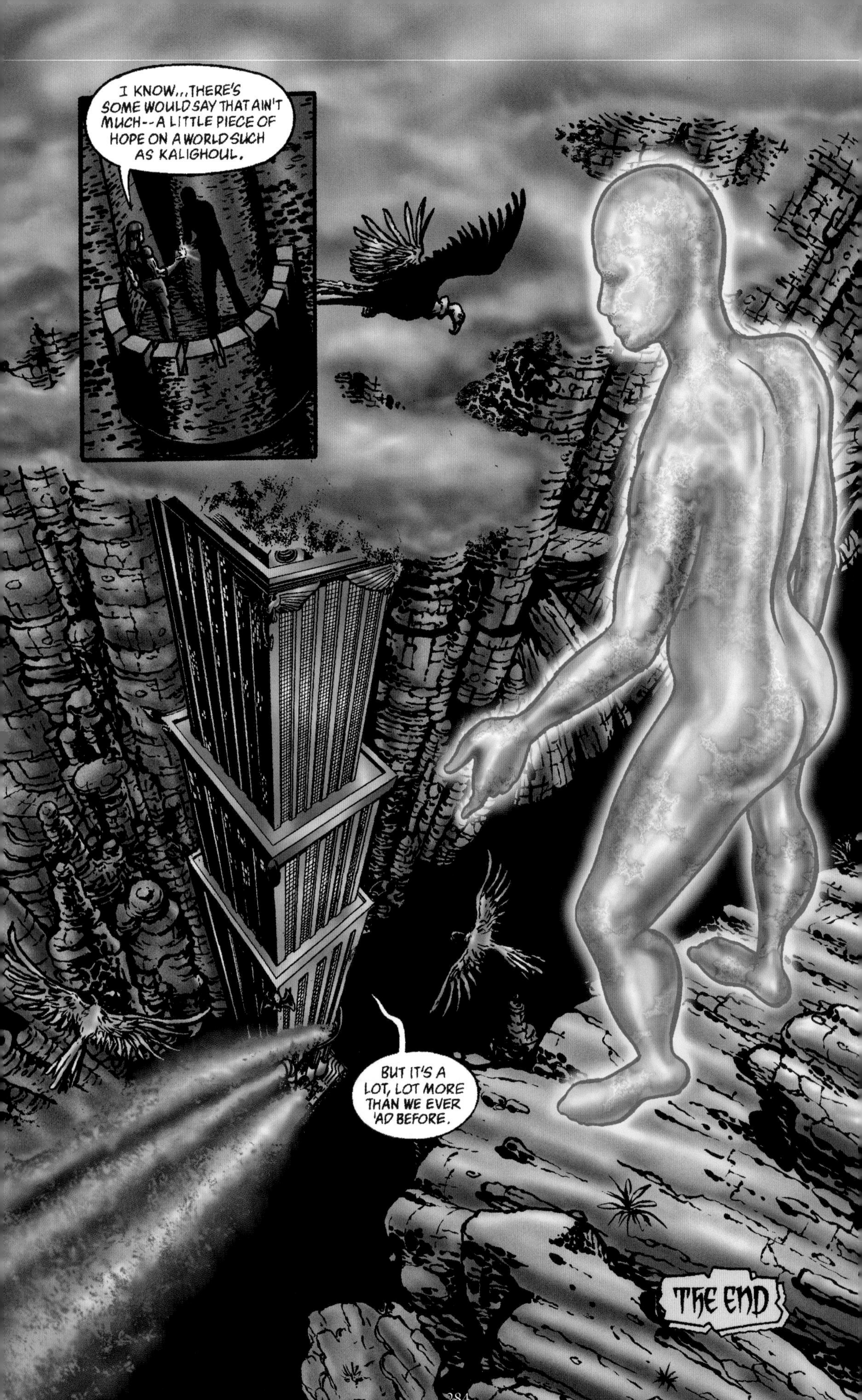
I KNOW,,,THERE'S SOME WOULD SAY THAT AIN'T MUCH--A LITTLE PIECE OF HOPE ON A WORLD SUCH AS KALIGHOUL.
BUT IT'S A LOT, LOT MORE THAN WE EVER 'AD BEFORE.
THE END

THE BOOK OF
TEKNOPHAGE

An Afterword by Jim Salicrup

In the beginning Laurie Silvers and Mitchell Rubenstein created the Sci-Fi Channel (which begat the Syfy). And it was good. And the Laurie and Mitchell said "Let there be Tekno•Comix." And behold, it was good too.

Laurie and Mitchell had a great concept for Tekno•Comix—use great talents such as Isaac Asimov, Leonard Nimoy, and others that they had met and worked with at the Sci-Fi Channel to create concepts for comicbooks. It was the early 90s, and they had also invited a hot new comics writer, Neil Gaiman, to contribute to this ambitious comics line. Never one to shy away from a challenge, Neil contributed several concepts—Lady Justice, Mr. Hero, Adam Cain, and Teknophage.

Unfortunately, following a big boom in comics in the early 90s, there was the inevitable big bust. Many of the new comics publishers launched around that time, were forced to shut down, including Tekno•Comix. In the intervening years, Neil Gaiman has become a literary superstar—an award-winning, best-selling author —while these comics have become virtually forgotten. And that's where Super Genius comes in. Over ten years ago, Terry Nantier, a pioneer publisher in the graphic novel field— his NBM has published everything from classic comic strip collections and translated European graphic novels to original works by such creators as Bryan Talbot and James Vance—and I started a new graphic novel publishing company called Papercutz. And Papercutz recently launched the modestly titled Super Genius imprint to publish material such as Neil Gaiman's Tekno•Comix.

We've already published Volume One of NEIL GAIMAN'S LADY JUSTICE. The LADY JUSTICE

comics may be surprising to many Neil Gaiman fans as the tone is very unlike most of Neil Gaiman's work, and more reflective of the comics and movies popular at the time they were originally published—comics such as Frank Miller's DARK KNIGHT, Alan Moore and Dave Gibbons's WATCHMEN, even Marvel's PUNISHER, and films such as *Natural Born Killers*. Not surprisingly, Lady Justice feels more Gaiman-like in the first story presented in this volume of NEIL GAIMAN'S TEKNOPHAGE. It's a story co-plotted by Neil, so that certainly makes sense. The story comes from NEIL GAIMAN'S WHEEL OF WORLDS #0 that introduced all of his Tekno•Comix characters. And what a story it is—it's like a giant jam session, featuring all of the creative teams that would produce the individual comics series starring Lady Justice, Mr. Hero, and Teknophage.

Aside from Neil's co-plotting credit on the WHEEL OF WORLDS story, none of the Tekno•Comix were actually written by Neil. Instead, talented writers and artists, such as Rick Veitch, Bryan Talbot, Angus McKie, Paul Jenkins, and Al Davison, as in the case of TEKNOPHAGE, were recruited to bring Neil's concepts to comicbook life. But as you can see on the previous and next pages, Neil was very involved in the development of the characters —even providing an initial pencil sketch of Teknophage as well as detailed feedback on sketches provided by Rick Veitch and Bryan Talbot—both very talented writers and artists themselves.

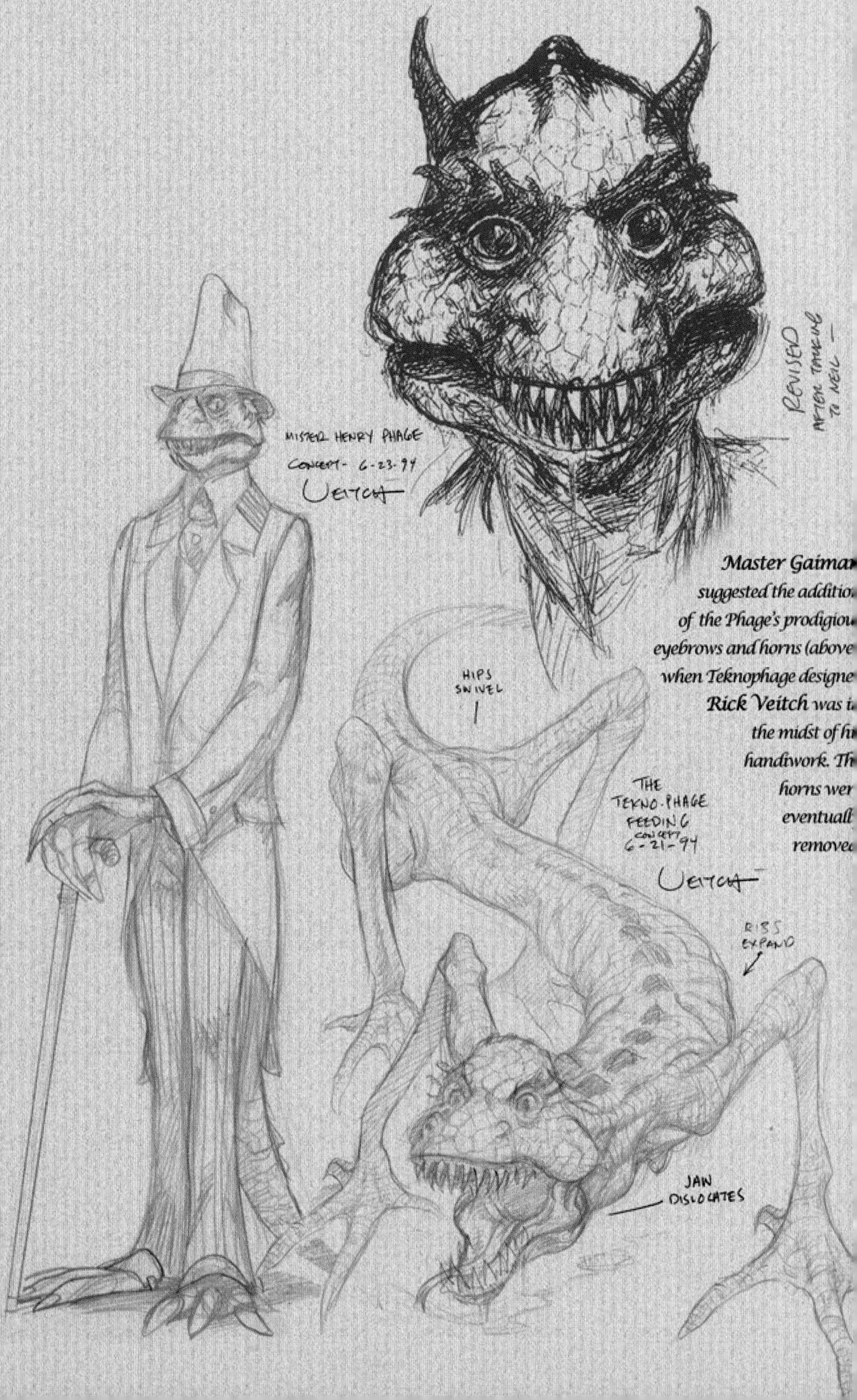
REVISED AFTER TALKING TO NEIL —
MISTER HENRY PHAGE
CONCEPT - 6-23-94
VEITCH
HIPS SWIVEL
THE TEKNO-PHAGE FEEDING
CONCEPT 6-21-94
VEITCH
RIBS EXPAND
JAW DISLOCATES

Master Gaima
suggested the additio
of the Phage's prodigiou
eyebrows and horns (above
when Teknophage designe
***Rick Veitch** was i*
the midst of hi
handiwork. Th
horns wer
eventuall
remove

*At left are Neil Gaiman's initial Teknophage sketces. **Bryan Talbot** gave the Phage his hypnotic gaze and forbidding manner (below).*

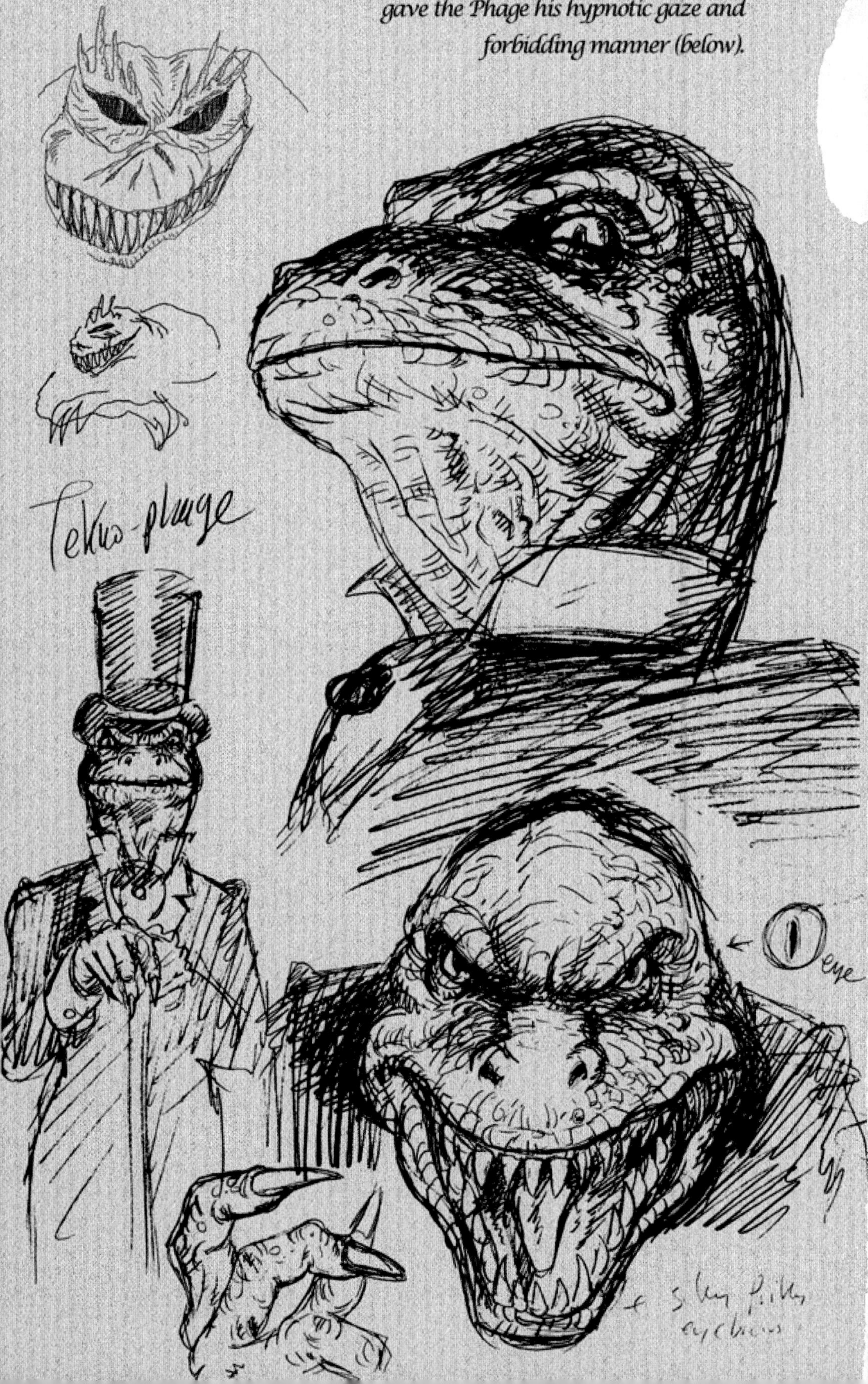

Tekno-phage
eye

THE WHEEL OF WORLDS story set the stage for all of the Gaiman-created Tekno•Comix characters, including Teknophage, who is right at the center of this Wheel of Worlds. This volume collects all ten issues of the original first series of NEIL GAIMAN'S TEKNOPHAGE comics for the very first time, and we think the comics' two main storylines benefit greatly from being altogether in one book. It's as if the comics were serializing two graphic novels and now they're together at last. The first TEKNOPHAGE graphic novel is by Rick Veitch and Bryan Talbot, while the second is by Paul Jenkins and Al Davison. The first graphic novel explores Kalighoul from a human perspective, while providing a biting satire of the capitalist system, while the second explores the religious elements of the series. While it may seem like it's all over for our favorite 65 million-year-old intelligent dinosaur, we promise he'll be back in NEIL GAIMAN'S TEKNOPHAGE Volume Two.

You also got to meet Mr. Hero and Lady Justice in this volume, and they'll both be back as well. Look for NEIL GAIMAN'S MR. HERO Volume One and NEIL GAIMAN'S LADY JUSTICE Volume Two.

So, start saving your Moolahbux, and beware of lizards offering you fruit!

Thanks, Jim Salicrup

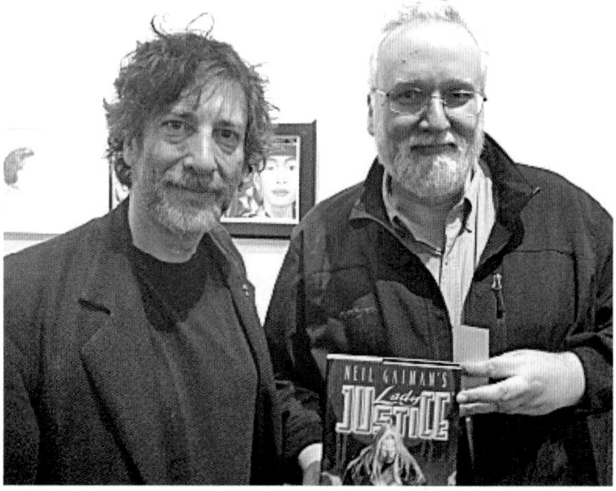
NEIL GAIMAN'S
Lady
JUSTICE

Neil Gaiman and Jim Salicrup with NEIL GAIMAN'S LADY JUSTICE Volume One.

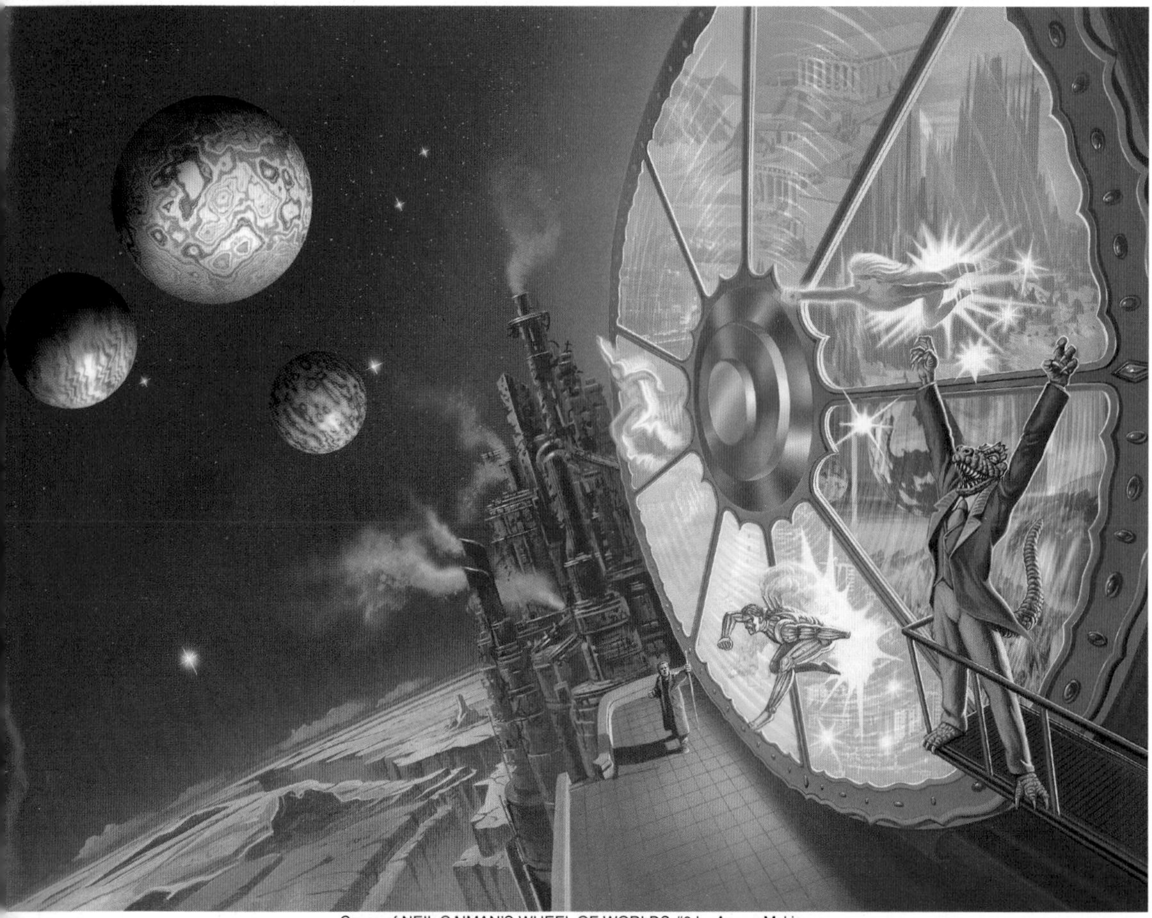

Cover of NEIL GAIMAN'S WHEEL OF WORLDS #0 by Angus Mckie